THE BLACK HUNTER

PIERRE VIDAL-NAQUET

The Black Hunter

Forms of Thought and Forms of Society in the Greek World

Translated by
Andrew Szegedy-Maszak

with a Foreword by
Bernard Knox

The Johns Hopkins University Press
Baltimore and London

In memory of
my brother Claude:
1944–1964

This book has been brought to publication with the generous assistance of the Andrew W. Mellon Foundation.

Originally published as *Le chasseur noir: Formes de pensées et formes de société dans le monde grec* by François Maspero, Paris, 1981, and La Découverte/Maspero, Paris, 1983. © Librairie Maspero, 1981

The Foreword is reprinted with permission from *The New York Review of Books* Copyright © 1983 Nyrev, Inc. Chapters 1, 5, 6, 10, and 13, translated by other hands, are reprinted here in revised form from *Myth, Religion, and Society,* edited by R. L. Gordon (Cambridge University Press, 1981). An English version of Chapter 14 appeared in *Journal of Hellenic Studies* 98 (1978).

The Johns Hopkins University Press
2715 North Charles Street
Baltimore, Maryland 21218-4363
The Johns Hopkins Press Ltd., London
www.press.jhu.edu

Library of Congress Cataloging-in-Publication Data

Vidal-Naquet, Pierre, 1930–
  The black hunter.

  Translation of: Le chasseur noir.
  Bibliography: p.
  Includes index.
  1. Civilization, Greek—Addresses, essays, lectures.
I. Title.
DF78.V5313   1986   938   85-45870
ISBN 0-8018-3251-9 (alk. paper)
ISBN 0-8018-5951-4 (pbk.)

Salut, chasseur au carnier plat!
A toi, lecteur, d'établir les rapports.
Merci, chasseur au carnier plat.
A toi, rêveur, d'aplanir les rapports.

René Char, Moulin premier

Contents

Contents

Foreword, by Bernard Knox

Ever since the turn of the century Paris has been the arbiter of fashion for the English-speaking world, and even though since the Second World War the dictates of its couturiers on skirt lengths have not imposed the universal conformity they once did, the methodologies launched by its intellectuals have all, in their turn, found industrious promoters and an enthusiastic clientele. Fashion, however, is a quick-change artist, and some of her intellectual creations no one would now want to be seen dead in. Even the most infatuated of sentimental leftists long ago gave up trying to explain Sartre's manic switches as he wriggled on the hook attached to the Party line, and almost everyone now realizes that Roland Barthes was too great a wit to have taken his own late work seriously (if *S/Z* is not a gargantuan parody of structuralist criticism, there is no excuse for it).

Epigones of Lévi-Strauss, of course, are still constructing diagrams which show the tortuous relationships between questionable opposites, and students of Derrida continue to write critical prose that is often a classic vindication of their master's basic contention that language is not an adequate instrument for the expression of meaning. These fashions too, mercifully, will pass, and there are signs that perhaps Paris is losing its power to impose instant ideologies: what seemed, a year or so ago, to be a distinct possibility that there would be a boom in the Freudian incoherencies of Lacan has turned out to be a false alarm.

In one particular field, however, which might be loosely defined as Greek cultural history, Paris has been exerting an enduring and steadily widening influence on the professional sector in England and the United

States. Its source is a group of scholars—Jean-Pierre Vernant, Marcel Detienne, Nicole Loraux, and Pierre Vidal-Naquet—who are not exactly an *école* (the senior member, Vernant, does not function as a *maître*) or even an *équipe,* for though they often publish collaborative work they have divergent viewpoints and interests. The main links between them are their cooperation in the direction of the Centre de recherches comparées sur les sociétés anciennes, their teaching and research functions in the Ecole pratique des hautes études (though Vernant moved on to the higher reaches of the Collège de France in 1975), and the general description "structuralist," which appears in the subtitle of a recent selection from their work in English translation.

Pierre Vidal-Naquet's name appears as joint author with Pierre Lévêque on the title page of *Clisthène l'Athénien,* and he shares with Vernant the authorship of *Mythe et tragédie,* to which he contributed two brilliant essays, but *The Black Hunter* is the first book dealing with classical Greek civilization to be issued solely under his own name. That name, however, has often appeared on books which appealed to readers who do not share his interest in the institutions of the ancient world; he was a leading figure, for example, in the campaign to expose and document the use of torture by the French army and police in Algeria. Between 1958 and 1977 he published a series of no fewer than four books which exposed the French army's systematic use of torture; the last of them, *Les Crimes de l'armée française,* was a selection of accounts by men who had served in the war which amply justified the book's uncompromising title.

This last book, Vidal-Naquet explains in the preface, is an *aide-mémoire.* For a people's memory, he points out, is not an automatic process, a "natural" phenomenon. It can be wiped out, as in the USSR, or maintained, as in the case of the museums and institutions that preserve the record of Nazi terror, or it can simply cease to function, lulled to sleep by the official voices of government, press, and television. "If the profession of historian has a social function," says Vidal-Naquet, in an ironically appropriate military metaphor, "it is to furnish cadres and benchmarks for the collective memory."

A collection of articles, prefaces, and essays, *Les Juifs, la mémoire, et le présent* (1981), explores the problem of Jewish identity and destiny all the way from a fascinating discussion of Josephus, the historian of the revolt that ended in the Roman destruction of Jerusalem, to the controversy over the "revisionists," French and American, who dismiss the Holocaust as Zionist propaganda. And in a long preface of over one hundred pages written for a translation of Josephus's *Jewish War,* Vidal-Naquet explores with penetrating political insight and formidable erudition the religious

and ideological chaos of first-century Palestine, a tangled skein which
seems so familiar that it is hardly a surprise to come across a Menahem
(who seizes the fortress of Masada in A.D. 66 and returns as king to
Jerusalem); one half expects to turn the page and find some form of the
name Arafat.

Vidal-Naquet has a talent for writing prefaces and he is often invited
to do so. He wrote the introduction to Detienne's book on early Greek
philosophy, *Les Maîtres de vérité dans la Grèce ancienne*, to translations of
Sophocles, the *Iliad*, and Aeschylus. He also contributed to the French
translation of M. I. Finley's *Democracy, Ancient and Modern* a substantial
essay on the use made of the Athenian democratic tradition by the French
revolutionaries of 1789–94 and to Pierre Savinel's translation of Arrian's
history of Alexander's expedition (1984) a substantial afterword (*postface*)
which discusses the position of the historian "between two worlds." *The
Black Hunter* does not contain any of these pieces, but it does consist
entirely of articles that have been previously published elsewhere; "in
Greek studies," Vidal-Naquet says in the Preface, "the article is much
easier for me than the book." The contents, written and published over
the course of twenty-three years (from 1957 to 1980), have here been
corrected, expanded, and rewritten to take account of criticism, fresh
insights, and new data.

The book is, however, not a haphazard collection of Vidal-Naquet's
scholarly articles; from his impressive output he has selected those essays
which deal with "forms of thought" and "forms of society" in the Greek
world or, rather, which attempt to establish a link between those two
subjects, "which are not here studied in themselves and for themselves."
Throughout this long text, each article with a solid sheaf of notes, the
argument maintains an unfailingly high level of interest; detailed discussion is not shirked, but it is conducted without pedantry; theory and
speculation abound but their formulation is concise and clear. In every
case, whether he is dealing with hoplite tactics, initiation periods, utopian fantasies, or mythical cities, Vidal-Naquet never loses sight of the
central concern of the book—its method.

For an example of the method at work one may as well choose what is
obviously the author's favorite piece, since he gives its title to the book.
"The Black Hunter" is a brilliant essay, which is already well known, not
only in French but in English and Italian versions. It is also the essay that,
as Vidal-Naquet states, marked a critical stage in his development, "the
discovery of structural analysis as a heuristic instrument." In it Vidal-
Naquet attempts to connect what is known about the Athenian *ephebeia*
with comparable institutions elsewhere (especially at Sparta but also in

Africa) as well as with the myth of Melanthos, the deceitful warrior, and a song sung by the chorus of women in Aristophanes' *Lysistrata* about a hunter-hermit called Melanion—*melas* means "black" and this is the black hunter of the title.

"Only connect," said Forster, and no one can fail to admire the brilliance of the connections Vidal-Naquet suggests; they give institutional solidity to a baffling but obviously important myth and insert in a coherent context historical and ritual details that meant little in isolation. The theory, presented with skill and eloquence, seems at first sight irresistible. But of course it has its flaws. The connection between myth and historical institution, to take one example, would seem stronger if our evidence for the Athenian *ephebeia* came from the sixth century B.C. instead of the fourth: critical readers will doubtless find other avenues of attack. In the end, some will be prepared to overlook weak spots in a brilliant interpretation which makes sense of many things that were obscure and connects in a meaningful pattern what previously were isolated and therefore puzzling facts. Others will prefer to settle, reluctantly in most cases, for the old uncertainty and imperfection, to live with unanswered questions and unrelated details rather than allow theory and occasional poetic license the benefit of the doubt.

Perhaps it is even a matter of national temperament. At the final session of an international conference on Greek myth held at Urbino in 1973, Vernant referred to some critical observations that had been made by the Regius Professor of Greek at Cambridge, Geoffrey Kirk, the author of two books on Greek myth which show an intimate acquaintance with, and a certain critical distance from, structuralist theory. He had written for the *Times Literary Supplement* a review of Vernant and Vidal-Naquet's *Mythe et tragédie* in which he remarked that the authors were both "extremely French." "Coming from a British pen," said Vernant, "the formula is at the very least ambiguous and I am not too sure how to take it. Perhaps I should turn it around and say that in his contribution to the discussion here, my friend Kirk has shown himself, in his positivism and prudence, to be 'extremely English.'" He added that empiricism, even if it is a spontaneous product and a natural inclination, is still as much a philosophy as any other and that it is a form of conceptualization which, if it remains merely implicit, is all the more likely to constrict and deform. He is of course quite right—if, that is, one can call "philosophy" an attitude which, having seen many theories come and go, is on its guard and which is prepared to accept the possibility that in this sublunar world the problems may have no final solution and the data may make less than perfect sense.

But there is one great advantage to being "extremely French": the
method is, as Vidal-Naquet says himself, "heuristic"—it discovers
things. And not even the most "English" reaction to Vidal-Naquet's
book could deny that it contains discoveries; exactly what the connection
is between the black ephebic cloak, Melanthos the tricky fighter, and
Melanion the woman-hating hunter may be disputed, but that there *is*
such a connection few readers of this book can doubt.

Discoverers have to be bold: one of Vidal-Naquet's great exemplars,
Lafitau, an eighteenth-century Jesuit who lived among the Algonquins,
Hurons, and Iroquois, is praised in this book for precisely that quality. In
his *Moeurs des sauvages amériquains comparées aux moeurs des premiers temps*
(Paris, 1724) he abandoned the customary attitude of writers on the
Americas, which was to measure their inhabitants by the standard of
classical antiquity. With what Vidal-Naquet terms an "incredible audacity" (*une incroyable audace*) he wrote that "if on the one hand the classical
authors had helped him understand the savages, the customs of the
savages had, on the other hand, lighted his way to an easier understanding and explanation of what was in the ancient authors."

Audacity has been characteristic of Vidal-Naquet's career from the
start; it marked his activities as a historian *engagé* in the political struggle;
it is visible at work in every page of this book, where, however, it is
tempered and checked by the historical conscience. As befits a man who
has learned from Vernant to reckon with the symbolic and social importance of civic space, the location of his office in Paris is wonderfully
appropriate. The rather dilapidated building which accommodates the
Centre de recherches comparées sur les sociétés anciennes is located on the
curve of Rue Monsieur-le-Prince. Upward the street climbs toward the
Odéon, a classic theater named after the building erected by Pericles to
commemorate the victory over the Persians. Downward it ends on the
Boulevard St.-Germain, where, in the midst of the surging traffic and
unnoticed by the pedestrians who wait for the bus, Danton stands on his
pedestal, shouting the words engraved below him on the stone: "De
l'audace, encore de l'audace, toujours de l'audace. . . ."

Preface

Let us establish at the outset what this book is not. There is a custom among scholars that, at retirement, they gather into one or more volumes their *scripta minora*, their *kleine Schriften*. Often it is the task of their students to make the collection posthumously, and above all it must be convenient and faithful. For the most part, the original pagination is preserved in the margin of the new printing. The Latin or German phrases convey their meaning well: these are "minor writings" as opposed to the "major works," those that had originally appeared in that noble form, the book.

For reasons that are my own and are probably not too "rational," in Greek studies the article is much easier for me than the book. I have tried to compensate for this failing, if that is what it is, by writing several studies over these last several years with the whole set in mind; indeed, with the subconscious idea that one day there would be this book. But even if this volume actually contains my most personal observations on the Greek world, it is neither *the,* nor exactly *a,* collection of my articles.

To begin with, not everything is included here. Among those topics omitted are the economic and social and institutional history of the Greek world, the history of the Jewish world and its contacts with Hellenism during the Hellenistic and Roman periods, the history of historiography, and, more generally, the history of the representations of the Greek world in Western thought. The same is true of research into tragedy, conducted in close collaboration with Jean-Pierre Vernant and saved for the books that appear under both our names.

Nor is this a case of a simple assemblage of works that have already been published. All the essays, with one exception, have been revised. Within what limits and according to what principles? I need not mention the physical unification, the correction of errors of detail, and the additional cross references to reinforce the internal coherence of these pages. Overall I had to deal with two symmetrically opposed facts. The chapters that now make up this book were written over a span of twenty-three years, from 1957 (the publication date of "Divine Time and Human Time") to 1980. During this period much was written, much was discovered, much was discarded, and I myself learned a great deal. Clearly it was unthinkable for me to publish here those opinions I no longer thought to be true. At the same time I could not reprint everything as if no time had passed. The final result is perhaps a little uneven. In some places I made extensive alterations, in others hardly any. The main criteria were the date of the original article and, above all, my own openness (greater or lesser as the case may be) toward the questions raised. Obviously when an essay set out to resolve an "enigma," I took into account as much as I could the subsequent literature on the subject, whether it accepted, extended, or contested my hypotheses. Often I could also adopt the results of such works as were written in response to my own; in other cases, by contrast, I could retain and develop my own conclusions. In disregard of a current rule, I have not indicated such changes—sometimes quite numerous—by special typographical signals. I do not wish thereby to claim a lucidity I have not always had: I am trying to write history, not to remake it. The texts from yesterday or the day before have not been dropped down Orwell's "memory hole." They are available to all, and anyone who finds the exercise amusing can trace the history of the variants in my texts. Moreover, when someone else's analysis has convinced me that I was mistaken, I have indicated as much in the notes. The essay on Epaminondas was written in collaboration with Pierre Lévêque and is reprinted here with his permission, for which he has my gratitude; it has not been altered, but it has been supplemented with an appendix framing the questions I am asking today.

Those articles on the most general topics are clearly those that have been least reworked. Nevertheless, I have always made at least a brief comment, augumented by a few references, to indicate how I think the problems should now be construed.

The Introduction is extracted from an encyclopedia article and has deliberately been given a programmatic form, cut off from a historical survey that would be useless here. In acknowledgment of these hard times, the amount of Greek has been significantly reduced.

This work of making-more-precise and bringing-up-to-date has not been easy. In fact, with various interruptions it has taken almost seven years, beginning with a thesis defense at Nancy on January 19, 1974, and continuing during a stay at Oxford, where I was invited by Anthony Andrewes at the end of 1976. I am not sure I would have finished it alone. In fact I was not alone; I could not have completed the project had it not been for the dialogue I have had over the years with Nicole Loraux. She has *made* this book with me in the course of scores of working sessions. Any expression of gratitude would fall short of that acknowledgment. I am very happy that this is being published at almost exactly the same time as her own books, *L'invention d'Athènes* and *Les enfants d'Athéna*.

Having said what this book is not, I must now tell what it does contain. It is called *The Black Hunter* not only because the essay of that title occupies a central position in the economy of the work as a whole but also because writing that piece marked a significant advance for me: the discovery of structural analysis as a heuristic device. Finally the black hunter travels through the mountains and forests, and I too approach the Greek city-state from its frontiers rather than its plains. Perhaps the subtitle conveys the meaning more clearly: "forms of thought *and* forms of society in the Greek world"; the coordinating conjunction indicates what is most important—the link I have tried to establish between two realms, which are not studied here by and for themselves.

In my work from the very beginning, I have had one goal: to bring into dialogue that which does not naturally communicate according to the usual criteria of historical judgment. I am not unaware that some of the comparisons I have put into play might appear as strange, if not so attractive, as the chance encounter "on a dissecting table, of a sewing machine and an umbrella" in Lautréamont's phrase. It is not obvious a priori that, in order to understand the treatment of women in Aristophanes' comedies and in Herodotus's history, one must first attend to the opposition between two very different types of slavery.

Forms of thought, forms of society. On the one side are literary, philosophical, and historical texts, mythical stories and descriptive analyses; on the other, social behavior: war, slavery, the education of the young, and the erection of commemorative monuments. On the one side, the imaginary field of the *polis,* on the other, what it includes of the real, the wholly concrete world of rituals, political decisions, labor—whose place in the imagination must also be revealed. In principle, what could be more abstract than a theory of space or more concrete than victory in battle? What I bring together can, quite legitimately, be the subject of independent studies, and I have had the opportunity to contribute to research in the two separate areas. It is their intersection that interests me here. Removed from the study of social practice, the structural analysis of myth can carry out a magnificent project by putting the myths into sets, having them reflect one another, and making them display their logical relationships. But then there is also the danger of taking refuge in what Hegel called the "the peacable realm of friendly appearances," a realm in which every compartment is filled as soon as it has been outlined. On the other hand, institutional, social, and economic history—such as that practiced in England by M. I. Finley and in France by Yvon Garlan, Philippe Gauthier, Claude Mossé, and Edouard Will—assumes its full value, in my view, only when it is linked with an analysis of the images that accompany and even pervade the institutions and practices of political and social activity.

The textual and the social. Several of the analyses to be found in this book begin with a text and have the ultimate aim of elucidating its meaning. However I am not among those, like Jean Bollack for example, who believe that meaning is immanent in a text, or that a text is explained only by itself. At the extreme, according to this school of thought (to whom we are indebted for some excellent work), the study of the text would have to be preceded by the elimination of all the accretions attached to it by tradition—and tradition begins with the Alexandrian philologists. Then, and only then, could the text glitter like a diamond in the rough, cut along its natural breaks. But is there such a thing as a pure text? I believe, on the contrary, that ultimately the text exists not only throughout its textual, political, social, and institutional environment but also in the tradition that has bequeathed it to us—the manuscripts and the studies by philologians, interpreters of every kind, and historians. I think this multi-dimensionality of the text is at the core of a multi-dimensional conception of history. Neither does the social exist in a pure state. Of course the conceptual is embedded in the social: a Greek tragedian does not write like Racine, and an Athenian general does not maneuver like Frederick II; but the social—as C. Castoriadis so well understood—is also imagination: so, for example, the creation at the time of Cleisthenes of the Athenian city-state with ten tribes, or the birth of tragedy. The social is density, but it is not *only* density. Even when the disjunction between the textual and the social is at its greatest, as for instance between the philosophical text produced by Plato and what Nicole Loraux calls "the Athenian history of Athens," the relation still exists. In this sense my work as a historian is linked with what Ignace Meyerson and Jean-Pierre Vernant have dubbed "historical psychology," but our paths are different. Meyerson and Vernant start from psychological categories and have shown that they are not everlasting, and in their quest they have dealt with texts and political and social institutions. I have proceeded from the opposite direction.

I should add that to make such relations manifest, to illuminate their meaning, does not result in the creation of a world unified under the gaze of the Form or "the development of the means of production." Unlike Descartes and the union of the body and the soul, I do not have the use of a pineal gland to allow me to articulate the two levels on which, broadly speaking, my analyses progress. Like many of my contemporaries I have learned from Marx (and not only from Marx) that men do not always do what they say and do not always say what they are doing; but I have tried to live this relation to Marx and to bring it over not as an absolute or a facile synthesis, not as teleology or the retrospective prediction of the future, but in the form of the incomplete, the fragmentary, the critical.

As a result, in my linkage of the imaginary and the social I do not find the unbroken thread of *logos* but, inescapably, the opaque. There is the temptation of transparency; it is one of the threats overhanging any study of fifth-century Greece precisely because *that world* tried to conceive of itself as perfectly clear: the simplicity, or rather the brutal distinctness, of social relations, the existence of political life in broad daylight. However, is the Athens of the tragedians perfectly congruent with that of the comic poets, the historians, the inscriptions, the monuments? And what right do we have to declare that, of the various sources, one is telling us the truth, the reality, while the other contains but the shadow? With what right will we unify all this without noting the breaks, the gaps, without at least using what Kant called "reflective judgment," which, unlike "determinant judgment," finds the universal on the basis of the particular?

It is this deep opacity of the social which, to my eyes, gives value to the effort expended to endow it with meaning, if it is true, as Jacques Brunschwig wrote, that "on the ruins of Absolutes—revealed, possessed or discovered" one must erect "in human time the modest devices of shared discourse and common work" (*Revue Philosophique* 89 [1964]: 179).

In my partiality I think that the fact that the plan of this book could have been different is not a proof of its incoherence but of its unity. Perhaps it might be useful to justify the organization as it stands.

The introduction sets out to define Greek discourse; more precisely, it defines a table of oppositions, a *systoichia,* which is, to some degree, the framework for such discourse. Cultivated and wild, master and slave, man and woman, citizen and foreigner, adult and child, warrior and artisan: these are some of the oppositions that the remainder of the book will put into play, without straining to enclose therein material that does not conform to the pattern.

There follow three studies on space and time, factors that will reappear in other portions of the book. Here it is not a question of space and time as conceived, for example, by Kant, as "necessary representations which function as the basis for all intuitions." As presented by the *Odyssey*, space figures into the opposition between the real and the imaginary, the gods, monsters and men, sacrifice and barbarism. After Homer it became the city-state's space, which generals had to take into account in their strategy, until the day Epaminondas's imagination shattered the rules that civic custom had codified. The study of time also leads from Homer to the crises of the fourth century, and brings into opposition and conjunction gods and men, as well as cyclical patterns and rising or falling vectors.

Youths and warriors. In this part of the book the problem is to see how two participants in the Greek polis locate themselves with regard to one another. On one side, the hoplite, who is officially the central figure, both the "real" hoplite who fights, and the hoplite of representations whose battle at Marathon in 490 would become a "tradition." The hoplite then, and on the other side the person destined to be a hoplite but not yet become one, the young man, the ephebe, who will succeed—or fail—as the "black hunter." Hoplite and ephebe, battle and military service, are exemplary social realities, but they are also studied here as figures of myth, the narrative of which antiquity has left us many written versions, and of mythology as an analytical discipline. Moving from one essay to the next in this section, the reader might notice a deepening in the investigation. I have deliberately put in texts that refer to one another in the chronological order of their publication.

Women, slaves, artisans. Both the actual and the imaginary city-state are studied in their relation to those who were forced into servitude, to women, who were excluded from political life save for serving the polis as slaves of Athena Ilias—if the rite is really as old as the tradition would have it, it is, as Arnaldo Momigliano once observed, the sole proof for the Trojan War—and finally to the artisans, who are liminal by comparison to the hoplites.

These social categories have their own history, which was occasionally phrased by the ancients in terms that have directed and misled the moderns; their internal oppositions (the Athenian slave is not the same as the Spartan helot, and he was not thought of and discussed in the same way); and their relations to one another in myth, tradition, and utopian thought, as well as in actual social life: one could be both woman and slave, both slave and artisan. For the comic poets the rule of women is not necessarily linked with rule by slaves. The social universe, even when it is turned upside down, retains its articulations; fables take different shapes in Argos, in Athens, in Sparta. The Athenian artisan has political rights that are denied to the artisan in Plato's imaginary city, which is set in Crete. The essays gathered in this section also make possible a different understanding of those that went before. Women, slaves, youths, and artisans comprise, by the time of Aristotle, a set to be defined in relation to the adult male citizen.

In the last section, "The city, vision and reality," the issues are rationality, Plato, Pheidias, and Delphi. The Platonic myths offer us two versions of the tale of two cities: Athens and Atlantis, two forms of the mythic past, the city of motionlessness and the city of history, the city of hoplites and that of marines, two forms of Athens. The age of Cronos, the age of Zeus: in the former, defined by the myth in the *Politicus,* men are governed by the gods and cannot live in cities; in the latter, men remember the gods but are on the path toward forgetfulness.

If the collection ends with "an enigma at Delphi," it is partly because according to Heraclitus F 93, "the master to whom the oracle at Delphi belongs neither reveals nor conceals; he indicates." Apollo does not act like men, who insist on yes or no answers, who do not recognize and do not wish to recognize either ambiguity or interferences. But there is something else; from Delphi, we see Athens differently, and especially from that unique base in honor of Marathon which Pheidias adorned with statues, and which shows us a different image from that which the city usually gives itself. Here, if we understand the text of Pausanias correctly, the Athenians portrayed another Athens. It is with this image that I wanted to close this volume.

A book of this type is the individual—signed—expression of a life composed of exchanges, debts, encounters, and lessons given and received. In this American edition I will not list all those to whom I am indebted. To my departed masters in France, Henri I. Marrou, André Aymard, Victor Goldschmidt, Henri Margueritte, and Roger Rémondon, I will add the names of those living scholars in America who welcomed me and my work, in particular Charles Segal and Froma Zeitlin. A return to France allows me to recall that Edouard Will, the chief French historian of the Greek world, had gone against the deeply entrenched customs of the universities and agreed to assemble a doctoral committee to judge a "dossier" that included ten of the essays collected here. I found invaluable his friendship and clear-sightedness, as well as those of the members of the jury—Claude Mossé, Jean Pouilloux, and

Claire Préaux (now deceased)—and its president, Roland Martin. I learned from Louis Robert how to use epigraphic texts. Over the past twenty years I have read, listened to, and become friends with Moses Finley and Jean-Pierre Vernant. The former has served as the "reality principle" for me, by which I don't mean to imply that I have to give a name to the "pleasure principle"; that would be to make a mockery of symmetry. Vernant has been and still is something else. Chance dictated that my first essay, "Divine Time and Human Time," was published in the same volume of the review that contained his study of the Hesiodic myth of the races. From that I learned about reading the texts, and I have learned ever so much more in seeing, coming to know, and listening to J.-P. Vernant. I need hardly add that I knew Louis Gernet only toward the end of his life, and that once again it was J.-P. Vernant who gave me this extraordinary opportunity. My wife, Geneviève, has lived through the gestation of these studies and "has allowed them to reach the position of security where I would wish to find them."

My old friend Manolis Papathomopoulos re-read my text with his double proficiency, both Hellenic and French. I have to thank him, and then all those who made this English-language edition possible. Bernard Knox, first of all, had faith in this book and gave it a memorable review in the *New York Review of Books*. Andrew Szegedy-Maszak worked on the translation with tireless patience, accepting all the additions and emendations I sent him from the beginning to the end of his work; Bernard Compagnon helped him with the first draft. Finally, Jeannie Carlier, herself a translator from English to French, read over the translation and made both the author and the translator beneficiaries of her *akribeia*.

Such a book could only have been brought to fruition in the Centre de recherches comparées sur les sociétés anciennes of the École des Hautes Études en science sociale, of which I have the honor to have succeeded J.-P. Vernant as director. My thanks to all its members; it is from this particular place that I speak.

THE BLACK HUNTER

By Way of Introduction:
A Civilization of
Political Discourse

Writing the history of civilization is beset by a double danger: a first approach makes it a kind of annex that would include art, fashion, funeral rites, cuisine, in a word everything that does not come under the heading of political history, or social and economic history, or the history of ideas; the second approach, in reaction to the first, assumes that all phenomena—religious, artistic, social, economic, and intellectual—that appear at the same time in the same group of people " have among them enough essential links to constitute an entity that is endowed with a particular unity and structure more or less like those of an organism."[1]

A variant of the organicist illusion, another temptation to which historians of Greece have often succumbed, consists of treating a civilization as if it were an unchanging essence. This leads the historian to reason as if the bands of "Indo-Europeans" who arrived around 2200–2100 B.C. in the peninsula that was to become Hellas, and who spoke a dialect that is the ancestor of both Classical and modern Greek, already possessed in embryo the qualities that would later permit the existence of Homer or Aristotle. Such reasoning entitles us to extend the study of Greek civilization up to our own time: from the Mycenaean tablets to the works of Nikos Kazantzakis there is complete linguistic continuity; from one generation to the next, there has been no break in understanding.

This is an abridged version of an article published in the *Encyclopaedia Universalis*, vol. 7. Paris, 1970, pp. 1009–18.

"Greek civilization," as discussed in the present work, corresponds to the birth, the growth, the maturity, and the crisis of the city-state, in other words, the period from the end of the Mycenaean world to the beginnings of the Hellenistic era.

"Birth and growth of the city-state": this immense and complex historical phenomenon can be approached from the perspective of economics and society, or from the perspective of historical narrative. Let us look provisionally at the logos as an event (événement-discours). The city lives its life and expresses itself through the logos, just as it is itself an utterance (parole) and an effectual utterance on the subject of the agora. We must try to analyze this discourse simultaneously in accordance with its language and our own. Every culture defines itself in relation to nature; every culture makes use of a grid to integrate and encode gods, humans, animals, and things. Usually this grid is covert and implicit, and it is the task of the ethnologist merely to decode it. In contrast, one of the most characteristic features of Greek civilization is that it places at the disposal of the investigator the pairs of oppositions that were explicitly its own. The "raw" and the "cooked" were simply the raw and the cooked. One does not have to infer them.[2]

The earliest texts of Greek literature, the Homeric and Hesiodic poems, provide an anthropological and normative definition, exclusive and inclusive, of the human condition. Man is excluded from the divine times of the Golden age; he exists only by means of agricultural labor carried out in the heart of the familial community, the oikos. Nor is man a cannibal: "Such is the law which Zeus son of Cronos established for men, that fish, beasts, and winged birds devour each other, since there is among them no justice."[3] The whole Odyssey proposes the same definition. The travels of Odysseus are voyages outside the land of men, where he meets with gods, the dead, cannibals, or Lotus-Eaters. Man—that is, of course, a Greek—is one "who eats bread."[4]

Sacrifice, a meal of meat, links and divides gods and men. The foremost sacrificial animal is the ox of the plow—accompanied by libations of wine and the symbolic destruction of grain. The gods receive the smoke from the bones and from part of the fat; they breathe in the spices. Men share among themselves the greater part of the meat. Thus the Greek is a farmer, a stock-breeder, and a cook,[5] but the whole range that separates the two extremes of culture and savagery will repeat itself in the sacrifice and in the pantheon itself. The gods of the night and of the underworld (such as the Eumenides) receive "pure" offerings, honeyed libations "without wine"; the animals sacrificed to them are burned completely. Those groups that forbade bloody sacrifice, like the

Pythagoreans, only offered up pure and "natural" vegetable products:　　3
milk, honey, and spices. Conversely, the cult of Dionysus, god of savage
nature, culminates in the eating of raw flesh (*ōmophagia*). At the other
extreme, the sacrifice of the ox, the companion of mankind, is a bor-
derline case of a murder that requires retribution. At the festival of the
Bouphonii, dedicated to Zeus Polieus at Athens, the killers of the ox (the
priest, the knife itself) had to be tried.[6] Since Dionysiac *ōmophagia* also
could result in murder (as in the *Bacchae* of Euripides), one can see that all
sacrifice finds its ideological limit in human sacrifice, which is a return to
savagery, a fall into the "primitive" world, the world of incest. At the end
of the fourth century, the Cynics, who urged a return to nature, condemned the consumption of cooked meat and advocated incest and cannibalism. Greeks experienced contact with nature in the wild during the
hunt. Herdsmen and farmers were only marginally hunters. An animal
that had been hunted could not, except in the most exceptional cases, be
sacrificed. As both myth and tragedy demonstrate, the hunter, in direct
contact with savage nature, plays a double role: the hunt is the prime
example of the break with nature, and the "culture heroes" of the Greek
legends are all hunters and destroyers of wild beasts, but the hunt also
reflects the savage part of man, and so, in the myths, the sacrifice of the
hunted animal is most often a substitute for the sacrifice of a human
being.

These archaic categories persist throughout Greek history and, especially from the end of the sixth century, are integrated into the violent
political conflicts that rock the city. The theme of the Golden age, that
vegetarian paradise, will be opposed to the theme of the misery of
uncivilized man. The cities will claim for themselves the origin of civilization, as Athens used the mysteries of Eleusis to appropriate the
"invention" of agriculture. For a brief, impressive moment in the fifth
century, the tearing away of humanity from savagery was attributed to
humanity itself (as by Democritus). But that did not last.[7]

The second opposition derives to some extent from the first: the
Barbarian is simply the non-Greek, that is to say the one who does not
know how to speak Greek, precisely as the German is, to the Russian, the
"mute." For Homer the word merely designates the neighboring Carians.
For Herodotus, in the fifth century, the relationship is more subtle:
Greece is the land of pleasant mixtures and of poverty; marvels, however,
gravitate toward geographical extremes, particularly gold, which is located at the four cardinal points. The march toward the extremes is also
the march toward the nonhuman. Barbarians are understood in Greek
terms to the degree that their customs are opposite. For example, Egypt:

4   "The Egyptians, who live in a singular climate, alongside a river that
exhibits a character different from other rivers, have adopted in almost all
affairs manners and customs opposite to those of other men." Later, in the
fourth century the historian Ephorus distinguished between two sorts of
Scythians, cannibals and vegetarians, two opposite sorts of the nonhuman.[8] Barbarians are origin as well as antithesis: for Herodotus, many
of the Greek gods come from Egypt, and the Carians are partially responsible for hoplite armor (which seems to be an error).[9] This strictly mythical level will be left behind. At the beginning of his account, Herodotus
himself intends to narrate "the great and wonderful exploits of the
Greeks as well as of the barbarians." The opposition of Greek/Barbarian
is not racial but cultural and social, that is, between the slaves of law and
the slaves of a despot, and it does not exactly replicate, for example, the
opposition Europe/Asia. The very notion of Hellenism is, moreover, a
triumphant accomplishment of the generation of the Persian Wars. Before becoming the victor at Marathon, Miltiades had been in the service
of the Great King, and his case is not an isolated one. In the fourth
century, the concept of Hellenism continues to be cultural: a Greek is
someone who has received a Greek education, which someone born a
barbarian is capable of acquiring. But this notion changes bit by bit. For
Aristotle, a barbarian is someone who, *by nature,* is fit to be a slave. The
cultural patterns that will function in the Hellenistic age are now in
place.

The master/slave opposition, although it has something to do with the
preceding ones, appears as a creation of the civilization of the city-state.
There are certainly some "slaves" in the Homeric world, but the words
used to designate them are often the same as those that describe servants
whom we would call "free." At the very bottom of the social ladder the
slave is joined by the *thete,* an agricultural worker who was not attached to
the *oikos.* The concept of the slave is only worked out as the concept of the
citizen is developed, which is to say that it is not completely clear before
the sixth century B.C. Solon repatriated the Athenians who had been sold
into slavery for debt; the same gesture distinguished the Athenians, who
could never again be slaves, from others. Henceforth, the slave will
always be a foreigner. In the Classical period the slave is ubiquitous; his
presence seems to be a fundamental fact of nature. The language of the
fifth century fails to distinguish between two kinds of slaves, those
bought in a market (from foreign dealers, or after the capture of a town)
and the rural dependents. Still, the difference is obvious, if only because
the latter have some political rights while the former have none at all.
One can imagine a city of helots: Messene became a city again in the

fourth century although for three centuries its citizens had been reduced to helots. One cannot imagine, even in utopia, a city of slaves. Greek theoreticians became aware of this difference, certainly from the fourth century on. Plato knows that "it is better not to have slaves from the same nationality nor, if possible, those who speak the same language."[10] To put it another way, a slave should preferably be barbarian. Thus we are brought back to our earlier pair of opposites.[11]

A Pythagorean table of opposites[12] places the female element on the side of the boundless, the pair (the even numbers), the multiple, the left side, the dark, etc., in the realm of the uncivilized, whereas the male embodies civilization. This opposition was preserved as long as the civilization of the city endured.[13] "Who can tell the high daring of the male, the shameless loves, that always lead to disaster, of women with insolent hearts? The bond which holds couples together is treacherously broken by that unmastered lust that overwhelms the female, among men as among beasts."[14] The Greek city, that men's club, had included in its catalogue of opposites an exclusively feminine kingdom, that of the Amazons. Aristotle compares the domination of the soul over the body to that of the master over the slave, humans over animals, and the male over the female, and writes, moreover, "even a woman or a slave can be good although the woman is for the most part an inferior being, and the slave entirely so."[15] Plato did not advocate the equality of men and women but insofar as possible an equal use of them. Still, although the democratic city could not conceive of an independent city governed by slaves, there do exist utopias—or better, fantasy lands—ruled by women. Yet the women in power in Aristophanic comedy (*Lysistrata* and *Ecclesiazusae*) own slaves. The difference we have already noted in the attitude toward slaves between Athens and Sparta on the one hand and between Crete and the agrarian cities on the other is here particularly striking; some legends draw a connection between slaves' power and women's power (the founding of Tarentum or of Epizephyrian Locri). At Gortyn in Crete a free woman could contract a legally valid marriage with a slave; the young Spartiate girls participated in the same training and the same contests as the boys. Elsewhere, the citizen is defined as not a woman, just as he is not a slave and not a foreigner.

In Plato's *Laws*, childhood and youth are the uncivilized part of life, which one must adapt by directing its strength toward the service of society as a whole. The elders who oversee the ideal city (the "nocturnal council") will thus be escorted by a retinue of "scouts" whose ferocity will have been tempered with the help of incantations. The "principle of seniority"[16] is typical of the Hellenic world. At Sparta, the highest

6   authority belongs to the council of the elders, the *gerousia*, on a level with
that of the kings and ephors and greater than that of the Assembly. In
Athens, members of the *boulē* had to be thirty years old, and in the
Assembly the older men had the right to speak first (a feature that one can
already find in Homer). The time between childhood and adulthood,
which is the time of war and political life, becomes a period of trial and
initiation like that practiced by "primitive" societies. The Spartiate
krypteiai (secret missions) are composed of the elite youths, who roam the
mountains in winter and steal, deceive, and murder the helots before
becoming, by a brutal reversal of values, hoplites. In Crete the "squads"
of youths are set against the "companies" of adult men. In the myths,
hunting alone or in small groups, as well as trickery, are the tests imposed
on the young men. The locus is neither the city nor the country, but the
frontier region. We have several examples of two cities staging contests
between youths in the border areas near the sanctuaries. In Athens the
ephebe is also called *peripolos,* "one who patrols around." The ephebia is
known above all as a secularized version of military service, lasting two
years and spent mainly in the frontier forts; it was reorganized by Lycurgus after the battle of Chaeronea (338 B.C.). In certain circumstances the
ephebe wears a black cloak as a symbol of seclusion. He cannot take part
in any legal action, either as plaintiff or defendant, except when it
involves the recovery of an inheritance, an *epiklēros* (a daughter who is sole
heir to a family's estate), or a family priesthood. Aristotle explains the
rule by saying that a young man must not be distracted during his
military service.[17] As an explanation of the origin of this custom, it is
absurd, but this laicizing of a religious custom is important in itself as a
testimony to the high degree of rationalization obtained among the Athenians.[18] At the peak of its power, on the eve of the Sicilian Expedition
(415 B.C.), the Assembly of Athens had seen Nicias and Alcibiades confront
each other in the name of the old and the young.[19] Such a debate would have
been unthinkable in any place other than the great democratic city. Here a-
gain the Athenian endeavor goes beyond the pre-established cultural schema.

   In the world described by Homer, the boundary between civilization
and savagery is drawn not between city and country, but between a
landscape that has been cultivated and one that has not. The presence of a
polis (a fortified place) or of a demos (a small group of people that one can
barely call a village) is less significant as a sign of civilization than the
working of fields, of which the Cyclops was ignorant. In Hesiod the
peasant thinks of the town as a distant realm, seat of the "bribe-devour-
ing lords." In the world of the city-state, untamed countryside, the *agros*,
continues to exist in the form of frontier areas inhabited by woodcutters

and migrant shepherds. We have seen that the *krypteia* and the ephebia were associated with such zones; in the *agros* a dialogue exists between Dionysus and Hermes. Hermes represents the civilizing action of the society that clears well-defined roads: he is the god of the space that is open in comparison to the enclosed space of the hearth (*hestia*), symbolized by the prytaneum. Dionysus, on the other hand, represents the unleashing of savage nature that can overrun even the wheat fields of Demeter—a story told in Euripides' *Bacchae*. Ideally, in the city the contrast between town and country is suppressed, and Plato concludes from this fact that everyone ought to reside both at the center and in the periphery. But this truth has different implications in Sparta and in Athens, with other cities occupying intermediate positions. At Sparta the city as such does not exist, for the monumental civic center is barely sketched in. The public land (*chōra politikē*) is divided into lots cultivated for the benefit of the full Spartan citizens, the *homoioi*, or "peers." The main relation therefore is not between the town and the country, but between the warriors and their dependent serfs—not to speak of the inhabitants of the towns in Laconia. At Athens, on the other hand, the demesmen cultivate the land, with, in the Classical period, many more slaves than is usually supposed. The rural demes are simultaneously parts of the larger polis and themselves little cities that mirror the metropolis. The Peloponnesian War and Pericles' policy of surrendering the countryside to the enemy in order to defend the city later contribute to a profound crisis in the relations between the city and the country that is reflected in the work of Aristophanes.

In the fourth century a new type of urban life develops—as illustrated, for example, by the houses at Olynthus—inasmuch as life assumes an increasingly private character. Paradoxically, the growth of the fleet and of maritime trade is responsible for Athens' stability and instability: for stability, because the rural small-holders, who had been incorporated into the city by Solon and Cleisthenes, made up a large part of the fleet's crew and profited from the revenues of the "Empire;" for instability, because these revenues were gradually concentrated within the city. To relieve the pressure created by large numbers of people displaced by war and political upheaval, especially the mercenaries, Isocrates recommends not a newly restructured city, but the conquest and colonization of Asia. That is what will come to pass.

In Book 18 of the *Iliad*, Hephaistos engraves on the shield of Achilles the images of a city at peace and a city at war: weddings, feasts, and legal

8   proceedings in the former; siege and ambush in the latter. The besiegers hesitate between two courses of action: should they destroy the city and its inhabitants, or should they accept a ransom of the city's wealth? The dilemma recurred frequently throughout Greek history. The problem is ancient—it already appears in the "banner" of Ur in the third millennium—but the Greek solution is original. The "Hoplite reform" at the beginning of the seventh century was both consequence and cause of a far-reaching political transformation. "The first constitution was based on the warrier class, and even, at its outset, solely on the cavalry."[20] Once he takes part in battle, the hoplite moves to participate in political life as well.[21] The fact of war becomes all the more important because the city's very existence is threatened by war. It has been said—with considerable exaggeration, to be sure—that for the Greeks the state of war was the rule and peace the exception; indeed until 386 B.C. most Greek treaties that we know of were temporary agreements that included an alliance: other states were either allies or enemies. Thus we could as well describe the Greeks' wars as peace continued by other means. Military and civic institutions were closely parallel.

    The battlefield is an arable plain, and the site is agreed on by the two sides. Until Epaminondas's innovative tactics at the battle by Leuctra (371 B.C.), elite squadrons were massed on the right of the line.[22] The battle consisted of the collision of the two lines, after which the victor did not pursue the enemy but erected a trophy made of the captured weapons. Even the war against the Persians conformed somewhat to these conventions. In the line of battle, the solidarity of the soldiers, each protected by the shield of his neighbor, reproduces the solidarity of the city. The Peloponnesian War strikes a blow at these traditions; bands of mountain guerrillas stage surprise raids on the hoplite forces, with devastating effectiveness. The concept of general war is balanced by the concept of "common peace," first imposed by the King of Persia (386 B.C.), then maintained by the various hegemonic cities, until the day when, at Corinth in 337 B.C., the king of Macedon imposes his arbitrage. In the meantime the city had invented new forms of warfare. A revolution like that of Epaminondas, who attacked from the left wing, implies both the conquest of the idea of geometric space with no direction privileged, and the influence of naval warfare, which had long since been stripped of such taboos. The mercenaries of the Athenian general Iphicrates discover for themselves "black" warfare, the kind of tricks and ambush which, during the great era of the hoplites, had been restricted to the youths. Xenophon, the champion of antique values, is also a skilled practitioner of the new techniques. When called upon to choose between the new, technological warfare and the older, citizen-based mode, Plato decides against the former, whose conditions he described so clearly in Book 2 of the *Republic*. Its evolution, however, went on without him.

The contradiction between art (*technē*) and science (*epistēmē*) is one of the most deep-seated in Greek civilization. In the context of what has been called "the human history of nature"[23]—that is, the history of the natural world as it has been shaped and comprehended by man—Greek civilization belongs to the artisan. When Plato wishes to give a mythological account of the creation of the world, he attributes it to a demiurge, that is, an artisan. The artisan is the hidden hero of Greek history. From the Ceramicus of Athens to the sculptures of the Parthenon, from the dockyards in Piraeus to the surgeons of the Hippocratic school, indeed at the foundations of all the creations of the Greek world, one discovers the artisan. Still, the social historian reaches a completely different verdict. For him, the category of "artisan" does not exist.[24] During the construction of the Erechtheion, citizens, metics, and slaves worked side by side; they were all artisans, but from the social point of view, what separates them is much more important than what unites them. Hephaistos, god of *technē*, or craftsmanship, is also the god with a crippled leg. Prometheus, the inventor, the hero of "crafty thoughts," underlines by his ambiguous identity as both the liberator of mortals and the enemy of Zeus, the Greeks' ambivalence toward their "specialists," who did not exist as such in society. A famous choral ode of the *Antigone* celebrates the inventiveness of man—as navigator, plowman, domesticator of animals, and hunter—who is also compelled to include in his knowledge the laws of the world and the justice of the gods, without which he becomes *apolis,* that is "city-less." For the city is itself the exemplary social fact, wholly apart from any participation in production. Thus it is not surprising that Greek language and thought had no unified category of "work."[25] There was not even a word that clearly denoted "a worker." Xenophon distinguishes *technitēs*, a professional artisan, from *geōrgos*, a farmer;[26] yet, by the Hellenistic era, *technitēs* came to mean an actor, a professional artist.

Two occupations, farming and warfare, manage to avoid the kind of exclusion from social life that characterizes *technē*. But for the Greeks agriculture is in fact a *ponos*, a labor, not strictly speaking a *technē*. Agriculture, says Xenophon, is not knowledge or ignorance, or the "discovery of some clever process,"[27] but rather virtue and attention. The paradox is that this same author, who was a genuine technician in military affairs, puts warfare and agriculture in the same category, since he feels that both engage the whole community, whereas other arts are the

10   province of specialists, and the city does not recognize specialists as such. Nevertheless, by the fourth century the evolution of military tactics has some dramatic consequences that the city can no longer control. The debate that matches Plato against the sophists is a special act in this drama of technology. The sophists did not want to be technicians, but teachers of *aretē*, civic virtue. To the extent that it is useful for the citizen the sophists will teach a technique, that of rhetoric. When Hippias of Elis boasted that he had made all the clothing he wore, he was not endorsing training in practical skills but the ideal of self-sufficiency (*autarkeia*).[28] Nothing could be more contrary to the principle of division of labor, which was occasionally acknowledged and described, but not chiefly as a process contributing to production. In order to discredit his opponents, Plato reduces them to the rank of technicians, explaining in the *Gorgias* that sophistic rhetoric is cookery, not medicine.

The philosophers constructed theories about contrasting "styles of life," whose origins are in fact to be found in the aristocratic era and the poets. For Tyrtaeus of Sparta, courage is set apart from everything else. A fragment of Pindar sets glory in opposition to wealth and to the mercantile spirit symbolized by seafaring.[29] When Xenophanes of Colophon writes in the sixth century about the victors at the Olympic Games, "Our wisdom (*sophia*) is worth much more than the might of men and horses,"[30] he means political wisdom. When the crisis of the city occurred, and perhaps even earlier among the Pythagoreans, the life of the mind (*theōrētikos*) is contrasted with the pragmatic life and even with the life devoted to pleasure (*apolaustikos*); but no one created, even to disparage it, the category of the "technical" life. Plato opposes the organized knowledge (*epistēmē*) of the person who contemplates the ideal form of a bed with the imitative action (*mimēsis*) of the person who actually constructs it. In other words, this opposition is co-extensive with the history of the city.

Greek civilization is a civilization of discourse, and particularly of political discourse. The Greek rationality that distinguishes and orders pairs of oppositions is a political rationality. Spoken language triumphs even in writing, at least until the fifth century. The fourth century first sees the triumph of the bureaucratic style, a style that only requires filling in the blanks. Political speech is necessarily antithetical, for a political problem has to be settled by a Yes or a No. Perhaps the frequency with which Greeks thought in alternatives and oppositions has no other origin. A work like that of Thucydides is divided into speeches and narratives of events; at every moment of his account he makes use of the antithesis between *logos* (speech) and *ergon* (action). His work shows *gnōmē* (rational prediction) in conflict with *tychē* (chance), that same Tychē that will become the great goddess of the Hellenistic cities. Peace is conductive to gnōmē, as war is to *tychē*. The words *nomos* (law, convention, custom) and *physis* (nature) sum up these opposing concepts well. What is imposed by men is of the order of *nomos*. Callicles, in Plato's *Gorgias*, will invoke *physis* to justify the violence of the tyrant. In contrast, the physician who wrote the *Treatise on Diet*[31] believed that if man is capable of imitating nature by laying down laws, it is because the gods have created and arranged a nature that men imitate without realizing it. Thus "nature" can be simultaneously a source of disorder and of order (as for the Ionian and Italian "physicists"). This fact alone allows Greek civilization to transcend the oppositions in which people have imagined it confined.

In the area of moral values a good example is the pairing of *dikē* and *hybris*, justice and transgression. This pair informs one whole level of Hesiod's *Works and Days*, especially the famous Myth of the Races.[32] By the time of Solon and Anaximander, *dikē* and *hybris* had become words in the civic vocabulary that could also be applied to the very structure of the universe. In tragedy, every hero—Antigone as much as Creon—is possessed by *hybris* that opposes the equilibrium achieved by the city. In Thucydides, however, such tensions seem to vanish, although it has been said that he merely transferred to history the values of tragedy. His Alcibiades would be the *apatē*, the deceptive temptation offered to the *hybris* of the Athenians,[33] but Thucydides rationalizes this fact and inscribes the tragic values in the actual universe. Such is the process of Greek civilization. Its motion is not repetition but innovation and renewal. On the pediment of the ancient temple of Athena at Athens (c. 560 B.C.) Heracles, the civilizing hero, contends with Triton under the gaze of a triple-bodied monster. Some 120 years later, on the Parthenon savagery is still present in the metopes' depiction of the battle between the Lapiths and the Centaurs, but on the east pediment the sun rises and the moon sets in accordance with a fixed pattern; whereas on the west pediment, the conflict between Athena and Poseidon explodes in the center of a composition framed by Dionysus and Cephisus. The themes are the same, but now an ordered nature predominates, and Dionysus is included in the ceremonies presided over by the king-archon. It is true that this will be short-lived. One could link the two anecdotes told by Plutarch about Pericles:[34] "by holding up his cloak between himself and the sun, he debunked the superstitious fear inspired by an eclipse; but, when he was sick, he used to wear an amulet that some women had hung around his neck."

Introduction

1. H.-I. Marrou, "Civilisation," 327.
2. C. Lévi-Strauss himself is clear on this point: "The results yielded by the analysis of primitive myths lie on the very surface, if I may say so, of Greek myths" (in R. Bellour, "Entretien," 176).
3. Hesiod, *Works and Days* 276–78.
4. See below "Land and Sacrifice in the *Odyssey.*"
5. See M. Detienne and J.-P. Vernant (eds.), *Cuisine.*
6. See J.-L. Durand, "Délit."
7. See below "Plato's Myth of the Statesman."
8. Hdt. 2.35; Ephorus, *F. Gr. H.* 70, F42. F. Hartog's whole book (*Miroir*) is a consideration of the possibility of being barbarian in Herodotus's work; the example he uses is that of the Scythians.
9. Hdt. 2.49-58 (the gods); 1.171 (the Carians). On the latter tradition, see D. Fourgous, "Invention des armes."
10. Plato, *Laws* 6.777d.
11. See below: "Were Greek Slaves a Class?"; "Reflections on Greek Historical Writing about Slavery"; "Slavery and the Rule of Women."
12. Preserved in Aristotle, *Metaph.* A5, 986a 22–64.
13. See N. Loraux, "Race des femmes."
14. Aeschylus, *Libation Bearers* 595–601.
15. Aristotle *Poetics* 1454a 19–20, *Politics* I 1254a 16–19.
16. I borrow this term from the title of the work by P. Roussel.
17. Aristotle, *Ath. Pol.* 42.5.
18. See below: "The Black Hunter" and "Recipes for Greek Adolescence."
19. Thuc. 6.8–18.
20. Ar. *Pol.* 4.1297b 17–20.
21. See below "The Tradition of the Athenian Hoplite."
22. See below "Epaminondas the Pythagorean."
23. As in the title of Moscovici's *Essai.*
24. See below "A Study in Ambiguity: Artisans in the Platonic City."
25. Cf. A. Aymard, "Hiérarchie du travail," and J.-P. Vernant, "Works" 1 and 2.
26. See Xenophon *Oecon.* 6.6.
27. Xen. *Oecon.* 20.2, 5.
28. Cf. Plato, *Hippias Minor* 368b–c and the Suda *s.v. Hippias autarkeia;* see also J.-P. Vernant, "Technological Thought."
29. Pindar F 96 (Puech); on this type of opposition see R. Joly, *Genres de vie.*
30. Xenophanes F 2 (Diels) in Athenaeus 10.413d.
31. Hippocrates, *On Regimen* 1.11.
32. See J.-P. Vernant, "Myth of the Races" 1 and 2.
33. See F. M. Cornford, *Thucydides Mythistoricus.*
34. R. Rémondon, "Bilinguisme," 146, based on Plut. *Pericles* 35, 38.

I   Space and Time

Land and Sacrifice in the *Odyssey:*
A Study of Religious
and Mythical Meanings

This is an essay about land. Perhaps paradoxically, I begin with some details taken not from Homer, but from Hesiod. Contrary to common opinion, both the *Theogony* and *Works and Days* can be used to elucidate not merely works composed after them but also those works that antedate them or are more or less contemporary with them—as is perhaps the case with the *Odyssey.*

I believe that the "myth of the races" and the myth of Pandora in the *Works and Days,* and the myth of Prometheus in that poem and in the *Theogony,* justify a definition that could be termed both anthropological and normative, both exclusive and inclusive. The exclusion is twofold. Hesiodic man is the man of the age of iron, which means in the first place that he is *not* the man of the age of gold, the mythical time when men "lived like gods," knowing neither old age nor true death: "They had all good things, and the grain-giving earth (*zeidōros aroura*) unforced bore them fruit abundantly and without stint. They pastured their lands (*erg'enemonto*) in ease and peace, with many good things" (*WD* 112–19). [1] The distinction between the age of gold and our own that I wish to study here—there are others—is that of work versus nonwork (agricultural work, of course). [2] As compared with the age of iron, the age of gold—the age of Cronos—is an absolute model; it is a condition the other ages can never hope to attain. The lot of the race of the age of gold during their

Published in an earlier version in *Annales, E.S.C.* 25 (1970): 1278–97; then in M. I. Finley (ed.), *Problèmes de la Terre en Grèce ancienne* (1973): 269–92.

lives is enjoyed by the race of heroes, or at least by some of them, after death: Zeus places them "apart from men" (*dich'anthrōpōn*) and apart from the gods, "under the rule of Cronos, at the ends of the earth." "And they dwell untouched by sorrow in the islands of the Blessed along the shore of the deep swirling Ocean, happy heroes for whom the grain-giving earth bears honey-sweet fruit flourishing thrice a year."[3] The age of gold in "time" is succeeded here by an age of gold in "space," in the islands of the Blessed, which are characterized also by the richness of the earth.

Elsewhere, in the myth of Pandora,[4] Hesiod summarizes in advance, as it were, the lesson of the myth of the races: "Before this the tribes of men lived on earth remote and free from ills and hard toil (*chalepoio ponoio*) and heavy sickness which bring the *Kēres* upon men: for in misery men grow old quickly" (*WD* 90–93).[5]

To have been excluded from the age of gold means that man is not a god.[6] But he is not an animal either; and the second exclusion bars him from *allēlophagia,* cannibalism: "For the son of Cronos has ordained this law for men, that fishes and beasts and winged birds should devour one another, for Right (*dikē*) is not in them" (*WD* 276–78). The practice of *dikē* is what enables man to escape from the animal state: man is the creature that does not eat its fellows.

The inclusions are closely related—simultaneously inverse and complementary—to the exclusions. The *Works and Days* itself is about the working of arable land and all that is implied by it: the planting of trees and the rearing of animals, especially for plowing. *Dikē* is a means of regaining—perhaps not the age of gold, for men are obliged to labor— but at least prosperity and fruitfulness in human beings, land, and flocks: "The earth gives them [i.e., those who practice *dikē*] a life of plenty, and on the mountains the oak bears acorns on high, and in the midst, bees. Their fleecy sheep are laden with wool; their women bear children resembling their fathers. They flourish continually with good things; and do not travel on ships, for the grain-giving earth bears them fruit" (*WD* 232–37).[7]

This human work is linked in turn to the possession (thanks to Prometheus) of fire for cooking, that fire which had previously been concealed by Zeus (*WD* 47–50). In revenge for the theft of fire, at Zeus's command Hephaistos made Pandora, who is both earth and woman (*WD* 59–105).[8] The hints contained in *Works and Days* are filled out by the *Theogony.* The quarrel between gods and men at Mekone has two carefully paralleled episodes.[9] The first incident consists of the primordial sacrifice of an ox and its unequal division, the gods receiving the smoke and men the flesh, which results in the confiscation of fire by Zeus and its theft by

Prometheus. Second, man is given the ambiguous gift of woman, to make up for the gods' acceptance of the state of affairs brought about by Prometheus. Arable land, cooking, sacrifice, and sexual and family life within the *oikos*—even, at one extreme, political life—form a complex, no element of which can be separated from the others. These are the terms that define man's estate, in between the age of gold and *allēlophagia*, cannibalism. [10]

The limits marked out here by Hesiod, with their characteristic features (which are also features of the crisis of this period) are repeatedly employed throughout subsequent Greek thought. From the end of the sixth century B.C. in particular, these patterns were taken up in the violent political disputes that divided the Greek world and led theorists to adopt contrasting "positive" or "negative" views of primitive man; the age of gold jostles against the theme of the misery of primeval man. One might be tempted—and some scholars have not resisted the temptation—to trace these disputes back to the time of Hesiod and to portray Hesiod himself as an opponent of progress. [11] It is not perceptibly more plausible to make him both a supporter of "chronological primitivism" (because he starts with an age of gold) and an opponent of "cultural primitivism" (in that he contrasts civilization with cannibalism). [12] For these two positions are in fact one.

It is not my intention to discuss this post-Hesiodic literature here. [13] I note simply, for reasons that will shortly become clear, that Hesiod's age of gold, the age of Cronos, the "vegetarian" age before cooking and before sacrifice, which is described for us in so many texts, [14] is also the period of cannibalism and human sacrifice in at least part of the tradition. Some of the texts that make this association between opposites may seem very late, [15] but we should not forget that as early as the fourth century B.C. the Cynics developed a theory of a "natural" way of life that both condemned the eating of dead flesh and cooked food and championed raw food, cannibalism, and even incest, the opposite *par excellence* of culture. [16] And it would be wrong to see this as merely a view held by theorists: Euripides' *Bacchae* oscillates between the atmosphere of paradise described by the messenger early on in his speech and the orgy of flesh-eating which culminates in the quasi-incestuous murder of Pentheus by his mother (*Bacchae* 677–768, 1043–47). Hesiod's Cronos is also a god who eats his own children (*Theog.* 459–67). [17] From this perspective, it is Plato who is "theorizing" when in the *Politicus* he chooses to define the age of Cronos as the time when cannibalism was unknown—a choice that happens to be the same as that made by Hesiod in his version of the myth of the races. [18]

18   If we begin from the other end, we find agriculture intimately linked with cooking, as for example in the Hippocratic treatise *On Ancient Medicine* 3 (ed. Festugière), where it is shown that the cultivation of cereals, which replaced the eating of raw foods, is founded upon a form of food that has to be cooked. An association between agriculture, family life, and the origin of civilization similar to that implied by Hesiod also occurs in the Athenian myths about Cecrops, who, guided by Bouzyges ("Ox-team Man"),[19] invented agriculture, and also invented the monogamous patriarchal family.[20] The purpose of this essay is to see whether such associations already existed in Homer.

When Odysseus realizes that he is at last on Ithaca, his first action is to "kiss the grain-giving earth in a greeting to his native land": Χαίρων ἦ γαίη, κύσε δὲ ζείδωρον ἄρουραν (*Od.* 13.354).[21] Now this is not merely the act of a man returning to his native land: it contains a fundamental point that deserves close analysis.

In talking about the *Odyssey*, we have to make further distinctions: not between the compositions of different bards detected by "analytic" critics in the light of criteria that differ with every scholar and produce results at once predictably divergent and fatally untestable, but between units that have a significance in the poem as we have it. To put it crudely, we cannot discuss Cyclops or Calypso in the same way that we discuss Nestor or Telemachus. In effect, as has often been recognized, the *Odyssey* contrasts a "real" world, essentially the world of Ithaca, but also Sparta and Pylos to which Telemachus goes, with a mythical world that is roughly conterminous with that of the stories in Alcinous's palace.[22] (Similarly, Shakespeare's *Tempest* contrasts Naples and Milan on the one hand with Prospero's magic island on the other.[23]) Odysseus enters this mythical world after his stay with the Cicones, a perfectly real Thracian people known to Herodotus (7.58, 108, 110), in whose territory he eats, fights, and plunders just as he might have done at Troy, and after a ten-day storm[24] that he encounters while rounding Cape Malea, the last "real" place on his travels before he gets back to Ithaca.[25]

Proof that this contrast is indeed relevant is supplied by the text itself. Telemachus's route never crosses that of Odysseus. There are two points of contact only between the two worlds. One is plainly magical: Menelaus tells Odysseus's son how he was informed by the magician Proteus, in Egypt, the land of wonders, that Odysseus was detained on Calypso's island (4.555–58; 17.138–44).[26] The other is the land of the Phaeacians, professional seamen who have been shown to occupy a strategic place at the junction of the two worlds.[27] I need hardly press the point. Odysseus's travels have nothing to do with geography, and there is more geographical truth in the "untrue" stories he tells Eumaeus and Penelope (14.191–359; 19.164–202)[28] than in all the stories in Alcinous's palace.[29] Crete, Egypt, and Epirus are real enough.

For Odysseus, leaving this fantasy world means leaving a world that is not the world of men, a world that is by turns superhuman and subhuman, a world in which he is offered divinity by Calypso but also threatened by Circe with reduction to the condition of an animal. And he must leave it to return to the world of normality. The *Odyssey* as a whole is in one sense the story of Odysseus's return to normality, of his deliberate acceptance of the human condition.[30]

There is therefore no paradox in saying that, from the Lotus-Eaters to Calypso by way of the land of the Cyclopes and the Underworld, Odysseus meets with no creature that is strictly human. There is of course sometimes room for doubt: the Laestrygones, for example, have an agora, the mark of political life, but physically they are not as men are, but giants (10.114, 120). Circe causes us to wonder whether we are dealing with a woman or a goddess: but finally, just as with Calypso, the humanity is merely in the outward form, in the voice. She is in truth *deinē theos audēessa*, the "terrible goddess with a human voice" (10.136; 11.8; 12.150, 449; cf. 10.228). Twice Odysseus asks himself what "eaters of bread" he has landed among—that is, what men; however, in each case the point is that he is not among "bread-eaters," but among the Lotus-Eaters and the Laestrygones (9.89; 10.101).[31]

There follows from this a signal implication, that the "stories" rigorously exclude anything to do with working the land, or with arable land itself insofar as it is worked.[32] The Thrace of the Cicones is the last cultivated land Odysseus encounters: there he eats mutton and drinks wine, and there he obtains the wine he later offers the Cyclops (9.45 ff., 161–65, 197–211).[33] Euripides' Odysseus, when he comes to an unknown land, asks Silenus, "Where are the walls and the city towers?" The answer comes: "Stranger, this is no city. No man dwells here" (*Cyclops* 115–16).[34] Here fortifications are the symbol of the presence of civilized humanity, or indeed of humanity at all. But Homer's Odysseus looks for cultivated fields, for the sign of human labor.[35] When the Achaeans reach Circe's island, they search in vain for the *erga brotōn*, the "works of men," that is, for crops. But all they see is scrub and forest, where staghunts can be organized (10.147, 150, 157–63, 197, 251). In the land of the Laestrygones, the sight of smoke might be taken as evidence of domestic hearths and the presence of human beings (10.99),[36] but there

20   is "no trace either of the work of oxen or of the work of men": ἔνθα μὲν
οὔτε βοῶν οὔτ' ἀνδρῶν φαίνετο ἔργα (10.98). The Sirens live in a meadow, as do the gods elsewhere (12.159).[37] Although Calypso's island is
wooded and even possesses a vine, this is never said to be cultivated
(1.51, 5.63–74).

There is one specifically human tree present in the world of the "stories": the olive, the tree of whose wood Odysseus built his bed, the fixed
point of his home (23.183–204). In fact, the olive is on occasion the
means of Odysseus's escape from danger, in several different forms. It
provides the stake with which he bores through the Cyclops' eye and the
handle of the axe with which he builds his boat (9.319–20; 5.234–
36).[38] And, although it is true that when he is with Aeolus, Circe, or
Calypso, Odysseus has plenty to eat, and that the poet playfully draws
attention to the vast difference between the gods' meals and those of men
(5.196–99), we are never told where the food comes from or who produced it.

A second exclusion is entailed by the exclusion of cultivated land: that
of the sacrificial meal, which we saw from Hesiod to be so intimately
related to the first. One could almost, in a sense, extend to the entire
world of the stories the remark Hermes jokingly makes to Calypso when
he arrives on her island: "Who would choose to cross this waste of
saltwater? There is not in these parts a single city of mortal men to offer
rich hecatombs to the gods" (5.100–102). But only in a sense. For the
sacrifice that Odysseus offers to the dead in accordance with Circe's
instructions and with lambs she has provided is performed in a trench and
is intended to provide blood for the feeding of the dead (10.516–40,
571–72; 11.26–47)—it is the opposite of a sacrificial meal, whose
purpose is to feed the living. And the same is true of the victims Odysseus
promises to offer the dead and Teiresias on his return: a barren cow and a
black ram (10.521–25; 11.29–33).

In the land of the Cyclopes, Odysseus's companions offer sacrifice
(9.231; *ethusamen*), as Polyphemus himself does not, but it is not a blood-
sacrifice because they are living on cheese (9.232).[39] And the sacrifice
they offer on the island just across from that of the Cyclopes—which is
abnormal because the victims are the sheep belong to Polyphemus, animals not reared by man—is rejected by Zeus (9.551–55); even when a
human community does sacrifice in nonhuman territory, the sacrifice is
improper.

We should now go back over Odysseus's journey and examine more or less in sequence the several types of nonhuman creature he meets. I take it for granted that Scylla and the inhabitants of the Underworld are not human: Achilles has made the point so that we shall not forget (11.488–91). Similarly, the Lotus-Eaters are not bread-eaters: they eat flowers, and the food they offer Odysseus's companions deprives them of an essential facet of their humanity, memory (9.84, 94–97). Except during the encounter with Scylla (12.227), Odysseus is constantly the man who remembers in the poem, the true man who stands out from his forgetful companions.

Much more difficult are the problems presented by the Cyclops episode. For here the mythical aspects with which I am concerned are conflated with a quasi-ethnographical description of pastoral peoples (nonhumanity may be just a different sort of humanity: savages)[40] and with an overt, realistic reference to colonization. If these men had been sailors, "they would have made their island a well-built place. The land is not bad; it would bear crops in each season. By the shores of the grey sea are soft, well-watered meadows, where vines would never wither, and there would be rich harvests every year, so rich is the soil under the surface" (9.130–35). This vision remains unfulfilled. The land of the Cyclopes is divided, it will be remembered, into two different areas. One is the "small island," which is utterly wild and where hunting is unknown. There Odysseus's companions find memorable sport (9.116–24, 131–35). The other is the land of the Cyclopean shepherds. Such a division implies a hierarchy: cultivators–hunters–shepherds, and it may be relevant to note that the same series recurs later in Aristotle (*Pol.* 1.8.1256a 30–40). But the Cyclopes are not merely barbarous herdsmen who lack political institutions and are ignorant of planting and plowing (9.108–15). Conditions on their land are very close to Hesiod's age of gold: "They do not plant or plow, but the earth provides them with all things: grain, vines, and wine from heavy clusters of grapes, which Zeus's rain swells for them" (9.109–11; cf. 123–24). Although they have sheep, they have no true draft animals: there are "no herds or plows" on the island (9.122). So it is, even if we may suspect that the vintages of the golden age lacked breeding (9.111, 357–59).

However, the real point is that the counterpart of the age of gold is cannibalism.[41] The details are so curious that it is impossible to believe that they are not intentional. Polyphemus brings in wood to make a fire for supper, but he does not use it: he is not an eater of bread, and even the humans he eats he does not cook as we might expect. He devours them raw, like a lion: "entrails, flesh, bones, marrow—he left nothing" (9.190–92, 234, 292–93).[42] Equally, he performs none of the actions characteristic of a sacrificial meal, for example the setting aside of the bones for the gods; and in any case the relations of these golden-age cannibals with the gods are fundamentally ambiguous. Homer stresses both that the Cyclopes trust in the gods (*pepoithotes athanatoisin;* 9.107)—which allows them not to plow or sow; and Odysseus will later have cause to rue the kinship of Polyphemus and Poseidon (1.68–73)—and that Polyphemus treats appeal in the name of Zeus Xenios [who protects strangers and guests] with total indifference: "The Cyclopes have no regard for Zeus who bears the aegis, nor for the blessed gods" (9.275–76). This detail bears a little further attention. The author of the *Iliad* seems to know of good Cyclopes, the *abioi* (without food), who milk mares and live on the milk, and are the "most just of men" (*Il.* 13.5–6). These men, now called *gabioi,* reappear as Scythians in Aeschylus's *Prometheus Unbound* (F 196 Nauck²).⁴³ They too are "the most just of men and the most generous to strangers. They possess neither the plow nor the hoe, which break the earth and score the plowland. Their furrows seed themselves [*autosporoi guai*] and give men food which never fails." Later, Homer's literary heirs elaborated the theme of the Cyclopes' way of life as part of the picture of the "noble savage,"⁴⁴ but the inheritance was not solely literary. When Ephorus (*FGrH* 70 F 42) contrasted two types of Scythians—actually referring to Homer's *abioi*—one of them cannibal, the other vegetarian (τοὺς δὲ καὶ τῶν ἄλλων ζῴων ἀπέχεσθαι: "they reject [all] living things"),⁴⁵ he was rationalizing and locating geographically a mythical opposition that is also an equivalent. The vegetarian is no less inhuman than the cannibal.⁴⁶

The island of Aeolus offers us another type of the nonhuman that is no less classic. The details are worth lingering upon for a moment. It is a "floating island" with bronze walls. There is naturally no cultivated land, although there is a polis, in perpetual banquet, but the feast is not sacrificial, and the bull in whose hide the winds are imprisoned is not offered to the gods (*Od.* 10.3–19). Of course it is incest that is the oddest thing about Aeolus's island: there is no exchange of women. The six daughters of Aeolus and his wife are married to their brothers (10.6–7). This is a closed world, where one banquets by day and sleeps at night (10.10–12). It is not a human *oikos.*

The Laestrygones look in some ways like another version of the Cyclopes, although the metaphor here is not hunting but fishing—they harpoon the Greeks like tuna fish and then eat them (10.115–16, 121–24). On Circe's island, nature presents itself at first as a hunting-park and Odysseus kills an enormous stag (10.168: *deinoio pelōriou;* 10.171: *mega thērion;* cf. 180).⁴⁷ Nonhumanity is here revealed in two forms, that of divinity and that of bestiality. The latter is itself twofold: Circe's victims are changed into wild animals, lions, and wolves, which nevertheless behave like domestic dogs (10.212–19). Circe has a drug added to the bread[48] served to Odysseus's companions, which turns them into pigs, although they retain their memory (10.239–43). Odysseus escapes this fate by taking with him a plant, the famous *moly,* which itself perfectly symbolizes the theme of reversal: "Its root is black, its flower the color of milk" (10.304).[49] Whereas Odysseus's companions regain their shape, the men who had been turned into wild animals do not. The episode thus contains a clear hierarchy: men–domestic animals–wild animals. This last category has no connection with humanity and cannot be restored to it even by magical means.[50]

The Cimmerians, whose land borders on the country of the dead, are nonhuman, in spite of possessing a demos and a polis, in that they never behold the sun, just like the dead (11.14–19). The Sirens are a fiercer version of the Lotus-Eaters. To surrender to their seduction means never to return home (12.41–45), but, like the Lotus-Eaters, they can be foiled. These are the only two of Odysseus's passages that he endures without harm. But if the Cyclops is to humanity what the raw is to the cooked, the Sirens belong to the rotten: their victims' corpses rot uneaten in the meadow (12.45–46).[51]

The episode of the herds of the sun, heralded in advance at the beginning of the poem (1.8–9), merits closer attention. The cattle and sheep are immortal, that is, they do not share the condition of the animals humans use for farm-work and sacrifice. Just as Calypso and Circe appear to be human, and just as the dead can pass as beings of flesh and blood at first sight, the herds of the sun appear domestic: they are protected only by the prohibition against sacrificing them. While Odysseus and his companions still have bread and wine, they respect the interdict (12.327–29), but with their supplies exhausted they must make a choice, between wild nature—to hunt and fish (the legitimate alternative, which Odysseus chooses: 12.330–32)—and the forbidden herds, which involves the sacrifice, the classification as "domestic," of animals that they have to capture, to bring in from the wild. This latter is the choice of Odysseus's companions (12.343–65). We should note how Homer emphasizes the sacrificers' lack of the essential requisites for proper sacrifice: the barleycorns (*oulai* or *oulochytai*) for sprinkling on the animal before its throat is cut are replaced by oak leaves (12.357–58),[52] the "natural" substituted for the "cultural"; the wine for the libations is similarly replaced by water (12.362–63).[53] The manner in which they perform the sacrifice itself also renders it an anti-sacrifice, and later, the

24   flesh, both raw and cooked, begins to groan (12.395–96). But of course: these herds are immortal; man's share of the sacrifice is the meat of the dead animal, the remainder passing to the gods. The herds of the sun are utterly unsuitable for sacrifice, and the companions of Odysseus do not escape unpunished for their sacrilege.[54]

The last stage of the hero's travels in the land of myth—he is now quite alone—sees him on Calypso's island, the navel of the sea (1.50). Here he is offered the possibility of becoming immortal, by marrying the goddess (5.135–36; 23.335–36). Now the point of this, as I have said, is that on Calypso's island the normal means of communication between men and gods, sacrifice, is unknown. Calypso can indeed dream of a code-breaking union, but she herself recalls earlier attempts that ended disastrously: Eos (Dawn) and the hunter Orion and Demeter and the farmer Iasion (5.121–28). And although the ancient allegorists understood the island as a symbol of the body, of the matter from which man's soul must free itself,[55] Homer's text scarcely supports such a reading. When he quits Calypso, Odysseus is deliberately choosing the human way over all that is nonhuman.[56]

In contrast to this world whose features I have just sketched, Ithaca, Pylos, and Sparta belong undoubtedly to the "grain-giving earth."[57] Although Ithaca, the "island of goats," is unable to support horses like Sparta (4.605–6), it is nevertheless a grain-producing land, and a land where the vine grows: "It has grain and wine in quantity beyond telling, rain in all seasons and heavy dews, a good land for goats . . . a land good for cattle" (13.244–46).[58] As a famous, and archaizing, passage affirms, it is for the king that "the dark earth bears wheat and barley, and the trees are heavy with fruit; the flocks bear without fail; the friendly sea brings forth fish under his good rule, and the people thrive under him" (19.111–14).[59] Odysseus's wheat, barley, wine, and livestock are, no less than Penelope, the prize in his dispute with the suitors. To return to Ithaca is thus to return to a land of grain. But Ithaca is not sufficiently land-locked: it is not here that Odysseus will one day meet death "far from the sea"; he will have to go beyond Ithaca, pressing on inland until men mistake an oar for a winnowing-shovel (11.127–28; 23.274–75).[60] There a threefold sacrifice to Poseidon will call a halt to his wanderings, and stability will prevail over movement.

Nor do I need to stress that Pylos and Sparta are corn-raising and stock-breeding countries (3.495; 4.41, 602–4, etc). But this fact does not make the three different places all of a kind. Pylos is the land of perpetual sacrifice, the model of a religious country: Nestor is sacrificing to Poseidon when Telemachus makes his appearance—all the ritual details are mentioned (3.5–9)—and a little later it is Athena's turn (3.380–84, 418–63).[61] At Sparta things are a little different, and we find features belonging to the world of myth. Menelaus's palace is different from Odysseus's but like that of Alcinous; with its decoration of ivory and amber, it is a residence worthy of Zeus (compare 4.71–75 and 7.86–90). At Sparta, as on Scheria, there are objects made by Hephaistos (4.615–19; 15.113–19; 7.91–94). Sacrifice at Sparta is retrospective: Menelaus mentions a hecatomb he had to make during the journey when he learned that Odysseus was on Calypso's island, which thus connects with the world of myth (4.352–53, 472–74, 477–79, 581–83). Again, unlike Odysseus's, Menelaus's destiny is not death, but that other golden age, the Elysian Fields (4.561–69).[62] And there is another respect in which Pylos and Sparta contrast with Ithaca: they are orderly kingdoms, where the sovereign and his wife are present, where the treasure-house is not looted, and where the ordinary rules of social life are respected. When Telemachus arrives at Sparta, Menelaus is celebrating the marriage of his son (4.3–14). In contrast, on Ithaca society is in crisis: the three generations of the royal family are represented by an old man (whose exclusion from the throne becomes slightly mysterious when we compare him with Nestor), a woman, and an adolescent youth, who is portrayed as slightly backward (1.296–97).[63] A society upside down, a society in a crisis symbolized by the revolt of the *kouroi*, the young aristocrats, and waiting for the reestablishment of order.

Sacrifice here turns out to be both the sign of the crisis and the means of its resolution. Who makes sacrifice on Ithaca? If our sole criterion is the use of the words *hiereuō* and *spendō* and related terms, the answer is everyone—both the suitors and Odysseus and his followers.[64] But if we examine the texts in which sacrifice is specifically addressed to the gods, we find that the suitors do not sacrifice. More precisely, one of them does suggest a libation to the gods, but this is Amphinomus, the one suitor whom Odysseus attempts to exclude from the coming massacre.[65] Antinous suggests a sacrifice to Apollo according to the rules, with the thighs burnt, but he is unable to fulfill his promise.[66] In contrast, on Odysseus's side, sacrifice, either retrospective or immediate, is perpetual. Eumaeus's piety is stressed: "The swineherd did not forget the immortals; he had a good heart" (14.420–21).[67] The comparison certainly suggests that we have to allow that *hiereuō* sometimes has a meaning that is not specifically religious.[68] More importantly, sacrifice is a double criterion in the *Odyssey:* of humanity, between humans and nonhumans; and of social and moral values, between human beings.

But there is in the human world of Ithaca at least one place directly

26 connected with the world of the myths—the complex consisting of the harbor of Phorcys, named after Cyclops' own grandfather (1.71–72; 13.96–97),[69] and the cave sacred to the Nymphs, the divinities of nature and of water. This cave has two entrances, one for the gods and the other for mortals (13.109–12). Appropriately enough, just near it is a sacred olive tree, under which Athena speaks to Odysseus (13.122, 372), and it is here that the Phaeacians leave Odysseus and his treasures.

Charles Segal has observed that the Phaeacians are "between the two worlds": they are placed at the intersection of the world of the tales and the "real" world, and their main function in the poem is to transport Odysseus from the one to the other.[70] When Odysseus comes ashore in Phaeacia, naked, after completing, or almost completing, his return journey home "without the help of gods or mortal men" (5.32),[71] he takes shelter under an olive tree. But this olive tree is remarkable: it is double, *ho men phyliēs, ho d'elaiēs*, both wild and grafted, oleaster and olive (5.477).[72] The very land of Scheria is double, comparable at once both with Ithaca, Pylos and Sparta and with the lands of the stories. Phaeacia contains all the characteristic elements of a Greek settlement in the age of colonization, physically framed as it is by the "shadowy peaks" that can be seen from afar (5.279–80). It has arable land distributed by a founder (*edassai arouras;* 6.10).[73] Its fields are beyond doubt the "works of men": *agrous . . . kai erg'anthrōpōn*, "fields and human tillage" (6.259)—exactly what Odysseus has looked for in vain in all his travels. It has a fortified citadel distinct from the fields: *polis kai gaia* (6.177, 191; also 6.3: *dēmon te polin te*). The country has wine, oil, and corn in abundance: Alcinous has a flourishing vineyard of his own (6.77–79, 99, 215, 259, 293; cf. 7.122–26). In sum, the Phaeacians are men just like other men, and they "know the cities and rich fields of all men" (8.560–61). When Odysseus lands in Phaeacia, he is returning to humanity. As he draws near to Nausicaa, he is likened to a lion that descends from the hills and kills livestock or deer, but when he leaves Phaeacia to return to Ithaca, he is likened to a tired plowman returning home (6.130–33; 13.31–35).

However, at the same time Phaeacia is sharply contrasted with Ithaca. There are no seasons in Alcinous's magic garden (7.113–32).[74] The west wind blows there perpetually, and the vine bears blossom and unripe and ripened grapes simultaneously. In effect, it is not ordinary orchard, but a golden-age land in the heart of Phaeacia. By contrast, Laertes' garden is normal: "each vine had its own time to be harvested, and the clusters of grapes were of every color, as the seasons of Zeus caused them to change" (24.342–44).[75] On the one hand, the age of Cronos; on the other, the age of Zeus.[76] The contrast can be developed. The dogs guarding Alcinous's house and the creations of Hephaistos in gold and silver are immortal, and naturally possess eternal youth; but everyone remembers the story of the dog Argo, whose life is exactly commensurate with the period of Odysseus's absence (7.91–94; 17.290–327).[77]

And what of sacrifices here? They are performed in Phaeacia much as they are at Pylos or on Ithaca. "We shall offer choice victims to the gods," declares Alcinous (7.191; cf. 7.180–81). Before Odysseus's departure an ox is sacrificed in the proper manner (13.24–27; cf. 50–56, libations to Zeus). And when the Phaeacians are threatened with destruction by Poseidon and Zeus combined, their fate turns on the result of the sacrifice that Alcinous decides to offer them: "and they prepared the bulls" (*etoimassanto de taurous;* 13.184). This is the last act of the Phaeacians recounted in the *Odyssey,* and we never discover their fate—the only case of a fate left in the balance. Yet, even here, the Phaeacians are not like other men. Alcinous can say: "When we sacrifice our magnificent hecatombs to the gods, they come and sit by us and eat with us" (7.201–3).[78] That sort of sharing has nothing in common with normal sacrifice, which, in contrast, separates men from the gods.[79] The Phaeacians are of course men: Alcinous and Odysseus remind each other of their mortality (7.196–98; 13.59–62), and the Phaeacians' last appearance in the poem clearly shows them facing the precariousness of the human condition, but they are also *ankhitheoi,* "relatives of the gods"—not merely a polite epithet, for Homer uses it twice only, and both times of them (5.93; 19.279). They were once neighbors of the Cyclopes and suffered from their attacks until Nausithoös set them "apart from men who eat bread" (*hekas andrōn alphēstaōn;* 6.4–8); indeed, in one sense they are the complete reverse of the Cyclopes.[80] All their human virtues, the practice of hospitality,[81] piety, the arts of feasting and gift-giving, are the inverse of Cyclopean barbarism. Moreover, the present disjuncture and previous proximity of the Phaeacians and the Cyclopes are signs of a more subtle relation: "We are intimates [of the gods]," says Alcinous, "like the Cyclopes and the savage tribes of the Giants" (*hōsper Kyklōpes te kai agria phyla Gigantōn;* 7.205–6)—those same Giants whom the Laestrygones are said to resemble (10.120). Proximity and kinship: surely an invitation to search in Phaeacia for both the pattern of the world of fantasy and its reverse.

After landing in Alcinous's country, Odysseus meets a girl washing clothes, who invites him to come and meet her father and mother (7.290–307). He had met another girl, elsewhere, drawing water from a spring, who gave him a similar invitation, but she was the daughter of the king of the Laestrygones. Both in the cannibal and in the hospitable

28   kingdom Odysseus meets the queen before he meets the king (10.105–15; 7.139–54; cf. 7.53–55). And is Nausicaa a girl or a goddess? A cliché, of course; but we must realize that she is a girl who looks like a goddess, while Circe and Calypso were goddesses who looked like girls (6.16, 66–67, 102–9; 7.291; 8.457).[82] Alcinous, and very discreetly Nausicaa herself, entertain ideas of her marriage to Odysseus, parallel to the goddesses' more energetically prosecuted plans. The seductive Sirens sing like bards of the Trojan War (12.184–91), just like Demodocus at the court of Alcinous, who brings tears to Odysseus's eyes (8.499–531). The first represent the perilous, Demodocus the positive, aspect of poetry.[83]

It will no doubt be objected that there is a limit to the number of utterly different situations a man like Odysseus can encounter. That is true, but there is one coincidence that is perhaps more than usually curious. Before meeting with his eventual carriers, the Phaeacians, Odysseus encounters another, who brought him to the neighborhood of Ithaca—Aeolus, master of the winds (10.21), who spends his time, like the Phaeacians, in feasting. In the course of both "returns" Odysseus falls asleep; disastrously after his sojourn with Aeolus, fortunately after Scheria (10.23–55; 13.78–92).[84] Now it will be recalled that Aeolus's family practice incest, and, if we are to accept the lines that introduce the genealogy of Alcinous and Arete, the same is true of the Phaeacian royal couple: 'Ἀρήτη δ' ὄνομ' ἐστὶν ἐπώνυμον, ἐκ δὲ τοκήων τῶν αὐτῶν οἵπερ τέκον 'Αλκίνοον βασιλῆα "Arete [the well adapted] is the name she is called, and she comes of the same parents as in fact produced the king Alcinous" (7.54–55; tr. Lattimore, slightly altered). The rest of the text as we have it (55–56) corrects the inevitable impression by claiming that Arete is not Alcinous's sister but his niece; but in this case there is some justification for invoking the hypothesis of interpolation.[85]

All the same, the "mythical" aspect of Scheria is counterbalanced by what I have termed the "real" world. I have already shown this for land and sacrifice, but the point can be extended to its entire social organization. The social institutions of Pylos, of Sparta, and of Ithaca particularly, are to be found on Scheria,[86] and the details of palace organization are identical in Ithaca and Alcinous's court: is it an "accident" that there are fifty servants in Alcinous's house, and the same number in Odysseus's (22.421–22; 7.103), and the same with everything else?[87] But these categories do not produce identical societies. For example, although there is at least one "angry young man" on Scheria, Euryalus, who insults Odysseus, he is compelled to apologize (8.131–415, esp. 396–415). One could hardly find a swineherd, a cowman, or a goatherd in Phaeacia, and there would be no chance of finding on Ithaca those professional sailors who steer infallibly without the aid of pilots (7.318–28; 8.555–63, 566; 16.277–31; cf. 16.322–27). Ithaca is an island whose men once went in ships, but it is in no sense a country of sailors, for all that Odysseus has acquired the necessary skill. Once back in harbor, he puts the equipment of his ship to purely static use—as when the ship's cable is used to hang the faithless servant girls (22.465–73).

Yet Phaeacia is at once an ideal and an impossible society: Homer, at the height of the Dark Age crisis of monarchy, pictures a king who can restore peace, who rules over twelve obedient vassals (8.390–91), over docile sons, over a wife whose role, despite claims to the contrary, is limited to intercession,[88] and over old men whose sole function is to give advice (7.155–66), and who are neither discarded like Laertes nor embittered like Aegyptius.[89] In this sense Alcinous's palace constitutes an ideal *oikos,* and yet it is impossible, as I have stressed. The Phaeacians are ignorant of physical struggle (8.246) and of political struggle as well: the stormy *agora* (political assembly) of Ithaca (2.6–336) should be compared with the agora in Phaeacia (8.24–49). On Ithaca, even a youth as inexperienced as Telemachus earns the label *hypsagorēs,* "assembly loud-mouth" (1.385, 2.85); and there can be little doubt that we have here a direct glimpse of historical reality. Both Pylos and Menelaus's Sparta, it may be argued, escape the crisis of monarchy, but both are orderly states, and the historical reality of crisis makes its appearance only when the logic of the story demands it. The crisis is on Ithaca, not necessarily everywhere in the world of men.[90]

But in that case, what is the difference between Phaeacia and Pylos or Sparta? The answer lies unhesitatingly in the land-based character of the latter. And this is the paradox: at the very moment at which a few Greek cities were embarking on the maritime adventure of colonization in the west, the poet of the *Odyssey* describes a city of sailors as something wildly utopian. In a sense, what Odysseus would like to restore on Ithaca is a system comparable to that existing among the Phaeacians, but he cannot succeed. He can never reproduce the perpetual feasting of the men of Scheria, with or without the gods' participation; in Book 24 he must seek a reconciliation with the families of the slaughtered suitors. The Phaeacians have cast him back into the world of men; their departure causes the images of anti-humanity that he encountered at every stage of his travels to vanish. Scheria may be the first utopia in Greek literature,[91] but we have not yet reached the point at which political utopias are to be distinguished from images of the golden age.[92] For the age of gold remains present in Phaeacia, and it is that element that distinguishes this

30   ideal society from another representation of the perfect city—that portrayed both in peace and war by Hephaistos on the Shield of Achilles in
Book 18 of the *Iliad*. Every scene here, from the ambush to the lawsuit, is
taken from the "real" world: the golden age must disappear; Odysseus's
journey must culminate in his return to Ithaca.[93]

NOTES

1. On the myth of the races, see J.-P. Vernant, "Myth of the Races," 1.
and 11.

2. Strictly, the contrast is between the "race of iron" and all the earlier ones.
Even the men of bronze, who "work with bronze" (*chalkōi d'eirgazonto;* 151) do
not "work" in the strict sense; they perform a military rite (cf. Vernant, "Myth of
the Races," 1.28). Only the "race of gold" is described explicitly as not working.

3. *WD* 167–73, restoring 169 (on the rule of Cronos) to its position in the
manuscripts [=173a Solmsen].

4. Vernant has demonstrated the close connection between this myth and that
of the races: "Myth of the Races," 1.18–19; similarly, "Myth of Prometheus,"
184–85.

5. Line 93, which I have restored here, is a quotation from *Od.* 19.360.

6. Commentators have perhaps been too quick to reject *WD* 108 as an interpolation (Lehrs, followed notably by Mazon [and Solmsen]). For the line introduces the myth of the races by connecting it with the myth of Pandora: "for gods
and men have the same origin": Ὡς ὁμόθεν γεγάασι θεοὶ θνητοί τ' ἄνθρωποι.

7. It is well known that these formulae appear frequently in the texts of oaths:
see in particular the oath of the Amphictyons in Aeschines *Ctes.* 111, and the oath
of the people of Dreros in *IC* 1.9 (Dreros) 1.85–89. And when *hybris* is triumphant, as at the end of the myth of the races, we are told that "the father will
no longer resemble his sons, nor the sons their father" (*WD* 182).

8. Cf. Vernant, "Myth of the Races," 1.18–19; P. Pucci, *Hesiod*, 82–135;
and especially N. Loraux, "Race des femmes," 44–52. Pandora is given to bring
"unhappiness to bread-eating men" (*pēm'andrasin alphēstēisin; WD* 82). It may be
relevant that *alphēstēs*, "bread-eating," which is a Homeric adjective, is formed
from the root *ed/*od, "to eat" and is a formation parallel (and in sense opposite)
to *ōmēstēs*, "raw-eating"; cf. Chantraine, *Formation*, 315.

9. The parallelism is emphasized by the repeated use of *epeita* in *Th.* 536 and
562. The whole affair takes place in the same period of time: "It was in the time
when the quarrel between gods and mortal men was being settled" (*hot'ekrinon-
to* . . . [535]). See Vernant, "Myth of Prometheus," and Detienne and Vernant,
Cuisine, 46–58.

10. Note that the Hesiodic accounts leave no space for a nomadic period in the
history of man; man is either a cultivator or no man at all.

11. A typical example is Havelock's book, *Liberal Temper,* the second chapter   31
of which, "History as Regress" (36–51), analyzes the "myth of the races" side by
side with the myths in Plato's *Politicus* and *Laws.* Needless to say, neither the idea
of "progress" nor that of "regress" was thinkable in Hesiod's time, for there was
no idea of "history" in our sense. This objection, however, does not apply to a
very useful book by a follower of Havelock, T. Cole, whose *Democritus* concentrates on a precise period and deals with genuine ideological disputes.

12. A. D. Lovejoy and G. Boas, *Primitivism,* 196.

13. The book by Lovejoy and Boas is certainly the most useful collection of
material for such a study. For the myth in the *Politicus,* see pp. 292–94 below.

14. One example (there are many others) is Empedocles, *Purifications* F 128
Diels-Kranz: In the reign of Kypris (Aphrodite), all sacrifices consisted of myrrh,
incense, and honey. Blood sacrifices, and indeed all eating of meat, were considered abominations. Plato's myth in the *Politicus* (272a–b) says much the same,
and vegetarianism is implicit in what Hesiod says. For a general survey, see
Haussleiter, *Vegetarismus;* also, more recently, M. Detienne, *Dionysos,* 56–62,
and D. A. Dombrowski, *Vegetarianism.*

15. For example, Euhemerus ap. Lactantius *Institutiones Divinae* 1.13.2: "Saturn and his wife and the other men of this time used to eat human flesh. Jupiter
was the first to prohibit the practice" (Euhemerus as translated by Ennius);
Dionysius of Halicarnassus, *Antiquitates Romanae* 1.38.2: "It is said that the
ancients sacrificed to Cronos according to the mode used in Carthage while that
city existed"; Sextus Empiricus, *Outlines of Pyrrhonism* (p. 190 Mutschmann):
"Some people sacrificed a man to Cronos in the same way that the Scythians
sacrificed strangers to Artemis." See Lovejoy and Boas, *Primitivism,* 53–79.

16. Cf. Diogenes Laertius, *Lives of the Philosophers* 6.34, 72–73; Dio
Chrysostom 10.29–30; Julian, *Orationes* 6.191–93.

17. On the subject of cannibalism and *allēlophagia* in Greek literature, see in
addition to the works already cited by Lovejoy and Boas and Haussleiter, Festugière, "Aretalogies."

18. See *Politicus* 272d–e: Οὔτ' ἄγριον ἦν οὐδὲν οὔτε ἀλλήλων ἐδωδαί, πόλεμός
τε οὐκ ἐνῆν οὐδὲ στάσις τὸ παράπαν: "There were no wild tribes among them [the
animals], nor cannibals; and war and political strife were completely absent."
The passage concerns animals, but the language employed is deliberately
"human."

19. See the vase described and illustrated by Robinson, "Bouzyges"; see also
U. Kron, *Phylenheroen,* 95–96.

20. Cf. the passages collected by Pembroke, "Women," 26–27 and 29–32,
and "Slavery and the Rule of Women" below.

21. The formula *kyse de zeidōron arouran* (he kissed the grain-giving earth)
occurs earlier, in the description of Odysseus's arrival on Scheria (5.463), but
naturally the first part of the line is different. The connection turns out not to be
accidental.

22. Cf. Segal, "Phaeacians," 17. The two separate worlds of the *Odyssey* are clearly delineated by G. Germain, *Genèse*, 511–82.

23. For the value of this distinction in the *Tempest*, cf. R. Marienstras, "Prospero."

24. To be exact, a nine-day storm; on the tenth day, they reach the Lotus-Eaters (9.82–84). "The number nine is used essentially to symbolize a period of time at the end of which, on the tenth day or year, a decisive event happens" (G. Germain, *Mystique*, 13).

25. "Der Sturm verschlägt den Helden ins Fabelland" (P. von der Mühll, "Odyssee," 720).

26. Menelaus has just returned, as Nestor puts it (3.319–20), from a region whence men rarely return.

27. Cf. Segal, "Phaeacians." There is one other place from which communication is feasible, but fails: Aeolus's floating island (10.3).

28. The second account to Penelope (19.262–307) contains a serious difficulty: Odysseus introduces the Phaeacians where they are clearly out of place, since Penelope does not yet know anything of Odysseus's adventures or his identity. Of the "interpolations" discovered by nineteenth-century critics, lines 273–86 are one of the few passages that almost certainly deserve to be rejected. In his first account, Odysseus heads for Crete after rounding Cape Malea (19.187), which is perfectly reasonable and restores "geographical" truth precisely at the point at which it was abandoned. Elements of "truth" slipped in among the "lies"—and contrasted with the "lies" that constitute the "true" tales—are fundamental to the Homeric story. See Todorov, "Récit," and L. Kahn, "Ulysse."

29. I hardly need add that I do not expect to discourage enthusiasts for Homeric "geography" and the "identification" of sites, although the sport has been aptly likened by J.-P. Darmon to the search for the rabbit-hole through which Alice entered Wonderland. Of course this is not to deny that Homeric wonders, like all wonders, bear some relation to the realities of their time, which means essentially the western Mediterranean (and perhaps in an earlier period, the eastern Mediterranean, if one believes K. Meuli, *Odyssee*). After all, there is presumably more resemblance between the wonders seen by Alice and Victorian England, than between that Wonderland and Manchu China.

30. "The movement of the *Odyssey* is essentially inwards, homewards, towards normality" (W. B. Stanford, *Ulysses*, 50); see above all Segal, "Phaeacians."

31. Similarly, Polyphemus "did not resemble a man who eats bread" (9.190–91).

32. This is a point overlooked by W. Richter, *Landwirtschaft*.

33. I cannot understand why Haussleiter thought that the Cicones were cannibals (*Vegetarismus*, 23). The text does not mention it.

34. Cf. Y. Garlan, "Fortifications," 255.

35. The use of the phrase *zeidōros aroura*, "grain-giving earth" (and life-giving as well), is not very satisfactory as a criterion, because Hesiod uses it of the golden

age. For what it is worth, of nine occurrences in the *Odyssey*, only three refer to a precise place (Ithaca: 13.354; Phaeacia: 5.463; Egypt: 4.22). The rest have a more general referent, roughly "here below."

36. There is also smoke coming from Circe's house (10.196–97), and when Odysseus approaches Ithaca after leaving the island of Aeolus, he can see men around a fire (*pyrpoleontas:* 10.30).

37. Cf. the Homeric *Hymn to Hermes* 72; Eur. *Hipp.* 74. On the *leimōn* see A. Motte, *Prairies,* and L. Kahn and N. Loraux, "Mort."

38. Cf. Segal, "Phaeacians," 45, 62, 63.

39. For the failed sacrifice of the Cattle of the Sun, see pp. 23–24 above.

40. The identification of the figures encountered by Odysseus with savage tribes is explicitly raised as a possibility in 1.198–99, where Athena, in the guise of Mentes, wonders whether he is the prisoner of men who are *chalepoi, agrioi* ("harsh," "brutish"), and when Odysseus himself asks what class of men the inhabitants of Cyclopia belong to: *hybristai te kai agrioi* or *dikaioi ēe philoxenoi,* "violent and brutish" or "righteous men who welcome strangers" (9.175–76). The same question recurs at 13.201–2, on Ithaca, before Odysseus recognizes that he is in fact at home, and earlier, when he lands on Phaeacia (6.120–21). See the excellent chapter on the Cyclopes in Kirk, *Myth,* 162–71, and also the semiological analysis by C. Calame, "Cyclopes."

41. It is scarcely sufficient to say, as does Haussleiter, that "the cannibalism of the Cyclops Polyphemus seems on the whole to be an isolated case" (*Vegetarismus,* 23 n. 2.). The incident deserves more than a mere footnote.

42. These and other details have been well stressed by Page, who compares Homer's Cyclops with the Cyclopes in folklore: *Odyssey,* 1–20.

43. Quoted by Lovejoy and Boas, *Primitivism,* 315. On the *abioi, gabioi,* or *hippomolgoi,* see also Nicolaus of Damascus, *FGrH* 90 F104.

44. The main texts are collected by Lovejoy and Boas, 304, 358, 411. The most curious of them is doubtless the speech Plutarch puts in the mouth of one of Odysseus's companions who was turned into a pig on Circe's island. Having tasted both human and animal existence, he praises the "life of the Cyclopes," comparing Polyphemus's rich earth with the thin soil of Ithaca (*Gryllus* 968f–87a).

45. Note also the *androphagoi* (man-eaters) in Hdt. 4.18, who live on the edge of the desert and are themselves at the limits of the human.

46. See p. 17 above. In the *Iliad,* when Achilles and Hecuba reach extremes of grief and anger, they fantasize about eating their enemies: 22.347; 24.212.

47. On Circe herself, see C. Segal, "Temptations."

48. There is no reason to alter the *sitoi* of the manuscripts at line 235.

49. In line 287, Hermes simply says to Odysseus that if he "carries this excellent remedy," *tode pharmakon esthlon echōn,* he will be safe. It is then not a charm to be used but a talismanic object.

50. It is Hermes, the god closest to humankind, who gives Odysseus the *moly,* and it is to Hermes that Eumaeus sacrifices a pig (14.435).

51. Cf. L. Kahn, "Ruse." For an analysis of the Sirens' song as a critical reading of the *Iliad* by the poet of the *Odyssey*, see P. Pucci, "Sirens." The grisly depiction of the situation on their island is Circe's, but when Odysseus himself tells the story, the skeletons have disappeared and the meadow is covered with flowers (12.159).

52. See Eustathius's comment on 12.359: καὶ τὰ ἑξῆς τῆς πολλαχοῦ δηλω-θείσης θυτικῆς διασκευῆς "and throughout the following description of the sacrificial preparations"; and on 357. On the role of the *oulai-oulochytai* in Homeric sacrifice, see J. Rudhardt, *Notions fondamentales*, 253.

53. The most curious feature of this episode is that normally water is used in Homeric sacrifice to prepare for the actual killing (it is contained in the *chernibes*, bronze vessels): cf. Rudhardt, *Notions fondamentales*, 254. Here, however, Homer does not mention water. Instead he concentrates on the libation of wine that follows the killing. This passage was noticed by Samson Eitrem (*Opferritus* 278–80), who believed that it presented evidence for a rite more ancient than blood sacrifice, as did the scattering of leaves attested in some funeral rituals: "They [Odysseus's companions] knew that in a previous period or in other places, this form had been used." Of course, when explained [!] in this way, the text loses all significance. Ziehen, by contrast, saw it as "an idea of the poet's, influenced by the situation" ("Opfer," 582).

54. In Herodotus, the legendary Ethiopians, who in the *Odyssey* feast with Poseidon, enjoy food that is the exact opposite of Odysseus's companions' sacrilegious feast. On a plain outside their city, the earth itself supplies them directly with the "Table of the Sun"—the boiled flesh of domestic animals (3.18). With their scented fountain of youth (3.23), the "long-lived Ethiopians" are scarcely mortal. Even their corpses do not smell unpleasant (3.24). In relation to the sun, they are guests, not utter strangers like Odysseus's companions.

55. Cf. F. Buffière, *Mythes d'Homère*, 461ff.

56. Cf. Segal, "Phaeacians."

57. The same applies to other countries that receive simply a bare mention. One of them, Syros, from which Eumaeus comes, presents a particular problem. It certainly produces corn and wine (15.406), but there is no illness or hunger there, and death comes without pain (407–11). It lies "where the sun sets" (404) and cannot therefore be the Aegean island of the same name. (I am grateful to F. Hartog for bringing this point to my notice.) I cannot here discuss the problem of the mysterious "Taphians."

58. For corn, see also 13.354; 20.106–10 (mills); for cows, 17.181. Odysseus also owns cows on Cephallenia (20.209–10).

59. On this text, which suggests a conception of kingship very archaic even in Homer's day, see Finley, *World of Odysseus*, 97–98.

60. See W. F. Hansen, "Journey."

61. Note the details: barley and lustral water, 3.440–47; the ritual cry of women, 450–52; cf. also 15.222–23.

62. In contrast, Odysseus says "I am not a god" (16.187).

63. Cf. Finley's remarks, *World of Odysseus*, 76. Despite the nineteenth-century arguments recently revived by Hirvonen (*Matriarchal Survivals*, 135–62), there is nothing in the treatment of Penelope to justify a reference to matriarchy, or even "traces" of it. Penelope's "special position" is to be explained simply by the absence of Odysseus.

64. See 2.56; 14.74; 16.454. 17.181; 17.600 [*hiereia*]; 20.3; 20.250–53.

65. See 18.414–28. Amphinomus is killed at 22.89–94; the hecatomb of 20.276–83 is anonymously offered, but clearly not by the suitors.

66. Liodes, the suitors' *thyoskoos*, is killed by Odysseus at 22.310–29, making it clear that the sacrifices performed in the past on the suitors' behalf have not been accepted. A *thyoskoos* is a seer; cf. J. Casabona, *Sacrifices*, 118–19.

67. See also 2.423–33 (Telemachus); 4.761–67 (Penelope); 14.445–48 (Eumaeus); 18.151 (Odysseus); 19.198 (Odysseus's "false" story); 1.60–62; 4.762–64; 17.241–43 (Odysseus's past sacrifices); 19.397–98 (list of sacrifices offered by Autolycus, the grandfather of Odysseus). And we should remember the sacrifices promised by Odysseus as well (pp. 20 and 24 above).

68. Casabona observes, "the idea of 'banquet' becomes predominant"—which is quite an understatement (*Sacrifices*, 23).

69. Cf. Segal, "Phaeacians," 48.

70. Cf. Segal, "Phaeacians," 17, and also 27: "The Phaeacians . . . while the instrument of Odysseus's return to the world of reality, are also the last afterglow of the fantasy realm he is leaving." I believe that the whole of Segal's case should be accepted, but without the "symbolist" and psychological language he sometimes employs. See also Segal's article, "Transition," 321–42; H. W. Clarke, *Art*, 52–56; and Hartog, "Les Phéaciens dans L'Odyssée."

71. Nonetheless he was helped by Ino-Leucothea and the river god of Phaeacia (5.333–53, 445–53).

72. The two trees share the same trunk. The ancient world unanimously understood *phyliē* as "wild olive" (see Richter, *Landwirtschaft*, 135). It is only in the modern world that a few critics have thought that a myrtle was intended (Pease, "Oelbaum," 2006).

73. Much has been made of this line by historians of colonization; see Asheri, "Distribuzioni," 5.

74. It must be clear that we cannot excise this famous description from the *Odyssey* on the staggeringly inadequate grounds that the "solid but narrow precincts" of the Mycenaean cities could never have had "room within their walls for the four acres of this orchard, double vineyard and kitchen-garden" (V. Bérard, in his C.U.F. edition, 1.186). It is instructive to note that the passage's utopian and mythical character was clearly recognized in antiquity; for example, Iamboulos's Hellenistic Utopia quotes lines 7.120–21 (Diod. Sic. 2.56). See A. Motte, *Prairies*, 121.

75. Cf. Segal, "Phaeacians," 47. Here there is a difficulty that I feel incapable of resolving. All the comparisons made in the present article tend, it seems to me, to support those who accept at least an overall "architect"—what Kirk calls a

36   "monumental composer," who gave the Homeric poems their present structure (Kirk, *Songs*, 159–270; to be supplemented by A. Parry, "Iliad," 175–215). This is also my position. But it must be admitted that there are many anomalies, especially in the language, in Book 24, and that it presents special problems (see Page, *Odyssey*, 101–36—an extreme view—and Kirk, *Songs*, 248–51). We also know that the Hellenistic critics Aristarchus of Samos and Aristophanes of Byzantium regarded the *Odyssey* as ending at line 296 of Book 23. If, for the sake of argument, we accept these criticisms as valid, does it follow necessarily that the parallel drawn between Book 7 and Book 24 is nonsense? For those who practice structural analysis on the basis of linguistic criteria alone, the question has little meaning; and indeed it is difficult to see why they should not "structure" a complex composed of the *Iliad*, the *Mahabharata*, and *Paradise Lost* . . . At this point the historian must make a graceful exit. But quite a different approach is possible. The work of Propp, and his immediate and later followers, suggests that, within a common cultural area, a complex of stories may be reduced to a few simple elements that may occupy a variety of different structural positions (Propp, *Morphology*; Brémond, "Message" and "Postérité"; and the whole of *Communications* 8 [1962]). It seems clear to me that, in the *Odyssey*, the motif of the golden-age garden is parallel to that of the garden cultivated by men; just as the motif of the hospitable girl is parallel to that of the girl who prepares visitors for death. I also believe that thematic analysis of the epic narrative of the kind practiced by the followers of Milman Parry leads in the end in the same direction (e.g., A. B. Lord, *Singer*, esp. 68–98), by showing that an ancient theme—and it is hard to imagine that the long-awaited meeting between Odysseus and Laertes could be anything but an ancient theme—may have acquired a fixed form only relatively late. These two approaches would benefit from mutual acquaintance.

   For these reasons, I do not believe that an *Odyssey* that is partially composite, historically speaking, cannot also be, from a structuralist point of view, homogeneous, although I admit that a strict proof has yet to be offered.

   76. More accurately, these are the equivalents to those states to which Hesiod and his successors gave the names "age of Cronos" and "age of Zeus"; for of course the land of the Cyclopes is also tended by Zeus (9.111, 358). Homer's Cronos is the father of Zeus and is imprisoned in Tartarus (*Iliad* 8.478–81).

   77. Eumaeus too has dogs that are quite real and that bark: 14.21–22.

   78. That is, the Phaeacians have the same privileges as the legendary Ethiopians (1.23–26); see also 6.203–5: "We are very dear to the immortals; we live in seclusion in the midst of the swelling sea, at the edge of the world [*eschatoi*], and no mortals visit us"; see S. Eitrem, "Phaiaker," 1523. The familiarity with the gods that is symbolized by shared feasts is correlated with isolation from mortal men.

   When Athena takes part in the first sacrifice offered by Nestor and his sons (3.41–44), she does so in disguise [as Mentor], whereas Alcinous stresses the fact that among the Phaeacians the gods do not assume disguise: *ou ti katakryptousin*

(7.205); they eat the sacrificial meal in common (7.203). Similarly, Poseidon is present at the Ethiopians' feast (*daiti parēmenos;* 1.26). It might seem as though Athena does the same in Nestor's palace (*ēlthe es* . . . *daita,* "she came to the feast"; 3.420); but after she has revealed herself by turning into a bird (3.371–72), she takes her share as an invisible divinity (3.435–36). Nestor and Telemachus do not therefore enjoy the same privilege as the Phaeacians.

79. On the contrary, in a Hesiodic fragment (F1 Merkelbach-West), sharing meals characterizes relations between mortals and gods prior to the establishment of sacrifice.

80. Cf. Segal, "Phaeacians," 33. J. Strauss-Clay makes the ingenious suggestion that the island that is home to the Phaeacians is none other than the island of goats, near that of the Cyclopes: "Goat Island"; she develops this theme of similarity between the two peoples in *Wrath,* 125–32.

81. The hospitality, though, is fairly ambiguous, for Athena, in disguise, warns Odysseus: "The people here do not welcome strangers or give a friendly reception to visitors from abroad" (7.23–33). Nothing in what follows justifies the warning, of course, but Nausicaa has just said that few mortals visit them (6.205 and note 76 above); and Athena covers Odysseus with a mist "in case one of the proud Phaeacians should cross his path, and insult him, and demand to know his name" (7.14–17). Peeping through the motif of the Phaeacians' hospitality is the image of a Phaeacia comparable to the land of the Cyclopes.

82. One sees here the problem that, in the Hesiodic poems, will belong to Pandora—the first woman at one and the same time resembles a young girl and looks like the goddesses; cf. N. Loraux, "Race des femmes," 45–49.

83. Cf. M. Detienne, *Maîtres de vérité.*

84. On the theme of sleep in the *Odyssey,* see C. Segal, "Transitions," 324–29.

85. A scholiast notes that "Hesiod" regarded Alcinous and Arete as brother and sister (cf. Schol. Od. 7.54 [I, p. 325 Dindorf] = Hesiod F222 Merkelbach-West); cf. also Eustathius on 7.64 [p. 1567]. This leaves two possible solutions: to agree with what the scholiast says, *touto machetai tois hexēs,* "this conflicts with what follows," and then—as has been done since the time of Kirchhoff, *Composition,* 54–56 (1869)—regard as interpolated lines 56–68 and 146 (where Arete is called the daughter of Rhexenor), or to accept that the poet gave the royal couple the appearance of incest, which was later corrected, so as to draw a parallel between Aeolus and Alcinous (see Germain, *Genèse,* 293).

86. Most obviously, of course, the king and queen: the same formulas are used to describe the royal couples' retirement for the night at Pylos and Sparta, and on Scheria: 3.402–3; 4.304–5; 7.346–47.

87. For example, there is a housekeeper on Scheria (7.166, 175; 8.449), as on Ithaca (17.94) and at Pylos (3.392); a nurse (7.7–12) as on Ithaca (19.353–56, 482–83); and a bard (8.261 et seq.) also as on Ithaca (22.330–31). The Phaeacian episode and the scenes on Ithaca have often been compared: note, for example, the arguments, so curiously similar despite the time lapse of 65 years and the

38   difference in the explanations offered (a mass of "interpolations" against oral composition) of Eitrem, "Phaiakenepisode," and M. Lang, "Oral Technique."

88. As will be seen by reading 7.146 et seq. free of the kind of preconceptions about matriarchy, such as to be found in Lang, "Oral Technique," 159–68.

89. Compare Echeneus's speech with that of old Aegyptius, 2.25–34.

90. A point made to me by M. I. Finley.

91. Cf. M. I. Finley, *World of Odysseus*, 100–102, 156.

92. M. I. Finley, "Utopianism," 178–92. I fully accept the general tenor of Finley's remarks here, but it should be remembered that by the time of the later Hellenistic period, utopias used a complex mixture of archaic and millenarian myths and political images (cf. L. Gernet, "City of the Future"). The situation was different in the fifth century B.C.; a utopia like that of Hippodamus of Miletus (Ar. *Pol.* 2.1267b 30 et seq.) cannot be explained by appeal to mythical thinking.

93. This study has given rise to several amplifications, notably H. Foley, "Similes," and S. Saïd, "Crimes."

2   Divine Time and Human Time

"For Hellenism . . . the passage of time is cyclical and not linear. Dominated by an ideal of comprehensibility that identifies the authentic and plenary entity with that which is in itself and remains identical to itself, that is, to the eternal and immutable, it considers motion and becoming as lower levels of reality, where identity is—at best—no longer grasped except under the forms of permanence and continuity, through the laws of recurrence."

In such words H. C. Puech summarizes a theory that, for all its traditional quality, still preserves a certain basis in truth.[1] My intention in the following pages, therefore, is not to take up arms against this interpretation and so deprive Judeo-Christian thought of the honor of having defined the historicity of man. To the extent that it is generally formulated in monolithic terms, however, this truism runs the risk of neglecting some of the facts.[2] Even when it is accurate, it is often presented in a hasty and superficial manner. When we teach that the ancients "recognized" only cyclical time,[3] do we wish to claim that they were ignorant of any other type of time, or that, with full knowledge of the facts, they rejected such alternative concepts? That is what only a broadly framed inquiry can prove. One must consider as many texts as possible—epic, tragic, historical, and even oratorical[4]—in addition to the purely philosophical.

Published in the *Revue de l'histoire des religions* (Jan.–March 1960), 55–80, with subtitle: "An Essay on Some Aspects of the Temporal Experience of the Greeks."

40   If classical antiquity really lived "in terror of history" (M. Eliade), this fact should be visible everywhere. One need only open a collection of inscriptions to find that it is nonexistent. When the Greek cities record at Delphi their victories in the Persian Wars,[5] when Pausanias records that he led the army at Plataea,[6] when, in celebrating the victory at Eion, the Athenians connect their present to the most distant past,[7] it could hardly be said that "human actions have no intrinsic, 'autonomous' value."[8] In these dedicatory inscriptions there is no trace of the "theocratic" conception of history that characterized the ancient Orient and that Collingwood has analyzed so well.[9] The city, by means of its writings, affirms its mastery over time. Finally, we should note that the discussion is biased if we speak comprehensively in terms of an "eternal return." In its literal sense, the eternal return is a specific doctrine whose place in Greek thought is real but limited. It is not even clear whether the whole discussion, as the young Pascal could have said, deals with "sticks and round." The subject of the present outline[10] is not so much to contrast cyclical time and linear time as to show what links were established, from Homer to Plato, between divine time and human time.[11]

Should the Homeric hero wish to have a wholly cyclical conception of time, he would not have the means to do so. His astronomical knowledge did not go beyond some extremely vague notions, even more primitive, some have claimed, than those of true "primitives."[12] The attempts to apply to the Homeric world traditional schemas—even when they manage to avoid error pure and simple—seem to lose track of the essential element, that is, human behavior.[13]

From the first lines of the *Iliad* we are put on the alert: the Muse is called on to tell a story from its beginning (*ta prōta*), and this story can only be understood by invoking the "will of Zeus" (*Il.* 1.5–6).

The plague in the Achaean camp is the inscription on the human plane of a divine decision, but this is something that is known only to the priest Chryses, Calchas the seer, and the poet himself. Thus the two levels of time are contrasted: divine:mythic and human:lived.

Later the Muses will be daughters of Memory, but for Homer they allow the poet to share in the gods' control over the confusion of the time and space of mortals: "Now, tell me, Muses, dwellers on Olympus—for you are goddesses, present everywhere, knowing everything; we hear only the din, and we know nothing—tell me who were the leaders, the captains of the Achaeans." At another place: "And now tell me, Muses, who was the *first* to take the bloody spoils, at the moment when [*epei*] the shining earth-shaker made the battle incline in their favor" (*Il.* 2.484–87; 14.508–10; see also 12.175 et seq.).[14] For the human observer, in fact, time is pure confusion. Achilles unsheathes and then replaces his sword without the onlookers understanding this temporal sequence. Invisible to the others, Athena has conversed with him, and her speech, in the words of R. Schaerer, "opens before him the perspective of time."[15] "Go, I tell you, and this is what will come to pass: one day he will offer you three times as many splendid gifts as a price for his insolence" (*Il.* 1.211–14). Thus the confusion of human time finds its explanation and its cause in the order of the time of the gods. "Tell me, in this world what do humans have in their minds? Only that which every day the father of gods and men decides to put there" (*Od.* 18.136–37).[16] This is doubtless a complex order, itself the result of a "compromise"[17] among the diverse forces that steer the world, but it *is* an order. It permits Homer to show Zeus weighing the "Keres" of Achilles and Hector in his scales and ascertaining that this is the "fateful day" (*aisimon hēmar*) for Hector as his pan descends (*Il.* 22.208–11).[18] Within the limits of this compromise the gods can tamper at will with human time, as when Athena rejuvenates or ages Odysseus (*Od.* 13.429 et seq.).

Thus, at the beginning of Greek literature, two types of time are contrasted, and one can already apply to them the epithets "tangible" and "intelligible." To what extent will this opposition be superseded?[19]

In fact, with the Hesiodic poems, the points of view undergo a considerable change. Whereas in the *Theogony* divine time is oriented along a linear series, the *Works and Days* of men are arranged as best as they can be in their degeneracy, around the rhythm of the seasons. For our purposes the *Theogony* is a primary text.[20] For the first time among the Greeks, the divine world is organized according to a "historical" myth:[21] a complex myth, to be sure, that can be broken down into two, perhaps three, "strata"[22] that in turn represent as many types of thought. The Hesiodic world at its origin (if one follows the order of the text) is a world without a creator, where natural forces break off, in units of two, from chaos and night, just as in the most classical Oriental cosmogonies. In a sense, these events unfold in linear time, but on closer inspection one can ascertain that this genealogical and chronological pattern is an overlay. Thus, there is no link between the offspring of Chaos and those of Gaia, who, moreover, produces most of her children without any "masculine" assistance.[23] (The same is true of Night.) From this primordial matter, on the other hand, there emerges a divine lineage perfectly set in time—linear time—the series formed by Ouranos and his descendants, Cronos and Zeus, which constitutes a dynastic history.[24] This series itself has a

42   goal: the victory of Zeus and his final accession to the throne of heaven. This victory is accomplished in time—that is, in uncertainty—and in his account of the last battle, against the giant Typhoeus, Hesiod takes care to tell us that the outcome was not decided beforehand.[25] Eventually, the triumph of Zeus is projected onto the past, and his will is fulfilled even prior to his birth.[26]

Divine history, therefore, has a "direction"; there exists a divine time, and, as for Homer, access to it is restricted to the disciples of the Muses. Given that there is this time oriented by and for the will of Zeus, will it not make the time of man lose its meaning, indeed its very existence? Homer's heroes are usually connected by family ties to the gods: "son of Zeus" is almost a polite compliment! Between gods and men, by contrast, the Myth of the Races erects an insurmountable obstacle (WD 109). Even the Race of Gold is not descended from the Immortals: it is created by them. The "decline"—interrupted only by the fourth age, the Heroic, which is the only one to have a historical nature[27]—is unstoppable from the earliest men to ourselves. The characteristic of the Race of Iron is precisely to live sorrowfully in time: "They will have no respite, either from suffering fatigue and misery by day, or, at night, from being tormented by the hard pains that the gods will send them" (WD 176–78). Hesiod's poem proposes a remedy for this situation: the monotonous repetition of agricultural labor. This is the first manifestation in Greek literature of the cyclical time that would be human time. A somewhat irregular cycle, after all, as in all primitive calendars: each month, each day, has its own benefits or drawbacks, all of which are of divine origin since the days are "sent by Zeus" (hēmata Diothen; WD 765).[28]

For those displaced persons, the lyric poets, such remedies remain altogether ineffectual. As for evil, it remains the same. Man is defined as "ephemeral" not because his life is short but because his condition is bound to time.[29] Time itself is nothing but the irregular succession of life's accidents. Archilochus alludes to this feeling in his famous line: "Be aware what rhythm men are subjected to" (F 66 Bergk),[30] and there is an echo in Bacchylides, "Tossed about by trivial cares, man has as his only lot the time he has to live."[31] From this fallen time, the lyric poets appeal to a time that is more noble, to the "avenging time" (F 4, line 16 Bergk) of Solon, which will reinstate justice, or to what Pindar grandly calls "the sole guarantor of genuine truth, Time" (ol. 10.65–67), which, by the very fact that it has passed, has made history. Outside time itself, Pindar invokes eternity; it is in his work that we find the first mention of the set of three lives that allows the sage to escape the time of mortals (ol. 2.123 et seq.).[32]

"I see clearly that all of us who live here are nothing more than phantoms or weightless shadows," says a character in Sophocles' *Ajax* (125–26). Like man in the lyric poems, the tragic hero is thrown into a world he does not understand. "One day can make all human fortunes rise or fall" (*Ajax* 131):[33] every tragedy of Sophocles is precisely the account of such a day. The quest of Oedipus, which takes a single day (*OT* 438), results in the victory of an unanticipated detective: "Time, which sees everything, has revealed you despite yourself. Today it accuses this marriage, in no way a marriage, where the begetter is also the begotten" (*OT* 1213 et seq.). The chorus of the *Trachiniae* defines human time: "For all men, joys and griefs follow one another in a circle; one could believe that he was seeing the wheeling stars of the Bear" (*Tra.* 129 et seq.);[34] thus time takes on a new dimension, "sovereign time" raised to divine status (*Tra.* 609).

According to a story that is utterly improbable but signals a "mental" shift, Thales the Milesian predicted an eclipse of the sun; in another case, profiting from his meteorological knowledge, he rented all the olive-presses and then made a fortune when the olive crop—as he had fore-seen—was particularly heavy (Hdt. 1.74; Ar. *Pol.* 1.11.1259a 9–19; DL 1.26).[35] Astronomical speculation would allow the Milesian school to construct a cosmological time that is rigorously cyclical. For Anaximander, "[the things that are] pay penalty and retribution to each other for their injustice according to the assessment of time" (F1 Diels, tr. Kirk and Raven). A vision "sprung from the conflict . . . of heat and moisture in the cycle of the year,"[36] but also a child of the city and its ideal of justice,[37] is thus extended to include the infinitely repeated genesis of the whole world.[38] The pairings of opposites in the *Theogony* are thus contained in a similar circle. The time of the gods has become cosmic time. Criticism of Hesiod, implicit in Anaximander, is explicit in Heraclitus. He proclaims the identity, at a higher level, of apparent opposites (Cf. FF 67, 88 Diels), and claims that "in the circumference, beginning and end coincide" (F. 103 Diels).[39] He also attacks Hesiod, "who did not understand either night or day; for there is an identity there" (F 57 Diels)[40] and who distinguished the days from one another in disregard of their fundamental equivalence (F 106 Diels).

If we also consider that, in the doxographic tradition, Heraclitus is supposed to have given evaluation of the "great year," the cosmic year,[41] we see that the essential features of the so-called Hellenic conception of time are settled in his thought.[42]

It is within such a framework that there developed the doctrine of the eternal return, in the precise sense of the term, but we are ill-equipped to

44   fix the date of its birth. The famous fragment of Eudemus contains the sole mention of its origin: "Will the same time return, as some claim, or not? One cannot say . . . . If we are to believe the Pythagoreans . . . I, with rod in hand, will again speak to you, who will again be seated as you are now, and it will be thus for all things; it is the characteristic of a numerically ordered [*eulogon*] time to be the same: there is only a singular and identical motion."[43] It is likely that a school that took an interest both in the problems of the soul and in the cycles of the stars could have arrived at this universal law. But when, and how? What role was played by the incontestably ancient speculation about reincarnation? Nothing known about ancient Pythagoreanism leads us definitely to attribute to it this vision of the world.[44] However, even if it is possible, with F. M. Cornford, to track down the traces of the "primitive" thought of Anaximander, it would be illusory to stop there.[45] Without speaking of the variants of detail, without mentioning the Eleatics' passionate denial of divine time, it is certain that more than a century later Democritus was thinking in a totally different fashion. The very idea of a multiplicity of worlds excludes cyclical time.[46] It seems that Democritus and his contemporaries, the sophists, would from then on emphasize uniquely human problems.

As a matter of fact, they were inspired by a tradition that was already very old. "The gods did not reveal everything to mortals from the beginning, but it is only by seeking, over time, that mortals find what is best" (Xenophanes F 18 Diels). The god of Xenophanes is thrown out of time into transcendence.[47] The idea of the cycle retains its full value from the point of view of cosmology,[48] but in parallel the human world has its own history, and it is no accident that this discovery is related to the criticism of Homer and Hesiod on the grounds of human morality (Xenophanes FF 1, 14).

The theme thus outlined takes a magnificent stride forward in the second half of the fifth century and crystallizes around the motif of the "first inventor."[49] Technology is no longer presented as the gift of the gods, nor even as the result of the "theft of Prometheus," but as the product of progressive and *datable* advances by humankind. The theme recurs almost obsessively in Herodotus, but it is the sophists, themselves inventors or teachers of *technai*, who seek out the human antecedents. Gorgias extols Palamedes, king of inventors.[50] Critias's Sisyphus goes much farther. "There was a time when the life of men was still in disorder" (F 24 Diels). The tragic passage that follows concerns nothing less than the simultaneous invention, by humans, of society and the

gods. One could not imagine a more complete reversal of Hesiod's 45
world.[51]

The place assumed by history in fifth-century thought leads us to
examine the historians themselves. They too speak and think like
"founders." Perhaps the first sign of the birth of history is the very
appearance of the name of the historian at the beginning of the works of
Hecataeus, Herodotus, and Thucydides.[52] As a result, there is scarcely a
problem more important for our study than to know how the historians
understood time.[53] "Polycrates," says Herodotus, "is the first of the
Greeks, so far as we know, to think of a maritime empire. I omit Minos of
Knossos and any others who might have ruled the sea before him, for I am
speaking of the 'first' in the time that is called human time" (Hdt. 3.122:
τῆς δὲ ἀνθρωπηίης λεγομένης γενεῆς).[54] Thereby, human history is set in
opposition to mythology;[55] the latter is discarded from the introduction
onward, when Herodotus recalls the divergent traditions about the origin of the conflict between Greeks and Asians and declares that he will
confine his own account "to him who was the first to undertake hostilities
against the Greeks" (1.5). Moreover, it is a flexible concept, this "human
time." If Minos is relegated to mythology, Egypt appears as the paradigm
of human history: 11,340 years have passed there without any divinity
appearing in human form. Although the sun has changed its course four
times, men continue to follow after one another (2.142). Nothing better
illustrates this immense perspective than the episode in which Herodotus
displays his predecessor Hecataeus. Hecataeus boasts to the Egyptian
priests that he is the sixteenth generation in a line of descent from the
gods; his interlocutors reply by showing him the statues of their predecessors, 345 in all, in succession from father to son (2.143–44).[56]
Human time means uncertainty and freedom, of which the most typical
instance is the scene prior to the battle of Marathon. Miltiades addresses
Callimachus: "It is up to you [en soi nyn . . . esti] to determine whether
Athens will be enslaved or free and so to leave behind, for all the time that
men will exist, a memorial such as not even Harmodius and Aristogeiton
left. . . . If we join battle before corruption touches some of the Athenians—and if the gods hold the balance level—we are in a position to
have the best of the fight" (6.109).[57] In view of this, do we have the right
to speak of cyclical time in connection with Herodotus?[58] He does allude
to the theory of "the wheel of incarnations" but only as an Egyptian
invention, not to take responsibility for it himself (3.123).[59] In reality,
what is archaic in Herodotus's work is less the conception of time than the
way it is put to use in historical writing. Characters address one another

outside of time. In many respects Croesus is an earlier version of Xerxes. The narrative is not organized chronologically; H. Fränkel could write, "For Herodotus, time is not the unique determinant for the contour of life, but rather a function of the event being recounted. Time flows when the event takes place, stops when there is a descriptive passage, goes into reverse when, after a son has been mentioned, the story of his father is told."[60] More precisely, the rich analyses of J. L. Myres have shown that the composition of Herodotus's work owes more to pedimental sculpture than to the frieze.[61] Nevertheless, in its lines of force, the inquiry does not depend on "the myth of the eternal return."

In a famous passage that describes the moral condition of Greece after the civil war in Corcyra, Thucydides writes: "Because of such strife there befell the cities such evils *as have occurred and will always occur* so long as human nature remains the same, but increasing and diminishing in strength and changing form according to the varying circumstances [*metabolai*] in each case" (3.82). For Thucydides, then, time fluctuates between being the "permanent" and the "changeable"; and, if it is mistaken to find in this text a purely cyclical concept of history, the opposite opinion is just as inexact.[62] When Thucydides himself defines his work, it is as a means "to see clearly both the events of the past and those of the future, which—thanks to their human character—will be similar or analogous" (Thuc. 1.22).[63] This is the force of the famous *ktēma es aiei* ("possession for eternity"). I think we may introduce here a distinction that was formulated by V. Goldschmidt in a completely different context, that is, logical time as opposed to historical time.[64] Thucydides' originality consists of having recognized both. He is the heir and disciple of Greek medicine, and according to a Hippocratic treatise one of the physician's most important tasks is "to predict—on the basis of the patients he sees, to know beforehand and to foretell, the events of the present, past, and future" (Hippocrates, *Prognostica* 1).[65] It is here that we find an explanation for the numerous passages in Thucydides that seem to reflect a cyclical concept of time. An argument projected onto the past and the general law of imperialism allow Minos to serve as a precursor, a prototype for Athenian imperialism; in the same way, Agamemnon's leadership of an armed confederation is like that of Brasidas and of Gylippus.[66] The analyses of J. de Romilly have demonstrated that Thucydides' narrative time is logical down to its smallest details. Relatively often, "simple chronological juxtaposition constitutes . . . a coherent and comprehensible series."[67] In addition, temporal series often intersect and fall into place so as to "reveal relations within the action that were invisible to the agents themselves."[68] Nevertheless, these remarks only make sense if we remember that for Thucydides, historical time is always intimately linked to logical time. The same facts are thus open to a double interpretation. If in certain respects Book 1 seems to be a collection of preludes, Thucydides insists from the very first lines that the Peloponnesian War was "the greatest upheaval [kinēsis] to have affected Greece and part of the barbarian world" (Thuc. 1.2); thus it is a unique event, to which nothing in the past is completely comparable. The same narratives that appear to show logic in action also attach the greatest importance to the occasions won or lost by one or the other of the adversaries.[69] Such dualism is not just a matter of style for Thucydides. One could easily show how it corresponds in his work to the great contrasts that characterize his vision of history: the oppositions between gnōmē and tychē brought to light long ago by Cornford (Thucydides Mythistoricus), between speech and action, between law and nature, perhaps even between peace and war.[70] The old dialogue between order and disorder within time, which already appeared in Homer, thus finds a radically new expression in Thucydides.[71]

It is in light of such facts that I must now give a rapid survey of the problem of time as it was posed by the men of the fourth century. The world of Plato and Isocrates differs in every way from that of Herodotus and the sophists—the gap having been opened by the terrible crisis described by Thucydides—yet the later age defines itself wholly by the standards of the earlier. Consideration of time can assume a radically new form in the fourth century, but it is nonetheless compelled to take into account the contribution of the preceding generation—even if only to make radical changes in its meaning. Even Plato cannot disregard time and history. Indeed, the appeal to history is a constant among the fourth-century writers, and especially among the orators. But it is an appeal, for the past becomes a source of paradigms. Someone like Isocrates can pretend to be unaware of any distinction between mythical time and historical time. Still better, the past becomes once again the time of the gods and of divine gifts.[72] The various eulogies of Athens compile memories and myths. In the fifth century, in the renowned Funeral Oration, Thucydides' Pericles did not look back beyond the generation of the Persian Wars. In the fourth century, the past is no longer the past, but rather the present as one would like it to be, that is, a bulwark against relentless evolution.[73] Nothing is more typical than Demosthenes' incessant invocation of the heroes of Marathon.[74] Perhaps the sole orator who

48 dares to attack the myth of ancestral greatness is Demosthenes' opponent, Aeschines; he is also the one who alludes to the changes in the world in the age of Alexander with the astonishing remark: "In truth, we have not lived the life of men" (Aeschines, *Ctes.* 132).[75] Under such conditions, the Time that is invoked in the epitaph for the fallen at Chaeronea is not historical time but "the divinity who oversees all things among mortals" and indeed is the only god mentioned by name.[76]

In Platonic thought, temporal experience is primarily that of linear time. The second hypothesis of the *Parmenides* consists of putting to the test of time the formula "If there is a One" (ἓν εἰ ἔστιν); the kind of time in question, a time that "advances" and is defined simply by the passage from before to after, can only be linear time.[77] Similarly, in the *Theaetetus* we find the same point in the hypothesis of Protagoras: knowledge is sensation and engenders universal motion, in other words the "coming-to-be" of Heraclitus, without the intervention of *logos* (*Theaet.* 155b–c), and, just as for Heraclitus, "becoming" is a linked series of opposites. "Everything that is born" is subject to this law (*Phaedo* 70d), whose truth Socrates comes to understand in his prison cell; on being freed from his fetters he experiences pain and pleasure in turn. "The two cannot simultaneously exist side by side in man, but in order to chase and catch one of them, we are almost always forced to catch the other as well, as if their double nature were attached to a single head" (*Phaedo* 60b). It is not possible, however, to use this sequence as a basis for knowledge. The One that takes part in time in the *Parmenides* is frozen in the moment, where it is at once older and younger than itself (*Parm.* 152b et seq.).[78] Containing all these contradictions and taking part in time, the One does undergo changes but only within "this strange nature of the immediate (*Parm.* 156d–e: (ἡ ἐξαίφνης αὕτη φύσις ἄτοπος)[79] outside of time." The analysis of linear time, then, results in this simultaneity of opposites, in the "indefinable dyad of the great and the small," which is for Plato the equivalent of the material world (Ar. *Metaph.* A 6, 987b et seq. Cf. *Phil.* 24c–d; *Tim.* 52d),[80] in other words the unknowable. Linear time means the death of time. Plato tells us so directly: "If generation were in a straight line only [εὐθεῖά τις εἴη ἡ γένεσις], and there were no compensation or circle in nature, no turn or return of elements into their opposites, then you know that all things would at last have the same form and pass into the same state, and there would be no more generation of them" (*Phaedo* 72b, tr. Jowett).[81] In fact, the demand for cyclical time springs from the level of sensation. In the *Phaedo,* when the discussion has not yet gone beyond the dialectical level of the image, when the hope of immortality is still just a wager based solely on "incantations" and "old traditions" (Pythagorean, in this case), Socrates declares that there needs to be an "eternal replenishment of generations, somewhat like a circle in their turning" (*Phaedo* 72a–b, 70c, 77e).[82] This is the premise that bestows security on the philosopher and the lawgiver. The philosopher will persuade his fellows either in this existence or in the other. "Quite a delay," he is told ironically. "This delay is nothing, in comparison with eternity" (εἰς οὐδὲν μὲν οὖν ὥςγε πρὸς τὸν ἅπαντα: *Rep.* 498d). The wise man tells the atheist, "My son, you are young, and the passage of time [προϊὼν ὁ χρόνος] will make you change your opinions on many issues and to hold views opposite to what you think now" (*Laws* 888a–b). This advice should be understood not only with the background of the "reconsideration camps" (*sōphronistēria: Laws* 908e), but again in terms of the great myth that describes the eternal "alteration of animate beings in accord with the order and the law of destiny" (*Laws* 904c). Even the death penalty, prescribed for unyielding atheists, cannot be the "ultimate punishment" (*Laws* 909a–c).[83] Thus a world made up of a regular alternation of opposites is an explicit feature of the Platonic system, but like any such element it can only be validated by means of a detour through the Form. Only then will the cycle of great eschatological myths become the process for the world. All generation is "because of the essence" (οὐσίας ἕνεκα: *Phil.* 54c).[84] Once the process of generation is organized in this way, the cycle of the seasons is "generation oriented toward the essence" (γένεσις εἰς οὐσίαν: *Phil.* 26a–b).[85] Such is also the case for time strictly defined, as in a well-known passage in the *Timaeus* (*Tim.* 37c–d et seq.).[86] Time is a creation, that is, a composite; it is "born" from the pleasure of the demiurge at the world he has made and which he wishes to make still more similar to his model. Thus there appears, along with the sky, "a certain moving image of eternity . . . which moves according to the law of numbers." Time is the means by which *genesis* becomes capable of approaching the realm of the Forms. Time is derived ontologically from the soul of the world, a self-propelling principle; therefore it is movement, but regulated and thereby canceled.[87] The planets were created to define the scale of time. Moreover, it is a multiple time. Each star is a gauge of time; each species "has its circle . . . within which it moves" (*Rep.* 546a). Still, this multiplicity is arranged in a hierarchy. As one descends the ladder of being, the material component grows larger, and the circles of the souls undergo "all possible breaks and injuries, and their rotation can scarcely continue" (*Tim.* 43d–e). Time becomes unhinged. The hierarchy is finally controlled by a shared standard, the Great Year, which occurs when all the circles together have resumed their original motion and when, in consequence, motion is abolished (*Tim.*

50   39d). This is the explanation of those instances, in the world and in human life, that seem to depend on linear time.. . . . The world is simultaneously very old and very young, since a periodic shift in the orbits of the planets gives rise to catastrophic changes (*Tim.* 22d). If the elderly are wiser than children, it is because for the former the revolution of the circle of the Same prevails over the revolution of the circle of the Other (*Tim.* 43b).[88] This process takes place "with time" (ἐπιόντος τοῦ χρόνου), that is, in imitation of eternity. In the composite that is man, like every living thing, time will be cyclical to the exact extent that the divine element overrides the material. This becomes totally clear in the *Laws*. The discussion takes place among three old men, of whom only one is a philosopher—although he doesn't say so—but whose age itself is enough to raise them to the level of the divine. Their conversation spirals in on itself, in a pattern of repetitions modeled on those of an ideal "music" (*Laws* 659c–d).[89] The loftiest notion accessible to the non-philosophers of Magnesia is that of the soul of the world, a soul that is separated from the ideal soul, as J. Moreau has shown, but still the source of cosmic time.[90] "Mankind are coeval with all time, and are ever following, and will ever follow, the course of time; and so they are immortal, because they leave children's children behind them, and partake of immortality in the unity of generation" (*Laws* 721c, tr. Jowett).[91] This participation has to be regulated. In the city of the *Laws*, cosmic time is engraved in the Constitution, in religious life, and in the very soil of the city, just as it was engraved on the tomb of the soldiers at Chaeronea. The citizens are divided into twelve tribes that are distributed among the twelve Olympian gods; the land is divided into twelve sections, both in the city and in the countryside. There are no fewer than three hundred ceremonies per year. Above all, the most important cult will be that dedicated to the stars (*Laws* 828b–c, 745b–e, 967a et seq.).[92] Between the cosmic cycle and the disturbance of the material world, Platonic history will be ordered in a manner rigorously parallel to time. At first sight, the time of history is no more than accident and disorder. Plato declares that "everything proceeds by drifting" (φερόμενα ὁρῶντα πάντῃ πάντως), "states are continually leaping among tyranny, oligarchy, and democracy" (*Letter* 7, 325e–26d). Such contradictory time gives rise to the most deadly of contradictions: permanent war (*Laws* 626a). But a philosophy of history cannot be based on chance—or on history. The naturalists—the intellectual heirs of Critias, Democritus, and Protagoras—err when they attribute the creation of the world to chance and the legislation of men to human skill or invention (*Laws* 889b–e). The prisoners of the cave struggle to "discern the objects

that pass by" and "to recollect as precisely as possible those that regularly went ahead, and those that followed after, and those that were together," for thus they would be most able to predict the future (*Rep.* 516c–d). Among the shades of the dead, therefore, Thucydides exerts a kind of royal power, and Herodotus too has pride of place. History is immense, but it is a cyclical history whose rhythm is set by periodic catastrophes (from which Egypt is spared not because it is the most human, but because it is closest to the divine [*Tim.* 21e–22b]).[93] For the one who espouses the "infinite, immeasurable" length of time, it is evident that "thousands and thousands of cities have followed on one another, and as many of equal size have disappeared. Have not these too known every type of government, over and over? Sometimes the small became great and the great small; sometimes the best turned into the worst, and out of the worst grew the best" (*Laws* 676b–c).[94] Such is the framework in which Platonic history develops. At heart, this will be neither a history of the good (progress), nor of evil (decline). If Books 8 and 9 of the *Republic* paint a Hesiodic picture of how the ideal city turns toward tyranny, and if the myth of the *Politicus* states that during the reign of Zeus (yet another allusion to Hesiod) men were on their way to the "region" of dissimilarity (*Pol.* 273d), these texts can only be understood in their own contexts.[95] The decay of the ideal city is the counterpart of its construction, which takes place outside of time. Pure good is succeeded by pure evil. The cycle of Zeus is the counterpart of the cycle of Cronos, another symbol of eternity.[96] In one case as much as the other, historical time is broken up and is no longer a composite.[97] There is certainly an order in the series of cities, but it is not historical.[98] Still, even within the framework of a purely human history, the philosopher remains free; in Plato, one could not seek out a meaning for history because history does not belong to the sphere of things that have meaning. Book 3 of the *Laws* contains a perfect illustration: there one finds again the great themes of the humanistic history of the fifth-century sophists, particularly that of technical and political progress of human inventiveness (*Laws* 677b et seq.).[99] Plato even returns to the distinction between mythic time and historical time that Isocrates had intermingled (*Laws* 683a). Mechanical progression allows humanity to pass from the family to the village, from the village to the town, from the town to the community of the polis, and with the polis, *phronēsis*. One also sees the emergence of "a plethora both of vices and of virtues" (*Laws* 678a). At all times—with the aid of *tychē*, favorable or unfavorable—Plato's people have the option to turn toward good or toward evil. Goodness will take the form of the Spartan Constitution, with its three strokes of historical good luck: the double kingship,

52   Lycurgus, the creator of the ephorate (*Laws* 691d et seq.). Evil is embodied in the choice made by the kings of Argos and Messene of a Constitution directed only at warfare—that is, the system of Sparta and Crete, by
the account of Cleinias the Cretan and Megillus of Sparta (*Laws* 686a et
seq., 625c et seq.). Janus-head of the same reality! The "historical"
section of the *Laws* ends with the decision to construct an ideal city.
Finally human time will have had significance only to the—quite improbable—extent that it yields a city entirely planned around divine
time. Still, another fundamental tenet of late Platonic philosophy is that
whatever time has made is sacred. Whatever has endured shares, in its
own way, in eternity. "Only a slow and cautious process of change, which
spreads progress over a long period of time" (*Laws* 736d) can avoid what
would be for an old city the calamity of reentering the cycle of
oppositions.

From Homer to Plato, gods and men play a continuous, uniquely
complicated game. Merely a game, empty of meaning? The problem
would deserve another study, longer and more involved than this one. To
our eyes the most striking fact is the fissure that began in the fifth century
between "science" and "history." On one side is espousal of a cosmogony
that, if it were to account for change, could only take a cyclical form; on
the other side is a belief that, step by step, humankind is moving away
from spiritual and material infancy. Is it an accident that this belief is
contemporary with the most dazzling period of Greek civilization? Pessi-
mism is already perceptible in Thucydides, and with him the idea of
repetition reappears in history. As a contemporary of the crisis of the
polis—Minerva's owl flies only at night—Plato summarizes and brings
together the contribution of his predecessors, for all the archaizing violence of his reaction. But Platonic thought, although it marks a turning
point, does not mark the end of the road.

NOTES

1. "Temps" 34; cf. "Gnose" 217–24. Discussions of the classic thesis are to be
found in the following works: M. Eliade, *Myth of the Eternal Return;* O.
Cullmann, *Christ and Time;* F. M. Cornford, *Principium,* 168ff.; I. Meyerson,
"Temps." On the other side, note should be made of A. Momigliano's essential
study, "Time," and the remarks in part inspired by the present essay, although
perhaps excessive, from R. Caillois, "Temps circulaire."

2. See the general comments of V. Goldschmidt, *Système stoïcien*, 49–64; F. Châtelet, "Temps de l'histoire," especially 363 n.1.

3. Cf. the original approach of B. A. Van Groningen, *Grip*.

4. So V. Goldschmidt, *Système stoïcien*, 50.

5. Meiggs and Lewis, *Selection* No. 27.

6. *Anth. Pal.* 6.197, reproduced in Meiggs and Lewis, *Selection*, 60.

7. See the comments of F. Jacoby, "Epigrams," 510–17 and N. Loraux, *Invention*, 60–61.

8. Eliade, *Eternal Return*, 18.

9. *Idea*, 14, cf. especially the analysis (16) of the victory stele of Mesha, king of Moab in the ninth century B.C. It would be easy to find other comparisons between Greek inscriptions and this type of "messages to the gods."

10. Much too cursory and systematically incomplete. It makes no sense, for example, to reexamine the "sophism of the Eleatics." Nor will I study time as it would be approached by a phenomenological study of Greek religion, as, for example, is done by Dumézil, *Temps et Mythe*.

11. When writing these lines I was unaware that for Vico, here under the influence of Diodorus Siculus, all human nations passed *seriatim* through the time of gods, heroes, and men. This is only an accidental concurrence of terms.

12. Cf. Nilsson, *Primitive Time*, especially 110ff. and 362.

13. The prime example is Onians' *Origins*, wherein the author tried to provide an etymological interpretation of the Homeric terms denoting time. One can raise two objections. First, the proposed etymologies are often unconvincing; second, there is no proof that the deduced meanings were the perceived meanings. For instance, even if one accepts the conjunction between *telos* (end) and *polos* (axis of rotation), it is hard to believe that the expression *telesphoros eniautos* (*Il.* 19.32) means "the totality of the circle of the year" (Onians, *Origins*, 443). On the risks involved in the method used by Onians, see also A. Meillet, *Langue*, 65–67, and J. Paulhan, *Preuve*.

14. F. Robert observes, "It seems that the divine element in poetic inspiration consists above all in the power to bring the mass of facts—in all its diversity—back to life, to retain, to solidify and to express a body of knowledge so extensive that one human memory would be unable to sustain it" (*Homère*, 13). See also Van Groningen, *Grip*, 99.

15. René Schaerer, *Homme antique*, 17.

16. A typical example: when Glaucos tells his own story (*Il.* 6.145 et seq.) he begins by remarking on the futility of such an undertaking with the famous image, "Like the generations of leaves, so are men"; he then connects his family with a deity.

17. Cf. F. Robert, *Homère*, 110ff.

18. It is well known that a day is something that falls from the sky (cf. Onians, *Origins*, 411). R. Schaerer has studied the image of the scale and its implications in Greek literature (*Homme antique*, *passim*); see also M. Detienne, *Maîtres de vérité*, 37–39.

19. One could push the analysis further and show, for example, the incoherence of Homeric chronology. Penelope does not age, Nestor is perpetually old. Is the latter case an instance of a law of "mythic time" as Van Groningen believes (*Grip*, 96), or on the contrary, as Gomme maintains (*Greek Attitude*, ch. 1), is it an example of the poet's difficulty in coming to grips with a "chronicle"? For the study of the other aspects of time in Homer, we may return to H. Fränkel, "Zeitauffassung." He makes the noteworthy observation that *chronos* is never a subject, but always denotes duration with a vague and affective quality (2–5).

20. The importance of Hesiod for the history of Greek philosophy, specifically for Ionian physics, has often been pointed out; cf. especially V. Goldschmidt, "Theologia"; Cornford, *Principium*, 193ff. At the time I published these pages I had nut read the study by J.-P. Vernant, "Myth of the Races," which is to be found in the same fascicle of *Revue de l'histoire des religions*. See also P. Philippson, *Genealogie*.

21. This is that "quasi history" that Collingwood simply calls "myth" (*Idea*, 15).

22. *Weltstufe* ("world-stages") in the coinage of P. Philippson.

23. P. Philippson, *Genealogie*, 10ff.

24. Ouranos-Cronos, line 137; Cronos-Zeus, line 457.

25. Καὶ νύ κεν ἔπλετο ἔργον ἀμήχανον ἤματι κείνῳ, καί κεν ὅ γε θνητοῖσι καὶ ἀθανάτοισι ἄναξεν (ll.836–37): "Then an incurable deed would have been accomplished on that day, and Typhoeus would have been king of men and gods." The dismemberment of Typhoeus recalls one of the oldest types of Oriental cosmogony, the murder of Tiamat by Marduk, a cosmogony that the king of Babylon regularly "re-enacted" (cf. Cornford, *Principium*, 218ff.).

26. Line 465; P. Mazon was unwilling to excise the line, since the *Theogony* "offers more than one example of this kind of contradiction" (*Travaux*, n. *ad loc.*).

27. There is a problem created by this interpretation of the decline. It was formulated by Mazon (*Travaux*, 60) and gave rise to different solutions from V. Goldschmidt, "Theologia" and J.-P. Vernant, "Myth of the Races," 1 and 2.

28. The foregoing is to be compared to the remarks of E. Benveniste, "Tempus": for the Latin peasant, time "is first of all the condition of the sky, the proportion of the elements that comprise the atmosphere and give it its character at the moment, and it is simultaneously the appropriateness of this meteorological situation to what [the peasant] is trying to do" (15). Such is the primitive meaning of *tempus*, closer to "weather" than to "time."

29. Compare Pindar *Pyth.* 8.95–97: Ἐπάμεροι τί δέ τις; τί δ' οὔτις; σκιᾶς ὄναρ ἄνθρωπος. "Beings bound to time: what is it, what is it not? Man is the dream of a shadow." The meaning of the word *ephēmeros* was clarified by H. Fränkel, "Ephemeros" and "Zeitauffassung," 23–29.

30. E. Benveniste, "Rhythm," showed that *rythmos* denotes "form at the moment it is assumed by that which is moving, mobile, fluid—the form of something that does not have organic form" (288).

31. 1.178–80 (with the emendation of Desrousseaux). See also the passages
cited by R. Schaerer, *Homme antique*, 135.

32. In a common play on words, eternity is symbolized by "the house of Cronos." Between the being that is tied to time and that which traverses the three paths lies an evolution that must be emphasized, but it is not yet a matter of the full-scale reincarnation spoken of by Herodotus (2.123). I will not broach the problems raised by representations of time among religious sects— especially in Orphism—on which subject I had been mistaken in the 1960 version; it was called to my attention by P. Boyancé.

33. Cf. H. Fränkel, "Zeitauffassung," 35.

34. Note the astronomical comparison, here evoking not regularity in order but regularity in disorder. See J. de Romilly, "Cycles," 150–51.

35. On the fabricated character of Thales' prediction, cf. O. Neugebauer, *Exact Sciences*, 142–43.

36. Cornford, *Principium*, 168.

37. See the general remarks in J.-P. Vernant, "Myth to Reason."

38. A largely conjectural survey of Anaximander's system is to be found in C. Mugler, *Deux thèmes*, 17ff.; see especially C. H. Kahn, *Anaximander*, 166–98.

39. This privilege is closed off to men, according to Alcmeon of Croton: "Men die, because they are not able to connect the beginning to the end" (F 2 Diels).

40. Cf. *Theogony* 123 et seq.

41. Cf. Aetius 2.32.3 and Censorinus 18.11 (= Diels 22 (12) A 13). See, however, G. S. Kirk, *Heraclitus*, 300ff. According to Kirk, the significance of the "great year" would not be cosmological but anthropological. If one accepts his argument, one must acknowledge that for Heraclitus there was a correspondence between human and celestial cycles.

42. Needless to say, within the bounds of this study we cannot trace the effects of Anaximander's discovery on the other Ionian or Italian "physicists." The thought of Empedocles, for example, is completely parallel.

43. Eudemus, *Phys.* B 3 F 51, quoted by Simplicius *Ph.* 732.26 (= Diels 58 (45) B 34). Thus this passage is preserved in a very late source. It is true that through this same Simplicius, a Byzantine from the sixth century, we have F 1 of Anaximander. Whether ancient or not, the text emphasizes that the eternal return is a radical position of certain theorists. See the commentary on this passage in T. Gomperz, *Ancient Thinkers* I, 140ff. Gomperz accepts the attribution to Pythagoreanism but notes, correctly, that reincarnation and the eternal return are not necessarily linked.

44. The development during the second half of the fourth century of what R. P. Festugière called the religion of "the cosmic deity" provides a date that is all the more likely, for, if Plato's thought on the subject remained only partial, Aristotle was familiar with the doctrine in all its purity (*Prob.* 17.916a 28 et seq.).

45. *Principium*, 168ff.

46. Cf. C. Mugler, *Deux Thèmes*, 145ff. The question is actually complex, and made still more complicated by the abundance of post-Epicurean sources. To confine our attention to the oldest sources, let us make the following statement: a single text (Ar. *Phys.* 8.1.251b 16 = Diels 69 (55) A 7) speaks of time in Democritus and then only to say that it is "ungenerated." Nonetheless, we should also note that it is Aristotle (*Phys.* 8.252a = Diels 68 (55) A 65) who chides Democritus for explaining natural facts by their history; elsewhere (*Phys.* 2.196a 24 = Diels 68 (55) A 69), no doubt alluding to Democritus, he criticizes those who explain the formation of the world by chance and the creation of living things by natural laws. Thus there could be a solution to the very complicated problem of the connection between physics and ethics in Democritus. In fact, for him human life is organized as a function of time, or rather against time (cf. FF 66, 119, 183, 203). Contrary to what I wrote before, it is certainly necessary to add to these references the fragments of the "Lesser Diacosmos" (Diels 68 (55) A 5, 135ff.). These passages contrast technical progress and moral progress in human history and partially resolve the dilemma by a consideration of politics. The attribution to Democritus now seems to me to have been proved by T. Cole, *Democritus*.

47. On the originality of Xenophanes' theology, see W. Jaeger, *Theology*, 38–54.

48. Cf. F 27: "Everything comes from the earth and ends in the earth."

49. The data on this question have been assembled in an exemplary fashion by A. Kleingünther, *Prōtos heuretēs;* see also P.-M. Schuhl, *Formation*, 348–50. An important subset of these legends concerns the first lawgivers; see A. Szegedy-Maszak, "Legends."

50. Among the sophists, the theme is closely connected to the discussions of nature and law.

51. This is also the subject of the famous chorus in *Antigone* (331 et seq.): "Many the marvels, but none so wondrous as man"; human technical prowess is extolled: "Language, thought swift as the wind, the aspirations that give rise to cities, all this he has taught himself." The end of the ode, however, remains faithful to traditional values (cf. C. P. Segal, "Antigone"). This process of thought underlies the extraordinary lists of inventions in Pliny, *H. N.* 7.57, and Clement, *Strom* 1.74. Similarly, Prodicus (F 5 Diels) links the discovery of gods with that of technology, while according to Protagoras (F 4 Diels) human life is too short to allow for a definitive statement about the existence of gods.

52. Cf. F. Jacoby, "Geschichtschreibung," 1–2.

53. See the indispensable article by M. I. Finley, "Myth."

54. In my understanding of the passage, it contrasts those men who are sons of men with those who are sons of gods, such as Minos.

55. In this case, the reference is to the "genealogies" in Hecataeus, although even these were limited to human "events." The same dialectic will be turned against Herodotus in the work of Thucydides.

56. It would be interesting to study the parallel opening of time and of

space in Herodotus. For the Ionian "physicists," space was symbolic and geometric; in Herodotus it retains numerous traces of such archaism, but there is a
clear transition toward a space that is not, as I used to believe, that of the
merchants. I wrote that this whole subject needed to be explored, and the task
has now been well done by F. Hartog in *Miroir*. He shows the overwhelming
presence—even in Herodotus's ethnology—of civic space on the Greek model.
See also W. A. Heidel, *Greek Maps*.

57. Cf. J. L. Myres, *Herodotus*, 52–54. Of course the gods do not always
hold the balance level, but the gods scarcely do more than confirm or support
human decisions. There is nothing more striking than to compare the intervention of Athena in the plenary council of the Achaeans with the Herodotean
account of the three meetings held by Xerxes concerning his dreams (7.8–19)
before divine intervention. The positions are the reverse of those in Homer; it is
on the human side that order, or rather clarity, is found. Whereas Homer was
writing from the height of Olympus, Herodotus knows about the gods'
thought only through the uncertain medium of oracles.

58. As, for example, in I. Meyerson, *Temps*, 339.

59. In the same way he has Croesus advise Cyrus that, "Human affairs are
on a wheel that revolves" (1.207).

60. "Stileigenheit," 85.

61. *Herodotus*, 79ff.

62. Cf. A. W. Gomme, *Commentary* I, *ad loc.*

63. I do not agree with Gomme (*Commentary, ad loc.*) that the future mentioned here would be the present for Thucydides' Greek reader.

64. "Temps logique."

65. The connection between Thucydides and medicine was defined by C.
N. Cochrane, *Thucydides*, and by many others afterward.

66. Cf. Grundy, *Thucydides*, 419, and J. de Romilly, *Histoire et Raison*, 276–
78. The latter observes, "It can be said that his account of events runs the risk
of being too rational, to the extent that it proceeds from a kind of unification of
history" (276). Although she is correct, I am not sure that—as she seems to
believe—it is a matter of a relative failure on Thucydides' part. It is so only
from the point of view of a modern historian. Nowhere is Thucydides closer to
the purpose he has set for himself. It is in this sense that Collingwood could say
that he was more the father of psychological history than of history proper
(*Idea*, 29ff.).

67. J. de Romilly, *Histoire et Raison*, 46.

68. J. de Romilly, *Histoire et Raison*, 58.

69. On the story of Gylippus's arrival at Syracuse, see de Romilly, *Histoire et
Raison*, 57.

70. Cf. Thuc. 3.82: "In times of peace and prosperity, cities and individuals
have better sentiments, because they are not confronted with dire necessities
[*anankas*]."

71. For a general overview, cf. de Romilly, "Progrès."

72. The passages have been analyzed by G. Schmitz-Kahlmann, *Beispiel*. It is odd to see what use Isocrates makes of the motif of the first founder. The theme is used to the advantage of city (cf. *Paneg.* 47 et seq.) yet the city itself owes everything to the gods (*Paneg.* 28 et seq.). Isocrates' historicism, like all historicism, is a sign of a present concern. Athens has to look like the semi-divine benefactor of Greece. The same should be the fate of the kings to whom he is appealing.

73. I can now refer to N. Loraux, *Invention*, Ch. 2.3 and 3, where there is also a copious bibliography.

74. All these facts have been well discussed by Van Groningen, *Grip, passim*, but he errs in thinking that we are dealing with a permanent feature of Greek thought. Moreover, it is characteristic that one of the rare passages in Demosthenes in which one sees the passage of time (*Phillip.* 3.47 et seq.) alludes to the progress of the only *technē* to undergo enormous development in the fourth century: that of warfare.

75. Cf. *On the Embassy*, 75.

76. Tod 2.176. As has been noted, the theme is common in the resolution of tragedies. I am not sure that this invasion of the human world by the god of time is really a sign of the optimism of the fourth century (as is maintained by A.-J. Festugière, *Dieu cosmique*, 155ff.). Our references to the orators deal only with historical time, but it would be very interesting to study the public speeches of the fourth century and to see how much the advance of commercial technology led to the disappearance of the old conception of time, a kind of monster that is difficult to bind in a contract. Cf. L. Gernet, "Time."

77. *Parm.* 155 et seq., as well observed by Cornford, *Parmenides, ad loc.*

78. Cf. also *Theae.* 155b–c.

79. It must be remembered that the "third hypothesis"—from which I have drawn this passage—is only an appendix to the second, whose conclusions (if there is a One, it partakes in all oppositions, notably those occasioned by time) are repeated at the beginning ; cf. Cornford, *Parmenides, ad loc.*, and L. Brisson, "Instant."

80. The argument originates with Heraclitus (cf. Diels 22 (12), A 22).

81. V. Goldschmidt has been able to show that the criticism of tragedy as an imitation of human life "made up of words that cannot be unsaid, irreparable actions, and events whose rigorous sequence is determined by the mechanical causality of development presupposes a criticism of linear time" ("Tragédie," 58). It might be pointed out to Goldschmidt that the kind of tragedy Plato has in mind is less that of Aeschylus and Sophocles—in which the final scene returns the action to divine time (as, for example, at the end of the *Prometheus Bound* or *Oedipus at Colonus*)—and more that of the "humanist" tragedy of Euripides.

82. Cf. V. Goldschmidt, *Dialogues*, 183–85.

83. This is Plato's opinion, at least from the *Republic* on. Neither the myth

of Er (*Rep.* 614b et seq.) nor the myth in the *Phaedrus* (246a et seq.) envisions
either eternal salvation (that is, in the case of the *Phaedrus,* the certainty that a
soul that has recovered its wings will not fall again) nor eternal punishment, as
discussed in the *Phaedo* (114d) and the *Gorgias* (614c et seq.); thus rescue from
time has ceased to be a possibility in Plato's eyes (but see *Rep.* 615d).

84. *Ousia* was earlier defined as *auto kath'hauto* (53d).

85. For the meaning of the expression, cf. L. Robin, *Platon,* 155.

86. This passage must not be approached without showing the elements of
Platonic thought that allow it to be understood. See the commentary of L.
Brisson, *Même et Autre,* 392–93.

87. This dependence does not appear in the *Timaeus,* due to the demiurgic
fiction. In the *Laws* (898d), "soul leads all things around." The motion is ob-
viously circular (*kat'arithmon kykloumenon;* 38a). There is no need to refute A. E.
Taylor (*Timaeus, ad loc.,* and 678–91) who speaks of Newtonian time, or C.
Mugler (*Deux Thèmes,* 59ff.) who speaks of "monodrome" time. Cf. Cornford,
Cosmology, ad loc., and J. Moreau, "Review of Mugler," 365–66.

88. It is only at the age of fifty that the philosophers of the *Republic* have the
right to contemplate the Good (*Rep.* 540a), that is, to move out of time. Hence
Plato's position is the opposite of Democritus's (F 183 Diels), that age would not
be able to make us wise. "We know that the problem of knowing 'whether
happiness increases over time' was constantly debated in the schools, well before
Plotinus devoted an essay to it" (V. Goldschmidt, *Système stoïcien,* 55).

89. See M. Van Houtte, *Philosophie politique,* 24. On the status of the old in
Plato's late work, cf. R. Schaerer, "Itinéraire dialectique."

90. J. Moreau, *Âme du monde,* 68.

91. Cf. *Sym.* 207a et seq.

92. Cf. O. Reverdin, *Religion,* 62–73, and P. Boyancé, "Religion astrale";
see also P. Lévêque and P. Vidal-Naquet, *Clisthène,* 140–46 and "A Study in
Ambiguity," below.

93. The famous encounter between Solon and the priest of Sais is parallel to
the meeting between Hecataeus and the priest of Ammon in Herodotus.

94. Herodotus does not believe that a transformation is reversible: "I will
go on in my story, paying attention to both great cities and small, for of those
that once were great most have become small, and those that were great in my
own time had been small before" (1.5).

95. See below, "Athens and Atlantis," p. 280, n.41; and "Plato's Myth of
the Statesman," p. 292ff.

96. Men in the age of Cronos are born elderly and die as infants.

97. Cf. V. Goldschmidt, *Religion,* 118–20, and L. Robin, *Platon,* 278.

98. On this point as on so many others, Aristotle made the pretense of
taking Plato literally (*Pol.* 7(5). 1316a et seq.). His lead was followed by K. R.
Popper, *Open Society I:* this lively book made Plato a precursor of Hegel, Marx,
and Hitler and has stirred up a controversy that is occasionally brilliant and

60 almost always futile (cf. G. J. de Vries, *Antisthenes;* R. Bambrough, *Plato, Popper;* R. C. Levinson, *Defense of Plato;* and the bibliography compiled in L. Brisson, *Platon,* vol. 3, p. 191).

99. In the myth of the *Politicus* (274c–d) human inventions are described in terms of divine gifts, the same reality being transcribed on two scales. In the *Politicus* Plato depicts an irreversible decline and so insists on the total dependency of his "primitives." From a Platonic point of view, however, an "invention" only has meaning to the degree that it is inspired by a divine model.

3   Epaminondas the Pythagorean,
     or the Tactical Problem
     of Right and Left

Epaminondas, a man famed for his learning and his philosophy.
                                    Plutarch, Agesilaus 27

ANTONY: *Octavius, lead your battle softly on*
        Upon the left hand of the even field.
OCTAVIUS: *Upon the right hand I; keep thou the left.*
ANTONY: *Why do you cross me in this exigent?*
OCTAVIUS: *I do not cross you; but I will do so.*
                    Shakespeare, Julius Caesar 5.1.16–20

If the two victories won by Epaminondas at Leuctra (371
B.C.) and Mantinea (362 B.C.) still pose difficult questions that offer a
broad field for the exercise of ingenuity and for disagreements among
scholars, there is one fact so secure that it scarcely arouses any discussion.
The Theban owed his success to a twinned revolution in tactics: adoption
of the oblique battle formation (*loxē phalanx*) and attack by the left wing
of the line. It is the second of these revolutions that we would like to help
analyze and explain.[1]

At Leuctra, with many fewer soldiers than his opponents, Epaminondas massed his best infantry across from the right wing of the enemy, who
were led by the Spartan Cleombrotus.[2] In a single phrase, Plutarch sums
up perfectly the shared element in the accounts of Xenophon and Diodorus: "At the time of battle, he drew his phalanx obliquely to the left"
(τὴν φάλαγγα λόξην ἐπὶ τὸ εὐώνυμον: *Pelopidas* 23). This maneuver,
utterly contrary to the military tradition of the Greeks, gained him the
victory.

Mantinea was a battle of allied forces, where Epaminondas's tactical
imagination was even more remarkable than at Leuctra. Mantinea was
also a more complex encounter; hence the divergent accounts among the
ancient writers.[3] On our specific problem, however, Diodorus and

This paper was written in collaboration with P. Lévêque and published in
Historia 9 (1960): 294–308.

Xenophon are in agreement. The description in Diodorus, probably following Ephorus, can easily be shown to have been modeled on the pattern at Leuctra. The strongest elements of Epaminondas's army (Thebans reinforced by Arcadians) are on the left wing, facing the right wing of the enemy, which is composed in the traditional way of the federation's elite (Spartiates and Mantineans). The account of Xenophon is certainly less precise, for it occurs in the last pages of the *Hellenica*, where the narrator is showing some signs of fatigue. Still, when he speaks of the federation's left wing, it is to locate the Athenians there and to indicate that Epaminondas massed against them only a thin screen of troops, whereas he used his stronger side to attack the enemy's right (*Hell.* 7.5.23). It was during the victorious onrush of his left wing, where the cavalry served as shock troops, that Epaminondas was to die.[4]

It is worth repeating that the deployment of one's best troops on the left was a true revolution in tactics, a complete break with tradition. In fact, prior to Epaminondas, the elite corps,[5] under the commander-in-chief,[6] always comprised the right wing; in case of a league battle, the right was manned either by the hegemonic city or by the city whose interests were most directly affected by the outcome.[7] At Marathon (Hdt. 6.111), for example, the only non-Athenian contingent is the Plataean, and it fights on the left. At Plataea, after having been compelled to accept Spartan command, the Athenians occupy the left (Hdt. 9.28).[8] At Delium (424) the Thebans are arrayed, conventionally, on the right (Thuc. 4.93). In the first battle of Mantinea, the Mantineans are on the right, the Argives in the center, and the Athenians on the left; Thucydides explains "The Mantineans held the right wing because the battle took place on their territory" (Thuc. 5.67).[9] Obviously, before Epaminondas, the right wing took the main role on attack.[10] This arrangement is so "natural" to the Greeks that when Xenophon describes the ideal battle— that is, between Cyrus and Croesus at the beginning of Book 7 of the *Cyropaedia*—he borrows a great deal from the genius of Epaminondas, but still maintains the primacy of the right side.[11] Epaminondas's daring in this respect had no immediate heir. From Granicus to Hydaspes, Alexander acquired tactical innovations along the line established by the Theban, but still he always led the charge from the right.[12]

Does this rule of land battles also hold true for naval engagements? The answer is more complicated, inasmuch as the fifth century, between Lade and Arginusae, saw naval tactics change much more quickly and fundamentally than land tactics. We know nothing about the deployment of the Ionians at Lade, where we find evidence of the first attempt at *diekplous* (breaking the enemies' line) (Hdt. 6.12).[13] At Salamis, just as at

Plataea and Mycale, the Spartans hold the right and the Athenians the   63
left (Hdt. 8.84–85). [14] Nonetheless, at the Battle of Sybota (433), on the
Corcyraean side the Athenians occupy the right as mere observers: facing
them, the Corinthians are on the left flank with the swiftest ships (Thuc.
1.48). [15] In this battle there is no longer any trace of the traditional order,
although Thucydides emphasizes its archaic quality (1.49). [16] Afterward,
little importance is given to the fact that at Naupactus the best of the
Peloponnesian ships are placed on the right wing (Thuc. 2.90). Could
Epaminondas have taken his inspiration from naval tactics? If so, we
would have to see more than just a metaphor in Xenophon's famous
description of Epaminondas at Mantinea, "leading his army with the
shock troops in from like the prow of a trireme" (ὁ δὲ τὸ στράτευμα
ἀντίπρῳρον ὥσπερ τριήρη προσῆγε: *Hell.* 7.5.23). Except for the expedition of 363, during which—to the best of our knowledge—he did not
participate in any real naval battle, Epaminondas's experience at sea does
not seem very significant. Before we can explain his bold innovation, we
must examine the origins and underlying motives of traditional tactics.

In approaching this problem we immediately confront a noted passage
in Thucydides that provides an adequate explanation in the opinion of
most commentators. [17] Describing the deployment of troops by the Spartan king Agis at the first battle of Mantinea (418) Thucydides says, "All
armies, when engaging, are apt to thrust outwards their right wing; and
either of the opposing forces tends to outflank his enemy's left with his
own right, because every soldier individually fears for his exposed side,
which he tries to cover with the shield of his comrade on the right,
conceiving that the closer he draws in the better he will be protected. The
first man in the front rank of the right wing is originally responsible for
its deflection, for he always wants to withdraw from the enemy his own
exposed side, and the rest of the army, from a like fear, follow his
example" (5.71, tr. Jowett). [18] On close reading, this mechanistic interpretation, although otherwise admirably coherent, provides a precise
explanation of only the most mechanical aspects of the Greek battle plan;
in no way does it allow us to understand why, in the same battle, Agis
took the precaution of stationing a few Spartans on the extreme right
(Thuc. 5.67). [19] To be blunt, it accounts for the movement of the armies
but does not explain the deployment of the line of battle. Let us suppose,
although it is far from certain, that Thucydides wanted to provide an all-
encompassing explanation. In itself such "rationalization" is not surprising, particularly within its own context. Indeed, the historian has just
suggested an explanation, no less rationalized, for the Spartan custom of

64   advancing to battle to the rhythm of flute music: "This is not a religious custom but a way to control the pace of the charge, without opening gaps in the ranks, as often happens to great armies when they attack the enemy" (Thuc. 5.70). Even if this were an adequate explanation for Thucydides' own time, it clearly fails to explain the origin of the convention he is describing.[20] Would not the same be true of the other explanation as well?

We feel that another passage in Thucydides is decisive in this regard. During the siege of their land in 427, some Plataeans make their escape in the odd garb that Thucydides describes as follows: "They were lightly equipped, and wore only the left shoe so as to have firmer footing in the mud" (Thuc. 3.22).

What is the value of Thucydides' explanation? Is it the bare foot, as some say, or the shod, as others claim, that prevents slipping in the mud?[21] In fact, by adopting a suggestion of Frazer (*The Golden Bough*), W. Deonna has shown that in sculpture, as in "life," the baring of one foot is part of a rite devoted to the chthonian deities; thus the passage in Thucydides can only be understood in connection with the many cases of *monokrēpides* (single sandals).[22] The historian is caught—pardon the expression—*in flagrante delicto,* in the abuse of rationalization.[23] The same is true of the long-accepted explanation of the primacy of the right side in military maneuvers before Epaminondas. We must move from the technical interpretation to the sociological.

There is general agreement about the preeminent role of collective representations in the opposition between right and left, which corresponds most often to the opposition between sacred and profane.[24] On the basis of "an almost insignificant asymmetry in the body"[25] human societies have developed a profoundly asymmetrical representation of space. Early Greece provides an excellent illustration of this fact[26] (which, moreover, goes well beyond the bounds of antiquity).[27] In Homer, for example, the right is always the side of active strength and of life; the left is the side of passive weakness and of death; the right emits life-giving and beneficial forces, whereas from the left emanate forces that are dispiriting and harmful. This has been well demonstrated by J. Cuillandre in the course of a long, minute analysis of the Homeric poems; although it occasionally founders on excessive subtleties, its overall argument remains wholly persuasive.[28]

From Homer, Cuillandre rightly moves on to compare the ancient Pythagoreans. The Pythagoreans actually systematized what was scattered throughout the *Iliad* and the *Odyssey.*[29] Aristotle's *Metaphysics* (*Metaph.* 1.5.986a 15 = Diels[7] 54 (45) B 5) has preserved for us a table of

correspondences (the famous *systoichia*), consisting of the ten essential   65
oppositions into which "certain Pythagoreans" compress all reality. The
unit right/left appears there, beside the pairs of limited/unlimited,
equal/unequal, unity/plurality, good/bad, and square/oblong. This is
evidently an ancient scale, in the eyes of Aristotle, since he specifies that
it was either borrowed by the Pythagoreans from Alcmeon of Croton or
by Alcmeon from the Pythagoreans.[30] The cosmos also is subject to this
general division of realities. According to Aristotle's *de Caelo* (2.2.284b 6
= Diels[7] 58 (45) B 30),[31] the Pythagoreans consider the sky a body that
has a right and a left side: "People are to be found who affirm that the sky
has a right and a left—I am thinking of those who are called Pythagoreans, for this theory belongs to them." Explicating this passage in his
commentary on the *de Caelo*, Simplicius provides some evidence derived
from a lost treatise of Aristotle's: "The Pythagoreans call good that which
is on the right, up high, in front; they call bad that which is on the left,
low down, and in back. Aristotle himself has recorded this in his collection of Pythagorean axioms."[32]

The primacy of the right is expressed in certain practices of the
"akousmatikoi": for example, the rules that require one to enter a sanctuary from the right, and always to put on the right shoe first (with the
opposite processes being performed from the left).[33]

Such qualitative topography recurs in the underworld as it is envisioned by some sects with "Orphic" or Pythagorean leanings. This is
what we learn from the symbolism of the Y: "At the crossroads of Hades
[*triodos*] there sit the judges of souls. They send to the right those whose
merits have made them worthy of entering the Elysian Fields; down the
road to the left, they drive the wicked who are to be thrown into
Tartarus."[34]

The dualism of left and right that is so clearly marked among the
Pythagoreans actually permeates all Greek thought throughout the fifth
century. For instance, according to a tradition shared by Parmenides,
Anaxagoras, Empedocles, and a physician of the Hippocratic school, the
conception of a boy takes place on the right of the uterus, and that of a
girl on the left.[35] Moreover, this was not an isolated belief among the
physicians of the Classical era. The right eye and the right breast were
thought to be stronger than their counterparts on the left;[36] for a preg-
nant woman, a connection was established between a male fetus and the
right breast;[37] and it was held that "it is dangerous to cauterize or make
an incision on the right, for as much as the right prevails in strength so
much do diseases on that side gain in intensity."[38] Such texts are even
more striking because they probably date from the beginning of the

fourth century[39] and because we know the huge place occupied by medicine in the *paideia* of Classical Greece.[40]

This tradition is so powerful that, in our opinion, it is enough to explain the Greeks' custom of making the right wing of the battle line carry the offense.[41] So, in fact, we are not too far from Thucydides after all, for it is "normal" that the right hand be the spear-hand and the left carry the defensive weapon, the shield.[42]

Under such circumstances there had to be a veritable revolution—during growth of the "enlightenment" that characterizes the age of Pericles[43]—to produce a challenge to a tradition that was still so vigorous. The criticism develops along three lines: *technē* (which might require the use of both hands),[44] the study of anatomy, and speculation about geometrical space. Greek physicians occupy a position of special importance in the progress of critical thought, at least with regard to *technē* and anatomy. When Diogenes of Apollonia describes the venous system[45] (making virtually no mention of the arteries), he constructs a network of veins that is completely symmetrical and based on the continual distinction—without any preference—between right and left.[46] Similarly, the "positivist" who is the author of the treatise *On the Doctor's Duty* declares[47] that one must "become accustomed to doing all things with each hand individually and with both together; indeed they are equals."[48]

Also basing his argument on reasons drawn from technology, and specifically from military technology, Plato (in Book 7 of the *Laws*) recommends the use of both hands: "The practice which now prevails is almost universally misunderstood . . . in that the right and left hand are supposed to be by nature differently suited for our various uses of them; whereas no difference is found in the use of the feet and the lower limbs; but in the use of the hands we are, as it were, maimed by the folly of nurses and mothers; for although our two arms are by nature balanced, we created a difference in them by bad habit" (794d–95d, tr. Jowett). Plato continues that this prejudice, dangerous enough in everyday life, is intolerable in the case of military training and the handling of weapons.[49]

Between 450 and 430[50] Hippocrates of Chios published the first *Elements of Geometry.* If geometrical study, as the Greeks conceived it, presupposes homogeneous space, the geometrician is not obliged to express this postulate explicitly. It was the Pythagorean Philolaos of Croton, the first to have written a public treatise about Pythagorean doctrine,[51] who Plutarch says defined geometry as ἀρχὴ καὶ μητρόπολις . . . τῶν ἄλλων (μαθημάτων) . . . "the base and mother city of the

other disciplines" (*Quaest. conv.* 8.2.718e = Diels⁷ 44 (32) A 7a). It was   67
also he, so far as we know, who was the first to declare the unity and
homogeneity of space.⁵²

This is implicit in a passage that Stobaeus attributes to Philolaos's
*Bacchae:*⁵³ Ὁ κόσμος εἷς ἐστιν, ἤρξατο δὲ γίγνεσθαι ἀπὸ τοῦ μέσου καὶ
ἀπὸ τοῦ μέσου εἰς τὸ ἄνω διὰ τῶν αὐτῶν τοῖς κάτω · ἔστι γὰρ τὰ ἄνω τοῦ
μέσου ὑπεναντίως κείμενα τοῖς κάτω· τοῖς γὰρ κατωτάτω τὰ μέσα ἐστὶν
ὥσπερ τὰ ἀνωτάτω καὶ τὰ ἄλλα ὡσαύτως· πρὸς γὰρ τὸ μέσον κατὰ ταῦτα
ἐστιν ἑκάτερα, ὅσα μὴ μετενήνεκται.—"The cosmos is one; it began its
becoming from the center, and, from the center, [continued to grow] in
the same way upward and downward. For what is above, in relation to the
center, is symmetrical to what is below. For to the things farthest below,
the center is as the things highest above are [to the center]; likewise for
the rest. Each of the two regions is in the same relation to the center, so
long as they do not shift position."⁵⁴ Here Philolaos shows himself a
heretical Pythagorean,⁵⁵ in that he affirms the relativity of the concepts
of high and low. To be sure, right and left are only alluded to in the phrase
καὶ τὰ ἄλλα ὡσαύτως "likewise for the rest." If, however, we recall that
the Pythagoreans linked the right with the high (identified with goodness) and the left with the low (as evil), the passage quoted above calls
into question the whole notion of a universe polarized along moral
lines.⁵⁶

The fragment from Philolaos inevitably calls to mind a passage from
the *Timaeus* (62c–d).⁵⁷ Plato puts the following words into the mouth of
Timaeus, another "Italian" philosopher: "It is quite a mistake to suppose
that the universe is parted into two regions, separate from and opposite to
each other, the one a lower to which all things tend which have any bulk,
and an upper to which things only ascend against their will. For as the
universe is in the form of a sphere, all the extremities, being equidistant
from the center, are equally extremities, and the center, which is equidistant from them, is equally to be regarded as the opposite of them all.
Such being the nature of the universe, when a person says that any of
these points is above or below, may he not be justly charged with using an
improper expression?" (tr. Cornford). There ensues a long speech in
which Timaeus refutes the theory of "natural" places,⁵⁸ and from which
we must cite at least these few lines: "In brief, since the Universe, as we
have just said, is spherical, it is inappropriate to call one place 'above' and
another 'below' " (*Tim.* 63a).

There is scarcely a dialogue in which Plato "Pythagorises" more than
in the *Timaeus;*⁵⁹ more to the point, we may note that the ancients
connected the *Timaeus* with the name of Philolaos.⁶⁰ In several sources—

otherwise divergent and showing signs of later influence[61]—we find the story of Plato in Sicily, buying one or more books either from Philolaos himself or from one of his relatives or disciples;[62] these books would enable him to write the *Timaeus*.[63] We readily admit that such stories might have been jealous slanders spread by Plato's detractors, notably Aristoxenus.[64] The comparison that we are emphasizing might help to explain the origin of such attacks.

At the transition from the fifth to the fourth century, then, the traditional conception of right and left had been badly battered. In the fourth century, Plato turned his attention both to the *technē* of the soldier, who should be able to handle arms with either hand, and to geometrical space. On the basis of his reflections, he demolished the traditional view, so he believed, beyond hope of repair. In the same period, Epaminondas stunned his adversaries by also discarding the preference traditionally accorded to the right wing. We can hardly doubt that these facts are connected, and our knowledge of the Theban situation around the year 400 lets us make the connection more precise.

Shortly after the Cylonian revolution, the Pythagorean community was driven out of Metapontum and scattered. Among them was Philolaos, who moved to central Greece and settled for a while in Thebes. A well-known passage of the *Phaedo*[65] tells us that the Thebans Simmias and Cebes, who were still young at the time of Socrates' death,[66] had been pupils of Philolaos. In addition, a firm tradition makes Epaminondas the devoted disciple of the Pythagorean Lysis;[67] the latter was himself a refugee at Thebes, and a passage in Plutarch describes him as Philolaos's companion in misfortune.[68] There is even one piece of evidence,[69] quite late to be sure,[70] that explicitly makes Philolaos the tutor of the victor of Leuctra, "who got the best of this battle from having been the disciple of Philolaos the Pythagorean." Whether Nonnos is giving us precious information or an error sprung from confusion, is it too much to assume that the young man "who took the greatest pleasure in study and spent his leisure time in discussion and philosophy" (Plut. *Pelopidas* 4)[71] could have shared in the intellectual project of the great Pythagorean?[72] In antiquity there was no doubt that the Theban hero made war as a philosopher. His contemporary, Alcidamas of Elea, noted that the Theban renaissance coincided with the accession to power of philosopher-rulers: "At Thebes, the city's prosperity was concurrent with the moment when its leaders became philosophers."[73] Six centuries later, Aelian asks in a rhetorical passage "whether philosophers were not also skilled in matters of war" (*Var. Hist.* 7.14) and answers in the affirmative, citing among others the example of Epaminondas. If we follow out our hypothesis, we

may conclude that Epaminondas showed that he was an extraordinary   69
tactician not in spite of his philosophy, but because of it.[74]

APPENDIX (1980)

Aside from a few insignificant details,[1] the foregoing text is the one
that was drafted in 1958 and published in 1960. For P. Lévêque and
myself, this study marked the beginning of a consideration of the connections between space and military and political institutions that led us,
several years later, to coauthor and publish *Clisthène l'Athénien*. With the
agreement of Lévêque, I am appending to our text a discussion that tries
to bring it up to date, to supplement it where necessary, and to say how I
now see the problems we had raised more than twenty years ago. Needless to say, if we were not still fundamentally confident about our conclusions, they would not have been included in the present volume.

This updating will generally follow the order of the article.

Recent work on Leuctra and Mantinea—valuable as it is for an en-
hanced understanding of the narrative of the two battles—does not,
however, modify what we know about Epaminondas and the attack by
the left wing.[2] Moreover, no one has provided us with a precedent that
would diminish the originality of the Theban leader. No such precedent
is furnished by the battle of Olpe (426), which was fought between the
Athenians, under Demosthenes and in alliance with the Messenians and
some Acharnians, against the Peloponnesians and Ambraciots.[3] On the
Athenian side, Demosthenes is conventionally on the right, with the
Messenians and part of the Athenian contingent. Although Thucydides'
account here is not a model of clarity, he does specify that on the other
line the Ambraciots of Olpe, "the best warriors from the area," held the
right wing, which was also the conventional position, since the battle is
on their territory; they are also distributed among the Peloponnesian
contingents. The fact that a Spartan leader, Eurylochus, occupied the left
wing with a few elite squadrons does not constitute a true exception to
the rule. The battle was won, very classically, by the victory of the right
wing of the Athenian army.[4]

With regard to the strange escape of the Plataeans, who had only one
foot shod, Yvon Garlan has noted that "none of the explanations, when
indeed one is proposed, seems sufficient."[5] Following Brelich,[6] one could
go much farther than we had suggested.[7] In Greek mythology, to have
only one sandal is unquestionably one of the characteristics of the heroes

who make safe the passage from the wilderness to the polis. So it was with the young Jason, in Pindar's *Pythian* 4, returning to his city Iolcos to expel the usurper Pelias; the latter "trembles on merely catching full sight of the single shoe, on the right foot." How does this ephebic custom—for the whole portrait of Jason is that of an ephebe[8]—contribute to understanding Thucydides' story? The besieged Plataeans who were trying to leave were hoplites, adults. Fleeing by night, outside the context of hoplite battle, they naturally return to using the equipment of the rites of adolescence. They had only a dagger and a breastplate and not the heavy hoplite armor. Thucydides certainly did not see things this way, and with the exception of the "absurd" detail of the single sandal, everything he said is perfectly "rational" or rationalizable. Nonetheless, there remains that detail, which he had the honesty to give us and which allows us to contradict him.

The posthumous glory of Robert Hertz continues to grow, and in the modern exploration of the symbolic world of human societies his study of right and left looks today like a pioneering work.[9] Following in the path he cleared, people have studied the opposition (or at least the distinction) between right and left in several societies. In Southern India, for example, it constitutes one of the elements of caste symbolism.[10]

Documentation has increased for the Greek world as well. In addition to the Orphic tablets that have already been mentioned,[11] there is now the gold plaque in the Getty Museum (Malibu, California); the deceased is invited to drink at the eternal spring, ἐπὶ δεξιὰ λευκὴ κυπάρισσος: "on the right, where the white cypress stands."[12] Above all, in his inquiry into "polarity" and "analogy" as modes of argumentation in Greek thought, G.E.R. Lloyd was led to include the opposition between right and left, along with the pairings of dry/moist, cold/hot, masculine/feminine, and several others.[13]

We tried to show that the military craft of Epaminondas presupposes an intellectual shift, or rather, in the terms of C. Castoriadis, a shift in society's image of itself.[14] This still seems evident to me, even if one can argue about the exact role played in the process by the Pythagorean philosopher Philolaos. To be honest, Philolaos's role strikes me as essentially symbolic; we suggested a name to represent this "mental revolution"—the opening of the city to geometrized space. That this did in fact take place seems to me indisputable. Today, however, it also seems to me

to have occurred in a much less simple and unitary fashion than I believed
twenty years ago. It is striking, for example, that Aristotle could be both
the theoretician of natural place and also the philosopher who refuted the
Pythagoreans by demonstrating the relativity of the concepts of right and
left (*de Caelo* 2.2.284b–85b).

There has also been further discussion of the real and supposititious
work of Philolaos.[15] According to G.E.R. Lloyd, for example, it is
Philolaos who is attacked in the Hippocratic treatise *Ancient Medicine*.[16]
What about the passage from the *Bacchae?* We reproduced the version in
the *Vorsokratiker* of Diels-Kranz, and we wrongly pronounced the emendations to be certain. The following change has been suggested in the
third clause: Τοῖς γὰρ κάτω τὸ κατωτάτω ⟨μέρος⟩ ἐστὶν ὥσπερ τὰ ἀνωτάτω καὶ τὰ ἄλλα ὡσαύτως. This yields, "To the things below, the very
lowest section is like the very highest, and similarly for the rest"; thus the
next statement would mean, "For both [the highest and the lowest] have
the same relation to the center, except that their positions are the inverse
of one another's." This does not alter the basic meaning of the passage.
What remains in dispute is its place in Philolaos's system. Its genuineness is rejected by some who accept the authenticity of most of the
fragments, but accepted by others.[17] I am not going to reenter the
argument, but for all concerned—myself included—it is a hypothesis
wholly outside the fragment itself that provides an answer.[18] Today I find
the question of minor importance.

Was Epaminondas a Pythagorean, and in what sense? Recent studies
confirm it, in brief or at length, but without ever addressing the question
of the connections between philosophy and military strategy.[19] Still, the
comparison demands attention if it is admitted that our sources inform us
about things other than themselves. To what extent has our hyothesis,
published in 1960, been accepted? The question needs to be asked, since
our essay had some significance for specialists in tactics as well as historians of philosophy and could also reach ethnologists and sociologists. In
the latter fields[20] our conclusions were readily welcomed, and the same
was true among certain historians of philosophy,[21] although not all. In an
elaborately detailed article, Kurt von Fritz referred to only one sentence,
where it was suggested, *cum grano salis,* that if one accepted the very late
testimony of Nonnos, Epaminondas had been the disciple of Philolaos. It
was here that von Fritz balked; the passage is not included in recent
collections of *testimonia*.[22]

There remain the historians of Greek cavalry and infantry. Only W. K.

72   Pritchett really took the trouble to read our work and pay serious attention to what we had to say about the military role of the two wings. He
does not, however, declare his own opinion on what he calls "the sociological or philosophical origin of associating the right wing with the
best troops."[23] Relying on Thucydides 5.71, he believes that a military
explanation can be provided for a military practice. J. K. Anderson
makes the friendly remark, "I do not believe that Epaminondas placed
his deep column on the left for metaphysical reasons, but see Pierre
Lévêque and Pierre Vidal-Naquet."[24] Space, a social construct if there
ever was one, must of course depend on metaphysics. . . . For a military
fact there has to be a military reason; having said that, one has said it all,
adopting the idea of our Medieval forebears that only like can act upon
like—an idea we have been freed from by some subsequent intellectual
developments.

Those who think this way would do well to push their reasoning to its
limit; Thucydides should not be enough for them, for he alludes to a
phenomenon that is neither technical nor military in a strict sense—the
fear that every soldier feels on seeing his right side exposed.[25] One critic
has found the perfect solution, materialist and military all at once: "If the
Greek armies leaned to the right, it was due to the simple fact that each
soldier in the battle line carried a 'big, heavy shield.'"[26] The willing
acceptance of such explanations—so easy, so "self-evident"—gives rise
to a sort of dread in the face of any explanation that depends on another
model. Thus G. Cawkwell, in a serious recent study, does take note of the
"revolutionary change"[27] we tried to account for, but on the verge of
explaining it he retreats and says nothing. In fact, this is a good example
of the mental habits—it must finally be said—that are ingrained in our
disciplines. "History, knowledge of Greek literature, and sociology can
furnish networks of explanation that are interconnected; a military event
is the product of several sets of 'causes' that are not altogether technical
and military"—this is easy to say, but much more difficult to have
acknowledged within a milieu where everyone thinks he owns some
property that he has to defend against trespass. To make the lines cross, as
we tried to do, provokes defensive reactions that we should have foreseen.
In 1949, Georges Dumézil, fighting on behalf of a project much more
far-reaching than ours, described the phenomenon in unforgettable
terms. Contrasting Latinists and Orientalists, with the latter representing a discipline more open to change, Dumézil wrote: "Unfortunately . . . these scholars [the Latinists]—for reasons stemming both from
the history of their field and from its current conditions—do not respond
to the progress of comparative methodologies with the same flexibility,

the same freedom, as do Orientalists of every type."[28] Specialists in the   73
Greek world could also use some limbering-up exercises.

Notes

1. The first revolution was drawn from a Theban tradition (cf. Thuc. 4.93).
2. The principal sources for the battle are: Xen. *Hell.* 6.4.1–16; Diod. 15.51–56; Paus. 9.13; Plut. *Pelopidas* 20–23. The basic modern bibliography is to be found in Kromayer-Veith, *Schlachtfelder* 4, p. 290, and Kromayer-Veith, *Schlachten-Atlas* 4, pp. 33–34 (and map 5, nos. 4 and 5); Glotz-Cohen, *Histoire grecque* 3, pp. 148–49; H. Bengston, *Griechische Geschichte*, 247 nn. 4 and 5.
3. Xen. *Hell.* 7.5.18–27; Diod. 15.84–87. Modern bibliography in Kromayer-Veith, *Schlachtfelder* 1, p. 24ff. and 4, p. 317ff., and Kromayer-Veith, *Schlachten-Atlas* 4, pp. 35–36 (and map 5, nos. 7 and 8); Glotz-Cohen, *Histoire grecque* 3, pp. 176–77; H. Bengston, *Griechische Geschichte*, 284 n. 4.
4. Our interpretation of the battle is that of J. Hatzfeld in his edition of the *Hellenica*, C.U.F. 2, p. 216 n. 1. In an unfortunate slip, however, he translates 7.5.23 (ἀπὸ τοῦ εὐωνύμου κέρατος—"from the left wing") as "from the right wing." Kromayer's reconsiderations do not affect our topic (most recently *Schlachten-Atlas*, n. 3 above). Later the Theban's tactics came to be represented as Theban tactics; hence Plutarch's rhetorical elaboration (*Quest. Rom.* 78.282e): "Indeed, once the Thebans had routed the enemy with their left wing and carried the day at Leuctra, they then continued to assign the hegemonic function to the left wing in all battles."
5. Clearly this is only the infantry; the cavalry was normally divided into two symmetrical groups.
6. The right is also the location of the polemarch at Marathon (Hdt. 6.111). It is the place of the king in tragedy (Eur. *Suppl.* 656–57) as well as in the Spartan army (Xen. *Lac. Pol.* 13.6). Other references for this question are to be found in an important article by K. Lugebil, "Staatsverfassung," 604–24.
7. The identification of command of the right wing with hegemony is especially emphasized by Plutarch, *Aristides* 16 (citing Hdt. 9.46): "The Spartans were willingly giving them possession of the right wing and were, in some way, handing over command"; cf. Plut. *Quest. Rom.* 78.282e. It is also worth recalling an odd anecdote recorded in Diodorus 1.67: In one of Psamettichus's campaigns, the Greek mercenaries are said to have been placed to the right of the king, to the great consternation of the Egyptians, who would have deserted (cf. Hdt. 2.30). On the authenticity of this episode, see the bibliographical information in J. G. Griffiths, "Three Notes," 144–49.
8. The Tegeans made a futile attempt to contend with the Athenians for the right to fight on the left (cf. 9.26). To mollify them, they were placed to the immediate left of the Spartans, as Herodotus makes clear: "To join them on the

74 line, the Spartans had chosen the Tegeans, with the additional purpose of honoring them for their courage." For technical reasons the Spartans then suggested to the Athenians—who had already fought against the Persians—to switch places with them so as to be face to face with the Persians. The decision was greeted with joy by the Athenians, who saw in it a Spartan cession of hegemony (cf. Hdt. 9.46 and Plut. *Aristides* 16). But the maneuver was thwarted by the Persians. The whole story was criticized as an Athenian fabrication by Plutarch (*de Malig. Herod.* 872a et seq.; cf. also W. J. Woodhouse, "Plataiai," 41–43).

9. In the same passage Thucydides explains that the Skirites (light-armed troops from a mountainous region in northern Laconia) occupy the left wing. But this is not exactly a "privilege," as in the translation by J. Voilquin and J. de Romilly. The historian simply says, "Alone among the Lacedaimonians they occupy that position in the line."

10. The ever-present possibility that both right wings could win led quite normally to some stand-offs; hence Xenophon's admiration for the behavior of Agesilaus at Coronea: having defeated the enemy's left wing, he swung around to defeat the right wing, which had overcome the men of Orchomenos (*Hell.* 4.3.16–19).

11. Xen. *Cyrop.* 7.1 (esp. 23–27). The Egyptians under Croesus are arranged in ranks 100-deep, in imitation of the Thebans at Leuctra "who had a formation with a depth of at least 50 shields" (*Hell.* 6.4.12) as opposed to twelve on the Spartan side. (We may note that as early as Delion the Thebans were arrayed in twenty-five rows: Thuc. 4.93.) Cyrus used chariots just as Epaminondas used his cavalry at Mantinea. At Cyrus's command, the battle was engaged in two stages, but each time beginning on the right. The first maneuver: engagement on the flanks to avoid encirclement by Croesus's army, which was broadly spread out; Cyrus attacked from the right, and only afterward did Artagersas engage from the left. The second: genuine combat was undertaken by Abradatas, who was specifically said to hold the right wing. There was an organic bond between the two wings that was one of the great tactical discoveries of the end of the fifth century; prior to Alexander, Epaminondas had known how to use it, although this in no way detracts from the originality of his attack from the left wing.

12. Cf. U. Wilcken, *Alexander*, 85, 103, 134, 182.

13. Cf. P. H. Legrand's edition of the *Histories*, C.U.F. 6, p. 13 n. 2.

14. It is an accident that the engagement begins on the left: before the advance of the barbarian fleet, the Greeks were ready to retreat when an Athenian, Ameinias of Pallene, fell upon an enemy ship and thereby gave the signal for battle.

15. Similarly in the battle of Sestos, Mindaros occupies the left wing with the swiftest ships (cf. Thuc. 8.104).

16. As Thucydides tells us explicitly, battle "in the old style" means one where the soldiers, massed on the bridges, play a more important role than the tactics of the ships. The order of the latter is not in question (cf. 1.49; 2.89; 7.62).

17. The traditional theory was expounded, for example, by W. Rüstow and H. Koechly (*Kriegswesen,* 126, 143). K. Lugebil does consider a sociological explanation but immediately rejects it, on the grounds that in classical battles the left wing is not the worst place but the second best ("Staatsverfassung," 605). This is unarguable: cf. for Marathon, Hdt. 8.148; for Plataea, Hdt. 9.26 et seq. (and Plut. *de Malig. Herod.* 872a, for whom the dispute between the Athenians and Tegeans is *peri tōn deutereiōn*); cf. also the case of Paralos in Eur. *Suppl.* 659 and that of Hyllos in Eur. *Heracl.* 671. Still it is clear that in a world divided between right and left, the center has much less importance. On the other hand, Kromayer and Veith make a distinction between the tilt to the right on offense and the custom of putting the best troops on the right (*Heerwesen,* 85, 94).

18. It is scarcely necessary to recall that the shield is held in the left hand. The explanation proposed by Thucydides has been sharply criticized by W. J. Woodhouse, who would like to assign a purely physical cause to the phenomenon: each man has to carry a heavy shield, which skews his gait to the right ("Mantinea," 72–73); *contra,* cf. A. W. Gomme, *Essays,* 134–35.

19. Strictly speaking, the right was held by the Tegeans. They probably got this privilege because the battle took place in Arcadia, in the land of their neighbors and traditional enemies, the Mantineans. We have seen that, for this same reason, the Mantineans occupied the right wing of the allied force. Moreover, their closest neighbors were other Arcadians.

20. Cf. especially the remarks in Pausanias 3.17.5 on the sanctuary of the Muses at Sparta—the Muses who protect flutists, lyre-players, and cithara-players, who keep time for the soldier's march.

21. Gomme's commentary on this point is rather odd (2., p. 283): "It is the naked right foot that prevents them slipping in the clay, not, as some have thought, the shod left foot (see Marchant). It would be normal to wear shoes of some kind for this purpose and in this weather; one was left off for a special reason. Arnold aptly quotes from Scott, *Last Minstrel,* canto IV.18: 'Each better knee was bared, to aid / the warriors in the escalade.'" It is astonishing to see knees compared to feet, escarpments to mud.

22. This is the title of an article by W. Deonna; see also his *Cornes gauches.* From these two studies the conclusion is drawn that, in all likelihood, the left side was dedicated to subterranean divinities. On the *monokrēpides* in sculpture, see W. Amelung, "Rito"; for the case of the shod left feet, cf. 131. A noteworthy feature of Deonna's study is the number of references to military life. In an obvious slip, the author writes (57) that only the right foot of the Plataeans was shod, and then establishes analogies between this fact and the *devotio* of the Romans. In reality, only a vast comparative inquiry would make possible the interpretation of an action whose ritual value is unquestionable. Paul Claudel's *Soulier de satin* is based on a similar rite. An equally religious explanation of "monosandalism" has recently been proposed by A. Brelich ("Monosandales," 469ff.): wearing one sandal would be a diminished variant of the imperfection of the lower limbs that often affects heroes, the imperfection being viewed as a

condition of perfection. For his remarks on the passage in Thucydides, see 473–74.

23. We do not wish to deny any value to Thucydides' explanation; what we are considering is a problem of origins.

24. We may refer to the classic study by R. Hertz, "Right Hand." In a recent article ("Main droite" 1), P.-M. Schuhl reminds us that Bichat was the first modern scholar to emphasize the importance of sociological explanations in the problems of right and left.

25. The phrase is R. Hertz's: "Right Hand," 21. It might need to be adjusted slightly.

26. The Greek language provides good evidence for the polarity between right and left by its use of the adjectives designating these concepts: cf. P. Chantraine, "Gauche."

27. For the whole question in antiquity, cf. the dissertation of a pupil of W. Kroll: A. Gornatowski, *Rechts*. Unfortunately, the author scarcely uses the enormous amount of textual material he cites. One could also study the problem in its modern context: in a book with the trappings of science (*Weg*), R. Kobler claims to show that the predominance of the right hand is an achievement of civilization—savages being left-handed—due to the handling of weapons.

28. *Droite et Gauche;* cf. the verdict of F. Robert in his review of J. Cuillandre.

29. "The Pythagoreans have simply defined and given shape to extremely ancient popular ideas" (R. Hertz, "Right Hand," 25 n. 50).

30. The very ambiguity of this statement seems to us to rule out the unhelpful hypothesis that makes the *systoichia* go back only as far as Philolaos: see A. Rey, *Jeunesse*, 374.

31. There follows a more precise statement of the theory: "As a result, it is quite odd that the Pythagoreans had spoken only of these two principles, right and left" (*de Caelo* 2.285a 10 = Diels[7] 58 (45) B 31).

32. P. 386.20 (Heiberg) = Arist. F 200 (Rose) = Diels[7] 58 (45) B 30. Simplicius goes on to observe that the idea of good and evil is primarily connected with right and left, much more so than with high and low or front and back.

33. Iambl. *Vit. Pyth.* 83 and *Protr.* 21.11 = Diels[7] 58 (45) C4, p. 464, and C6, p. 466. To these passages one can compare the curious observation in Plutarch *de Vit. Pud.* 8, that when crossing their legs the Pythagoreans took care never to put the left above the right. In all these examples, it is the *beginning* of the action that must be performed from the right, the divine side; cf. A. Delatte, *Études*, 300, and J. Cuillandre, *Droite et Gauche*, 470.

34. F. Cumont, *Lux perpetua*, 279–80. For the depiction of the Pythagorean Y on funeral steles, see F. Cumont, *Symbolisme funéraire*, 427; C. Picard, "Représentation" and "Marchand d'huile," 154. The texts confirm the systematic character of this topography. They have been collected by Gornatowski, *Rechts*, 48ff. The best known is the famous "Orphic" tablet from Petelia (Diels[7] 1 (66)

17), which has the instructions that one must avoid the spring located to the left of the abode of Hades and go to the right toward the Lake of Memory. On the whole question, see E. Rohde, *Psyche*, 444 n. 4. The research of J. G. Griffiths, "Three Notes," and S. Morenz, "Rechts," allow these observations to be extended to the Egyptian concept of the judgment of the dead. Hence it is worth noting the opposite opinion held sway for a long time: cf., for example, Widemann, *Geschichte Aegyptens*, 135. It has even been possible, as a result, to write that for the Egyptians the left was the place of honor: cf. B. A. van Groningen, *Herodotos Historien* 1, p. 121.

35. This is the source for the line in Parmenides, "To the right the boys, to the left the girls" (Diels⁷ 28 (18) B 17). The doctor of the *Aphorisms* 5.48 (545 Littré) is more cautious: "Male embryos tend to be situated on the right, and females more often on the left." Bourgey dates the *Aphorisms* to the end of the fifth century (*Observation*, 36–37). Comparable texts from the whole of antiquity have been collected by Gornatowski, *Rechts*, 39–44. Cf. also A. Rey, *Jeunesse*, 444.

36. *Epidemics* 2.6.16 (136 Littré).

37. *Aphorisms* 5.38 (544 Littré).

38. *Diseases* 3 (154 Littré). Similar "facts" still appear in Aristotle. Thus, among the animals, the better is to the right (*de Part. An.* 665b 22 et seq.). In man the heart is on the left to compensate for the unusual chill on that side (*de Part. An.* 666b 7).

39. So Bourgey, *Observation*, 33–41.

40. Cf. especially W. Jaeger, *Paideia* 3, 445ff.

41. It is worth remembering that in the *Iliad*, it is Achilles who occupies the extreme right of the Achaean camp, while Ajax holds the extreme left: cf. J. Cuillandre, *Droite et Gauche*, 18ff. When we recall the roles played by these two heroes in epic and tragedy, the arrangement scarcely seems accidental.

42. Cf. J. Cuillandre, *Droite et Gauche*, 471, and the anthropological discussion in n. 4.

43. The *Aufklärung* (enlightenment) in the second half of the fifth century is ably discussed by P.-M. Schuhl, *Formation*, 318ff.

44. "It is because of the use of his hands that man is the most rational of the animals, according to Anaxagoras," says Aristotle (*de Part. An.* 687a8 = Diels⁷ 59 (46) A 102).

45. Diels⁷ 64 (51) B 6; cf. J. Zafiropulo, *Diogène d'Apollonie*, 86ff.

46. The same could be said of the treatise *On the Places of Man*, although it seems to date from the middle of the fifth century (Bourgey, *Observation*, 37). These references render all the more striking the errors of Aristotle mentioned above.

47. *On . . . Duty* 4 (Kuehlwein). The text seems to date from the beginning of the fourth century (Bourgey, *Observation*, 33–34). On the treatise and the spirit that informs it, see Bourgey, *Observation*, 60–61.

48. These brief remarks on *technē* would require an inquiry into the use of both hands in the working methods of Greek artisans.

49. Here Plato is arguing like a pragmatic legislator, as in the *Republic*, where he justifies what has been called his feminism by arguments that are essentially practical (5.455a et seq.). The passage from the *Laws* quoted above has been commented on by P.-M. Schuhl, "Main Droite" 2. Schuhl has shown that it is all the more impressive since, in several other places, Plato agrees with the Pythagorean tradition on the problem of right and left. We may also note that in the *Politics* Aristotle finds it enough to cite Plato's opinion (2.1274b 12—but according to Newman the passage is a gloss); for his own part, he observes reasonably that the right hand is more skillful, but that everyone can become ambidextrous.

50. P. H. Michel, *Pythagore*, 247.

51. Demetrius *ap.* D. L. 8.85 = Diels⁷ 44 (32) A 1; Iambl. *Vit. Pyth.* 199 = Diels⁷ 14 (4) 17.

52. For reasons that would take too long to detail here, we consider the fragments of Philolaos to be authentic, but we know that the contrary opinion has long prevailed. We will not revive a dispute that is already very old, since it dates back, in its main features, to an article by Bywater, "Fragments." E. Frank, whose hyper-criticism brought down so many Pythagoreans, went so far as to consider Philolaos a "mythical personage," a literary fiction created by Plato and used by a clever fabricator as the author of the *Peri Physios (Sogenannten Pythagoreer, passim*, and 294 n. 1). Reaction against such excesses came especially from E. Zeller and R. Mondolfo (*Filosofia* 1.2, pp. 367–85), and G. de Santillana and W. Pitts in a rapid but forceful treatment ("Philolaos"). Spuriousness is still alleged by J. E. Raven (*Pythagoreans*, 93ff.), and by Kirk and Raven, *Presocratic Philosophers*, 307–11. Two concise synopses, both favoring authenticity, are to be found in P. Wuilleumier, *Tarente*, 566–73, and P. H. Michel, *Pythagore*, 258–61. It is enough to note here that the principal argument in favor of authenticity is the weakness of the claims on the other side, which are too often infused with the impassioned logic that gives life to such debates. Thus P. Tannery insists that there is no mention of the *Peri Physios* earlier than the first century B.C. ("Fragments philolaïques"). This, however, means he is forgetting a citation in Aristotle (*Eth. Eud.* 2.8.1225a 30 = Diels⁷ 44 (32) B 16), allusions that are unmistakable in the *Phaedo* (86a) and probable in the *Philebus* (17d et seq.), and the apparent influence of this book on a work of Speusippus (*Theolog. Arithm.* 82.10 de Falco = Diels⁷ 44 (32) A. 13). One often forgets that Aristotle was not a historian; on the subject see the fair comments of E. Zeller, "Philolaos." As for the most recent of the skeptics, J. E. Raven, he insists on two main points (cf. Kirk and Raven, *Presocratic Philosophers*, 309–10). First of all, he says, even if Mondolfo did succeed in explaining all the anomalous details, he cannot dispel "what might be thought the strongest of all arguments against the fragments, the unduly large number of such suspicious or unusual features" (309). But this is to forget that, in the

hypothesis being advanced, the "suspect" details are only suspected details.
Pushing the case to its limits, one could impugn the existence of Napoleon on
the grounds of the number of those who saw a solar myth in his story. Secondly,
says Raven, the Philolaic fragments bear too close a resemblance to what Aristotle writes about the Pythagoreans. The argument is dubious when one exam-
ines the indicated passages, and moreover it can easily be turned upside down.
It is time to put a stop to this nonsense—opportunely denounced by V. Goldschmidt, *Système stoïcien,* 50–52—which consists, for example, of suggesting
that a certain maxim of Democritus has a Platonic ring to it. No one has yet
been able to explain why a fabricator, whether inspired by Aristotle or not,
would have made Philolaos into a dissident Pythagorean, when such dissidence
only had meaning and interest in the period during which he lived and wrote.

53. Stobaeus, *Flor.* 1.15.7 = Diels[7] 44 (32) B 17. The text is classed
among the genuine, although as Diels notes the title of the work is probably of
Alexandrian origin. As for its transcription into *koinē,* the occurrence is too
frequent to pose any problem and could have taken place in any era. The
emendations suggested by Diels are indisputable, at least in their main lines.
Cf. an earlier commentary on this fragment by A. Boeckh, *Philolaos,* 90ff. See
also Chaignet, *Pythagore,* 234. In Stobaeus (*Flor.* 1.15–16) the text from Philolaos is preceded by a passage from a doxographic manual by Aetius (*Placita*
2.10.1 = Diels, *Dox. Gr.* 339) that attributes to Pythagoras, Plato, and Aristotle a cosmology based on the distinction between right and left, conterminous with a criticism implying the relativity of the notions of height and
depth in the cosmos. All too clearly, this makes inept use of Plato (*Tim.* 62c)
and Aristotle (*de Caelo* 2.2.284b et seq.) and, no doubt, of our passage from
Philolaos.

54. This passage should be compared with two sections from the doxographic manual of Aetius, which contains about all we know of Philolaos's
cosmology (2.7.7 and 3.11.3 = Diels[7] 44 (32) A 16, 17). Mention is made
there of "high," but this highness is defined as *periechon,* enveloping. This
envelope is what Philolaos calls Olympus. The term *kosmos* is reserved for the
substellar world. The detail is problematic but does not imply a contradiction
with F 17, as Diels suggests, especially since *kosmos* is used in its broad sense in
FF 1, 2, and 6.

55. On the innovations of Philolaos's thought within Pythagoreanism, cf.
M. Timpanaro Cardini, "Cosmo." With regard to the problem of the motion of
the earth, the innovations are confirmed by Aetius 3.13.1–2 = Diels[7] 44 (32)
A 21.

56. This calling-into-question is not so surprising in that Philolaos—de-
cidedly not very faithful to the Aristotelian *systoichia* that has bizarrely been
attributed to him—introduced alongside the pair even/odd the result of their
blending, the even-odd (*artioperitton*), which is probably unity (Diels[7] 44 (32) B
5); cf. Ar. *Metaph.* 1.5.986a 17. On the subject, see P. H. Michel, *Pythagore,*
335.

57. The comparison with the fragment from Philolaos was already made by A. Boeckh, *Philolaos*, 92. Aristotle rejects this argumentation (*de Caelo* 2.2.285a 30).

58. That is, for the most part, the theory that will be held by Aristotle. Evidently, if it were not in the *Timaeus*, numbers of scholars would have thought this passage post-Aristotelian.

59. This is demonstrated, with a bit of exaggeration, in the commentary of A. E. Taylor. It is well known that for several years criticism has tended to give Pythagoreanism a major place in the formation of the Platonic system. See, for example, V. Goldschmidt, *Cratyle*, 117ff.; P. Boyancé, "Euthyphron," 146ff., "Religion," 182ff., "Religion astrale," 312ff. At the École Pratique des hautes études, Henri Margueritte has long pursued analogous lines of research.

60. Whence the unhelpful suggestion by C. Ritter that identified Philolaos as the mysterious fifth character in the *Timaeus* (*Untersuchungen*, 174).

61. They are collected in Diels[7] 44 (32) A 1 and 8. Hermippos's narrative in D. L. 8.85 goes so far as to mention the price of 40 Alexandrine minas!

62. On the different versions of this story, cf. A. E. Taylor, *Commentary*, 39–40; J. Burnet, *Early Greek Philosophy*, 280ff.; P. Wuilleumier, *Tarente*, 568. It is not possible to agree with Burnet that none of these texts would suggest that the book was by Philolaos himself: cf. at least Hermippos in D. L. 8.85.

63. From the first quarter of the third century, the story was exploited by the lively satire of Timon the Sillographer, as evinced by these verses preserved by Aulus Gellius (3.17.4)—where Philolaos is not named—"You peddled a little book for a lot of money and with the proceeds you learned how to write the *Timaeus*."

64. Cf. Burnet, *Early Greek Philosophy*, 281.

65. 61d: "Haven't you been instructed on this type of question, you and Simmias, who have lived near Philolaos?"; 61e: "I myself heard Philolaos when he was staying among us." Thus the two Thebans were members of a Pythagorean society directed by Philolaos (cf. Xen. *Mem.* 3.11.17, and Robin, *Notice du Phédon*, C.U.F., xiv).

66. Their youthfulness is confirmed by *Phaedo* 89a, and this detail allows us to fix the date of Philolaos's stay in Thebes around 400 B.C. If we accept Apollodorus's statement (*ap.* D. L. 9.38) that Philolaos was a contemporary of Democritus, who was born between 460 and 457 (*ap.* D. L. 9.41), Philolaos was about sixty years old when he was in Thebes.

67. Corn. Nep. *Epaminondas* 2.2; Cic. *Or.* 3.139, *Off.* 1.155; DS 10.11.12; Plut. *de Daim. Soc.* 16; Paus. 9.13.1; Aelian, *Var. Hist.* 5.17; D. L. 8.1.5; Porph. *Vit. Pyth.* 55; Iambl. *Vit. Pyth.* 250. Diodorus (16.2) knew an aberrant version of this tradition in which Philip of Macedon joins Epaminondas as a disciple of Lysis; cf. A. Aymard, "Philippe," 418 n. 4. Still, Diodorus's foolishness does not give one the right to consider the meeting of Epaminondas and Lysis a pure literary fiction (E. Frank, *Sogenannten Pythagoreer*, 294 n. 1). On Lysis, cf. P. Wuilleumier, *Tarente*, 564–65.

68. *de Daim. Soc.* 13; Philolaos and Lysis are the sole survivors of the burn-

ing of the sect's building in Metapontus. On the different versions of this story, see P. Wuilleumier, *Tarente*, 564 n. 3.

69. Nonnos, *Commentary on the Speech of St. Gregory against Julian* 1.19 (*Patr. Gr.* 36, pp. 993–94).

70. The abbot Nonnos, commentator on St. Gregory of Nazianzus, seems to belong to the beginning of the sixth century; cf. E. Patzig, *De Nonnianis commentariis*, 30.

71. It is true that this image of Epaminondas as a philosopher is perhaps a bit forced, as contrast with a Pelopidas who is purely military: cf. Bersanetti, "Pelopida," 86ff.

72. The chronology is less of an obstacle in that we are completely ignorant of the date of Epaminondas's birth; cf. Swoboda, "Epaminondas," col. 2675.

73. Quoted by Ar., *Rhet.* 2.23.1398b 18. The passage is part of a series of enthymemes, quasi syllogisms based on similarity.

74. It is true that the Athenian sailors had not needed a philosopher to abandon a tradition that they had had to adopt (cf. above, p. 62ff.). But the open sea, recently conquered, was a space less charged with taboos than the land. In a speech to the men that he attributes to the Athenian general Phormio (2.89), Thucydides shows admirably that at sea there were possibilities for maneuver available to experienced sailors that were unknown to those who fought on land. The oldest Greek innovation in naval tactics was the *diekplous*, an operation in which each ship slipped between two enemy vessels and then did an about-face. The turning itself implies the abandonment of the primacy of the right wing.

NOTES FOR APPENDIX

1. Standardization and updating of references, correction of some details, replacement of several Greek quotations with translations.

2. The most important studies are those by W. K. Pritchett, *Topography* 1, pp. 49–58 (for Leuctra), and above all by J. K. Anderson, *Theory*, 192–224.

3. Here I am answering an objection raised by Raymond Weil.

4. Thuc. 3.106–8; later than Epaminondas, there is a clear example of attack by the left wing (with reinforcement) under Alexander in the war not against an equal but against the Illyrian rebels (Arrian, *Anabasis*, 1.5.3).

5. *Poliorcétique*, 121 n. 6.

6. "Monosandales," 473–74.

7. Here I am recapitulating the main points of a talk given in February 1977 at l'Arbresle. N. Loraux has independently reached conclusions very close to mine.

8. *Pyth.* 4.96; I return to the character of Jason as ephebe in "The Black Hunter," p. 108 below.

82   9. See M. Matarasso, "Robert Hertz"; in another connection, Hertz's study is placed at the head of an essential anthology edited by R. Needham, *Right and Left*. As an example of the analysis of a symbolic constellation, see P. Bourdieu, *Esquisse*, 45–69 and 211–18 (the Kabyle house as an inverted world).

   10. F. Zimmerman, "Géométrie."

   11. Pp. 76–77, n. 34 above.

   12. J. Breslin, *Prayer*, with referral to parallel texts at 8–9.

   13. *Polarity*, 37–41, and "Right and Left," where there is a complete catalogue. His remarks on Parmenides have been disputed by O. Kember, "Right and Left."

   14. C. Castoriadis, *Imaginaire*.

   15. The authenticity of the majority of the fragments is upheld in the collection by M. Timpanaro Cardini, *Pitagorici* (for our fragment, cf. 237); the same author, however, thinks that nothing in this fragment admits the relative character of right and left. The one who has done the most work to demonstrate the authenticity of the tradition about Philolaos is W. Burkert, *Lore*, 218–98; likewise, K. von Fritz, "Philolaos."

   16. "Who is attacked?"

   17. This is the reading accepted by both W. Burkert, *Lore*, 268, and by J. Mansfeld, *Peri Hebdomadōn*, 62–63; in place of *meros* the manuscripts have *megas*, which makes no sense.

   18. W. Burkert (*Lore*, 268ff.) argues for authenticity and compares Hippocrates, *Peri Hebdomadōn*. J. Mansfeld, whose work tries to show that this treatise is quite late, obviously adopts the opposite position. For a geometric interpretation of the *kosmos* of Philolaos, see R. E. Siegel, "Hestia."

   19. So M. Fortina, *Epaminonda* (Turin, 1958), 3–6. This author, whose monograph we had been unable to consult, mentions the attack by the left wing only very briefly (31, 97). The piece by M. Sordi, "Epaminonda," goes into greater depth. Sordi stresses the passage in Diodorus (15.52–54) where Epaminondas, as philosopher, attends to the dismissal of an unfavorable omen. Although this is only one tradition, no one tells similar anecdotes about, for example, Iphicrates or Charidemos.

   20. Cf. M. Matarasso, "Robert Hertz," 141, 146; F. Zimmerman, "Géométrie," 1393, who states, "The direction of predominance can be reversed, and the left will be given honorability."

   21. P.-M. Schuhl, "Epaminondas"; G.E.R. Lloyd, "Right and Left," 186; V. Goldschmidt, *Système stoïcien*, 233.

   22. K. von Fritz, "Philolaos," col. 456.

   23. *War* 2, 190–93 (the quoted passage is on 192).

   24. *Theory*, 322 n. 45.

   25. Cf. J. de Romilly, C.U.F., 154 n. 1.

   26. W. J. Woodhouse, "Mantineia," 72.

   27. G. Cawkwell, "Epaminondas," 261.

   28. G. Dumézil, *Héritage indo-européen*, 247.

II   The Young, the Warriors

4 The Tradition of the Athenian Hoplite

At the beginning of his book *Cadmos et les Spartes*, F. Vian makes what I think is a fairly good summary of recent work on the "warrior function" in the Greece of the polis: "It can be maintained without paradox that the social organization of Classical Greece does not recognize the category of war. If the cities naturally have military institutions, they do not comprise groups of specialists in this activity (except at Sparta). Early on, the nobles kept as one of their privileges that of seeing to the national defense, and then—especially under democratic rule—the responsibility slowly came to be shared by the citizens at large."[1] This formulation is a little extreme and could be corrected in two ways. At Sparta there certainly is a group that specializes in military activity, but if this group of "peers" does not merge with the complex aggregate of "Lacedaimonians," at least it is identified with the whole city of the Spartiates.[2] Spartan *agōgē* simultaneously confers full citizenship and warrior status.

Conversely, when the "nobles" kept for themselves the "privilege" that Vian refers to, it seems to me that their "nobility" was utterly inseparable from their character as warriors.

Still, it is no less true that for Athens, especially in the Classical period, military organization merged with civic organization; it was not as a warrior that the citizen governed the city, but it was as a citizen that the Athenian went to war. Perhaps there was a time, as described by M.

An earlier version was published in J.-P. Vernant (ed.), *Problèmes de la guerre en Grèce ancienne* (Paris and The Hague: Mouton, 1968), 161–81. The revision has benefited from the advice of Philippe Gauthier and Sally Humphreys.

Detienne, when the Assembly was primarily the gathering of warriors, called together, for example, to discuss the division of spoils.[3] There has been a long search for "survivals" from this time, but the project has proven futile.[4] To be sure, warlike organization was once a model, but in the first analysis it is no longer so in the Classical era. Claude Mossé has given several clear examples that prove that the army and the navy of the Greek cities were modeled on the polis.[5] This was obvious at Salamis, where it was not the fleet that saved the city but the city that took up residence on the ships, sheltered by the famous "wooden walls" of the prophecy. It was still true for the mixed force, in which Athenian citizens were not the majority, that Nicias commanded in Sicily. Even more impressive is the example of the motley band of mercenaries in the *Anabasis;* after the death of the generals who had recruited them, the mercenaries elected their *stratēgoi* and deliberated in assembly and, in short, behaved—in Taine's expression—like a "traveling republic." We are dealing with a distinctive trait of the Classical city-state. We might add, by the way, that this feature survived into much of the Hellenistic era, not only at Rhodes, but in scores of small villages, whose inscriptions from the third to the first century B.C. display their pride in their civic militias. But even where the citizen-soldier gradually became something of an archaic dream, as in fourth-century Athens, the principle remains obvious, almost too obvious.

Since we are speaking of Athens, let us begin with the Athenian hoplites, the backbone of the army, the quintessence of every citizen-army. From Aristotle and the *Constitution of Athens* to the more recent authors of textbooks, general or specialized, people have enjoyed sketching the harmonious picture of this heavy infantry and its organization.[6] To tell the truth, recent authors have sometimes yielded to the temptation—unknown to Aristotle, who was describing what he saw—of jumbling together two centuries of historical evolution and of analyzing the army of Marathon with criteria drawn from sources from the end of the fifth, or even the end of the fourth, century. Historical reality turns out simplified, but also unacceptably homogenized.

In Aristotle's time, the Athenians liable to military service (there being no distinction between the hoplites and other branches) were divided into forty-two age groups, with the service starting at age 19 and ending at 60 (*Ath. Pol.* 53.4, 7). Fairly simple cross checking, verified by contemporary testimony and scholia, allows us to single out the two youngest groups (*neōtatoi* or *ephēboi*) and the ten oldest (*presbytatoi*), with the remainder making up the bulk of the force.[7] No doubt this division is ancient, since it was known to Thucydides, although he applied it solely to those Athenians with the qualifications for hoplite duty.[8]

An ingenious device was in operation at the time of Aristotle: each of the forty-two ranks had its own eponymous hero, and these heroes (ἐπώνυμοι τῶν ἡλικιῶν, ἐπώνυμοι τῶν λήξεων) served not only to summon the conscription classes but also to designate the public arbitrators (*diaitētai*). This magistracy appeared in 403–2, and its members were recruited from among those Athenians who were sixty years old. At the end of their sixtieth year, they passed into the class of elders, and the cycle of the forty-two years was over for them. Their eponymous hero thereupon became available to the ephebes entering their nineteenth year.[9] We do not know when this system started, but Aristotle spoke of it as something that had already functioned for some time. We are equally ill-informed about the potentially very useful list of heroes' names,[10] of which we know only one with complete certainty.[11]

But then who were the Athenian soldiers, the citizen-soldiers? In Aristotle's time, citizenship and enlistment in the rolls of the army are one and the same thing. Citizen rights are extended only to those young men who are "registered among the number of *dēmotai* at the age of eighteen" (Ar. *Ath. Pol.* 42.1). Although Aristotle does not use the term, it is generally admitted that enrollment is recorded in the *lēxiarchikon grammateion,* the registry kept by each deme.[12] In this period the registry included all future citizens, all the ephebes. But may one move back from Aristotle's time to Cleisthenes' great reform at the end of the sixth century, the reform that rendered Athens democratic? Such was certainly the opinion of the historian—the ideologue—who produced the fourth-century draft of the "decree of Themistocles," of which a copy was found in Troizen.[13] Describing the city's preparations on the eve of the battle of Salamis, he specifies that the Athenians were enlisted for service in the fleet on the basis of the *lēxiarchikon grammateion.* But this text is mostly a reconstruction on which one can scarcely rely.[14]

Can one take the opposite tack, beginning with a *lēxiarchikon grammateion* limited to hoplites alone and then imagining its progressive extension to all able-bodied Athenians eligible for conscription, including the thetes? I used to think so—following scholars like T. Toepffer and C. Habicht[15]—but no longer. For the time being, modern theories about this institution do no more than reflect the incurably random and contradictory character of the ancient evidence.[16] The oldest document, an inscription dating from the Archidamian War, is too mutilated to provide any firm conclusions.[17]

88   There remains, however, another category of documents: the epitaphs
of the fifth century, the lists of soldiers fallen on behalf of Athens. By no
means are these transparent documents, putting us in direct contact with
the social realities of the fifth century, but at least, as N. Loraux has
shown, they give us a better view into the problem of Athenian identity.[18] There is no indication that thetes were excluded from these lists.
The word 'hoplite' appears at most one time,[19] yet the lists do mention
certain marginal groups: slaves, *isoteleis* (metics with certain additional
privileges), plain foreigners, and even bowmen fighting on foot or on
horseback, whether Athenian or barbarian. In the last case, the opposition is not just between citizens and foreigners; it is as if there survives on
these lists a trace of the old distinction between the archer and the regular
soldier, which is attested by several texts and is apparent on many
vases.[20] This opposition is equally pervasive in the institutions; archers,
those "poor devils,"[21] are not allowed to pay their share following the
same procedure as other soldiers.[22] One inscription even sets apart an
inhabitant of Eleutherae, which is a frontier outpost whose status in
relation to the city of Athens is not altogether clear.[23] It calls to mind the
custom reported by Aristotle that prohibited citizens living in the
vicinity of the frontier from taking part in public deliberations when they
dealt with the neighboring city (*Pol.* 7.1330a 20).

Who then were the "Athenians" who died on behalf of Athens? The
question occurs to Thucydides himself as he tallies the dead after the
battle of Delium (424). The word "Athenians" is used in a double sense:
contrasted with the Boeotians, it means the whole contingent; contrasted
with the light-armed troops (*psiloi*) it means only the hoplites, for it was
the latter who constituted the nucleus of the citizen army (Thuc.
4.101.2).[24]

What remains indisputable and undisputed is that until the Peloponnesian War hoplite service was not required of all. Whatever had been the
exact function of the *lēxiarchikon grammateion*, it was the catalogue of
hoplites that informed the city about the number of men it could call on
to form its regiments of heavy infantry,[25] with each man paying for his
own equipment. There is nothing simpler and (relatively) better understood than the process whereby such men were mobilized. The decree of
conscription was posted in front of the monument to the eponymous
heroes that was built in the last quarter of the fifth century.[26] Depending
on circumstances, mobilization would be partial or total. Aristophanes'
farmer complains at seeing his name reappear too often on the lists,
alongside the instruction—dare we call it laconic?—Αὔϱιον δ' ἔστ' ἤξ-
οδος, "departure tomorrow" (*Peace* 1181), and he curses his leader, "the

goddamn taxiarch" (*Peace* 1171). In principle, however, those citizens
who had not yet gone on a campaign should have been summoned first
(Lysias, *For the Soldier* 15).

Post-Cleisthenic Athens was the city of the ten tribes, and this basic
division is recapitulated in the army: "The people, under arms, always
exist as an image of the Cleisthenic city."[27] At the top were the *stratēgoi*
and then the taxiarchs, who command the ten hoplite units, each of
which, in 431, numbered 1300 men (Thuc. 2.13). The ten *taxeis* were
subdivided into *lochoi,* possibly corresponding to the trittyes. During
battle, the soldiers are marshaled by tribes, in an order that is not left to
chance; the funeral orations for those fallen on behalf of the polis were
delivered before ten coffins of cypress wood (Thuc. 2.34); the epitaphs
clearly take most careful note of a citizen's membership in his tribe.[28]
Thus we see the outlines of an ideal model for a hoplite republic. Let us
rapidly examine a few of its most important features.

Athenian hoplites are men who themselves pay for, and hence are able
to pay for, their heavy armor, so heavy that they need a "bearer" to
accompany them; they belong to the three highest classes in the Solonian
hierarchy. They make up an army of small-holders: the hoplite republic is
one of farmers. This kind of army, just like the Spartan, is well suited to
only one kind of combat: in the open, phalanx against phalanx, with the
site having been agreed on by both sides. This latter feature, moreover, is
typical of the whole Greek world during the Persian Wars. In Herodotus,
Mardonius the Persian expresses his amazement: "I have been told that
the Greeks customarily throw themselves into wars that are utterly mad,
without deliberation or prudence; once war is declared, the adversaries
seek out the most convenient and most level terrain and gather there to
fight. Even the victors suffer grave losses, and there is no need to mention
the losers. They are annihilated."[29] Such an army is meant for a war that
is seasonal, beginning in spring and subsiding in autumn.

On the other hand, this kind of army is as poorly suited as possible for:
1) pursuit of the enemy; 2) siege warfare—the hoplites who conduct the
siege of Potidaea make it drag on and on,[30] and 3) mountain warfare—
the hoplites under Demosthenes in Aetolia are slaughtered by the
mobile, light-armed enemy (Thuc. 3.96–98).

Each of these features is equally evident in the other large Greek cities
that had made their hoplite corps the instrument of the "warrior function." Still, Athens is set apart by one outstanding idiosyncrasy: nowhere
else is the ideology of nonprofessionalism pushed so far. In a famous
passage in Thucydides (2.39), Pericles declares: "Our military training is
in many respects superior to that of our adversaries. . . . We rely not

upon management or trickery, but upon our own hearts and hands. And in the matter of education, whereas they from early youth are always undergoing laborious exercises which are to make them brave, we live at ease, and yet are equally ready to face the perils which they face. . . . If then we prefer to meet danger with a light heart but without laborious training, and with a courage which is gained by habit and not enforced by law, are we not greatly the gainers? Since we do not anticipate the pain, although, when the hour comes, we can be as brave as those who never allow themselves to rest; and thus too our city is equally admirable in peace and war" (tr. Jowett).[31] We should sense the supreme insolence of the foregoing remarks and observe how profoundly they challenge the ideal of a hoplite republic. By arguing from such evidence, Wilamowitz rejected the very idea that obligatory military service could have been instituted at Athens prior to the time of Lycurgus: "That is an institution strikingly remote from *eleutheria,* from *parrhēsia,* from the ζῆν ὡς ἄν τις βούληται—'living as one wishes to' of which the Athenian demagogues are so proud. Anyone who does not shake his head (in negation) at the first glimpse of such an institution is a complete stranger to Athenian life and thought—no matter how many thick volumes he may have written on these topics."[32]

Without going to such an extreme, we may still ask when there existed this army of ten tribes—the republic of hoplites and farmers created by Cleisthenes' reforms—and when the body of hoplites was truly the main military force at Athens. The answer, I believe, is simple and clear, and the ancient tradition unanimous: practically for the first time, and surely for the last time, Athens adhered to the ideal plan I have just described at the time of the battle of Marathon in 490, seventeen years after the great reform.

Although I say that the ancient tradition is unanimous, that certainly does not mean that it is exempt from critical scrutiny.

In the fourth century, Plato, as a loyal supporter of the hoplite army and land warfare, fashioned a unique diptych contrasting the shame of Salamis with the glory of Marathon and Plataea (*Laws* 4.707a–d). One of the most significant achievements of modern research has been to show that in the fifth century an analogous controversy divided admirers of the first and second Persian Wars. One of the so-called Marathon epigrams extols men of dauntless heart ('Εν ἄρα τοῖς ἀδά[μας ἐν στέθεσι θυμός]) because they formed the battle line against the enemy's multitudes before the gates of the city (hότ' αἰχμὲν στέσαμ πρόσθε πυλõν ἀν[τία μυριάσιν]). This poem was undeniably inscribed *in the time of Cimon,* around 465, during a period of aristocratic ascendancy and *after* the text that doubtless

describes the second Persian War and glorifies those who "on foot and
aboard swift ships saved all Greece from seeing the day of enslavement"
(Ἔσχον γὰρ πεζοί τε[καὶ ὀκυπόϱον ἐπὶ νεõ]ν Ἑλλά [δα μ]ὲ πᾶσαν δού-
λιο[ν ἔμαϱ ἰδẽν]).[33]

In discussing Marathon, then, we are partially in thrall to a tradition
that in all likelihood vigorously exaggerated some aspects of the battle.
But this tradition is itself an ancient historical datum of primary importance; therefore, deliberately, we will remain faithful to it here.

Marathon thus appears as an exemplary battle.[34] For the Athenians it
is hoplite battle in its pure form, "with spear and shield, soldiers standing firm side by side."[35] The cavalry providentially missing from the
Persian force does not appear on the Athenian side either.[36] Athens'
hippeis (knights) fight on foot. Before Cleisthenes, Athens might have had
a corps of ninety-six horsemen, two per naucrary (Pollux 8.108). If this
squadron in fact existed, it took no part in the battle. Nor did light-
armed troops, whose absence has sometimes aroused suspicion.[37]
Pausanias indicates that alongside the Athenians and Plataeans there were
slaves, who had been freed in advance. Their dead were placed in the
tomb of the Plataeans,[38] but we do not know what role they played—
mere bearers, perhaps, armed as hoplites at the last minute to reinforce
the center of the Athenian line.[39]

The battle itself conforms in the strictest sense to the rules of archaic
and classical combat. The nominal commander of the Athenian army
naturally holds the right wing: "It was a rule for the Athenians that the
polemarch direct the right wing" (Hdt. 6.111).[40] Plutarch even provides
a curious detail.[41] It was the tribe Aiantis that occupied the right flank of
the line; Plutarch offers the explanation that this tribe was *prytanis* at the
time of "Miltiades' decree." Unfortunately, this decree is a notorious
fourth-century forgery, not to mention that it was only much later that
the prytanizing tribe came to be included in the prescripts of decrees.[42]
If, however, the original statement is correct, it can be explained almost
too neatly by the fact that Aiantis was the tribe of the polemarch Cal-
limachos of Aphidna and that Marathon is located in the territory of
Aiantis.[43]

The perfect arrangement of the battle, however, masks a profound
imbalance that the probable enlistment of slaves at the last minute will
render explicit. At Marathon the Athenians numbered nine thousand,
joined by one thousand Plataeans.[44] It is likely that these nine thousand
Athenians represented all the available eligible men between the ages of
eighteen and sixty, within the confines of the hoplite census—that is,
within the three highest categories in the Solonian hierarchy.[45] However,

the Cleisthenic constitution of 507 involved, in principle, the integration and mobilization of all sources of strength—the process that endowed the history of fifth-century Athens with the "modern" features that are so impressive. We can accept that the population of Athens, which was growing rapidly, was about thirty thousand citizens at the beginning of the fifth century. In 483, at the time of Themistocles' "naval law," forty thousand Athenian men and adolescents were entitled to claim a share in the treasure discovered at Laurion;[46] with the age of puberty being set at sixteen, this implies that overall there were more than thirty thousand potential combatants. Faced with a formidable danger threatening the very existence of the city, the young democracy managed to "mobilize" less than a third of its available manpower: the profligacy has something appalling about it.

In a series of upsets that imbue it with drama and interest, Athenian history in the fifth and fourth centuries consisted of first making full use of its complement of citizens, then going well beyond that. As early as the Sicilian Expedition, the Athenian army was about as Athenian as Napoleon's *grande armée* was French; finally, in the fourth century the citizen-soldier disappeared before the mercenary. The republic of hoplites (Theramenes) or of farmers (Phormisios)[47] was a political platform that prevailed for a short time in 411. The "five thousand" hoplites of 411 were, we are told, nine thousand[48]—an odd recurrence of the figure for Marathon. But this program—which enticed intellectuals like Euripides and, later on, Isocrates, Plato, Xenophon, and Aristotle—was conceived in direct opposition to democratic practice.[49]

It is impossible to dwell at length on the changes that Athenian military organization underwent between Marathon and the aftermath of Chaeronea; I will supply only the gist. The manpower so incompletely used at Marathon came to be fully employed not in the Athenian army but in the fleet. Athens' navy employed more than thirty-six thousand men at Artemisium, of whom at least thirty-four thousand were Athenians, and of this latter number, according to the calculation of J. Labarbe, only one thousand seven hundred thirty-four hoplites were called to fight as such.[50] The tally at Salamis was similar.[51] Themistocles' "naval policy" can only be understood as putting to use a hitherto unused resource. Let us not conclude that this was the only option. At Plataea, Sparta is said to have furnished thirty-five thousand helots with light arms, thus deploying a total contingent of forty-five thousand men—an enormous number. At the same time, the Athenians, who once again were probably using all their available hoplites, fielded only eight thousand men (Hdt. 9.28–29).[52] As yet there had been no change in the ground forces.

Nonetheless, an evolution took place, originating largely in the Peloponnesian War. The causes were more complex, inasmuch as Athens was not alone and the art of war developed more or less at the same rate in all Greek cities. I would insist, however, on the importance of one influence: the maritime model and the new skills it represented and inspired. Naval strategy first copied land strategy but then rapidly became much less simple, with its innovations like *diekplous* or *periplous*, and the Peloponnesian War marked the disappearance of the traditional primacy of the right wing.[53] When Xenophon compares Epaminondas's shock troops at Mantinea to "the prow of a trireme" (*Hell.* 7.5.23), there may be more to it than a banal metaphor. The two domains, however, seem separate: Pericles plans to defeat the Peloponnesians because all "that affects the fleet is a matter of skill" (τὸ δὲ ναυτικὸν τέχνης ἐστίν) (Thuc. 1.142) and *technē*—like the Athenians who embody it to the highest degree, in the eyes of their adversaries—implies continual innovation.[54] Once again in the fourth century, as Isocrates regretfully justifies the choice made by Themistoclean Athens, he will explain the contrast between land power and sea power: the former involves *eutaxia* (the practice of order), moral discipline (*sōphrosynē*), and obedience (*peitharchia*), while sea power is based on the various *technai* (*Panath.* 116). But Pericles himself advises the Athenians: "We have gained more experience of fighting on land from warfare at sea than they of naval affairs from warfare on land" (Thuc. 1.142, tr. Jowett). Let us not forget that there were no—rather, there were fewer and fewer—men who fought only at sea or only on land. Instead there were men who were sometimes soldiers, sometimes sailors. The fleet was simultaneously a model and an agent of imbalance, the destroyer of the old organization. If the fleet allowed the employment of the thetes who had no place at Marathon, it also paradoxically mobilized the upper class. A group of those who regularly served as hoplites was set aside for the duties of the trierarchy.

In which directions did the basic transformations develop? With regard to the use of manpower, the example of the fleet was followed grudgingly, under the pressure of military exigencies, but followed nonetheless. A major factor was clearly the incorporation of thetes among the hoplites, which means that the state provided armor, just as it provided the trierarchs with hulls and rigging. In fact, we know very little about this incorporation, but thetes *epibatai* ("hoplite-marines") did go on the Sicilian Expedition (Thuc. 6.43).[55]

94   The metics pose fewer problems than one would think: in the fifth century, they were Athenians of lower rank; they were the bran of the grain, while the Athenians were the kernel, and foreigners the husk.[56] Therefore it is natural that as hoplites they would, in principle, be grouped with the young men who were not yet admitted to the assembly (the *neōtatoi*) and with the old men now incapable of active service (the *presbytatoi*); they were usually relegated to garrison duty (cf. Thuc. 2.13). In an emergency, however, they took part in distant campaigns; as early as 424 at Delion, the strategos Hippocrates had charge of metics and "whatever foreigners were present" (Thuc. 4.90, 94).[57] Despite the example of Marathon, the use of slaves was much rarer. The clearest instance, in the fifth century, did not involve the army but the fleet at Arginusae.[58] Later on the Athenians enlisted slaves in the army, especially after Chaeronea.[59]

The latter is only one aspect of the diversification of the Athenian army. Although there are others as well, we must be careful not to exaggerate their effect, for the powers of conservatism remain strong in spite of everything. We will note, in passing, the growth of a corps of archers,[60] and of light-armed troops in general—a process that was very slow[61]—and the equally slow development of groups of specialized warriors, recruited largely from abroad,[62] and of a cavalry.[63]

Beginning with the last phase of the Peloponnesian War, and still more in the fourth century, the evolution became much more marked: the growth of professionalism at every level,[64] from the generals to the men at arms, as a result of the return of large numbers of mercenaries.[65] Battle became much more costly as the spirit of competition gave way to the desire for utter destruction; meanwhile the war of "raids"—of "commandos" and "guerrillas"—whose heroes were peltasts, came to rival open combat. Dionysius the Elder, who made great use of siege engineers,[66] Iphicrates, and Epaminondas illustrate in various ways the changes that culminate in the action of Philip of Macedon. The contrast with the past is so brutal that Demosthenes, otherwise indifferent to historical evolution, frames a stunning contrast between war in days gone by, which was seasonal and principled, and contemporary war, permanent and waged by any means (*Philippic* 3.47–50). The short treatise of Aeneas Tacticus illustrates in its own way the violent world of the fourth century.

In the great period of the citizen-soldier, the "warrior function" had not disappeared; in a word, it had embraced the whole city-state, whether the combat was on land or sea. If there is now an ideological interpretation of the warrior function as a type of political thought that

assigns the task of defending the city to certain specialized groups, it is a
striking fact that this ideology reappeared in its full glory during the
Peloponnesian War—even though the hoplite did not hold the foremost
place in this restoration (as seems to have happened in 411). Thus there is
a myth of the cavalry, which was fostered by a long aristocratic tradition
and also by the democracy in its efforts to acquire a cavalry that was not
just for show. The amazing *parabasis* of Aristophanes' *Knights* (424) is
directed against Cleon, against hoplites, and against the aggressive democracy; after a jumbled evocation of Marathon and Salamis, the speech
draws toward an encomium of the knight as a soldier and as a man: "For
ourselves we claim the defense of the city, gratis, nobly, and for the
national gods as well. Aside from that we ask for nothing, nothing but
one small favor: if peace ever returns and puts an end to our labors, do not
begrudge us our long hair and a strigil to scrape our limbs" (*Equ.* 576–
80). Xenophon was the heir of this tradition.

The fourth century went much farther, and I will say just a few words
about Plato. In the *Laches,* which is one of the "Socratic" dialogues, there
are two *stratēgoi*—Nicias, the well-known politician, and Laches, who is
already a professional soldier—and their discussion concerns the advantages and disadvantages of *hoplomachia* (fencing) and, in general, the
science of arms. Nicias argues for this approach on the basis of a diversi-
fied conception of tactics, which includes not only battle lines but also
individual combat. Laches rejects this approach, citing the example of
the Lacedaimonians, that is, a completely socialized concept of martial
courage denying the role of *technē.* He is the defender of traditional
hoplite combat and, in order to make it a better model for all combat, he
scrupulously avoids mentioning it by name (*Laches* 181e–84c). Socrates'
contribution consists of demolishing both of their arguments, refuting
the traditional view as well as the more "scientific" and "technical"
definitions of courage.[67] Thus, once Laches defines the courageous man
as the one who battles the enemy while keeping his position in line—
which was the traditional Spartan ideal from Tyrtaeus on[68]—Socrates
answers by invoking "the example of the Scythians" who "I am told, fight
as well in retreat as they do in pursuit." Once this example is dismissed,
as pertaining to troops and customs that are non-Greek, Socrates adduces
the example of the Spartans themselves, who staged a tactical retreat at
Plataea (*Laches* 190e–91c).[69] This text is important because it is a suc-
cinct outline of the whole criticism of the traditional idea of courage and
military life that is developed so expansively in Plato's last work, in the
first three books of the *Laws.*

Now we reach one of the crucial points in the Platonic drama. *Technē* first appears as characteristic above all of naval warfare, and it is for this reason that Plato abjures it, in the name of just those traditional values that he criticizes so sharply in the *Laches* (and in the *Laws*). Describing the seafaring fate of the Athenians, he writes, "Better for them to have lost many times over the seven youths (handed over to the Minotaur), than that heavy-armed and stationary troops should have been turned into hoplite-marines, and accustomed to be often leaping on shore, and again to come running back to their ships; or should have fancied that there was no disgrace in not awaiting the attack of an enemy and dying boldly; and that there were good reasons, and plenty of them, for a man throwing away his arms and betaking himself to flight—which is not dishonorable, as people say, at certain times" (*Laws* 4.706b–c, tr. Jowett). It is precisely because naval victories are due to *technai* that Plato condemns them (*Laws* 707a–b).

Land warfare, however, has itself become the business of specialists, and no one knows it better than Plato. It is the establishment of precisely this fact that makes the "elementary city" of Book 2 of the *Republic* pass through the stages that will result in the "ideal" city, of warriors and then of philosophers. "The principle, as you will remember, was that one man cannot practice many arts with success. . . . Is not war an art? . . . Nothing can be more important than that the work of a soldier should be well done. But is war an art so easily acquired that a man may be a warrior who is also a husbandman, or shoemaker, or other artisan? . . . How will he who takes up a shield or other implement of war become good all in a day, whether with heavy-armed or any other kind of troops?" (*Rep.* 2.37a–d, tr. Jowett).[70] Then how is one to reconcile the citizen-army, which is traditional for all the Greek cities, with the reality of *technē*, which, appearances notwithstanding, invalidates both the Spartan hoplite and the Athenian? The Platonic "solution" is the whole of the *Republic;* that is, the city is fundamentally *one,* but divided into three castes, with the central one being that of the warriors. Power belongs to the philosopher, who is himself molded by education in war. Plato will give a spatial representation of this image in the prologue to the *Timaeus* and in the *Critias,* where he symbolizes the Acropolis of early Athens by the body of warriors whose essence never changed (*Crit.* 112b).[71] At the end of his life, however, when he had to choose between military *technē* and the traditional concept of the city, Plato discarded the technological radicalism of the *Republic* and, in the *Laws,* came around in his way to the plan for a "republic of farmers." Technical training persists only in some aspects of the education of the future hoplite-citizen. Unlike the tradi-

tional hoplite, the hoplite of the city of Magnesia will have to be able—
like a Scythian archer—to use both hands equally (*Laws* 7.794d–95d).[72]

Shortly after Plato's great renunciation of the professional soldier, the
atmosphere of "moral and intellectual reform" that characterized the
aftermath of Chaeronea and the administration of Lycurgus returned
Athens once again to the ideal of the citizen-soldier. This occurred by
means of the elevation of an institution whose roots undoubtedly sprang
from the archaic forms of the "warrior function": the ephebia. There is
controversy about the ephebia, but it is perfectly pointless. To maintain,
with Wilamowitz,[73] that the ephebia was a totally artificial institution
created in 336–35 is not defensible now and never has been.[74] Nevertheless, it is almost as dangerous to confuse the institution described in
Chapter 42 of the *Constitution of Athens* and identified by a few slightly
earlier or contemporary inscriptions[75]—one that evinces a conscious
political plan—with the ephebia of the earlier period about which little
is known, or with the *neōtatoi* whom Thucydides mentions, or even with
the "ephebes" among whom the young Aeschines found himself around
372.[76]

There is no question about the archaic quality of the "ephebic oath"—
a major epigraphic discovery has allowed us to see one of the official
texts.[77] The oath was sworn in the sanctuary of Aglauros, an old deity
that was *kourotrophos* (in charge of raising boys).[78] The organization of the
ephebia can recall a time when categories of age divided the human
groups of the city,[79] but it is precisely a matter of recall. Even an official
document like the ephebic oath ought not to be studied solely in the
context of the date of its drafting, real or conjectured, but also in the
context of its publication, in this case in the deme of Acharnia at the time
of Lycurgus. The text appears on the same stele as the fictional "oath of
the Plataeans," and we know that an orator like Aeschines liked to refer to
it, along with the "decree" of Miltiades or that of Themistocles recently
found at Troizen (Dem. *On the Embassy* 303).[80] That is, for the ephebia it
is difficult to distinguish the archaic from the archaizing.

In any event, Aristotle's ephebia involves the whole citizenry and
comprises a preparation for hoplite service.[81] The arms provided by the
city, which appear on the "stele of the oaths," are a spear and a round
shield, which form part of a hoplite's equipment (*Ath. Pol.* 42.4). Under
the form it eventually took, which is about all we know of it, the ephebia
is inconceivable without the innovations we noted above, particularly the
admission of thetes into the hoplite corps with the state supplying their
equipment.[82]

We must admit, I think, that certain archaic aspects of ephebia at the end of the fourth century were renovations and generalizations. They still *do* exist, but to advance our understanding of the problem, we must, like C. Pélékidis, take it to another level.

According to Aristotle, during their two years of garrisoning and service, the ephebes "cannot go to law either as defendants or as plaintiffs, unless it is a matter of upholding an inheritance, arranging the affairs of an heiress, or a priesthood related to the *genos*" (Ar. *Ath. Pol.* 42.5). These two years of seclusion have plausibly been connected with the latency period that marks the transition from childhood to adulthood in a number of societies.[83] In Athens, however, the latency period, which can be compared to the Lacedaimonian *krypteia*, works on two different levels. An ephebe—on the civic scale, an adolescent who has reached the age of eighteen—is also a boy who has reached *hēbē*, or puberty. But, from early antiquity onward, Athens also recognized a legal puberty, a sexual maturity that endowed Athenians with the particular privilege of sharing in the silver of Laurion—(ἔμελλον λάξεσθαι ὀρχιδὸν ἕκαστος δέκα δραχμάς) "they proposed to share out the total at the rate of ten drachmas for each sexually mature male" (Hdt. 7.144)[84]—that is, age sixteen. That is why the expression *epi dietēs hēbēsai*, "two years since puberty," *hēbē*, means to be age eighteen, hence an ephebe.[85] Then he entered a new transitional period—of a paradoxical sort, since eighteen marks full majority—which resulted, at the end of "military service," in the acquisition of full civil rights. It seems likely, as C. Pélékidis saw, that this two-stage puberty corresponded, from Cleisthenes on, to the two different registries we spoke of, one for the deme and the other for the phratry.[86]

We know all too little about the phratry,[87] although people have freely said that after Cleisthenes' creation of the demes the phratry becomes a frozen, "disconnected" institution.[88] Nothing is less certain; on the contrary, it seems that the phratries were reorganized at the time of Pericles, in connection with the famous law that set the requirements for citizenship.[89] The phratry continued to evolve, and it is hard to say whether the customs of the demes influenced it, or vice versa. There is only one document that affords us a glimpse into the workings of a phratry in the first half of the fourth century; it is the inscription ascribed to the Demotionidai.[90] For the admission of some (at least) new members, it prescribed a moratorium of one year, like the latency period in the ephebia, between the offering of the *koureion* at the festival of the Apaturia and the vote of the members of the phratry (Τὴν δὲ διαδικασίαν τὸ

λοιπὸν ἔναι τῶι ὑστέρωι ἔτει ἢ ᾧ ἂν τὸ κόρεον θύσῃ, τῇ Κορεώτιδι
'Απατορίων): "Henceforth let the admission take place one year after the
sacrifice of the *koureion,* on the day *Koureōtis* of the Apaturia."[91]

There has been a great deal of argument about the *koureōtis* but it is
now agreed that the offering of the *koureion,* the young man's hair,
corresponds to puberty.[92] On the occasion of the *Oinistēria* and prior to
the sacrifice of hair, it is the ephebes-to-be (οἱ μέλλοντες ἐφηβεύειν) who
offer Heracles a bit of wine.[93] But the allusion to shearing (πριν ἀπο-
κείρασθαι) seems to prove that the issue here is not civic ephebia, which
one enters at the age of eighteen, but traditional puberty, which was
recognized at the age of sixteen within the framework of the phratry.[94]

The Apaturia was the festival of the phratries, and it was there that the
new ephebes were enrolled and that their fathers swore on their behalf
that they were true Athenians, sons of Athenians.[95] From its earliest
appearance in history, the phratry had a military character: Nestor arrayed his men by phratries (*Il.* 1.362–63).[96] Better yet, the etiological
myth that was supposed to explain the origin of the Apaturia takes the
form of a border-duel between the Athenian king Thymoites, later replaced by Melanthos (the ancestor of the Codridai), and a Boeotian king,
Xanthos; Dionysus Melanaigis, bringer of *apatē,* stood next to Xanthos
and by his mere presence brought about the Boeotian's defeat.[97]

In the next chapter I will return to the significance of this myth. H.
Jeanmaire had little difficulty in detecting a "succession motif": through
his victory, Melanthos, Thymoites' champion, earned the right of succession to the throne,[98] and the myth presents him as the father of Codros,
the last king of Athens. For now it is enough to stress the story's location
on the border. We know that in their oath the ephebes swore to "the
boundary-stones of the fatherland, the wheat, the barley, the vines, the
olive trees and the fig trees."[99] Moreover, in the Classical era their
"military service" was spent primarily in the frontier outposts; one piece
of late evidence (128 B.C.) shows them performing a sacrifice on the
border to the gods of Attica.[100] This clue might reinforce the interpretation that identifies the ancient ephebia, initiation into a warrior's life,
with the time when a young man prepares himself for entry into a
phratry; thus the Classical ephebia is seen as an adaption of archaic
institutions. Be that as it may, in the fourth century the resurgence of the
ideology of the warrior function—finding renewed expression in the
reorganization of the ephebia—was not so much a case of the survival of
an ancient custom, but instead reflected the crisis of the city of Athens,
precisely to the extent that the whole city was an agent of war.[101]

The Young, the Warriors

1. F. Vian, *Cadmos,* 5.

2. I suggest that we reject once and for all the translation "equals," which does not convey the sense of the Greek *homoioi.* Both Herodotus and Thucydides played on the use (quotidian or institutional) of this word: cf. N. Loraux, "Belle Mort," 107.

3. Géométrie." Among the attempts that have been made to reconstruct this distant past, I think that the most fruitful—sometimes bold but always brilliant—is the book *Couroi et Courètes* by H. Jeanmaire.

4. P. Briant (*Antigone,* 279–350) has disposed of the theory, which I myself echoed in 1968, that presented the assembly of soldiers as a political and judicial institution fundamental to Macedonian kingship.

5. Cf. C. Mossé: "Archidamos," "Armée et Cité," "Rôle de l'armée," "Rôle politique."

6. Henceforth the basic work is W. K. Pritchett, *War,* which one can supplement with J. K. Anderson, *Military Theory.* Among the older treatments, the most useful remains J. Kromayer and G. Veith, *Heerwesen.*

7. Cf. C. Pélékidis, *Éphébie,* 48.

8. Thuc. 1.105 and 2.13; in the latter passage the historian clearly shows that he considers both the *presbytatoi* and the *neōtatoi* as hoplites, by grouping with them the metics who were serving as hoplites. The episode from the Megarian War, described in the earlier passage, is the subject of a long commentary by Lysias, *Epitaphios* 49–53. His emphasis on the age of the combatants allows him to consider them exceptional hoplites. Cf. N. Loraux, *Invention,* 136.

9. This follows from Ar. *Ath. Pol.* 53.4; the other texts about these eponyms are essentially *Etym. Mag.* (after *Etym. Genuinum*) *s.v.* "Eponymoi"; *Suda, s.v.* "Eponymoi." See also schol. ad Demos. 21 *Meidias* 83, which informs us about the arbiters chosen from those in their sixtieth year; "sixty" translates a justified emendation of "fifty" by E. Koch, "Lexiarchicon grammateion," 16. Cf. C. Pélékidis, *Éphébie,* 100 nn. 1 and 2.

10. In any case, they must not be confused with the hundred heroes whom Cleisthenes used as eponyms for his tribes; the error is made by C. Pélékidis, *Éphébie.*

11. Cf. C. Habicht, "Neue Inschriften," 143–46. Commenting on a dedication from 333–32 discovered near the Pompeion and dedicated by the ephebes of the tribe Aiantis, Habicht proves that the hero Mounichos—under whose protection the ephebes won their victory—can only be the eponymous hero of that conscription class of ephebes. As a result, I think I can establish a second identification. In fact, Mounichos is the eponym neither of a deme nor of a tribe, but of a month (and a festival) of the Attic year. Another character, Panops, is so defined by the tradition reflected in Photius and Hesychius (*s.v.* "Panops": "*Hērōs attikos kai en tois epōnymois*"). We are ill-informed about this hero, who is mentioned only by Plato (*Lysis* 203a). Lycurgus (F 3 Durrbach) does indicate that "the other Greeks" use the name *Panopsia* for the festival that corresponds to the fourth

month of the Attic year, the festival called by the Athenians *Pyanopsia*. Under such circumstances, is it not tempting to identify twelve of the forty-two eponyms with the more or less artificial heroes of the twelve months of the Attic year? I cannot press this suggestion farther, since another interpretation is possible: H. Jeanmaire has called attention to the initiatory quality of the festivals celebrated in Mounichion and Pyanopsion and has himself related these customs to ephebic initiation (*Couroi*, 244–45).

12. Cf. C. Pélékidis, *Éphébie*, 87.

13. R. Meiggs and D. Lewis, *Selection* no. 23, 11, 29–30; like M. H. Jameson, the discoverer of this document ("Provision," 399–400), Meiggs and Lewis believe that it provides direct information about Athens in 480. My opinion is different and rests on the comments of J. and L. Robert, "Bulletin" (1961) 320 and (1962) 135–43. Whatever the objections that can be raised about certain details, the studies by P. Amandry ("Themistocle") and C. Habicht ("Falsche Urkunden") seem to me to be essentially irrefutable.

14. As does H. van Effenterre in "Clisthène," 11, an article that in other respects convinced me that I was mistaken about some essential points.

15. J. Toepffer, "Gemeindebuch,"; C. Habicht, "Falsche Urkunden," 5–6.

16. The evidence is collected in E. Koch, "Lexiarchicon grammateion"; J. Toepffer, "Gemeindebuch"; H. van Effenterre, "Clisthène." For the most part it consists of definitions from the lexicographers. The passage in Aeschines (*Tim.* 103) does not prove, as I once thought, that only those who owned a *klēros* were registered on the *lēxiarchikon grammateion*.

17. I. G. 1^2 79.11.5–7. The traditional reading of this text was modified by B. D. Meritt, *Studies*, 26, partially followed by H. van Effenterre, "Clisthène," 11.

18. N. Loraux, *Invention*, 32–37, on the basis of the fundamental studies by D. W. Bradeen, "Casualty Lists" and *Agora* 17.

19. *Agora* 17, no. 23; *hopl(itai)*.

20. See "Recipes for Greek Adolescence," p. 142 below. That the same is true of vases will be shown by a work of F. Lissarrague (to be published).

21. F. Hiller von Gaertringen, "Voreuklidische Steine," 668.

22. This is proven by I. G. 1^2 79.

23. I. G. 1^2 948. Other examples bearing on frontier locations are to be found in D. W. Bradeen, "Casualty Lists" 3, p. 150.

24. Cf. N. Loraux, *Invention*, 34.

25. The passages have been collected by F. Lammert, *Katalogos*. Demosthenes (13.167.4) still knows of soldiers "outside the catalogue."

26. On the role of this monument as the center of civic life, cf. P. Lévêque and P. Vidal-Naquet, *Clisthène*, 72; for the date, see "An Enigma at Delphi," n. 7, p. 316 below.

27. G. Glotz, *Histoire Grecque* 2, p. 342.

28. There are some necessary details in N. Loraux, *Invention*, 23.

29. Hdt. 7.9; cf. also the demarcated site, the closed field of the mythic

combat between Nestor and Eurythalion in Ariaithos of Tegea, *FGrH* 316 Fl. For a commentary on the passage in Herodotus, see Y. Garlan, *Poliorcétique,* 20–22.

30. See Y. Garlan, *Poliorcétique,* esp. 106–8.

31. Cf. N. Loraux, *Invention,* 152–53.

32. *Aristoteles* 1, p. 191.

33. The passages are quoted with commentary in R. Meiggs and D. Lewis, *Selection* no. 26, where there is also a bibliography. The basic article is by P. Amandry, "Epigrammes de Marathon." See "An Enigma at Delphi," n. 64, p. 321 below.

34. I think the best reconstruction is by W. K. Pritchett, *Marathon,* whose discussion of the topography is completed by the same author's "Marathon Revisited." See also the analysis by J. Labarbe, *Loi navale,* 162–72. On the tradition about Marathon, see also N. Loraux, "Marathon."

35. Aristoph. *Wasps* 1081–83. On the hoplite's armor at Marathon, which can be seen on the stele of the hoplite Aristion, see W. K. Pritchett, *Marathon,* 172–74.

36. Hence the proverbial expression *chōris hippeis* recorded in the *Suda;* cf. W. K. Pritchett, *Marathon,* 170–72.

37. K. J. Beloch, *Geschichte* 2.1, p. 21; 2.2, p. 80.

38. Paus. 1.32.3, 7.15.7; cf. K. W. Welwei, *Unfreie,* 22–35, 41.

39. J. Labarbe, *Loi navale,* 170.

40. On this priority of the right wing, which is virtually unbroken in land battles prior to Epaminondas, see "Epaminondas the Pythagorean," above.

41. *Quaest. conviv.* 628a–29a.

42. Cf. C. Habicht, "Falsche Urkunden," 20.

43. Cf. W. K. Pritchett, *Marathon,* 147–48 and n. 79.

44. See the discussion, with confirmation of the figures, in J. Labarbe, *Loi Navale,* 162–68.

45. Ibid., 172.

46. Ibid., 199–211.

47. On these two concepts, see R. Goossens, *Euripide,* 556–59, and C. Mossé, *Fin,* 251–53.

48. Cf. Lysias, *Polystratos* 13.

49. Aristotle, for example, explains that the decline of Athens was due to the death of the *gnōrimoi,* who, through the time of the Peloponnesian War, formed the hoplite corps (*Pol.* 5.1303a 9–10: cf. *Ath. Pol.* 26.1). For other references, see P. Spahn, *Mittelschicht,* esp. 7–14.

50. J. Labarbe, *Loi navale,* 182; see, however, the discussion by H. T. Walinga, "The Trireme."

51. Labarbe, *Loi navale,* 188.

52. Regarding the light-armed troops, the passage in Herodotus is ambiguous and difficult to interpret. I concur with the commentary of J. Labarbe, who

believes that the Athenians, unlike most of the Greeks, had not provided light-armed troops (*Loi navale,* 190).

53. The main references are given in "Epaminondas the Pythagorean," pp. 62–63 above.

54. Cf. Thuc. 1.71, which explicitly notes the conjunction between innovation, *technē,* and Athens. This is an instance of a speech with pragmatic goals. In contrast, in the Funeral Oration anything related to *technē* is passed over in silence.

55. Nonetheless, the distinction between such hoplites and those in the "catalogue" remains in force. Harpocration (*s.v. thētes kai thētikon*) quotes a fragment from Antiphon—"he speaks of making all the thetes hoplites"—but we do not know who is the subject of the sentence or its exact implications: in any case, during the Peloponnesian War it concerns a recent event, since it is mentioned in Aristophanes' *Daitaleis,* quoted under the same rubric.

56. Cf. Ar. *Acharn.* 502–8 and the commentary by J. Taillardat, *Images,* 391–93.

57. Doubtless this refers to citizens from allied cities who were present in Athens. M. Clerc has assumed so (*Métèques,* 43), and proof was furnished by P. Gauthier, "Xénoi," 51–52. On the metics and hoplite service, see now D. Whitehead, *Metic,* 82–86.

58. Cf. Xen. *Hell.* 1.6.24; the inscription I.G. 11. 1951 is not, as was believed and as I used to say, the obituary for Arginusae but a naval catalogue; cf. Y. Garlan, "Esclaves grecs 1," which is based on an unpublished dissertation by D. R. Laing.

59. Lycurgus (*Against Leocrates* 41) comments disparagingly on the inclusion of slaves and foreigners; the former are freed, and some among the latter are naturalized citizens, while those Athenians who had been punished with *atimia* (loss of civil rights) are re-enfranchised. On this episode see also Hyperides FF 27–29 (Jensen).

60. See A. Plassart, "Archers."

61. In 424 Athens did not have, and had never yet had, light-armed troops trained for combat: cf. Thuc. 4.94.

62. During the Sicilian Expedition, the slingers were Rhodians, the archers Cretans, and the light-armed soldiers Megarians (Thuc. 6.43).

63. The Athenians brought no more than thirty horsemen to Sicily. The basic book on the development of the Athenian cavalry is still A. Martin's *Cavaliers;* see also J. K. Anderson, *Horsemanship,* 140–54, and for an overview of the fourth century, *Theory.*

64. The specialists in "military affairs" made their appearance; among them are the sophists Euthydemus and Dionysodorus, who turn up in the dialogues of Xenophon and Plato.

65. It is enough to refer to the book by H. W. Parke, *Mercenary Soldiers,* and the study by A. Aymard, "Mercenariat."

66. See Y. Garlan, *Poliorcétique,* 156–59.

67. It is significant that Socrates himself mentions hoplite combat (*hoplitikon*) as being only one part of military skill (*Laches* 191d).

68. This had been Socrates' behavior at Delium, alongside Laches himself (*Sym.* 221a–b).

69. Behind this dialogue there is certainly reference to Herodotus, both in what concerns the Scythians (4.120–27) and in regard to the Spartan ideal (7.104, 9.71); on these passages see F. Hartog, *Miroir,* 70, and N. Loraux, "Belle Mort."

70. See "A Study in Ambiguity," p. 233 below.

71. Cf. "Athens and Atlantis," p. 269 below.

72. On this passage, cf. "Epaminondas the Pythagorean," p. 66 above, and P.-M. Schuhl, "Main droite" 2.

73. *Aristoteles* 1, pp. 193–94; on this dispute, cf. C. Pélékidis, *Éphébie,* 7–17.

74. See L. Robert, *Études,* 306.

75. See "The Black Hunter," pp. 106–8 below, with bibliography.

76. *On the Embassy* 167. Aeschines served as *peripolos,* in the forts of Attica.

77. Cf. L. Robert, *Études,* 296–307; subsequent bibliography is in C. Pélékidis, *Éphébie,* 110–13; see also "The Black Hunter" below, p. 121, n. 1.

78. H. Jeanmaire, *Couroi,* 308; cf. also R. Merkelbach, "Aglauros." On the sanctuary cf. J. Bousquet, "Aglaurides," 664.

79. In addition to Jeanmaire's study, there is the fundamental essay by P. Roussel, "Principe d'ancienneté."

80. For the complete collection of such documents produced by fourth-century historiography, I refer once again to C. Habicht, "Falsche Urkunden."

81. Nonetheless the ephebes learn not only "to fight like hoplites, but also to shoot with the bow, hurl the javelin and use the catapult" (*Ath. Pol.* 42.3). The innovations from the end of the fifth century, and those of the fourth, are reflected in ephebic service.

82. The other group of Athenians whom the state supplied with arms were the war orphans (cf. Plato, *Menex.* 248e–49d). G. Mathieu ("Éphébie") insisted rather too strongly on the importance of this institution for the origins of the fourth-century ephebia; a new document was published by R. Stroud, "Theozotides"; cf. N. Loraux, "Thucydide," 61–64.

83. See P. Roussel, "Review of A. Brenot."

84. The meaning of this expression has been clarified by J. Labarbe, *Loi navale,* 61–73.

85. Cf. J. Labarbe, *Loi navale,* and C. Pélékidis, *Éphébie,* 51–60.

86. The parallelism is well established in the fourth century. Cf. for example, Isaeus 2.14: an adopted child explains how his adoptive father straightened out the situation by introducing him into his deme, his phratry, his *orgeōn* (religious brotherhood): "He inducted me into his phratry, in the presence of these very men, and he had me enrolled in his deme and his brotherhood."

87. From now on the essential study is by D. Roussel, *Tribu,* 93–157. The

most important earlier bibliography is to be found in C. Rolley, "Thesmophor-
ion." In showing that nothing allows one to derive the civic phratry from a
putative pre-civic phratry, Roussel has confirmed me in the skepticism I had
already expressed against theories like those of M. Guarducci (*Fratria* 1 and 2).

88. M. Guarducci, *Fratria* 1, p. 17: "Organismo separato del ceppo com-
mune dello stato" ("an organism separate from the common body of the state").

89. Cf. A. Andrewes, "Philochoros."

90. I.G. 11, 1237; R. Dareste, B. Haussoullier, T. Reinach, *Recueil des
inscriptions juridiques grecques* 2, no. 29; Dittenberger, *Sylloge³* no. 921. The
Demotionides were a phratry whose seat was in the deme of Decelia. See also
D Roussel, *Tribu*, 141–47, who does not, however, touch on the problem
raised here.

91. *Sylloge³* 921.26–28. Using some worthwhile arguments, A. Andrewes
has attempted to show that this *diadikasia* was in some ways exceptional and
that the procedure, far from being standard in all phratries, was not even the
rule in the one addressed in this document ("Philochoros," 3). But how are we
to understand *to loipon* "henceforth," if the established rule does not, as Dittenberger claims, have a general application? Whatever the situation, this rule,
which was adopted in 396/5, was abrogated around 350 (cf. Menexenos's
amendment at lines 115–16).

92. Cf. J. Labarbe, "Coureion."

93. Hesychius, *s.v. Oinistēria;* Pollux 6.22; Photius *Lex. s.v. Oinistēria.* The
Oinistēria probably took place on the occasion of the Apaturia (cf. L. Deubner,
Feste, 233, qualified by the reservations of C. Pélékidis, *Éphébie,* 63–64).

94. The participants in the feast of the Apaturia had shaved heads (cf. Xen.
Hell. 1.7.8), but the significance of this evidence is unclear.

95. *Etym. Mag. s.v. Apatouria.*

96. A. Andrewes presents the phratry as a creation of the aristocratic state of
the ninth and eighth centuries ("Phratries").

97. The essential reference is Hellanicus in *FGrH* 323a F23; all the sources
I know of are cited in "The Black Hunter," n.15, p. 122 below.

98. Jeanmaire, *Couroi,* 382.

99. The ephebic oath in C. Pélékidis, *Éphébie,* 113, 119–20.

100. O. W. Reinmuth, "Ephebic Inscriptions," 224, 228, and C. Pélékidis
Éphébie, 271.

101. I cannot end these pages without recalling the firmness with which
Max Weber knew how to define the ancient city, in contrast with the medieval
city, as an association of warriors (*The City,* 196–226). However, no matter
what D. Roussel says (*Tribu,* 123, 131 n. 2), I never suggested, in referring to
Weber, that "the city was above all a military establishment of men organized
for war."

5 The Black Hunter and the Origin of the Athenian *Ephebia*

TO M. I. FINLEY

> *We have seen nothing;*
> *We are beastly-subtle as the fox for prey,*
> *Like warlike as the wolf for what we eat;*
> *Our valor is to chase what flies . . .*
> Shakespeare, Cymbeline 3.3.39–42

Before, and even more since, the discovery of Aristotle's *Constitution of Athens*, the Athenian ephebia has been a subject of controversy. This two-year "military service" is described by Aristotle in Chapter 42 of his little treatise. But was it an entirely artificial creation resulting from Lycurgus's policies, as Wilamowitz maintained, or was it rather an extremely ancient, even archaic, institution, of the kind likened by nineteenth-century scholars to the Spartan *krypteia?*

The argument has grown stale now, and as a result of the analyses and discoveries of the past thirty years it is easy enough to reach agreement on two points.[1] First, no one would now claim that the ephebia in Lycurgus's time was in every respect an ancient institution: the Athenian politician reordered and rationalized whatever existed before his time. Second, everyone would now agree that the ephebia of the fourth century B.C. had its roots in ancient practices of "apprenticeship," whose object was to introduce young men to their future roles as citizens and heads of families—that is, as full members of the community. I hardly need remind the reader of the role played by comparative ethnology in the realization of the significance of initiatory rituals in the ancient world; as early as 1913 Henri Jeanmaire based his own work on such studies, and only a little later Pierre Roussel commented upon a text of Aristotle (*Ath. Pol.* 42.5) in similar terms.[2] We know that the ephebe "cannot go to law

---

This is a considerably revised version of the original article. I have taken account of several points that have been made to me, especially by O. Picard, and of the criticisms of Maxwell-Stuart, "Black Coats."

either as a defendant or as a plaintiff, unless it is a matter of upholding an inheritance, arranging the affairs of an heiress, or a priesthood related to the *genos.*" Aristotle's own explanation is simple: the ephebes must not suffer any distraction from their military service, but this sort of explanation is valid only for Aristotle's own time. Roussel observed, "the *ephebia* is much more than a period of military service. It is the period of transition between childhood and complete participation in the life of the society. . . . There is so much evidence from other societies, including Sparta in Greece itself, that young people led a life apart for a period of time before their definitive admission into the social group, that one is inclined to see an example of the practice here."[3]

"Definitive admission" meant for the young citizen essentially two things: marriage, and entry into the hoplite phalanx (or later, becoming a sailor in the Athenian navy). So long as these two conditions remained unfulfilled—and the second was especially important in Classical Athens—the young man's relation to the polis was ambiguous. He both was and was not a member.

The ambiguity is strikingly illustrated at the level of topography—remembering that the organization of symbolic space does not always coincide with actual geography. When Aeschines the orator mentions his own ephebic generation (around 370 B.C.), he says that he served for two years after childhood as "*peripolos* of this land" (*On the Embassy* 167). When Plato came to copy the institution of the ephebia, he made his *agronomoi* circle round his city, first in one direction, then in the other (*Laws* 6.760b),[4] thus taking literally the etymological meaning of *peripolos,* "one who circles round." In the fourth century B.C. the ephebic *peripolos* was normally stationed in the frontier forts: Panacton, Deceleia, Rhamnus, and so on.[5] That might perhaps be entirely natural for lightly armed young men,[6] who were called upon to fight only under exceptional circumstances,[7] and would then obviously be used on patrol (which is another possible translation of *peripolos*). And yet these young men are associated with foreigners and with citizens of recent date: Aeschines served as a *peripolos* and, as a *neos,* with young men of his own age and with mercenaries (*On the Embassy* 168). Thucydides mentions *peripoloi* twice, first in association with Plataeans (Athenian citizens of recent date) at a night ambush near Nisaea in 425 (4.67–68), and later he says that the man who murdered Phrynichus in 411 was a *peripolos,* his accomplice being an Argive (8.92.2). Other sources too state that Phrynichus's murderers were foreigners.[8]

The same word could then designate both the young men of Athens and foreigners in her service. Both are marginal to the city (although the ephebe's marginality is temporary). But the ephebes' relation to the world of the frontier is complex. As young soldiers, they occupy the frontier zone of the city, which is expressed physically in the ring of fortlets (as in Crete, where there is epigraphic evidence for a clear-cut distinction between the full citizens and the young men, who occupy the *phrouria,* the *oureia,* the frontier area),9 when they take the oath that makes them full hoplites, they mention the boundary-stones that separate Athens' territory from her neighbors'. With these stones are associated wheat, barley, vines, olives, and fig trees—in a word, the world of cultivation. 10

A short discussion of a non-Athenian poetic text may make it easier to understand this. The finest evocation of the duality of the Greek ephebe is no doubt the Jason of Pindar's fourth Pythian ode. Pelias, the old king of Iolcos, was appointed to "die by the hands of the noble sons of Aeolus or their unrelenting schemes":11 Ἐξ ἀγαυῶν Αἰολιδᾶν θανέμεν χείρεσσιν ἢ βουλαῖς ἀκάμπτοις. He had been told to beware "at all costs the man with one sandal" who should pass from "a lofty retreat" to "the sunny plain"—"stranger be he or townsman" (*xeinos ait'ōn astos;* 75–77). And indeed Jason comes from afar, where he had been brought up in wild nature by Chiron the centaur and his daughters. He is a foreigner and is received as such, but he is also a citizen, speaking of himself as such to his fellow citizens: *kendoi politai, phrassate moi sapheōs* (117). He is a qualified ephebe, twenty years old, belonging to two worlds, with two javelins, and dressed both in the clothing of Magnesia and in the leopard-skin of the wild man: ἐσθὰς δ' ἀμφοτέρα νιν ἔχεν / ἅ τε Μαγνήτων ἐπιχώριος ἁρμόζοισα θαητοῖσι γυίοις, / ἀμφὶ δὲ παρδαλέᾳ στέγετο φρίσσοντας ὄμβρους. ". . . and a twofold guise was on him. A tunic of Magnesian fashion fitted close his magnificent limbs, and across it a panther's hide held off the shivering rains" (tr. Lattimore). The hair that the Athenian ephebe cut as a mark of entry into manhood still hangs down his back (82–83).

This prolonged adolescence is removed from the world of social reality and belongs to the realm of myth. Let us return to Athens, where the ephebe's ambiguity—at the level now of its institutional reality—can be seen as double. As Jules Labarbe saw, there were really two ephebic structures: the official ephebia, which was a civic military service, and a more archaic one through which one gained admission to the phratry. Hence the expression *epi dietēs hēbēsai,* which means 1) to be an ephebe in the civic sense, that is, to have reached the age of eighteen; and 2) as the literal sense suggests, to have attained the *hēbē,* to have been an ephebe for two years. 12 Labarbe showed that the first ephebia was marked ritually by the sacrifice of the *koureion* (the young man's long hair) at the age of sixteen. I may add that in one case at least admission to the phratry was not ratified until one year had elapsed from the date of the offering of the hair. [13]

The sacrifice of the hair took place at the time of the *Koureōtis,* the third day of Apaturia, the great festival celebrated by the phratries of the Ionian world, which took place in the month of Pyanopsion (September–October). This month was marked by a series of festivals that have been shown, by Jeanmaire in particular, [14] to have been festivals celebrating the return of the young men from the campaigns of the summer. It was through studying the etiological myth connected with the Apaturia that I was led to formulate the ideas presented here.

The myth is known from many texts dating from the fifth century B.C. right down to the Byzantines Michael Psellus and Johannes Tzetzes, who are of course simply restating older sources. The texts do not for the most part come from the principal ancient works of literature or history; although alluded to by Strabo and Pausanias, the myth is recounted only by Konon (an extremely obscure Hellenistic mythographer), Polyaenus, and Frontinus; otherwise it is a matter of scholiasts' remarks and entries in ancient lexica. [15] In view of the state of the sources, it is hardly possible to define "ancient" vs. more recent versions of the story, and I will therefore try to indicate the most important variants.

The scene is the frontier between Athens and Boeotia: an *eschatia,* a mountainous area that is the "end" of a city's territory, and whose inhabitants are always at loggerheads with their neighbors over the border. Such places existed on the borders of all Greek states. [16] They were the terrain of hunters and shepherds, frontier zones constantly in dispute. And they were necessary to Greek cities if only for training the young soldiers for war. [17]

A conflict broke out between the Athenians and the Boeotians. In some versions, over Oenoe and Panacton, in others over the frontier deme Melainai. The fourth-century historian Ephorus (quoted by Harpocration) says that the dispute was *hyper tēs Melanias chōras:* "over the area called Melania." I will observe simply that at Panacton there was an annual sacrifice to mark the Apaturia (*Sylloge*[3] 485). The Boeotian king was Xanthos (or Xanthios, or Xanthias), which means "the fair one." The Athenian king was Thymoites, the last of the descendants of Theseus. It was agreed to settle the dispute by means of a duel, a *monomachia.* But Thymoites stood down, according to a scholiast on Aristophanes' *Frogs* and another on Aelius Aristides' *Panathenaicus,* because he was too old. Another warrior came forward and was according to some versions promised the succession in return. His name was Melanthos (or Melanthios), "the black one." So the Black One was to fight the Fair One.

As they were fighting, Melanthos suddenly cried out, "Xanthos, you do not play according to the rules [*synthēkai*]—there is someone at your side!"—and as Xanthos looked round in surprise, Melanthos took his chance and killed him. The sources differ over details of what happened. Polyaenus and Frontinus say it was a ruse pure and simple; Halliday compares it to Tom Sawyer's trick when he cries out "Look behind you Aunty!" and thus escapes the beating she was about to administer.[18] The *Lexica Segueriana* makes Melanthos pray to Zeus *Apatēnōr* (Zeus "of wiles"). Most mention an intervention by the nocturnal Dionysus of the black goatskin, *nykterinos kai melanaigis*, to whom Plutarch seems to allude (*Quaest. Conviv.* 6.7.2.692e). The myth has his cult founded at Eleutherae, in this same frontier area. Afterward, the victor Melanthos became king of Athens.

In every source, the Apaturia is explained by paronomastic etymology. The festival is supposed to commemorate this *apatē* (wile, deception), whether the inspiration of the deception is ascribed to Dionysus, to Zeus, or to Melanthos himself.[19] The sources offer this explanation even though the scholiast on Aristophanes' *Acharnians* 146, as well as the grammarian quoted by the *Suda s.v. Apatouria*, knew an explanation: *Apatouria = Homopatoria*. Today we would say that the *a* of *Apatouria* is a copulative: the festival of the Apaturia is the festival of those who have the "same father"—in other words, the festival of the phratries.

Over the years there have naturally been many attempts to explain this myth. First, of course, historically—many such, from Johannes Töpffer's *Attische Genealogie*[20] to Felix Jacoby's great commentary on the Atthidographers, the historians of Attica. We are assured that Melanthos was a historical personage, a Neleid, the father of Codros, who, thanks to another *apatē* (disguising himself as a peasant), managed to get himself killed and thus ensured the safety of Athens in accordance with the oracles' prophecy. Melanthos is also described as the "ancestor" of the phratry of the Medontidae. Attempts have even been made to pinpoint the story's date—Wilamowitz put it not earlier than 508 B.C. because the frontier was only established then.[21] And Jacoby, while not denying the mythical nature of the story, envisaged the possibility of a real frontier skirmish.[22]

But it was Hermann Usener who first attempted to provide an overall explanation of the myth.[23] He pointed out that this was a duel between the *Black* and the *Fair*, as a few ancient authors realized: Polyaenus quotes, or invents, an oracle given before the encounter, which runs: τῷ

Ξάνθῳ τεύξας ὁ Μέλας φόνον ἔσχε Μελαίνας. "Having wrought the
death of the fair one the black one seized Melainai." ["Melainai" means
"the black country."] Usener saw the duel in symbolic terms, as a ritual
combat between winter and summer, an interpretation welcomed by,
among others, Lewis Farnell and Herbert Rose.[24] But it fails to explain
what needs to be explained: the link between the duel and the festival
itself. The same applies to Nilsson when, in a variant of the theory, he
suggested that this *agōn* linked with the worship of Dionysus was one of
the earliest forms of tragedy.[25]

Many years later, in *Couroi et Courètes,* Henri Jeanmaire offered an
entirely different view.[26] He saw the duel between Xanthos and Melanthos as a ritual joust, perhaps followed by a procession, through which a
claimant to the throne declared himself master of the territory. The name
of Melanthos is replaced in Pausanias (9.5.16) by that of Andropompos
(the "leader of the procession"); and according to Plutarch (*Quaest. Graec.*
13.294b–c) it was in a similar way—a duel involving a trick almost
identical with ours—that Phemius, king of the Aenianians, established
his claim to the valley of the Inachus. It also recalls the famous—
legendary—battle between Pittakos and Phrynon at the time of the war
over Sigeum between Athens and Mytilene.[27]

But to my knowledge only Angelo Brelich has really attempted to
explain the possible relationship between this myth and the Apaturia,
the festival of the phratries during which the ephebes were received into
the phratry after consecrating their hair. In particular he stresses the
frequency with which duels between young men take place in frontier
districts and observes that Dionysus (whom he identifies with Dionysus
Melanaigis) is described sometimes as *hēbōn* ("with his beard starting to
grow"). But he fails to push his interpretation much further than this.[28]

For my part, I was struck by three points that require explanation.
First, that the story takes place in the frontier region, just as it is to the
frontier region that the Athenian ephebes are sent, and that in their oath
they swear to protect the boundary-stones of their country. The second
point is the story's stress on the *apatē,* the trick. Why should the ephebes
be offered a model of behavior contrary to that which they swear in their
oath to observe? We have single combat (*monomachia*) and trickery contrasted with fair hoplite fighting on even terms. (Let it be noted in
passing that the very name Melanthos was probably evocative for a reader
of Homer: just as Dolon is the cunning wolf in the *Iliad,*[29] so in the
Odyssey Melanthios or Melanthieus is a treacherous goatherd [17.212,
22.159, 161, 182, etc.], and his sister Melantho is a treacherous servant
[18.321–22]. Their father is called Dolios, "the cunning one."[30]) Third,

I was struck by the stress on black in the story: *melas* (adj.), stem *melan-*. We find the name Melanthos, the location, which in some texts is called Melainai, and Dionysus of the Black Goatskin (*Melanaigis*). And this is not the only occurrence of an association between the Athenian ephebes and the color black; at least on certain solemn occasions, they wore a black *chlamys* (a short cloak) that was replaced, thanks to the generosity of Herodes Atticus, by a white one in the second century A.D.[31]

In his discussion of the inscription that provides this last item of information (I.G. 11² 3606), Pierre Roussel showed that the black *chlamys* was supposed to commemorate Theseus's forgetfulness: that ephebe of ephebes forgot to change the black sails on his ship for white ones on his return from Crete.[32] But etiology is not explanation, and George Thomson understood this black garment as a sign of ritual exclusion.[33] And there is certainly something very peculiar about this predominance of black—we have only to refer, for example, to Gerhard Radke's conscientious catalogue to understand just how startling, indeed shocking, a ritual victory for black might be in a festival celebrating the entry of young men into the community.[34]

It may help to formulate these problems more precisely if I now digress in order to discuss the Spartan *krypteia*, an institution that has often been compared to the Athenian ephebia, and which, although it involved a much smaller number of young men, was indeed parallel to it in some respects. It is well known that we have a very small number of sources for the *krypteia*,[35] but the scholiast on Plato's *Laws* 1.633b says explicitly that it was a preparation for military life. And Koechly argued as early as 1835 that this training was to be compared to that of the Athenian *peripoloi*;[36] a point made even more clearly by Ernst Wachsmuth, who lucidly observed that this military apprenticeship took the special form of a helot-hunt.[37]

A brilliant article by Henri Jeanmaire elucidated the fundamental characteristics of the *krypteia* by means of comparison with certain African societies: compulsory isolation of certain young men around the time of puberty; living in the bush; even the killing of helots—all these can be paralleled in black Africa, in the initiation ceremonies and secret societies of Wolf-men and Panther-men. But if this is so, what is the military role of the *krypteia?* Jeanmaire's reply was unequivocal: "The whole of Spartan military history cries out against the idea of turning the Spartan hoplite into a tracker in the bush, clambering over rocks and walls."[38] And he added wryly that if the *krypteia*, with its camping out in the mountains, had really been a training for military life at the time of the battle of Thermopylae (480 B.C.), Ephialtes' path—by which the

Persians surprised the Spartans—would have been discovered and guarded.

To my mind, Jeanmaire was both profoundly right and profoundly wrong. What he failed to understand was that the *krypteia* was by no means completely unrelated to the life of the hoplite: the two were symmetrical opposites. A list from what the sources tell us shows:

1. The hoplite is armed to the teeth; the youth in the *krypteia* is *gymnos*, which means either that he carried no arms at all (Schol. to Plato's *Laws* 1.633b) or that he had only a dagger (Plut. *Lycurgus* 28.2).

2. The member of the phalanx is opposed to the youth on his own or living in a small group.

3. The fighter in the plain is opposed to the youth who runs wild in the mountains.

4. Plato's youth in the *krypteia* did his training in the middle of winter; the hoplite fought in summer.

5. The trustworthy hoplite cheered on by Tyrtaeus (seventh century B.C.) is opposed to the cunning killer of helots.

6. The man who fights in the light of day is opposed to the youth who fights by night.

7. The scholiast on Plato's *Laws* says that the youth in the *krypteia* ate whatever he could find, living from hand to mouth, probably without ever finding time to have anything cooked; whereas the hoplite is above all a member of a common mess, the *syssition*.

8. The members of the *krypteia* stayed in the areas that became, in a sense, the frontiers of enemy territories—for the ephors annually declared war on the helots in a ritual comparable to the Roman declaration of war by the *Fetiales*.[39] (In contrast, the full hoplites were obliged to remain, in peacetime, close to their *syssitia*, that is, close to Sparta itself.)

In sum, with the hoplite, order (*taxis*) reigns;[40] in the *krypteia* there is nothing but cunning, deception, disorder, irrationality. To borrow Lévi-Strauss's terms, one might say that the hoplite is on the side of culture, of what is "cooked," while the *krypteia* is on the side of nature, of the "raw," bearing in mind of course that this "nature," the side of nonculture, is itself to some degree socially organized.[41] And we might apply this point more widely: for example, in Crete we find *agelai* of young men, which Pierre Chantraine interprets as the "herds of animals that are driven along,"[42] as opposed to the *hetaireiai*, the "brotherhoods" of mature men. And I could go on, but I have said enough to indicate how, by a procedure that Lévi-Strauss would term a logical inversion, the *krypteia* dramatizes the moment when the young elite Spartan leaves his childhood behind him forever.

In his *Polarity and Analogy,* Geoffrey Lloyd has brilliantly shown how the principle of polarity played a fundamental role in the reasoning of Greek thinkers of the Archaic period. Indeed I believe that his conclusions could easily be extended to include the Classical period itself: how can we understand Thucydides, for example, without using the notion of polarity? Rational decision (*gnōmē*) is for Thucydides the opposite of chance (*tychē*), and discourse the opposite of action, just as the hot is the opposite of the cold or the dry of the wet in Milesian cosmological thinking. My intention here, as must already be evident, is to detect evidence of polarities expressed not in book-thinking but in social institutions; and I propose to do that without touching upon whether "thought" and "institutions" are the effective consequences of one single entity, the Lévi-Straussian "human mind."

I think we may generalize and extend what I have already said in discussing the Spartan *krypteia:* for we must recognize that in Athens and in many other parts of the Greek world—above all in Sparta and Crete, where very archaic institutions were preserved until well into the Hellenistic period—the transition between childhood and adulthood (the period of marriage and fighting) is dramatized both in ritual and in myth by what we might call the "law of symmetrical inversion." Indeed, since the publication of Arnold van Gennep's *Les Rites de passage* in 1909, many rituals of status-transition have been analyzed in these terms.[43] I may remind the reader that in Argos, young women sported a (false) beard when they got married (Plut. *de Mul. Virt.* 4.245 et seq.); and that in Sparta, when a girl was to be married, she was "handed over to a *nympheutria* who shaved her hair, dressed her in a man's clothes and shoes, and made her lie down all alone on a mattress in the dark" (Plut. *Lycurgus* 15.5). The two cases are parallel, as is obvious when we remember that, according to Herodotus (1.82.7) adults in Argos had to be entirely bald, while in Sparta they had to let their hair grow long. We have here then a kind of double inversion.

But we must return to Athens, and look again at the festival known as the *Oschophoria* (held on the seventh day of Pyanopsion).[44] This is a particularly interesting festival because its etiological myth is concerned precisely with Theseus's return from Crete after killing the Minotaur, and the conflicting emotions he feels—glad because he has been victorious, filled with grief at his father's death (Plut. *Theseus* 22.4). And it was precisely this death that the ephebes' black *chlamys* was believed to commemorate.

The traditional sources for the Oschophoria diverge markedly from one another. I do not propose to analyze them exhaustively[45] but will simply emphasize some points that have sometimes been neglected. First of all, an essential role in the Oschophoria is played by an outlying *genos* (a group of relatively wealthy families claiming descent from a single ancestor), that of the Salaminians, who had moved to Attica. It was this *genos* in particular that provided the youths (*neaniai*) who carried the vine branches complete with bunches of grapes (*ōschoi*) and who were in consequence called the *ōschophoroi*.[46] Second, the first event of the festival was a procession (*parapompē*) from Athens to the shrine of Athena Skiras at Phaleron. Now the word *skiron* means "lime" and so "badlands"; and Felix Jacoby has shown that the names *Skiras, Skiros,* and *Skiron* were generally given to outlying districts that either were or had been at some time in the past frontier areas.[47] Thus Skira is another name for the offshore island of Salamis; Skiron is a village on the old boundary between Athens and Eleusis, and so on. The procession to the shrine of Athena Skiras was made up of boys (*paides*) led by two boys *disguised as girls* carrying the *ōschoi;* these boys are referred to as *paides amphithaleis*.[48] Plutarch explains the transvestism by saying that among the seven maidens whom Theseus took with him to Crete there were two boys disguised as girls (*Theseus* 23).[49] I cannot here venture to tackle the very complex problems presented by the festivals connected with Athena Skiras (Oschophoria, but also Skira or Skirophoria): the sources are so confused that it is hard to tell which of the various festivals they refer to. I will simply point out that Athena Skiras seems to have been linked significantly with the custom of dressing up: it is during her festival that Praxagora and her friends decide in Aristophanes' *Ecclesiazusae* to dress up as men and wear false beards (and it so happens that one of the characters has a husband who is a Salaminian).[50] In the *Life of Solon* (8–9) Plutarch gives two versions of how the Athenians seized Salamis (otherwise known as Skiras) from the Megarians. In one of them the beardless young men disguise themselves as women, and Plutarch says a festival was established on the promontory Skiradion after the seizure (although he links its details to the second story, which, while involving a deception, contains no transvestism).

Besides the procession and the boys' transvestism, the Oschophoria featured a race (*agōn, hamilla*) between ephebes carrying *ōschoi*. Most of our information about this is derived from Proclus's *Chrestomathia*.[51] The course ran from the temple of Dionysus to Phaleron. The competitors were either two representatives from each of the ten tribes, each pair running separately, or else twenty youths, two from each tribe, all running against each other. The victor drank the "fivefold cup," a mixture of oil, wine, honey, cheese, and flour. After the ceremonies at Phaleron, and in particular the rituals of seclusion and the *deipnophoria* (food-carrying), there were libations, followed by a revel (*kōmos*) that brought the participants back to Athens. It is evident from Plutarch (*Theseus* 22.3) that this revel was accompanied by a herald, and that the return journey too was explained by reference to Theseus's return from Crete (he was supposed to have stopped at Phaleron in order to sacrifice). In the story, Theseus's herald precedes him with the news of success and discovers the death of Aegeus, which he reports to Theseus, who is still outside Athens. Theseus's party then entered Athens loudly lamenting, but still the bearers of happy news. For this reason, says Plutarch, it is not the herald himself who is crowned at the Oschophoria, but his staff (*kerykeion*); and cries of joy, "Eleleu," alternate with keening, "iou, iou," in commemoration of Aegeus's death.[52]

The structure of the Oschophoria is thus marked by a series of oppositions. The most blatant is that between male and female, which is clear in the procession itself (boys dressed as girls versus the youths), but also in the contrast between the procession (boys dressed as girls) and the race (*dromos*) between the ephebes—the race of course is nothing if not virile: in Crete the *dromeus* is a mature man,[53] and in Lato, in particular, the word for leaving the *agela* to become a man is "running out" (*egdramein: I.C.* 1.16 [Lato], 5.21), and according to Aristophanes of Byzantium an *apodromos* was a young boy not yet allowed to take part in the public races.[54] The race during the Oschophoria is indeed exactly parallel to the *staphylodromia* during the Spartan festival of the Carneia, which was also a festival of the phratries: it was a race in which five unmarried young men from each tribe ran against one another.[55] Third, joy is opposed to grief, as is shown by Plutarch's *Theseus* 22.3, which has been considered, wrongly I think, to be a later interpretation.

It is well known that in archaic Greek societies, as well as in other societies, dressing up as a woman, as in the procession at the Oschophoria, was a means of dramatizing the fact that a young man had reached the age of virility and marriage. The classic example in Greek mythology is the story of Achilles on Skyros, dressed up as a girl but unable to control himself at the sight of a weapon.[56] But it can be demonstrated that it is not the *kind* of disguise that is important, rather the *contrast* that it underscores. The opposition between light and dark, for example, is no less significant: young men not yet adult are known sometimes to have been called *skotioi* ("of the dark"; Schol. to Eur. *Alcestis* 989); the *neaniai* (youths) of the Oschophoria are called *eskiatraphomenoi*, "brought up in the dark" (Plut. *Theseus* 23.2; Proclus, *Chrestomathia* 89 [p. 56 Severyns]).[57] Both Malla and Dreros in Crete seem to have held ceremonies of admission to the adult age-classes that involved ritual nudity before the conferring of hoplite arms. The young men are called *azōstoi*, which Hesychius defines as "those who are without arms." At Dreros they were called *panazōstoi* and *egdyomenoi*, "those who have no clothes," and the latter term occurs also at Malla.[58] Similarly, at Phaestus there was a festival called the *Ekdysia* ("clothes off"): the etiology here is a story about a girl who turned into a boy—which forms a link between the two sets *boy:girl* and *naked:armed*.[59]

It is perhaps worth noting finally that the sexual inversion of any young man about to become an adult is clearly related to these facts: it is enough to mention Ephorus's well-known story about the rape (*harpagē*) of a young Cretan boy, who is taken by his lover into the country (of course!) for two months, for a life of relaxation and *hunting*. It is on his return to town that he receives the arms that make him a hoplite (*FGrH* 70 F 149 [from Strabo 10.4.21: 483C]).

I come now to the theme of the hunt, which appears in the title of this paper, and which I still have to explain and, if possible, justify. Pierre Chantraine has noted that hunting is linked fundamentally with the *agros* in Greece, the land that lies beyond the cultivated area, that is, with the *eschatiai*, the borderlands of Greek cities.[60] Plato calls his ephebe, the person who defends the frontier area, an *agronomos* (*Laws* 6.760e–61a). More generally, hunting was so normal for heroes, whom the ephebes emulated, that F. Orth remarked that "heroes are hunters and hunters heroes."[61] In a sense, hunting is firmly on the side of the wild, the "raw," of night,[62] and the skills employed in the Spartan *krypteia* were those of hunting. But only a sense; we have to make certain distinctions.

My starting point is a well-known text on education, from the end of Plato's section on education in the *Laws* (7.822d–24a). Using the method demonstrated in the *Sophist*, Plato introduces here a whole series of distinctions. Each time he speaks of a left side, the side of evil, and a right side, that of good. Fishing depends upon the use of nets: it therefore falls squarely on the left. One ought then to restrict oneself to the hunt and the capture of quadrupeds (*thēreusis te kai agra;* 824a). However, here, too, he makes a distinction: one is not allowed to hunt at night with nets and traps. All that seems to be permissible is the type of hunting that conforms to the ethos of the horseman and the hoplite: coursing the animal or killing it with a lance—both of which are kinds of hunting that involve the use of one's bare hands (although bird-catching is tolerated *en agrois*, "beyond the area of cultivation"). "But as for the man who hunts by night, the *nyktereutēs*, with only nets and traps, let no man allow him to hunt anywhere" (824b).

When faced with a text of this kind, we must of course allow for Plato's dichotomizing method and for his moralizing tone. Perhaps we should allow for a similar tone when Pindar describes Achilles killing deer without dogs, and without guile or nets, but simply by running faster than they (*Nemean* 3.51–52)—although it reminds us of the Cretan *dromeus*. But there are several texts that draw a contrast between two types of hunting: adult hunting, where the spear is used rather than the net, and which takes place by daylight, sometimes in a group, and which is in keeping with the hoplite ethos; and hunting by night, a "black hunt" based on the use of the net. The heroic prototype of the group hunt is of course the hunt of the famous black Calydonian boar. Now it has been observed that "the use of nets is not a feature of pictorial representations of the Calydonian boar hunt," any more than it is of the literary accounts.[63] And for this reason: the Calydonian boar hunt is a hunt involving the adult heroes of Greece. Similarly, Hegesandros reports a Macedonian custom stipulating that no man could dine reclining until he had killed a boar without the aid of net or snare (Athenaeus, *Deipn.* 1.31.18a). Poor Cassander had to wait until he was thirty-five before he could enjoy this privilege—distinguished hunter though he was. We may put the point slightly differently: unless he had accomplished some signal exploit, a young man could not be a full participant in the communal meals that were a feature of so many archaic or marginal societies.

Two Spartan customs neatly illustrate how integral hunting was to the hoplite ethos. According to Plutarch, anyone who took part in the communal meals had to present the table with the choicest parts of his sacrifice, or if he had been hunting, with part of the bag (*Lycurgus* 12.4). One was allowed to dine at home if the sacrifice or hunt had finished late, but the others had to come along too (*tous d'allous edei pareinai*). And Xenophon informs us that hunting-dogs and horses were common property, while any food left in the mess after dinner had to be kept in a special place for any hunters who were delayed (*Lac. Pol.* 6.3–4).

In contrast to these heroic and communal exploits, hunting by oneself and with nets seems often to be typical of the adolescent. This is indicated by many texts, although it is true that many are late. According to Oppian, it was Hippolytus, the prototype of the youth who is unmarried and who refuses to marry, who invented the hunting-net (*Cynegetica* 2.25). In the story of young Philios, the first task imposed on him was to

kill a lion *aneu sidērou*, "without an iron weapon." And he slew it not with
a net but with a typical trick (*apatē*)—he made it drunk (Antoninus
Liberalis, *Metamorphoses* 12). It is in such terms, perhaps, that one might
explain why on the Chigi vase in the Villa Giulia in Rome there is a line of
men creeping through the undergrowth, over against the line of horsemen and the line of hoplites (the Chigi vase is Late Corinthian). And it is
by reference to the same oppositions that we can understand why Nestor
has two different initiations into the art of war in the *Iliad*, first as a young
man, lightly armed, taking part in a cattle raid at night, and then as a
heavily armed adult (*Iliad* 11.670–762).[64]

But I want to argue that the essential evidence for the role of the hunt
in the various stages of a young Greek male's life is provided by a figure
whom it is high time that I dealt with: the Black Hunter, Melanion. In
the *Lysistrata*, the chorus of old men sing:

> Let me tell you a little story
> I heard when I was a boy
> How there once was a youth [*neaniskos*] called Melanion, who
> Was so appalled at the prospect of women he flew
> To the mountains rather than marry.
>   And he hunted hares
>   And set his snares
>   With his dog there
> And never came back for anyone!
> [781–96, tr. Dickinson]

Melanion appears here as an ephebe, but a sort of ephebe *manqué*—a
kind of Hippolytus in fact, as Wilamowitz makes clear in his commentary.[65] If we looked no further than this chorus, we should have here a
version of the widespread myth of the gloomy solitary hunter who is
either a misogynist or who tries to insult Artemis, and who, in either
case, flouts the social rules. It is the well-known type of the hunter
Orion—who was indeed, according to Oppian, the inventor of hunting
by night (*Cynegetica* 2.28–29).[66]

But look further we must. Putting the story of Melanion back into its
mythical context, we can bracket it with the story of a young girl, the
Arcadian Atalanta, who was a huntress and who excelled in running.[67]
The legend is set near a frontier mountain, Mount Parthenion, between
the Argolid and Arcadia. Pausanias says that the nearest village was
called Melangeia (8.6.4). Like Melanion, Atalanta was brought up in the
mountains, suckled by a bear (Artemis's animal). Euripides characterizes

her as *misēma Kypridos* (F530 Nauck²) "hated by Aphrodite"—a social failing parallel to Melanion's. Theognis describes her as "the blonde Atalanta who strides over the mountain peaks, fleeing from the desire of marriage" (1291–94). For Hesiod she is the "light-footed Atalanta" (FF 73.2; 76.5, 20 Merkelbach-West)—the maiden who escapes from the Centaurs' attempts to rape her (Apollodorus, *Bibliotheca* 3.9.2). Aelian knows of her only that she is a virgin (*VH* 13.1), just as all that is known of Melanion in Aristophanes' chorus is that he refuses to marry. In Apollodorus's well-known version, she returns home and challenges any comer to a race, stipulating that it shall be an armed race. She thus trepasses on male preserves twice over. Xenophon says that Melanion won her hand thanks to his skills as a hunter (*Cynegeticus* 1.7), but a widespread mythological tradition (in Apollodorus, for example) had it that Melanion beat Atalanta and won her for life by means of a feminine *apatē*—dropping Aphrodite's three golden apples, one at a time. Both of them were depicted on Cypselus's chest at Olympia (Pausanias 5.19.2). During that period of their lives that was more or less unexceptionable, they both took part in the Calydonian boar hunt: they appear together, for example, on the "François vase"—Atalanta all light in color, Melanion all black (in keeping with pictorial convention), and with a white hound about to spring on a black boar. They had a son, whose name, significantly enough, was Parthenopaeus.[68] However, once again they violated sexual rules by having intercourse in a shrine sacred to Zeus or Cybele, the Mother of the Gods, and then they were transformed into lions, because, it is said, lions are unable to have sexual intercourse.[69]

The Athenian ephebe is in a sense the true heir of the Black Hunter. The Black Hunter is, as I have observed, an ephebe *manqué,* an ephebe who may fail at every turn.[70] And many Attic vases depict a young ephebe setting off with his hound: perhaps they do indeed, in their own way, represent the young man on the threshold of adult life.

It is time to draw this paper to a close. In historical terms, the ephebe in Archaic and Classical Greece was a pre-hoplite. By virtue of this, in the symbolic enactments that are the rites of passage, he was an anti-hoplite: sometimes a girl, sometimes a cunning hunter, sometimes black. It is not in the least surprising that a mythical figure like Melanthos should have been considered a model for the ephebe.[71] At the technical level, the ephebe is a light-armed soldier, an anti-hoplite who ensured the perpetuation, often unseen, of a mode of fighting that is both pre- and anti-hoplite, and that reappears in the light of day (and of history) during the Peloponnesian War and in the fourth century B.C.[72] Creature of the frontier area, of the *eschatia,* he guarantees in his hoplite oath to protect

Fig. 1.   Horsemen and guerrillas; the Chigi *olpê* (Rome, Villa Giulia, no. 2279); *ca*.
625 B.C.

the boundary-stones of his country, and with them, the cultivated fields, the wheat, barley, olive trees, vines, and figs.[73]

We might extend this study of the ephebia to a consideration of the role of the warrior in Greek mythology. Long before the introduction of hoplite warfare into Greece and Rome, the warrior's function in Indo-European society was twofold. On one side was order, which later led to the development of the phalanx and the legion, and on the other, disorder and the exploits of the individual. As Georges Dumézil has stressed, these personal exploits, through which the young warriors won recognition, derived from their *furor, lussa, celeritas, menos,* from their fighting spirit, but the exploits of the Irish Cuchullain, which made his return journey from the frontier zone so difficult and dangerous, were also tricks.[74] In just the same way it is by a trick, in Livy's account, that Publius Horatius defeated the three Curiatii (1.25.7–12). There is a striking parallel in Herodotus's story of the battle between three hundred young Spartans and three hundred young Argives in the frontier area of Thyreatis (1.68).[75] Young Horatius may thus be distant cousin to the Black Hunter.

NOTES

1. For the controversy, see Wilamowitz-Moellendorf, *Aristoteles* 1.193–94; L. Robert, *Études,* 297–307 (with the official text of the ephebic oath); H. Jeanmaire, *Couroi;* C. Pélékidis, *Éphébie* (with full bibliography); H.-I. Marrou, *Education,* 163–68, 521–22, 539–44. Reinmuth has shown from the inscriptions that the ephebia existed in 361 B.C., considerably before the period of Lycurgus's domination of Athenian political life (*Ephebic Inscriptions,* 123–38). To be sure, the date of the inscription that Reinmuth relies on has been questioned by F. W. Mitchell ("Ephebic Inscription," 233–43), but the scholar who found the stone, M. Mitsos, was in a position to defend Reinmuth (cf. J. and L. Robert, "Bulletin" (1976), no. 194). Most important of all, Philippe Gauthier has shown decisively in his discussion of Xenophon's *Ways and Means* 4.51–52 (which had not hitherto been adduced in the debate) both that the ephebia antedates Lycurgus—the *Ways and Means* was written in 355 B.C.—and that, prior to Lycurgus, it was not a duty imposed on all young male citizens (*Poroi* 190–95).

2. Jeanmaire, "Cryptie"; Roussel, "Review of A. Brenot."

3. Roussel, "Review of A. Brenot," 459.

4. See "A Study in Ambiguity," p. 232 below.

5. On the *peripoloi* generally in the Greek world, see L. Robert, *Hellenica,* 10,

283–92; we may add two recent items from Acarnania and Epirus: cf. J. and L. Robert, "Bulletin" (1973), nos. 229 and 260.

6. Xenophon thus uses the verb *peltazein* rather than *hopliteuein* (*Ways and Means* 4.52), the *peltē* being a light shield (and *hopliteuein* referring to the performance of military service equipped with heavy hoplite armor, especially the shield, *hoplon*). Cf. P. Gauthier, *Poroi*, 192–93.

7. Young men were used to fight only under exceptional circumstances, and so are normally specifically mentioned: note the episode in the first Peloponnesian War, a battle against Megara involving the *neōtatoi* (the young men not normally called up) and the *presbytatoi* (the older men no longer normally called up). Cf. Thuc. 1.105.4, Lysias, *Funeral Oration* 50–53, and the comments by N. Loraux, *Invention*, 136.

8. Lysias, *Against Agoratos* 71; *Sylloge³* 108 = Meiggs and Lewis no. 85; I am not concerned here with the mutual inconsistencies of these passages.

9. See *IC* 1.9 (Dreros), 1.126–27; and for *oureuō*, "to be a young soldier in the frontier forts," van Effenterre, "Fortins crétois." Thucydides 5.41.2 offers a clear-cut, official distinction between the frontier areas and the territory proper of Argos and Sparta (H. Bengston, *Staatsverträge*, 192).

10. Cf. G. Daux, "Deux stèles d'Acharnes," 78–90; J. and L. Robert, "Bulletin" (1966), no. 165.

11. The text sets formal combat against stratagem, an opposition whose significance is discussed below.

12. "Koureion"; for the mèaning of the expression *epi dietēs hēbēsai*, cf. J. Labarbe, *Loi navale*, 67–75, and C. Pélékidis, *Éphébie*, 51–60.

13. This is the so-called "Ruling of the Demotionidae"—*Sylloge³* 921, lines 27–28 (= Sokolowski, *Lois sacrées* (1969), no. 19, with bibliography).

14. *Couroi et courètes*.

15. Here is a list—assuredly incomplete—of the "sources" (an inadequate term, as will at once be realized, for most of these texts): Hellanicus, *FGrH* 4 F 125 = 323a F23 (Scholiast T on Plato, *Symposium* 208d) with Jacoby's commentary; Ephorus, *FGrH* 70 F 22 (= Harpocration *s.v. apatouria* [1, pp. 42–43 Dindorf]; Konon, *Diegeseis* in *FGrH* 26 F 1, 39 (*Melanthos*); Strabo 9.1.7 (393C); Frontinus, *Strategemata* 2.5.41; Polyaenus, *Strategemata* 1.19; Justin 2.6.16–21; Pausanias 2.18.8–9, 9.5.16; Eusebius, *Chronicon*, 56 (ed. Schoene); John of Antioch in *FHG* 4, p. 539, no. 19; Proclus, *in Timaeum* 21b (1.88.11–90.12 Diehl); Nonnus of Panopolis, *Dionysiaka* 27.301–7; Michael Apostolios, *s.v. apiōn es Apatouria* in *Corp. paroemiogr. gr.* 2, p. 294 (ed. Leutsch and Schneidewin); Michael Psellus, *De actionum nominibus* 40 (= Migne, *PG* 122, cols. 1017d–20a); Tzetzes, *Comm. in Aristophanis Ranas* 798a (4.3, pp. 907–9 Koster); Lycophron, *Alexandra* 767 with scholia (ed. Scheer); *Etym. Magn. s.v. apatouria* (cols. 336–37 Gaisford), and *s.v. koureōtis* (1522–23 Gaisford); *Lex. Seg. s.v. apatouria* (in Bekker, *Anec. Gr.* 1, pp. 416–17); Scholiast on Aelius Aristides 1 *Panath.* 118.20 (3, pp. 111–12 Dindorf); Scholiast on Aristophanes, *Acharnians* 146 (7 Dubner), and *Peace* 890 (315 Dubner); *Suda s.v. apatouria* (1, no. 2940 Adler),

Melanthos (3, no. 458 Adler), *melan* (3, no. 451 Adler), and *Xanthos* (3, no. 8 Adler); George Syncellus in *FHG* 4, p. 539. These sources have recently been assembled and discussed by F. Nieto, *Acuerdos belicos* 2.15–20 (no. 3).

16. Cf. L. Robert, "Lesbos," 304–5.

17. The ritual nature of the training has been demonstrated by A. Brelich, *Guerre, Agoni;* cf. Garlan, *War,* 29–31

18. "Xanthus-Melanthos," 179.

19. There is more here than a mere etymological play on words. As Pauline Schmitt shows, according to Pausanias (2.33.7) there was on the island of Sphaeria, near Troizen, a temple of Athena Apaturia, which played an important part in the initiation of young girls. The "original" *apatē* is the union of Poseidon and Aethra, mother of Theseus; cf. P. Schmitt, "Athena Apatouria," 1059–73.

20. Published in 1889, 225–41.

21. "Oropos," 112 n. 2.

22. *FGrH* 3 b Supp. 2: 50 [on 323a F 23].

23. "Göttliche Synonyme," 365–69 (= *Kl. Schr.* 4.292–97), following a suggestion by Maas, "Review of Toepffer," 805 n. 13. Cf. also Usener, "Heilige Handlung," 301–13.

24. L. R. Farnell, "Dionysia"; *Cults,* 130–31, 134–36. Farnell's theory was very like Nilsson's, discussed above (p. 111), which of course he did not know. Cf. also A. Cook, *Zeus* 1. 689; H. J. Rose, *Handbook,* 131–33.

25. "Ursprung," 674–77 (*Opuscula Selecta* 1.61–110, 111–16).

26. *Couroi,* 382–83; see also Y. Garlan, *Guerre,* 15–17.

27. The sources are in E. Will, *Korinthiaka,* 381–83.

28. *Guerre, agoni,* 56–59. Marie Delcourt's remarks in *Pyrrhos,* 18, are completely unfounded, being based upon factual mistakes.

29. L. Gernet, "Dolon"; see A. Schnapp-Gourbeillon, *Lions,* 104–31, and F. Lissarrague, "Dolon."

30. Dolios himself is a sympathetic figure: *Od.* 24.222–25, 387–90, 397–411.

31. This point has been challenged by Maxwell-Stuart, "Black Coats," 113–16. He tries to minimize the significance of Philostratus, *Lives of the Sophists* 2.550, according to which the ephebes wore in assembly and in public processions a black *chlamys.* His criticism does not carry conviction because, although he is familiar with Roussel's article ("Chlamydes noires")—which to my mind is decisive—he persists in thinking that *I.G.* 11² 1132 (honorific inscription for Herodes Atticus) refers to Herodes' father, Claudius Atticus, whose vow Herodes was fulfilling. But Roussel showed that the text in fact refers to Theseus: it says "the son of Aegeus much to his dismay forgetting his father . . ." (*lēthēn patros akeomenos/ Aigeideō;* 20). Moreover there is no way of showing that this inscription refers to the mysteries of Eleusis. On the other hand, I have taken account of two points by Maxwell-Stuart and removed a reference to Xenophon, *Hellenica* 1.7.8 (which I interpreted wrongly) and the evidence of the vases (which I misrepresented).

32. "Chlamydes noires."

33. *Aeschylus*, 107.

34. *Farbe;* cf. B. Moreaux, *La nuit.*

35. See Plato, *Laws* 1.633b and the relevant, and very important, scholia on it; Heraclides Ponticus, *FHG*, 2, 210; Plutarch, *Lycurgus* 28; note too Plutarch, *Cleomenes* 28, which mentions one Damoteles, who was in Cleomenes' army the head of the *krypteia* (that is, in charge of ambushes). Cf. Koechly, *Cryptia*, 1.586–87.

36. [Mueller, *Geschichten* 2.302]; Koechly, *Cryptia* 1.587–88.

37. *Alterthumskunde* 1.462, 2.304. It would be diverting to compare these "military" interpretations in the nineteenth century with the liberal, not to say Louis-Philippian, one of Henri Wallon, the "father of the French Republic," for whom the *krypteia* was essentially a police operation.

38. "Cryptie," 142.

39. Plutarch, *Lycurgus* 28.4 (quoting Aristotle). For a defense of the seriousness of this tradition, see M. I. Finley, "Sparta," 165 with n. 9, 176–77.

40. At the level of ideology, of course; the actual social organization of the Spartiate hoplite body is more complicated than this, as Nicole Loraux reminds me (cf. "Belle mort").

41. See Lévi-Strauss, "Triangle," and more generally *The Raw and the Cooked;* N. Yalman, "The Raw," also R. Jaulin, *Mort sara,* 40–119 and 141–71, the astonishing account of the author's "initiation" by a tribe in Chad; and, on another type of opposition between the "naked" and the "heavily armed" warrior, Dumézil, *Mythe et Epopée* 1.63–65.

42. *Études*, 32–33.

43. On the concept of inversion, one could quote the whole of Lévi-Strauss's work; see also Pembroke's important paper, "Women."

44. On the Oschophoria, see A. Mommsen, *Feste*, 36, 278–82; A. R. van der Loeff, "De Oschophoriis"; L. Deubner, *Feste*, 142–46; A. Severyns, *Recherches*, 243–54; H. Jeanmaire, *Couroi*, 346–47, 524, 588; Jacoby, *FGrH* 3 b l, pp. 285–304, 3 b 2, pp. 193–223; P. Faure, *Cavernes*, 170–72.

45. The entire literary tradition on the Oschophoria and Skira is printed in Jacoby *FGrH* 3 b 1 (Suppl.), 286–89, in his commentary on some of the most important passages (Philochorus, 328 FF 14–16). The only significant inscription relevant to the Oschophoria is that belonging to 363 B.C., which gives us the record of an agreement between the two segments of the Salaminian *genos* that had been in dispute (first published with a full commentary by W. S. Ferguson, "Salaminioi"; conveniently reprinted in F. Sokolowski, *Lois sacrées, Suppl.* no. 19).

46. See Sokolowski, *Lois sacrées*, 50, line 49. The same *genos* provided two female *deipnophoroi* (food-carriers), who brought food to the young people "shut away" during the seclusion ceremonies in Phaleron. Cf. Nilsson, "Salaminioi."

47. *FGrH* 3 b 2 (Suppl.), 200–203. The sanctuary of Athena Skiras is said

126   to be "outside the city" (*ex tēs poleōs*): *Etym. Magn.* p. 717.28 [=*FGrH* 3 b 1 (Suppl.) 287, no. 7].

48. *Amphithalēs* has two meanings: "a child with both parents alive," and "one who cuts and handles green branches or twigs in rituals or processions"; cf. L. Robert, "Amphithalēs."

49. Here Plutarch is quoting the Atthidographer Demon [c. 300 B.C.]; Proclus, *Chrestomathia* 88–91 (56–57 Severyns) [= Photius, *Bibliotheca* 239].

50. *Eccl.* 18–25, 38; cf. also *Frogs* 204. These points seem to have gone unnoticed.

51. Proclus, *Chrestomathia* 91–92 (57 Severyns): Εἴπετο δὲ τοῖς νεανίαις ὁ χορὸς καὶ ᾖδε τὰ μέλη, ἐξ ἑκάστης δὲ φυλῆς ἔφηβοι διημιλλῶντο πρὸς ἀλλήλους δρόμῳ ("the chorus followed the young men [the procession with the two boys dressed as girls] and sang the songs; ephebes from each tribe competed against each other in a running race"); see also the scholiast on Nicander of Colophon, *Alexipharmaka* 109 [36 Abel and Vari: "*Oschophoroi* means at Athens boys who carried sacred branches and who competed by tribes; they ran with vine-branches from the temple of Dionysus to the temple of Athena Skiras."]. The inscription of the Salaminioi, quoted above (cf. n. 45), apparently alludes to this competition (*hamillos*) in lines 61–62: "Each party (i.e., the two segments of the Salaminian *genos* whose dispute is here resolved) shall perform in turn the sacrifice which precedes the contest" (cf. W. S. Ferguson, "Salaminioi," 37).

The literary tradition is hopelessly confused, since the sources seem to mix up at least four festivals, the Oschophoria, the Skira, the Skiraphoria, and the Thesmophoria. The first and last of these took place in the month Pyanopsion (September–October) and the Thesmophoria was confined to married women. But what about the Skira? Aristodemus of Thebes, a late Hellenistic Boeotian writer, assigned the ephebic race, which I have assigned to the Oschophoria on the authority of Proclus, to the festival of the Skira, which was connected with Athena Skiras, just as the Oschophoria was (*FGrH* 383 F 9, from Athenaeus, *Deipn.* 11.495 e). The scholiast to Aristophanes, *Ecclesiazusae* 18 (315 Dubner) says that the Skira was a June festival (12 Skirophorion). If so, it is impossible to suppose that the youths carried *ōschoi*, bunches of *ripe* grapes. I cannot therefore agree with Jacoby when he writes: "Our tradition is perfectly clear: the procession is attested for the Oschophoria, the race for the Skiraphoria" (or the Skira, perhaps), and then clarifies this "tradition" by arguing that part of Proclus's text is interpolated (*FGrH* 3 b 1 [Suppl.], comm. on 328 FF 14–16). Additional support for my interpretation is provided by the existence at Sparta of a ritual race very close to that described by our sources, linked to a festival of the phratries (the Carneia), and in which the runners carry bunches of grapes in just the same way (cf. p. 116 above).

On the Skira, see Dow and Healey, *Calendar*, 16–17, 33, 39–41, 44, revising and commenting upon *I.G.* 11² 1363 (though the book must be used with caution: cf. J. and L. Robert, "Bulletin" [1963], no 217, and the authors they cite, especially Jean Pouilloux and Georges Roux).

52. See also Aristodemus of Thebes, *FGrH* 383 F 9, and Proclus, *Chresto-mathia* 91–92 (57 Severyns).

53. R. F. Willetts, *Aristocratic Society,* 11–14.

54. "(They call the ephebes) *apodromoi* in Crete because they do not yet take part in the running races": ἀλλὰ δηλαδὴ ἀπόδρομοι ἐν Κρήτηι, οἱ μήπω τῶν κοινῶν δρόμων μετέχοντες ἔφηβοι . . .—Eustathius, *Comm. in Hom. Il.* 2.630.9 Van der Valk, quoted by Willetts, *Aristocratic Society,* 11 n. 5.

55. J. E. Harrisson, *Themis,* 234, cf. 321.

56. See H. Jeanmaire, *Couroi,* 354–55; M. Delcourt, *Hermaphrodite,* 5–27, where many examples are collected; B. Bettelheim, *Symbolic Wounds,* 109–21.

57. It will be recalled that there were festivals, such as the *Pannychis* during the Panathenaia, from which all but the young were excluded, and which were held at night (cf. Euripides, *Heracleidae* 780–83); note too the ritual mentioned by Herodotus 3.48, discussed by P. Schmitt, "Histoire de tyran," 226–27.

58. See *IC* 1.9 (Dreros), 1.11–12; 98–100 (p. 85); 1.19 (Mallos), 1.17–18, with Guarducci's commentary on pp. 87, 232; cf. E. Schwyzer, "Eid," and van Effenterre, "Serment."

59. Antoninus Liberalis, *Metamorphoses* 17 [Leukippos]; cf. the commentary by M. Papathomopoulos in the Budé edition (1968); R. F. Willetts, *Cretan Cults,* 175–78.

60. *Études,* 40–65.

61. "Jagd," *RE* c. 559. The main work on hunting in classical Greece remains Otto Manns, *Jagd.* There is some information to be gleaned from J. Aymard, *Chasses romaines* (mostly about Roman hunting). See also A. Brelich, *Eroi* (index s.v. *caccia*). When this article was first published, I did not know K. Kerenyi's "Dio Cacciatore," which raises a number of the problems discussed here. The still unpublished thesis by A. Schnapp, *Représentation,* reworks the question; see his article, "Immagini di caccia." Finally, see A. Brelich, *Paides* 198–99, and H. W. Pleket, "Collegium," which is thought-provoking.

62. In the well-known opposition between hoplite and archer in Euripides' *Herakles,* the archer is rejected, since he hunts wild animals (lines 153–58).

63. Cf. P. Chantraine, *Études,* 64–65, relying on P. de la Coste-Messelière, *Musée de Delphes,* 130–52 (though Immerwahr, *Atalanta,* 52–54, points out that this feature does occur on Roman representations of the hunt on sarcophagi; and see now G. Koch, *Die mythologischen Sarkophage*).

64. See the definitive commentary on this passage by Bravo, "Sulan," 954–60.

65. *Lysistrata,* 169–70.

66. Originally Orion is also a destroyer of wild animals, a killer armed with a mass of bronze (cf. *Od.* 2.572 et seq.). According to Plutarch, Aristaeus was the first hunter "to set traps for animals" (*de Amore* 757 b).

67. The literary texts concerning Atalanta are given, for example, by W. Immerwahr, *Atalanta.* Bowra's article, "Atalanta," although devoted to Swinburne's poem, is suggestive, but the fundamental discussion is now G. Ar-

128   rigoni, "Atalanta." See also M. Detienne, "Panther," esp. pp. 25–34, 40–52. On the episode of the apples, see J. Trumpf, "Aepfel," 20.

68. "A half-child man" (*andropais anēr*) says Aeschylus, *Septem* 533; the very name Parthenopaeus means "with a face like a girl's."

69. Apollodorus, *Bibliotheca* 3.9.2; Ovid, *Metamorphoses* 10.560–607; *Vatican Mythographer* 1.39 (ed. Mai); Hyginus, *Fabulae* 185; Servius in *Vergil. Aeneid.* 3.113. The sources differ concerning the name of Atalanta's husband.

70. This type of figure in myth should be compared with the whole range of those who refuse transition. That is a subject that has not yet been explored.

71. Starting from here, I have tried to show that one can interpret Sophocles' *Philoctetes* in terms of the ephebia ("Le *Philoctète* de Sophocle et l'éphébie" and cf. n. 144 below).

72. Xenophon's work on war and hunting reveals this modification of the hoplite tradition extraordinarily well. Many sentences—for instance those that advise the training of youths and older men for war by the practice of hunting—have a polemical significance that has hardly been noticed.

73. This is as far as I go along with the remarks of Pleket, "Collegium," 294 on the ephebe as hoplite-in-the-making. On the ephebic oath as a hoplite oath, see P. Siewert, "Ephebic Oath."

74. See Dumézil, *Horace*, 37; *Aspects*, 23; also F. Vian, "Fonction guerrière." In the properly Roman context, several studies by J.-P. Morel have thrown new light on the role of the *juventus* (the age-class of young men) in the age-class structure (cf. "Pube praesenti," "La Juventus," "Pantomimus," and "Jeunesse.")

75. After the battle, Othryades, the sole Spartan survivor, set up a trophy while the two surviving Argives returned to Argos with the news of victory; both sides could thus legitimately claim to have won.

6 Recipes for Greek Adolescence

I hate travel and explorers.
Claude Lévi-Strauss

In 1724 a book appeared in Paris by the Jesuit Joseph François Lafitau that was entitled *Moeurs des sauvages ameriquains comparées aux
moeurs des premiers temps.*[1] A modest enough title, but the contents constitute a kind of landmark in the historiography of the ancient world.
Lafitau was a missionary, born (1670) in Bordeaux into a family of rich
merchants and bankers. From 1712 to 1717 he lived in Canada with P.
Garnier, who knew the Algonquins, Hurons, and Iroquois well. As an
ethnologist who had worked in the field, Lafitau was of course neither the
first missionary nor the first European to favor the conquering West with
the benefit of the knowledge he had acquired. Reflection and discovery
went hand in hand. In effect, ethnology had established itself since the
sixteenth century as a science of barbarian societies, conceived now as
static in relation to a world swept up in the flux of history. Lafitau's
originality lay elsewhere.[2] Arnaldo Momigliano has put it well: his book
"revealed to the world the simple truth that also the Greeks had once
been savages."[3] To be sure, Thucydides had made almost exactly the same
point: "One could point to a number of . . . instances where the manners of the ancient Hellenic world are very similar to the manners of
barbarians today" (1.6.6). But Thucydides had been forgotten. De-
precating the conquest of America, Montaigne—who was yet at mo-
ments so close to historical relativism—wrote: "Why did not so noble a
conquest fall under Alexander, or the ancient Greeks and Romans: and so

First version published in J. le Goff and P. Nora, *Faire de l'histoire* III (Paris,
1974) 137–68.

great a revolution and mutation of so many empires and nations, fall into hands that would have gently leveled, rooted up and made plain and smooth whatever was rough and savage amongst them, and that would have cherished and propagated the good seeds that nature had there produced; mixing not only with the culture of land and the ornament of cities, the arts of this part of the world, in what was necessary, but also the Greek and Roman virtues, with those that were original of the country?" (*Essays* 3.6, tr. Cotton). Indeed Lafitau went further than Thucydides, by comparing not only the distant past of the Greeks with the world of the savages, but also Classical Greece itself. In his own way, the Jesuit was drawing a line under the debate between Ancients and Moderns. The Greeks, the Romans, even up to a point the Jews (in a sense more decisive still), lost the cultural privilege they had been granted by the scholars of the Renaissance and the seventeenth century. "I declare," he wrote with extraordinary temerity, "that if the ancient authors have afforded me illumination to substantiate several happy solutions regarding Savages, the customs of Savages have afforded me illumination the more easily to understand, and to explain, several matters to be found in the ancient authors." In saying that, Lafitau was taking the opposite line to another founding father of anthropology, the Spanish Jesuit José de Acosta, author of a *Historia natural y moral de las Indias*, published at Seville in 1590 and almost at once translated into French and English [by Edward Grimston, 1604]. De Acosta's epistemological rule, except in matters religious, was that the Greco-Roman world remained *the* civilization. To be sure Lafitau, learned missionary that he was, found himself, in true classical fashion, an ancient patron: "The science of the manners and customs of different people is so useful and interesting that Homer deemed that he should make it the subject of an entire poem. Its purpose is to celebrate the wisdom of his hero Ulysses who, seeing himself after the siege of Troy carried ever further from his homeland Ithaca by the wrath of Neptune, profits from different mistakes in his voyage to instruct himself in the manners of the nations at which the anger of the winds obliged him to touch, and to derive from each what was in it good and praiseworthy" (*Moeurs* 1.3). But these nations are not only the imaginary peoples that Odysseus describes in the palace of Alcinous, they are the Greeks themselves, seen both as the creators and as the objects of a science.

The frontispiece to Lafitau's work (fig. 2) is an emblematic engraving. How did he himself interpret it?[4] The writer (apparently a woman) is seated at a writing desk in ancient dress. She is busy, "comparing a number of ancient monuments, pyramids, obelisks, pantheons [statues

Fig. 2. The historian confronting Time, between pagan symbols and Christian iconography; the frontispiece to Lafitau's *Moeurs des sauvages amériquains*.

132   combining the attributes of several gods], medallions, ancient texts with
a number of accounts, maps, voyages and other curiosities of America,
among which she is sitting." In particular one can make out one such idol
on the ground, an Artemis of Ephesus lying on its side. Two putti help
her in this task. One holds in his left hand the caduceus of Hermes and in
his right a Red Indian pipe; the other holds an Iroquois "turtle" against
some sort of rhomb or rattle from a statuette from the Hellenistic East.
Higher up, above Adam and Eve, the risen Christ and the Virgin Mary
after the Assumption, surrounded by angels,[5] flank the dazzling Host on
an altar. Finally, Time takes the writer back "to the source of all" and
makes her "as it were palpate the connection between all these monuments and the origin of man, between them and the essence of our
Religion." I do not know whether Lafitau imagined that Time, with his
wings and scythe, was a figure from antiquity; today of course we know
that it is not.[6] Father Time, descended from ancient Saturn and the
medieval figure of Death, owes his iconography to the Renaissance: he is
contemporary with the men who witnessed the "Great Expansion," and
Lafitau's draftsman stresses his vitality rather than his destructive aspect
(the scythe is not at work). The Jesuit saw no contradiction between the
action of Time and comparison between, as we might say now, the
"diachronic" and the "synchronic."

Comparison between the customs of the Indians and the Greeks is
legitimate because Indians and Greeks are each descended from Adam
and Eve. The scene is given unity by the figures and symbols of Judeo-
Christian myth. Moreover, Lafitau makes his own attempt to historicize
the myth by having his Indians be the distant cousins both of the Greeks
and of their barbarian neighbors. (Here again he differs from his predecessor de Acosta, who thought indeed that the American Indians came
from the Old Continent—he had guessed the existence of the Bering
Strait—but stressed that these ancestors can hardly have been anything
but "mas hombres salvages y cazadores, que no gente republica y pulida"
[savages and hunters rather than a refined and civilized polity][7]—"savages and hunters," the very redundancy of the phrase is characteristic.)
But Lafitau could hardly ignore (and did not) the fact that even before his
own century, and in particular after the Great Expansion, the possibility
of another Adam, or of several other Adams, had been raised, sometimes
to justify the enslavement of the Indians, but sometimes to assert that
they were free of original sin.[8] The death of God, so close to Lafitau's
work, while it cut away the top of his picture, in a way left things as they
stood. Is that why we now have the right to *compare*, that is, as it were, to
annul, Father Time?

Nineteenth-century evolutionary theory, in its own way structuralist,
injected a dose of secularism into Lafitau's schema. At Stuttgart, in 1861,
Johann Jakob Bachofen published his *Das Mutterrecht*. Right from the
start, the Swiss scholar relied on a now famous passage from Herodotus
(1.173): in Lycia the men took the name not of their father but of their
mother—which is what the Iroquois, among others, also did. Now
Lafitau knew this text; indeed he had collected all the texts he could find
on what we must after him call "matriarchy" and "matrilinearity."
Gynecocracy, the Rule of Women," he observed, "was practically universal" (1.71). His first reaction on comparing Lycians, Iroquois, and
Hurons was to suppose that the American Indians were descended from
the Lycians (1.64). He was a little doubtful on account of the claimed
universality of matriarchy in the ancient world, but having no change of
theory at hand, finally concluded that "the larger part of the inhabitants
of America stemmed originally from those barbarians who dwelt on the
mainland of Greece and the islands" (1.82–83), before the arrival of the
Greeks. Bachofen did not need such a hypothesis. For him, all mankind
has passed through a stage of "matriarchy," a stage of comforting contact
with nature that reproduces the mother's breast and that precedes the
cultural break brought about by patriarchy. Even earlier than Bachofen
and apparently without knowing Lafitau, L. H. Morgan had likened the
Lycians to the Iroquois.[9] When the time came for a synthesis in 1877
(*Ancient Society*), God, incessantly on Lafitau's pen, makes an appearance
on the very last page, where Morgan pays homage to these "savages,"
these "barbarians," whose patient toil was "part of the plan of the Supreme Intelligence to develop a barbarian out of a savage, and a civilized
man out of this barbarian." A hesitant enough appearance, but all the
same necessary. For the parallelism of social evolutions is explained at
least partly by the presence in all men, if not of a gleam of original
Revelation, then at least of the "primary germs of thought" that the
transition between one stage of social evolution and another allows to
develop.[10] Secularized by Engels (*Origin of the Family* was published in
1884), Morgan's schema makes comparison both legitimate and straightforward. To compare two societies, it is necessary and sufficient to determine their coordinates on the graph of social evolution. The Iroquois are
at the lower margin of the state of barbarism whose upper margin is
represented by Homeric Greece. Fine, but what about all the innumerable institutions that Lafitau knew perfectly well could exist in quite
different societies? Must we, for example, forbear to compare the warrior
societies of the medieval West and Homeric society on the grounds that
one, in Marx's and Engels' terminology, belongs to a social formation

founded on slavery, and the other to the "feudal" period? Even if we do make the sacrifice, the problem refuses to go away. We have to make a choice: either we say, with the Soviet version of Marxism in particular, that all human societies have passed or will pass through the same stages (which is just not true[11]), or we restrict the occurrence of "feudalism" simply to the medieval West and Japan, which involves an extraordinary constriction of the comparative field, one that would disallow a whole series of studies whose very existence proves that you cannot make something true simply by believing it.

Although I have cited Lewis Morgan, it was not, unfortunately, his work, the work of a man who had received a double education, Iroquois and American, and who, in spite or perhaps because of that, insisted upon the unity of the human family, that dominated such interest as anthropologists had in the Greek world. Six years before *Ancient Society*, in 1871, there the first edition of Edward B. Tylor's *Primitive Culture* appeared, and it was through Tylor and his followers, above all Andrew Lang (1844–1912) and J. G. Frazer (1854–1941), that Greek studies were decisively influenced by the work of anthropologists,[12] after the collapse of Max Müller's "comparative mythology."[13] Of course there were many points on which Morgan and Tylor were agreed, but their views were at heart different. Right at the beginning of his book, Tylor, while allowing for the existence of good savages, sets up an opposition between savagery and civilization—that is of course Western imperialist civilization. But comparison is justifiable because of *survivals* (an older notion significantly adapted by Tylor) from the savage world at the heart of the civilized: "If we choose out in this way things which have altered little in a long course of centuries, we may draw a picture where there shall be scarce a hand's breadth difference between an English plowman and a Negro of central Africa."[14] There is a fundamental unity between the lower *classes* of the West and the inferior *races* of the world; in Tylor's day English royalty could not yet be compared with African chiefs. Moreover Tylor made a point that is the origin of many theories of totemism: "The sense of an absolute physical distinction between man and beast, so prevalent in the civilized world, is hardly to be found among the lower races."[15]

What was the place of the Greek world seen through the evolutionary spectacles of the nineteenth century? It is crisply defined by Andrew Lang, a key figure of the age, at once a journalist, a historian on the grand and the small scale and a foremost anthropologist. It went without saying that, from the age of Homer, the Greek world belonged utterly to civilization. After all, from then on there were royal houses. But it was equally obvious that the Greeks were conscious of having been savages. Their rituals and myths are full of odd things, from human sacrifice to cannibalism. Here the notion of survival combined with evolution plays a crucial role: the Greeks *had been* savages, they were so no more; their myths are survivals from the past,[16] and mythology *tells* what their ancestors did. Comparison was compatible with hierarchization.

The synthetic systems of the Romantic period and the Age of Positivism are now mere rotted hulks or etiolated to the point of unrecognizability. Let us take a look at a slightly later period: at a time when the kings of anthropology were Frazer on one side and Malinowski on the other. What fresh basis for comparative study could a historian have found? Frazer was a fact-gleaner. Starting from the Greco-Roman world, which he knew admirably well, he was an indefatigable footnoter of Pausanias and Ovid without ever explaining what it was that permitted him to compare the Priest-King of Nemi slain by his successor, Christ dying on the Cross, or the God-King of Pharaonic Egypt. Malinowski dedicated himself to an unprecedented effort of reflection upon the functioning of a single Melanesian society, over-hastily equated with the Savage *tout court*.[17] For the historian, the choice might properly appear ruinous. And yet, of the two, from the time of Salomon Reinach to our own, it was undoubtedly Frazer who was, in France and elsewhere, the more influential. With hardly an exception (M. I. Finley's *World of Odysseus* being one) the central concept that we owe to Malinowski (and refined by his successors, above all Radcliffe-Brown), "social function," has hardly been put to use by historians of the ancient world. To be sure, it was not a clear or a crisp notion, and it has properly been stressed that "function" has two senses for Malinowski: an organicist sense—an institution is an element that has a function, a role, in a social aggregate— and a logistic or symbolic sense—mythology has a symbolic function in the structuring of social relations.[18] But there was here an open door that almost no one stepped through. One may be allowed to regret this at a time when anthropology has, once again, rocketed in the most divergent directions, of which "structuralism" is just one, although the one that, even allowing for fashion, attracts many historians most strongly.

How are we placed now? The latest research, so far from making the historian's choice easier, simply makes it more painful, because every historian today knows that what he studies is properly speaking neither the unique nor the universal—even if the universalism of the "human mind" has replaced Frazer's empirical universalism. We all know as historians that the truth of the history of a Breton village is not to be found in the simple history of a Breton village, but also that the diverse metahistories that crowd us, from a more or less refurbished Marxism to psychoanalysis, from the philosophy of the price-curve to that of universal logic, will never relieve us of the obligation to get back to our village.

Structural anthropology is one of these metahistories, one of the Siren voices—surely one of the most exciting and stimulating. Based on the Saussurian model of language, it privileges the synchronic over the diachronic and offers the most complete challenge ever thrown to a discipline that believed that there was no peeping over the walls of time, unless it was for some rhetorical or pedagogic purpose to paint what the dissertation-scribblers call a "picture." Yet this challenge does not abolish those offered by earlier generations, it is simply added to them. For it is not enough to assert, even to prove, as structuralism attempts not unsuccessfully to do, that the "human mind" is a universal logical agent, to restore to the historian the security he has lost and that, one must hope, he will never rediscover. For the "human mind" is not in itself the object of history, and anyway the ethnologists who postulate, even prove, its universality do not claim that it is, if it be that their undertaking is "the reintegration of culture in nature and finally of life within the whole of its physio-chemical conditions."[19] The "logic of the living," which is also that of things in themselves,[20] is not answerable to historical reason, which is constitutive, not constituted, and which unendingly makes and remakes its operational fields, its "scenarios."[21]

Conversely, we cannot appeal to the uniqueness of every event in time and take refuge in the bosom of Singularity. The historian cannot isolate himself in such a view. The individual occurrence is properly unintelligible if it is not set in some relation. The Breton village is in Brittany, France, the West; it is also in the Celtic world: studying its folklore may force one to study Irish or Welsh folklore; and it may not be entirely profitless to take a look at the folklore of the Auvergne or of Provence.[22] At any rate the historian is condemned at every moment to define his contexts, and the contexts of his contexts, and his definitions are always provisional—"Greek culture" is a context, but a potentially illusory one if the Greek world is isolated from the Thracian or the Illyrian, to say nothing of the Mediterranean. The historian is doomed to operate simultaneously on the spatial and on the temporal axes; and if he adopts provisionally "universal" categories like the Raw or the Cooked, it is always to make them dynamic.

In his own way, Lafitau understood and anticipated the dilemma: "The customs and manners of nations could well guide us to more refined understanding of these manners and customs. But some among them were general, instituted upon the earliest ideas which the fathers of the

peoples communicated to their children and which were among the
majority integrally preserved, or at least without marked alteration notwithstanding their separation in space and their lack of communication.
Such are the ideas related to most of the practices of collective life.
Assuredly from them one can derive no conclusions. In making the
comparisons which are proper, therefore, I will not scruple to cite the
customs of what peoples soever they be, without claiming to draw any
conclusions other than the sole relation of these customs with earliest
antiquity. It should then only be in the matter of certain distinctive and
characteristic features of the peoples newly discovered, in relation to
those peoples of antiquity of whom the historians have preserved to us
some knowledge, that one could hazard some conjectures, bringing these
distinctive features together and comparing them one with another"
(1.44–45). Of course "the general" no less than "the distinctive" have
varied since the Jesuit missionary. All the same, the extraordinary thing
is that such a text might serve as well as a motto for the work of Georges
Dumézil as for that of Claude Lévi-Strauss.

Among all the many human institutions that Lafitau sought to relate
to one another, there is one that ethnography was to take up in remarkable fashion—initiation. To adopt a recent definition, initiation is "a
body of rites and oral teachings whose purpose is to produce a radical
modification of the religious and social status of the person to be initiated. In philosophical terms, initiation is equivalent to an ontological
mutation of the existential condition. The novice emerges from his
ordeal a totally different being: he has become *another*."[23] Even before
Lafitau the initiations that are, even today, best known and best studied,
had been perfectly rehearsed and identified: the means by which the
young "savage" entered upon the adult community. So Robert Beverley,
author of *The History and Present State of Virginia*, retails the rituals
undergone by the young Indians.

> The choicest and briskest young men of the Town, and such only as have
> acquired some Treasure by their Travels and Hunting, are chosen out by the
> Rulers to be Huskanawed; and whoever refuses to undergo this Process, dare
> not remain among them. Several of those odd preparatory Fopperies are
> premis'd in the beginning; which have before been related; but the principal
> part of the business is to carry them into the Woods, and there keep them
> under confinement and destitute of all society for several months; giving them
> no other sustenance, but the Infusion, or Decoction of some Poisonous Intox-

icating Roots; by virtue of which Physick, and by the severity of the discipline, which they undergo, they become stark, staring Mad; in which raving condition they are kept eighteen or twenty days.

[On their return to the village] they must pretend to have forgot the very use of their Tongues, so as not to be able to speak, nor understand anything that is spoken, till they learn it again. Now whether this be real or counterfeit, I don't know; but certain it is, that they will not for some time take notice of any body, nor any thing, with which they were before acquainted, being still under the guard of their Keepers, who constantly wait upon them every where, till they have learnt all things perfectly over again. Thus they unlive their former lives, and commence Men, by forgetting that they have ever been Boys.[24]

But Lafitau improved this initial interpretation in two ways. He allowed into the category of initiations not merely admission into the community but acceptance into smaller groups (secret societies), religious and shamanist initiations, and the like. And in the spirit of the general program of his inquiry, he compared the Indian initiations with those known in classical civilization—the Mysteries of Eleusis as well as Spartan and Cretan education systems—and even medieval, for he treated the ritual of admission to knighthood as an initiation—yet another stroke of daring.[25]

It was not indeed until 1909, with the publication of Arnold van Gennep's *Rites de passage,* that this framework was further enlarged and that the first steps were taken toward the elaboration of a formal structure of analysis, the French folklorist demonstrating that the enormous body of rituals like these could be classified under three headings: rituals of separation, rituals of exclusion, rituals of (re)-incorporation.

This classification obviously presupposes in addition, indeed in first place, an articulation of time and space peculiar to *rites de passage.* Time first. Its rhythm is not that of the continuum, invented by mathematicians: "The idea of Time . . . is one of those categories which we find necessary because we are social animals rather than because of anything empirical in our objective experience of the world."[26] Time in rituals of status-transition is also a human creation: the year is punctuated by the rituals and the ritual itself causes the initiate to pass from the ordinary to the extraordinary and back again to the ordinary, now consciously accepted. For the ritual to operate also at the level of conceptions of space, it must itself be broken up: "human" space, in which social life is lived, against "marginal" space, which may be a symbolic sacred area, "the bush" whether literal or figurative, forest, or mountain[27]—it hardly matters, provided it be perceived as *other:* "heaven" and "hell" in children's hopscotch is a good, if extreme, example. So time and space are "binary" (that is, each organized into two mutually exclusive—and inverted—categories), although the ritual rhythm, as defined by van Gennep, is threefold. Edmund Leach defines three roles men find themselves playing in this kind of ritual action: formality, masquerade, and role reversal.[28] In the context of initiation of young men into warrior life, for example, the three terms will be represented by warrior uniform, by disguise (of which countless types are found at the point of marginality), and by the inversion that temporarily turns the man into a woman, and that also causes him to behave in exactly the opposite manner from how he is to behave in "normal" life.

It would be possible to exemplify this rhythm among the Australian aborigines no less than among Africans or among the Amerindians, but as long as we remain on this very general level, we are not actually within the realm of the historical, or the "sublunary" to use a term Paul Veyne has borrowed from Aristotelianism. Let us see what becomes of these concepts—and they are indeed concepts—in a particular historical society, that of Archaic and Classical Greece.

Recent excavation by Swiss archaeologists at the site of the Greek city of Eretria, on the island of Euboea, has revealed among other things a small necropolis surrounding the tomb of a prince or king, datable to the late eighth and early seventh century—precisely the period of the emergence of the Archaic city.[29] The tombs excavated form two groups: to the west we find only incineration; to the east, inhumation. It is not a case of change of fashion, since the two groups are contemporary; nor is it a matter of competing funerary customs, such as one finds elsewhere—for example, at the Kerameikos at Athens in the ninth century. We have rather a deliberate and significant opposition at the symbolic level: the inhumations are of children, the incinerations of adults. Both sexes are represented in the two groups. Their opposition is signaled in the group of incinerations by the presence of arms in the one case, and of jewelry in the other. Claude Bérard, the excavator, makes the point: "Inhumation was the practice at Eretria until just before adolescence, cremation being reserved for marriageable girls and married women, and for youths and men able to use the lance and take their place in battle."[30] Trying to determine the age at which the appropriate funerary practice changed, Bérard suggests that at Eretria, and very probably in many other places, it was about the age of sixteen.[31] The mere account of the archaeological finds (is an account ever innocent, though?) directs us to the search for a ritual of status-transition that dramatized for the Greek adolescent the transition between nature and culture, or, if you wish, between the raw and the cooked, in the most concrete sense. The ritual is relatively well known; at Athens in the Archaic and Classical periods, as Claude Bérard notes, it is identified with admission into the phratry. The distinctive occurrence on the third day of the Ionian festival of the Apaturia (the festival of "those who have the same father"—that is, of classificatory "brothers") was an initiation ceremony, the *koureōtis:* the name derives from the shearing (*koura*) of the flocks and of men, and it probably connotes also the young warrior (*kouros*). At Athens, the sacrifice of the *koureion* (probably the offering of the hair itself), which marked the admission of the ephebes into the phratry, took place at the age of sixteen.[32]

One point, however, reminds us that we ought not to neglect the "diachronic" aspect. The opposition between cremation and inhumation employed at Eretria and elsewhere to denote the opposition between childhood and adulthood obviously cannot predate the introduction of cremation into Greece, which did not happen until after the collapse of the Mycenaean world.

Nevertheless, the discovery, due as we saw to Lafitau, of initiation rituals in Greece parallel to those of "primitive" societies, has stimulated, especially in the twentieth century, a very large amount of work recently synthesized by the Italian historian Angelo Brelich in his *Paides e Parthenoi* (1969).[33] Jean-Pierre Vernant, using the evidence of the mythical tradition especially, has analyzed a number of different religious festivals, summarizing his results as follows: "If for a boy the significance of the rites of passage was to mark his accession to the condition of a warrior, for the girls who took part alongside them in these same rites and who were also often subjected to a period of seclusion, the initiatory trials had the force of a preparation for marriage. Here again both the link and the polar opposition between the two types of institution are noticeable. Marriage is for the girl what war is for the boy: for each of them these mark the fulfillment of their respective natures as they emerge from a state in which each still shared in the nature of the other."[34] This is the explanation, for example, of the fact that the Athenian ephebes wear the "black *chlamys*," not always perhaps, but at least at the solemn occasion of the procession to Eleusis to be initiated into the mysteries,[35] before they put on, after swearing the hoplite oath, the hoplite panoply,[36] and it also explains why the festivals and myths frequently dramatized a young man's entry into adulthood by having him put on female disguise, and a girl's into womanhood by means of a male charade.[37] Here of course we remember Leach's three terms: formality, masquerade, role reversal.

The male rituals of the ephebia in particular allow us to define a twofold structure: on one side the hoplite, who fights by day, in ranks, face-forward, supporting his fellows, on the level plain; and on the other the ephebe (or the Spartan *kryptos*) who fights by night, unaided, resorting to tricks of the kind deplored by hoplite and citizen values, skulking on the frontiers—all in all acting in a manner quite the reverse of how he must behave when he is integrated into the polis.[38] Surely we have here Culture on one side, Nature on the other; on one side Savagery (or femininity), on the other Civilization. Like many other Greek thinkers, Plato defined childhood as the savage time of human life (*Tim.* 44a–b; *Laws* 2.653d–e, 666a–c). The Greeks made the principle of polarity one of the cornerstones of their mode of representing the world.[39] No less than us, they were capable of representing the oppositions that articulated their world (in the form of a table with two columns). Thus the Pythagoreans, according to Aristotle, "recognized ten principles, which they list in two parallel columns:

limited	unlimited
equal	unequal
unity	plurality
right	left
male	female
still	moved
straight line	curved
light	dark
good	bad
square	oblong"

[*Metaphysics* 1.5.986a 22–26]

One could easily extend that list by looking at different aspects of Greek culture: master/slave, Greek/barbarian, citizen/foreigner, even Apollo/Dionysus perhaps. Here again ancient thought largely anticipated modern structural analysis: think for example of how Aristotle asks himself how far the sets adult/child, man/woman, master/slave, employer/craftsman coincide, and the senses in which they do not (*Pol.* 1.1259a 37 et seq.). And do we need to be reminded of the propensity of sophists, tragedians, and philosophers to contrast, oppose, and compare *physis* (nature) and *nomos* (law, custom)?

These and other pairs may be considered to constitute the framework of the discourse of the Greeks, but the structural anthropologist and the historian cannot both deal with them in the same manner. For example, if we take the opposition between ephebes and hoplites, fledgling warriors

142   and adult warriors, the comparatist will observe, from the work of
Georges Dumézil, that the opposition between the *naked* (i.e., not heavily armed) warrior, the ephebe fighting unaided, and the warrior integrated into some group and fully armed, is much earlier than the set
ephebe/hoplite, since hoplite warfare makes its appearance in Greece
only early in the seventh century, and that the opposition can be traced
elsewhere in the Indo-European world. The opposition is the same, but
the words used to describe it are not. Thus in the Indian epic, the "heavy"
warrior is an archer, while in Greece the bow belongs to the savage.[40] It
will be objected that the Indo-Europeans, or at least their conceptions,
are nevertheless historical, yet Dumézil, in studying a ritual of warrior
initiation at Rome, makes use not only of Indo-Iranian and Irish evidence, but also of evidence from Canadian Indians: "It is British Colum-
bia, the East coast of Canada, which, *by virtue of a coincidence we cannot
explain,* best helps us to see the meaning of the Indo-Iranian legends
about a three-headed monster" (emphasis added).[41] The explanation, if
indeed it is possible, is here fatally ahistorical: no historian can postulate
a collocation including Red Indians, Indo-Iranians, and Romans. Such a
collocation is in fact the human race itself—or better still, the "human
mind." The Greek historian, on the other hand, is concerned with a
datable reality, the hoplite, and with another datable reality, an institution first attested epigraphically in 361–60 B.C., and whose working is
explained some thirty-five years later by Aristotle; that is, the institution
called at Athens the ephebia, and its parallels in the rest of the Greek
world.

One characteristic of the history of ancient Greece, from the beginning
of our knowledge of it, is an extraordinary unevenness of development—
an unevenness so marked that for an Athenian of the fifth century some
indisputably Greek peoples were thought of as "savages" (cf. Thuc.
3.94), almost as the Brazilian Indians were by their sixteenth-century
conquerors. Following Thucydides, modern historians see the opposition
between Sparta and Athens, between the type of conservatism and of
rejection of history on the one hand, and the city, which by contrast chose
in the fifth century to identify itself with historical change on the other,
as one of the major features of the Classical period. In view of that, what
of male and female initiations? To put it another way: what differences are
there between the two in terms of the sets child/adult and girl/boy
(alternatively male/female)?

The ephebia as described by Aristotle is a form of civic military
service.[42] For the philosopher, the two-year period of service is in no
sense a period of isolation preparatory to integration into the civic com-

munity: he says expressly that the admission of a young man into the deme-lists *precedes* the period of probation and is not its consequence. One point only suggests something other than the mere performance of military obligations: "During these two years of garrison duty, they wear a *chlamys,* and they are free from all financial impositions; they cannot be involved in a lawsuit, either as plaintiff or as defendant, so that they will have no excuse for absenting themselves. The only exceptions are cases concerned with an inheritance or with an heiress; or when a man has to take up a priesthood hereditary in his family" (*Ath. Pol.* 42.5). The *chlamys* is understood not to be the dress of ritual seclusion but to be like the military uniform of our own day. Aristotle also understands the debarment from litigation in purely secular terms, and it is obviously extremely significant that he can take this approach naturally. The question of origins is a different problem. Long ago it was observed that "the seclusion of the young, in the period immediately prior to their definite inclusion within the society, is so well attested in all kinds of different societies and, in Greece, in Sparta, that one is inclined to discern a trace of it here."[43] To be sure, but what exactly do we mean by "trace"? Is the *function* of an institution in a society to be confused with *origin?* Is the B.A. degree to be explained by its medieval origins? Of course not, no more than Aristophanic comedy is to be explained by a seasonal ritual of fertility as the Cambridge school would have it.[44] Of course there are inertias and repeats in society, but it does not live in the past. The past is influential only inasmuch as it is present in the structures of thought, manners, and interpretations. To return to the ephebia, it is obvious that in Aristotle's time the ordinary understanding of the ephebes' stay in the frontier forts was not as an exclusion of the young men prior to their entry, or reentry, into the polis, but as garrison service. When Thucydides mentions in passing that the *peripoloi* ("those who go round"), that is, the ephebes, went on a *night attack* near Nisaea in 424 together with the new Plataean citizens (4.67), there can be no doubt that the ephebes are not (yet) citizens like other citizens and that they are associated with irregular activities in war; all the same, we must show that such an interpretation was current at the time. In any case, it is obvious that it no longer was so in Aristotle's time.

If we look at the historical changes we can obtain some idea of what happened. The earliest ephebia was set in the context of the phratry, an Archaic institution, certainly reactived in the fifth century, but whose rule was diminished markedly after the Cleisthenic reforms (508 B.C.) by the demes. One became an ephebe in the civic or military sense of the word at eighteen, but one became an ephebe in the phratry at sixteen. It was within the phratry that there took place the rituals of status-transition that mark the entry into adulthood, the most important being the offering of the child's long hair.[45] But in myths, comedy, in the work of a philosopher like Plato, and even, as I have tried to show, in an entire tragedy of Sophocles, the *Philoctetes*,[46] there is preserved something else—the "trace" of an initiatory ritual in which the young man, as a guileful "black" hunter, was sent out to the frontier area until he should perform the "exploit" symbolically imposed upon the young men in Archaic societies. Rituals of this type were real enough in Crete, where even in the Hellenistic period the official vocabulary of a city like Dreros makes a distinction between city, country, and the frontier forts, and where the educational institutions set the "flocks" (*agelai*) of adolescents against the brotherhoods (*hetaireiai*) of the adults—nature against culture (cf. p. 113 above). In Athens these institutions had been for the most part detached from the city-state, in a civic world that had been profoundly affected by rationalism—one might almost say secularized. And so Brelich, hardly one to avoid comparison with "Archaic" societies, in his discussion of the Athenian ephebia concluded that "the original initiatory elements we can discern in it came to be voided of their original functional integrity."[47] The principle of "elders first" endured of course. In the Athenian Assembly, the old men had first right to speak. In the course of what was perhaps the most crucial debate ever held in the Assembly, whether or not to deploy almost all its forces in the expedition to Sicily (415 B.C.), Nicias appeals to the old men as a group to resist the crazy ideas of Alcibiades and the young men with him, attempting thus to swing the traditional mechanism of age-classes into action. Alcibiades asks the Athenians not to be afraid of his youth: the city is made up of young and old, and *together* they can win (Thuc. 6.13, 17, 18). Alcibiades carried the day, although the Athenians were to regret it. At least his speech suggests that the city is an inclusive *totality* that to a significant degree cancels the opposition between age-classes.

"Old" Nicias thought of a city in which the young held power more or less as an inversion, a topsy-turvy world. The comic poet Aristophanes, imagining a utopia in which everything is turned upside down—in *Lysistrata* or *Ecclesiazusae* (*Women in Assembly*)—makes the women of Athens responsible for the decisions of government. In *Lysistrata* (411 B.C.) the wives of the Athenians have seized the democracy. They decide to go on a sex-strike if peace is not made. In their justification, the chorus of women use the language of assembly meetings to declare:

It's open to anyone to praise
The city and I to the end of my days
Shall love her for giving joy to a gentle child.
  I was only seven when I
  Carried the Sacred
  Vessels; and at ten I
  Bore the Temple Mill;[48]
Then in yellow I acted the Little Bear at Brauron,
  And, growing taller,
  And lovelier, took care
  Of the Holy Basket—it was heaven!
[638–47, tr. Dickinson]

The declaration looks at first sight like a list of female initiations, in which there were several stages, rather like the system for boys at Sparta.[49] But no such thing existed, and we must understand this speech as ideological: Athenian women were not properly speaking citizens, and young girls were not citizens-to-be whom the city had to take through stages of an educative initiation. The Athenian polis was founded upon the exclusion of women, just as, in other respects, it was founded upon the exclusion of foreigners and slaves. The sole civic function of women was to give birth to citizens. The conditions imposed upon them by Pericles' law of 451 was to be the daughter of a citizen and of a citizen's daughter. The chorus in *Lysistrata* is arguing *as if* the women of Athens were in fact the citizens. The stages referred to are those of a fictitious cycle. Most of them have nothing whatever, or virtually nothing, to do with rituals of status-transition: there were only two *arrēphoroi* ("bearers of the secret symbols"), chosen from among girls of noble birth. They were responsible for weaving the *peplos* (robe) of Athena Polias, and they played a key role in the highly secret ritual of the Arrephoria (or Arretophoria).[50] As for the "grinders of grain," they prepared the flour and bread for the sacrifices in the cult of Athena. The most important duty of the *kanēphoroi* was to carry baskets in the solemn Panathenaic procession. In short, these are duties undertaken by young girls in the service of the community, even if some of them reveal characteristics of initiation rituals—the special dress and seclusion of the *arrēphoroi*, for instance—there is no question here of a regular institution affecting an entire age-class;[51] rather, the city at each festival renews its contact with divinity. The women of Athens are not altering their status.

The case of the little "Bears" in the sanctuary of Artemis at Brauron is very different and much more complex. The very name of the animal that the girls represent is that of the divinity, Artemis, goddess of wild nature. The evidence of the scholiasts for the cult and that of other sanctuaries of Artemis in Attica, and archaeological evidence going back to the first half of the fifth century,[52] permit no doubt about the general character of the ritual: it involved a seclusion preceding—by a considerable period of time—and preparing for marriage. The scholiast Harpocration, for example, tells us that the girls had to "become bears before marriage, (in honor of) Artemis of Mounychia or of Artemis of Brauron." The explanation offered by the etiological legends for this obligation involve an original killing of a bear by some boys, the retribution for which was at first a human sacrifice and later the ritual of substitution performed by the girl-bears.[53] Variants or no, the myth is not difficult to explain: in exchange for the very advance of culture implied by the killing of wild animals, an advance for which men are responsible, the girls are obliged before marriage—indeed before puberty—to undergo a period of ritual "wildness." Study of the pottery evidence from Brauron reveals that the rituals in honor of the goddess involved (sequentially?) nakedness and the wearing of a special form of clothing (the "crocus," a saffron yellow robe)—perhaps as a means of dramatizing the transition between savagery and civilization. But it remains true that only a very few Athenian girls could become "bears"; the very size of the sanctuaries enforces the conclusion. The Aristophanes scholion that gives the most detailed account says both that the "bears" were girls who had been "chosen" and that the goddess had determined—at the original institution of the ritual—that no Athenian girl might marry before she had become a bear in her service.[54] We must then allow that, even if the little bears represent the female community, in the sense in which the Boule represents the city, they constitute an "elite" of the chosen and that initiation was confined to them. Moreover, such a pattern is well known to anthropologists as the pattern of a "secret society," a small group that fulfills a function for the public weal, the precondition being a special degree of initiation.

Let us return to Vernant's parallel, which we used as a model: "Marriage is for the girl what war is for the boy," a formulation that evidently can be applied to innumerable societies. We can now see just what happened in Athens. As regards boys, the ephebia as a ritual of entry into adolescence is separated from the ephebia as compulsory military service for all: at this level, there are no longer any groups privileged by birth, wealth, or membership in some priestly family. At most, considerations of family order—establishing one's inheritance, saving an *oikos* from the threat of "escheat" by marrying an *epiklēros* (heiress)—could relieve one of obligation.[55] Depending on his wealth, a young Athenian would later serve as a rower in the fleet, as a cavalryman, or as a hoplite, but in each case he would have served as an ephebe and have sworn an oath based upon the hoplite ethic: "I will not abandon the man who stands next to me in the battle lines." Initiatory rituals proper are to an extent separate from the process of entry into the civic community. It is obvious that nothing of the kind existed for girls: certainly marriage involved well-known rituals of status-transition (being carried over the threshold by the husband), and it bestowed the right to take part in ceremonies specifically for women, the Thesmophoria,[56] which was the only forum that brought women together as citizens of Athens for the one kind of political activity (if one can call it that) allowed them; but age-class initiation properly so called, if it ever had been a collective experience, developed in a direction opposite to that of male initiations: it involved only a tiny group of initiates who could represent the city only by metonymy.

The image of Sparta transmitted to us by the ancient texts, particularly those deriving from Athens, is that of a society that refused historical change and suspended itself in the changelessness of the "Constitution of Lycurgus."[57] Such modern scholars as have not capitulated to the "Spartan mirage" have directed themselves to "normalizing" Sparta's oddness—Arnold Toynbee would have it as one of his "civilizations." To normalize is the resort both of Jeanmaire in his *Couroi et Courètes* (1939), where he discerns "beneath the mask of Lycurgus" a society exactly comparable with African societies, and of M. I. Finley, in showing that the three fundamental aspects of classical Sparta—the agrarian infrastructure, with the hierarchy of *homoioi* (the "Peers"), *perioikoi* (free but non-Spartiate inhabitants), and helots; the governmental and the military structure; the system formed by the rituals of status-transition, education (the *agōgē*), age-classes, collective eating, etc.—were not developed and instituted at a stroke; and that the "sixth-century revolution" that gave to classical Sparta its characteristic stamp was a complex process of innovation, transformation, and revival of features and institutions apparently transmitted from remote prehistory.[58]

What was true of the Athenian ephebe *at the level of myth* is true of the Spartan *kryptos in practice:* the *kryptos* appears in every respect to be an antihoplite. The *kryptoi* were young men who left the city to roam, in secret and in isolation, "naked" (that is, not heavily armed), through mountains and countryside, feeding themselves as they might, assassinating helots under cover of night—the helots against whom the Ephors, to ensure that no pollution attached to such killings, declared war each year. According to the scholiast on Plato's *Laws* 3.633b, the period of seclusion lasted an entire year, although Plato himself expressly remarks that it occurred in winter. We have only to invert this text to find the rules that governed the manner of life and the moral and social behavior of the hoplite, whose virtues otherwise compose the very fabric of Spartan life: collective living and eating, fighting in the open, on the flat, in summer—a mode of fighting founded upon the face-to-face encounter of two sets of phalanxes. And yet, just as only a tiny number of Athenian girls played the part of "bears," only a tiny number of Spartiates followed this mode of life, which Jeanmaire compared to the "lycanthropy" known particularly in Africa.[59] Plutarch noted that it was "the most astute" (*tous malista noun echein dokountas; Lycurgus* 28.2) young Spartiates who were chosen for this ritual of status-transition; and it is probable that, once they became adults and full warriors, it was the *kryptoi* who composed the elite formation of three hundred "cavalrymen" concerned above all with police duties.[60] In other words, it is impossible to detach the *krypteia* from the practical part it played in Spartiate society, a role that must have been developed for the most part from the eighth century, the date of the conquest of Messenia; that is, to maintain in every way possible a repressive regime faced with the endemic rebellions of the subject population of Messenia and of Laconia itself. The *kryptos,* like the ephebe of Athenian myth, is a guileful hunter—but he hunts helots.[61] The temporary "wildness" of the *krypteia* is an utterly socialized, even political, wildness: it functions directly to maintain the political and social order.

At first glance, the education (*agōgē*), which was the precondition for the entry of a Spartiate into full citizenship, has every appearance of being a system of initiatory rituals of "primitive" type that remained, in the Classical period and even thereafter, fully effective. Indeed Sparta is the only Greek city for which we at least know the names of the different age-classes that articulated childhood, youth, and adolescence.[62] According to a Roman historian, "Lycurgus laid down that the children should be brought up not in the area of the city but in the fields, so that they might pass their early years not in luxury but in toil and suffering; and he directed that they should return to the city only when they had become full-grown men" (Justin 3.3.6). "Bush" versus city, childhood versus adulthood: the oppositions look transparent. But if we look more closely, things are not so clear. First, one surprising point seems to have escaped notice: it seems difficult, not to say impossible, to fix precisely the point at which the young Spartiate became a full adult.[63] We know of course that around twenty or twenty-one the Spartiate *eirēn* (i.e., ephebe) became a *sphaireus* (ball-player) (Pausanias 3.14.6). But this moment does not seem to have been made particularly dramatic: nothing at Sparta recalls the oath of the Athenian ephebes when they became hoplites, although such an oath is found in other societies in several respects closer to Sparta than to Athens, for example in Crete. A text of Xenophon has sometimes been used to prove the existence of such a status-transition at this point,[64] but it says nothing of the kind—indeed quite the reverse: "In respect of those who have passed through the period of adolescence and are now eligible even for the highest public offices, the other Greek states no longer insist that they should keep fit, yet lay upon them nevertheless the obligation to go on campaign; Lycurgus on the other hand laid down that for men of this age hunting was the perfect thing, so long as it did not interfere with any public obligation, so that they too would be able to sustain the physical hardship of campaigning no less than those in the flower of youth" (*Lac.Pol.* 4.7). It is hard to tell whether adulthood at Sparta was an extension of childhood; or whether childhood was rather an anticipatory preparation for the life of an adult and a soldier. At any rate, in contrast to what happened elsewhere, for example in Crete, marriage is in no way the point at which adolescence comes to an end; for several years after his marriage, the husband continued to live in barracks and saw his wife only in secret (Xen., *Lac. Pol.* 1.5; Plut., *Lycurgus* 15). Moreover, whereas in other Greek cities it was the offering of the child's long hair that marked the end of adolescence, in Sparta it was customary for the adult males to wear their hair long (Hdt. 1.82; Plut., *Lycurgus* 1). The offering of the hair is a ritual of status-transition because it involves a "before" and an "after"; to keep one's hair is different, because that can hardly be betokened by a ceremony. And search as one may through the successive ordeals undergone by a young Spartiate, the most notorious of which is the cheese-stealing beneath the lash at the altar of Artemis Orthia, for the ghosts of initiations and even of fictive deaths, not one of these ordeals is in the least decisive.[65]

In contrast, a patient reading of the well-known texts that describe the *agōgē*, Xenophon's *Constitution of the Lacedaimonians*, and Plutarch's *Life of Lycurgus*, reveals one striking fact. Childhood at Sparta has two connotations: "savagery" and hoplite culture, since the child is at one and the same time a small animal and a pre-hoplite. That is the mark of the extent to which properly military institutions "consumed" Spartan education. The vocabulary—so far as we have any direct knowledge of it—is characteristic. For the groups of young men, two words were used in antiquity: *agela* (flock), and the word *ila*, which really means the group of young soldiers.[66] Xenophon's description is particularly telling: the children are simultaneously introduced, like the *kryptoi*, to guile, stealing, and activity by night, but they also mix with the adults at the *syssitia*, the common meals (*Lac.Pol.* 2.5–8, 5.5; cf. Plut. *Lycurgus* 12).

150   One ritual deserves special emphasis: from time to time, two battalions (*moirai* = *morai*, a term used in the Spartan army) of Spartan "ephebes" met at Platanistas in Sparta. The fight was simultaneously hoplite and "wild," since the combatants were allowed to resort to a number of expedients, including biting, which were ordinarily forbidden, and it was preceded by the sacrifice to Enyalios, the god of Bloody Fight, of two dogs, that is of the most domesticated animals—in fact, to be more precise, of two puppies (Plut. *Quaest. Rom.* 111.290d). It was preceded too by a fight between two boars, wild animals if ever there were, but in this case *ēthades*, which means "tame." The victory of the boar belonging to one or the other camp usually ensured the victory of its group of young men.[67] It all looks as if "the wild" and "culture" were not enemies whose hostility had to be dramatized, but two opposed principles that it was appropriate as far as possible to bring together.[68] It was the *kryptoi* alone who had the privilege of dramatizing this opposition.

As early as Lafitau it had been noted that the status of women at Sparta was different from elsewhere in Greece; Lafitau even used the word "gynecocracy" in this connection (1.73). One might say in general that in the most archaic of archaizing Greek cities the opposition between the sexes was stressed less heavily than in a democratic city, such as Athens. In the latter, female power is an issue only in comedy and in utopian thinking; at Sparta or Locris and elsewhere it forms part of the historical-legendary tradition associated moreover with power being seized by slaves (cf. p. 209 below). In the particular case of Sparta, and of what little we know of its "female initiations,"[69] we know that the Spartiate woman underwent on her marriage rituals of inversion comparable to those known elsewhere in the Greek world. The girl "was put into the care of a woman called a *nympheutria,* who shaved her hair, dressed in the clothes and shoes of a man, and settled her down on a mattress stuffed with leaves, all alone and without light" (Plut. *de Virt. Mul.* 245 et seq.; *Lycurgus* 15). However, generally speaking, what we know of a girl's childhood and adolescence gives less the impression of being a preparation, punctuated by rituals, for marriage, than an imitation of institutions for males—not that the Spartan woman prepares herself for war, like the female citizens of Plato's *Republic* and *Laws,* but the only specifically female duty that remains is the obligation to produce fine children. The Spartiate family is scarcely an institution of the city, which on the contrary took great pains to restrict family life to the bare minimum.

At any rate, the impression given by the few ancient texts is not so much of a parallelism between the education of girls and that of boys[70] as of a direct reproduction: there were *agelai* of girls as well as of boys

(Pindar F112 Snell); nakedness was obligatory for girls in certain ceremonies as it was for boys (Plut. *Lycurgus* 14–15); both sexes had to
perform physical exercises and compete (Xen. *Lac.Pol.* 1.4)—it would
be easy to go on. Certainly the reproduction was not complete: little girls
and teenagers were not organized into age-classes: in many cults the girls'
role was different from the boys'; boys alone underwent ordeals to test
endurance, such as that at the altar of Artemis Orthia; and the *krypteia*
was strictly confined to males, just as were all the properly political
institutions of ancient Sparta. The Spartiate girl was in a real sense a boy
manqué.

It will probably now be clear where the comparison between Athens
and Sparta has led us—a comparison that I am not the first, nor the last,
to make. In each case the lexical items of the language of initiation are
doubtless the same, and it is easy enough to find in them the opposed
pairs that modern anthropology has taught us to discover, but their
articulation into phrases is radically different—so much so that one
would almost want to say that the opposition between Athens and Sparta
at the level of practice is nearly as strict as it is in Thucydides' speeches.
Yet this opposition is evidently the consequence of a historical development that accentuated, instead of reducing, the differences. No doubt
Greek society is a "historical" society, and we know some have contrasted
" 'cold' and 'hot' societies; the former seeking, by the institutions they
give themselves, to annul the possible effects of historical factors on their
equilibrium and continuity in a quasi-automatic fashion, the latter reso-
lutely internalizing the historical process and making it the moving
power of their development."[71] But Sparta is the exact archetype of a
society that refuses to internalize history and that is, for all that, in
comparison to the other Greek states, the consequence of a complex
historical evolution. The question now is, having borrowed from the
anthropologists ideas they themselves took over, with changes, from
structural linguistics, should we in turn not require of them the same
holism that they have properly demanded of us: that they should give the
same weight to the diachronic dimension as to synchronic analysis?[72]
Unless we make that demand, what significance could be attached to the
system of signs within which we encapsulate the societies we study—
ignoring their scientific import, of course, which is supra-historical, not
to say supra-ethnological—but the deposit or the spoor that each of them
leaves behind in the form of texts, artwork, or ruins? Edgar Morin has a
nice comment on the strange world of tourist guidebooks: "It is a kind of
gigantic Luna Park. The country is stripped of its sociology [and of its
history] for the sake of its ethnology, its archaeology, its folklore and its

152   oddities."[73] We can admire the work of ethnologists past and present—they have enormously increased the historian's "proper" field. But without history can ethnology be anything but a day-trip—first class?

NOTES

1. [*Customs of the American Savages compared with the Customs of Earliest Times*] cited in the second edition, 4 vols., *duodecimo*. The book was translated into Dutch in 1751 and into German in 1752, and finally into English in 1974, by W. N. Fenton and E. Moore, 2 vols. (Toronto: Champlain Society).

2. See especially K. Kaspar, *Indianer*, and the authors he cites, notably A. van Gennep, "Contributions"; some additional information may be found in M. Duchet, *Anthropologie et Histoire*, 14, 15, 72, 99, 101, 105, and especially the chapter "Discours ethnologique." Cf. also E. Lemay, "Nouveau Monde," and S. Pembroke, "Family," 277–79.

3. *Studies* 141.

4. *Moeurs* I: "Explanation of the engravings and figures in the First Volume"; for a detailed commentary using an important bibliography, see M. de Certeau, "Lafitau."

5. It is hard to say whether the bearded figure below Mary is a prophet or whether, more probably, it is the Eternal Father addressing himself to Adam and Eve. Lafitau makes no comment. [The Iroquois "turtle" was the emblem of one of the three common Iroquois clans, the Turtle, the others being the Wolf and the Bear.]

6. Panofsky, *Iconology*, 69–93.

7. J. de Acosta, *Indias*, 34. The French translation of 1598 (p. 50) is a mollification of the original.

8. Cf. L. Poliakov, *Mythe aryen*, 125ff.

9. L. H. Morgan, "Descent," 145; cf. S. Pembroke, "Women," 3.

10. L. H. Morgan, *Ancient Society*, 4 ["As we re-ascend along the several lines of progress toward the primitive ages of mankind and eliminate one after the other, in the order in which they appeared, inventions and discoveries on the one hand and institutions on the other, we are enabled to perceive that the former stand to each other in progressive, and the latter in unfolding, relations. While the former class have had a connection, more or less direct, the latter have been developed from a few primary germs of thought. Modern institutions plant their roots in the period of barbarism, into which their germs were transmitted from the previous period of savagery. They have had a lineal descent through the ages, with the streams of blood, as well as a logical development."]

11. See, for example, the discussions in R. Garaudy (ed.), *Mode de production asiatique;* M. Godelier, "Préface"; P. Vidal-Naquet, "Avant-propos"; G. Sofri, *Modo di produzione asiatico;* P. Anderson, *Absolutist State*, 397–431; and now S. P. Dunn, *Fall and Rise*.

12. Note the sort of "manifesto" edited by R. R. Marett, *Anthropology and the Classics* (1908), involving five classicists [Arthur Evans, Gilbert Murray, F. B. Jevons, J. L. Myers, W. Warde-Fowler] and an anthropologist-historian, Andrew Lang. The manifesto summarized the work of a generation.

13. See H. Gaidoz, "Mythologie comparée," cols. 97–99. On this and several other changes, see Detienne, "Repenser," 72–77.

14. *Primitive Culture*, 1.7. Chapters 3 and 4 are devoted to "Survivals in Culture." On Tylor and his contemporaries, see P. Mercier, *Histoire de l'anthropologie*, 50–79; there is some information on Tylor's concept of "survival" to be found in M. T. Hodgen, *Survivals*, 36–66, and especially J. W. Burrow, *Evolution*, 228–59.

15. Tylor, *Primitive Culture*, 1.469.

16. A. Lang, *Myth, Ritual and Religion*, 2.255–88. Note the respect accorded to Lafitau: "[He] was perhaps the first writer who ever explained certain features in Greek and other ancient myths and practices as survivals from totemism" (1.73). For a critical modern view, see Detienne, "Gnawing."

17. Cf. E. Leach, "Frazer and Malinowski," 360–67.

18. M. Panoff, *Malinowski*, 109.

19. Lévi-Strauss, *The Savage Mind*, 247.

20. See Lévi-Strauss's finale in *L'homme nu* (559–621), which argues the point in striking fashion.

21. See P. Veyne, *Histoire*.

22. For an example that is not from Britanny but from Poitou, see J. Le Goff and E. Le Roy Ladurie, "Mélusine," 587–622.

23. M. Eliade, *The Quest*, 112.

24. *Virginia* 3.8 Par. 32 (pp. 39–41).

25. *Moeurs* 1.201–56; 2.1–70, 283–88.

26. E. Leach, *Rethinking Anthropology*, 125; on van Gennep and *rites de passage*, see N. Belmont, *Van Gennep*, 69–81.

27. It has been demonstrated by A. Margarido, "Textos Iniciaticos," that in initiation rituals the same area can be sometimes the world of the wild and sometimes the humanized world; indeed the function of rituals of initiation is to humanize both the age-classes and the "wild."

28. E. Leach, *Rethinking Anthropology*, 135.

29. See C. Bérard, *Eretria III*, and the discussions occasioned by his work in *Société et Colonisation eubéennes* (especially the remarks of Auberson, Mele, Martin, and Lepore), although I think that Bérard has answered their objections ("Herôon"). Cf. also the remarks of C. Rolley, "Fouilles à Érétrie"; more generally A. M. Snodgrass, *Archaeology and the Rise of the Greek State*

30. C. Bérard, *Eretria III*, 50. At Marathon the adult male Athenians were cremated, but the Plataeans and slaves who fought, but not on the same basis, were buried: cf. D. Kurtz and J. Boardman, *Burial Customs*, 246, and the conclusions of N. Loraux, "Mourir," 810.

31. Archaeologists have habitually ignored burials of children and adolescents because the bodies were laid just beneath the surface—although they have carefully recovered the remains of babies (which were placed in amphorae) and of adults (which were placed in cinerary urns). But *somebody* must have died between the ages of two and eighteen; cf. C. Bérard, *Eretria III*, 52.

32. See J. Labarbe, "Koureion"; J.-P. Vernant, "City-State Warfare"; and P. Vidal-Naquet, "The Tradition of the Athenian Hoplite" and "The Black Hunter," pp. 98 and 109 above.

33. Of special importance are H. Jeanmaire, "Cryptie," and *Couroi;* M. P. Nilsson, "Grundlage" (= *Opuscula Selecta* 2.826–69); P. Roussel, "Principe d'ancienneté" and "Chlamydes noires"; G. Thomson, *Aeschylus;* and Brelich himself, *Guerre, Agoni* and "Initiation." On *Paides e Parthenoi* (as well as on earlier work by Nilsson, Jane Harrisson, Jeanmaire, etc.), see C. Calame, "Philologie et Anthropologie"; C. Sourvinou-Inwood, "Review of *Paides.*" More recently, J.-P. Vernant, *Myth and Society;* P. Vidal-Naquet, "The Tradition of the Athenian Hoplite," pp. 98–99 above.

34. Vernant, "City-State Warfare," 23; on marriage, cf. Calame, *Choeurs,* 1.239–40 and P. Schmitt, "Athéna Apatouria."

35. See P. Roussel, "Chlamydes noires," 163–65; Maxwell-Stuart, "Black Coats," 113–16; and Vidal-Naquet, "The Black Hunter," p. 112 above.

36. See Vidal-Naquet, "Philoctetes," 175–76, where there is an account of the earlier discussions.

37. There is an extensive literature, but note L. Gernet and A. Boulanger, *Génie grec,* 39–40; Jeanmaire, *Couroi,* 442; Delcourt, *Hermaphrodite;* Vernant, "City-State Warfare," 21–25; and Vidal-Naquet, "The Black Hunter," pp. 116–17 above.

38. See Brelich, *Guerre, Agoni,* and also P. Ellinger, "Gypse" (a study of a particularly radical form of myth about warrior-ruses or stratagems).

39. See G.E.R. Lloyd, *Polarity and Analogy.*

40. See G. Dumézil, *Mythe et Epopée,* 1.63–65; and J. Le Goff and P. Vidal-Naquet, "Brocéliande," 273–75. In the Greek world, as in the medieval, there were bows and bows; the bow drawn by Odysseus at the end of the *Odyssey* is the type-case of the bow classified "positively."

41. *Horace et les Curiaces,* 128.

42. See the very detailed commentary on *Ath.Pol.* 42 by C. Pélékidis, *Éphébie,* 83–86, cf. 87–152; also Brelich, *Paides,* 216–27; for the date, p. 121, n. 1 above.

43. P. Roussel, "Review of A. Brenot," 459.

44. For example, F. M. Cornford, *Attic Comedy,* especially 53–69.

45. See "The Tradition of the Athenian Hoplite," p. 98 above.

46. "Philoctetes," whose fundamental conclusions I stand by, despite the arguments of V. de Benedetto, "Il Filotette."

47. Brelich, *Paides,* 227.

48. [Literally, "I ground the grain for our *Archēgetis.*"] Who is this patroness

(*archēgetis*)? With a number of commentators I had believed that it could only be
Athena. Still, there are some good reasons why it could be Artemis, and more-
over neither the order nor the punctuation of the passage are at all certain; cf. C.
Sourvinou-Inwood, "Lysistrata 641–647." Most recently, M. B. Walbank, in
"Artemis," argues that the whole passage actually concerns the cycle at Brauron.

49. See Brelich, *Paides*, 229–30, who properly criticizes the assumption; I
continue to agree with Brelich despite the arguments of C. Calame, *Choeurs*,
1.67–69.

50. The fundamental text is Pausanias 1.27.3; the evidence is collected (and
given a bizarre commentary) by Cook, *Zeus*, III.165–91, and especially by W.
Burkert, "Kekropidensage," who indeed emphasizes the initiatory aspects of the
cult, but fails, I think, to relate it to the transition between one age-class and
another. On the number of *arrēphoroi*, see Brelich, *Paides*, 233, 282.

51. Although Aristophanes chooses to present the situation as if it were, for
dramatic and comic reasons that have not really been understood; see N. Loraux,
"Acropole comique."

52. For the sanctuaries, see Brelich, *Paides*, 247–49; for the inconclusive
archaeological "evidence," L. G. Kahil, "Artémis attique," I and II, "Artémis de
Brauron"; and now C. Montepaone, "Rituale munichio" and "Arkteia."

53. The two periods are sometimes telescoped into one.

54. See Brelich, *Paides*, 263–64.

55. ["Escheat" is a feudal, not an ancient legal term, and is technically
inappropriate because of course the land did not revert to the crown in classical
Athens in default of direct heirs. Nevertheless the word conveys a sense of the
danger of a family's land being dispersed beyond its control in such a case. The
French is "tomber en déshérence." An *epiklēros* was a woman who, on the death of
her father, found herself the sole surviving direct heir, and who in Athenian law
was compelled to marry her nearest agnatic kin—R. Gordon's note.]

56. Cf. M. Detienne, *Gardens*, 78–81, and Detienne and Vernant, *Cuisine*,
183–214.

57. See especially E. N. Tigerstedt, *Legend;* and E. Rawson, *Tradition.*

58. M. I. Finley, "Sparta," 161–77. ["Beneath the mask of Lycurgus" is the
title of chapter 8 of Jeanmaire's *Couroi et Courètes.*]

59. Jeanmaire, *Couroi*, 540–69.

60. Jeanmaire, *Couroi*, 542–45.

61. Cf. W. Wachsmuth, *Alterthumskunde* 1.462, 2.304.

62. Most recently, Brelich, *Paides*, 116–17.

63. In Thuc. 2.39.1 Pericles plays on the doubt about Sparta for the benefit of
the Athenians when he declares that the Spartiates "by dint of harsh training
pursue the state of manhood [or manly things] while still youths": cf. N. Loraux,
"*Hébè* et *Andreia*," 6.

64. Brelich, *Paides*, 125.

65. *Paides* 136; the text is Xen. *Lac. Pol.* 2.9—the custom is not to be
confused with what it became in the Roman period, a mere spectacle.

66. Plut. *Lycurgus* 16.4–5; Xen. *Lac. Pol.* 2.11. Nilsson, "Grundlagen," 312 [=*Opuscula Selecta* 2.831] is of the opinion that Plutarch's *agela* is a translation of *ila*. The official title, attested epigraphically, of the group-leader was *Bouagos*, "Herdsman."

67. Pausanias 3.14.8–10, 20.8. One of the competitions among the young men that we know from the dedications to Artemis Orthia was called by a name that indisputably means "hunt"; the others seem to have been musical competitions; cf. Brelich, *Paides*, 175.

68. We might pursue the play of these institutionalized metaphors: thus, as Nicole Loraux has noted ("Belle Mort," 116), in the last stages of the battle at Thermopylae the three hundred Spartiates—that is, the former *kryptoi* now serving as *hippeis*—fought "with their hands and with their teeth" or "like boars sharpening their tusks": Hdt. 7.225.3, Aristophanes, *Lysistrata* 1254–56.

69. See Brelich, *Paides*, 157–66, and Calame, *Choeurs* 1.251–357.

70. See Brelich, *Paides*, 157.

71. Lévi-Strauss, *The Savage Mind*, 234.

72. I would note among the best efforts in this sense N. Wachtel, "Poma de Ayala," and R. I. Zuidema, *Cuzco* (with a preface by Wachtel).

73. E. Morin, *Politique de l'homme*, 223.

III Women, Slaves, and Artisans

Were Greek Slaves a Class?

Did slaves constitute a class within Greek society? The question is less trivial than it may appear, and to frame it in this way requires the historian of Greece to clarify certain points.

It seems to me that our modern notion of social class is bound to three distinct sets of phenomena, which I will now outline empirically and impartially.

1. A class is a group of people who occupy a well-defined place on the social scale. This is what we express in our everyday language when we speak of the *grande bourgeoisie* or the *petite bourgeoisie*, the alleged "middle class" or the "lower classes." We are familiar with the empiricist subtlety with which this vocabulary is used by Anglo-Saxon scholars. It is no accident that it is an English author, Hill, who wrote a book entitled *The Roman Middle Class*,[1] devoted to Roman knights—although C. Nicolet has demonstrated that, until the Augustan era, they did not constitute a class but an order.[2]

2. A social class occupies a specific place in the system of production. This is the principal contribution of Marxism and needs no further emphasis here.

3. Finally, a social class implies the awareness of common interests, the use of a common language, and united action in the social and political arena. This concept too we owe to Marx, and it will be enough if I simply refer to the famous passage in the *Eighteenth Brumaire* about the small-holding French peasantry: "an enormous mob whose members all live in the same situation but without being united to one another by

complex ties." Everyone knows how Marx concludes by playing on the two meanings of the word "class": "to the extent that millions of families live under economic conditions that separate them from one another and oppose their way of life, their interests and their culture to those of other classes of society, they do constitute a class. But to the extent that peasant small-holders have only local solidarity, and the identity of their interests fails to create any genuine community or national bond or political organization, they do not constitute a class."[3]

It would be very easy to take these three concepts—status, the system of production, and consciousness—and try to apply them to Classical Greece and its slaves, but before we indulge in this little game, we might take a detour, perhaps to render the game pointless. My first point can be summed up as follows: we are accustomed to portraying ancient society as made up of masters and slaves—Marx himself said so at the opening of the *Communist Manifesto*—but we have to acknowledge that: 1) this was not always the case, and 2) that even in the Classical era two kinds of society confronted each other, and only one can be considered "slave-holding" in the proper sense of the term.

In Greek the slave is a *doulos*. Even though the word appeared as early as on the Mycenaean tablets, in the form *doero,* its presence does not mean that Mycenaean society recognized a neat, definitive break between the free and the enslaved. In fact, *doero* seems to have a number of denotations. Beginning with the *doero* pure and simple and the *doero* of the gods there are subtle distinctions: for example, one woman is said to be the daughter of a *doero* and of a woman belonging to the class of potters. The facts are so confusing that the Soviet historian J. A. Lencman, although utterly convinced that Mycenae was a "slave society" and that it therefore made a radical distinction between slave and free, could write about the *doero* that, were it not for the word itself, we would have no serious reason to view the *doero* as a slave.[4] Under such circumstances, why not move on?

In Homeric society—or rather, in what we mislabel Homeric society, that is, the society evoked and envisioned by the Homeric poems—slaves *do* exist: kidnapped women, prisoners of war, slaves acquired in rudimentary commerce. Still, the slave is not alone at the bottom of the social ladder, and he is by no means the worst off. As M. I. Finley has often said and has proved superlatively well, the most wretched of all is not the slave.[5] Instead, it is the agricultural laborer, who has no means of support but his own labor and no permanent tie to the household, the *oikos:* that is, the *thete*. For Homeric society, as for the Mycenaean, there is a full spectrum of conditions between freedom and slavery.

Let us now leap across the centuries to the Classical period. We find a pair of antagonistic models that confronted each other in theory and in practice: Athens and Sparta. This is a very crude simplification, of course, for Sparta has some unique features that keep it from being an oligarchic state; nonetheless, what is true for Sparta is often roughly true for Thessaly or Crete as well.

At Athens there prevails the wondrous simplicity we first became familiar with in secondary school. There are citizens, metics, and slaves; within the respective ranks there are, to be sure, distinctions of wealth, of locality (city or countryside), and, I might add, of age, since the Athenian "constitution" contrasts the "young" and the "old."

It is obvious that there are enormous differences within the world of the slaves. A policeman, a civil servant, a miner, a shopkeeper, and a farmworker are not all the same thing; but legally, from the standpoint of personal status, their differences are minor (at least in the fifth century). The best proof of this claim I find in an experiment carried out by more than one Athenian. Suppose there is a man whose claim to citizenship is contested. He first stands trial before the assembly of his deme. If they declare that he is not a citizen, he will be reduced to the status of a metic, thereby preserving his personal freedom. But suppose that he refuses to accept this verdict and, by means of *ephesis,* transfers his case before the popular tribunal, the *Hēliaia.* If he loses his appeal there, he will be sold as a slave. Conversely, before a freed slave can even hope for citizen status, he will have to be satisfied with the freedman's usual lot, metic status. In brief, this is neat, simple, and complete; at the same time it shows that the three abstract categories of Athenian society—citizen, resident alien, and slave (that utter foreigner, that *outsider* as Finley calls him)—were the actual experiences of Athenian life.

It hardly needs to be mentioned that none of these three categories comprises a class according to any of the concepts we have outlined. This is the case even if we agree with C. Mossé that in the fourth century there arose a group of wealthy men that comprised both citizens and naturalized foreigners (including former slaves).[6]

Our handbooks also speak of a tripartite division of society in Sparta— the "peers" (*homoioi*), the *perioeci,* and the helots—but this division is not at all congruent with the Athenian model. The helot and the *homoios* mark two extremes, but they do not allow us to say either that the "peers" fit perfectly into the category of liberty or the helots into slavery. We can disregard the *perioeci,* about whom we know virtually nothing except that they were inhabitants of the cities incorporated into the Lacedaimonian state. Despite their title, the *homoioi* do not form a homogeneous social unit, even in the fifth century. Indeed there were specialized groupings

162 within the *homoioi:* the youths in the *krypteia* who demonstrated their prowess in the countryside;[7] the three hundred *hippeis* (horsemen) who were under the command of *hippagretai* and, despite their name, traveled on foot; and the *agathoergoi* mentioned by Herodotus (1.67), who were recruited annually in groups of five from among the *hippeis* in order to carry out secret missions. Moreover, once the young Spartiate had completed the *agōgē*, Spartan training, he was eligible to become *homoios,* but not all did so; in the fifth century there were a growing number of "half-castes," a multiplication of categories, some of which might date back to early antiquity. For example, there were the *hypomeiones,* Spartiates who lacked a *klēros,* an inherited plot of land; there were also those who had been demoted for military reasons and formed a separate group called *trēsantes*—"tremblers."[8] There was just as little uniformity among the helots. A helot could be a *mothax,* defined by the ancient sources either as a slave born within the household or as a helot brought up among the Spartiates and subjected to the same *agōgē* as the future "peers." Once manumitted, the helot became *neodamōdēs*—a new member of the *damos*—without becoming *homoios.* In brief, Spartan society encompassed a range of conditions that did not afford a clear delineation of the boundaries of freedom and slavery; on closer examination, even the "peers" were not free men in the Athenian sense of the term. Heavily qualified, this also seems to be true of other rural societies, notably the Cretan. There too a spectacular variety of terms was used to designate subservient groups and sometimes groups of citizens "with full franchise." Therefore we must not let ourselves be deceived by the fact that in one fifth-century text the same word, *douleia,* simultaneously denotes the slaves at Athens and the helots at Sparta (Thuc. 5.23).

Now let us put our social groups into motion. What role did slaves play in the exceptionally violent social conflicts—especially in the fourth century—that agitated the two types of society? The most extraordinary account of class conflict in Classical Greece is probably the one offered by Plato in Books 7 and 8 and the beginning of Book 9 of the *Republic.* Although a professed admirer of Sparta, Plato had "data" that were essentially Athenian and Sicilian. In Sicily he observed the behavior of a military tyranny. He borrowed material from a revised and corrected version of fifth- and fourth-century history and presented it in the guise of the ideal republic's progression through timocracy, oligarchy, democracy, and tyranny. What role do slaves play in all these "events"? A meager, not to say nonexistent, one. How did Plato handle the topic that seems most important to us, the explanation meant to account for the birth of democracy? His analysis was, above all, military. He alluded to

the almost complete inability of an oligarchy to wage war: either the
rulers will have to arm the people, who will then become more fearsome
than the enemy, or, failing to do so, will make it all too obvious in the
battle that they are indeed *oligoi*, few in number. Plato provided a
powerful image (*Rep.* 8.556d) of a rich man and a poor man side by side in
the battle line: the rich man is pale and stout; the poor man, sunburnt
and wiry, thinks to himself, "Those people manage to keep their wealth
only because others are too cowardly to take it from them." Democracy
arises, Plato said, "when the poor defeat their enemies and then slaughter
some, exile others, and take an equal share in the government and
magistracies with those who are left." Not a word about slaves. Plato
limited his comments on slavery to the metaphorical partition of human
personality into three parts—reason, courage, and base desires—wherein the first and second are slaves to the third. He defines the *dēmos* as being
composed of land-owning peasants (*autourgoi*), the idle (*apragmones*), and
the well-to-do; clearly, slaves have no place in this scheme. They make
their appearance at a later stage, with the arrival of tyranny. Then, Plato
claimed, the tyrant removes slaves from their masters and emancipates
them in order to raise them to equality with citizens, who are thereby
reduced to servile status (*Rep.* 8.569a–c). In fact, this political ploy was
occasionally put into practice and is the subject of a recent study.[9]

Plato's description is fully confirmed by what we know of Athenian
history, with the possible exception of the very first stages of the democracy in the sixth century, when the distinction between free men and
slaves was not so firmly entrenched as it was, say, from the end of the sixth
century on. Was there, then, a collective demand among slaves that
would make them a "class" according to the third of the definitions I give
above? No, not even in the most dramatic episodes, such as the mass
defection of twenty-five thousand slaves in the wake of the Spartan occupation of Deceleia (Thuc. 7.27). Those who escaped were primarily
artisans, *cheirotechnai* (those who work with their hands), and doubtless a
number of miners. These slaves made no demands, either for political
power in Athens or collective access to citizenship. Those who were
Greek certainly reclaimed their original citizenship, and, naturally, all
reclaimed their liberty, but no one nurtured the ambition of becoming
strategos or archon. In several individual instances in the fourth century,
some slaves could and did have such ambition, but it was never a matter
of a joint undertaking by a group of slaves.

Does this imply that the slave's role was unimportant? Fundamentally,
it was he who made possible the clearly defined rank of the citizen. The
classic example, from the sixth century, is Chios, the city where demo-

cratic institutions first appeared and where, according to Theopompus, slaves were first acquired from abroad. In Finley's well-known formulation: "One aspect of Greek history, in short, is the advance, hand in hand, of freedom *and* slavery." [10]

The slave made the social game feasible, not because he performed all the manual labor (that was never true) but because his condition as the anti-citizen, the utter foreigner, allowed citizen status to define itself. In addition, the slave trade—indeed, all trade, the monetary economy—made it possible for an exceptional percentage of Athenians to be citizens. In other words, the interpretation I am defending here is exactly the opposite of that propounded in the nineteenth century by Henri Wallon and Fustel de Coulanges. Even in the twentieth century, the great historian Corrado Barbagallo wrote a famous book in which it was explained that the existence of slavery corrupted, even poisoned, social relations among the different classes. [11] In my opinion, this interpretation has it completely backward: I do believe that the contrast between masters and slaves is the fundamental contradiction of the ancient world, but at no time do these masters and slaves collide at the level of ongoing social practice. To make my point more clear, let me take an example from outside the ancient world. In fourteenth-century Florence, and most of the medieval Italian cities, the basic contrast was between the *città* and the *contado*. As one leaves the gates of Florence, one enters a space totally different from that of the town; a countryman, a *contadino*, is not usually a citizen of Florence. There is no question that Florence partly lived off her exploitation of, and domination over, the countryside, but this fundamental opposition did not impinge on her social struggles, which were essentially limited to factions within the city.

Let us turn our attention to rural societies like Sparta, Thessaly, or Crete. The contrast is stunning. It finds expression in a simple example: at the time of the second Persian War, both Athens and Sparta mobilized all their available manpower. Athens' fleet was manned by more than thirty thousand citizens; at Plataea, Sparta furnished five thousand hoplites chosen from the *homoioi*, about the same number of *perioeci*, and thirty-five thousand helots. This one fact reveals the fundamental difference between the two systems. Except in a truly extraordinary emergency, Athens never mobilized the slaves; if they were used in the army, they were manumitted. The result is that, removed as the helot may have been from the full citizen, he still played a role of great significance in the political drama. Political action by the helots was possible at Sparta; political action by Athenian slaves was inconceivable.

At Sparta the political demands went in two possible directions: the

first is secession, the dream of the Messenian helots that came true after
Epaminondas's campaign cleared the way for the reconstruction of Messene; the second, just as important, is full integration into Sparta. Instances from the fourth century are well known; I want to emphasize an
episode from the fifth century, from the time of the Peloponnesian War,
recounted by Thucydides (4.80). One day the ephors issued a solemn
proclamation to encourage those helots who believed that they had done
the most service to Sparta to identify themselves, with a view to being
freed. As the ephors hoped, the bravest and worthiest came forward. Two
thousand were selected and manumitted and joyfully crowned their
heads. Then they vanished without a trace. I feel that this episode
illustrates equally well the power of the helots' demands and the violence
of the repression directed against them, for Sparta's very existence was
threatened by helot revolts. At Athens, one fugitive slave mattered little;
at the time of the Decelean War, the flight of twenty thousand slaves was
a catastrophe, but even twenty thousand escapees could be replaced by
the purchase of others. At Sparta there was no question of buying additional helots, because a helot was not an item for sale in a market; this is
why a helot uprising challenged the whole Spartan order. At the end of
the third century and the beginning of the second, the tyrant Nabis tried
to solve the Spartan dilemma. He even indulged himself in an explanation delivered to Flaminius, in a speech that Livy reports: "Our lawgiver
did not wish our city to be in the hands of a few citizens—what you call
your Senate—nor to be dominated by one or two orders; rather, he
believed that by equalizing wealth and honor, it would have many men
who would take up arms for their country" (Livy 34.32.18). [12] What a
sweeping claim! The plan that Nabis proposed, under the aegis of
Lycurgus, was in reality nothing but the plan put into effect by Athens in
the sixth century. Nabis was obviously a little late, and, if I may say so,
all that was missing was everything that had made Athens' development
possible—slaves, to begin with. It is clear that the same word, *doulos,* can
signify widely differing social realities. But perhaps most curious of all is
the realization of how long it took for people to become aware of this
difference. When did it finally happen? The answer is easy: in the fourth
century, with the demise of societies like the Spartan, Cretan, or Thessalian. Then there arose the theoreticians, like Plato and the members of
Aristotle's school, who inquired into the bizarre circumstances that put
man "between the free and the enslaved." [13] But this very moment—
seemingly the triumph of the classical model of chattel-slavery—was the
advent of a whole new set of problems. In the Hellenistic world the labor
force, which supported both the Greek cities and the monarchies, was no

longer the slave corps of the Classical city but was an immense mass of dependent peasants from Egypt or the Orient. It is these whom Aristotle called "slaves by nature."

I will not address such problems here but instead limit myself to a brief comment. The phenomenon of slave rebellions, in the second century and the beginning of the first, should not make us believe that from then on there existed a slave class in the modern sense of the word, consolidating all or most of the servile population. A revolt like that in Sicily in 139–133 B.C. was primarily an uprising of herdsmen: armed herdsmen in a country with a long tradition of conflict between farmers and stock-breeders, where latifundia had assumed the character of enormous live-stock enterprises. Such a revolt, in my opinion, is essentially the same as those analyzed by E. Hobsbawm in his *Primitive Rebels*. 14 The ideal of a classless society was never seriously propounded. The leader of the re-bellious slaves even declared himself king; he issued money under the name of Antiochos, and his coins bore the image of an old Sicilian divinity, Demeter of Enna. If his regime had survived, there is not the slightest doubt that the rebels would have owned slaves. 15 When slaves in the Hellenistic-Roman period were not socially ground down as they were in the Classical city, their activity found its limits in the organiza-tion of a city. The historian Nymphodoros of Syracuse provides some evidence for the Hellenistic period in the form of a tragic story, which will also furnish my conclusion. 16 The scene is set in Chios, the first city to see purchased slaves. The slaves there staged a mass defection, and among them was a sort of Robin Hood named Drimacos; after a variety of adventures, he offered the people of Chios a solution to the problem. He ratified an armistice that put a limit on "reparations." Every storehouse that had been (somewhat) plundered would be marked with a seal to protect it from another attack. As for the fugitive slaves, he proposed to return those who fled without justifiable cause. "If they had valid reasons for leaving," he said, "they will stay with me; if not, I will return them to you." The number of slaves to join the exodus promptly became much smaller. Those whom Drimacos kept were organized along military lines and came to fear him much more than their former masters. Drimacos remained so virtuous that, in his old age when the Chians had put a price on his head, he asked his best friend to cut off the aforementioned head and thus win the sizable reward that had been promised. The citizens of the island finally turned this model rebel into a hero, who appeared in their dreams whenever there was unrest among the servile population.

The story does not reveal if he posted at the gates of his camp the motto adopted by the hero of Orwell's *Animal Farm*, something along the lines of "All slaves are equal, but some are more equal than others."[17]

NOTES

1. *Middle Class.*
2. *Ordre équestre.*
3. *The Eighteenth Brumaire*, p. 187; I give here the whole of the passage from Marx to reply to some objections that were raised, notably by G.E.M. de Sainte-Croix, "Karl Marx," 30–31 and *Class Struggle*, 63–65.
4. *Esclavage*, 181.
5. Cf. *The World of Odysseus*, pp. 53–55—the claim, however, is disputed by A. Mele, *Società*, 107ff.
6. C. Mossé, "Classes," 27–28.
7. See "The Black Hunter," pp. 112–14 above.
8. See N. Loraux, "Belle Mort," 108–12.
9. C. Mossé, "Rôle des esclaves."
10. Theopompus *FGrH* 115 F 122; M. I. Finley, "Slave Labour," 164.
11. C. Barbagallo, *Il Tramonto*.
12. Cf. C. Mossé, "Nabis."
13. See "Reflections on Greek Historical Writing about Slavery," below, and M. I. Finley, "Between Slavery and Freedom."
14. E. J. Hobsbawm, *Primitive Rebels*.
15. At the time of the second slave revolt in Sicily, beginning in 104 B.C., the city of Morgantina was besieged by slaves under the command of "king" Salvius, and both besiegers and besieged promised freedom to the slaves in Morgantina who would join their side (Diod. Sic. 36.4.5–8). This episode qualifies Diodorus's general statement that poor freemen willingly joined the rebels (Diod. Sic. 36.11); in the first case we have a factual account, in the second perhaps just a theoretical assertion. On this event, see M. I. Finley, *Sicily*, 139–45, and A. Momigliano, *Alien Wisdom*, 33–34.
16. *FGrH* 572 F4, quoted in Athenaeus 6.265c–66e. On this passage, cf. S. Mazzarino, *Pensiero storico*, 49–50, 505 n. 363. The attempts by A. Fuks, "Slave Wars," to date the events are unpersuasive.
17. M. I. Finley explicitly accepts the argument developed in this essay (*Ancient Slavery*, 77). I remain unconvinced by the objection of Y. Garlan in his valuable study, *Les esclaves en Grèce ancienne*, 217–24.

8   Reflections on Greek Historical
Writing about Slavery

The sixth book of Athenaeus's *Deipnosophists* is a treasury of evidence for the terminology and history of slavery in Greece. [1] Athenaeus quotes a passage from the historian Theopompus of Chios that justly can be seen at the heart of recent discussion of slavery: "The Chians were the first Greeks, after the Thessalians and Lacedaimonians, to use slaves, but they did not acquire them in the same way. For the Lacedaimonians and Thessalians, as will be seen, constituted their slave-class (*douleia*) out of the Greeks who had earlier inhabited the territories which they themselves possess today; the Lacedaimonians taking the land of the Achaeans, the Thessalians, that of the Perrhaebians and Magnesians. The people reduced to slavery were in the first instance called *helots,* in the second *penestae.* But the slaves (*oiketai*) whom the Chians own are derived from non-Greek peoples, and they pay a price for them" (*FGrH* 115 F122 in Ath. 6.265b–c: Loeb ed., trans. Gulick). [2]

Why do I assert that this famous text forms the core of all the treatments of slavery? In comparing the above fragment from Book XVII of the *Philippica* with the inscription known as the "Constitution of Chios," [3] M. I. Finley made his renowned observation that, "One aspect of Greek history, in short, is the advance, hand in hand, of freedom *and* slavery." [4] Moreover, our passage makes a perfectly clear distinction be-

---

Published in 1973 in the *Actes du Colloque 1971 sur l'esclavage* (Paris: Annales litt. de l'Université de Besançon), 25–44; translated in 1979 with some corrections in L. Sichirollo (ed.), *Schiavitù antica e moderna* (Naples: 159–81).

tween the two types of "slavery" familiar to the Greeks: on one side, the "helotic" and, on the other, the "commercial" (or "chattel-slavery" to Anglo-Saxon scholars; in French *l'esclavage marchandise*). The distinction in Theopompus's text rests on a set of neat oppositions:

1. Chronology—with the old slavery *before* (and still earlier, no slavery at all), the new slavery *after*.
2. "National" origin (so to speak)—the "early" slaves are Greek, while the "later" are barbarians.
3. Method of acquisition—the early slaves were reduced to servitude by military conquest, but the later were purchased for a sum of money in a market.

In 1959 D. Lotze published a book whose title is borrowed from a phrase used by Pollux, the Alexandrian grammarian, to try to define those who are "between free men and slaves."[5] Since then a good part of the scholarly discussion has been devoted to assessing the value of Theopompus's distinction between the two "slaveries." (Even to say "two" slaveries is an abuse of language, since one of the categories, chattel-slavery, is a perfectly clear condition, whereas the other by its very nature resists clear, distinct definition.) The works that have explored this terrain are known to all.[6] My own attempts to develop the argument have led me in two directions. Taking up a suggestion of C. Mossé,[7] I have tried to show that the two categories of slaves are radically opposed to each other in the political realm.[8] The utter political inertia of chattel slaves—even when they were concentrated in relatively large numbers, as in the Athenian mines at Laurion—is the countertype of the noteworthy political activity undertaken by helots, penestae, etc. An alliance of the miners at Laurion with Athenian thetes to bring about a more radical democracy is unimaginable. In contrast, in Sparta in 397 B.C., Cinadon tried to unite all the lower segments of Spartan society against the *homoioi*. In Xenophon (*Hell*. 3.4.4–11) the ephors' informant tells them, "Those actually in the plot . . . were not very many, though they were trustworthy; it was rather the case, the leaders claimed, that they were in the plot with everyone else—helots, freedmen (*neodamōdes*), inferiors (*hypomeiones*) and perioeci—since all these people showed clearly enough, if there was ever any mention of the Spartan officer class, that they would be glad to eat them up raw" (tr. Warner, Penguin ed. sl. mod.). This contrast in behavior seems to me to be basic. Whenever the question arises, in connection with the Classical period, of unrest or slave revolts with political aims (that is, not purely for the personal freedom of the participants), it is a safe bet that those involved are the "slaves" in Theopompus's "earlier" category, even if our authors do not explicitly say so.[9] The difference between their respective activity and inactivity is also reflected in military affairs: helots *did* serve in the Spartan army, while some slaves *could* be enlisted in the Athenian army, but only in rare, emergency situations, and such service entailed manumission.[10]

My second approach has been quite different, proceeding by way of myth, legend, and utopianism.[11] I took as my starting point the fact that the Greek city-state was based on the exclusion of women, slaves, and foreigners (and also, provisionally, youths). Then I tried to see what role was *shared by women and slaves* in imaginary situations, in the "upside-down world" where we are presented with a kind of reversal of "normal" society. When we are in Sparta, Argos, Locri—in brief, any land with "helotic" slavery—the upside-down world is controlled by *women and slaves*. By contrast, Aristophanes' *Ecclesiazusae* depicts a society where women hold power but slaves continue to work the land. Similarly, in the *Lysistrata* not a single female slave or metic takes part in the seizure of the Acropolis. There is, there can be, no question of slaves in power.[12]

Now I would like to assay the validity of this opposition by means of a third approach, through historiography. The text of Theopompus that provided a starting point is located in a specific historical moment. It can be roughly assigned to the 330s, around the end of the reign of Philip and the start of Alexander's expedition[13]—precisely the time that Greece was getting ready to impose servitude not on other Greeks but on barbarians. This was also the moment that Aristotle, who had left the Academy in 347, working out his theory of the "slave by nature," took a keen interest in the helots of Sparta and the "perioeci" of Crete. It is easy to trace the posterity of a text like that of Theopompus. In the next generation, Timaeus also speaks of the introduction of slaves "bought for money" not at Chios, but in archaic Greece among the Locrians and Phocians; they did not replace Greeks who had been enslaved but youths who had performed household tasks (*FGrH* 566 FF 11–12 in Ath. 6.264c–d, 272a–b, and Polyb. 12.5.1 et seq.). Athenaeus VI is in itself sufficient evidence for the interest displayed by historians and philologians—especially around the time of Aristophanes of Byzantium—in servile statuses that looked like curios or fossils.[14] To find the antecedents of such views is not nearly so easy.

Still there are many signs that in the time of Theopompus, although there was no truly historical consideration of the origins of slavery, there were numerous discussions of the best possible forms of slavery and, consequently, of the comparative merits of helot-slavery and chattel-slavery. Perhaps the clearest evidence appears in Plato's last work, the *Laws*,[15] published posthumously (347), in which Plato observes that "the question of menials is difficult in every regard" (τὰ δὲ δὴ τῶν οἰκετῶν χαλεπὰ πάντῃ) (*Laws* 6.776b). The difficulty is not purely theoretical, inasmuch as human chattel is "less convenient" (777b). "For almost all the Greeks the type of helotism adopted by the Spartans offers a topic of discussion and argument, with some finding the institution acceptable and others not. There is less argument about the slavery practiced by the Heracliots after their subjugation of the Mariandynians or about the serf population (*penestikon ethnos*) of the Thessalians" (776c–d). Plato is explicit about the practical reason underlying such debates: the continual revolts of the Messenians have shown what a city gets by having slaves from a cohesive group, especially if they speak the same language (777c–d). If servile labor is to be used correctly, the slaves must have been, so to speak, socially fragmented; that is, they should neither come from the same homeland nor share the same language (777d). In other words, they should be foreigners,[16] taken from an area large enough to preclude national cohesion among them. Thus Plato casts his vote in favor of chattel-slavery, thereby fulfilling in the *Laws* the consequences of the axiom he had postulated in the *Republic:* Greeks must not be reduced to slavery (*Rep.* 5.469c). This was a commonplace, no doubt; but—with the precision characteristic of the *Laws*—Plato proves his originality by applying to it the opposition that Theopompus would later draw between helots and slaves bought on the open market. Aristotle's treatment of this point is little more than a recapitulation (*Pol.* 1.1255a 28; 2.1269a 35 et seq.; 7.1330a 25 et seq.),[17] as he too recommends the acquisition of slaves from a nonhomogeneous group, in order to avoid the dangerous revolutions that had threatened both Sparta and Thessaly.

However, no one prior to Theopompus put this contrast into historical perspective, distinguishing the *earlier* (helots and penestae) from the *later* (slaves bought for cash).

Let us then return to that essential text, for on reflection it reveals a number of peculiarities. As we have seen, Theopompus identifies the "bought" slave as non-Greek and the "archaic" slave as Greek. This first equation certainly raises the problem of accuracy. In the light of the most recent studies, we can be sure that the large concentrations of slaves (e.g., at Laurion) were chiefly comprised of non-Greeks,[18] but it is not true that commerce was the sole method of acquiring such slaves. A major role was played by domestic breeding, piracy, and above all, war. More importantly, many Greeks (and Plato himself) could envision enslavement as the boundary of their own individual fates. In moving back from the

fourth century to the fifth, and paying particular attention to the tragedians, we find that enslavement was far from limited to markets and
barbarians. Instead, it appeared as a kind of individual catastrophe that
could befall anyone, Greek or foreigner. [19] The insistence of Theopompus
and his successors on *purchase* is due to some relatively clear general
causes: the very uneven growth of economic activity based on profit, what
Aristotle calls *chrēmatistikon,* or, in other words, the whole fourth-century transition toward the Hellenistic enterprise, and its corollary, the
multiplication of sources of servile labor outside the Greek world.

If we wish to avoid generalities, we must first ask how the origins of
slavery were depicted prior to Theopompus. [20] We can answer this question by showing that, for those cities where slavery really played a
fundamental role, the problem of its origins was phrased in terms of
earlier or *later.* The *earlier,* however, was not located, as it was for Theopompus, in true history, but in legend or myth.

The oldest evidence leads to the very wellsprings of Greek historiography, where Herodotus contrasts a tale of his predecessor, Hecataeus, with
an Athenian tradition. [21] At issue is the reason for the Pelasgians' leaving
Athens to go to Lemnos. According to Hecataeus, the Pelasgians were
unjustly expelled from the land the Athenians had given them as payment for having built the original walls of the Acropolis. The Athenian
version, a precious fragment of folklore, is different: "The Pelasgians
used to leave their settlement under Hymettus and come after the Athenian women and children [22] when they went to fetch water from the Nine
Springs. *Neither the Athenians nor any of the other Greeks had household slaves*
(*oiketai*) in those days, so their own daughters used to go for the water;
and whenever they did so, the Pelasgians, regardless of decency or respect, used to rape them" (tr. de Selincourt, Penguin). Timaeus puts
work by youths prior to servile labor. Here Herodotus consolidates,
within a mythic *earlier,* the work of women and of children. [23] To say that
"once upon a time, work was performed by women and children" is to
connect slaves with others *excluded* from the Greek city, women and
children: using a myth, this defines a social hierarchy, [24] but it is not
historical writing. Moreover, the comic poet Pherecrates, a contemporary of Aristophanes, provides corroborating evidence. Athenaeus preserved four lines from his comedy *The Savages* that describe primitive life
before civilization: [25] "Then, no one had any slave, not a Manes nor a
Sekis, [26] but women had to undertake all the domestic chores. From dawn
til dusk, it was the women who had to grind the grain; they made the
whole village echo with the sound of millstones." The use of "village"
(*kōmē*) is interesting: it denotes an *earlier* time that is pre-urban.

Let us go a little farther back, to a mythical time, the Hesiodic Golden age frequently described by the Athenian comic writers, of which Athenaeus himself observes, "When the poets of Old Comedy tell us of life in early times (περὶ τοῦ ἀρχαίου βίου) they explain that then there was no need of slaves" (Ath. 6.267e). There follow some interesting quotations, such as this from the *Ploutoi* of Cratinus: "Their king long ago was Cronos, and they used to play games with loaves of bread" (Cratinos F165 [Kock] in Ath. 6.267e). It goes without saying that no slave was responsible for baking this bread. Another citation, even odder, is drawn from Telecleides' *Amphictyons,* conjuring up a land of milk and honey, where slaves existed but did not have to work: "They played dice with the vulvas of sows and other dainty morsels" (Telecleides F1 [Kock] in Ath. 6.268b–c). It is often said, and on occasion I myself have written,[27] that Greek uptopianism had no notion of the abolition of slavery. I think that this is correct, inasmuch as a utopia defines itself through a radical critique of existing society and through the construction of a society meant to be rational—even if absurdly so, as in the *Ecclesiazusae.* But the statement about slavery is not true when the utopia is merely a transfer into the future of a discussion about the Golden age. Here, too, Athenaeus quotes a valuable text that pertains to an imaginary future but which he rightly classes among the descriptions of the Golden age. Two characters from Crates' *Thērioi* (*Wild Beasts*) are conversing about the future: "A: So nobody will own a slave, male or female. B: What? Will an old man have to wait on himself? A: Of course not, for everything I will create will be able to walk," and hot water will make its own way from the sea to one's wash-basin.[28] This is not the transformation of seawater into lemonade predicted by Fourier, but, blended with the folklore motif of the "magic table," it foreshadows the famous passage in Aristotle: "If every instrument could accomplish its own work, obeying or anticipating the will of others, like the statues of Daedalus, or the tripods of Hephaestus, which, says the poet, 'of their own accord entered the assembly of the gods', if in like manner, the shuttle would weave and the plectrum touch the lyre without a hand to guide them, chief workmen would not need servants nor masters slaves" (Ar. *Pol.* 1.1253b 32–38; tr. Jowett).[29]

In any case, whether one turns toward the past or toward the future, for the slave-holding city a time without slaves is outside of history; it is in a pre-civic *earlier* or a post-civic *later* and even, to a great extent, before or after civilization itself. It is remarkable that the only serious attempt by a Greek historian to reconstruct Greece's past through rational deduction—I mean Thucydides' *Archaeology*—makes no mention of the origins of slavery. I think that this is in itself enough to highlight the originality and the novelty of the question posed by Theopompus, but it is also an invitation to inquire whether speculation about *another form of slavery* could not have been the source of the crisis to which Theopompus bears witness.

The theory he uses to explain the origin of helots and penestae is based on the idea of conquest; as such it resembles the one expressed or implied (Athenaeus's citations are far from being uniformly straightforward) by several fourth-century and Hellenistic authors who wrote about Sparta, Thessaly, Crete, and Pontic Heraclea.[30] Archemachos of Euboea, for example, tells the following story: When the early Boeotians, under pressure from Thessalian invaders, were getting ready to take over the region that was to become Boeotia, one group decided not to migrate. Its members struck an accord (*homologia*) with the Thessalians and agreed to become their slaves, on the condition that they would neither be driven from the land nor killed. This theory of the original contract for servitude has a number of variant versions: like earlier authorities, Posidonios of Apamea explains that the Mariandynians became "slaves" of the Heracliots under the provision that they would neither be evicted nor sold abroad.[31]

One could claim that this theory met with immense success; with some modifications, it is often invoked by modern historians to explain the origins of helotism. Of course they do not adopt the anecdotes about the servile contract, but most of them do claim that helots, penestae, klerotes, etc., are the descendants of pre-Dorian peoples. In this respect the historians are the heirs of Theopompus, Ephorus, and several others. Naturally, most of the evidence concerns Sparta and the beginnings of helotism—*as perceived by the Greeks*—of which I now wish to speak. I do not intend to treat the question in depth nor to revive the debate that had engaged Kahrstedt and Ehrenberg before H. Jeanmaire's *Couroi et Courètes*, which magisterially dismissed both of them at once. In spite of the efforts of F. Kiechle,[32] I am very doubtful that the matter will ever be finally settled. As P. Roussel said, "It is impossible to prove that the perioeci were not Dorians and that the enslavement of the helots resulted solely from the complete takeover of the land by the invading forces."[33] Not a *single one* of the pre-Dorian traces that we have been able to detect in the written or spoken language of Laconia can be ascribed specifically to the helots; this should be enough to settle the question, or rather to show that it is unanswerable. With considerable insight, for once, A. J. Toynbee observed, "There are at least four different and mutually irreconciliable accounts of the date and the circumstances in which the helotage originated. This indicates that all four accounts are guesses, and that there was no authentic record."[34]

But even if the problem is fundamentally insoluble, the discussions of slavery's origin deserve to be studied in all their manifestations, including those of which we know only that there is no hope of their being true. (A similar situation obtains with regard to the French theory, common from the seventeenth to the nineteenth centuries, that made the nobility the descendants of the conquering Franks and the common people the descendants of the vanquished Gallo-Romans.)[35] We can establish a few basic guidelines; the first one, at least, concerns history as such and not just historiography.

1. The fourth-century Athenian was surprised by the subservient condition to which Greeks like the helots and penestae were relegated. Our reaction should be exactly the opposite. What is surprising, even amazing, in the Mediterranean world of the first millennium is not the subjugation, but the freedom—for example, the liberty attained by Athenian peasants from Solon on. When we attempt to understand what the Greeks tell us, we must do so against this unique background of liberty and liberation.

2. The interesting phenomenon to which we ought to devote our attention here is that at some particular times, but not at others, the Greek historians asked themselves about the origin of helotism. We must try to find the Why? behind such inquiry.

3. That Spartan society was divided among helots, perioeci, and homoioi was as much a given for the ancients as it is for us. When it came to understanding and explaining it historically, the Greeks found themselves in essentially the same situation as we do. To be sure, we have the advantage of archaeology, but up to now archaeology has not uncovered many helots, and it will not be able to explain how they came to form a social group. But, with that one (rather negligible) difference, the Greeks proceeded as we do, constructing their arguments on the foundation of facts: *helots exist, perioeci exist.*

Once it is decided that the questions are worth asking, the number of answers is not unlimited. True, the problem is less simple than I have indicated here. In particular, the Greeks had to allow for the existence of *two kinds* of helots: the Laconian and the Messenian, the latter in permanent rebellion to "re-create" Messene, while the former's demand was instead a revolutionary transformation within Lacedaimonian society. The Greeks also had to take into account a tradition for which Tyrtaeus's poems provide the earliest evidence: the formation of Sparta resulted from an invasion, carried out by the Dorians under the leadership of the

176   Heraclidae, of a land that was formerly Achaean and whose capital was Amyclae.

Once this has been established, however, the historians of antiquity argue like their modern counterparts. It is striking, for example, to see a contemporary scholar like F. Gschnitzer setting up the problem of the origin of the perioeci in terms of logical alternatives: either the perioeci were Spartans who lost their rights or they were non-Spartans enclosed within the Lacedaimonian state under specific conditions.[36] It is as if historical reality were always subject to the logic of exclusive options.

Starting from the three postulates I have just mentioned, what are the possible solutions to the question of the Spartan system?

    1. One could avoid the question entirely.

    2. One could claim that the differentiation of Lacedaimonians into three social categories began from within, as the result of historical evolution or of a dramatic event that resulted, for example, in the issuance of a decree.

    3. One could also say that the perioeci and helots were the descendants of conquered peoples, without making this claim apply to all helots (since the Messenians formed a special category).

    4. One could also state that perioeci and helots did not have the same origin, with one group raising a historical problem and the other not.

I am simplifying, of course, and it would be easy to complicate matters,[37] but broadly speaking the hypotheses I have just summarized are those that were formulated by the Greek historians.[38]

What about Herodotus? For him the Dorians were a migratory people, whom his deep-seated Hellenism led him to contrast with the Ionians of Athens, who to be sure were autochthonous but also Pelasgian—Hellenized Pelasgian rather than Greek (Hdt. 2.17; 1.56). The Dorians forced all pre-Dorian peoples of the Peloponnese to depart, with only three exceptions, all different: the Arcadians did not leave (Hdt. 2.171; 8.73); the Achaeans left Laconia in order to take over the region of the Peloponnese that was to become Achaea (thereby displacing the resident Ionians) (Hdt. 8.73; cf. 1.145 and 7.94); the Cynurians, located at the border of Argos and Sparta, became Dorianized (Hdt. 8.73). In addition to the Dorians (possessors of "many renowned cities"), the Peloponnese was appropriated by the Aetolians of Elis, the Dryopians of Hermione and Asine, and—on the west coast of the peninsula—by the Lemnians, otherwise known as Paroreatai (Hdt. 8.73). Herodotus also recognized the Messenians, and without expressly saying so, he presented them as being as Dorian as the Spartiates, present at the time the conquest occurred, at the birth of the twins Procles and Eurysthenes who founded the two royal dynasties (Hdt. 6.52). Herodotus made several allusions to what we now call the Third Messenian War, which he depicted as being more or less continuous since the end of the Persian Wars (Hdt. 3.47; 5.49; 9.35, 64). But he *never* merged the Messenians with the concepts of helotism, and when he did refer to helots, it was always as men in a specific condition at present; he never suggested the least interest in the origin of this condition (Hdt. 6.58, 75, 80–81; 7.229; 8.25; 9.10, 28–29, 80, 85).

Thucydides argued in a slightly different manner. He too was familiar with the Messenians and specified that they spoke not only Dorian but also the exact same dialect as the Lacedaimonians (Thuc. 3.112.4; 4.3.3). In describing the insurrection of 465 (?), which he ascribed to the helots and the perioeci of Thouria and Aithaia, he added that, "most of the helots were descended from the ancient Messenians, who had been reduced to slavery, and so all of them came to have the name of Messenians" (Thuc. 1.102). With respect to the non-Messenian helots, Thucydides omitted any reference to a non-Dorian origin; it was the Athenians, not the helots, whom the Spartans distrusted as belonging to a different ethnic group, and this suspiciousness was the reason they sent back the Athenian expedition directed against the rebellious helots on Mt. Ithome (Thuc. 1.102.3). To sum up, Thucydides did not inquire at all into the origins of the non-Messenian helots, whom he mentioned frequently in connection with the tight control to which they were subjected (see especially 4.80).

In the fifth century, however, the first theories on the origin of the Spartan helot system appeared, and it is striking to see how men writing at the same time arrived at exactly opposite conclusions.

Antiochos of Syracuse, for example, traced helotism back to the First Messenian War, but he said "Those of the Lacedaimonians who did not take part in the expedition (against the Messenians) were declared to be of servile status and called helots." So, in this version, some Lacedaimonians were reduced in the course of time to a lower rank[39] that was comparable to what the Classical period knew as the "tremblers" (*tresantes*), cowards denoted in rank because of their lack of courage.[40]

The other theory, based on the idea of conquest, made its first appearance, chronologically speaking, in the modest form of a quotation from Hellanicus of Lesbos preserved in Harpocration's *Lexicon:* "Helots are the Spartans' slaves, but not by birth; they were the first from among

178   the inhabitants of the city of Helos to have been captured."[41] The theory
of conquest is introduced by means of a pun linking *Hēlos*, a Laconian
city, with *helot*. Although Hellanicus's testimony stood alone in the fifth
century, the same hypothesis had considerable success in the following
century. We have already seen that Theopompus (who adopted the absurd
story about Helos) also referred to the Dorian conquest. From his contemporary Ephorus, another student of Isocrates', Strabo[42] preserved a
long fragment whose content is as follows: During the Dorian invasion,
most of the Achaeans abandoned the land, which was then divided into
six sections (corresponding to the six *morai* of the Classical Spartan army).
One of these, Amyclea, was given to Philonomos, the Achaean who had
handed over the country and persuaded its leader to emigrate (cf. Strabo,
8.5.5). Sparta became the seat of royal power, but local kings were
dispatched to govern each of the regions. Due to the scarcity of men
(*leipandria*) the local kings were invited by the Heraclidae to offer the
status of fellow-inhabitant (*synoikos*) to any foreigner who asked for it.
These foreigners, called helots[43]—who were also the subjects and perioeci of the Spartiates (ὑπακούοντας δ' ἅπαντας τοὺς περιοίκους Σπαρ-
τιατῶν)—nonetheless acquired legal equality with their masters; they
had the benefits of citizenship and of access to the magistracies. In the
next generation, King Agis deprived them of such citizenship and imposed a payment of tribute on them. All of them acceded to the new order
except the people of Helos, who seceded; once they had been vanquished,
they were declared to be of servile status, with the reservation that their
owners would not be allowed either to free them or to sell them abroad.
In sum, this is the starting point for the theory of contractual slavery that
we have already encountered. Moreover, the historical myth created by
Ephorus has the advantage of accounting for the existence of both helots
and perioeci. Both groups are "foreigners," first admitted to the center of
Lacedaimonian society and then lowered to their respective stations. We
might even suspect that Ephorus was trying to reconcile two traditions,
the one portraying perioeci and helots as victims of conquest, and the
other presenting them as demoted Spartiates. But what did Ephorus
understand by "foreigners"? Fragment 117 (which we have just analyzed)
does not specify a meaning with any precision, and if we stick to it, we
would be under no obligation to see these "foreigners" as Achaeans.[44]
However, Fragment 116, about the Messenians, removes any doubt:
"When Cresphontes took possession of Messene, he divided it into five
cities and located his royal residence in Stenyclaros, in the center of the
country. To the other cities—Pylos, Rhion, Mesola, and Hyameitis—he
sent kings, and he granted all the Messenians equal rights with the

Dorians. But this offended the Dorians, and he changed his plan; Stenyclaros alone had the rank of city, and he gathered the Dorians together
there." This account leaves no room for ambiguity: "foreigners" are non-
Dorian, the aboriginal inhabitants of the land, since it is difficult to
imagine that what was true for Messene was not also true for Sparta.

With various modifications, Ephorus's account had great influence.
Pausanias, for example, used a related version in ascribing the creation of
helotry to King Alcamenos, several generations after King Agis (Paus.
3.20.6).[45] In sum, Pausanias is a precursor of F. Kiechle, who also sliced
the Dorian conquest into many sections.

In the fourth century, however, this interpretation—which Ephorus
had not invented—was far from being unanimously accepted. In the
Republic, hence before Ephorus, Plato considered the transformation of
the model city into a "timocracy" of the Lacedaimonian type, and he
summarized the constitution of ancient Sparta as follows: "There was a
battle between them, and at last they agreed to distribute their land and
houses among individual owners; and they enslaved their friends and
maintainers, whom they had formerly protected in the condition of
freemen, and made them subjects (*perioeci*) and servants (*oiketai*); and they
themselves were engaged in war and in keeping a watch against them"
(*Rep.* 8.547b–c; tr. Jowett).[46] There is not the slightest hint of an
"Achaean" origin for the perioeci and helots, nor will one find it in Book
III of the *Laws,* in which Plato describes the establishment of the three
Dorian cities Sparta, Messene, and Argos; internal evolution is the sole
explanation for Sparta's success and the rapid decline of the two other
cities (*Laws* 3.683a et seq.).

Turning to Isocrates, we find that he was familiar with several different
interpretations and used them according to the needs of a particular
speech. The *Archidamos* of 366 presents the imaginary argument of a
Spartan prince, who identified the Messenians as Dorians whose ancestors
were made subject to the Lacedaimonians as punishment for having
assassinated their founding king, Cresphontes. However, Archidamos
refuses to equate the "Messenians" recently freed by Epaminondas with
the Messenians of long ago. "In fact the former are helots located on our
borders" (*Archidamos* 16, 28, 87). This version is compatible with the
theory of conquest. But in the *Panathenaicus* (written in 342–39, hence
after the corresponding book of Ephorus), Isocrates tells a completely
different story that counterbalances the version in Plato's *Laws.* While
Messene and Argos were undergoing an evolution similar to that of the
other Greek cities, i.e., from oligarchy to democracy, Sparta was characterized by persistent *stasis.* Instead of absorbing their people into the

community, the Spartiates made them *perioeci*: (Τὸν δῆμον περιοίκους ποιήσασθαι, καταδουλευσαμένους αὐτῶν τὰς ψυχὰς οὐδὲν ἧττον ἢ τὰς τῶν οἰκετῶν.)—"They made the people (*dēmos*) into perioeci, enslaving their spirits no less than those of slaves (*oiketai*)." What does this last expression signify? Why is there an allusion to the enslavement of the spirits of the people and a comparison with the treatment of slaves? Isocrates cannot be referring to the perioeci alone, because he specifies that the Spartans reserve the right to execute these people without trial, a remark that can only apply to helots. The passage makes sense only if we see that the author has lumped together all dependent populations, perioeci and helots (*Panath.* 170–80),[47] and that he might allude equally well to the presence at Sparta of chattel-slaves of the classical type (a likelihood in the fourth century).[48]

This completes our survey of the historical explanations for helotism. We can easily see the profound disjunction between them, as a set, and Theopompus's account of the origins of slavery. Whatever the explanation might be, helotism is always presented as having its origins not *before* history but *within* history. Whatever the explanation may be, the men it concerns are always presented as having once been free. It is no accident that Theopompus, who explains how the victims of the Dorian invasion became helots, also tells us that during the Messenian wars a certain number of helots, called *Epeunaktoi*, took the place in the Spartan bunks of those "peers" who had fallen in battle (*FGrH* 115 F171 in Ath. 6.271c–d).[49] In this case, the phenomenon of enslavement is reversible. A helot was once free and can become so again; in no way is he a slave by nature. In contrast, free men are not bought and sold, but slaves are; only before history was there a time without slaves. Their fate cannot be reversed.

At the end of the sixth century, Greek historiography had arisen within the framework of the city, and the city served as its reference point. Helots had their place because they participated (at the lowest possible level) in the Spartan state; chattel-slaves, on the other hand, were *private property*, even when owned by a city, and thus were much more difficult to fit into history. It is just Theopompus—whose major work, the *Philippica,* indicates by its title that it focuses on the person of the Macedonian king—who signals a turning point in the field.

Must we add that, at least for the historians, the helots and their like are Greek, while the other slaves are barbarian? Someone might offer the Mariandynians, among others, as a counterexample, and we must reply to such an objection.

Let us begin with a hypothesis. As we consider the factors contributing to the Hellenization of non-Greek peoples during the Classical age, shouldn't we assign an important place to the rural slavery imposed on some of them? Probably the earliest example we could adduce is that of the Cyllirioi of Syracuse; Herodotus tells us that shortly before Gelon seized power, these people joined with the *dēmos* to expel from the city the Gamoroi, the oligarchs (7.155). One would search in vain for a single instance of an alliance between the *dēmos* of a Greek city and free Siciliots. Still the most remarkable case might be that of the Mariandynians of Pontic Heraclea, about whom we are relatively well informed—possibly Clearchos the tyrant of Heraclea was a pupil of Plato and Isocrates.[50]

The fifth century knew the Mariandynians as a barbarian people, Bithynian or Paphlagonian, on whose territory the Heracliots founded their city, and who also owned the cave of Cerberus.[51] Although they are often depicted as non-Greek, one might say they are "familiar" barbarians, as the Carians were in Homer's time.[52] Their barbarian nature never completely vanishes.[53] The Mariandynians remain *barbaroi*,[54] but the geographer Strabo does not really know what to make of them. Are they Cauconians, a people known to Homer but since disappeared, or are they Bithynians, whose dialect and race they share (Strabo 12.3.2–9)? Neither does Strabo know, except indirectly, about Mariandynians working the land on behalf of the citizens of Heraclea.

As we have seen, fourth-century historiography puts them in the same category as the helots and penestae, and Theopompus himself seems to group them among those people who entered into what we have called "slavery by contract" (*FGrH* 115 F388 in Strabo 12.3.4).[55] Doesn't such a classification imply that they were largely Hellenized? This hypothesis is bolstered by two sets of facts. Heraclea's history shows signs of great upheaval during the Classical period, as evinced by Aristotle's numerous allusions to revolutions there (*Pol.* 5.1304b 31, 1305b 4, 1305b 36).[56] Heraclea was certainly remarkable, in that at times it could support a sizable fleet, despite a meager citizen population; it could do so, says Aristotle, thanks to the large number of "perioeci and peasants (*geōrgoi*)"—that is, Mariandynians (*Pol.* 7.1327b 10–15).[57] But did this situation persist throughout the fourth century? A passage in Aeneas Tacticus, to which D. M. Pippidi has called attention,[58] reveals that Heraclea underwent a far-reaching constitutional reform of the Cleisthenic type. To improve their supervision of the wealthy, the commoners replaced the earlier system—three Dorian tribes, each with twelve centuries (*hekatostyes*)—with an arrangement of sixty centuries, implying the likely existence of ten tribes. Can we not assume that such a reform would be accompanied by an expansion of the citizen body, without which it would lose a great deal of its meaning? At least this is a hypothesis one can suggest. In 364 the tyrant Clearchos seized power with the support of the *dēmos*. He enforced a redistribution of land, freed the slaves of the wealthy, and enacted compulsory marriages between slaves and the daughters of the aforementioned aristocracy.[59] Who were these slaves? Very probably the Mariandynians, some of whom at least would have been manumitted.[60] The business about the marriage is also a commonplace found only in connection with cities having rural dependents.[61] Can we not conclude that the slaves who were married to the Heracliot women were Hellenized barbarians? We can at least ask the question.

But we can also approach the problem by another route. From Herodorus in the fifth century to the Hellenistic-Roman period and Promathidas, Amphitheos, Nymphis, Domitius-Callistratus, and Memnon, Heraclea possessed a whole school of historians and mythographers;[62] the fragments are preserved primarily in the scholia to Apollonius's *Argonautica*, since one episode is set among the Mariandynians.

This mythography tells us nothing about the Mariandynians as rural dependents, but what it does tell us is just as interesting at another level. After landing on the shore of Asia Minor, the Argonauts encountered two kinds of barbarians, and the unmitigated hostility of the Bebrycoi of Mysia is balanced by the boundless friendliness of the enemies of the Bebrycoi, the Mariandynians, whose king, Lycos, sealed a treaty with the Greeks in the temple of *Homonoia* (Harmony) (Ap. Rhod. *Argon.* 2.352 et seq., 722 et seq.)—possibly a mythic transformation of the original contract of servitude. The theme of the noble barbarian is common enough (recall the legend about the founding of Marseilles). What is more interesting is that the myth stresses the reasons behind the friendly welcome: King Lycos is son of Dascylos and grandson of Tantalus, hence the nephew of Pelops of Phrygia; it is to honor Pelops that Lycos extends a welcome to the heroes of the *Argo* (Nymphis *FGrH* 432 F4 in *Schol. ad Ap. Rhod.* 2.752).[63] Especially in the Hellenistic period, kinship with Greek gods and heroes was certainly one of the expressions of Hellenization,[64] so that King Lycos can be seen as the retrojected hero of the Mariandynians' Hellenization.

If this is true, the case of the Mariandynians is no exception to the rule, and they can be described in the same terms as helots or penestae. A historical explanation is given for their entry into servitude because the condition was not thought of as eternal; some of them, at least, were judged worthy of leaving it.

Now we can see the conclusions toward which this study has tended, and we may summarize them concisely. In Theopompus's analysis, historical consideration of slaves of the helotic type served as the model for speculation about the beginnings of chattel-slavery. The latter was, in any event, wholly without precedent.

The causes of what we might call the preeminence of the helots are not difficult to uncover. It would be futile to look for the slightest sign of crisis within the chattel-slave system that was in effect throughout the Classical period.[65] On the other hand, it could be said that the permanent crisis of the old rural variety of dependence is one of the most important aspects of Greek history from the Archaic age on. When the Messenian helots rebelled in the fifth century, it was not a novel event.[66] Well before the end of the century, the penestae of Thessaly began their agitation (Xen. Hell. 2.3. 36).[67] In the fourth century the whole political and social equilibrium of the chief archaic city, Sparta, was destroyed. The event that most certainly led historians to speculate about the fate of the helots was the construction of Messene, which was conceived of and lived in from 369, as a rebirth; it caused extraordinary trouble within the Greek world, particularly as it beckoned to the Messenian *diaspora* scattered from Naupactus to Sicily. Even Crete no longer seemed to be the sanctuary it had been for so long. Aristotle ascribed its earlier security to its position as an island—"in Crete the class of *perioeci* remains tranquil, whereas the helots frequently rebel"—but he promptly added, "the recent arrival of an army from abroad has forced everyone to become aware of the weakness of Cretan institutions" (*Pol.* 2.1272b 15–23).[68]

Thus writing the history of helots is an offspring of systemic crisis, but we can extend our conclusions still further. The rural mode of dependency that the Greeks found in Asia—from which their cities and kingdoms greatly profited[69]—is fundamentally no different from what the Greeks knew at first hand in helots and penestae. It would also be interesting to examine to what extent Hellenistic conquest was an achievement of the same Greek peasants whom the troubles of the fourth century had partially liberated and had partially forced out of their traditional social framework.[70] An example is the Cretan archers. That raises the question whether the enslavement of barbarians—Aristotle's "slaves by nature"—was not a consequence of the freeing of this group of Greeks.

But that is another story.

NOTES

1. In its essentials this essay is the one that was presented orally at Besançon. Of course I have taken into account the remarks that were made during the

184 discussions as well as the works by P. Lévêque, C. Mossé, and J. Ducat that have appeared since its publication.

2. On Theopompus in general, see A. Momigliano, "Teopompo," reprinted with some bibliographical supplements in *Terzo contributo* 1, 367–92.

3. The latest edition is by R. Meiggs and D. M. Lewis, *Selection* no. 8; today this text is dated ca. 570. See, however, C. Ampolo, "La *boulē demosiē.*"

4. "Slave Labour," 164, restated in *Slavery*, 72; see now *Ancient Slavery*, 67–92.

5. D. Lotze, *Metaxy;* cf. Pollux 3.83.

6. See M. I. Finley, "Servile Statuses," "Between Slavery and Freedom"; D. Lotze, "Woikees"; C. Mossé, "Rôle des esclaves"; P. Oliva, "Helots"; R. F. Willetts, "Servile System." Naturally these authors are far from agreeing with one another, even—above all—when one or another appeals to Marxism. Thus P. Oliva sees as "undeveloped" a form of slavery that Willetts justifiably finds radically different from classical slavery, but when Willetts himself speaks of "serfs" he creates a conflation with Medieval Europe. Willetts has reconsidered the problem in a later article ("Terminology," 67–68); in spite of his comments, I do not see what would stop him from using the word "bondsmen" instead of "serfs."

7. In "Rôle des esclaves."

8. P. Vidal-Naquet, "Économie et Société," 127ff.; also "Were Greek Slaves a Class?" above.

9. See below the case of the troubles of Pontic Heracleia in the fourth century. We can also refer to the tradition about the founding of Ephesus as reported by an unknown historian, Malakos, *FGrH* 552 Fl in Ath. 6.267a–b. In this version Ephesus was founded by one thousand rebellious slaves from Samos who, after a pact, obtained the right to emigrate. If this story has the slightest historical foundation, it can only mean rural dependents; this was well observed by M. Sakellariou, *Migration grecque*, 127.

10. See Y. Garlan, "Esclaves grecs," 1.

11. See "Slavery and the Rule of Women," below.

12. For an analogous comparison between woman and artisan, see "Study of an Ambiguity," p. 240 below; on Lysistrata, see N. Loraux, "Acropole comique."

13. For the dating of the *Phillipica,* see W. R. Connor, *Theopompus,* 5.

14. See some of the references below. A. Momigliano has suggested to me an interesting direction for research along the lines of the passage from Theopompus. At least two historians from the end of the Hellenistic age—Posidonios of Apamea (*FGrH* 87 F38) and Nicolaus of Damascus (*FGrH* 90 F95)—collected anecdotes about the miseries visited upon the Chians in consequence of the invention of chattel-slavery. We should probably give the same interpretation to the story of the slave revolt directed by Drimacos, as recounted by Nymphodoros of Syracuse (*FGrH* 572 F4). These texts (cited in Ath. 6.266e–f) are characteristic of the emotional reaction prevalent in certain intellectual circles at the

end of the Hellenistic era, in response to chattel-slavery. For the story of Drim-acos see p. 166 above.

15. See. G. R. Morrow, *Plato's Law of Slavery,* 32–39.

16. I will return later to the problem posed by the Mariandynians, the Bithynian dependents of the Heracliots.

17. On the theory of the natural slave and its limitations, see V. Gold-schmidt's slightly paradoxical article, "Théorie aristotélicienne."

18. See primarily S. Laufer, *Die Bergwerkssklaven.*

19. See V. Cuffel, "Concept of Slavery."

20. Henceforth when I speak of slavery without further clarification, it will always be chattel-slavery that I mean.

21. Hdt. 6.137, quoting Hecataeus (*FGrH* 1 F127).

22. All the manuscripts but one contain this latter detail, which most editors have suppressed. Indeed, it is the women and the women alone whom the Pelasgians will abduct. But it is natural that in his depiction of mythic times Herodotus assigned domestic labor to *women and children,* i.e., to the group of non-men, rather than to women alone. I might add that such a passage helps us understand how a word like *pais* could denote at the same time "child" and "slave"; for analogies in the Roman world, see J. Maurin, "Puer."

23. This is not an instance of the opposition between outdoor work, which in Greece is the duty of men (unlike in Egypt, according to Hdt. 2.35), and inside work, which belongs to the condition of women. Here again women and children are presented as substitutes for workers of servile status.

24. As is shown by Aristotle (*Pol.* 1. 1253b 1 et seq.).

25. Pherecrates F10 (Kock) in Ath. 6.263b.

26. Manes is a typical Phrygian name; as for Sekis ("little servant"), it is a characteristic "slave name." See O. Masson, "Noms des esclaves."

27. See "Slavery and the Rule of Women," pp. 207–8 below.

28. Crates F 14 (Kock) in Ath. 6.267e–f.

29. In fact this famous passage is almost an explicit echo of comic situations.

30. For example: Archemachos (third century?) *FGrH* 424 F1 in Ath. 6.246a–b; Callistratos (disciple of Aristophanes of Byzantium, second century) *FGrH* 348 F4 in Ath. 6.263d–e; Philocrates (fourth century?) *FGrH* 601 F2 in Ath. 6.264a; Sosicrates (second century) *FGrH* 461 F4 in Ath. 6.263f.

31. *FGrH* 87 F8 in Ath. 6.263c–d. See below for Ephorus's analogous theory about the origin of the helots and for Theopompus's theory about the Mariandynians. The theme is taken up again, with some others, by J. Ducat, "Hilotisme," esp. 5–11.

32. *Lakonien.*

33. *Sparte,* 20. The controversy about the genuineness of the Dorian Invasion has recently broken out again. I have no intention of taking part in the debate except to note that the presence of Dorian dialect on the Myceanaean tablets seems incontrovertible (cf. J. Chadwick, "Dorians").

34. *Problems,* 195.

35. For comparable examples in English historiography, see M. I. Finley, *Ancestral Constitution.*

36. F. Gschnitzer, *Abhängige Orte,* 146–50.

37. All the same, we may say from now on that the victims of the Dorian Invasion could either have emigrated as a group of could have partially remained on their ancestral land.

38. Research in this area has been greatly facilitated by the fine book by E. N. Tigerstedt, *Legend.*

39. *FGrH* 555 F 13 in Strabo 6.3.2. Ἐκρίθησαν δοῦλοι καὶ ὠνομάσθησαν εἵλωτες.. Despite the objections of P. Lévêque (*Terre et Paysans,* 115), I do not see how this passage can be viewed as anything other than an account of the origins of helotism. The story has two stages: 1) the decision is made that the "unworthy" are to be reduced to servile status; 2) these slaves take the name of helots.

40. Hdt. 7.23; Plut. *Agesilaus* 30, *Lycurgus* 21.2; Thucydides is surely alluding to this position in 5.34; on the *tresantes,* see N. Loraux, "Belle Mort," 111–12.

41. *FGrH* 4 F188 in Harp. *s.v.* εἰλωτεύειν; see Jacoby's commentary *ad loc.* The etymological story connected with Helos was known to Theopompus (*FGrH* 115 F13 in Ath. 6.272a) as well as to other authors, mentioned by J. Ducat, "Hilotisme," 9.

42. *FGrH* 70 FF116–17 in Strabo 8.4.7 and 8.5.4. Jacoby's commentary eliminates all the hesitations that this passage could initially arouse.

43. Meineke suggested that the mention of the helots be moved after that of the town Helos.

44. This was the argument, for example, of L. Pareti, *Sparta arcaica,* 190–91.

45. Plutarch has another candidate, King Soös (cf. *Lycurgus* 2.1).

46. This passage is difficult to interpret since it operates on two levels: on the one hand, Plato tells how the citizens of the model city, who owned everything in common, proceeded to the distribution of land and the specialization of the ruling caste in a purely military role; on the other hand, he is giving his own version of the establishment of the Spartan state. We may add that the "citizen" status of the members of the lower classes in the Platonic city is extremely dubious, and Aristotle gleefully emphasizes the real or imaginary contradictions in the text (*Pol.* 2.1264a 25 et seq.). But such a remark, in itself, would have to make us acknowledge that Plato is here following a "historical" version of Spartan history.

47. This passage has been subject to varying interpretations: C. Mossé believes that it is to the perioeci and to them alone that Isocrates is alluding ("Périèques"); J. Ducat disagrees with my interpretation, while granting my point that there is "perhaps some confusion (more or less deliberate in a violently polemical work) with the status of helots" ("Hilotisme," 9).

48. Plato alludes to the presence of slaves, as in *Alc.* 122d (which C. Mossé brought to my attention). Nonetheless, one could interpret the passage differently and conclude that there Isocrates is speaking about slaves in general.

49. Cf. S. Pembroke, "Locres," 1246. Theopompus compares these *Epeunak-toi* with a servile group in Sicyon, the *Katōnakophoroi*, F176 in Ath. 6.271d.

50. Cf. Memnon, *FGrH* 434 F1 in Photius *Bibl.* 224.

51. Hecataeus, *FGrH* 1 F198; Hdt. 1.28, 3.90, 7.72; Xen. *Anab.* 6.2.1. All the documentation on the Mariandynians is now collected in D. Asheri, "Herakleia Pontike," 17–23.

52. See Pherecrates F68 (Kock) in Ath. 14.653a, where jokes are made about their dialect and its attendant confusions; on the dirges attributed to them, see Nymphis *FGrH* 432 F5 in Ath. 14.619b–20c. Pausanias also knew of a dedicatory offering at Olympia, given by the Megarians and Boeotians, the founders of Heraclea, "on the Mariandynian barbarians" (5.26.5).

53. Cf. for example the anonymous author of the *Periplous of the Euxine Sea* 27 (*G.G.M.* 1, p. 408). Eustathius, among others, makes some comment about their use of the poison aconite (*Comm. ad Dion. Periegetes, G.G.M.* 2, p. 354).

54. The latest evidence is a funerary inscription from the imperial period preserved by Constantinus Porphyrogenetes in the *Book of Themes* (C.I.G. 3188) in connection with the career of a proconsul; the inscription places the land of the Mariandynians between Galatia and Pontus.

55. The passage in Strabo does not state explicitly that Theopompus is responsible for this claim. For his part, Callistratos declares that they had been given the name "tribute-carriers" (*dōrophoroi*) to avoid the bitter connotations of the word "menials" (*oiketai*); cf. *FGrH* 347 F4 in Ath. 6.263d–e.

56. On the history of Heraclea and especially the tyranny of Clearchos, there is a brief summary in W. Hoepfner, *Herakleia Pontike*, 9–14; see also D. Asheri, "Herakleia Pontike"; the basic work on tyranny is still H. Apel, *Tyrannis*.

57. For Aristotle the word *perioeci* almost always means dependent rural populations; cf. R. F. Willetts, "Interregnum," 496.

58. *Aen. Tac.* 11.10–11; D. M. Pippidi, "Luttes politiques."

59. See Justin 16.3–5. If, for Justin, the *plebs* is clearly the *dēmos*, his *senatores* are much more likely to be the *oligoi* and not the *bouleutes*.

60. Cf. C. Mossé, "Rôle des esclaves," 357–59.

61. To the examples recounted in "Slavery and the Rule of Women," pp. 209–12 below, there can be added the case of Nabis, who also enforced marriages between helots and Spartiate women; on these events, cf. *Polyb.* 16.13, 1, and the studies by C. Mossé, "Nabis," and B. Shimron, "Nabis." I support this claim for the most part, despite the objections of D. Asheri, "Mariage forcé."

62. The fragments of their works are collected under the numbers 31 and 430–34 in Jacoby; on the Mariandynians and their iron mines, see L. Robert, *Asie mineure*, 5–10.

63. It is a possibility, but only a possibility, that Herodotus had also referred to this kinship: *FGrH* 31 F49. Unfortunately the text is both cryptic and corrupt.

64. The finest example known to me is the unpublished inscription discovered by H. Metzger in the Letoön of Xanthos (third century) that sets up a

188   common genealogy between the Lycians and the Dorians from the metropolis. We know the Lycians were among the populations that were the most thoroughly Hellenized. See, in general, D. Musti, *Syngeneia*.

65. For reasons that escape me, this sentence has occasioned some violent dispute; see, for example, D. Musti, "Valore de scambio," 170–71. It seems to me that the meaning is clear: Classical antiquity went for centuries without a major confrontation between free men and slaves.

66. See, however, the reservations of J. Ducat, "Hilotisme," 24–38, and his study "Mépris des hilotes."

67. Cf. C. Mossé, "Rôle des esclaves," 354–55.

68. On this invasion, possibly that of Phalaikos and his mercenaries in 345 or that of Agis in 333, see the discussion in H. van Effenterre, *Crète*, 8off.

69. See P. Briant, "Laoi."

70. It is enough to glance at the prosopography in M. Launey's thesis, *Armées hellénistiques*, to see the importance of the rural regions of old Greece in the zones of recruitment.

9   The Immortal Slave-Women of Athena Ilias

In 1911 Adolf Wilhelm published, with detailed commentary, an inscription that had been discovered in 1895 near Vitrinitsa (Oiantheia?) in Western Locris. It has been known ever since by the name he gave it, *die Lokrische Mädcheninschrift*—"the inscription of the maidens of Locris."[1] This text enjoys a well-deserved fame. It is framed as an agreement; on one side are the city of Naryka in Eastern Locris and the Aianteioi (descendants of Ajax son of Oileus),[2] and on the other are the Locrians. It is a straightforward document, probably from the early part of the third century,[3] about a custom attested to by numerous literary texts. The Locrians sent young girls to the temple of Athena at Ilion in the Troad[4] in order to expiate the crime committed by Ajax son of Oileus: during the sack of Troy he had tried to rape Cassandra, daughter of Priam and inspired prophetess of Apollo. The text presents the tribute as a simple "liturgy," thereby secularizing (so to speak) or at least politicizing an ancient custom. The Aianteioi and the city of Naryka deliver the maidens but receive in exchange a number of negative and positive privileges, such as priority in access to courts of justice and dispensation from the requirement of providing hostages. The girls' parents are given compensation for their clothing and upbringing (*kosmon kai trophan*:

Published in *Le Monde grec, Hommages à C. Préaux* (Brussels: 1975, 496–507. The study has been reworked with the help of comments I have received from Benedetto Bravo, Philippe Gauthier, Victor Goldschmidt, and Christian Le Roy, all of whom have my thanks.

l. 10). As happens all too often, the text is mutilated at exactly the points where one would least want it to be. If we read the Vitrinitsa inscription independently of the literary tradition, what do we learn about this peculiar payment of maidens? In lines one and nine, it is simply a matter of "young girls" (*tas kora{s}, tān korān*), but we know from the use of the dual in lines ten and twenty-three (*korain*) that the girls go in groups of two, both now (line 10) and in the past; in line twenty-three it is stated that justice will be rendered, to the greatest possible extent, to the earlier pairs of maidens (ἐπιδικῆσαι τοῖν πρόσθ[ε]ν κὰτ τὸ δυν[ατόν]). Unfortunately, in line ten, where the length of the girls' service to Athena was certainly specified, the stone is broken; we find only that each of the girls is to be given an allowance of fifteen minae for clothing and expenses until . . . (καὶ τοῖν κόραιν ἑκατέραι πεντεκαίδεκα μνᾶς ἐν κόσμον καὶ τροφὰν παρέχειν, ἔντε κα . . .).[5] Here we can only respect the silence of the stone and hope that some day another copy of the decree will be found in Locris or somewhere else.

But there *is* a wealth of literary evidence from poets, historians and chroniclers, geographers, authors of specialized treatises, mythographers, and scholiasts.[6] Can't we use their testimony to fill in the lacuna?

Obviously the aim of the present study is not to consider all this material as a whole. That has been done quite thoroughly. The tradition does inform us about the points that the epigraphic text, by its very nature as an official document, does not address: Ajax's crime, and its immediate and long-term consequences, and the punishment imposed for one thousand years on the Locrians, who were thought to be accomplices in the deed. The earliest direct evidence is found in Aeneas Tacticus and goes back to the middle of the fourth century. It shows that the tradition is already well established: between the Locrians and the residents of Ilion there exists a sort of *agōn*. The former try to get their maidens into the sanctuary of Athena and, according to Aeneas, always succeed; the latter try to stop them. Several authors (Timaeus, Lycophron and the scholia, Plutarch, Pseudo-Apollodorus, Aelian, and Tzetzes, whose account is almost identical with that of Pseudo-Apollodorus) place special emphasis on the pitiable situation of the Locrian girls who become slaves to Athena after having escaped death. Their life is said to be dreary and their funerals degrading. As for Saint Jerome, he finds it enough to note that their chastity never occasioned the slightest scandal.

The texts I have mentioned show that there was some controversy about the origin and the exact nature of the service performed by the maidens at Ilion. I do not, however, intend to go into all the details of this dispute. When did the expiatory rite begin? At the end of the Trojan War, most of the texts calmly assert. But Strabo indicates that it was a topic for debate and, trusting in the opinions of learned men from other cities in the Troad, believes that it could not possibly date from a time before the Persian occupation. Which cities, which groups supplied the girls? All the Locrians, by means of a lottery? (So say Lycophron, Callimachus, Pseudo-Apollodorus, and the scholiast on the *Iliad*.) Or was it a group of one hundred noble families, who also used selection by lot? (Thus Polybius.)[7] Or was it the kingdom of which Ajax had been leader, as is claimed by Servius (citing Aeneas Tacticus) whose observations conform to the *Mädcheninschrift?* I will not try to raise these problems again; still less will I pass judgment on the "historical" or "archaeological" background of the ritual.[8] My intent is much more modest—to think about the term of the service of the Locrian maidens at Troy. As we have seen, the Vitrinitsa inscription sheds no light on this point, and it has long been observed that the literary tradition is split in two.[9] One set of texts claims that the young Locrians had to serve the goddess until they died. Lycophron makes this unmistakably clear in lines 1150–61 of the *Alexandra,*[10] where Cassandra declares:

. . . As for you, the whole house of Ileus, race of Hodoidacus,   1150.
because of my defiled nuptials, all of you—
in grave expiation to the Gygean goddess Agrisca [Athena]—
will have to pay for one thousand years a tribute of maidens
and leave here to grow old those whom the lot will select!
For them, strangers in a strange land, a tomb without honor,   1155
a wretched tomb, which the waves on the beach will obliterate
until, on sterile wood, Hephaistos scorches their limbs with his fire
and scatters into the sea the ashes
of her who will be flung from the towers of Trauron!
Others will enter by night   1160
equal in number to those who will die . . . [11]

The same holds true in the *Epitome* of Pseudo-Apollodorus, who introduces an additional picturesque detail: "The Locrians returned home, not without difficulty, and three years later, when a plague struck Locris, they received an oracle commanding them to appease Athena of Ilion and to send, for one thousand years, two girls as suppliants. The lot fell first on Peribea and Cleopatra. . . . After their deaths, the Locrians sent others, entering the city by night,[12] for fear of being killed if they were discovered outside the sanctuary. Thereafter, the Locrians sent infants with their nurses (μετέπειτα δὲ βρέφη μετὰ τροφῶν ἔπεμπον). Once a thousand years had passed, after the Phocian War [which ended in 347–46 B.C.], they stopped sending suppliants." These last details are picked up, either directly or from a common source, by J. Tzetzes, who attributes them (probably by mistake) to Timaeus[13] and repeats them in his own commentary to lines 1141–45 of the *Alexandra:* "The first Locrian girls to arrive at Troy were Peribea and Cleopatra. At first the Locrians sent young girls, and later one-year-old infants[14] in the company of their nurses." Tzetzes too puts the end of the rite after the Phocian War.

Finally, the same tradition appears in the anonymous poet cited by Plutarch:[15] "Without a cloak, barefoot, like slaves, with shaven heads, they clean up the area around Athena's shrine, even when they have reached extreme old age (καὶ εἰ βαρὺ γῆρας ἱκάνοι)." Must we add to this list[16] the name of the historian Timaeus (c. 300 B.C.) cited by the scholiast on Lycophron? For now I will find it sufficient to translate the passage that, on first sight, actually resembles what Lycophron says: "Timaeus states that the young girls, two in number, who arrived [at Ilion] were slaves in the sanctuary of Athena. If one of them should die, another came to replace her (ἑτέραν παραγίνεσθαι ἀντ' αὐτῆς). The one who died was not buried among the Trojans but was cremated with uncultivated wood, and her bones were thrown into the sea."

There is another set of texts that claims, by contrast, that the girls were sent out and replaced *each year*. This *might* be the information provided by our earliest source, the *Poliorceticus* of Aeneas Tacticus (mid-fourth century B.C.). Explaining that the people of Ilion fail to prevent the Locrian maidens from entering their territory, he adds: 'Αλλ' οἱ Λοκροὶ προσέχοντες τῷ λαθεῖν, λανθάνουσιν ἀνὰ ἔτεα πολλὰ εἰσάγοντες σώματα. This can be translated as follows: "But the Locrians, striving to act without being seen, over the years brought in a large number of such people without anyone's knowing."[17] Strabo's version is absolutely clear. Telling the story as the citizens of Ilion do, he writes: Αἱ γοῦν Λοκρίδες παρθένοι μικρὸν ὕστερον ἀρξάμεναι ἐνεπέμποντο κατ' ἔτος. "Shortly after (the sack of Troy) Locrian virgins were sent over every year." So too Aelian: Ὁ Ἀπόλλων φησὶ πρὸς Λοκροὺς μὴ ἂν αὐτοῖς τὸ δεινὸν λωφῆσαι, εἰ μὴ πέμποιεν ἀνὰ πᾶν ἔτος δύο παρθένους ἐς τὴν Ἴλιον τῇ Ἀθηνᾷ Κασάνδρας ποινὴν ἕως ἂν ἰλεώσητε τὴν θεόν. "Apollo tells the Locrians that their trouble will not end unless they send, every year, two virgins for Athena at Ilion, as punishment for the crime committed against Cassandra, until they have appeased the goddess." Similarly, Servius, citing Aeneas Placidus: "For the story is that Minerva was not satisfied with the penalty imposed only on Ajax for the rape of Cassandra, in her temple, but through an oracle she commanded that every year a girl from Ajax's royal line be sent to Troy as a sacrifice."[18] Finally, the ancient scholion on line 1411 of Lycophron's *Alexandra* is just as clear: Ἔχρηεν ὁ θεὸς ⟨β'⟩ παρθένους ἐνιαυσιαίας εἰς Τροίαν τῇ 'Αθηνᾷ ἀποστέλλειν ἐπὶ ᾳ ἔτη. "The god demanded, through an oracle, that two girls[19] be sent annually to Athena in Troy."[20]

How can we explain this double tradition? Wouldn't the likeliest, the "most natural," solution be to acknowledge that the doubling corresponds to an evolution in the ritual itself? Thus A. Wilhelm argued that, "The difficulty is certainly to be resolved by conceding that at different times the service took different forms."[21] The ancient sources do not say so *directly*, but we can see that some authors, *not among the first of the tradition*, did follow this line of reasoning. What chronological guidelines have they preserved for us? Several texts inform us that the service required of the Locrians was to last a total of one thousand years, beginning, of course, with the return from Troy.[22] All such texts belong to the *first* tradition I discussed (I do not mean to say that it is the earliest), the one that has the maidens growing old and dying at Troy. One text alone formally denies that there was a fixed term for the whole liturgy.[23] This same text, regrettably damaged, alludes to a deliberate interruption in the practice. The Locrians are then stricken with a new sign of divine displeasure (sterility of the land) and so decide to reinstate the offerings; however, thinking that "it was punishment enough" (ἀρκοῦσαν εἶναι δοκοῦντας τὴν τιμωρίαν), they resolve that they will no longer send *two* maidens but *only* one. We can discard a useless suggestion of Plutarch's, "It is not long ago that the Locrians stopped sending maidens to Troy." But what is "not long ago" (οὐ πολὺς χρόνος)? Does it refer to Plutarch's own time? If so, we are into archaeology or tourism. Is he simply quoting his source? What is this source?[24]

Two texts, closely related—we are in the realm of Byzantine erudition—speak both of a change in the ritual (instead of girls, infants are sent with their nurses) and of a definite termination "after the Phocian War." The latter point raises some difficulties. First of all, the *Mädcheninschrift* proves[25] that several decades after the end of the war in question (347–46) the service was still in existence, although perhaps in a new form. Second, the text itself poses some problems. Tzetzes' version reads Χιλίων δ' ἐτῶν παρελθόντων μετὰ τὸν Φωκικὸν πόλεμον ἐπαύσαντο τῆς τοιαύτης θυσίας.[26] That is, "One thousand years having passed [after the return from Troy], after the Phocian War they put an end to the sacrifice." But no matter what date is adopted by the ancient scholars for the fall of Ilion, the millennium of the Trojan War cannot coincide with the end of the Third Sacred War; it must come later.[27] It is hard to understand how two chronological indices that contradict each other can be given in succession. It has also been asked whether the reading Τρ-ωικόν should not be substituted for Φωκικόν.[28] Then the text would simply say that the Locrians waited for one thousand years to pass after the fall of Troy to be quit of their obligation. We must suspend final judgment, because the principle of *lectio difficilior* argues for the retention of Φωκικόν, since the Phocian War is less well known than the Trojan War; nonetheless, it is worth recalling that the debate exists.

There remains one text of prime importance for any discussion of chronology: Aelian. In fact the text is so badly mutilated that at first glance it appears absurd. What does it say? Aelian first tells the story of Apollo's oracle and its demand for the annual shipment of girls to Athena Ilias and then says, "The maidens sent to Troy grew old and died there (κατεγήρασαν),[29] since those who were to succeed them did not arrive.[30] The women then began to give birth to crippled and deformed infants."[31] When the Locrians inquire at Delphi, the oracle first dismisses them, and then, on their insistence, reminds them of the omission of which they are guilty. Thereupon the Locrians turn to Antigonus and "leave it to him to designate which city in Locris had to send the tribute" (τιθέντας τὴν κρίσιν ὑπὲρ τοῦ τίνα χρὴ Λοκρικὴν πόλιν πέμπειν δασμόν). The king ordered that "the question should be settled by lot" (προσέταξε κλήρῳ διακριθῆναι).

How have modern scholars reacted in the face of this jumble of texts and their divergent accounts of what Casaubon called a *historia nobilissima?* I do not wish to go into the details of a colossal bibliography, which I do not claim to know thoroughly; I will merely say that the whole of the discussion of chronology has revolved around the possible dates of the "interruption in the practice" "after the Phocian War" and its resumption "under King Antigonus." But which Antigonus? The three possible candidates have each had their supporters.[32] Antigonus Doson (king from 227 to 221) seems to be ruled out; the *Mädcheninschrift,* which is earlier than his reign, seems to be from after the revival of the ritual, if in fact such a revival did occur. There remain Antigonus the One-Eyed (r. 306–1) and Antigonus Gonatas (ruler of Macedon from 276 to 239).[33] If a choice *has* to be made, the best candidate is Antigonus the One-Eyed, who was master of the Troad and who, from before 306, controlled even if he did not create the federation of the cities of the Troad around the sanctuary of Athena Ilias.[34] Once this hypothesis is established, an *explanation* of the chronology becomes possible. If we combine the texts of Pseudo-Apollodorus and Tzetzes (end of the liturgy after the Phocian

War), a welcome suggestion from Diodorus (who tells us that Naryka, home of Ajax, was destroyed by the very Phocians in 352 [Diodorus 16.38.5]), and the text from Aelian, it seems likely although perhaps very bold to say, that the old ritual, interrupted in the middle of the fourth century, could have been reestablished by "King Antigonus" several decades later. What then of the two major traditions I have analyzed? Must we not assume, in principle, that the one corresponds to the earlier custom and the other to the renewed practice? Granted, but which is the earlier and which the later? Disturbingly, the modern authorities are split into two factions. Must it be admitted that in the Archaic and Classical period the "payment" was annual and that it became permanent in the Hellenistic period?[35] But how is this thesis to be reconciled with the testimony of Strabo, who has plenty of knowledgeable informants on matters concerning Asia Minor? Must we think, in contrast, that a life-sentence was humanized during the Hellenistic period and changed into a one-year term?[36] This theory makes it hard to take into account our earliest evidence, the text of Aeneas; even if it is almost contemporary with the temporary break in the service, it deals with the period prior to this break.

By far the most ingenious explanation is the one proposed by A. Momigliano. The annual term is well attested to in the Hellenistic epoch (in Strabo, Servius, the scholion to line 1141 of the *Alexandra,* and Aelian). It is also likely for the Archaic and Classical periods (Aeneas), although one could also imagine a somewhat longer obligation that would have been made less stringent after its reinstatement.[37] But then how can we explain the version in Lycophron and (in Momigliano's reading) in Timaeus? Must we believe that Cassandra the prophetess prophesied something that did not come to pass? The solution would be as follows: Timaeus (end of the fourth century) and Lycophron (at the very beginning of the third century) would have been writing precisely during the period of the interruption of the liturgy. "The appropriate period for their literary activity is in the gap between the suspension of the tribute and its revival."[38] Thus there is room for baroque exaggeration, and, with Lycophron serving as a source, poets and mythographers gladly adopt his version of the facts.

Still, I think that even this explanation, so convincing at first sight— and, *a fortiori,* the other hypotheses I have mentioned—do not pay sufficient attention to an essential feature of ancient scholarship, particularly that of the Hellenistic and Roman eras. As Momigliano knows better than anyone, the ancients were, like us, readers *of texts.* When they presented a new version of one event or another, it was not always because they had discovered a new document or a new tradition but because they had done a good, or often a bad, job of reading a *text,* and because they wanted to appropriate, to refute, or to synthesize *texts.*

Long ago J. Vürtheim provided an excellent example of a critical reading of the works of the ancient scholars.[39] How can we explain the tradition, ascribed to Timaeus, of the infants' being dispatched to Troy along with their nurses, the same tradition that appeared in Tzetzes and Pseudo-Apollodorus? Quite simply by the fact that the παρθένοι ἐνιαυσιαῖαι,[40] that is, the girls performing one year of service, were thought to be girls one year old, thereby allowing the substitution of "babies" (βρέφη) for "maidens" (παρθένοι). In a stroke, a moving anecdote disappears from the tradition. One can probably use an analogous argument to explain the scholion on line 1159 of Lycophron's *Alexandra,* according to which the Locrians first sent *two* girls to Ilion and later only *one.* In his readings the scholiast must have encountered the tradition reported by Servius, *unam puellam,* and wished to square this "information" with what he knew from other sources.

Momigliano attaches great importance to the text of Aelian, whose mention of "King Antigonus" really does give us a new, precious bit of information; but this too is no longer immune to a reductive criticism.[41] Let us read it again. Apollo declares to the Locrians that "their misery will not cease unless they send two maidens a year to Ilion for Athena." Thus Aelian belongs to what I have called the second tradition. But the text continues, "the girls sent to Troy grew old and died there, since those who were to succeed them did not arrive." This "aging" of the maidens is precisely one of the points emphasized by the authors who follow the first tradition: e.g., Lycophron uses the participle γηροβοσκοῦσαι, "nurturing until old age," and the poet cited by Plutarch speaks of "burdensome old age." Is it not obvious that Aelian tried, as best he could, to reconcile the two traditions he found in the documents?

Is it possible to go much farther than these small points of detail, to show—in a word—that it is possible to reduce the seemingly insurmountable barrier between the two traditions? I think the answer is yes, and it is a study by C. Préaux that sets us on the path.[42] The lease of a flock called "iron livestock" is a well-known type of contract, widely evidenced in the ancient and modern Mediterranean world, and especially well represented in the papyri of Hellenistic-Roman Egypt. "The lessee commits himself to replace any animal that dies or disappears, so that the flock is called *athanatos,*[43] immortal." What holds true for flocks can also hold true for men; we have the famous example of the Persian squadron of "immortals," of which every member who fell ill or died had to be replaced to keep the number constant (Hdt. 7.83, 211).[44] Evidently this is the kind of immortality that Homer alludes to in describing the doves that carry ambrosia (the drink of immortality) to Zeus and that are snagged on the high peak of the Planctes:

'Αλλά τε καὶ τῶν αἰεν ἀφαιρεῖται λὶς πέτρη·
ἀλλ' ἄλλην ἐνίησι Πατὴρ ἐναρίθμιον εἶναι

Each time the bare rock takes one of them,
which Zeus must replace to restore their number
[Od. 12.64–65).[45]

Claire Préaux had the vision to recall that contracts for immortality were equally available to men in the Classical age. The irrefutable example she cites is drawn from Xenophon's *Way and Means* (355 B.C.; 4.14–15). Nicias, son of Niceratos, the fifth-century Athenian general, in all likelihood "once owned one thousand men in the silver mines; these he leased to Sosias the Thracian on the condition that Sosias pay one obol per day per man and always maintain their number at full strength" (ἐφ' ᾧ ὀβολὸν μὲν ἀτελῆ ἕκαστον τῆς ἡμέρας ἀποδιδόναι, τὸν δ' ἀριθμὸν ἴσους ἀεὶ παρέχειν). Thus Sosias commits himself to replace, at his own cost, any slave belonging to Nicias's company who might disappear. Since it concerns such an important effective force and the manpower at work in the mines, this clause is obviously not purely rhetorical.

I am suggesting that a contract of this sort is to be found at the origin—if not of the relation between the Locrians and Athena Ilias, which is much more complex—at least of the double tradition that I have analyzed. What is the foundation shared by the two systems? It is that Locrian girls, two in number (recall that the figure appears in both sets of stories), must always be present at Ilion. The fragment from Timaeus, which has been subject to overinterpretation, expresses this idea with simplicity: εἰ δέ τις ἀποθάνοι, ἑτέραν παραγίνεσθαι ἀντ' αὐτῆς: "If one of them should die, another arrives to replace her."[46] But the decisive evidence is a passage in Lycophron, although he is the least judicial author imaginable. In lines 1160–61 of the *Alexandra* he describes what happens when one of the maidens dies of old age: he says: ἄλλαι δὲ νύκτωρ ταῖς θανουμέναις ἴσαι ἵξονται . . . "Others will come by night, in number equal to those who have died."[47] Aside from the detail about nocturnal arrival, we have exactly the conditions specified in the contract between Nicias and Sosias. No matter how the "maidens" died: from the blows of the people of Ilion, stoned to death, as some texts claim; from old age, as Lycophron, Plutarch, and Aelian imagine; from illness or accident during their journey; or, quite simply, if they leave once they have finished their term of service, as the other tradition has it. No matter. They must be replaced. And it is up to the Locrians to do so.

As in the contract analyzed by Préaux, it is not a matter of *parechein* but of *pempein*,[48] not of providing but of sending, of conveying. The idea of *pompē* is not far off, but the theme of perpetual presence at Ilion is unmistakable in all our texts. Can we imagine what happened after this shared starting point? One of the traditions emphasized what made the offerings to Athena most like the "lease of iron livestock" and the Nicias–Sosias contract—the idea of a constant number of slaves; ἧτε δοῦλαι, "like slaves" says the poet cited by Plutarch, and ἐδούλευον, "they were slaves" observes the fragment from Timaeus.[49] Lycophron transformed Ajax's crime into an offense against the laws of marriage and gave rhetorical amplification to his idea by depriving the "maidens" of the joys of marriage and motherhood. The other tradition, by contrast, in its insistence on the annual character of the service, rather diluted it, changed it into a more ordinary liturgy. We have seen that the Vitrinitsa inscription also tends in this direction.[50] Under such circumstances, one might well reason as Momigliano did: among the different terms that could have been included in the primitive contract, the preference in the Hellenistic age (after the intervention of "King Antigonus") would have been for a relatively swift method of replacement.

If, however, my analysis is correct—that is, if our tradition is accurately explained by the image of a contract for "immortality" (limited to one thousand years)—I do not think we have any hope of reconstructing the initial agreement. An annual offering is not impossible, and we might compare the procedure of the Hyperborean rites at Delos,[51] but what would justify our calling it aboriginal? The alternative, from the tradition exemplified by Lycophron, embodies enough baroque excesses to make one uneasy. It is better to admit our ignorance and say that the first contract was such that it could give rise to the twofold tradition.[52] At least, that is all I have tried to prove.

NOTES

1. A. Wilhelm, "Mädcheninschrift"; the text of the inscription is now reprinted in I.G. IX.1²3.706 (G. Klaffenbach), and in H. Schmitt, *Staatsverträge*, 3, no. 472, pp. 118–26, which also has the essential bibliography. A study of particular importance, above all for the establishment of the text, is A. Nikiskij,

"Aianteia." A recent study of the purely religious and ritual aspects of the sending of maidens to Troy is F. Graf, "Mädchen."

2. The exact status of the *Aianteioi* cannot be precisely defined—tribe or phratry, no one knows. With reason A. Wilhelm merely says "The *Aianteioi* are, at first sight, the lineage of Ajax, the whole group of his descendants" ("Mädcheninschrift," 172). It is not possible to cite the text from Servius, quoted below, to make the *Aianteioi* a tribe.

3. Before 272, according to H. Schmitt, who notes, along with other authors, that there is no mention made of the Boeotian League, to which the Opuntian Locrians belonged at this time (*Staatsverträge* 3, p. 125). According to Klaffenbach, the script is from the beginning of the third century. I will not address this question here.

4. Strictly speaking, the text mentions only the sending of maidens, without specifying their destination—at least in the part of the document that is preserved.

5. Until their marriage, according to A. Wilhelm, who makes the following restoration: ἔντε κα ἐν 'ἀνδρὸς ἔλθη ("Mädcheninschrift," 220). Other attempts at restoration have been made, and they are to be found in the critical apparatus in the edition by Schmitt, *Staatsverträge* 3, p. 121. Schmitt himself has justifiably left the space blank. In addition to the maidens' marriage, or concurrently with it, the other possibilities are: their arrival at Ilion, their return to their homeland, or the end of the obligation imposed on the Locrians after the crime of Ajax.

6. There follows a list, which I hope is complete: Aen. Tact. *Poliorc.* 31.24; Timaeus, *FGrH* 566 F146a (quoted in *Ancient Scholia to Lycophron, ad* 1155) and b (dubious, quoted by Tzetzes, *Lycophronica, ad* 1141); Lycophron, *Alex.* 1141–73, the Scholia to 1141 (quoting Callim. *Aitia* 1, F35 Pfeiffer), to 1172 (quoting Timaeus) and the commentary by Tzetzes to 1141 (citing Timaeus and Callimachus)—1162; Polyb. 12.5.6–9; Strabo 13.1.40.600–601 (relying on Demetrios of Skepsis); Plut. *Delays in Divine Justice* 12.557d (quoting an anonymous poet); [Apoll.] *Epit.* 6.20–22; Aelian *Var. Hist.* F47.2, 205–6 Hercher (reconstructed from several passages in the *Suda*); Iambl. *Vit. Pyth.* 42; St. Jerome, *Against Jovinian* 1.41; Serv. *Comm. ad Aen.* 1.41 (quoting the historian Annaeus Placidius); *Scholia A D ad Il.* 13.66 (quoting Callimachus's *Aitia*). A. Wilhelm and the authors who have treated the *Lokrische Mädcheninschrift* in detail have obviously made note of all these passages, which were, to the best of my knowledge, first collected and commented on by I. Casaubon in a note to his edition of Aeneas, as a continuation of his edition of Polybius, Paris, 1609, 89; republished in Leipzig, 1818 (*Aeneae Tactici Commentarius . . . rec. Is. Casauboni*) with supplements, 243–44. It should be noted that Casaubon knew the passage from St. Jerome, which has not been cited by the recent authors. One can find a convenient collection and translation of the majority of the texts in A. J. Reinach, "Origine." Except when greater specificity is called for, I shall henceforth refer to the ancient texts solely by the name of the author.

7. On the passage in Polybius, see S. Pembroke, "Locres," 1250–55. His

interpretation, which makes short work of the Locrian pseudomatriarchy, seems to me to be decisive.

8. See, for example, a good discussion in L. Lerat, *Locriens,* 19–22. On the archaeological evidence, of whose existence I am quite doubtful, see W. Leaf (following Brückner), *Troy,* 126–44; the same author has collected the texts in Appendix C, 293–96. Another archaeological inquiry, utterly mad, is G. Huxley, "Troy VIII"; the author believes that he has "recovered" the ashes of the Locrian maidens. But the ashes had been thrown into the sea.

9. On this point the best discussion is by A. Momigliano, "Locrian Maidens"; I owe a great deal to this article, although in the end I adopt a different position.

10. I am not going to reopen the debate on the dating of the *Alexandra,* which I, with numbers of good scholars, locate in the first third of the third century.

11. The translation is from the French of A. J. Reinach, "Origine," 26–27.

12. This detail renders all the more absurd the hypothesis of G. Huxley, which is based on the existence of a *temenos extra muros* ("Troy VIII"). In fact, during the Hellenistic period the temple of Athena was in the northern part of the site but definitely *within* the city.

13. The attribution to Timaeus has been called into doubt, with some very good reasons, notably by Wilamowitz, *Ilias,* 387–88. Jacoby summarizes the debate in his commentary to Timaeus F146. In the quotation from Tzetzes, Jacoby himself athetizes the name of Timaeus. Tzetzes also cites Callimachus, but if this remark has any value it might bear only on the legend as a whole.

14. Or *eniausia*—see above for the content of this adjective.

15. There are so many guesses about his identity (a cyclic poet, Euphorion, Callimachus) that I refuse to take sides.

16. As for example in A. Momigliano, "Locrian Maidens," 51.

17. The text and its translation raise several problems: 1) Following Wilhelm ("Mädcheninschrift," 175) I have adopted Sauppe's conjecture substituting *hoi Lokroi* in place of *oligoi*—an emendation that the recent editors of Aeneas (Oldfather and Dain) have wrongly neglected to mention. It is quite likely paleographically and yields better sense. 2) The manuscript has *anetea* with a *signum corruptionis* on the first *e.* Orelli and the subsequent editors of Aeneas were right to interpret it as *ana etea* or *an'etea.* But it is the meaning of the expression that is in question. Oldfather and A. M. Bon understand "year by year"; Momigliano writes, "The words *an'etea* must not be pressed unduly" ("Locrian Maidens," 50), and indeed this is not a case of *ana panta etea* as in Hdt. 8.65 or *ana pan etos* as in Hdt. 1.136, 2.99, 3.160. In this spirit, I have translated it as "in the course of the years." There could be some hesitation about the function of *polla,* and Oldfather suggests that the adjective could refer to *etea* (in a note, p. 169 Loeb ed.). This seems less than likely, for the idea of extended duration is introduced in the preceding phrase with the expression *ek tosoutou chronou.* At any rate, as Momigliano notes, the text of Aeneas is irreconcilable with the "first" tradition I have just invoked. I still uphold my interpretation of this passage, despite the objections of F. Graf, "Mädchen," 66 n. 30.

18. Note that Servius breaks with the rest of the tradition by speaking of a *single* maiden; the ancient scholion on Lycophron's *Alexandra* 1159 states that on the second occasion the Locrians sent only one servant for Athena, thinking that that was punishment enough: πέμπειν οὐκέτι β', ἀλλὰ μίαν, ἀρκοῦσαν εἶναι δοκοῦντας τὴν τιμωρίαν.

19. The figure is a restoration by E. Scheer.

20. Some authors, whose purpose was different, did not take part in the controversy; Polybius, Iamblichus, St. Jerome, and the scholiast on the *Iliad*.

21. "Mädcheninschrift," 219.

22. See Lycophron, the scholiast on *Alexandra* 1141, the scholiast on Homer, the *Epitome* of Pseudo-Apollodorus, St. Jerome, Iamblichus, Tzetzes on *Alexandra* 1141.

23. That is, the scholiast on *Alexandra* 1159: ὁ δὲ χρησμὸς οὐκ εἶχεν ὡρισμένον χρόνον "the service did not have a fixed time limit," which shows that the tradition employed by the scholiast is far from being homogeneous.

24. There is nothing to be gained from citing that eternal stopgap, Posidionius, as does Schmitt (*Staatsverträge* 3, p. 125).

25. Unless one agrees with C. Robert that the inscription does not refer to the sending of maidens to Ilion but to a sanctuary of Athena in Western Locris (*Heldensage*, 1274); but this theory is highly improbable.

26. The clause in the *Epitome* ends, "they stopped sending suppliants (*hiketidas epausanto pempontes*)."

27. Jacoby makes a good point in his commentary on Timaeus F146: even with the chronology in Douris, who gives a date for the end of the Trojan War that is clearly earlier (1334/1333) than those used by other ancient scholars, it is not possible to place the end of the Third Sacred War one thousand years after the sack of Troy. Is it because the date of the ancient tradition seems so chronologically uncertain that St. Jerome writes that the Locrian maidens had been sent to Ilion *per annos circiter mille?* Casaubon already relied on the *circiter* to reconcile Timaeus's statement and what he himself knew about the chronology. E. Manni proposed another solution to the problem: the Phocian War should be identified with the Gallic attack on Delphi (278 B.C.), which would coincide more or less with the millennium of the Trojan War according to Herodotus (*Locridi*). Regrettably there is no evidence that a Gallic raid was ever called "Phocian War."

28. So far as I know, the first person to make this conjecture was L. Sebastiani in his edition of *Lycophron* and the scholia of Tzetzes (Rome, 1803, p. 297); he took it so much for granted that he did not think it necessary to alert his reader that it was not the reading of the manuscripts. The conjecture is upheld by C. G. Müller citing Casaubon's argument in a note to his edition of the same texts (Leipzig, 1811, 939 n. 29). Since then it has been ignored, except by Leaf ("Troy," 132) and rejected without discussion by A. Momigliano ("Locrian Maidens," 49 n. 2).

29. On this meaning for *katagēraskō*, see the comments by P. Treves in an appendix to his article, "Consenesco," 149–53.

30. A sentence is certainly missing; clearly the text cannot mean the *first* maidens sent to Troy (cf. A. J. Reinach, "Origine," 35).

31. Evidently this means the women of Locris, not the *hierodoulai* of Troy, as was the opinion of A. J. Reinach, "Origine," 35.

32. Cf. A. Wilhelm, "Mädcheninschrift," 186–87.

33. Schmitt aligns himself with the former (*Staatsverträge* 3, p. 125) and Momigliano with the latter ("Locrian Maidens," 52–53).

34. The earliest document "confirms the existence of the confederation and its links with Antigonus a little before 306 and a little after" (cf. L. Robert, *Monnaies en Troade*, 20–22). Antigonus the One-Eyed—the beginning of whose career is the subject of a recent monograph by P. Briant, *Antigone*—was well known for his intervention in the affairs of the Greek states; cf. for example the renowned inscription on the synoecism of Teos and Lebedos (Dittenberger *Sylloge*³ 344). It is surprising to find Momigliano saying "King Antigonus' arbitration, in its present form, is better explained if Ilium did not belong to his sphere—that is, if Antigonus is Antigonus Gonatas" ("Locrian Maidens," 53 n. 1). F. Graf also comes out for Antigonus Gonatas, on the grounds that the time of Antigonus the One-Eyed would be too far removed from the period when the decree of Vitrinitsa was issued ("Mädchen," 64). But under any circumstances there exists an interval of several dozen years, and it is hard to see what difference twenty years more or less would make.

35. This is the thesis developed by P. Corssen, "Sendung," 197–98; he is thereby led to restore line ten of the *Lokrische Mädcheninschrift* as ἔντε xα [ζώηι].

36. Most recently this thesis is adopted by Schmitt, *Staatsverträge* 3, p. 123.

37. It is an ancient notion that one proceeds from the harsher to the milder: Casaubon (*Aeneae Tactici*) wrote: Puto verum esse quod dixit Timaeus [i.e., Tzetzes] de tempore, quo immane institutum, mitescentibus in dies magis magisque hominum ingeniis, omitti coepit.

38. "Locrian Madiens," 52.

39. J. Vürtheim, *De Aiacis origine*, 110. His argument is accepted by A. Wilhelm, "Mädcheninschrift," 184, and by A. Momigliano, "Locrian Maidens," 50 n. 2. On the other hand, Nikitskij thought that the mention of βρέφη ἐνιαύσια μετὰ τῶν τροφῶν αὐτῶν—"infants one year old with their nurses"— could have arisen from the confusion between *trophos* (nurse) and *trophē*, the upkeep guaranteed to the maidens in the Mädcheninschrift ("Aianteia," 15). But this posits, unnecessarily, a contamination between the literary tradition and the epigraphic documentation.

40. The expression appears in the ancient scholion to *Alexandra* 1141.

41. The composite nature of the passage in Aelian has been well observed by Nikitskij, "Aianteia," 16.

42. C. Préaux, "Troupeaux." Before Préaux, A. Wilhelm had already made this comparison (*Poroi*, 26).

43. Préaux, "Troupeaux," 161. The bibliography on this institution is pro-

vided by J. and L. Robert, "Bulletin," 1976 no. 327 and by P. Gauthier, *Poroi*,
139. In addition, J. Triantaphyllopoulos, "Varia graeco-romana," 183–84.

44. I have not made special inquiries into the origin of the term "Immortals" that is applied to the members of the Académie Française, but it is well known that they owe this epithet not to the quality of their writing, which is variable, but to their number, which remains constant.

45. This example from Homer was not cited by J. Triantaphyllopoulos, "Varia graeco-romana," who does mention some others that are not all persuasive. Nonetheless, I agree with him that in the famous episode of the Cattle of the Sun (*Od.* 12.127–30) Homer plays on the implications of the two possible meanings of immortality. Plato makes use of an analogous pun in *Rep.* 10.611a: ". . . the souls will always be the same, for if none be destroyed they will not diminish in number. Neither will they increase, for the increase of the immortal natures must come from something mortal, and all things would thus end in immortality" (tr. Jowett). Thus group immortality and personal immortality are associated in an inverse order to that in Homer. But who will say which was the earlier concept? Cf. also *Tim.* 41d and *Phaedo* 61a–e, where there appears the theme of men as a flock protected by divinity. My thanks to V. Goldschmidt for having drawn my attention to these passages.

46. Also Tzetzes, *Schol. ad Lycophron Alexandra* 1141: καὶ πάλιν οἱ Λοκροὶ ἑτέρας ἔστελλον.

47. This is undoubtedly the meaning of the expression, as the Scholiast understood perfectly: ὅσαι γὰρ ἀπέθνησκον, τοσαῦται ἀντ' αὐτῶν ἐστέλλοντο ἐν Τρῳάδι παρὰ τῶν Λοκρῶν ("As many as died, so many were sent in their place to the Troad by the Locrians"). "Ebensoviel wie die Toten," was Wilamowitz's translation (*Ilias*, 387). Since the Renaissance the error has frequently been made to render the phrase as "Like the dead." On this subject see the judicious remarks by Reinach, "Origine," 26 n. 3, and Momigliano, "Locrian Maidens," 51.

48. This verb appears in nearly all the Greek texts; the exceptions are Aeneas, who speaks from Ilion and not from Locris, and Polybius, who uses the verb *apostellein*. Servius says *ad sacrificium mitti*, which translates the idea of *pompē*. Nikitskij is probably correct in having restored *pempsein* in line 2 of the *Mädcheninschrift*.

49. I say "one of the traditions" because I am reluctant to use Aeneas's term *sōmata*, as he dubs the Locrian maidens. Undoubtedly the word *sōma*, when used in reference to humans and without an adjective to qualify its meaning, most often denotes slaves, but there are some exceptions (cf. the discussion in P. Ducrey, *Prisonniers*, 26–29). Even within the tradition that has the "young maidens" growing old in Ilion, their status is not clear. For Pseudo-Apollodorus they are "suppliants"; Lycophron and Tzetzes insist on the lowliness of their duties. A. J. Reinach conveyed all that in his use of the word "hierodulie" ("Origine," *passim*).

50. Therefore, among the restorations that have been suggested for line 10,

204   the one that I find most rewarding is by Nikitskij: ἔντε xα [ἐπανέλθωντι]" until
they return."

    51. Cf. Hdt. 4.32–34, commented on by P. Bruneau, *Recherches*, pp. 39–44.

    52. The objection raised by F. Graf ("Mädchen," 66 n. 29) shows that he thought that my intention had been to reconstruct the original contract, but it was nothing of the sort.

Slavery and the Rule of Women in
       Tradition, Myth, and Utopia

To Simon Pembroke

This essay is an attempt to bring together two different approaches. The first is the straightforward use of social history, of the work done in recent years on the category of unfree persons defined by Pollux as "between free men and slaves": *metaxy eleutherōn kai doulōn*, such as the helots of Sparta, the *penestae* of Thessaly, and the *klarōtai* of Crete. The outcome of this work has been well summarized by M. I. Finley: ancient society passed from a state in which personal status was distributed along a continuum, with the free man at one end and the nonfree at the other, to one—the model or ideal type being classical Athens—in which the distinction between citizen and slave was clear-cut, crisp, and absolute.[1]

Of course, if we look only at the Spartiate *homoioi* (peers) and at Athenian citizens, we can maintain, as is often done, that the difference between the democratic city and the one Plato called "timocratic" is merely one of degree. The two types of city (three if we include property-based oligarchies) are founded on the principle of equality, differing only in the number of those who possess full rights. But the case is different if we consider the social formation as a whole.

Developing this argument, I have tried to show elsewhere that the political nullity of the Athenian slave—whom it is totally impossible to

This is an extensively revised version of a study published in C. Nicolet (ed.), *Recherches sur les structures sociales dans l'Antiquité classique* (Paris: C.N.R.S., 1970), 63–80; translated with numerous additions and corrections in L. Sichirollo (ed.), *Schiavitù antica e moderna* (Naples, 1979), 117–36.

imagine demanding the right to hold political office—contrasts with the genuine political activity of the helots and *penestae*.[2] One element of Spartan history, right down to the time of Nabis [r. 207–192 B.C.], is helot rebellions and demands. Plato took the point in the *Laws* (6.777d): "[If the slaves are to be docile] they will not be taken from within the same country (*patriōtas*) nor if possible from the same language community (*asymphōnous*)."

I want here to test these conclusions, not with material from political and social history, but from myth analyzed in the manner championed by Claude Lévi-Strauss. Of course the Greek myths, which have come down to us through a scholarly tradition, require subtle treatment. For the sake of simplicity I shall make a distinction between myths of origin, or myths about the development of order, and legends. In Greece, the former went through three stages: 1) cosmological-cum-social myths, 2) purely cosmological myths, and 3) properly civic myths.[3] By this means each city pictured for itself the transition "in the beginning" from chaos to order and from Nature to Culture. The legendary tradition incorporates mythical elements but is felt and described as historical. The *utopia* stands on the frontier between the mythical and the social, and it concerns us here inasmuch as what it retains is as important as what it rejects. As Lewis Mumford has observed, the Greek utopian writers "could (not) . . . admit, even as a remote ideal, the possibility of breaking down permanent class divisions or doing away with the institutions of war. It was easier for the Greek utopians to conceive of abolishing marriage or private property than of ridding utopia of slavery, class domination and war."[4]

The justification for examining the place of slaves together with that of women is this. The Greek city in its classical form was marked by a double exclusion: the exclusion of women, which made it a "men's club"; and the exclusion of slaves, which made it a "citizens' club." (One might almost say a threefold exclusion, since foreigners also were kept out; but the treatment of slaves is no doubt merely the extreme case of the treatment of foreigners.) It is of course true that these two exclusions are not precisely of the same order. But Aristotle at least granted a connection between the position of women and that of slaves. In a passage dealing mainly with Sparta, he remarked that women make up "half the city" (*to hēmisy tēs poleōs*) and that the lawgiver must therefore bear them in mind; and he went on to compare the different dangers that stem from overindulgence (*anesis*) toward slaves and toward women (*Pol.* 1.9.1269b 7 et seq.). In each case the threat is political in a direct and immediate sense: indulgence toward helots leads them to revolt and to demand equality;

and if women rule the rulers, they therefore rule the city (καίτοι τί διαφέρει γυναῖκας ἄρχειν ἢ τοὺς ἄρχοντας ὑπὸ τῶν γυναικῶν ἄρχεσθαι: 2.9.1269b 33–34). He returns to this question in a discussion of tyranny and democracy (5.11.1313b 32–39). Here the danger is the same but it is less directly and immediately political: laxity toward slaves (*doulōn anesis*) or women's rule in the home (*gynaikokratia . . . peri tas oikias*) leads the democratic city into tyranny—which means neither the rule of slaves nor the rule of women, strictly speaking. Aristotle simply explained that, under tyrants, women and slaves do not conspire because, as under the previous democracy, they are treated with laxity.

It may also be remarked that for Aristotle the distinction between master and slave, as well as that between male and female, were of the same order as the distinction between body and soul, between that which commands and that which obeys (*Pol.* 1.5.1254a34–b16). And elsewhere he commented, "Both a woman and a slave can also be good; but a woman is perhaps an inferior being—and a slave utterly worthless" (καίτοι γε ἴσως τούτων τὸ μὲν χεῖρον, τὸ δὲ ὅλως φαῦλόν ἐστιν: *Poetics* 15.1454a 20–22). The nuance is worth remembering.

Were there traditions in Greece about the rule of slaves or the rule of women? If so, is there any connection between them? On the first point, if we set aside such famous but obscure episodes of Hellenistic history as the "City of the Sun" founded by Aristonicus (Eumenes III) of Pergamum,[5] or the anecdote about Chios reported by Nymphodorus of Syracuse,[6] evidence in myth for the city of slaves (*Doulopolis* or *doulōn polis*) is thin. To a Greek the very expression was of course contradictory. A character in the *Anchises* of Anaxandrides (a writer of Middle Comedies, mid–fourth century B.C.) puts the point succinctly: "Slaves have no city, old man"—Οὐκ ἔστι δούλων ὦγαθ' οὐδαμοῦ πόλις. (F 4 [*CAF* 2.1371] = Athenaeus *Deipn.* 6.263b). There are references in historians, comedians (quoted, unfortunately, only by lexicographers), and paroemiographers to a "city of slaves," a place where all one had to do to become free was to bring a stone.[7] This city is barely distinguished in the tradition from the City of Crooks (*Ponēropolis*)[8] or from the one in which there is only one free man, the priest.[9]

The one interesting feature of these texts is the location ascribed to this city of slaves. Sometimes it is placed in barbarian territory (Egypt, Libya, Syria, Caria, Arabia); sometimes in Crete.[10] And what interested Sosicrates and Dosiadas, who both wrote *Histories of Crete,* was precisely the different terms used for "slaves"—or rather the statuses "between slave and free"—on the island, the place par excellence in antiquity where technical terms of this kind were developed.[11] *Not one text* locates a city of

208   slaves in any part of Greece where slavery in the strict sense existed—
that is, chattel-slavery based on slave-trading. [12] That implies that when
the Greeks wanted to describe a city of slaves they could choose only
between complete marginalization (barbarian countries) and locating it
in a country where a "slave" was not quite a slave. There is a sense in
which Naupactus (founded in the mid–fifth century by helots who had
fled from Messenia) and other cities established by the Messenians, and
Messene itself (refounded in 369 B.C. after Epaminondas's expedition)
might be added to Cretan *Doulopolis*. Yet even when they had become
helots, the Messenians continued to be thought of as Greeks and Dorians,
just like the Spartans themselves. Pausanias claimed not only that they
had not lost their Dorian dialect even after three centuries of exile for
many of them, but also that, in the Empire, it was the purest Doric in the
Peloponnese (4.27.11). The right of these really peculiar "slaves" to a
political existence or revival, a right they repeatedly asserted, could be
legitimated by means such as these. [13]

And what of women? Research in this area has been greatly stimulated
by the work of Simon Pembroke on Greek traditions about "matriarchy." [14] In the last century, Bachofen, followed by Engels and many
others, saw matriarchy as a universal stage in the history of man. Its
"survivals"—such as the institutions of Lycia described by Herodotus
(1.173)—were seen as evidence for an earlier period. Pembroke has
shown that the ancient sources do not stand up to critical examination
and that the Lycian inscriptions, for example, show no trace of a matriarchal system. But he has also explained the logical structure of the
concept of matriarchy itself: whether we are talking about the Amazons
or the Lycians, it is the Greek polis, that men's club, that is being defined
by historians and its "ethnographers" in terms of its opposite. [15] There is a
splendid example of this technique of inversion, or reversal, in Herodotus's statement that the institutions of Egypt are exactly the opposite of
those of the Greeks (2.35). The imaginary polity of the Amazons is the
inverse, set in a precise location, of the Greek city. Lemnos, the island
notorious for its "atrocities," is also characterized as "ruled by women." [16]
The chorus in Aeschylus's *Libation Bearers*, referring to Clytemnestra, [17]
picks up expressions from the *Agamemnon:* the "man-woman" (*Ag.* 10–
11, 350; cf. 259–60) and the "female that kills the male" (*thēlys arsenos
phoneus: Ag* 1231)—human monsters who have failed to pass the barrier
separating savagery from civilization:

The female force, the desperate
love crams its resisted way

on marriage and the dark embrace
of brute beasts, of mortal men.
[599–601; tr. Lattimore]

The word rendered here as "the female force" is *thēlykratēs*, an adjective that can mean both "which conquers women" and "where the female has power"; the first example then given (631–34) is that of the Lemnian women, whose "power" took the form of the murder of their husbands.

However, the tradition does include female power exercised honorably. But the relevant texts speak not of Athens (see p. 216 below) but of Sparta, which was of course the male city par excellence—but also the city Aristotle believed to be threatened politically by a takeover by women, as we have seen (p. 207 above). Plutarch records a famous witticism by Gorgo, wife of Leonidas and, according to Herodotus (5.51), the woman who prevented Cleomenes from supporting the Ionian revolt against the Persians. To a woman who observed, "You Spartan women are the only women who give men orders," Gorgo was supposed to have replied, "Yes, because we are the only women who give men birth" (Plut, *Lycurgus* 14.8; cf. *Apothegm. Lac.* 227e, *de Mul. Virt.* 240e). And it was Sparta, not Athens, that provided Plato's model when he gave women their place in his *Republic*.

In view of all this, it is perhaps worth inquiring whether there was an ancient tradition in any way linking the exercise of power by women and by slaves. I argue that such a tradition did indeed exist, and in at least four forms.

The first is connected with a well-known historical event, the defeat of Argos by the Spartans at the battle of Sepeia, which has been dated variously between 520 and 490 B.C.[18] Our earliest source is Herodotus (6.77, 83), who prefaces his account with a Delphic oracle in verse predicting a drama in which "the female will prevail over the male and win glory among the Argives": Ἀλλ' ὅταν ἡ θήλεια τὸν ἄρσενα νικήσασα ἐξελάσῃ καὶ κῦδος ἐν Ἀργείοισιν ἄρηται. Argos is defeated and loses all its men. "Many Argive women," the oracle proclaims, "will tear at their faces"—that is, will be in mourning. The slaves take control of the affairs of state until the young Argive citizens reach manhood. The "slaves" thereupon flee to Tiryns, whence they are ultimately driven out by the Argives. In this account the two elements, rule of women and rule of slaves, are present but are kept separate: the first occurs in the oracle while the second appears in the historical account. This scheme disappears in the later versions, which no doubt involve an alteration of the original material; but this hardly matters, since my task is not to reconstruct the "facts" but to understand the logic of the myths. What is important is that, even in Herodotus, Argos is an upside-down world, where the female has overcome the male and the slaves are in power.[19]

Plutarch (de Mul. Virt. 4.245 et seq.) gives his own gloss to Herodotus in quoting him as saying that when the city lost its men the "slaves" married the Argive women; he also introduces, from the historian Socrates of Argos, a new character, Telesilla, a poetess. She organizes the women of Argos to defend the city, dressing them up in men's clothes— which later gave them the right to put up a commemorative monument to Enyalios, the god of warriors (245c–e). Most important of all, he says that this episode was the origin of a festival still celebrated in Argos, the Hybristika, which commemorates the women's courage, and in the course of which men and women wear each other's dress (245e–f).

Pausanias's version is different again (2.20.8–9). According to him, Telesilla called upon all those who could take part in the defense of the city—women, old men, young boys, and slaves (oiketai): in other words, all those normally excluded from fighting for the polis.[20]

But who exactly were these slaves? Aristotle's own mention of this "servile interregnum" says nothing of women at all: he observes simply that the Argives "had been forced to admit into the city a certain number of perioikoi": ἠναγκάσθησαν παραδέξασθαι τῶν περιοίκων τινάς. (Pol. 5.3.1303a 6–8). It has been shown that Aristotle generally uses the word perioikoi to mean rural dependants or bondsmen rather like the helots of Laconia.[21] And in fact there can be no doubt but that our sources' Argive "slaves" are to be identified with the occupants of the servile status-category known in Argos as the gymnētai: those who were "naked" by contrast with those who wore the hoplite panoply. Equally important, when Aristotle wants to give a comparable example from Athens, he speaks not of the recruitment of slaves but of hoplites from outside the register—that is the thetes, the citizens of the lowest category in terms of property.

A tradition known from much later texts offers a parallel so precisely conforming to the Argive episodes as to be suspicious. This time we are at Cumae, in Magna Graecia, where in 505–4 Aristodemus made himself tyrant, put to death or exiled the aristocrats, and bestowed their property, their wives, and their daughters upon the slaves who had murdered their masters.[22] That left, according to our principal source, Dionysius of Halicarnassus, only the fate of the male children to be determined. At first, Aristodemus thought of putting them all to death, but after appeals from their mothers, and the latters' new lovers, decided to send them off to the fields to lead servile lives of agricultural or pastoral labor. The world is turned upside-down: the young aristocrats take the place of the "slaves," whom they now serve. So far we can interpret the story in common-sense terms, but what follows is rather odd. These young slaves in the fields are brought up as girls: long curly tresses, kept in a net; embroidered dresses; living in the shade of parasols, with endless baths and perfume (Dion. Hal. *AR* 7.9.4 Jacoby). It is hard not to suppose a ritual comparable to the Argive *Hybristika* or the *Oschophoria* in Athens (see pp. 115–16 above). There comes a time when the "sons"—who seem, as in Argos, to be all of an age—rise in revolt and with the help of the exiles suppress the tyrant (*AR* 7.9.6). It is Plutarch who supplies the dimension of the episode relevant to the theme of the rule of women: Xenocrite, the daughter of an exile, became Aristodemus's mistress, and it was she who persuaded the young men to overthrow the tyrant (c. 491– 90), together with an unnamed women of Cumae who remarked to them that Aristodemus was the sole man (*anēr*) in the city (Plut. *de Mul. Virt.* 26.262c–d).

Here again servile power and female power are linked, the women ensuring the continuity of legitimacy. But it is less easy to say what precisely the "slaves" were, although the "helot-type" is more likely than the "Athenian" type, given that these men seemingly lived in the fields and made an effort to act politically or collectively.

My third example comes from the well-known tradition about the origins of Epizephyrian Locri in Southern Italy, a colony founded by the mainland Locrians, whether Opuntian or Ozolian is unclear.[23] The foundation of the city was the subject of an acrimonious debate, reported by Polybius, between Aristotle (or more probably the author of the Peripatetic *Constitution of Locri*) and the Sicilian historian, Timaeus of Tauromenium. Polybius reports the debate as part of his own polemic against Timaeus.[24] Aristotle said that Locri had been founded by riffraff, runaway slaves and slave-dealers; in reply, Timaeus argued that in the very early period "it was not the national custom of the Greeks to use slaves bought with money."[25] No doubt repeating Aristotle, Polybius then tells the story of how, when the Locrians were the allies of Sparta in the Messenian War (presumably the first war), they were prevented— perhaps by an oath, as in the legend of the foundation of Tarentum (p. 212 below)—from having intercourse with their wives. The wives then turned to substitute husbands, the slaves; and it was these women and slaves who later became the first colonists of Italian Locri. Consequently, hereditary nobility in the colony was derived originally not from the men but from the women: Πάντα τὰ διὰ προγόνων ἔνδοξα παρ' αὐτοῖς ἀπὸ τῶν γυναικῶν οὐκ ἀπὸ τῶν ἀνδρῶν ἐστιν (Polybius 12.5.6). We also know that some of the female founders of Locri belonged to the hundred noble families who had the "privilege" of sending two girls each year to serve Athena of Ilion.[26]

Irenically minded readers will doubtless observe that it is not impossible to reconcile Aristotle and Timaeus, at least in terms of the coherence of the tradition. Certainly a famous inscription, the bronze plaque from Galaxidi [in Ozolian—western—Locris], seems to prove the existence of helotage in Locrian territory at an early date (early fifth century B.C.).[27] The inscription gives the regulations for the colony established by the Eastern Locrians at Naupactus, and prescribes as the penalty for a magistrate who refuses justice to a plaintiff the confiscation of his property, the land itself together with its "slaves" (woikiatai): Καὶ χρέματα παματοφαγεῖσθαι, τὸ μέρος μέτα Ϝοικιατᾶν (lines 43–45). Notwithstanding that Hesychius identifies the oikiētēs (which occurs only here) with the chattel-slave (oikiētēs: ōnētos doulos), there can be little doubt but that the Locrian woikiatas, whose position is linked closely with the citizen's land-allotment, is more like that of the Cretan woikeus: he is in effect a helot. So there is no reason not to accept that in the tradition followed by Aristotle and Polybius, the Locrian "slaves" who married their mistresses were in a category similar to that of the Argive gymnētai.

The women's role is no less important, although Polybius does not say, as has been claimed, that at Epizephyrian Locri nobility descended through the female line: he says simply that originally in the Locrian "nobility" there was a group of women; they were citizens, and many of them of good families, and their husbands were "slaves."[28] He explains by reference to the same tradition the fact that a procession, which he says was taken over from the Siculi, was led by a girl and not by a boy (12.5.10–11).

This connection between female citizens and "slaves" recurs in a legendary tradition whose variants are far more complex, that of the foundation of Tarentum.[29] Although all the sources agree in describing the founders of Tarentum as a minority felt to be undesirable in their country of origin, Sparta, and who were called Partheniai, there were at least three versions. The oldest is represented by Antiochus of Syracuse, a contemporary of Thucydides.[30] He says that during the first Messenian War the Spartans disenfranchised those of their number who had not taken part in the fighting: they were declared slaves (ekrithēsan douloi) and thereafter termed "helots," as were their descendants, the Partheniai. The latter plotted together, but were discovered by the ephors and were then expelled from the city and sent to Italy. This version contains two myths, one about the foundation of Tarentum, the other about the origin of

Spartan "slavery": the original helots are supposed to have been *tresantes* ("tremblers"), those Spartiates who had failed in war and so been disenfranchised.[31]

Strabo rejects this version in favor of one followed by the fourth-century historian Ephorus and consequently by many others, whether directly or indirectly.[32] The Spartans were at war with Messenia and had sworn not to return home until they were victorious. But the war dragged on and the next generation could not be born. It was decided that the young men, who had not taken the oath, should return home to Sparta and all of them should have intercourse with all the young women (*parthenoi*) so far as possible: συγγίνεσθαι ταῖς παρθένοις ἁπάσαις ἅπαντας.[33] It was the offspring of these promiscuous unions, *who knew their mothers but not their fathers*, who received the name *Partheniai*. In other words, the *Partheniai* were the result not of normal marriage but of a sort of original scramble.[34]

The third and simplest version is analogous to that of the foundation of Epizephyrian Locri: while the Spartiates were away fighting, their wives slept with their slaves, and the *Partheniai* were the resulting bastards.[35]

There are some further texts that are not quite parallel to any of these versions. A rather elliptical passage of Aristotle seems to suggest that the *Partheniai* suffered from some kind of political discrimination without there being any question about their birth (*Pol.* 5.7.1306b 27–31).[36] To make things even more complicated, a fragment of Diodorus Siculus published in 1827 (8.21) gives a composite account of a rebellion that occurred in Sparta after the First Messenian War.[37] The most important group of rebels were the *epeunaktai*, who are defined by Hesychius as *synkoimētai*, "bedfellows"; they were responsible for the plot and later got in touch with Delphi in order to found a colony. The other group was the *Partheniai*, who came to terms with Sparta as soon as the conspiracy was discovered. It is tempting, but unprovable, to suppose that the second are the sons of the first.[38] They are often confused, all the more easily in view of Hesychius's equivalent for the very similar word *epeunaktoi: Partheniai*. But Theopompus does explain the identity of the *epeunaktai* (although he calls them *epeunaktoi*): they were helots who during the Messenian War—he does not say which one—took the place of the dead Spartiates, not in their marital beds but "on their beds in camp": *epi tas stibadas*.[39] It is important to understand that in the myths relating to Sparta, a slave could substitute for a citizen in his basic duty, that of fighting.

Although these versions are very different, they have one constant: the women ensure the continuation of the population. In short, the *Par-*

theniai are the sons of young *women* before they are the sons of *men*. The versions disagree only about the identity of their fathers, and yet as a whole they are quite coherent. In the first case (Antiochus) they are cowards, in the second (Ephorus) *young* men, in the third (Heracleides) "slaves": and, perhaps, for Aristotle, political inferiors. In the first case they are made distinctive by a moral judgment; in the second by their place in the system of age-classes; in the third by a social judgment; and in the fourth by their places in the political hierarchy. The variants have a common theme: the fathers of the *Partheniai* both are and are not of the city—they are *marginal*. Exactly the same was true of the Argive "slaves" and of the husbands of the women who founded Locri; the normal hierarchy is inverted.

Other texts on the foundation of Tarentum make this inversion explicit, although it is unfortunate that they are often contaminated by traditions about the foundation of Rhegium.[40] An oracle is said to have advised the founding fathers to settle where they saw a she-goat mounting a buck,[41] or where they saw rain falling out of a clear sky (Paus. 10.10.6).[42] Both are ways of suggesting an inverted world. The parallel texts about Rhegium explicitly direct the founder, Antimedes of Chalcis, to a place where he saw "the male mounted by a female"[43]—which takes us right back to the oracle Herodotus says was given to the Argives (p. 209 above).

All the same, this topsy-turvy world, which gives extraordinary prominence to women and to "slaves," is an imaginable one. Whereas at Athens the exceptional use of slaves in war was logically followed by their emancipation,[44] in Sparta there was nothing unusual about helots fighting—as in the case of Theopompus's *epeunaktoi* (cf. Hdt. 9.29, Thuc. 4.80, etc.). Similarly, the Code of Gortyn provides for the possibility of a marriage between a male slave and a free woman: "If the slave (*dōlos*) goes to the free woman and marries her, their children will be free; but if the free woman goes to the slave and marries him, their children will be slaves."[45] Moreover, although in the classical period Spartiate marriage-rules did not explicitly permit such liaisons, they at least gave both husband and wife the right to take a substitute partner (Xen. *Lac. Pol.* 1.7–8). And there was at Rome, in a religious context, an association between slaves and women: at the *Saturnalia* masters (*domini*) served their slaves (*servi*), while at the *Matronalia,* wives were honored by their husbands and prepared a feast for their *male* slaves[46]—yet another detail that makes archaic Rome look more like Sparta than Athens.

It was inconceivable in Athens that an Athenian woman might marry a slave, and in general the Athenian attitude toward marriage was much stricter.[47] With the exception of the special case of heiresses (see p. 155, n. 55 above), marriage in Athens involved the transfer of a young woman from one *oikos* to another. In Sparta, on the other hand, well-known texts indicate that a Spartiate woman could belong simultaneously to two households (Xen. *Lac. Pol.* 1.7–8; Plut. *Lycurgus* 15). Even crisis measures were different: a tradition that may go back to Aristotle says that when there was a scarcity of men, the law permitted male citizens to get children by a *citizen* woman other than their wife.[48] It was naturally only a matter for citizens—there was no question of the law allowing the recruitment of substitute husbands from among the metics or the slaves, even though the metics regularly served in the army.

A good illustration of the contrast here between Spartiate and Athenian practice is provided by Herodotus's parallel accounts concerning the island of Lemnos, one of which relates to the Spartans, the other to the Athenians (4.145; 6.137–38). In the first, some descendants of the Argonauts and the women of Lemnos come to Sparta, saying that they are the indigenous Minyans (that is, from prior to the Pelasgians); the Spartiates welcome them and exchange wives with them. But the strangers turn arrogant, and it is determined to put them to death. The "Minyans" are then saved by their wives, who change clothes with them, and they escape to the mountains dressed as women.[49] Eventually they become the colonists of Thera. In the other story, the Pelasgians have been expelled from Athens for insulting the daughters of the Athenians. They move to Lemnos and in revenge take with them some Athenian women whom they use as concubines. The women bring their children up according to Athenian ways, speaking Attic Greek, and in the end are massacred with their children.[50] The story is plainly an inversion of the Spartan one; at Sparta marriage with foreigners leads to colonization, while in Athens concubinage with foreigners leads to destruction—to one of the versions of the "crime of the women of Lemnos." And the value judgments in the two societies are symmetrically inverse.

At least after the law of 451 B.C., marriage in Athens stands midway between two equally repellent extremes. One extreme is of course incest: "Can a bird that eats bird's flesh be pure?" asks Danaus in Aeschylus's *Suppliant Women* (226). The other is revealed by Theseus's outrage at an Argive who on the advice of an oracle from Apollo had married his daughters to a boar and a lion, two wild animals, to Tydeus and Polyneices, foreigners both:

Theseus: To strangers, then, you wedded Argive girls?
Adrastus: Yes—Tydeus and Polyneices, of Theban stock.

Theseus: How did you come to want them for your kin?
Adrastus: Puzzling riddles of Phoebus lured me on . . .
that I give my daughters to a boar and a lion . . .
Theseus: They were beasts? You gave your girls to them? . . .

Theseus: First, bowing to Phoebus's words, like one who thinks
the gods exist you gave your girls to strangers:
A mating of fair with foul to hurt your house!
Wrongdoer's bodies should not be joined to the just . . .
[Euripides, *Suppliant Women* 135–45, 219–24, tr. F. W. Jones]

As a traditional place of refuge—even if only for the Neleids of Pylos supposed to have fled there before going on to settle in Ionia[51]—Athens did of course have some myths very similar to those of Sparta. But in the classical period there is not a word about marriage with a foreign male, and the democracy put an end, at least in principle, to the inverse process, marriage between an Athenian citizen and a foreign woman (which had been very common among the aristocrats), by the law of 451.

Although it is found only in late sources, we can reconstruct one myth to tell us about two matters, the origin of male democracy and the origin of Athenian marriage.[52] According to Varro (quoted by St. Augustine, *Civ. Dei* 18.9), in the time of Cecrops there occurred a dispute between Athena and Poseidon as to which of them should be patron of Athens. An oracle told the king to put the choice of patron divinity to a vote among all the inhabitants, including women, "for at that time it was customary in those parts for even women to have their say in public votes" (*mos enim tunc in eisdem locis erat ut etiam feminae publicis consultationibus interessent*); and because there were more women than men, the choice fell on Athena. The men took their revenge by deciding that "from henceforth the women of Athens shall not vote; that children shall no longer be known by their mother's name; that the women shall not be called 'women of Athens.'" Thus in the classical city there are no "women of Athens"— only the wives and daughters of the "men of Athens." That remains the case even in the comedy that reverses their roles: in the *Thesmophoriazusae*, Aristophanes speaks of the *dēmos* (people) of women, and of the council of women, but never of the *dēmos* of the women of Athens (335–36, 372–73).[53] The second decision is explained by those texts that make Cecrops the inventor of marriage.[54] Cecrops's usual epithet "double-natured" (*diphyēs*) was normally explained by saying that he was part man, part animal; but these texts account for it by saying that, as the inventor of marriage, he taught that each man had both a father and a mother.

According to Clearchus, before that sexual unions took place at random and no one knew who his father was, which implies that individuals were known by their mother's name only. So Cecrops's role here is that of a culture hero—and indeed the scholiast on Aristophanes' *Plutus* (773) says as much: "he brought the Athenians out of savagery to civilization" (ἀπὸ ἀγϱιότητος εἰς ἡμεϱότητα ἤγαγεν). The rule of women in Varro's report (the women not only vote, they are in the majority) thus corresponds to the state of nature, to the original scramble. We have already seen that the same features recur in the accounts of the foundation of Tarentum; but what is "in the beginning" for Tarentum is at Sparta part of "history" and is used to legitimate a number of actual practices in society.

The passages just discussed do indeed tell us about the Athenian account of the origin of marriage and the exclusion of women from the body politic, but they have nothing to say about the connection—or inversely, the distinction—between the status of women and that of slaves. And it is on this point that Athens can be seen to be the exact opposite of Sparta or Locri.

It will be clear from what I have already said that in a topsy-turvy world like that of the legends about the First Messenian War, slaves' getting above themselves might occur with a temporary tracing of descent through the female line. Now in the late fifth century B.C., classical Athens also had its topsy-turvy worlds, above all in Aristophanes' utopian comedies. The hoopoe in the *Birds* has a bird slave and when Euelpides expresses surprise at this, the slave tells him, "I think he likes to be reminded he was a man" (70–75). In *Lysistrata* the women take over the Acropolis (345 et seq.) and at once the theme of topsy-turvydom makes its appearance in an oracle (which recalls Herodotus's Argive oracle):

> When all the Swallows gather into one place, eschewing the
> Hoopoe-birds and their amorous pursuits, then is come the end of
> all Evils, and it is ordained by Zeus the Thunderer that the low shall
> be exalted over the high (*ta d'hypertera nertera*).
> [770–73; tr. Dickinson][55]

All the same, Lysistrata at one point calls for a Scythian archer, and slaves appear on several occasions (18, 184, 241).

But of course my best evidence here comes from the *Ecclesiazusae*. The play is based upon a double transvestism, first that associated with the festival of Athena Skiras (the *Skiraphoria*), when women dressed up in beards (18, 25, 38, cf. p. 115 above), but also the comedy's own: the

218   Athenian women disguise themselves as men in order to vote themselves into power in the Assembly. The communist system they start is presented as the fulfillment of democracy and involves the sharing of all wealth visible and invisible, including slaves. It is forbidden that some should have much and others nothing at all. But of course the land itself will be worked by slaves—while their masters relax and wait for their dinners (593, 602, 631, 651–53; cf. *Plutus* 510). Now all this is reasonably familiar; perhaps less so are the sexual implications of this feminist-communist democracy. For the women propose to equalize sexual opportunity (944–45)—for the young citizens, naturally: of male slaves, not a word. In contrast, the female slaves are expressly excluded from citizen-amours; they have to make arrangements with male slaves (725–27).

Aristotle's point remains true then: there *is* some difference between women and slaves (cf. p. 207 above). An Aristophanic utopia can put women on top, just as Plato later can set them almost on the same level as men. But chattel-slaves are simply not part of the city at all. And I would say that myth, legendary tradition, and utopias as well respected this state of affairs even though it was of recent date.[56] A myth accounts for the reduction of the status of women in Athens to being one brick in the wall between savagery and disorder on the one hand, and civic order on the other. But the distinction between free men and slaves simply was not a "problem" of this kind. On the other hand, in archaic societies (of which Sparta is the best known), the situation is different. Slavery was understood there as having an origin in history (I have discussed one of the traditions in this connection, but there are many others), and on many occasions the status of women and the status of slaves are seen as linked. Each occupies a variable position on the continuum between the free and the nonfree.

I began by observing that Athens and Sparta can be seen as logical opposites; I hope this study serves to reinforce the point.

NOTES

1. M. I. Finley, "Between Slavery and Freedom," 249; cf. also D. Lotze, *Metaxy.*

2. "Économie et société," 127–49; and "Were Greek Slaves a Class?," p. 162ff. above; cf. C. Mossé, "Rôle des esclaves," which I found very useful.

3. Cf. J.-P. Vernant, *Origins.*

4. "Utopia," 277; cf. Finley, "Utopianism," 178–92.

5. On this point, see L. Robert, *Villes,* 264–71; J.-C. Dumont, "Aristonicos," 189–96; Finley, "Utopianism," 183–84.

6. In Athenaeus, *Deipn.* 6.265c–66e; cf. "Were Greek Slaves a Class?," pp.
166–67 above; and, for an attempt at a historical interpretation of this affair, A.
Fuks, "Slave Wars" (whose conclusions are quite dubious.)

7. Hecataeus of Miletus *FGrH* 1 F 345 (from Stephanus of Byzantium). See
also Cratinus F 208 (*CAF* 1, p. 76, quoted by Stephanus of Byzantium); Eupolis
F 197 (*CAF* 1, p. 312, quoted by Hesychius); Ephorus, *FGrH* 70 F 50 (quoted in
the Suda); Mnaseas of Patrae, quoted in the *Appendix proverbiorum* 3.91, *s.v. mē eni
doulōn polis* (*Corpus paroem. gr.* ed. Leutsch and Schneidewin, 1, pp. 433–34 =
FHG 3, p. 155, F38); Sosicrates, *FGrH* 461 F 2 (quoted by the Suda); Pliny *HN*
5.44; Olympianus, quoted by Stephanus of Byzantium, *s.v. doulōn polis* (237
Meinecke); Apostolius 6.35 (*Corpus paroem. gr.* 2, p. 371 *s.v. doulōn polis*). Most of
these references are to be found conveniently in three lexica, *s.v. doulōn polis:*
Hesychius, 437 Schmitt; Stephanus of Byzantium, 237 Meinecke; the Suda, no.
1423, 2, p. 133 Adler.

8. Pliny *HN* 4.41; Plut. *de Curiositate* 10.520b; this was a fabulous city,
supposed to have been founded by Philip of Macedon in Thrace.

9. Hecataeus *FGrH* 1 F 345.

10. Our source, Ephorus (*FGrH* 70 F 29, from Athenaeus *Deipn.* 6. 263 et
seq.) says that around the town of Kydon there were festivals in which no free
man could enter the city and "the slaves are in control of everything" (*hoi douloi
pantōn kratousi*). We also have the information from Stephanus of Byzantium.

11. Sosicrates *FGrH* 461 F 4; Dosiadas *FGrH* 458 F 2–3; cf. Vidal-Naquet,
"Économie et Société," 128 n. 46.

12. Possible counterexamples are the slave camp on Chios mentioned by
Nymphodorus (see Fuks in n. 6 above), or the slave kingdom set up in the second
century B.C. round Enna in Sicily; but these were institutions created by slaves,
not "cities" described as servile.

13. See "Reflections on Greek Historical Writing about Slavery," p. 183
above.

14. See Pembroke, "Last"; "Women"; "Locres" (which deals with the traditions concerning Epizephyrian Locri and Tarentum). His arguments are not
affected by the dissertation by K. Hirvonen, *Matriarchal Survivals*, which anyway
ignores them.

15. See now M. Rosellini and S. Saïd, "Usage des femmes."

16. See the texts assembled by Dumézil *Lemniennes*, at least one of which uses
the term *gynaikokratoumenē* ("ruled by women") in connection with Lemnos:
Apollodorus, *Bibliotheca* 1.9.17.

17. On Clytemnestra in Greek tragedy as the usurper of male powers, see J.-
P. Vernant, "Hestia" (in *Myth and Thought*) and F. I. Zeitlin, "Misogyny."

18. There is a vast, although often worthless, literature on this topic. There
are, however, two useful articles I may mention: S. Luria, "Frauenpatriotismus,"
and R. F. Willetts, "Interregnum" (as well as a summary of the problem in R.
Crahay, *Littérature*, 172–75). This text of Herodotus, and many other parallel
ones, including several of those discussed here, have now been dealt with by my

220   friend David Asheri in "Mariage forcé." His common-sense perspective is very different from my own, but his full collection of evidence may allow a reexamination of the problem. Let me also mention the (often misdirected) criticisms of my article by R. Van Compernolle, "Doulocratie."

19. See R. F. Willetts ("Interregnum," 502): "It is well to bear in mind that *hē thēleia ton arsena nikēsasa* [the female victorious over the male] represents a proverbial idea for topsy-turvy conditions."

20. However, he also quotes Herodotus's oracle at 2.20.10.

21. Willetts, "Interregnum," 496.

22. The major sources are Dion. Hal. *AR* 7.2–12, esp. 7.9.1–11.4 Jacoby, and Plut. *de Mul. Virt.* 26.261e–62d. [Further references are to be found in H. Berve, *Tyrannis* 2.611, although his discussion (1.160–63) is not illuminating.] See now D. Asheri, "Mariage forcé," 22–23.

23. See the discussion by L. Lerat, *Locriens* 2.22–25; he favors the western (Ozolian) Locrians.

24. Polyb. 12.5–11; the passage of Timaeus appears as *FGrH* 566 F 12. An account similar to Polybius's (i.e., Aristotle's) is given by the scholiast to the second century A.D. geographer, Dionysius Periegetes, 366 (= *GGrM*, 2, p. 495 line 30). See F. W. Walbank, *Commentary* 2 *ad loc.;* and especially Pembroke, "Locres," who subjects these texts to careful scrutiny; and also Sourvinou-Inwood, "Votum," 188–94. The long analysis by R. Van Compernolle ("Tradizioni") loads the rules of positivist history on the tradition in Aristotle and Polybius in order to deny it any value; his study does not overlap mine.

25. More or less the same expression occurs in Athenaeus, *Deipn.* 6.264c; 272a (=*FGrH* 566 F 11).

26. The essential document is the inscription "of the Locrian maidens" (reprinted in Schmitt, *Staatsverträge* 3, no. 472), brilliantly elucidated by A. Wilhelm, *Die Lokrische Madcheninschrift*. See "The Immortal Slave Women of Athena Ilias," p. 189ff. above.

27. Reprinted in Meiggs and Lewis, *Selection* no. 20 (pp. 35–40); they strangely omit the important commentary in *IJG* 1.180–92 (no. 11). See also L. Lerat, *Locriens*, 29–31 and 141–42—which I am close to here.

28. The point is firmly established by Pembroke, "Locres"; he also shows that no support for matrilineal descent in Locris can be derived from the epigram in *Anth. Pal.* 6.265 (= 2801–2 Gow and Page). L. Lerat also found not the slightest trace of matrilineal filiation among the Continental Locrians (*Locriens* 2.139–40).

29. Sources and bibliography are to be found in P. Wuilleumier, *Tarente,* 39–47; J. Berard, *Colonisation,* 162–75. I have relied heavily on Pembroke's discussion of this tradition ("Locres," 1241–49). See also M. Corsano, "Sparte et Tarente."

30. *FGrH* 555 F 13 from Strabo 6.3.2; cf. "Reflections on Greek Historical Writing about Slavery," p. 177 above.

31. Hdt. 7.231; Plut. *Agesilaus* 30, *Lycurgus* 21.2; cf. Loraux, "Belle Mort," 105–20.

32. Ephorus *FGrH* 70 F 216 from Strabo 6.3.3. Among the many imitators of Ephorus, whether direct or indirect, see especially: Polyb. 12.6b.5; Dion. Hal. 19.2–4; Justin 3.4.3–11.

33. Similar expressions occur in Justin: *promiscuos omnium feminarum concubitus* (indiscriminate couplings by [or with] all the women); and Dionysius of Halicarnassus: ἐκ τούτων γίνονται τῶν ἀδιακρίτων ἐπιμιξιῶν παῖδες (sons were born from these indiscriminate couplings). Note also Servius *ad Vergil. Aen.* 3.551: *sine ullo discrimine nuptiarum* (there were no rules at all in these sexual encounters)—but he makes the fathers slaves.

34. On such practices in Herodotus, see M. Rosellini and S. Saïd, "Usages," 955–66, 995–1003.

35. Scholia ([Acron] and Porphyrion) on Horace *Odes* 2.6.12; Servius *ad Vergil. Aen.* 3.551; *ad Vergil. Eclog.* 10.57; Heracleides Ponticus *Peri politeiōn* 26 (in *FHG* 2.209) = Aristotle F 611.57 Rose.

36. Aristotle has just been emphasizing the dangers facing oligarchies "when the mass is composed of men who are ambitious to be equal [to their superiors] in valor": ὅταν ᾖ τὸ πλῆθος τῶν πεφρονηματισμένων ὡς ὁμοίων κατ' ἀρετήν. "For example, in Sparta, the group called the *Partheniai*, who were descendants of the *homoioi* and whom the Spartans sent to Tarentum after catching them in a conspiracy": Οἷον ἐν Λακεδαίμονι οἱ λεγόμενοι Παρθενίαι (ἐκ τῶν ὁμοίων γὰρ ἦσαν) οὓς φωράσαντες ἐπιβουλεύσαντας ἀπέστειλαν Τάραντος οἰκιστάς. The sense of the expression ἐκ τῶν ὁμοίων here is unclear. As well as "descendants of the *homoioi*" it could mean "who belonged to the *homoioi*," but that would make the passage meaningless. On my interpretation, it may be regarded as just compatible with Ephorus's account and even with that of Antiochus of Syracuse.

37. Another passage in Diodorus (15.66) more or less follows Ephorus. Justin 3.5, which is parallel to Diodorus 8.21, refers explicitly to the Second Messenian War.

38. Commentators on this passage usually confuse them; credit for distinguishing them must go to Pembroke, "Locres," 1245–47.

39. Again, for the argument see Pembroke, "Locres."

40. See G. Vallet, *Rhegium,* 68–77; J. Ducat, "Récits"; N. Valenza Mele, "Hera," especially 512–17, which restates and sharpens the conclusions drawn here; similarly, D. Musti, "Locri."

41. Cf. Dion. Hal. 19.1.3–2.1 (Jacoby); the buck-goat motif is gradually bowdlerized to a (male) wild-fig tree enveloped by a (female) vine.

42. The "clear sky" is Aithra, the wife of the founder of Tarentum, Philanthos. She weeps while holding her husband's head in her lap (Paus. 10.10.7).

43. Diod. Sic. 8.23.2; Heracleides Ponticus, *Peri Politeiōn* 25 = *FHG* 2.220; Dion. Hal. *AR* 19.2.

44. Aristophanes, *Frogs* 694–95 with scholia; Lycurgus, *Against Leocrates* 41; cf. L. Robert, *Études,* 118–26; Y. Garlan, "Esclaves grecs"; K. W. Welwei, *Unfreie.*

45. *Opuien,* which in the language of the Athenian comedy-writers means

something like "to fuck," is in the Code of Gortyn the technical term for the marital union. The exact status of the *dōlos* has been the subject of endless discussion, since the laws of Gortyn mention another slave, the *woikeus*, who is, everyone agrees, similar to the Spartan helot. H. van Effenterre concludes that *dōlos* indicates the juridical aspect and *woikeus* the social aspect of the same individual (*Crète*, 92); Finley, developing a point of Lipsius's, argues for the simple equivalence of the two ("The Servile Statuses," 168–72). The latest editor of the code, R. F. Willetts, is more hesitant: "the word *dōlos* is sometimes synonymous with *woikeus* and sometimes denotes a chattel-slave" (14); a *dōlos* could, for example, be purchased in the agora (col. VII. 10). My own conclusion is that by the time the Gortyn Code was written down, social reality had altered (in particular because of chattel-slavery), but the vocabulary had not followed suit exactly.

46. The texts are Macrobius, *Saturnalia* 1.12.7; Johannes Lydus, *De Mensibus* 3.22 (Wunsch); Justin 43.1.3–5 (for the Saturnalia); and Macrobius and Johannes Lydus *ibidem* (for the Matronalia); cf. Dumézil, "Roman Religion," 2.618.

47. See J.-P. Vernant, "Marriage."

48. Diogenes Laertius 2.26; Athenaeus *Deipn.* 13.556a–b quoting the *Peri Eugeneias* ("On Good Birth") attributed to Aristotle; Aulus Gellius, *Noctes Atticae* 15.20.6, 18, 21. On this matter see J. Pépin in P.-M. Schuhl (ed.), *Aristote*, 123–25; on the authenticity of the "decree" quoted by Hieronymus of Rhodes, see A.R.W. Harrison, *Law*, 1.17. Athenaeus and Aulus Gellius, but not Diogenes Laertius, speak of a second marriage. [The reference is to Athens.] D. Asheri ("Mariage forcé") is mistaken in adding to this list an excerpt from the second discourse on slavery by Dio Chrysostom (15.3). According to this rhetorical text, during a period of *oliganthropia* some Athenian women had children whose fathers were foreigners, but such children were not citizens.

49. Dumézil regarded this myth as the etiology of a Spartiate ritual with a procession and disguise (*Lemniennes*, 51–53); see also Pembroke, "Locres," 1266.

50. Dumézil (*Lemniennes*, 11–12) sees here an etiology for a ritual of separation and initiation. My own interpretation is not intended to be exclusive, I am simply trying to stress why this account is Athenian.

51. For an analysis of these legends, see M. Sakellariou, *Migration grecque*.

52. Most of this reconstruction is owed to Pembroke, "Women," 26–27 and 29–32.

53. See N. Loraux, "Le nom athénien" in *Les Enfants d'Athéna*.

54. Clearchus quoted by Athenaeus, *Deipn.* 13.555d (= *FHG* 2, p. 319, F 49); Justin 2.6; Charax of Pergamum (*FGrH* 103 F 38); John of Antioch in *FHG* 4, p. 547, F 13.5; Nonnus of Panopolis, *Dionysiaka* 41.383; scholia on Aristophanes, *Plutus* 773.

55. See Willetts, "Interregnum," 496.

56. It is not possible to say exactly when. It was a process that ended only with

Pericles' law of 451. Clearly, it we could credit all "Laws of Solon" quoted by Plutarch, one could point to an implicit contrast between two passages in the *Solon* (21.4 and 1.6), between the provision of the law on wills that disqualifies the testator who acts "under the influence of a woman" (*gynaiki peithomenos*), and the law that forbids slaves to oil themselves for exercise in the gymnasium or to practice pederasty with citizen minors. This second restriction is twice repeated by Plutarch (*Convivium* 152d, and *Amatorius* 4.751b). There is an epigraphic parallel, for in the inscription concerning the "Mysteries of Andania" (*Sylloge*[3] 736, line 109 = Sokolowski, *Lois sacrées* no. 65), there occurs the expression *doulos de mētheis aleiphesthō:* "no slave may oil himself."

These "Laws of Solon" are not to be trusted, but they do provide a good illustration of the text of Aristotle cited earlier. It is true that Plutarch said immediately afterward in the *Amatorius* that Solon "did not forbid sexual relations between slaves and (free) women"; but this negative affirmation, if I may call it that, is not to the point here, because the context shows clearly that for Plutarch himself it was merely a matter of an inference drawn by Protogenes in the dialogue, not of a tradition believed to be ancient.

A Study in Ambiguity:
Artisans in the Platonic City

The subject of this essay is the status of artisans in Plato's final political construction, the *Laws*, and at first glance it does not appear at all ambiguous. A passage from Book 8 seems to be as clear and categorical a statement as one could ask for: "This is the principle by which we must control that which pertains to men following skilled professions [*dēmiourgoi*]. In the first place, let no *epichōrios* [i.e., no citizen of Magnesia] devote his efforts to artisanal [demiurgic] activities; neither let any servant of *epichōrios* do so" (Laws 8.846d).[1] Plato immediately justified his law by explaining that no one can practice two professions at once. To be a citizen is a profession, which is to cultivate virtue (ἡ τῆς ἀρετῆς ἐπιμέλεια: *Laws* 8.847a); it is exclusive of any other. Thus Plato's law is twofold, affecting both artisans and citizens. In no case may citizens be artisans. Those who break the law are to be subjected to public outrage (*oneidos*) or civil disgrace (*atimia*), which are the gravest moral sanctions at the city's disposal. As for the artisans, they are forbidden to pursue two professions at the same time, either directly or indirectly, under pain of being fined or exiled. To put it another way, a blacksmith cannot simultaneously be a carpenter; nor is he allowed to be an entrepreneur in carpentry, with others working wood for his profit (*Laws* 846e–47b).

The first version of this chapter was published in B. Vincent (ed.), *Les Marginaux et les Exclus dans l'histoire*, Cahiers Jussieu 5, Paris, U.G.E., coll. 10–18, pp. 232–61.

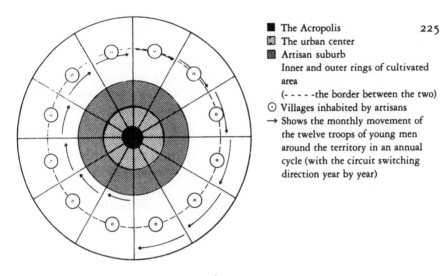

■ The Acropolis
▩ The urban center
▨ Artisan suburb
  Inner and outer rings of cultivated area
  (- - - - -the border between the two)
⊙ Villages inhabited by artisans
→ Shows the monthly movement of the twelve troops of young men around the territory in an annual cycle (with the circuit switching direction year by year)

Fig. 3. The Spatial Organization of the City of the *Laws*

This passage contains no surprises. A. Diès quite correctly refers the reader of his edition of the *Laws*[2] to two parallel passages in the *Republic*. In Book 2 Plato established the principles of what has been called division of labor, which I prefer to call division of trades.[3] "Of course the farmer himself will not make his own plow, if it must be well made, nor his mattock, nor his other agricultural tools; neither will the mason make his own tools, and he too needs many; the same is true for the weaver and the shoemaker" (*Rep.* 2.370c–d).[4] In Book 3 the philosopher returned to the principle of the single profession by advancing once again the rule of quality: "Has not this question been decided by the rule already laid down that one man can only do one thing well, and not many; and that if he attempts many, he will altogether fail of gaining much reputation in any?" (*Rep.* 3.394e; tr. Jowett) The result is that in the Platonic city, unlike the Athenian republic in its greatest years, "the shoemaker will be a shoemaker and not a pilot too; the farmer will be a farmer and not a judge in addition; the soldier will be a soldier and not also a businessman; and so throughout" (*Rep.* 397e).

Among the characters who meet in Plato's dialogues, there was one, Protagoras, who vigorously propounded the opposite point of view. He was required to explain how it is that in a city like Athens the opinion of a carpenter or a blacksmith or shipowner carries political weight without anyone's intervening to protest their lack of expertise (*Protag.* 319d).

Protagoras based his reply on the famous myth he recounts in the dialogue that bears his name: in addition to the *technai* uniquely his own—in fact there is only one skill for each person—every one of us has received a portion of *technē politikē,* political skill, as a gift from Zeus to men (*Protag.* 322c). In the words of G. Cambiano: "Only one skill, different from that of the artisans, can assure the required cooperation that makes possible the social use of the other skills with the advantages they imply. That is political *technē.* Such is the central hypothesis of the myth told by Protagoras."[5] It must be added that the theory developed by Protagoras serves as the basis for democracy, that is, the very thing that Plato rejects.

For Plato's Protagoras the democratic city possesses an educational function beneficial to all.[6] Compared to an uncivilized man, an educated man—even if a criminal—looks like an artisan (*dēmiourgos*) of justice (*Protag.* 327c). Let us set aside for the moment the equivocal use of the word that denotes an artisan. We will return to it later. Plato's solution in response to Protagoras is well known. If everyone is to carry on his own business within the city, it is appropriate that activities be separated. In the *Republic* artisans and farmers[7] form the third class, or, to put it in Dumézilian terms, they represent the third function in the model city (warriors being the second and philosophers the first). We may proceed to the *Timaeus* and the *Critias,* to the preface and the main text respectively, where Plato claimed to set the city of the *Republic* (*Tim.* 19c) in motion and put it into history; the crucial difference is that the gods take the place of philosophers at the city's helm. Plato promptly reaffirmed the principle of the single profession (*Tim.* 17c–d); and one notes without the least surprise that, in the primitive and mythic Athens of the *Critias,* the Acropolis is dominated by the sanctuary of Athena and Hephaistos and is occupied solely by warriors (*Critias* 112b).[8] The farmers and artisans have to content themselves with the periphery.

If I now turn to what is customarily called the literature on the subject, I will not gather much that is new. In his great treatise of quasi-historical sociology devoted to the *Laws,* G.E.R. Morrow provides only one short chapter in which he paraphrases the passage that served as our starting point and compares the lot of the artisans with the more exacting one of the merchants. In a book addressed to *Platone e le tecniche,* G. Cambiano's treatment of the *Laws* does not go much farther; he merely notes that in this dialogue, "the artisan continues to be more appreciated than the merchant and the slave, but he enjoys no rights of citizenship and exercises no power in the city."[9] Picking up the vocabulary of the *Protagoras,* he adds that the *technē politikē,* which had been restricted to the possessors of wisdom in the *Republic,* is henceforth distributed among all citizens (i.e., all landowners). [10] Finally, M. Piérart—who joins many others in trying to compare "theory and reality" in the *Laws*—gave our passage a brief chapter whose purpose is to compare artisans in Plato with those, little understood, in Gortyn. [11] For all their ingenuity, such efforts do not bring us much closer to Plato's final position on the subject of the artisans' role within the city.

Of course there is one question that all commentators on Plato have had to confront: the brutal contrast between the social standing of the artisans and the metaphorical status of artisanry. Whenever Plato wishes to cite an activity correctly defined in its goals, he refers, directly or indirectly, to artisanal activity. [12]

At a level that goes beyond the metaphorical, the weaver was explicitly singled out by Plato as the paradigm of the political person, someone who possesses the science of government (*Pol.* 305e). [13] Plato had already eliminated the seemingly "natural" exemplar of the shepherd. Indeed in the *Laws* it is explained quite forcefully that politics is a matter of *technē* and not of nature (*physis*) (*Pol.* 275b–c; *Laws* 10.889d–e). Nonetheless, the king is set in opposition to the whole class of professionals, including the weaver: "In the city all the arts that produce an object (*dēmiourgousi*) either great or small must be classed among the secondary skills. Without them, to be sure, there would be neither *polis* nor politics, but on the other hand there is no aspect of the art of ruling that we can attribute to them" (*Pol.* 287d). [14] It is paradoxical that the philosopher uses the weaver as a model for the king, for in Greek anthropology weaving is an essentially feminine activity; [15] one of the closest parallels to Plato's text is the famous speech in which Lysistrata explains that the art of politics and the art of weaving a cloak for the people are one and the same (*Lys.* 574–87). [16]

I will come back later to another artisan who has also occasioned speculation, the demiurge in the *Timaeus*. However, in spite of the value and interest of several general and particular studies that qualified this position, Plato seems to take a place of honor in the broad current of Greek thought that denies any mark of nobility to demiurgic activity. Thus Edgar Zilsel observed that—Pheidias, Apelles, and Zeuxis notwithstanding—antiquity considered "the tongue, not the hand, as inspired by the gods"—*nur die Zunge, nicht die Hand als göttlich inspiriert*. [17]

But isn't this rule at least partially the result of an optical illusion? A recent book has rediscovered an almost forgotten mental category that pervades the entire history of Greek culture; it might be called "cunning intelligence"—*mētis*. [18] The gesture of the artisan, whether potter or weaver, is as surely an expression of *mētis* as is the near-feral cleverness of the hunter, the scout, the fisherman, or the young soldier lying in ambush. Plato has his place in the story of *mētis,* and the authors of this book adduce the example of Eros in the *Symposium:* like any number of the intermediaries that mark an area between the apparent and the ideal, Eros is one of the grandchildren of Metis, the goddess swallowed by Zeus. [19] But when the discussion turns to the long concealment of *mētis* and to understanding why "in studies of the Greeks pursued by scholars who claim to be their heirs, there has been a prolonged silence on the subject of the intelligence of cunning," it is still Plato who is held responsible, if it is true that "the concept of Platonic truth, which has overshadowed a whole area of intelligence with its own kinds of understanding, has never really ceased to haunt Western metaphysical thought."[20]

And yet one cannot repeat too often that the vast majority of Platonic writings do not describe the universe of forms but our world. On closer examination the passages about artisanship, despite their seeming transparency, should have spawned a bit more uncertainty. The uncertainty should have begun,[21] in some rare cases did begin, with the two key terms *technē* and *dēmiourgos.*

Technē is certainly one of the most ambiguous, flickering terms in the Platonic lexicon. Plato is aware of it in the *Cratylus,* when he pretends that its etymology is from ἐχονόη (*hexis nou*), the fact that reason is innate in us (*Crat.* 414b)—thereby giving the word an elevated interpretation. This does not stop Plato, at the "culmination of this dialogue," from moving straight from *technē* to *mēchanē,* from art to artifice (*Crat.* 415a)[22]—that is, to the most humble kind of *mētis.* As G. Cambiano justly observes, "in the Platonic view, *epistēmē, dynamis* and *technē* comprise a system of concepts that mutually reinforce and define one another."[23] The *Republic,* for example, puts under the control of mathematics a unit composed of *technai, dianoiai,* and *epistēmai:* skills, intellectual processes, and sciences. Among the skills is that *technē polemikē* (*Rep.* 7.522c), art of warfare, whose very existence signals the turning point of the dialogue. It is precisely because war is a profession that Plato separates its practitioners, who will be the guardians of the Republic, from those who pursue other occupations—those other occupations that will be proscribed for citizens in the *Laws* (*Rep.* 2.374a–d).

The word *dēmiourgos* has a complex history in Greek. In the course of an evolution that we can trace from Homer on, it sometimes designates the highest magistrates of certain cities—often but not always Dorian—and sometimes the artisan personnel.[24] For our purposes it is not very interesting that a professional grammarian like Hesychius[25] notes as a curiosity the two meanings of a word whose etymology derives from "the one who concerns himself with the *dēmia*, things having to do with the *dēmos*."[26] It is much more striking to see how Gorgias, and Aristotle after him, played on the two senses of the term: there are the makers of mortars and, at Larissa, there are "demiurges" who are makers of citizens (Ar. *Pol.* 3.1275b 29 et seq.).[27] Thus in the fifth and fourth centuries there was an awareness of the linguistic ambiguity. Indeed, the Platonic *dēmiourgos* is surely the technician, the artisan as such—rhapsode, physician, painter, or sculptor,[28] all persons who share a craft linked to the material world; but the *dēmiourgos* is also the Creator in the *Timaeus,* as well as the Lawgiver in the *Cratylus* and the *Laws:* "Surely the artisan who is to be deemed worthy of any regard at all ought always to make his work self-consistent" (*Crat.* 389a; tr. Jowett).[29]

The use of this word in the passage from the *Laws* with which we began is all the more impressive since another term was available to denote "artisans" in the strict sense; that is, the adjective *banausos* (and the substantive *banausia*) whose pejorative connotation is vivid.[30] For example, Plato uses the latter word, in conjunction with *dēmiourgia,* in a passage in the *Republic* where he explains that philosophy is pursued by many people whose occupations have rendered them unfit for the task; their bodies have been deformed by their work in crafts and professions (ὑπὸ δὲ τῶν τεχνῶν τε καὶ δημιουργιῶν), and their souls have been ruined by artisanal occupations (συγκεκλασμένοι τε καὶ ἀποτεθρυμμένοι διὰ τὰς βαναυσίας: (*Rep.* 6.495d–e). *Dēmiourgia* debases the body, but it is the soul that is injured when a person is a *banausos.* Perhaps the distinction deserves some emphasis, since it shows that Plato's use of the word *dēmiourgos* is not entirely innocent.

But it is time to establish our demiurges in the land of the city of Magnesia in Crete. It is impossible, however, to approach the problem directly. Because it is essential for the argument, we must first recall how Plato locates the citizens in the city-state; the citizens are the owners of, or rather those who have been assigned to (*geōmoroi*), the five thousand forty lots into which the civic territory has been divided, with a man and his allotment forming a partnership (γενόμενα ἀνὴρ καὶ κλῆρος συννομή: (*Laws* 5.737e). At the center of the land lies the city proper; both it and the plain (*chōra*) are then subdivided into twelve sections (*merē*), to which there is added a thirteenth reserved for the gods: Hestia, Zeus, and Athena, who will occupy the central acropolis (*Laws* 745b–c). Each section is simultaneously allotted to one god and to a twelfth of the population, called a *tribe,* with some effort to allow for the varying quality of the land; the individual lots, in turn, are divided in two. The point is to apportion the occupied land in two concentric zones, one around the city and the other extending out to the borders. Plato says that, "everyone shall have two habitations, one near the center and the other near the edge of the territory" (*Laws* 745e).[31] Thus the allotments will be near the urban habitation at one place and, at the other, the rural settlement situated on the country's frontier. This arrangement will do as much as can be done to nullify the separation between city and countryside and to ensure the intense unity of the city-state, both *asty* and *chōra*.[32]

Still, this system concerns only the citizens, and the city of Magnesia is not inhabited solely by its citizens and their dependent women, children, and slaves. Let us turn again to Book 8 and to the instructions Plato gives after he has discussed the distribution of the fruits of the land "by the Cretan method," among all inhabitants: citizens, their families and slaves, artisans and foreigners in general, whether in residence (as metics) or simply passing through. For foreigners, and for them alone, a market must be established (*Laws* 8.847e–48c).[33]

Plato then moves on to the problem of housing: Τὸ δὲ μετὰ τοῦτο αὐτοῖς οἰκήσεις δεῖ χωρὶς διατεταγμένας εἶναι (*Laws* 848c 6), which Robin translates correctly as "What we must discuss next is the separate residences that should be assigned to the people." The word *autois* does not refer only to the citizens;[34] the preceding phrases certainly refer to the population as a whole. To say that Plato is concerned here only with housing for the citizens is to claim that he has forgotten that he already dealt with the basic problem in Book 5; cf. G. R. Morrow: "There is a lack of clarity here, however, which suggests that these details had not been worked out fully in Plato's mind."[35] But nothing in the text requires that we accuse Plato of senility. What does he say next? There are to be twelve villages (*kōmai*);[36] one in the center of each of the twelve districts into which the land has been divided (*Laws* 8.848c 7). The villages lie halfway between each citizen's allotted properties near the city and near the border.

Within each village, just as in the central city, the first area to be marked off is public and religious, for the temples and the agora; this allows for the organization of the cult of the principal deities (Hestia, Zeus, and Athena), the cult of Magnesia's own gods, and that of the patron god of each district (i.e., of each tribe) (*Laws* 848d). On the high ground around the temples, houses are to be erected that will also serve as fortifications to be used by the garrison (*Laws* 848d–e). The troops on active duty are the only citizens to reside (albeit temporarily) in the villages. Plato specifies that settlement of all the remaining territory (τὴν

δὲ ἄλλην χώραν κατασκευάζειν πᾶσαν: *Laws* 848e) will be accomplished
by dividing all the artisans into thirteen units (*merē*), with one in the city
being distributed among the twelve segments of the citizen population
(εἰς τὰ δώδεκα μέρη τῆς πόλεως ἁπάσης: *Laws* 848e 5).[37] These artisans
are not to live in the actual urban center, but around the periphery in a
suburban ring (καὶ ἐν κύκλῳ κατανεμηθέντας . . . : *Laws* 848e 5–6). The
twelve other groups will take up residence "in every village," where
"those sorts of craftsmen useful to the farmers" (τὰ πρόσφορα γεωργοῖς
γένη τῶν δημιουργῶν: *Laws* 848e 6–7) are to be settled. As a result, the
villages situated in the center of each district will have a permanent
population made up of artisans. Thus as one moves from the center
toward the periphery, one will encounter in succession:

1. the political and religious center (rather more religious than
political); the zone reserved for the sovereign deities;
2. the city as such, divided into twelve sections corresponding to
the twelve tribes;
3. the "suburbs," also divided into twelve sections and occupied by
one of the thirteen demiurgic units;[38]
4. the first set of properties allotted to all the 5040 citizens and
corresponding to their urban residences;
5. twelve villages, set in a corona around the center of the territory,
occupied by the gods and citizen-soldiers but inhabited too by artisans, the latter thus being made useful to the farmers both in their
urban and their frontier residences;
6. a border zone forming the outermost ring, where each citizen
will possess a country house.[39]

Thus the artisans—a mobile group if ever there was one—are tied
down. Like the Athenian metics, they live "in the demes," but they are
not demesmen. There can be no doubt that by such an arrangement Plato
wished to stress the dependency of this social group. Some symmetries
are too obvious to be overlooked. There are twelve tribes that share the
territory, but the gods occupy a thirteenth location in the very heart of
the country. The artisans themselves are also divided into twelve groups,
plus one that encircles the city: the divine center is counterbalanced by
the demiurgic suburb.

At this stage of our discussion we have verified D. Whitehead's claim
that Plato accomplished what Athens had been unable to do—to concen-
trate absolutely all technical activity in the hands of noncitizens. But
Whitehead is also right in adding the qualification that it is too simplistic to characterize the philosopher as an enemy of the artisans.[40] After
all, they do surround the city.

I think we will obtain a clearer understanding of the artisans' installation within the cityscape if we compare them to another group, whose position Plato established in Book 6. They are the guardians of the *agros*, the *agronomoi*, who can be likened to Athenian ephebes and whom Plato himself compared to Spartan youths in *krypteia* (Laws 6.760b–63c).[41] The young men are recruited from among the *neoi*, the 25- to 30-year-olds in Plato's system (*Laws* 6.760c), and they form twelve units, since there are twelve tribes. Every tribe will make an annual selection of five "wardens," and each such group in turn will enlist a dozen young men. Thus there will be a total of one hundred forty-four *neoi*.[42] But the function of these tribal representatives is to negate the tribe, inasmuch as it represents spatial fragmentation, and to embody the space of the city-state as a whole. Each squadron (in the military sense of the term) spends one month in every sector so that within the year it makes a thorough tour of each sector of the *chōra*—one year in one direction, and one year in the other. The squads pay particular attention to the frontier zone (*Laws* 760e) and thus become a mobile defense around the fixed centers outlined above. Again, the parallels are striking: the mobile artisans are set in a fixed place, while the *neoi*, destined to become the elite of the city, are temporarily put in motion. Plato has linked the two groups. Those in charge of the *agronomoi* also make decisions about the artisans in the *chōra*, "determining how many of them, and of what type, each place requires; and where they are to live so as to be least annoying and most useful to the farmers" (*Laws* 8.848e–49a). The urban artisans are under the jurisdiction of the head magistrates (*astynomoi*).

Plato can now determine the position of the metic in his city. In fact, a metic *is* an artisan, because he must already have a profession in order to settle in the city. Unlike the Athenian metic, he does not pay a residency tax, but he is not permitted to remain for more than twenty years without special dispensation. A metic's son is subject to the same regulations: he too must have a *technē*, and his twenty-year sojourn begins at the age of fifteen (*Laws* 850a–b).[43]

At this point in my discussion the reader might well ask why I spoke of the *ambiguity* of the artisan's status. But Plato addresses precisely this question in Book 11 of the *Laws*, and this passage seems to have the sole purpose of contrasting merchants and artisans. Against the former all conceivable precautions are to be taken. Not one of the five thousand forty land-holders is allowed to work for someone inferior to him. But by

far the most servile profession is retail trade (*kapēleia*), which only metics
will be allowed to engage in (*Laws* 11.919d–e).

When Plato now reconsiders the case of the *dēmiourgoi* (*Laws* 920d–
22a), he speaks of them in terms very different from those he used in Book
8. "To Hephaistos and Athena is dedicated the class of artisans whose
combined skills have organized our lives"; to Ares and Athena are dedicated the other practitioners of the *technai* that have to do with military
matters or the construction of fortifications. Let us pause for a moment at
the tutelary divinities, the triad of Hephaistos, Athena, and Ares. Athena has a mediating function, which is explained by the fact that her
character is both technician and warrior, and warrior because of technical
ability.[44] But the pair that Plato puts in charge of the artisans is also the
one that dominates the city in the *Timaeus* and the *Critias*—and that
requires our attention. The artisans are thereby in parallel with, and to
some extent contrasted to, the warrior function. But what does the
warrior function consist of? Here Plato's use of language is extraordinary,
for the military consists of οἱ τὰ τῶν δημιουργῶν σῴζοντες τέχναισιν
ἑτέραις ἀμυντηρίοις ἔργα— "those who, by means of other skills[45] with
a defensive purpose, ensure the preservation of the products made by the
artisans." The purpose of the "warrior function" is thus to protect the
work of the artisans, and so a parallel can be drawn between artisans and
soldiers. Both are *dēmiourgoi* in the etymological sense of the term (no
matter that the etymology is false), in that both serve the people: Οὗτοι
δὴ πάντες χώραν καὶ δῆμον θεραπεύοντες διατελοῦσιν— "All these continue through life serving the country and the people" (*Laws* 11.920e; tr.
Jowett). Plato goes so far as to compare *agōn* and *misthos,* the citizens'
battle on behalf of their country and the artisans' salary (*Laws* 920e 5–6).
An amazing passage. It seems that, in speaking about the artisans, Plato
was aware of the importance of their role in a city like Athens and was
defending them against his own principles.[46] In any event, he drew
certain conclusions from his introduction. He set up the artisans' rights
and duties: they have the duty to carry out their tasks to perfection, and
they have the right to be paid. (They even have the extraordinary right to
collect interest if payment is delayed!) The artisans' salary is placed under
the protection of Zeus *poliouchos* ("protector of the city") and of Athena,
for these gods are partners (*koinōnous*) in the Constitution (*Laws* 921a–
b).[47] Once again there appears the comparison with soldiers, all the more
peculiar because the soldiers of the *Laws* are not professionals like those of
the *Republic*. Here the soldiers are called *dēmiourgoi* of defense; whether
common troops or specialists they form "another class of artisans" (οἷον
ἑτέροις οὖσιν δημιουργοῖς: *Laws* 11.921d 5). Yet another comparison

234   reappears: the soldiers' *timai* (honors) are their *misthoi* (salary) (*Laws* 921e
1). The warrior and the artisan become an inseparable pair. The former
protects the work of the latter and, as a citizen and the possessor of a
technē, becomes his alter-ego. As for the artisan, he cannot receive more
stirring praise than to be compared to the warrior. The marginal figure
we were considering at the beginning of this essay has practically become
a central actor in the city-state of the *Laws*. Thus the aforementioned fact
that the very author of the Constitution—Plato himself—can compare
himself to a demiurge no longer comes as a shock.

From these observations, I think we can go much farther in uncovering
a little known facet of Plato's thought. We can even formulate hypotheses
that apply to the whole of Classical Greek civilization.

Let us return to the *Timaeus* and the *Critias*. Mythical Athens is
consistent with the outline in the *Republic,* but Plato did introduce two
important; characteristic variations. The first has to do with the spatial
and chronological framework of the two groups of dialogues. The encounter described in the *Republic* takes place in Piraeus, the symbol of
democratic and mercantile excesses, on the feast day of Bendis, a Thracian goddess. Plato noted at the outset that there are two processions, one
Athenian and the other Thracian (*Rep.* 1.327a–28b). The settings of the
Timaeus and *Critias* are not specified, but the date is the "panegyric" of
the goddess (*Tim.* 21a), that is, the Panathenaea, the prototypical Athenian festival, conducted under the patronage of Athena Polias. In Critias's own narrative he mentions an epic poem that has been recited to
him on the day of the Apaturia (*Tim.* 21b), a festival that is Ionian and
especially Athenian. A fragment from the Atthidographer Istros informs
us that during the sacrificial rites of the Apaturia the Athenians staged a
torch-race (*lampadophoria*) in honor of Hephaistos the Firebringer (*FGrH*
334 F2).[48] Hephaistos is not the only god involved in the Apaturia, but
the comparison we have just made becomes meaningful if we recall that
Athena and Hephaistos, the artisans' patrons in the *Laws*, also possess
and preside over the Athens of early myth (*Critias* 109c).[49] The great
innovation of the *Republic,* a separate caste of philosopher-kings, is missing from the *Timaeus* and *Critias*. The summary of the *Republic* recognizes
only one category of guardians; according to Plato, their soul is "philosophical to the highest degree" (*Tim.* 18a), but they do not have to go
through the *cursus* of the apprentice philosopher. In mythic Athens the
place of philosophers is taken by divinities: Athena, both warrior and
philosopher (*Tim.* 24c), and above all the pair of Athena and Hephaistos.

Plato says that the latter couple unites *philosophia* and *philotechnia* (*Critias* 109c), the latter word being a Platonic coinage of high significance. Of course the pairing itself is not Plato's creation, since it appears in the myths of Erichthonius and of Pandora.[50] What is important is that Plato has countered Atlantis, where *technē* runs wild, with the example of a just city wherein *technē* also reigns but is controlled by a goddess who is philosopher, warrior, and technologist. We can be still more precise. What is the temple of the two deities that Plato sets on the peak of the Acropolis (*Critias* 112b)?[51] He is certainly not thinking of the Parthenon, the Erechtheion, or any of the other buildings that adorned the Acropolis of his day. Can we not assume that Plato transposed the Hephaisteion, now wrongly called the Theseion, from the hill overlooking the Agora where it still stands? According to Pausanias, it used to house a statue of Athena side by side with that of Hephaistos (Paus. 1.14.6).[52]

But let us proceed to the principal character in the *Timaeus*, the demiurge himself,[53] and begin with the well-known facts. He is father, *ho gennēsas*,[54] which is to say that he conforms to the Hesiodic model in which creation occurs through sexual union. But this father does not have a consort, and Plato does not spend time on this role. Like the legislator in the *Laws*, the demiurge is a founder and colonizer of cities. It is he who places the human soul on the Acropolis and the choleric spirit "at the sentinel's post" (*Tim.* 69d–70b)[55] and so on.

The demiurge is above all an artisan in the proper sense of the term, and L. Brisson's detailed analysis has shown that he uses all the artisanal techniques available in Plato's time: smelting and metallurgy, iron-working and welding, the craft of the carpenter and the potter, painting, wax-working, weaving, and agriculture.[56]

All that is clear enough. What is less understood, in my opinion, is that all these skills form a meaningful hierarchy. It is startling to see how consistently Plato makes the demiurge use what we would call "state-of-the-art" technology to create the elements that are most important in the aforementioned hierarchy. At the peak of creation, the world-soul is produced by the finest metallurgy, with its techniques of refining, alloying, even lamination (*Tim.* 35a et seq.). The human body, by contrast, is produced by the relatively less complex work of the potter (*Tim.* 73e). The altogether humble tasks—such as the implantation of the soul in the body, deployment of the circulatory system, or grafting of skin onto the body—are consigned to the level of agricultural technique (*Tim.* 41e, 73c, 76c, 76e, 77c, 91c).[57]

At this point a serious problem arises,[58] for Greek tradition contains numerous texts that make the farmer superior to the artisan.[59] In his own way Plato shared this outlook. He certainly said that *geōrgia* (farming) is a *technē* (*Euthyd.* 291e, for example). True, artisans and farmers are together in the third class of the *Republic* and in the lower orders in the *Critias* and the preface to the *Timaeus,* but it is different in the *Laws.* The citizen of Magnesia is not a professional soldier, although praise of the soldier is obsessively linked with praise of the artisans. The citizen is an individual land-holder, and we have seen how the artisans were located in the city so as to be useful to the *geōrgoi.* It is true that Plato almost sneaks in the observation that, strictly speaking, agricultural labor is confined to slaves (*Laws* 7.806d–e), but this simply reveals that the difficulty lies at the heart of the *Laws* or within the very word *geōrgos;* throughout Greek history the word simultaneously denotes both the person who owns land and the person who tills it.

If my argument holds, there seem to be two value systems colliding within Plato's writings. The one, to some degree official and public, links the self-affirmation of the citizen to possession and cultivation of land and thus privileges the *geōrgos* over the *dēmiourgos.* The other is covert (although it comes to the surface in the *Timaeus* and the *Laws*) and presents the activity of the artisan—like Prometheus's or Hephaistos's—as the center of human action and its highest exemplar. Given the dramatic relation between Plato and his age, this is not the first time such a tension can be discerned.[60]

What we can actually read, through Plato, is the drama of the artisan in Greek civilization. To repeat what I have already said:[61] in this civilization the artisan is the hero, albeit a hidden hero.[62] From the epic poems sung by the ἀηδοῖ, those "demiurges" mentioned in the *Odyssey* (*Od.* 17.385), to the creations of sculptors, there are hardly any great works of Greek culture that are not, in one way or another, demiurgic. Doctors are *dēmiourgoi.* The builders of the Erechtheion are *dēmiourgoi,* the citizens, metics, and slaves commemorated in a famous set of inscriptions. All this Plato conveyed in making the creator of the world an artisan on a colossal scale. Why then was there such a deep chasm, in the Classical age, between the social and political personae of the artisan? The gap existed, and it becomes visible as one tries to define its dimensions; take, for example, the case of the architect, who is unquestionably an artisan in his own right, yet is separated from other artisans because he is also a magistrate and the designer of civic space.[63] It is obvious that the gap, such as it was in the Classical age, is itself the product of a history. That *technē* has a history is clear to all, but *mētis*—that mental category that, as we have seen, includes the artisan's gesture—also has a history of its own. It is remarkable that in the ten centuries from Homer to Oppian, "The entire semantic field within which the concept of *mētis* is set, and the network of its various meanings has remained virtually unchanged."[64] This does not mean, however, that the social role of the man, or god, with *mētis* also remained unchanged. The full story ranges from Chiron (whose name derives from *cheir*, "hand"), the mythical centaur who, on the edge of the wilderness, tutored young heroes, to the fifth-century *cheirourgos*, the doctor who also had to use both his hands.[65] Detienne and Vernant have demonstrated it convincingly: in archaic mythology, one of the necessary conditions for sovereignty is possession of *mētis* (as, for example, in the thunderbolts forged by Zeus by the giant blacksmiths, the Cyclopes).[66] Neither does artisanal *mētis* mar the character of a Homeric king like Odysseus. Of course he is not a demiurge, but he did construct his own bed. Against Polyphemus he is a man of *technē*, and when he stabs the Cyclops' eye with a stake that he himself has carved, his action is metaphorically that of a carpenter and a bronze-smith (*Od.* 9.387–94).

But what, in the Classical period, was the situation in Athenian democracy? Occasional, even frequent, comment has been made about a rise in the artisans' social standing,[67] but it seems that such a depiction actually disguises the confusion of several levels.

It is perfectly true that in the fifth century—in a work like that of Democritus, but also in Aeschylus's *Prometheus*, in Anaxagoras, and many others as well—we can see an acknowledgment of the decisive role of *technē* and artisanal skill in the historical liberation of man from the constraints of nature.[68] But there is an abyss between recognizing the importance of technology—by saying for example, as Anaxagoras did, that "man is the most intelligent of the animals because he has hands"[69]—and recognizing artisans as a social group holding independent political power, subject to increase or diminution in the course of political and social struggles. What evidence, then, could we adduce? Not much. We may disregard Plutarch's story that Theseus first divided the Athenian populace into three groups: Eupatridae, Geomoroi, and Demiourgoi (the latter characterized primarily by their number) (Plut. *Theseus* 25). A well-known passage from Aristotle's *Constitution of Athens* says that in 581–80 a compromise sorted the ten archons into three units: five Eupatridae, three Geomoroi, and two Demiourgoi (*Ath. Pol.* 13.2). Nothing, however, is more dubious than the historicity of this episode; L. Gernet has proven that it emerges directly from fifth- and fourth-century theorizing.[70] One piece of evidence, admittedly speculative, remains. This is the ideal city—the first of the genre according to

238   Aristotle—of the talented Hippodamus of Miletus, who envisioned a city of ten thousand citizens divided into three autonomous and equal sections: artisans, farmers, and soldiers (Ar. *Pol.* 2.1267b et seq.). This is indisputably an intellectual breakthrough that goes well beyond political and social reality.

In fact even the theorists of democracy are a long way from basing it on the class of artisans. This is true for Protagoras, the greatest of such thinkers, and thanks to Plato, the least obscure. In the myth discussed earlier,[71] he justifies the fact of democracy, which is that every artisan can be relied on to give his opinion in political affairs. Protagoras does not place the foundation of democracy on the possession of *technai* but on the superior qualification of *technē politikē.*

No city of the Classical period thought of itself as a city of artisans, nor did it think of artisans as a group or an independent entity. What did the Athenian artisans have in common? Perhaps one festival, the *Chalkeia,* celebrated in the month of Pyanopsion (October). We know very little about it. Was it a festival for all Athenians or just for artisans? Was it dedicated to Athena, to Hephaistos,[72] or to both? Our sources fail us, and it is difficult to pass final judgment.[73]

Athens did have a district called Ceramicus, just as Corinth had its potters' quarter. No matter what Medieval comparisons spring naturally to mind,[74] we have never found, and never will, a collective action with political goals staged by the potters of Athens or Corinth. In Archaic or Classical Miletus there was never an *Arte della lana;* there did exist a guild of musicians, the *Molpoi* (*Sylloge*[3] 57; 272), but it is not the same thing.

Far from the artisans' participating in the direction of the city, even a democracy, it is the city that exerts control over artisanal activity. In the city of Thasos, for example, a crucial role was played by trade in wine bottled in amphorae. Y. Garlan and M. Debidour have recently offered a conclusive demonstration that, at the end of the fourth century and the beginning of the third, the famous "amphora stamps" were not potters' marks but seals issued to each artisan by a magistrate; the latter was probably the *keramarchos,* who supervised all the workshops on behalf of the city. In sum, this is a phenomenon like coinage, and some of the aforementioned stamps are borrowed from monetary emblems.[75] On the other hand, there is to the best of my knowledge one instance in Greek historical writing, and one alone, of a planned *concerted* revolt, in which there participated, if not artisans as such, a subordinate segment of the population whose weapons were the tools (*organa*) of artisans. At the dawn of the fourth century, Cinadon planned to upset Spartan institutions from top to bottom, and he explained to the person who would eventually inform on him, "All tools which are used for work in agriculture, forestry, or stonework are also weapons, and most of the other industries, too, use implements which are perfectly good weapons" (Xen. *Hell.* 3.3.7; tr. Rex Warner).

What conclusion can we draw from a comparison of Homeric man and the citizen-soldier of fifth-century Athens? Values compatible with the royal function are marginalized, if not discarded. Pericles, as strategos, does not have available to him the *mētis* of Odysseus. The techniques of night warfare, ambush, and the hunt are relegated to the ephebe, the prehoplite period of life.[76] There does exist one area where *technē* triumphs, where its link with *mētis* is clearly perceived: naval warfare, in which imagination has free rein and where space does not impose the traditional rules of combat,[77] but the Athenian sailor is a technician only for the duration of a campaign, and the values of hoplite battle continue to dominate ideology. Only in the fourth century, in the time of Plato and Xenophon, did *mētis* join with the technical ability of the mercenary to reclaim its primacy in the plan of battle.[78] But this triumph of a certain type of technician had no effect on the political and social role of the class of skilled workers, precisely because this class never constituted a political force.

We might borrow from S. Moscovici[79] one of the concepts that will enable us to think the problem through. Indeed we must make a distinction between two levels: that of the history of nature, i.e., the relation between man and the material world of which he is part; and that of social history, covering the human classes and groups that come into contact with each other. These two levels are far from being wholly congruent. What can we say about Greece? In terms of the history of nature, there is certainly an artisanate, whose importance one would have to be blind not to see. But the major invention of the Greeks, the city-state and its concomitant political activity, also causes the abasement of artisanal activity. The same men who work side by side on the site of the Erechtheion, for equal pay[80] (no matter here who was the *real* beneficiary of the slave's salary), resume, when they leave, their ranks as citizens, metics, or slaves. Those who were united at the technical level find themselves separated at the political level. Sometimes the Athenian vase-painter will indicate the difference between the free artisan and the slave artisan; for example, he can attach to the portrait of the artisan the signs of athletic activity that above all denote liberty.[81]

Greek civilization could, so to speak, live out such a contradiction without being aware of it, but the greatness of a body of work like Plato's lies in bringing it to light. One of the ironies of the history of ideas is that

240   Plato, that "reactionary" aristocrat, sometimes passes for a feminist, which he certainly was not, but, in advance of Aristotle he had simply observed that women comprise half of the city and he had drawn conclusions more radical than those his disciple would formulate.[82] In likening artisans to women I am not indulging in a simplistic comparison.[83] The Greek woman and *technē* share a reciprocity that is extremely ancient. Is not Pandora constructed by Hephaistos (Hesiod, *Theog.* 571, *WD* 61)?[84] In Homer, doesn't Thetis teach metalworking to Hephaistos (*Il.* 18.395 et seq.)?[85]

In Book 10 of the *Republic* Plato seems to remember the claim in Euripides' *Medea* that women are *tektones sophōtatai*, "expert artisans" of evil; he describes the posthumous fate of Epeios, the famous artisan who built the Trojan Horse, as "taking the form of a woman artisan" (εἰς τεχνικῆς γυναικὸς ἰοῦσαν φύσιν) (*Rep.* 10.620c).[86] Plato was even less an admirer of artisans than he was a feminist, even if he did declare that the person who sings about the beauty of a bed is farther removed from the Form than the person who constructs the bed (*Rep.* 10.569b et seq.); yet Plato did understand that while poets might perhaps be driven out of the Republic, it is much more difficult to expel the artisans.[87]

NOTES

    1. For my understanding of the *Laws* I owe a great deal to the translation by L. Robin and A. Diès.

    2. 91 n. 1.

    3. Cf. M. I. Finley, "Aristotle," 27–28.

    4. The overall Greek tradition emphasizes the quality of products and not their quantity; Plato took exception to this view in only one passage, saying that "things will be made in greater quantity, and of better quality, and more easily, if everyone makes only one kind of thing" (*Rep.* 2.370c). This is certainly an extraordinary insight, and I am grateful to G. Salviat for having pointed this passage out to me, but it cannot erase the fact that in the whole of his work Plato argues like the other Greek thinkers; that is why I speak of the division of trades rather than the division of labor, as do G. Cambiano (*Tecniche*, 170–201) and many others. I will have more than one occasion to refer to this important book, at times with other criticisms.

    5. G. Cambiano, *Tecniche*, 16.

    6. Cf. G. Cambiano, *Tecniche*, 19–21.

    7. Plato grouped them together but distinguished them clearly from one another. Hence one should respect the distinction and not, like Chambry, for example, translate *Rep.* 2.371 as "laborers and other artisans" but as "farmers and artisans as well"; the same applies to *Tim.* 17c.

8. See "Athens and Atlantis," p. 269 below.

9. G.E.R. Morrow, *Cretan City*, 139–48; G. Cambiano, *Tecniche*, 244. There is a good chapter on the artisans as foreigners in the *Laws* in D. Whitehead, *Metic*, 129–35.

10. Cambiano, *Tecniche*.

11. M. Piérart, *Platon*, 41–47.

12. For the metaphors, see P. Louis, *Métaphores*, 203–7; for the direct use of technical references, Cambiano's book provides a full catalogue.

13. On the concept of the paradigm, see V. Goldschmidt, *Paradigme*.

14. The weaver is mentioned in *Pol.* 288b.

15. Cf. L. Gernet, "Ancient Feasts," 42 n. 118, and "Law and Prelaw," 163. Gernet draws on the Code of Gortyn 2.51, 3.26.

16. Cf. J. Taillardat, *Images* no. 684, and N. Loraux, "Acropole comique," 171, 191–92.

17. E. Zilsel, *Geniebegriff*, 27; my thanks to M. I. Finley for having drawn my attention to this book.

18. M. Detienne and J.-P. Vernant, *Mètis*. To the literature on *mētis* one should now add L. Kahn, *Hermès*.

19. *Mètis*, 144; cf. Symp. 202b–4c.

20. *Mètis*, 317–18. The second part of the quotation reproduces the last sentence in the book, but I have taken the liberty of shifting it from the interrogative to the affirmative.

21. In addition to G. Cambiano, *Tecniche*, mention should be made of the article by P. de Fidio, "Demiurgo," and the first chapter of the book by L. Brisson, *Même et Autre* (27–106). There are also useful observations in H. Joly, *Renversement*.

22. N. Loraux called my attention to this passage, which is one of the turning points of the *Cratylus*.

23. G. Cambiano, *Tecniche*, 90–91. On the semantic field that includes *technē* and *epistēmē*, the principal work is J. Lyons, *Structural Semantics;* its analyses ought to be completed with a consideration of the concept of *mētis*.

24. Out of the considerable bibliography, I note especially K. Murakawa, "Demiourgos," whose conclusions are taken up by L. Brisson, *Même et Autre*, 88–97; F. Bader, *Démiourgos*, esp. 133–41; P. de Fidio, "Demiurgo," 234–40.

25. *S.v. dēmiourgos;* cf. F. Bader, *Démiourgos*, 133.

26. F. Bader, *Démiourgos*, 136; Bader convincingly refutes the traditional interpretation of "the one who works for the people."

27. Other examples in Aristotle of the demiurgy as a political institution are *Pol.* 4.1291a 33, 5.1310b 22. A special case is the difficult passage in Plato's *Republic* (4.433d) where it is a question of that virtue, justice, which is to be found in all who do their own work and participate in the city: καὶ ἐν παιδί καὶ ἐν γυναικὶ καὶ δούλῳ καὶ ἐλευθέρῳ καὶ δημιουργῷ καὶ ἄρχοντι καὶ ἀρχομένῳ— "In a child, a woman, a slave, a free man, *an artisan*, the ruler and the ruled." The order of the words poses a problem that is not resolved by eliminating the

mention of slaves (as is the opinion of C. Despotopoulos, "Esclavage"). Before the free men, Plato naturally mentions those who are provisionally or definitely excluded from citizenship: women, children, slaves. The location of the *dēmiourgos*, after the free man but before the ruler, is what creates the problem. P. de Fidio also cites *Rep.* 1.342e, where rule and demiurgy are associated ("Demiurgo," 238).

28. Cf. *Ion* 531c, *Protag.* 327e, *Rep.* 7.529e for rhapsodes, doctors, and painters and sculptors, respectively.

29. The legislator is defined as the artisan who appears most infrequently among men; cf. V. Goldschmidt, *Cratyle*, 147. The quotation above is from *Laws* 5.746d; cf. the commentary on this passage by G.E.R. Morrow, "Demiurge."

30. Cf. P. Chantraine, "Artisan," where *banausos, dēmiourgos,* and *cheironax* are compared and contrasted.

31. The first sentence is a summary of 745c–e.

32. On this passage cf. J.-P. Vernant, "Space," 231–33.

33. I am summarizing this very difficult passage, which I do not claim to have understood in all its details.

34. A. Diès translates, "Après cela, il faut disposer, pour les citoyens, des habitations séparées" (After that, it is necessary to arrange separate dwellings for the citizens). His whole interpretation of the passage is a web of imprecisions. In his translation for the Penguin Classics, T. J. Saunders writes, "Next, the population should have houses grouped in separate localities."

35. *Cretan City*, 126.

36. By no means twelve neighborhoods ("quartiers") which is Diès's absurd translation.

37. I understand the passage as follows: the urban artisans form twelve groups, each of which is assigned to one of the tribes represented in the city and representative of the city as a whole. Plato did not identify the official who divides the artisans into thirteen groups. In Athens the polemarch distributed the metics into ten units, corresponding to the number of tribes (Ar. *Ath. Pol.* 58).

38. Bisinger, *Agrarstaat*, 72, conjectures that Plato was inspired by the existence of a suburb of Gortyn, the Latosion, which was reserved for freedmen and foreigners and the like (*I.C.* 4.78). This idea has been adopted by R. Willetts, *Aristocratic Society*, 40.

39. The sketch illustrating my description (p. 225) was drawn at the Superintendency of Campobasso under the direction of Alain Schnapp, whom I thank, along with Bruno d'Agostino.

40. D. Whitehead, *Metic*, 132.

41. The comparison with those in *krypteia* occurs at the end of the passage; cf. C. Pélékidis, *Éphébie*, 25–30.

42. In fact the passage I interpret in this way (*Laws* 6.760b–c) is in awful condition; for a detailed commentary on the various hypotheses and emendations, see M. Piérart, *Platon*, 260–67. It is his conclusions that I eventually adopted.

43. Cf. the comments by L. Gernet, pp. cxvii–cxix of the introduction to his translation of the *Laws* in the Budé series.

44. See M. Detienne and J.-P. Vernant, *Mètis*, 177–258. For the twofold nature of Athena, as warrior and technician, see for example the *Homeric Hymn to Aphrodite* 10–15.

45. Not "by new techniques" (Diès). The word *heteros* implies a term-to-term opposition.

46. Also against the very ideology of the democratic city, as it is manifested in official pronouncements wherein *aretē* consistently displaces *technē* (cf. N. Loraux, *Invention*, 213–14).

47. For the most part in the *Laws* the collection of interest is forbidden; see L. Gernet, *Laws*, pp. clxxxiii–clxxxiv.

48. Cf. Jacoby's remarks *FGrH ad loc.*, 286. The passage does not specify on what day of the Apaturia the procession in honor of Hephaistos took place, but the allusion to sacrifice indicates that it might be the day of the Koureōtis, which is mentioned in *Tim.* 21b.

49. In the prologue to the *Timaeus*, it is said—in reference to the myth of Erichthonius—that the goddess received from Gaia and Hephaistos the seed from which the Athenians sprang (*Tim.* 23e).

50. For a meticulous analysis of the mythological background, see L. Brisson, *Critias*. On Erichthonius and Pandora at Athens, see N. Loraux, *Enfants, passim*.

51. Protagoras's myth also links the two divinities. Prometheus makes his way into the Acropolis of Zeus and, in the workshop of Athena and Hephaistos, steals the technology of fire and the other *technai*, the domains respectively of Hephaistos and Athena (*Protag.* 321d–e). Once again, Plato constructed a theory by confronting the great adversary he raised for himself, Protagoras.

52. See "Athens and Atlantis," p. 269 below. On the Hephaisteion, see H. A. Thompson and R. E. Wycherley, *Athenian Agora* 14, 140–49, and J. Travlos, *Bildlexikon*, 261–62 (with bibliography).

53. I take my starting-point from the detailed analysis of the role of the demiurge in L. Brisson, *Même et Autre*, and the insightful comments in P. de Fidio, "Demiurgo," 244–47.

54. See, for example, *Tim.* 28c, 37c, 41a–b. Unlike L. Brisson, I think this paternity is a serious issue.

55. Cf. L. Brisson, *Même et Autre*, 50–51.

56. Cf. L. Brisson, *Même et Autre*, 35–50.

57. L. Brisson writes, "This metaphor of sowing seed is present everywhere in the infusion of souls on the stars or into the human body" (*Même et Autre*, 49).

58. Contrary to the remarks by L. Brisson, "That [the agricultural activity of the demiurge in the *Timaeus*] creates no difficulty, for in the Platonic city artisans and farmers are continually presented together as forming the third class" (*Même et Autre*, 48).

59. Cf. J.-P. Vernant, "Work 1," 248–55.

60. See below, "Plato's Myth of the Statesman."

61. See "A Civilization of Political Discourse," p. 9 above.

62. The number of studies has been growing, but only from a very recent date. In addition to the books already cited by L. Brisson, G. Cambiano, and M. Detienne and J.-P. Vernant, see A. Burford, *Craftsmen* (the best overall synthesis), F. Frontisi-Ducroux, *Dédale*, Z. Petre, "Représentation," and, for the iconography, J. Ziomecki, *Représentations*. Beginning from the last book there could be a whole study, parallel to this present one. Finally one should note the very important third chapter, entitled "Les artisans de la Parole," in the book *Parole* by J. Svenbro (141–212). Svenbro shows that the poets at the end of the Archaic age and the beginning of the Classical period were "artisans" in a sense that was wholly un-metaphorical.

63. See Z. Petre, "Architecte."

64. M. Detienne and J.-P. Vernant, *Mètis*.

65. See G. Cambiano, "Main."

66. *Mètis*, 68–79.

67. Recently, for example, in one section of the book by G. Cambiano (31–34) devoted to "L'ascesa sociale degli artigiani e dei technici." Cf. also A. Carandini, *Archeologia*, 153–66 (partially influenced by Cambiano).

68. The fundamental documentation is collected in G. Cambiano, *Tecniche*, 26–79, who is perfectly right to stress Plato's debt to this fifth-century tradition; more specifically on Democritus, see T. Cole, *Democritus*.

69. Ar. *de Part. Animal.* 687a 8–9 (=Diels 59 A 102). It is typical of the fourth century that Aristotle reacted against this definition by saying, "what is reasonable, rather, is to say that man has hands because he is the most intelligent."

70. L. Gernet, "Archontes." I was mistaken to have collaborated at one time in criticizing this definitive article (P. Levêque and P. Vidal-Naquet, *Clisthène*, 74 n. 3).

71. That this myth is an authentic expression of Protagoras's thought is a point on which I agree with, for example, G. Cambiano, *Tecniche*, 17–22.

72. Hephaistos and Athena are linked in one of the primary myths of the city of Athens, the birth of Erichthonius, but this does not necessarily imply that Athens' origin was thought of as falling under the sign of *technē;* for this episode the depictions on Attic vases do not make Hephaistos a blacksmith. Cf. N. Loraux, *Enfants*, 135–37.

73. The sources are collected in Deubner, *Feste*, 35–36. The most explicit epigraphic document is a decree from 277/276 (I.G. 2² 674.16), which mentions only Athena. The historian Phanodemos, on the other hand, speaks of Hephaistos (Harp. *s.v. Chalkeia*). The *Suda* (*s.v. Chalkeia*) mentions two periods in the history of the festival, the first civic, the second reserved for the artisans alone, under the patronage of Athena and Hephaistos. There are several factors that make me hesitant about the "corporate" nature of this festival: the presence of the two aforementioned divinities, the civic role that they play in Athenian mythology, and the *Suda*'s mention of the presence of *Arrēphoroi* and priestesses of

the goddess with the *peplos*. The lexicographic passages are collected in A. Adler, *Lexicographi Graeci* 1.4 *s.v. Chalkeia;* to the latter add Pollux 7.105, which assigns the festival to Hephaistos. I plan to make a detailed study of the feast of the *Chalkeia.*

74. Such comparisons are attacked by M. I. Finley, *Economy,* 137–38.

75. Y. Garlan, "Timbres amphoriques" 1, and M. Debidour, "Timbres amphoriques" 2; in the former see especially the conclusions on pp. 265–66, and in the latter pp. 271–75.

76. See "The Black Hunter," p. 121 above; and also A. Schnapp, "Territoire de chasse."

77. Cf. M. Detienne and J.-P. Vernant, *Mètis,* 296–99.

78. See "The Tradition of the Athenian Hoplite," p. 94 above. Here we could cite the whole *oeuvre* of Yvon Garlan.

79. S. Moscovici, *Nature,* whose analyses strike me as important.

80. R. H. Randall, Jr., "Workmen"; M. Austin and P. Vidal-Naquet, *Economic and Social History of Ancient Greece* (English version), 106, 276–82. A. Carandini, *Archeologia,* refers to this last study, but his conclusions seem to be the opposite of ours.

81. Cf. J. Ziomecki, *Représentations,* 131–32.

82. We should note, moreover, that it is in relation to Sparta (and not Athens) that Aristotle made this remark, so that its application is limited, even though it is presented as having universal value (*Pol.* 2.9.1269b 12 et seq.).

83. See the passage from the *Homeric Hymn to Aphrodite* cited above (n.44). In her role as technician, Athena presides over the work both of artisans (*tektonas andras*) and maidens.

84. See N. Loraux, "Race des femmes," esp. 47–49.

85. Cf. M. Detienne and J.-P. Vernant, *Mètis,* 146, for amplification on Thetis as a metalworker in certain commentaries.

86. To be compared with Euripides, *Medea* 409.

87. See T. J. Saunders, "Artisans." In this essay Saunders levels what he intends as a devastating attack on my analysis, but, in my opinion, he has confused Plato's city-plan with an English-style garden.

IV   The City, Vision,
      and Reality

12   Greek Rationality and the City

Is it still possible to invoke "Greek rationality" as if it were an ideal we could use for inspiration? Not so long ago the answer would have seemed self-evident: our reasoning, our conception of truth based on the principle of identity, had its origin in Greece, in the development of thought that was born in Ionia and came to maturity with Plato and Aristotle. This is a commonplace, but it too has its history. We recall, for example, the utter contempt for the Greeks—those magpies, those irrational rationalists—that was expressed by the lover of clear ideas and founder of the "Freethinkers" Union, Voltaire.

We need not linger over such a history, but we ought to remember that a manifest, complex assault has come to be directed against the very idea of exemplary Greek rationality. What are its main lines of attack? Our conception of reason and our image of Greek thought have both been profoundly altered.

I am poorly qualified to expand on the first of these two themes. However, it seems to me that modern science could not fail to overturn our conception of rationality. Bachelard, the interpreter of the *Nouvel Esprit Scientifique,* speaks of "giving back to reason its turbulence and aggression"; he showed that the principle of identity applies only in one particular area of rational activity, just as the geometry created by the Greeks, the Euclidean system, is only one of many possible geometries put into practice by modern mathematics since the time of Riemann and Lobatchevsky.

Published in *Raison présente* 2 (1967), 51–61.

A parallel course is being followed in a wholly different region. Modern ethnology has shown that the Western thought that arises from, or is supposed to arise from, the Greeks, was in fact the result of a specific process of evolution. Even if Claude Lévi-Strauss, a more faithful disciple of nineteenth-century universalism than he seems to be, finds in "primitive thought" the laws of "the human mind," the undertaking is fraught with paradoxes and with consequences for our study.

We know that what Lévi-Strauss finds among the "primitives" is not, strictly speaking, "primitive thought" but "thought in a primitive condition;" it consists of actual "practico-theoretical logic," which in turn is based on the principle of identity in the form of the double opposition: A is A :: A is not not-A. "The logical principle," he says, "is always to be *able* to oppose terms which previous impoverishment of the empirical totality . . . allows one to conceive as distinct."[1] Totemism, for example, is a grid conveying a message. Every totemic system presupposes an ideal "totemic operator" who codifies nature and provides a global interpretation, *at the level of the unconscious,* which will be deciphered by ethnology. Such unconscious logical processes will thus create difficulties for Greek rationality, and the Western reasoning that is its offspring, because they are only "particular cases." At the same time, however, assumptions about the unconscious also preserve the Greek and Western points of view in all their dignity, since the "human mind" in general, that creator of forms, is—as Paul Ricoeur has shown—nothing other than an avatar of Kantian understanding.[2]

Thus it is on another level that Lévi-Strauss calls into question the Greco-Occidental model. The true paradox and the true difficulty reside elsewhere. They appear, I think, in the ambiguity of the notion of structure and its oscillation between the conscious and the unconscious, or more precisely in the fact that Lévi-Strauss deliberately downplays an opposition between the conscious and the unconscious. Any social organization is a language written in a code that one has to know how to decipher; every language is thought and ultimately presupposes a systemic organization of the world. Therefore a totemic organization is in no way inferior, in its wealth of signification and thought, to the most elaborate of philosophical systems, or the most articulate Greek cosmology.

But let us state the matter simply, perhaps even coarsely: the question is exactly whether every fact of language *is* a fact of thought, in the active sense of the word.

In every linguistic code there are *thoughts*, but there is not necessarily *a* thought. I think it is impossible to dismiss the difference between Leibniz's "small perceptions" and perception itself, between language and purposeful speech. For Lévi-Strauss and his disciples, structure is sometimes patterning and sometimes patterned—hence the ambiguity. Ancient Greek had a vowel graduation, of Indo-European origin, to mark the difference between singular and plural in the aorist tense (*ethēka, ethemen*); this fact, along with many other marvels, can be put into a structure. But does that imply a "linguistic operator" who put thought to work? A language of Oceania makes use of nine duals, which implies a very subtle classification of the different categories of dualist relations. Is this an autonomous act of thought? Most importantly, is it a fact of consciousness? Does it imply that radical separation from nature which we, from the Greeks on, have identified as *thought?*

I am ready to agree with the recent statement by J.-F. Lyotard: "Primitives do speak, unquestionably, but in primitive speech; they are stingy in their use of language. . . . 'They don't believe that language should be used indiscriminately, but only in certain specific frames of reference and somewhat sparingly' [Lévi-Strauss, *Structural Anthropology*, 67]. They are like Brice Parain's peasants and Balzac's provincials; they would speak about what is before them in the evidence of a quasi-perception, the evidence with which their culture endows things and people. As a result the universe of language does not have for them, as for us, the task of clarifying, restoring or establishing the meaning of reality. . . . And so primitive speech is not necessarily a discourse about reality . . . but *existence pursued by other means.*"[3]

Lévi-Strauss himself says, "The Omaha Indians consider one of the main differences between themselves and the white to be that 'Indians never pick flowers'"[4]—i.e., to put in vases, but also "for botanical study." I do understand that for Lévi-Strauss language is the experience of the difference between "nature" and "culture." Let us grant him his explanation of totemism and accept his definition of it as an "application," an intellectual activity, "of the animal and vegetable world to society."[5] Even if the identification of animal and vegetal is only an episode in logical thinking, and even if—in binary logic—it cannot be separated from the distinction of the human from animal and vegetable, it still remains far removed from science and philosophy. The latter begin precisely when language is separated from what it wants to explain, when there is recognition of the fundamental importance of the distinction between signifier and signified. In his own way Heraclitus explains the same thing in his famous saying, "The master to whom the Delphic oracle belongs neither tells nor conceals; he indicates" (F 93). What was the fundamental experience that allowed the Greeks such a separation, the decisive "denaturation" of thought?

It is not only our traditional, positivistic conception of science and scientific thought that is under strenuous attack but also our portrayal of Greece and Greek thought. Fortunately, we no longer imagine the Greek thinkers as pure rationalists constructing a pure understanding in the sky. A century of Hellenic studies has succeeded to a great extent in moving Greece farther away from us rather than bringing it closer. The question is whether the Greek mind operated with the same models and motives as ours. In particular, current research constantly runs into the following problem: if Greek reason discovered mathematics, why did it fail to discover its application to science? Today some scholars go so far as to ask whether Greek reason actually partakes in what we now call the rational.

Since Nietzsche, modern philology has favored the exploration of the so-called hidden zones of the Greek spirit, opposing Dionysus to Apollo. At the beginning of his very fine book, *The Greeks and the Irrational*, E. R. Dodds tells the following story, which exemplifies a certain modern mentality:

> Some years ago I was in the British Museum looking at the Parthenon sculptures when a young man came up to me and said with a worried air, "I know it's an awful thing to confess, but this Greek stuff doesn't move me one bit." I said that was very interesting; could he define at all the reasons for his lack of response? He reflected for a minute or two. Then he said, "Well, it's all so terribly *rational*, if you know what I mean."

Dodds goes on to discuss—often brilliantly, sometimes more arguably—both the nonrational aspects of Greek thought, "shamanism" or "maenadism," and the attempts of Greek reason to overcome the "hidden forces." Going beyond this anecdote and this approach, we must remember that, especially under the influence of Heidegger, our current vision of Parmenides and Heraclitus has only the most tenuous links with "rationalism," as elsewhere with "humanism." Instead of a series of reasonings and mediations, we now emphasize the fundamental experience of truth as the disclosure of being in the *exaiphnēs*, the "suddenness" of the *Parmenides'* third hypothesis (however misinterpreted) and Plato's Seventh Letter.

No matter that such exegeses are often quite mad; what is sure is that we can no longer think of Reason springing forth, like Athena, from the universe of myth, with Thales and Pythagoras suddenly dealing with concepts "without recourse to matter, in a purely intellectual fashion" (Proclus). In fact, for an entire historical school the problem we are used to setting up as "from myth to reason" does not arise. This is what F. M. Cornford tried to show throughout his fundamental life's work, including the posthumously published *Principium Sapientiae*.[6] In the passage from myth to reason, myth was not left behind, and what we call "reason" for the Greeks is often myth.

Cornford intended to combat the theory of the "Greek miracle," and so he wished to restore the bond of historical continuity between philosophical reflection and mythic-religious thought. Between the Hittite and Babylonian myths and Anaximander's cosmogony, Hesiod's *Theogony* supplies the missing link. There is no basic difference among the following three stories:

1. The Babylonian foundation myth in the *Enuma Elish,* which describes the slaughter of the monster Tiamat by the god Marduk and the creation of the world by Marduk out of the corpse.

2. The *Theogony*'s myth of Zeus's killing Typhon and drawing out, if not the world, at least the winds.

3. Anaximander's cosmogony, in which the different qualities, such as hot and cold, dry and moist, and so on, emerge two-by-two from the *apeiron* (the infinite).

Cornford went even farther, in pointing to the role of myth in a work that we think of in many respects as one of the major accomplishments of Greek reason, the history of Thucydides. To the author of *Thucydides Mythistoricus,* a crucial feature of the *History of the Peloponnesian War* is its laicization and rationalization of Aeschylean tragedy: it is Xerxes' *hybris* (excess) that leads him to Salamis, just as Agamemnon's *hybris* leads him to his death, and the *hybris* of Alcibiades, a victim of *atē* (ruinous fate), that leads the Athenians to Sicily. In detail, Cornford's analyses are often very acute and can be accepted as they stand. In order for a myth to be rationalized, it still must have some function; we must still explain why Thucydides was not satisfied with myths in their unadorned state, and why he expressly rejected myth, even in the form it took in Herodotus. Even if we grant Cornford all his claims, we will only have rephrased the problem.

What is worth retaining from the twofold attack on the naive vision of Greek rationality? Perhaps, most basically, that rationality, Greek or other, must be restored to its historical setting. It is within Greek history that we will have to look for the fundamental traits that explain a number of phenomena; the *voluntary* renunciation of myth; the evolution from unconscious organizing structures—however "logical" in Lévi-Strauss' sense of the term—into a resolute endeavor to explain both the workings of the universe (by the Ionian and Italian "physicists") and the functioning of human groups (by the historical reasoning of Herodotus, and still more of Thucydides). What are the "patterns of intelligibility" that animate an Anaximander, an Empedocles, or a Thucydides? What are the rules of Greek social practice that find expression in the very specific language of history or Ionian physics—in the same way, as Lévi-Strauss demonstrated so wonderfully well in *Tristes Tropiques,* that the social regulations of the Caduveos are replicated in the designs that these same Caduveos etch on their bodies?

The work of J.-P. Vernant offers a clear answer to such questions.

In the "Oriental" societies with which the Greeks had contact (principally Egypt and Mesopotamia), "Oriental" myth had a precise function and clear-cut models of intelligibility. Cosmogony, like history, reflected a particular type of social relations, conducted by the king as much with the world of nature as with the world of men. As shown in the well-known works of A. Moret, R. Labat, and H. Frankfort, the king served to link men and nature, guaranteeing the security of the former and the order of the latter. The fact that this "royal theology" was not always historically experienced as such in no way diminishes its importance for the history of thought.[7] Within the confines of this kind of thought, history appears not as an explicatory narrative but as bulletins from gods to mortals, as the operation of a divine plan in the human realm. The cosmogony elevates the king as creator of order to the divine level. The *Enuma Elish* (literally: "when far above") is a ritual poem repeated annually at the festival of the new year in Babylon. During the celebration the king renewed his sovereignty just as Marduk renewed his own every year by killing Tiamat; in the same way, in another place, the pharaoh renewed his kingship during the festival of Sed.

Did the Greeks have experience of this kind of sovereignty? We must be cautious and not engage in a search for "pure" varieties of "Oriental" society in Crete and Mycenae. Scholars have been able to prove that even in Mesopotamia tensions existed between the urban economy and society on the one hand and those associated with the royal palace on the other, tensions that were based on control by the king or the temple over the plains.[8] Despite some extremely dubious archaeological interpretations, there may be some value in Henri van Effenterre's hypotheses about the existence in Crete of another center of power in addition to the palace.[9]

Nonetheless, such considerations must not distort what is obvious. The decipherment of Linear-B moves the first signs of Greek language back in time by about seven centuries, and it allows us to examine the language over thirty-five centuries of continuous evolution, from the archives of Knossos, Pylos, and Mycenae to Kazantzakis. It does not, however, permit the belief—often maintained with disarming naïveté— that a similar continuity obtains in the realm of institutions and social life. The person who inhabits the palaces of Knossos, Phaestos, Mallia, or Palaeokastro, who packs the products of his fields into jars (*pithoi*), oversees stock-breeding and keeps his accounts, might be god, priest, or king (the term will always be mistranslated), but whoever he may be, he will always be inscrutable to future generations; and I do not mean only the age of the city-state but already what is called the "Homeric world"—no matter what the power of memory or the legendary traditions that are to form or deform the figure of a Minos or an Agamemnon.

The Mycenaean world crumbled at the end of the thirteenth century. We do not know the exact causes, and we are also ignorant of the role played by what modern scholars used to call the "Dorian Invasion." The material catastrophe was immense, and today its extent can be easily ascertained at sites in the Peloponnese and Crete, but the "crisis of sovereignty" was even more decisive. Greece was now a world freed from the omnipresent lord (*wanax*); after a long separation, the villager and the warrior-aristocrat came face to face, belatedly reunited at the end of the eighth century (the work of Hesiod serving as a *terminus post quem*). Out of this reunion arose the classical polis. We will not make the attempt here to deal with the insoluble problem of the origins of the polis. What led to this extraordinary situation? I mean that a community could publish decrees—the earliest, I think, in Crete—containing formulae that, although often repeated throughout ten centuries of history, still inspire my admiration in their testimony to the sovereignty of a group of equals: "Resolved by the city, resolved by the people, resolved by the council and the people." I will only say that for a clear view of this evolution one must understand that it was, so to speak, double-barreled. In the first stage— for which we have better information for Sparta and the Cretan cities, because these communities scarcely changed—the principal agents of change were warriors, the young soldiers who accompanied the Homeric king, the *kouroi*.

Henri Jeanmaire had the admirable insight that for Homer the only purely political institutions[10]—assembly, council, and monarchy it-self—were military institutions. Before Jeanmaire, Engels had invented the idea of "military democracy," but for want of documentation he was unable to place it in real historical perspective. From roughly the end of the eighth century on, youths wore the *uniform* of the hoplite, most elements of which had already been assembled, beginning in the My-cenaean era or thereabouts.

Thus what we call the "hoplite reform" is not a shift in technique but the result of a shift in society.[11] From now on, it is the *phalanx* that fights, not the individual. We are still in the presence of an aristocratic social order, but it is an aristocracy of equals. The young companions of the Homeric king gradually succeed in claiming, if not supremacy, at least a place and a part of what is from now on the political arena.

I mentioned the "double-barreled" process: the second stage belongs to democracy. Discussions of Greek oligarchy and democracy frequently make it appear as if they were differentiated only by degree, by the number of active participants. But if there is such a thing as the "Greek miracle," it is not to be found in the sky over Attica or in the colonnades of the Parthenon. Rather, it is that the city-state no longer consists solely of warrior-aristocrats, who profit from the labor of the Spartan helots or Thessalian penestae, but comes to include the small-holding peasants who work their own land. In Athens, beginning with Solon's reforms, every "Athenian" is a free man, and every free man has the calling to be a citizen, a process that will be completed by Cleisthenes' reforms. It is this development alone, the expansion of the concept of the citizen, that made possible the growth of other social categories. The latter comprise both slaves—in the proper sense of the term, those who are bought and sold and are "foreigners" par excellence—and metics. Athens is the classical example, but analogous phenomena took place in Ionia—de-spite contact with first Lydian then Persian monarchy—Chios, Samos, and Miletus.

Perhaps now we have a better view of what has been called "the spiritual world of the polis."[12] The originality of the Greek city-state is not in that it is a society that obeys rules—every society answers to this definition—nor in that the rules form a coherent system, which is a law not only for social groups but also for the very study of such groups. The originality does not rest even in the fact that the members of the society tend to equality and the distribution of power, for that is true for any number of "primitive" societies. In his book *Ancient Society* Lewis Morgan depicts Cleisthenic Athens as both the initiation of a new world, of civilization, and as the completion of the "barbarian" stage of human history, the classically tribal society that he saw in the "democracy" of the Iroquois. In Greece such phenomena rose to the level of consciousness; the Greeks were aware of the "crisis of sovereignty" even if only in comparing themselves to the empires nearby.

An oft-noted sign of this transformation is the alteration, after nearly four centuries of eclipse, in the role of writing. It is no longer a privilege of palace scribes but a public skill; it no longer serves privately to keep accounts or describe rites reserved for initiates, but publicly to record religious and political *laws* available to all. Still, Classical Greek civilization is not a civilization of literacy—or, to be more precise, a shift in that direction does not emerge until the fourth century—but a civilization of speech; it is not paradoxical to say that from then on writing was one of the forms of speech.

The city-state created an entirely novel social space, a public space, centering on the *agora* and its common hearth, the place where problems of general interest were argued and where power was no longer located in the palace but in the center, *es meson*. It is "in the center" that the orator stands, the one who is supposed to speak in the interest of all.[13] This space corresponds to the pattern of civic time; the most striking example is provided by Cleisthenes' prytanic year, radically distinct from the religious calendar and divided into as many prytanies as there are tribes in the city.[14]

Within the city-state, speech in the form of persuasion (*peithō*) becomes the most basic political tool. Although it can, of course, be trickery and deceit, it is no longer the ritual utterance. The oracle itself is not a command but a particularly solemn form of speech, rooted in ambiguity. It enters into the contentious debate about what decisions or laws should be made; that was evident on the eve of Salamis when Themistocles interpreted Delphi's prophecy about "wooden walls" as meaning the fleet. Therefore, despite so many antagonisms, despite so many holdovers from the past, religion too shares in its own way in a progressive humanization. If the cult statue become purely human, it is in that it becomes an *eikōn*, an image whose ritual function is to be seen. Needless to say, this is only one aspect of Greek religion; civic religion is counterposed by the universe of the sects and of the mysteries. This twofold representation is echoed in philosophy itself, until the time of Aristotle, balanced as it was between exhibition or public "scandal" (from Empedocles to Socrates) and the retreat into the gardens of Academos, between the exoteric and the esoteric.

At this point let us examine to what extent the spiritual world, which we have sketched in broad strokes, is reflected in the thought of the Greek philosophers. To tell the truth, it has often been maintained that their works conveyed something other than their manifest content. In the Presocratics scholars sought and sometimes found sexual mysteries and symbols, such as those discovered by Bachelard when he "psychoanalyzed" fire. There was also a less successful quest for direct signs of economic transformation and social change. Almost invariably such efforts resulted in palpable absurdities. The English Marxist George Thomson compared the struggle of opposites in Greek philosophy with the most archaic social structure and the balance, within the tribe, of two opposing clans and intermarriage. [15] Unfortunately there is not a single text to confirm the existence of such a structure in Greece.

On the other hand, another type of research is becoming more and more prevalent, in the work of scholars like P. Guérin, G. Vlastos, and J.-P. Vernant: [16] between "economics" and philosophy there is room for a privileged mediation that represents the Greeks' most important experience, political life.

Examples are easy to find. There is the passage from Alcmeon of Croton who defines health in the body by alluding to the concept of *isonomia*, while illness is the result of monarchy, of tyranny exercised by one element over the others. There are the extant portions of the work of Anaximander, in itself witness that we are not in the realm of mere imagery. The infinite, *apeiron*, is both a reality separate from all the constituent elements of the universe and their inexhaustible source of energy. Aristotle tells us so: if one of the elements were not subject to law, the world would not enjoy its characteristic egalitarian equilibrium. The famous fragment of Anaximander defines the order of the world by showing that the elements engage in a mutual exchange of *retribution* and *justice* for the *injustices* that they commit against each other according to the order of time. [17]

After the publication of J. Bollack's great book on Empedocles, [18] I would like to take the opportunity to emphasize what we can learn from the philosopher from Agrigento. There have been several demonstrations of the "archaic" or "primitive" aspects of his work: for E. R. Dodds he was a "shaman"; L. Gernet showed that being the master of wind and rain, he was a fairly good image of Frazer's "magician king." [19] For a long time the universe of Empedocles was portrayed as passing through a series of distinct phases from the absolute unity of the *sphairos* to the utter diversity of the *Cosmos,* from the reign of Love to that of Hate. Bollack has proven that this depiction, which is actually Gnostic, was wrong. Instead of a cycle, there is at the very heart of the universe a continuous coexistence of love and hate. This is a dramatic expression of the problem of unity and diversity in the city that Plato and Aristotle will examine.

The destruction of the divine sphere (*sphairos*) is the division of power and the division of the elements—Fire, Earth, Air, and Water—comparable to the allotment of the world among the Homeric gods; the concomitant construction of the *sphairos* is equality's expression of power, replacing the dispersion of the elements with equilibrium. The sea balances the sum total of fire, and an anti-sun counters the sun; blood itself, that gathering of "spheromorphic" elements, is composed, so to speak, of equals. As for Anaximander each element (like the citizen in the city-state) exercises power *in turn,* but the equality of each element's share destroys what is excessive in its individual supremacy. "At one and the same time everything is full of light and of lightless night, both equal."

I hardly need specify that I do not mean to reduce philosophical thought to being a projection of politics. The political world furnished thought with the vision of an order both created and to be created, but from Parmenides on philosophical thought rapidly developed its own language and its own problems. Purely political theory underwent a parallel development; in the hands of the sophists, those professors of politics—who share Protagoras's sense that politics is possible because choice is a natural skill for the citizen—political thought underwent in its own way the influence of Ionian and Italian physics.

What of the historians? Too often we forget that they too had a role to play in the birth and growth of Greek reason.[20] Hecataeus of Miletus, the first historian, says "I record what I believe to be true, for the stories of the Greeks are numerous and, it seems to me, foolish." The work of Thucydides is the supreme expression of historical reason, and of reason constituting history. We know how Lévi-Strauss systematically uncovers the binary structures concealed within myths. In Thucydides they are not hidden, and it is easy to retrieve superimposable pairs: rational decision (*gnōmē*) and chance (*tychē*), speech (*logos*) and action (*ergon*), law and nature, peace and war. Thus history takes the form of a huge political confrontation; statesmen's plans are challenged by the plans of other statesmen, and also by the test of reality, of *tychē* and *ergon,* and of that nature about which Thucydides made the curious remark early in Book 1 that it shared in the upheaval of the human world—as if the Peloponnesian War had occasioned earthquakes.

I think I have said enough, for now, about the ambition of political reason; it is an overmastering enterprise that, in the fifth century, had the goal of placing everything under the rule of law, since the outline I have just given could be extended to several other areas, such as medicine. In a sense the Greeks held all activity to be political activity.

J.-P. Vernant has established that what gave Greek reason its strength also created its weakness: it is uniquely dependent on the ideal of the free citizen. While the oft-mentioned "technological failure" of Greek thought undoubtedly has an economic and societal cause (in slavery), it also has an intellectual basis. In the machines it contrived, Greek reason did not see instruments for the transformation of nature but *copies* of man, hence marvels (*thaumata*).

It is as if the Greeks pushed to its absolute limit the distinction between nature and culture, or to use their own terms, between nature and law; they took an interest in machines only as prodigies of legalism. Vernant made the very good point that there, too, political models, derived from the sophistic, played a fundamental part. The sophist teaches his pupil that in politics the weaker argument can overcome the stronger. To the extent that he pays attention to nature, the Greek thinker does not ask it for instruction but rather gives it instruction; sometimes he masters it—he never submits to it.

In the *Mechanics,* for example, Aristotle analyzes the principle of the reversal of force that occurs when a winch transforms circular motion into linear motion. He locates it in the "sophistic" ambiguity of the circle: "It is because the circle is itself a contradictory reality, indeed the most remarkable thing in the world, bringing together in the same nature several opposites. Thus it is in motion in one direction and in another, and it is at the same time concave and convex, mobile and stationary" (*Mech.* 847b–48a).[21] In brief, it is in itself a logical reality, a sophistic argument.

This being the case, is it surprising that the Greeks made decisive progress in the technical realm chiefly as it was applied to warfare? That was the only *technē* that seemed to them to impinge on the fate of the city-state.

So much for the synchronic limits—let us now say a word about the diachronic limits of the political reason we have been trying to describe. The end of the sixth century and the beginning of the fifth marked a period of equilibrium between the nascent democracy and political theory. In the course of the fifth century and above all in the fourth, with the gradual development of "the internal stresses of triumphant Hellenism" (A. Aymard), we see reason, the child of the city, turning back to the city, delivering a critical examination and, in large measure, turning *against* the city. The philosopher, sometimes starting out as a religious sectarian (most notably among the Pythagoreans) and often linked to aristocratic factions, concludes that the city-state does not live up to the ideal of justice that it spawned. So, for example, it uses arithmetic equality—a citizen = a citizen—rather than geometric equality, based on proportion, as urged by the philosopher.

All this culminates in the Platonic paradox. For Plato, man himself is a polis in which antagonistic forces clash; as for the philosopher's city-state, its model is no longer the empirical city but the order of the universe; relations are turned upside down. Set aside by the real city, Plato took refuge in "that *Republic* inside ourselves" that is the topic of the dialogue *On Justice*.[22]

NOTES

1. C. Lévi-Strauss, *The Savage Mind*, 75.

2. "Structure et Hermeneutique"; on the ambiguities in Lévi-Strauss's conception of the "human mind," see the works of E. Leach, especially "Lévi-Strauss." On the totemic operator, see Lévi-Strauss, *Totemism*.

3. "Indians," 3.

4. *The Savage Mind*, 42–43.

5. Lévi-Strauss, *Totemism*, 101.

6. Here I am very close to the comments by J.-P. Vernant, "From Myth to Reason"; see also *Origins*. On the insoluble problem of the Oriental background, see the optimistic book *Orient* by M. L. West.

7. See G. Posener, *Pharaon*, and the works implicitly or explicitly criticized therein: A. Moret, *Royauté pharaonique;* R. Labat, *Monarchie assyro-babylonienne;* H. Frankfort, *Kingship and the Gods*.

8. See A. L. Oppenheim, *Mesopotamia*, ch. 2.

9. "Politique et Religion"; now see *Mallia* 1, pp. 189–95 and in general, *Cité*, 96–121, the most adventurous of all Van Effenterre's demonstrations.

10. H. Jeanmaire, *Couroi*.

11. Cf. M. Detienne, "Phalange."

12. J.-P. Vernant, *Origins*, ch. 4.

13. Cf. M. Detienne, "Géométrie," for a good explanation of the military origin of the concept of centrality.

14. Cf. P. Lévêque and P. Vidal-Naquet, *Clisthène*.

15. G. Thomson, *The First Philosophers*.

16. See P. Guérin, *Justice;* G. Vlastos, "Equality"; J.-P. Vernant, "From Myth to Reason."

17. See the essential work by C. Kahn, *Anaximander*.

262   18. J. Bollack, *Empédocle.*
           19. L. Gernet, "Origins."
           20. See F. Châtelet, *Naissance.*
           21. Cf. J.-P. Vernant, "Technological Thought."
           22. For a general consideration of the problems raised in this chapter, see the recent work by G.E.R. Lloyd, *Magic,* 226–67.

13

Athens and Atlantis: Structure
and Meaning of a Platonic Myth

Harold Cherniss once observed of the problem of Atlantis,
the subject of so much debate since classical times, that "it is easier to
conjure the djinn out of the bottle than to get him back in again."[1] At the
beginning of the *Timaeus* and in the unfinished dialogue *Critias,* Plato
describes, in the form of a tradition learned by Solon from the priests of
the goddess Neith at Sais in Egypt and passed on by him to his relative
Critias, one of the "Thirty Tyrants" and Plato's uncle,[2] the institutions,
the political geography, and the history of two cities that disappeared
almost nine thousand years earlier—prior to the last of those catastrophes
(universal conflagration or general flood) that recur regularly on this
planet (*Tim.* 22d–23e)—proto-Athens and Atlantis.

What is the point of this description? Socrates and his friends have just
been through the fundamental characteristics of the Platonic city as put
forward in Books 2 to 5 of the *Republic:* the group of Guardians, both male
and female, separate from the rest of the population; the community of
women and children; the rational and secret ordering of sexual relations
(*Tim.* 17b–19b). Socrates then says that he would wish to see a real city of
such a kind in existence; in a word, to place it in the actual world, the
world of war and international relations. Does that mean to place it in
history, in our sense of the word? No indeed; it means constructing one of
those mechanical models that Plato so loved to work out and that allowed
him to dramatize an abstract discussion.[3]

The first version published as "Athènes et l'Atlantide," *REG* 77 (1964)
420–44.

But the conflict between proto-Athens and Atlantis is a model in a second sense besides. For in Plato any paradigm presupposes that there is a structural homology between pattern and product, between reality and myth.[4] Thus, in the *Politicus,* the ruler is defined in terms of the image of the weaver, because the ruler of a state is a weaver, a craftsman who works with his eye fixed on the divine model. The problems involved in the accounts of the *Timaeus* and the *Critias* are endlessly more complex: The city whose fundamental institutions are described in the *Republic* provides the paradigm for the constitution of proto-Athens, so that the description of Atlantis, of its empire and the final catastrophe that engulfed it, is determined by its relation to the fixed point provided by the just city. But this "Tale of Two Cities" is itself intimately linked to the physics of the *Timaeus,* as Plato expressly says. One cannot enterprise, as the *Critias* does, a detailed account of this human history without first defining man's place in nature—in that nature laid bare for us by the physiologue of Locris (*Tim.* 27a–b). Physics itself, because its object belongs to the world of becoming, can only ground a "probable myth" (*Tim.* 29d). But the narrator has known through contemplation that "being which is eternal and which has no share in the world of becoming" (*to on aei, genēsin d'ouch echon*), just as the demiurge has, who understands not through "opinion linked to sense-impressions" (*doxa met'aisthēseōs*) but through "intelligence combined with reasoning" (*noēsis meta logou*)—in short, what is in the truest sense "the same" (*Tim.* 28a). For that reason, his account is no less founded in truth, worthy of the goddess whose festival is being celebrated (i.e., Athena). Socrates could even characterize it as "a true account, not merely an imaginative fiction" (*mē plasthenta mython all'alēthinon logon; Tim.* 26e).

There are then three rules for the historian who wishes to understand the myth of Atlantis. He must not sunder the two cities that Plato has linked so closely together. He must constantly refer himself to the physics of the *Timaeus.* And consequently, he must relate the historical myth whose structure he is trying to explain to Plato's "idealism." The success of a properly historical interpretation depends entirely upon the extent to which this preliminary task is performed.[5]

Although for Plato it is proto-Athens that is the paradigm, Atlantis has attracted enormously greater attention thanks to the simultaneously circumstantial and imaginative character of the myth.[6] In antiquity his account was taken in various ways: sometimes as a story that might agreeably bear imitation, as did Theopompus in the fourth century, substituting for Solon's meeting with the priests at Sais a dialogue between Silenus and King Midas, and for Atlantis a warlike city (*Ma-*

chimos), for Athens a reverent one (*Eusebēs*).[7] Alternatively, it could be made the occasion for a lesson in geography, a speculative mode—more nicely discriminate of language than of reality—encouraged by Hellenistic philology; Strabo at any rate was amply justified in his criticism of Poseidonius's credulity, and in his comment—recalling Aristotle's on Homer—that the continent had been done away with by its own maker.[8] We know much less about philosophical interpretations, which we hear of almost exclusively through Proclus's *Commentary on the Timaeus;* he observed, intelligently enough, that the beginning of the *Timaeus* was a presentation, in the form of images, of the theory of the Universe (*tēn tou kosmou theōrian: in Tim.* 1.4.12 Diehl). His own interpretation and those of his predecessors are sometimes lunatic, but at least did not divorce Athens from Atlantis and related the myth systematically to the *Timaeus's* physics, for all their failure to eschew realist hypotheses (*in Tim.* 1.75.30 et seq.). But these philosophers, soaked in a social and religious world completely different from Plato's, simply did not comprehend the political aspects of his thought. Later still, a Christian geographer turned Solon into Solomon and accused Plato of distorting an account he had got from the Chaldaean oracles.[9]

If a "realist" reading made little headway in the ancient world, the case since the Renaissance has entirely altered. In the late seventeenth century, and in the eighteenth, Atlantis became the focus of great debate: was Plato's continent the New World, America? Was it the land whence civilization for Christians had developed—was it Jewish Palestine? Or was it rather an anti-Palestine, watershed of the Arts and Sciences, that could be located in Siberia or the Caucasus? The first stirrings of modern nationalism played their part too.[10] A Swede, Olaf Rudleck, marshaled a learning of almost inconceivable weight in order to prove that Atlantis could lie nowhere but in Scandinavia.[11] And of course the quest passed from the hands of scholars to those of would-be scholars,[12] and so to mythomaniacs and charlatans, those who, even to this day, "discover" or peddle Atlantis anywhere between Heligoland and the Sahara, between Siberia and Lake Titicaca.[13] The "realist" reading has been exterminated in science. But has it really disappeared? Failing a submerged continent, we are often assured, Plato might have known a tradition that more or less faithfully reproduced a memory of an actual historical event or a local saga.

As early as 1841, Thomas-Henri Martin, in his justly famous *Etudes sur le Timée de Platon,* in spite of placing Atlantis in the region of the "Island of Utopia," wondered whether Plato had not been thinking of an Egyptian tradition.[14] Since Evans' discoveries, it is of course Crete that has provided most ammunition; it was practically inevitable that the bull-sacrifice in the oath of the kings of Atlantis should point someone to the land of the Minotaur; and the destruction of the fabulous kingdom has been assimilated into the fall of Knossos. [15] It is simply unfortunate that such claims remain completely undemonstrable, but one is compelled to wonder whether any progress has been made in the interpretation of the text since Olaf Rudbeck when one finds an archaeologist declaring that the site of Atlantis is amazingly similar to that of Lake Copais—with just one problem: "The greatest discrepancy is the fact that Atlantis according to Plato lay far to the West, while the Copais basin is in the midst of Greece."[16]

At the heart of these lucubrations lies a weird image of the philosopher: Plato the historian, whose "sources" have to be looked into, as one might in the case of Herodotus or Diodorus Siculus. But Plato did not think in terms of "sources," of what Herodotus called *opsis* and *akoē* (eyewitness and hearsay), but precisely in terms of models. [17] And the inquiry into these "models" has been a good deal less enthusiastic than the search for "sources." And where there has been inquiry, one could hardly call the method employed empirical; which compels me now to turn to these arguments and comment upon them.

Many scholars have compared the island of Atlantis with the Phaeacians' Scheria. [18] And the parallelism cannot be doubted. After all, the kingdom of Alcinous, with its idealized patriarchal monarchy and its palace filled with marvels, is the first utopian city in Greek literature. [19] At least, that might have been the impression of a fourth-century Greek. Again, it is important that we have a utopia connected with the sea. Scheria, like Atlantis, is a city of sailors: "They, confident in the speed of their running ships, cross over the great open water, since this is the gift of the Earthshaker to them . . . (*Od.* 7.34–35; tr. Lattimore). The kings of Atlantis were descended from the union of Poseidon and a mortal woman, Kleito, while Alcinous and Arete were the descendants of the union of Poseidon and the nymph Periboia (*Critias* 113 d–e; *Od.* 7.56 et seq.). The one temple on Scheria is consecrated to the god of the sea, as is the one temple described by Plato (*Od.* 6.266; *Critias* 116d–17a). Homer speaks of two springs, as does Plato (*Od.* 7.129; *Critias* 117a).

The local color, then, is epic; and Plato actually notes at the very beginning of the *Timaeus* that Solon, had he so wished, could have equaled Homer and Hesiod (*Tim.* 21c). The names of some of the kings of the great island are borrowed from Homer. [20] But here Homer's world is inverted: the land that bids welcome has become an empire from which will set sail the armies determined upon the destruction of Greece; the

parallelism does not explain everything—even if it ought certainly to
figure in any discussion of Plato's relation to Homer.

Then again, Paul Friedländer and Joseph Bidez after him have stressed
the many reasons for supposing Atlantis, which Plato sets at the western
edge of the world, to be an idealized transposition of the East and of the
world of Persia.[21] It is certainly plausible that Plato's description of the
walls of the capital city and the city itself may have been inspired by
Herodotus's description of Ecbatana and Babylon (Hdt. 1.98, 178; *Critias* 116a et seq.). The Greeks thought of an Oriental king as a lord of the
waters. Herodotus describes the legendary heart of Asia, a plain, en-
circled by mountains, giving rise to an imaginary mighty river that
flowed through the mountains in five branches until the Great King built
five sluice-gates that he alone could open (3.117).[22] I hardly need recall
what he says about the Nile, about Egypt and the Pharaohs. The massive
irrigation works undertaken by the kings of Atlantis (*Critias* 117c–d)
and the scale of the kingdom itself are sufficient indication that Plato is
thinking here primarily not of the tiny world of the Greek city-states but
of the universe of Oriental despotism. Such an interpretation might
obviously lead one, as it has many,[23] to view the struggle between Athens
and Atlantis as a mythical transposition of the struggle between Greeks
and barbarians, and the Persian Wars in particular. One can even show, as
I do not think it has been, that Plato was directly influenced by Herodotus. For in the *Timaeus* he says: "And he told my grandfather Critias
(according to the story the old man used to repeat to us) that there were
great and admirable exploits performed by our own city long ago, which
have been forgotten through the lapse of time and the destruction of
human life" (20e; tr. Cornford). This is how Herodotus begins his history: "These are the researches of Herodotus of Halicarnassus which he
publishes in the hope of thereby preserving from decay the remembrance
of what men have done, and of preventing the great and wonderful
actions of the Greeks and the Barbarians from losing their due meed of
glory . . ." (1.1; tr. Rawlinson). For his part, the historian tried to be fair
to each of the warring sides.[24]

But if the model is really the Persian Wars, then Plataea here comes
before Marathon. Athens starts out as leader of the Hellenes, but she wins
the victory alone, and she alone sets up the trophy and liberates the
Greeks and the subjects of Atlantis's empire (*Tim.* 25b–c)[25]—those very
cities and peoples over which the Athens of history had extended her sway
after the war. Should we find that surprising? The second Persian War
was for Plato marred by the naval engagements at Artemisium and
Salamis (*Laws* 4.707b–c). When he discusses the matter, it is certainly

not to praise Themistocles' daring and the decisive role of the fleet. While Xerxes made his preparations to invade Attica, "[The Athenians] considering that there was no salvation for them either by land or by sea. . . . One chance of safety remained, slight indeed and desperate, but their only one. They saw that on the former occasion they had gained a seemingly impossible victory, and borne up by this hope, they found that their only refuge was in themselves and in the Gods." (*Laws* 3.699a–c; tr. Jowett).26 But Plato's remodeled Athenians do not get on board their ships; his Athenians defeat the seafaring men of Atlantis not on the sea but on land. An odd Athens, and an odd "Orient." But a closer look at the texts leads us, without rejecting what we have learned, to a more complex interpretation of the struggle between the two cities. Plato's Athens meets and vanquishes Atlantis; in so doing, she really overcomes herself. That may sound strange, but let us look once more at the facts and at the texts.27

On the west face of the pediment of Pheidias's and Iktinos's Parthenon was represented the mythical dispute between Athena and Poseidon. I think it no exaggeration to say that this dispute was one of the mythical foundations of Athenian history. The ironical funeral speech in the *Menexenus* declares: "Our country is worthy to be praised, not only by us but by all mankind; first and above all, as being dear to the gods. This is proved by the strife and contention of the gods respecting her" (237c; tr. Jowett).28 The passage is directly contradicted by one from the *Critias:* "In the days of old, the gods had the whole earth distributed among them by allotment. *There was no quarreling;* for you cannot rightly suppose that the gods did not know what was proper for them to have, or, knowing this, that they would seek to procure for themselves by contention that which more properly belonged to others." (109b; tr. Jowett). According to this, it was Dikē who shared out the allocations. Athens was assigned to Athena and Hephaistos, and Atlantis became the realm of Poseidon (*Critias* 109c, 113c). The two divinities worshipped together in the Erechtheion are thus separated; and Plato similarly separates and opposes the two Greek forms of power: the Athenians, stemming from the seed of Hephaistos and Gaia (*Tim.* 23e), inherited power on the land; the kings of Atlantis, children of Poseidon, power by sea. But that very fact reveals to us that Plato is presenting his native city from two different points of view: the city of Athena and the olive tree is identified with proto-Athens, and the city of Poseidon, lord of horses and the sea, is realized in Atlantis.

Let us take a closer look at the topography and the institutions of this idealized Athens. It is essentially an enormous acropolis, which includes, besides the classical Acropolis, the Pnyx and Lycabettos, and thus extends as far as the Eridanus and Glissos rivers; and it is covered in earth. It is thus very different from the harsh rock that Plato knew (*Critias* 111e–12a). Its summit forms a level area enclosed by a *single* wall (*heni peribolōi*: 112b)[29] and is where the second class of the population, the warriors, live. The craftsmen and the farmers live outside and work the fields beyond. Plato describes the class of warriors (*to machimon genos*) characteristically by means of an expression denoting what never changes: it is *auto kath'hauto*.[30] Civic space is organized in a manner quite unlike that of the classical city. There is no Agora to be the *meson* (center) of political life; no temple that might be the prototype of those built in the fifth century. To the north, there are common barracks, refectories suitable for use in bad weather, and temples. To the south, gardens, gymnasia, and summer refectories (112b–d). In the middle is the sanctuary of Athena and Hephaistos, an evident transposition from the Hephaistion that still dominates the Agora today, and in front of which Pausanias records that there stood a statue of Athena (which we know, like that of Hephaistos, to have been the work of Alkamenes)—a conjunction he found unsurprising in view of the myths of Erichthonius.[31]

What does this divine pair signify here? The Homeric Hymn to Hephaistos sang of the God: "With Athena of the glittering eyes he taught men on earth wondrous crafts" (20.2–3). But this is not the only *technē* that may be relevant: "Hephaistos and Athena, who were brother and sister, and sprang from the same father, having a common nature, and being united also in the love of philosophy (*philosophia*) and art (*philotechnia*), both obtained as their common portion this land, which was naturally adapted for wisdom and virtue" (*Critias* 109c; tr. Jowett).[32] Hephaistos and Athena thus guarantee the close relationship between the two classes, guardians and producers, of proto-Athens.

I have already observed that this Athens is land-based. The term really applies to Attica as a whole, more extensive than Plato's city, since it reached down to the Isthmus of Corinth (*Critias* 110e).[33] It is a land wonderfully fertile, covered with fields and forests, "able in those days to support a vast army, exempt from the labors of the soil" ("Critias 110d–11e), thereby permitting soldiers to be soldiers only, as Plato hoped, having seen the development of military *technē* and professionalism, while at the same time he was eager to reconcile this evolution with the ideal of the citizen-soldier, as even Sparta had failed to do (cf. esp. *Rep.* 2.373a et seq.). To the very end of its history, the city of the *Timaeus* and the *Critias* is a republic of land. When the terrible cataclysm comes, its army is swallowed by the earth, whereas Atlantis is engulfed by the sea (*Tim.*

25d). It goes without saying that in his account of prehistoric Athens Plato devoted no space to the life of the sea. The country is surrounded by sea, but there are no harbors. A republic of the land: a republic united and unchanging. Unity is the foundation of all Plato's constitutions,[34] and here it is ensured by the divine pair and by the community of women and offspring. Plato stressed this unity and the lack of change even in tiny details: there is only one spring, and its water is of a temperature equally convenient in summer and winter.[35] Changelessness appears in the number of warriors, which so far as possible shall not alter; and in the way in which the constitution and the organization of the land has been ordained once and for all.[36] And, more jokingly, in the art of house-building, which the inhabitants pass down "to others like themselves, always the same" (*Critias* 112c).[37]

One might ask whether there is any further connection between this structure based on the land, this unity and changelessness, beyond the connections that are obvious. In the cosmology of the *Timaeus*, of the four elements, it is precisely earth that cannot be transformed: οὐ γὰρ εἰς ἄλλο γε εἶδος ἔλθοι ποτ' ἄν (*Tim.* 56d). Movement in this cosmology consists in the commingling, at every level, of the principle of changelessness, "of the indivisible Existence that is ever in the same state," the Same, with "the divisible Existence that exists in bodies," the Other (*Tim.* 35a et seq.).[38] One might see prehistoric Athens as the political manifestation of the Same. The tenor of the myth is no less evident at a political level. It is not by chance that Plato takes Solon as the intermediary for his knowledge of this Athens: by the mid–fourth century the Archon of 594 had become the grand old man of the moderates, the supporters of the *patrios politeia*.[39] The great cataclysm deprived Athens of the greater part of her land. The small remainder, of first-rate quality, was a token of what once was (*Critias* 110e), just as among the Athenians of Solon's day, "a little of the seed" of the Athenians of former days was preserved (*Tim.* 23c). Athens was not then "lost," if the word means anything in Plato's philosophy, but the city Plato describes was the antithesis of the real city of the fifth and fourth centuries—in a word, an anti-Athens.

In the *Politicus* Plato presents, in the form of a myth, two cycles in the universe.[40] At times, "God in person accomplishes the movement of the universe, putting his own hand to the wheeling of its circles" (tr. Taylor). The world then comes to know what the poets have called the age of Cronos, men under the sway of divine shepherds. "Sons of the earth," men lead a life exactly the reverse of ours: they are born greybeards and die babies. Then the cycle goes into reverse and God abandons the helm. At first men succeed reasonably well in organizing things, "but in process of time, as forgetfulness comes over (the world), the old discord prevails ever more and more." The threat is then that the world will be swallowed up "in the boundless place of unlikeness" (*eis ton tēs anomoiotētos apeiron onta topon; Pol.* 273d).[41] God takes a hand, and the world reverses itself once again. In Books 8 and 9 of the *Republic* Plato outlines an analogous shift, from timocracy to oligarchy, from oligarchy to democracy, from democracy to tyranny: the ideal model is progressively distorted, yet each type preserves elements of the preceding constitution. Equally, each stage is a little further removed from the ideal of unity: democracy is like "an emporium of constitutions where one can choose the model he likes best" (*Rep.* 8.557d; tr. Cornford). And Plato is especially fond of the adjective *poikilos* to describe democracy and its logical consequence, tyranny (*Rep.* 8.557c, 558e, 561e, 568d). These two forms of constitution push "diversity," "chiaroscuro," to the very limit.

In order to characterize this "chiaroscuro" quality—or, in a different image, this *apeiron,* this lack of limits—Plato uses oppositions, big and little, hot and cold, pitched and unpitched, etc.:

> Wherever they are present they exclude any definite quantity. They always imbue activities with greater strength over against greater mildness and conversely, rendering them more or less whatever it may be (*to pleon kai to elatton apergazesthon*), and ruling out definite quantity. . . . If they do not obliterate definite quantity, but allow degree and measure to appear in the midst of more or less, or strongly and mildly, they in fact abandon the territory they occupied. For in admitting of definite quantity they would no longer strictly be hotter or colder. For the hotter goes on without pause, and the colder in the same way, while a definite quantity comes to a particular point and goes no further. So on the present argument the hotter and at the same time its opposite would come out as indeterminate. [*Philebus* 24c–d; tr. Gosling][42]

It is easy to recognize in this passage the well-known "indeterminate dyad" (*dyas aoristos*) of great and small, by which Aristotle defined the material principle in Plato; and of course the Other of the *Timaeus.*[43]

It is in this last dialogue that we find, in close mutual relationship, the two cycles that are sundered in the *Politicus.* The circle of the Same corresponds to the movement of the stars, and moves from left to right, while the Other, divided into seven unequal circles (the planets), moves from right to left. But the turning of the Other is brought about by the turning of the Same, which it imitates (*Tim.* 36c et seq.).[44] The harmony of the universe can thus be accounted for, but also the unforeseen eventualities to which it is subject.

If proto-Athens is the political expression of the triumph of the Same, what of Atlantis? I do not say that it *is* the political expression of the Other, because the Other does not exist in itself. What is subject to coming into being and is visible (*genesin echon kai horaton*) is an imitation of the model (*mimēma de paradeigmatos*), which is itself alone intelligible and eternal (*noēton kai aei kata tauta on; Tim.* 48e–49a).[45]

To grasp what Atlantis is, it would be sensible first of all to look once again at the fate of Athens. The prehistoric city lost what gave it permanence: "For the fact is that a single night of excessive rain washed away the earth and laid bare the rock" (*Critias* 112a); "in comparison with what then was, there remain only the bones of the wasted body . . . the mere skeleton of the land being left" (111b). It became the rock that Plato describes thus: "The whole country is only a long promontory extending far into the sea away from the rest of the continent" (111a).[46] Athens is therefore condemned to seafaring and all that that involves—political change, commerce, imperialism. But is not that the fate of Atlantis? Is this extraordinary world, this island "larger than Libya and Asia together" (*Tim.* 23d),[47] and whose Homeric and Oriental characteristics we have explored, *Athenian?*[48] Early in his account, Plato has recourse to a very odd expedient to explain why the names he is going to use are Greek: "You must not be surprised if you should perhaps hear Hellenic names given to foreigners" (*hoia kai tēide onomata; Critias* 113b). The story told to Solon came to him from the Egyptian tongue and was then turned into Greek. An entirely pointless thing to say, unless the point is precisely to intimate that "Hellenic names given to foreigners" might reveal realities no less similar. The structure of Athens is fixed once and for all; that of Atlantis, by contrast, is a continuous creation. First of all, it is on an island, and it has a fertile plain, like that of Athens, that is close to the sea. Above this plain is a mountain, inhabitaed by a couple, Euenor and Leucippe, "born from the earth" (*Critias* 113c-d).[49] In the beginning, then, Atlantis was of the earth, and Poseidon, lord of the island, before he became god of the sea, was a divinity of the soil. To keep his affair with Kleito secret, however, he fashioned around the mountain two circular enclosures of earth, and three of sea; but Plato remarks, "no man could get to the island, for ships and voyages were not yet thought of" (*Critias* 113d-e). The coexistence between earth and water nonetheless became from that moment a fundamental aspect of the structure of Atlantis. A spring rises in the island's center, no longer as a *single* source that could be used at any time of year as at Athens, but as two fountains, one hot, the

other cold, which the god himself caused to flow, just as he caused the 273
famous "sea" of Erechtheus to exist at Athens (*Critias* 113e, 117a; cf.
Hdt. 8.55).[50] Indeed, water appears on Atlantis in a rather less likely
way, too: its soil is rich in every conceivable metal, and especially in gold
and the mysterious metal orichalcum (114e); and in the *Timaeus* (58b et
seq.) Plato tells us that metals, and the purest metal, gold, in particular,
are merely varieties of water.[51]

The coexistence between earth and water, which is in itself significant,
is only the most striking aspect of a dualism that Plato stresses constantly
and that proves that the structure of Atlantis is constituted by the play of
the *apeiron*, of non-identity.

The island refuge in the center is five stades across; then there comes a
stretch of water one stade wide, and then two groups of enclosures of
earth and water, two and three stades across respectively (*Critias* 115d–
16a).[52] Thus we have a sequence that is more or less that of an inverted
fugue: 5(3+2), 1,2,2,3,3; anyone who leaves the island's center rapidly
enters the world of doubleness.[53]

Closely corresponding to the five enclosures that protect the island are
the five pairs of twins Kleito bears to Poseidon. In giving the tally of these
twins (one of which bears both a barbarian and a Greek name: Gadeiros-
Eumelos), Plato carefully distinguishes elder from younger (*Critias*
113e–14d). Again he records that some of the buildings were simple
(*hapla*) and others of different stones (*poikila*); some of the cisterns were
open to the sky and others covered over; and that "twice in the year they
gathered the fruits of the earth," making use of rain during the winter,
and in the summer water from the canals. The kings held their meetings
"every fifth and every sixth year alternately, thus giving equal honor to
the odd and to the even number" (τῷ τε ἀρτίῳ καὶ τῷ περιττῷ μέρος ἴσον
ἀπονέμοντες; *Critias* 116b, 117b, 118e, 119d).[54] When he describes in
the *Timaeus* the formation of the natural world, from the World-Soul to
man, and from man to fish, Plato is also describing the advances of
nonhomogeneity, which is supreme in nature (*physis*). Nature appears in
Atlantis in all its limitlessness: trees, different sorts of plants, fruit,
animals, and in particular the elephant, "the largest and greediest of the
animals" (*Critias* 115a). This structure has a history: the ten sons of
Poseidon give rise to ten royal dynasties, and these dynasties perform
construction works that link the center of the island to the sea beyond
(*Critias* 115b–16a).[55] The kings build bridges and open the land to
seafaring (117e).[56] They improve the plain by means of a grandiose
system of canals (118a–e).[57] They provide themselves with a large army
(119a–b).[58] And, finally, they lay out in the center of the island a

274   monumental area complete with a palace, a sanctuary of Poseidon, and
even a horse-racing circuit, as one might expect on an island consecrated
to that god (*Critias* 116c–17a). Plato gives us figures for most of these
undertakings: the temple, for example, was "a stade in length, and half a
stade in width, and of a proportionate height" (*symmetron;* 116d). If we
convert that into *plethra,* we get 6:3:2—a simple example, one of many,
of a play on the ten primary numbers, and above all, on the number 10, of
which Atlantis provides many instances. [59]

The descendants of Poseidon established a political system of sin-
gularly mixed character (*Critias* 119b–20d). Within his own domain,
each king is sovereign, with power over life and death, which might
correspond as well, to the ideal situation in the *Politicus* (292d–97b), in
the case of a philosopher, as to tyranny in the opposite case. As a group,
the ten kings constitute an oligarchy or aristocracy, which governs collectively in accordance with the precepts engraved by the first kings on a
column of orichalcum at Poseidon's behest. [60] When justice has to be
done, these rules are ensured by the legendary oath, which consists
essentially in the pouring of the consecrated blood of a bull, the characteristic means by which nonphilosophers are able to maintain a constitutional ordinance. [61] And when a member of the royal family is to be put to
death, it must be decided by a majority verdict. From its institutions,
Atlantis might then appear to be one of those successful mixed constitutions described in the *Politicus,* the *Timaeus,* the *Philebus,* and the *Laws;*
and indeed, for many generations, "the kings were obedient to the laws,
and well-affectioned toward the god, whose seed they were"—they even
thought "lightly of the possession of gold and other property, which
seemed only a burden to them" (*Critias* 120e–21a). [62] But the divine
element withered, and the kings were filled "with unrighteous ambition
and power" (*pleonexias adikou kai dynameōs;* 121a–b). [63] And it was then
that, to punish them, Zeus called together the company of the gods to
the center of the universe, to a place "which . . . beholds all created
things" (*hē . . . kathora panta hosa geneseōs meteilēphen*) and that. . . . "
The dialogue breaks off (121b–c), presumably because everyone knew the
outcome. [64] The history of Atlantis thus reveals the same advance toward
disunity that we have seen in its physical structure.

At this point it is appropriate to stress, more than I have done so far,
the Athenian aspects of the mighty island. Cleisthenes' reforms divided
Athens into ten tribes, and it is into ten parts that Poseidon divides his
own domain (*deka merē kataneimas: Critias* 113e). [65] When Plato wrote of
orichalcum, the metal that played so large a part in the prosperity of the
kings of Atlantis, he mentioned that it was "more precious in those days

than anything except gold" (114e).[66] The description of the harbors and
their fortifications is greatly indebted, as has often been noted, to the
complex Kantharos, Zea, Mounychia, the naval yards (*Skeuothēkē*), and
the arsenal. The naval dockyards of Atlantis had triremes lying in them;
and Plato observed of the ports: "they were full of vessels and merchants
coming from all parts, who, from their numbers, kept up a multi-
tudinous sound of human voices, and din and clatter of all sorts night and
day" (*phōnēn kai thorybon pantodapon:* 117e).[67] In other words, just like the
Piraeus.

Unlike the royal palace, the temple of Poseidon is described at length.
And in spite of its exotic decoration, it is astonishingly like the Parthenon. In the sanctuary stands the statue of Poseidon, mounted in a
chariot and surrounded by a hundred sea-nymphs on dolphins; he is "of
such a size that he touched the roof of the building with his head" (116d),
just like Pheidias's statue of Athena Parthenos.[68] All these statues were of
gold. We are reminded of what Pericles says in Thucydides: "The gold
with which the image of the goddess was overlaid . . . weighed forty
talents pure" (2.13.5). All around the temple are statues, and in particular those of the wives of the ten kings (the ten eponymous heroes of
Cleisthenes' city?); and Plato remarks, curiously enough, that there were
"many other great offerings of kings and of private persons, coming both
from the city itself and from the foreign cities over which they held sway"
(*Critias* 116e–17a)—as though he were thinking of Pheidias's two Athe-
nas on the Acropolis, Athena Promachos, set up by command of Pericles,
and Athena Lemnia, which took its name from the Athenian cleruchs of
Lemnos who dedicated it.[69]

Finally, and most important, Atlantis became an imperial power:
"Now in this island of Atlantis there was a great and wonderful empire
which had rule over the whole island and several others, and over parts of
the continent" (*Tim.* 25a; cf. *Critias* 114c). Not satisfied with all this, its
leaders embarked on an overseas expedition. Their clash with prehistoric
Athens brought upon them a catastrophe comparable to that suffered by
the Athens of history in Sicily, or recently experienced by her at the time
when Plato was writing the *Timaeus* and the *Critias,* at the hands of her
rebellious allies.[70]

But we still have to explain, if we are able to conclude the demonstration, why Plato should so oddly have mixed Athenian with Oriental
features in his historical myth. In the *Laws* he analyzes briefly the two
constitutions that "are two mother forms of state from which the rest may
be truly said to be derived" (3.693d): the despotism of Persia, and
Athenian democracy. The account is unhistorical, but Plato's description

of their development (*Laws* 3.694a–701b) establishes a strict parallel between the two of them, strikingly reminiscent of the history of Atlantis: the same just, if precarious, equilibrium in the beginning, the same disastrous evolution, which leads, in the first case, under the impulse of gold and imperialism, to the despotism of an absolute ruler; and in the second, after the Persian Wars, and then the abandonment of the old *mousikē* (moral education) to "theatrocracy." I need hardly add that the Persian king had by the fourth century become enormously influential in the Greek world, whether directly or through the use of satellites.

We can now understand the true significance of the praise of Athens in the *Timaeus* and the *Critias*. The technique is common in Plato.[71] In the *Phaedrus* (278e–79a–b) he praises the young Isocrates, who at the time was actually an old man and Plato's opponent.[72] In doing so, he calls attention away from the real Isocrates to a possible Isocrates, the philosopher-orator that he was not. The Athenian Stranger in the *Laws* raises a protest when his Spartan and Cretan interlocutors account for the institutions of their countries by appealing to military necessity; and Plato then gives us a philosophical Sparta and a philosophical Crete out of his imagination: "the order of them is discovered to his eyes, who has experience in laws gained either by study or by habit, although they are far from being self-evident to the rest of mankind like ourselves" (*Laws* 1.632d; cf. the philosophical Sparta in *Protagoras* 342b–e).

Nevertheless, the moral of our story is complicated. Athens is triumphant. The city of Unity defeats the city that has allowed itself to be taken over by disunity and by heterogeneity. The waters close over Atlantis. Their absolute victory halts the advance of nonidentity. But Athens loses her foundation in earth and becomes Atlantis.[73] Is this "serious"? "I say that about serious matters a man should be serious . . . only God is the natural and worthy object of our most serious . . . endeavors" (*spoudēs axion; Laws* 7.803c). But Plato has just said that if "human affairs are hardly worth considering in earnest . . . yet we must be earnest about them—a sad necessity constrains us" (803b). Man is nothing but a puppet in the hands of God, a plaything made by God for his own pleasure (*theou ti paignion memēchanēmenon; * 1.644d et seq.; 7.803c). And so man pays God homage by "playing the most beautiful games he can" (*paizonta hoti kallistas paidias;* 7.803c). Myth and history, like all things that come from imitation, are among these games. As the *Timaeus* has it: "A man may sometimes set aside meditation about eternal things, and for recreation turn to consider the truths of generation which are probable only; he will thus gain a pleasure not to be repented of, and secure for himself while he lives a wise and moderate pastime"

(*metrion . . . paidion kai phronimon*) (*Tim.* 59c–d). All the same, the game
is worth it: at the beginning of the dialogue, Critias craves his hearers'
indulgence by saying that he is going "to speak of high matters" (*hōs peri
megalōn mellōn legein; Critias* 106c). It is more difficult, he says, to speak of
men than of the gods, because a man is always demanding when a painter
undertakes to paint his portrait (107d). Pointless—if Plato were not
saying to his contemporaries what Horace once said to his own and so
many later philosophers have repeated: *de te fabula narratur*.

NOTES

1. "Review of Gegenschatz," 251 (= *Selected Papers* 200).
2. The undoubted chronological difficulties of this filiation are discussed by J.
K. Davies, *Families*, 325–26. For my part, I am inclined to think that Plato took
a perverse delight in its implausibilities. Is the character who gives his name to
the *Critias* the one who joined the Thirty Tyrants or his grandfather? If the latter,
there would be three Critias's in six generations: the "tyrant," his grandfather,
and his great-great-grandfather. In my opinion, it seems natural that the tyrant
Critias converse with Hermocrates, who was also a well-known political figure at
the end of the fifth century (leader of the Syracusan opposition in Thucydides).
Moreover, this same Critias was also an important theorist in political
philosophy.
3. Cf. P. M. Schuhl, *Fabulation*, 71–105.
4. Cf. especially V. Goldschmidt, *Paradigme*, 81ff.
5. The task has but rarely been either sketched or attempted. I find it extraordinary, for example, that these problems are scarcely even mentioned in the great
commentaries on the *Timaeus* by Taylor (1928) and Cornford (1937). But note E.
Gegenschatz, *Atlantis* (1943), who at least sees that there is a problem.
6. There was for long astonishingly little written on proto-Athens—one
exception was O. Broneer, "Early Athens," although he was mainly interested in
archaeology and the history of religions; now see H. Herter, "Urathen." In
contrast, recent work on the *Critias* reveals a spate of studies of Atlantis; see H.
Cherniss, *Platon I*, 79–83; and L. Brisson, *Platon III*, 266. This recent material is
conveniently synthesized in E. S. Ramage (ed.), *Atlantis*. For an account of the
fantasies, see L. Sprague de Camp, *Lost Continents*.
7. See *FGrH* 115 F 75 (a fragment of Theopompus's *Meropia*, his account of
the human condition, a sort of narrative fiction; the basic source is Aelian, *VH*
3.18).
8. Strabo 2.3.6 (102C); 13.1.36 (598C). For references to interpretations of
Atlantis since antiquity, see P. Couissin, "Mythe," and especially E. S. Ramage,
"Perspectives."
9. Cosmas Indicopleustes, *Christian Topography* 452a 11 et seq. Winstedt. W.

278   Wolska rightly points out that Cosmas's Platonic references are full of mistakes (*Cosmas*, 270); this Byzantine monk is at least strongly skeptical of the historicity of Plato's account. For other hints of the myth of Atlantis in patristic thought, see Ramage, "Perspectives," 24–27.

10. Here I am summarizing my essay, "Hérodote et l'Atlantide."

11. *Atland*, esp. 1.144–302. Rudbeck energetically attacks those who simply assumed that Atlantis was America. On Rudbeck, see E. Simon, *Réveil national*, 269–84 (a reference I owe to H.-I. Marrou), as well as the heavily documented study by J. Svenbro, "Idéologie gothisante."

12. Having had occasion to read Pierre Benoit's monstrous fiction, I confess that at first I took the geographer Berlioux to whom he often refers to be the spontaneous product of Benoit's imagination. That was simply ignorance. I am now able to refer the reader to the *Annuaire de la faculté des lettres de Lyon*, 1 (1884), 1–70, for an article by E. F. Berlioux, "Les Atlantes—Histoire de l'Atlantis et de l'Atlas primitif, ou Introduction à l'histoire de l'Europe," which is one of Benoit's sources. And one might recall that this piece was written at about the same time as the French colonization of the Sahara.

13. P. Couissin's *Atlantide* provides an amusing account of this literature. Since then, the spate shows no signs of diminishing. The reader will forgive me for not citing the authors of this stuff, in spite of their sociological interest, and notwithstanding that among them are to be found eminent men: a Lutheran pastor, a colonel, and a lieutenant-colonel.

14. *Dissertation*, 332.

15. So far as I know, the first scholar to produce this argument was K. T. Frost, "Critias" (1913). A more complex form of the same hypothesis (legend replacing a historical tradition) appears in W. Brandenstein, *Atlantis*. Finally, according to S. Marinatos (*Legend*), Atlantis is indeed Cretan, but only after a detour through Egypt—which makes the legend labyrinthine; cf. J. V. Luce, *Lost Atlantis*, and "Sources." Perhaps these authors should have thought a little more about Proclus's observation: "the theologians often put Crete when they mean the Intelligible" (*in Tim.* 1.118.25 Diehl).

16. Needless to say the article, by R. L. Scranton, is called "Lost Atlantis found again?" (the quotation on p. 160). Since A. Schulten, people have also looked for Atlantis in Tartessus. For another enterprise centered in Spain, this time in Cadiz, see V. Bérard, *Calypso*, 262–86. It contains this argument in connection with the sacrifice of bulls in the oath of the kings of Atlantis (p. 281): "Must we note that Cadiz still has its Plaza de toros, to which people bring, from the neighboring continent, the savage herds of Geryon?"

17. I need hardly say that in making this point I am not criticizing those studies that attempt to relate Plato's "information" to the real institutions of his own day, of which Gernet's introduction to the C.U.F. edition of the *Laws* is an admirable example. A. Vincent has in fact shown what can be done by comparative means in relation to the oath of the kings of Atlantis: "Sacrifice," cf. also

Gernet, "Law and Prelaw," 167ff. It is necessary, however, to show how this "information" relates to Plato's thought, and I would criticize R. Weil for only half performing that task: *Archéologie,* esp. 31–33.

18. See M. Pallottino, "Atlantide," who, however, unfortunately combined sensible observations with much more problematic theses concerning Atlantis and Crete.

19. See M. I. Finley, *The World of Odysseus,* 100–102, 156; and "Land and Sacrifice in the *Odyssey,*" pp. 26–28 above.

20. For these names, see L. Brisson, "Critias," 422–24.

21. P. Friedländer, *Plato,* 273–77; J. Bidez, *Eos,* App. 2, 32–34.

22. On the "hydraulic" aspects of oriental despotism, see my "Avant-propos" to the French translation of K. Wittfogel, *Oriental Despotism.*

23. So A. Rivaud in the C.U.F. edition, 252.

24. I am pretty sure that Plato even borrowed the name Atlantis from Herodotus. The latter places his Atlantes at the western edge of what he knew of the bulge of the Sahara; of which he says that it extends still further west, beyond the Pillars of Hercules (4.184–85). These Atlantes lived on a mountain in the shape of a column. It was enough for Plato to push the geographical myth a little farther by transferring his island "in front of the straits which are by you called the pillars of Hercules" (*Tim.* 24e).

25. On the relation of the Platonic account to the "Athenian history of Athens," see N. Loraux, *Invention,* 300–308.

26. There is no need to stress the disdain that the aristocratic Plato felt for the sea and everything connected with it: see J. Luccioni, "Platon et la Mer," and R. Weil, *Archéolgie,* 163.

27. The thesis is not entirely new. Various Athenian features of Atlantis have been noted, especially by A. Rivaud (C.U.F. edition, 249–50), P. Friedländer, *Plato,* vol. 1, 273–77, and a number of others, mentioned in H. Herter, "Atlantis." Among the latter, the most important and most original is also the earliest: G. Bartoli (*Explication historique*), to whom I refer in my essay "Hérodote et l'Atlantide." For a comparison of the imperialism of Atlantis with that of Athens, see C. Kahn, "Menexenus," 224. In a recent monograph, W. Welliver writes quite seriously that: "Many others have noticed these and other parallels between Atlantis and Persia or Athens; none, so far as I know, has suggested this purpose of Plato's in reflecting both in the same mirror" (*Timaeus-Critias,* 43 n. 8).

28. Note that according to tradition the arbitrator of the dispute was Cecrops, whom Plato makes one of the military leaders of his proto-Athens (*Critias* 110a).

29. The expression suggests a circular enclosure.

30. Rivaud unaccountably translates "separate from the rest"; if the expression is indeed translatable, it means rather "always identical to itself."

31. On the statuary see O. Broneer, "Early Athens," 52, and H. A. Thompson and R. E. Wycherley, *Athenian Agora XIV,* 140–49.

32. Plato does not mean to suggest that Athena is a pure philosopher. On the contrary, statues of Athena as warrior prove to him that in those days women fought just as men did (*Critias* 110b).

33. Northward, the frontier reached as far as the peaks of Cithaeron and Parnes, and included the territory of Oropus.

34. Cf. Aristotle *Politics* 2.2.1261a 15 et seq.: Λέγω δὲ τὸ μίαν εἶναι τὴν πόλιν ὡς ἄριστον ὂν ὅτι μάλιστα πᾶσαν· λαμβάνει γὰρ ταύτην ὑπόθεισιν ὁ Σωκράτης: "I am speaking of the premise from which the argument of Socrates proceeds, 'that the greater the unity of the state, the better.'" There are many comparable Platonic passages; see above all *Rep.* 4.462ab. Of course no tribal organization like that of classical Athens impairs the unity of the city of the *Critias* and the *Timaeus*. On the tribes in the city of the *Laws*, see "A Study in Ambiguity," pp. 229–30 above.

35. This is how I understand the phrase *eukras ousa pros cheimōna te kai theros* (112d; with J. Moreau in his Pleiade translation); unlike Rivaud, who translates, "equally healthy in summer and winter," thus simply omitting the idea of blending—which occurs in relation to the seasons (*hōras metriōtata kekramenas:* 111e; cf. also *Tim.* 24c: *tēn eukrasian tōn hōrōn*).

36. *Critias* 112d: "And they took care to preserve the same number of men and women as could already perform, or could still perform, military service— that is to say, about twenty thousand." A moment earlier, we learned that the Athenians were "the leaders of the Hellenes, who were their willing followers." As in so many other cases connected with the description of prehistoric Athens, we find here a borrowing from the vocabulary of the funeral oration; cf. N. Loraux, *Invention*.

37. All this is well understood by Proclus, *in Tim.* 1.132 et seq. Diehl.

38. Like Rivaud, I adopt here Burnet's text, which treats the words αὖ πέρι as an ancient interpolation; see however the objection by L. Brisson, *Même et Autre*, 270–75. I think that even if he is right, my argument is not substantially undercut, for the Same and the Other remain fundamental elements in the structure of the World-Soul.

39. Cf. Lévêque and Vidal-Naquet, *Clisthène*, 118–19, and the authors cited there. E. Ruschenbusch ("Patrios Politeia," 400) has noted that all the allusions to Solon in the Attic orators are, with three exceptions, later than 356 B.C., the date of Athens' defeat in the Social War and the break-up of the second Athenian Empire. The *Timaeus* and the *Critias* can be dated precisely to this period.

40. *Politicus* 269c–74e; on the relation between the structure of this myth and Empedocles' thought, cf. J. Bollack, *Empédocle*, 133–36; also my "Plato's Myth of the Statesman," pp. 292–93 below.

41. I cite the text of the manuscripts. The indirect tradition (Proclus, Simplicius) usually cites the passage with the substitution of *ponton* for *topon*, which has been accepted by many editors, for example A. Diès, who translates, "in the bottomless Ocean of dissimilarity." The passage has been much debated; cf. especially J. Pépin, "Mer," 257–59. My preference for *topon* is merely ascetic,

since *ponton* is too suitable for my thesis for me not to be conservative. There is no
doubt that the earlier images of the pilot, the helm, and the storm might
naturally evoke the image of Ocean (as Diès says); no less naturally, however, they
might have inspired a correction.

42. Note that Plato here uses the dual number throughout.

43. On the role of the *apeiron* in Platonic teaching, see the very clear discussion by K. Gaiser, *Ungeschriebene*, 190–92. The second hypothesis of the *Parmenides* is a study of the dilution of the One in the world of the Dyad; cf. also *Theaetetus* 155bc.

44. The same characteristic divisions of the World-Soul are reproduced at each level of the hierarchy of souls. Each of the two circles is formed, according to fixed proportions, from the substance of the Same, of the Other, and of that which results from their blending. It is its position in the universe that determines the primacy of the circle of the Same. See L. Brisson, *Même et Autre*.

45. I omit here any discussion of the *chōra*, the material receptacle that makes it possible for differentiation to proceed.

46. Plato at once goes on to make a comparison with islands.

47. There is nothing unusual in a comparison between imperial Athens and an island; Pericles tells the Athenians at the beginning of the Peloponnesian War to behave as if they were islanders (Thuc. 1.92.5). The same image is used by the "Old Oligarch" (Pseudo-Xenophon, *Const. Ath.* 2.14) and by Xenophon (*Poroi* 1).

48. Others have seen here, perhaps rightly, reminiscences of Plato's visit to Syracuse; cf. G. Rudberg, *Platonica*, 51–72.

49. The earliest inhabitants of Atlantis were thus autochthonous, just as the inhabitants of Attica were (*Critias* 109d). Plato underlines the point by giving one of the kings of Atlantis the name Autochthonos (113c). Deliberate play on the etymology of proper names is characteristic of the entire account of Atlantis: Euenor is "the good man," Leucippe "the white horse" (of Poseidon), their daughter Kleito "renown," and so on; cf. L. Brisson, "Critias," 421–24.

50. I have already mentioned this Homeric reminiscence (p. 266 above): a good example of the many-layered significance of Platonic texts.

51. Stones, of which there are so many in Atlantis, are similarly the result of passing earth through water (60b et seq.). These scientific ideas about the origin of metals surely have a mythical background. One is reminded of the first lines of Pindar's *Olympian 1*: Ἄριστον μὲν ὕδωρ, ὁ δὲ / χρυσὸς αἰθόμενον πῦρ / ἅτε διαπρέπει / νυκτὶ μεγάνορος ἔξοχα πλούτου "Best of all things is water; but gold, like a gleaming fire by night, outshines all, pride of wealth beside" (tr. Lattimore). There are of course no precious metals in proto-Athens, and they are anyway forbidden by the laws (*Critias* 112c).

52. See the diagram in Lévêque and Vidal-Naquet, *Clisthène*, 137. Note also the role played by double and triple intervals in the structure of the World-Soul (*Tim.* 36d); the double interval corresponds to the octave, the relation 3:2 to the fifth.

53. Nicole Loraux has called to my attention the fact that this doubleness is implicit in the doubly autochthonous origin, male and female, of the inhabitants of Atlantis. This is quite a remarkable innovation as compared to the Athenian myth of autochthony, which applies solely to men (see Loraux, *Enfants*).

54. Equal and unequal, like hot and cold, dry and wet, were part of the famous table of opposites (*systoichia*) that Aristotle attributes to the Pythagoreans (*Metaph.* 1.5.986a 15—for the table, see p. 141 above). I think that the interpretation of Plato's many numbers in his account of Atlantis in Brumbaugh's stimulating book (*Imagination,* 47–59) is highly debatable. I do not think that Plato intended to provide a world badly constructed in terms of an archaic mathematics. But Brumbaugh is right to stress the role of the numbers 6 and 5 in Plato's description: there are five pairs of twins, and five enclosures; the central island is five stades across; the relation between the total area of the rings of water and that of the rings of earth is 6:5; the statue of Poseidon shows him driving six horses (116d); the central level area measures 6,000 stades square (118); it is rectangular, not square, which puts it on the "bad" side of the aforementioned table of opposites. The number six and its multiples play a fundamental role in the military organization (119ab). I have no desire to interpret these points in detail here, but simply note that Plato himself stresses that the opposition between 5 and 6 is a form of the opposition between the equal and the unequal, which is to say, according to the Pythagorean table of opposites, between good and evil.

55. The kings build both the canals and the bridges at the same time, thus ending the earlier isolation of Kleito's island. This is yet another step in the progress of disunity.

56. Cf. C. Gill, "Origin," 8–9.

57. Note that in the *Laws* (3.681d et seq.), the constitution under which men colonize the plains after the cataclysm is "one in which all other forms and conditions of polities and cities are mingled together" (quoting *Iliad* 20.216–18).

58. This army has both Greek and barbarian characteristics: hoplites and chariot-fighters exist side by side. It is wrong to claim, as does Rivaud (*Laws*, C.U.F.), that slings were also a barbarian weapon; note the Rhodian slingers mentioned by Thucydides, 6.93.

59. The number 10 is the sum of the first four primary numbers, and corresponds to *tetraktys,* on whose role in Pythagoreanism and in Plato, see Lévêque and Vidal-Naquet, *Clisthène,* 100, and the works by Boyancé, Delatte, and Kucharski cited here; also K. Gaiser, *Ungeschriebene Lehre,* 118–23, and the Aristotelian texts cited on p. 542. See also J. Brunschwig, "Review of Kucharski." For Plato, the *tetraktys* is a form of *genesis* (e.g., *Tim.* 53e), to say nothing of the construction of the World-Soul in the form of a double *tetraktys* (*Tim.* 32b–35bc). It seems to me, in the case of the *Critias,* that the genesis of numbers corresponds closely to the play of *physis.* These comments have not proved persuasive to L.

Brisson, who has, I fear, too rationalist a conception of Platonism to entertain speculation about numbers; cf. "Critias," 430.

60. One is reminded of the *kyrbeis* on which the laws of Solon were engraved.

61. The role of the oath in the constitution of Atlantis is analogous to that of incantations and myths in the *Laws*. To echo an expression from E. R. Dodds, the object is to stabilize the Inherited Conglomerate (*The Greeks and the Irrational*, 207).

62. There is probably nothing in the typology of social disharmony in *Republic* 8–9 quite so surprising as the analysis of the role of gold. Gold did not exist in the timocratic city of the Spartan type (8.547b–48b), but it makes its appearance in the oligarchic city, where it provides the basis of the right to rule (8.550de) and becomes the object of envy on the part of those who have lost their position and who found democracy (8.555b et seq.): but it is not enough to level rich and poor, and a lust for gain drives the latter into the arms of the tyrant (8.556 et seq.).

63. Note that this is the language commonly used to describe imperialism.

64. Similarly in the *Odyssey* (12.154–84), the fate of the Phaeacians, guilty of enabling Odysseus to reenter the world of men, is not specified; the story ends with a sacrifice of bulls.

65. On the significance of this division, see Lévêque and Vidal-Naquet, *Clisthène*, 96–98, 110–11, 135–36, 141–42, which offer analyses of the texts, particularly from the *Laws*, that allow us to define Plato's reactions to the institutional innovations of Cleisthenes.

66. There is an evident reference to the silver of Laurion.

67. *Thorybos* is a word regularly employed by Plato to describe what goes on in democratic assemblies: see, for example, *Rep.* 6.492bc. In the *Timaeus*, the union of the soul with the body also involves a *thorybos* (42c). In contrast, true and eternal reason (*logos ho kata tauton alēthēs*) occurs silently, without a sound (*aneu phthongou kai ēchēs;* 37b). The discussion in the *Republic* takes place in the Piraeus, after a procession in honor of a foreign goddess, in the house of the arms-manufacturer Cephalus, in the midst of a boisterous gathering of young people: philosophy is the last thing they care about. That being so, should we not see the very first words of the dialogue—*Katebēn chthes eis Peiraia,* "I walked down to the Piraeus yesterday"—as an image of the philosopher's descent back into the cave? That was the suggestion of Henri Margueritte (during his seminars in the École pratique in 1952–53).

68. See C. Picard, *Manuel, Sculpture*, II. 1, p. 174 n. 2.

69. See Pausanias 1.28.2. I am indebted for most of these remarks on the archaeology to Pierre Lévêque; see also our *Clisthène*, 138.

70. *Tim.* 25a; cf. also *Critias* 114c. There is nothing novel to the view that the *Timaeus* belongs to Plato's last dialogues, but it was recently challenged by G.E.L. Owen, "Place," which, in my opinion, was decisively answered by Cherniss, "Relation." By means of a comparison with the myth of the *Politicus*, C. Gill arrived at the same conclusion ("Critias and Politicus").

71. This was well demonstrated by R. Schaerer, *Question*.

72. There is little point in referring here to the many discussions of this text; cf. the remarks of J. Bollack, *Phaidros,* 152–53.

73. The eschatological myth of *Laws* 10.903e–4e depends upon an analogous reversal.

14

Plato's Myth of the Statesman,
the Ambiguities of the Golden
Age and of History

To A. Andrewes

> And close your eyes with holy dread
> For he on honey-dew hath fed,
> And drunk the milk of Paradise
> Coleridge, Kubla Khan

In the treatise *de Abstinentia* that the neoplatonist Porphyry
devoted to justifying abstention from foods of animal origin, there is a
long quotation from *Life in Greece* (*Bios tēs Hellados*) by the Peripatetic
Dicaearchus (end of the fourth century B.C.), who was a direct disciple of
Aristotle.[1] This book is known to represent a sort of cultural history of
Greek humanity from the very earliest times.

In its essentials, the text tells us that the Golden Age, or age of
Cronos, referred to by the poets, principally by Hesiod in his *Works and
Days* (from which Dicaearchus quotes lines 116–19: "And they had all
good things, the grain-bearing earth [*zeidōros aroura*] itself produced an
abundant and generous harvest, and they lived off their fields in peace and
joy, amidst countless boons . . ."), that this marvelous epoch was a
historical reality: "If it is to be considered as having actually existed
(λαμβάνειν μὲν αὐτὸν ὡς γεγονότα) and not as idle fiction (καὶ μὴ μάτην
ἐπιπεφημισμένον), if all that is exaggeratedly fabulous (τὸ δὲ λίαν μυ-
θικόν) in this tradition" has been eliminated "in order that it might be
reduced, by means of reasoning, to a natural meaning." This would mean
reconciling what is apparently unreconcilable, that is to say, a basically

---

This chapter was published in French in the volume entitled *Langue, discours,
société. Pour Émile Benveniste* (Paris: 1975), 374–91. It has been translated in
collaboration with Maria Jolas, and I have taken this opportunity to revise it and
make a few slight changes. I want to thank those who have been so kind as to read
it, especially V. Goldschmidt, G. E. R. Lloyd, C. Gill, and Nicole Loraux.

pessimistic view of the history of humanity with all that the historical-sociological investigations of the fifth century (Democritus, Protagoras, Thucydides) taught Greek thinkers about the hardships and afflictions of the first human beings, and which would hardly correspond to the vision of a Golden Age.[2] It would also mean taking into account the contribution, in the fourth century, of the new medical thinking, which was particularly centered on a scrupulous system of dietetics.[3] In actual fact, according to Dicaearchus, the Golden Age coincided with the origins of human life, and by the Golden Age must be understood a time when neither property nor its corollaries, social conflict and war, existed. The Golden Age is marked, however, not by infinite abundance, but by frugality, simple living, and simple eating. The excellence of dietary habits that are perfectly consistent with the most advanced teachings of medical science is explained by the scarcity (*spanis*) of the earth's natural products. Such simplicity is referred to in a proverb quoted by Dicaearchus (and many others) as symbolizing the simple life: *halis dryos*. Let's have done with the oak, it says, i.e., with the acorns on which primitive humanity fed. This break with the traditional diet is successively expressed in the invention of pastoral living (accompanied by war and hunting), then of agricultural society (accompanied by all the political regimes known to the men of the fourth century). A text of this kind in itself would deserve a lengthy analysis, one that could and should include confrontation of this passage with a contemporary document, the *Peri Eusebeias* (*On Piety*) by Theophrastus, which we also know essentially through Porphyry's *de Abstinentia*. It would be worthwhile, too, to prolong the analysis to include the utopias and historical constructions of the Hellenistic period: Iambulus's philosophical tale (Diodorus 2.55–60), or Polybius's sixth book. Here, however, my intention is more modest, and I shall use the Dicaearchus text not to look foward but, on the contrary, to look backward, to see what he has acquired and what he conceals.

Let me note immediately that Cronos, the father of Zeus, under whose patronage Dicaearchus, following numerous others, places the felicitous—if simple—beginnings of humanity, is an extremely ambiguous divine personage.[4] Indeed, Theophrastus, who in *On Piety* outlines a history of the religious practices of humanity, also places the first human eras in a period of vegetable consumption and non-vegetable sacrifice. But the Cronos he tells about is also a terrible, apparently cannibalistic, god; the god to whom the Carthaginians offer children in sacrifice.[5] Theophrastus's entire account, in his references to primitive humanity, closely mixes vegetarian, idyllic features with sanguinary references to anthropophagy and cannibalism. Human sacrifice immediately "succeeds" vegetable sacrifice. Animal sacrifice only appears at the following "stage," as a substitute for human sacrifice (Porph, *de Abst.* 2.27, p. 156). Needless to say, in studying these texts we have every right to read in palimpsest logical opposition for historical succession, nor is it very hard to demonstrate that Dicaearchus and Theophrastus have historicized myths that are older in time than they are. But can we consider as negligible the fact that these philosophers should deliberately have situated the fables they tell us in the human era? Dicaearchus and Theophrastus see humanity's advance since the time of the oak and the acorn, which for Dicaearchus too is the time of Cronos, as a continual, historical evolution toward the age of cities and empires, the empire of Athens or of Alexander. The fourth-century historian, Ephorus, proceeded in the same manner, except for the fact that, in his works, vegetarianism and anthropophagy did not succeed each other in time, but were contiguous in space. Protesting against the historians who, "because they know that the terrible and the marvelous are startling," attribute ferocity to the entire Scythian and Sarmatian communities, he demonstrated that these people have very dissimilar customs: "For whereas some are so cruel that they even eat human beings, other abstain from eating any living creature," and he added, "one should also tell the opposite facts and describe their patterns of conduct" (*FGrH* 70 F 42 = Strabo 7.3.9; tr. H. L. Jones).

In order to be convinced of the very marked difference between this type of historical or geographical portrayal and the schemas of the archaic epoch, we need only to return briefly to this epoch, that is, to Homer and Hesiod. Here there is no question of describing either succession or contiguity. It is undoubtedly important to note that Hesiod's text is presented in narrative form, but as J.-P. Vernant has ably shown, Hesiod's myth of the "races" does not define a "history of the decadence of humanity, but a series of statuses that is founded on the distinction between *dikē* and *hybris,* the golden 'race' being the supreme accomplishment of *dikē.*"⁶ The very fact that the "races" disappear entirely once their time has run its course shows that for Hesiod there is no continuity between the Golden Age and our own, in which *hybris* and *dikē* are mingled. Properly speaking, we are not *descended* from the men of the age of Cronos.

It may be added, however, that Homer and Hesiod define this status of humanity now implicitly, now explicitly, as being intermediate between the world of the gods, which was touched by the Golden Age, and the world of bestiality characterized by anthropophagy. "This," says Hesiod, "is the law prescribed for men by the teachings of the son of Cronos,

288   namely that fishes and beasts and winged fowl devour one another, for right (*dikē*) is not in them" (*WD* 276–78). Consequently, the very one who, according to Hesiod and later tradition, was at the origin of the status of social man, Prometheus, who furnished fire for cooking and introduced sacrifice, was also responsible for the break with the gods and with wild beasts. As Marcel Detienne recently wrote: "In one case, by the invention of sacrifice, Prometheus assures passage from the communal repasts of gods and men in the Golden Age to the meat diet; in the other, by bringing fire and inventing various techniques, Prometheus wrests humanity from savagery and bestiality."[7] But it is not enough to pose this question in terms of binary logic. What we shall have to discuss is ambiguity. Not, of course, "primitive" ambiguity, such as the ambiguity that Freud situated at the "origins" of language, when contradiction was nonexistent. Emile Benveniste made short shrift of this myth and re-called that "if we assume the existence of a language in which *large* and *small* are identically expressed, it will be a language in which the distinc-tion between *large* and *small* has literally no meaning and the dimensional category is nonexistent, not a language that permits a contrary expression of dimension."[8] But, as Benveniste further points out, "what Freud asked in vain of *historical* language, he could have asked of the myth to a certain extent . . ."[9] and in reality it is evident that in archaic times the Golden Age of Cronos is also an age of bestiality; witness Homer's Cyclops, to whom the earth furnishes everything with the generosity described by Hesiod, but who remains nevertheless the cannibal with whom we are all familiar.[10]

   Greek thought, which was an offspring of the city-state, contested this ambiguity and tried to mitigate its importance—"Greek thought," or at least an entire current of it. The *Prometheus* of Protagoras, in the myth told by Plato, and which may well hark back to the thought of the great Sophist,[11] does not separate men from gods. Better still, from the mo-ment man has at his disposal the *technē* stolen from Athena and Hephaistos, he possesses his "share of the divine lot" (*Prot.* 322a), a share that is moreover insufficient for the requirements of urban life, which is only made possible when Zeus and Hermes confer upon humanity the gifts of *aidōs* and *dikē*. This introduction to the strictly civic and political dimension summarizes, in its way, the mutation that had taken place since the time of Homer and Hesiod. For the Archaic poets, the human status that they defined with the help of the oppositions that I pointed out earlier was a technical and social status; the political dimension, although not lacking,[12] was only one aspect of this status. For the thinkers of the Classical epoch, a separate place had to be reserved for that greatest of all inventions, which is the mark of civilized life: the triumphant polis.

But let us return to the fourth century, which we left in the middle of a discussion about Dicaearchus and Theophrastus. As is well known, this was a period of crises, political and social change, subversive activity, and reexamination of values. The question of the Golden Age, therefore, is not only a theoretical problem that one tries to integrate into the historical discourse. The age of Cronos, "life in the time of Cronos," as it is called, is a slogan for philosophical and religious sects that are not satisfied, or are no longer satisfied, with the existing civic order. In this domain, to be sure, the transgression goes much further back than the fourth century, but it was at this epoch that, in the dual religious and philosophic context that characterized it at the time, this transgression was systematically organized. 13

As Detienne has clearly shown, 14 transcendence of the civic order can be oriented in two opposed directions: "upward" or "downward." If upward, an attempt is made to implant in "our" world the virtues of the Golden Age. Beginning with the Archaic epoch, this tendency was expressed by the Orphics and the Pythagoreans. If downward, on the contrary, an effort to enter into contact with bestiality is given expression through practice and even more by means of the Dionysical phantasm of *ōmophagia*, or through consumption of raw food that could lead finally to cannibalism. However—and this is what makes the problem so interesting—these two forms are always liable to interfere with each other; certain works of tragedy, in fact, throw particular light on this interference. 15 Thus, at the very end of the fifth century, the tragedy of the *Bacchae* shows the women companions of Dionysus living in a paradisiacal world that the messenger described to Pentheus as follows: "On their heads they put garlands of ivy and oak and flowering bryony. One grasped a thyrsus and struck it into a rock from which a dewy stream of water leapt out; another struck her rod on the ground and for her the god sent up a spring of wine; and those who had a desire for the white drink scraped the ground with their fingertips and had jets of milk; and from out of the ivied thyrsi, sweet streams of honey dripped" (*Bacchae* 702–11; tr. G. S. Kirk). In opposition to his idyllic scene, in the same account given by the messenger, there is the description of the Bacchae leaving the mountain for the plain of Demeter, carrying off children and lacerating cattle, as prelude to the final murder, which was to be the incestuous and as it seems cannibalistic murder of Pentheus by his mother. What unifies these two contradictory states is, however, clear: in the first as well as in the second, there is no separation of human beings from animals, or this separation has ceased. The Bacchae of the Golden Age, instead of suckling their own children, which they abandoned, gave suck to fawns and wolf-cubs (*Bacchae* 701–2). The bestiality of the mad Bacchae was such that precise details do not even need recalling.

Our epoch, which is not lacking in propaganda and advertising for both "natural water" and "pure" foods (which the Orphics recommended), which abounds as well in neo-naturist sects, is particularly well placed to understand, it seems to me, what the eruption upon the scene of those who demanded a Golden Age here and now meant for the fourth century. Among so many sects in confrontation, there was one, however, that made its choice, and which in absolute seriousness decided in favor of a return to savagery. I refer of course to the Cynics. True enough, no one would argue today, as C. W. Goettling did in the last century, that the thought of the Cynics is the philosophy of the Greek proletariat[16]—in itself an absurd expression—but there is no disputing the fact that Cynicism marvelously expresses one aspect of crisis in the classical city. Indeed, it is characteristic that the founder of the sect, Antisthenes, was not a full-fledged Athenian, but of bastard birth, the son of an Athenian and a woman of Thrace, one of the group that met in the Cynosarges gymnasium, reserved for *nothoi* (bastards);[17] as we would say today, a "marginal" figure. The lifestyle that the Cynics were supposed to adopt was based on deliberate transgression of all interdictions, especially those of a dietary or sexual nature, upon which society is founded: hence the defense of raw versus cooked, of masturbation and incest versus a regulated sexuality, and in fact, of cannibalism. We are not surprised to learn that Antisthenes had written two treatises on the Cyclops, and Diogenes a tragedy on Thyestes (Diogenes Laertius 6.17, 18, 73, 80). The enemy of the Cynics was the civilizing hero of Aeschylus and of Protagoras, Prometheus.[18] In short, to borrow from Plutarch, the intent was "to brutalize our lives," *ton bion apothēriōsai* (Plut. *De esu carnium* 995c–d). We should not be surprised, therefore, that the Cynics should have adopted as their own the slogan *eleutheria hē epi Kronou*, "freedom as in the time of Cronos,"[19] which they situated in an age of "primitive" savagery, not one of vegetarianism and Orphic foods. The Golden Age is the age of Polyphemus and the "cyclopic life," praise of which may be found, for instance, in Plutarch's *Gryllus*, which allows the victims of Circe to speak, in order to proclaim their happiness. This is a theme of Cynic origin.

At the crossroads of these fourth-century crises, concerning which the Cynics' subversiveness bears such eloquent witness, Plato's philosophy appears to be at once a document about the crisis and an effort to solve it, at least theoretically. To the extent that the Golden Age was actually at the heart of contemporary discussion, it is through this discussion that we must study what becomes of this theme in Plato's hands, as for instance in the *Statesman* myth (268d–74e). But first let us recall briefly the location of the dialogue in which the myth appears. The discussion taking place between Socrates the younger and the stranger from Elea, a discussion that had been conducted by means of successive dichotomies, had reached an impasse: the definition of the Statesman as a shepherd of the human flock. The myth, which occupied here the "role of criteri-on,"[20] contains a warning against "angelism,"[21] which could lead us to confuse divine with human statesmen, the Golden Age with the cycle of Zeus; not that the identification of king and shepherd is an erroneous one, but it may be applied to too many different personages for it to be usable.

The myth is introduced by a preamble (268e–69c) that appears to have been curiously neglected by commentators. Actually, Plato regroups three "stories from the old days" before combining them into a single narrative. The first tells of the strange phenomenon that marked the quarrel between Atreus and Thyestes, an episode that is mentioned in very numerous sources.[22] The two brothers are in dispute as to which will occupy the throne. A supernatural event occurs in support of the claims made by Atreus, when a lamb with golden fleece is born in his flock. But Thyestes, who is the lover of Atreus's wife, with her complicity steals the miraculous lamb. At this point, Zeus intervenes with an even more prodigious event, which is decisive: he reverses the course of the sun and the Pleiades. This, at any rate, is the most widespread version: there is another one, which was known to the Latin poets and perhaps to Sophocles, but to which Plato makes no direct allusion, which is that, out of horror at the criminal feast organized in honor of Thyestes, the divine ruler changed the sun's course.[23] Let us note right away why the use of *this* legend is a bit strange. In order to shift from one solar cycle to the other, Plato did not have to mention those strange "shepherds," Atreus and Thyestes, nor was he obliged to recall the miracle that had taken place in favor of the organizer of a cannibalistic feast. Herodotus knew that the sun had "changed its dwelling-place four times, twice by rising where it now sets, and twice by setting where it now rises" (2.142),[24] and he had used this legend to enhance another myth, which concerned the perenniality of Egypt. In the *Timaeus* and elsewhere, Plato wisely remembered this lesson.[25]

The second tradition used by Plato was the one concerning the men said to have been born from the earth (the *gēgeneis*) before the appearance of sexually differentiated reproduction. Without enumerating here the many instances in Greek warrior mythology in which this type of birth is utilized to represent brute force,[26] I shall merely recall that the "sons of the earth" appear on two more occasions in the work of Plato: first, in the *Republic*, where they are the heroes of the famous "Phoenician story" about the "fine lie" that was told to persuade the citizens of the "ideal city" that they were all children of the same mother, the earth, but that some were of gold, others of silver, and the remainder of bronze (*Rep.* 414 et seq., 468e–f). And again, in the *Sophist* (248c, cf. *Laws* 727e), in which the *gēgeneis* are the people defined as *spartoi te kai autochthones*, that is, sown in the earth and sprung from it, the "materialists," whom Plato contrasts with the "friends of Forms" in this dialogue, which is exactly contemporary with the *Statesman*.

The third "tradition" is the one that treats of the time of Cronos.

Plato returns to the question of royalty, which is identified with the Golden Age, in the *Laws*, written when he was a very old man. We shall simply note here the mention he made of it in a much earlier dialogue, the *Gorgias*. In the myth that ends this dialogue, referring to the way in which the judgments of men were arrived at in the time of Cronos and the very beginnings of Zeus's reign, that is, to the legal instrument that determined whether one had or did not have the right to enter into the sphere of the Islands of the Blessed, Socrates cites an observation to the effect that it had been an era of injustice, since the living judged one another at the end of their lives. Zeus decides to put an end to these errors and Prometheus is charged with depriving men of their former knowledge concerning the moment of their death. From now on, it is men's souls that will be judged, and the souls of Minos, Rhadamanthus, and Aeacus will pronounce the judgments.[27] This amounts to saying that Prometheus helps men to assume their mortal status, and that the age of Zeus is opposed to the age of Cronos in the same way that the age of just judges is opposed to the age of arbitrary judges. Plato's Cronos is not a simple personage, and there exists at least one other example of the ambiguous nature of Cronos. In *Republic* 2 (378a) the Cronos myth is presented as a typical example of the kind of story that should not be told to children.

We are warned in advance, as it were, that a certain ambiguity will appear in the myth itself. Let us recall briefly how the myth functions; I use the word "functions" because, as has already been demonstrated by Schuhl, Plato had in mind a technical model to which the text makes implicit reference.[28] He supposed that the cosmos is actuated by "two circular movements that are deployed successively in opposite directions, and which engender both worlds: in opposition to our era, the divine age, and carried forward by its own momentum, the actual course of things."[29] These two consecutive states of the world are separated by a reverse movement, *metabolē*, characterized now by divine control of the course of the world, which then runs quite independently, the way the circle of the Same does in the *Timaeus:* now by relinquishment of divine control—the world has turned in the opposite direction and is sailing toward "the endless ocean of dissimilarity" (εἰς τὸν τῆς ἀνομοιότητος ἄπειρον ὄντα πόντον: 273e). As J. Bollack very aptly says: "What Plato's myth develops in opposite directions, in order to examine them, is both aspects of the same world, which actually coexist, and not the stages of a cyclic evolution." One might ask how the two worlds oppose each other inside the myth. One of these worlds is undoubtedly the age of Cronos, with the features that, since Hesiod, have been attributed to it: infinite fertility of the earth, a harmonious relationship between men and animals, absence of anthropophagy (271e). That the humanity of the time of Cronos was not a political humanity is also in accord with the earliest accounts, although Plato lays special emphasis on this aspect of the myth in favor of his own argumentation, according to which God made humanity in the same way that today humanity breeds animals, "but there was no constitution and no possession of either women or children" (271e–72a). In passing it might be noted that only male humans are born from the earth, women and families being necessarily part of organized life. In the last analysis, this implies the city-state. In this respect, the picture of life in the time of Cronos, contrary to what has been frequently argued,[30] is radically different from that of the *city-state,* which is situated far back in history, the ideal Athens of the *Critias.* To this general view, Plato adds features that are his own: the human beings of the time of Cronos led their lives in reverse; men were born from the earth, and they were born old. The bodies that come out of the earth remember nothing (272a) and have white hair,[31] just as the men who, according to Hesiod, will be born at the end of our age, will also have white hair (*WD* 181). The cycle of their lives, like the White Queen's in *Through the Looking Glass,* is the opposite of ours. These men in reverse are therefore not citizens, but do they live according to philosophy? Plato asks this question, but he answers it only indirectly. "If they were so busy gorging themselves with food and drink that they only exchanged with one another and with animals such fables as are now told about them, in that case . . . the question would be easily solved" (272c–d). Fables? The fables of Hesiod, no doubt, but also those that Plato himself referred to in the preamble to the myth in which, here again, we find a remarkable discordance inside the beautifully symmetrical whole. It is certainly not enough to say, as P. Friedländer does, that Plato is commenting ironically on the little confidence to be placed in all human descriptions of the Golden Age.[32] The Paradise of the Golden Age was definitely an animal paradise. Humanity, including the humanity of the philosophers, in on the other slope of the mountain, on the side of the cycle of Zeus. The pastoral vocabulary[33] that was used to describe the time of Cronos was followed, during the Zeus cycle, by a political vocabulary. The world that God had abandoned[34] had *kratos* over itself (273a): it is *autokratōr* (274a).[35] Our humanity, therefore, is the humanity that must brave the necessity and even the savagery that immediately followed the catastrophe created by God's departure (274c). In short, it is the humanity of the Protagorean myth, except for one important point: nothing was stolen. The gifts of the gods and those of Prometheus are considered of equal value.

I say "our humanity," and I must immediately correct myself. For one of the great difficulties that the myth poses is that of deciding how the status of "our" world should be defined. When Plato says *nyn* (in 272b and 271e), what exactly is he designating? Is it the world of the myth, the world dominated by innate desire, the *symphytos epithymia* (271e), the world "framed in the prodigality of nature," as Shakespeare would have put it, the world evolving logically toward dissimilarity and dissolution? Or is he speaking of a mixed world, the world of the *Timaeus*, the world that is founded on the collaboration of reason with necessity? One is tempted, for instance, to give this interpretation to the passage in which Plato defines the world as a mixed one: "Now what we know by the name of Heaven and World has indeed been endowed by the author of its being with many blessed conditions; none the less it partakes of body also, whence 'tis impossible it should be internally exempt from change, though 'tis true that, so far as it may, it moves in one place with a uniform and single Motion" (269d–e; tr. Taylor). And Plato adds, as I understand (with L. Robin), that the world has received a share of the circular movement (*anakyklēsis*) that, "of all movements is the least possible alteration of the original movement."[36] Here, it is true that what follows clarifies Plato's meaning, namely that whereas in the *Timaeus* the circle of the Same and the circle of the Other function together, one in one direction, one in the other, one incarnated in the fixed astral bodies, the other in the planets,[37] here the world's movement is now forward, now backward. But this logical solution does not remove all the ambiguities; it fails to take into account the fact that one of the states of the cosmos, the one placed under God's immediate direction, is an anti-world, a

world in reverse, and that this reverse state corresponds exactly to an
obverse right state, to a world in which the temporal order is the one that
we know. It will no doubt be objected that philosophy is just that: "the
world in reverse," that to read reality philosophically is to see in it the
contrary of what it appears to be. The lesson is certainly Platonist, but it
would still be necessary to explain the following curious fact: the divine
gifts, those made by Prometheus, Athena, and Hephaistos, were granted
to humanity[38] at the very time in the cycle when God was supposed to
have withdrawn entirely from the world. We are therefore obliged to
admit that the ambiguity of the text is not a matter of chance but is
located at its very center. However, it is also true that in Plato's reference
to the difficulties encountered by humanity when it is left to its own
devices, we find no arguments to prove that our philosopher was merely a
man who worshipped the past, for whom the Golden Age was situated at
the beginning of history. On this point, we must disagree with those
commentators who, with K. R. Popper and E. Havelock, have represented Plato as the theoretician *par excellence* of decadence.[39] We can never
insist enough on the following important fact: in the *Statesman*, the
Golden Age is radically severed from the city-state. And Plato does
undoubtedly tell us that the world was most mindful of the teachings "of
its maker and father" (273a–b) at the beginning of the Zeus cycle.
Cosmology does not follow the same rhythm as anthropology. Protagorean progress, that is, the progress that wrested men from dependence and from the war that animals waged against them advanced in the
opposite direction to that of the evolution of the Cosmos;[40] but Plato did
not so easily rid himself of Protagoras as one might think. For philosophy,
science, and the city are, implicitly, also situated in the Zeus cycle.[41]
Certain interpreters have undertaken to go further than I do here. E.
Zeller, in a passage of his *History of Ancient Philosophy,* understood the
description of the men of the Golden Age as an ironic criticism of
Antisthenes' naturalist philosophy.[42] G. Rodier refuted this interpretation,[43] and his arguments have been generally accepted. However, if one
agrees that there is a kind of shadow over the Platonist Golden Age, one
is inclined to think that Zeller's intuition was not entirely absurd. At the
time Plato wrote the *Statesman*—the date is not known, but it evidently
precedes the "resignation" revealed in the *Laws*[44]—he was not trying to
escape from the city, either by means of the Golden Age, or, needless to
say, by means of a return to savagery.

And yet, does there exist in his last work the element that would be
needed to explain, or at least to initiate, the historical treatment of the

Golden Age that, at the end of the century, was to characterize the work of Dicaearchus? We shall try to answer this question.

The universe presented in the *Statesman* in fragmented form, with both cycles of the myth I have just discussed, in the *Laws* becomes one of the "mixed" pieces, for which the *Timaeus*, the *Philebus*, and the *Sophist* furnish the theory; the story that Plato outlined in Book 3 of his last work is also a "mixed" one. It would be vain to try to find in this story *one* single "meaning," either positive or negative. Through a series of felicitous accidents and divine interventions, the story could just as well end with a successful mixture, such as the Spartan constitution,[45] as with the disaster that struck Argos and Messene (*Laws* 690d–91b). The historical investigation ends, as we know, with the decision to found an ideal city-state that, in relation to the city in the *Republic*, would be *mia deuterōs*, second in oneness (*Laws* 739e).[46] In this ultimate effort, what is the position attributed to the age of Cronos? It is introduced at the exact moment when the Athenian, speaking to the imaginary colonists, is about to explain that "God should be for us the measure of all things, absolutely supreme, and far superior, I think, to what man is said to be." And in fact, in the *Laws*, the city-state, which is a theocracy "in the etymological sense of the word,"[47] only has the appearance, although it is reproduced down to the minutest detail, of a classical city, that is to say, of a group based on the responsibility of each citizen. The traditional institutions and magistratures perform only more or less fictitious functions; sovereignty is elsewhere. The reference to the age of Cronos (713a–14b) has been presented as a mere "extract" of the myth of the *Statesman*.[48] Of course, considering the fact that we are in a period of recomposed time, Cronos is situated so far back in history (*eti protera toutōn, pampoly:* 713b) that it is impossible to speak of a human time that began with the Golden Age. But as regards the myth of the *Statesman*, there are three essential differences. First, just underneath God's direct control, there is a government of demons, religious personages whose duties are limited by the *Statesman* to administering animals. In addition, the reign of Cronos, although characterized by the "abundance without toil" that, since Hesiod, had been part of the tradition, possessed nevertheless political institutions and a political vocabulary. The age of Cronos included *poleis* (713d–e) and divine rulers (713d). There was not only material abundance but abundance of justice, *aphthonia dikēs* (713e), and the political regime was characterized by "good legislation," *eunomia*. Plato even notes the existence of precautionary measures to prevent revolution (713e). Finally, the pastoral image, which in the *Statesman* is objected to as being unsuitable, is taken up by the Plato of the *Laws*.

After playing upon the different meanings of the root *nem*, then explaining that since oxen are not appointed to be the lords of oxen, men need not be the lords of men, he remarks that what we call the *law* is the *dianomē tou nou* (714a). It is therefore legitimate to say that the best ordered among existing city-states are copies of the forms of "authority and administration that obtained in the time of Cronos," ἀρχή τε καὶ οἴκησις . . . ἐπὶ Κρόνου (713b).

The age of Cronos is paradigmatic in relation to the best of present-day cities, just as the city in the *Republic* is paradigmatic in relation to the city in the *Laws* (739e). But Plato makes no further mention of the ideal city, except to say that it is inhabited by gods, or the children of gods. Does it necessarily follow that, even in the *Laws*, Plato had rallied to the cause of "soft primitivism," that is, to idealization of the early ages of humanity,[49] in short, that he believed, to quote K. R. Popper, that "the 'model,' the *original*, of its stage of perfection can be found in the remotest past, in a Golden Age that existed at the dawn of history"?[50] True enough, when Plato writes of the discovery of agricultural techniques, the gifts of Demeter and Kore, through the intermediary Triptolemus, he makes very specific allusions to Orphic traditions: "There was a time when we dared not eat even beef, when the sacrifices offered to the gods were not living creatures, but cakes or fruit dipped in honey, and similar *pure* offerings, such as those that required us to abstain from meat, in the belief that it was blasphemous to eat meat, or to soil with blood the altars of the gods" (782c). Thus the models for the lives we call "Orphic" refer back to a distant past (*Orphikoi legomenoi . . . bioi*). Nor is there any lack of "historical" warrant for a life that was in opposition to the Orphic life. "That men offer other men in sacrifice is illustrated by numerous examples that have survived until this day": Τὸ δὲ μὴν θύειν ἀνθρώπους ἀλλήλους ἔτι καὶ νῦν παραμένον ὁρῶμεν πολλοῖς (782c). Actually, before the invention of agriculture, living creatures,[51] as is still the case, devoured one another assiduously. Thus the most remote past presents a very different picture from that of only Orphic life, which moreover can hardly be considered to be a model. The author of the *Epinomis*—whether it is or is not Plato—later returned, in fact, to this point, explaining that the interdiction of anthropophagy must be put in the same category as the invention of agriculture and *technai*, that is to say, in a secondary category (975a–b).

There remains to be examined, however, the famous passage in Book 3 of the *Laws* that describes humanity's fresh beginnings after the catastrophe, and the patriarchal life that Plato describes, with the help of Homer's Cyclops, but without referring to cannibalism.[52] A savage life, as

298   explicitly stated, but a just and simple one. Plato confronts Protagoras once more by pointing out that the absence of art is not a decisive obstacle to human happiness. But when he compares these "noble savages" with his own contemporaries, Plato observes that they showed greater simplicity (*euēthesteroi*), were more courageous (*andreioteroi*), more temperate (*sōphronesteroi*), more just (*dikaioteroi*) than we are (679e). Justice, temperance, courage . . . the traditional virtues from which Plato made a theory of virtues in the *Republic,* are here, except for the greatest of them all, wisdom (*sophia*), which is the virtue of the mind, the virtue of philosophers, of possessors of knowledge (*Rep.* 428e–29a). Wisdom replaced by simplicity, in the dual sense of this word, is an ambiguous compliment.[53]

But Plato explains himself clearly on this subject: our world, which was born of historical evolution: "cities, constitutions, arts and laws," is "an abundance of vice and also of virtue" (*pollē men ponēria, pollē de kai aretē; Laws* 678a). Primitivism, so far from being a slogan, is merely a last resort, and the simplicity of patriarchal life is not viewed with any greater illusions as regards its basic features than the elementary city of the *Republic,* which is founded solely on necessity, and which Plato's brother Glaucon, in spite of the happiness supposed to obtain there, describes as a "city of swine" (*Rep.* 372d). There remains the fact that, although Plato resisted to the end the different mirages of the Golden Age that flourished once again in the epoch that followed, there was no lack of tension— between happiness and science, between the city of men and the city ruled by God (as, shall we say, in the *Laws,* through the intermediary of the philosophers disguised as elders in the "nocturnal council"), between history and intelligible Forms—tension that seems to end in a breach.[54] It has justly been said that although the Platonist city itself represents the "finest of all dramas" (*Laws* 817b), "this drama that has been lived seems to be void of all dramatic elements; nothing that is irreparable can happen to the soul; the drama comprises neither tragic adventures nor even a *dénouement* since it does not end in death."[55] Actually, the real Platonist tragedy lies elsewhere: in the very place occupied by Platonism, in the ambiguity of history.

NOTES

1. Porphyry, *de Abstinentia* 4.2, pp. 228–31 Nauck. The Dicaearchus text forms no. 49 of the collection of the fragments by F. Wehrli (see also FF 47, 48, 50, and 51, which are from the same source but are not direct quotations). Our

text is also reproduced (with translation) in A. O. Lovejoy and G. Boas, *Primi-tivism*, 94–96.

2. Here I shall simply refer readers to T. Cole's fundamental book, *Democritus*.

3. Here I have in mind especially the things we have learned from J. Bertier in her edition of the Mnesitheus and Dieuches fragments (Leyden: 1972).

4. I have briefly explained this elsewhere; cf. "Land and Sacrifice in the *Odyssey*," pp. 17–18 above.

5. *De Abstinentia* 2.27, p. 156, corresponds to F 13, p. 174, of the W. Poetscher edition (Leyden: 1964).

6. See his "Myth of the Races" I and II.

7. "Gnawing," 57.

8. "Remarks," 71.

9. "Remarks, 72.

10. See "Land and Sacrifice in the *Odyssey*," pp. 21–22 above.

11. Cf. for instance what E. Will says on the subject, *Le Monde grec*, 482. A detailed demonstration is presented in the unpublished thesis by R. Winton, Cambridge.

12. Here I recall the famous lines from the *Odyssey* (9.112–15) on the lack of deliberative institutions among the Cyclopes.

13. Aristotle has provided testimony that is probably valid for his own epoch when he states that, in the tradition of the Athenian peasants, the tyranny exercised by Pisistratus seemed like the age of Cronos (*Ath. Pol.* 16.7).

14. In his article quoted above (n. 7, "Gnawing"), the entire analysis may be considered a commentary on Aristotle's formula: "he who by nature and not by accident is without a city is either base (*phaulos*) or more powerful than a man is" (*Pol.* 1.1253a 4).

15. See N. Loraux, "Interférence."

16. "Eine Schule, welche recht für die Proletarier Athens gerechnet war": "Kynosarges," 169.

17. Diogenes Laertius 6.1.13; *Lex. Rhet.* Bekker, 274; cf. S. C. Humphreys, "Nothoi."

18. Cf. Plutarch, *Aquane an ignis sit utilior* (956b; Dio Chrysostom, 6.25, 29–30. The anti-Prometheus is Heracles.

19. Cf. [Diogenes] *Ep.* 32; Lucian, *Drapetai* 17; and T. Cole, *Democritus*, 151 n. 10.

20. V. Goldschmidt, *Dialogues*, 259. On the role of the myth that treats of the search for a human *eidos*, see S. Benardete, "Eidos," esp. 198.

21. V. Goldschmidt, *Dialogues*, 260.

22. They have been collected by J. G. Frazer in his edition of the Pseudo-Apollodorean *Library*, 2. 164–66; the most important texts dating from before Plato are Euripides *El.* 699–730, *Or.* 996–1012.

23. Cf. A. C. Pearson, *Fragments* 1, p. 93.

24. Cf. C. Froidefrond, *Mirage égyptien*, 143.

25. Cf. Froidefrond, *Mirage*, 276–342.

26. See for instance F. Vian *Cadmos* and "Fonction guerrière," concerning which, however, I do not accept the historicity of the interpretation.

27. *Gorgias* 523b–e; on the negative aspects of Cronos, see also *Rep.* 378a.

28. P. M. Schuhl, "Politique."

29. J. Bollack, *Empédocle*, 133. I also recommend the excellent analysis in p. 135 n. 1; cf. preceding this, V. Goldschmidt, *Platonisme*, 104. It has occasionally been argued that instead of *two* cosmic cycles, there were three stages: the age of Cronos, the age of the world in reverse, and the age of our world, which is a mixed one. This interpretation is endorsed by A. Lovejoy and G. Boas, *Primitivism*, 158, and independently by L. Brisson, *Même et Autre*, 478–96. This hypothesis can be supported by such texts as *Statesman* 269d, in which "our" world is described as a mixed world in terms that *Timaeus* himself would not disclaim, but the description is incompatible with a close reading of the myth.

30. Among others by G. Rodier, "Politique."

31. Which is how we should understand an expression in the *Statesman*, 273e: τὰ δ' ἐκ γῆς νεογενῆ σώματα πολιὰ φύντα.

32. *Plato* 1, 206.

33. Cf. the use of *nemein, nomeuein,* and of the noun *nomē* in 271d–72a, 274b; see E. Laroche, *Racine "nem,"* 115–29, and, briefly, E. Benveniste, *Vocabulaire* 1, pp. 84–86. The "pastoral" value did not enjoy priority, but at the time of Plato it was very clearly sensed.

34. The proximity of these two expressions, "abandoned by God" and "cycle of Zeus," underlines once more the brilliant ambiguity of Plato's text. Both are supported, naturally, by precise passages (272b, e, etc.). It is nevertheless true that Plato underlines the fact that the region of Zeus was merely a *logos,* here "hearsay" (272b), and that while the God abandoned direct administration of the world, he continued to occupy an observation post (272e).

35. The prehistory of the word *kratos* in the Homeric epoch has been studied by E. Benveniste, *Vocabulaire* 2, pp. 57–83. The author makes a statement of essential importance to us: "*Kratos* is used exclusively for gods and men" (78).

36. On this point I am correcting the interpretation of A. Diès and of many other scholars who understand *anakyklēsis* as "reversal of revolution" (Taylor), cf. the note by L. Robin, *Platon* 1456 n. 46. The usual translation is incompatible with the text that follows, which sees the world turning *now* in one direction, *now* in the other.

37. The essential text is *Timaeus* 36b–d; for details I shall simply recall the above-mentioned thesis by L. Brisson, *Même et Autre.*

38. True enough, one can hesitate about the exact meaning of what Plato is saying in 274c: *ta palai lechthenta para theōn dōra,* which are "the gifts of the gods mentioned by tradition," a tradition that Plato does not necessarily assume as his own; but between the invention by men of the arts and *technai,* and their definition as divine gifts, both of which are "traditional," Plato evidently chose the version that was most opposed to humanism (cf. *Menex.* 238b, in which this choice is given preference over the "lay" tradition of the Athenian funeral oration).

39. E. A. Havelock, *Liberal Temper;* K. R. Popper, *Open Society* 1, esp. pp. 19–25 and 39ff. For a convenient summary of the discussions prompted by Popper's book, see the selection made by R. Bambrough, *Plato, Popper;* also V. Goldschmidt, *Platonisme,* 139–41.

40. A similar opposition may be found in Epicurean philosophy, cf. the classic study by L. Robin, "Progrès."

41. V. Goldschmidt is right to call attention to this point: "The city, the material origins of which lie in needs, in the inability of individuals to achieve self-sufficiency, and in blind Necessity, seems to be of no use in the next world. There does not exist in Plato the equivalent of the 'city of God' " (*Platonisme,* 120). However, although in Plato's writings science is by rights separable from civic institutions, it remains true, as we have seen, that the men of the Golden Age do not seem to have been scientifically active.

42. *Philosophie* 2, p. 324 n. 5.

43. "Politique," n. 42.

44. It will be recalled that Wilamowitz had given this title to the chapter devoted to the *Laws* in his *Plato* 2, pp. 654–704. The *Statesman* is generally dated to the period immediately following Plato's third visit to Sicily (361); hence before the final crisis of the Athenian empire.

45. A god creates the dual royalty, a "human nature united to a divine nature" establishes the gerousia, a "third savior" invents the ephorate. "And so, thanks to these proportions, the royalty of your country, a balanced mixture of the ingredients that were needed, saved itself and brought salvation to others" (*Laws* 691d–92a).

46. Here, as I was taught to do in the past by H. Margueritte, I have retained the text of manuscripts A and O, and rejected Apelt's uninspired conjecture τιμία δευτέρως "next in honorability," which has been retained in the Des Places edition. Concerning the question of unity as the basic principle of Plato's *Republic,* cf. Aristotle *Pol.* 2.1263b 30 et seq.

47. V. Goldschmidt, *Platon,* 113.

48. E. Des Places edition of the *Laws* 2, p. 61 n. 2.

49. Literally speaking, this expression is unsuitable, since for Plato humanity begins again, it does not begin.

50. *Open Society* 1, p. 25.

51. *Ta zōia:* this can hardly refer to animals exclusively, since they are not the only creatures concerned by the invention of agriculture.

52. The quotation from *Od.* 9.112–15 occurs at *Laws* 680b–c; cf. J. Labarbe, *Homère,* 236–38.

53. The simplicity and naïveté of early legislation was also to become a theme for Aristotle; cf. *Pol.* 2.1268b 42. I want to thank R. Weil for having reminded me of this text.

54. This study begins with an attempt to show that the breach took place after Plato's time.

55. V. Goldschmidt, *Platonism,* 98.

15   An Enigma at Delphi

"Delphi still has its enigmas. Some of them will probably never be solved, and we must certainly agree with E. Bourguet that 'the last Pythia took her secret away with her.'" So begins a collection of essays that has caused the spilling of a great deal of ink—and a little bile—and from which I have borrowed the title for this essay. [1]

My intent is more modest than that of Jean Pouilloux and Georges Roux; it is simply to provide historical clarification for a passage in Pausanias that has occasioned multiple discussions before, during and after the "great excavation."

Having arrived at the entrance to the sanctuary of Apollo and passed through the *peribolos*, Pausanias describes in succession the bull of Corcyra, the statue-base of the Tegeans and that of the Lacedaimonian admirals (ex-voto for Aigospotami), the wooden horse offered by the Argives in memory of a battle against Sparta over Thyrea, and, finally, the "Marathon base."

The passage that deals with this last offering can be read as follows:

Τῷ βάθρῳ δὲ ὑπὸ τὸν ἵππον τὸν δούρειον δὴ ἐπίγραμμα μέν ἐστιν ἀπὸ δεκάτης τοῦ Μαραθωνίου ἔργου τεθῆναι τὰς εἰκόνας. Εἰσὶ δὲ ᾿Αθηνᾶ τε καὶ ᾿Απόλλων καὶ ἀνὴρ τῶν στρατηγησάντων Μιλτιάδης. ᾿Εκ δὲ τῶν ἡρώων καλουμένων ᾿Ερεχθεὺς καὶ Κέκροψ καὶ Πανδίων [οὗτοι μὲν δὴ] καὶ Λεώς τε καὶ

Published in *Revue historique* 91 (1967) pp. 281–302. Alain Schnapp was of great assistance in completing the present version.

Ἀντίοχος ὁ ἐκ Μήδας Ἡρακλεῖ γενόμενος τῆς Φύλαντος, ἔτι δὲ Αἰγεύς τε καὶ παίδων τῶν Θησέως Ἀκάμας· οὗτοι μὲν καὶ φυλαῖς Ἀθήνησιν ὀνόματα κατὰ μάντευμα ἔδοσαν τὸ ἐκ Δελφῶν· ὁ δὲ Μελάνθου Κόδρος καὶ Θησεὺς καὶ Φιλαῖός ἐστιν, οὗτοι δὲ οὐκέτι τῶν ἐπωνύμων εἰσί· τοὺς μὲν δὴ κατειλεγμένους Φειδίας ἐποίησε καὶ ἀληθεῖ λόγῳ δεκάτη καὶ οὗτοι τῆς μάχης εἰσίν·² Ἀντίγονον δὲ καὶ τὸν παῖδα Δημήτριον καὶ Πτολεμαῖον τὸν Αἰγύπτιον χρόνῳ ὕστερον ἀπέστειλαν ἐς Δελφούς, τὸν μὲν Αἰγύπτιον καὶ εὐνοίᾳ τινὶ ἐς αὐτόν, τοὺς δὲ Μακεδόνας τῷ ἐς αὐτοὺς δέει.

4   Πανδίων correxit in margine Riccardianus gr. 29: Δίων Fb Pc Vn ‖5 οὗτοι μὲν δὴ omiserunt Vindobonensis hist. gr. 51 Parisinus gr. 1399 Lugdunensis B.P.G. 16 K (non uidi) et seclusit Schubart ‖ καὶ Λεώς correxit Porson (καὶ Λεών Palmerius): Κελεός codd. (expunctum in Riccardiano) ‖ 9 Φιλαῖος (uel Φιλέας) correxit Curtius: Φιλεύς Fb Pc Vn Φυλεύς deteriores quidam et editores ante Spiro Νηλεύς Gœttling.

On the base below the wooden horse is an inscription that says the statues were dedicated from a tithe of the spoils taken in the engagement at Marathon. They represent Athena, Apollo, and from those who served as strategoi, Miltiades. Of those called heroes [by the Athenians] there are Erechtheus, Cecrops, Pandion, as well as Leos, and Antiochus, son of Heracles by Meda, daughter of Phylas; there are also Aegeus and Acamas, one of the sons of Theseus; these heroes gave their names to the tribes of Athens, in obedience to a Delphic oracle. There are also Codros the son of Melanthos, Theseus, and Philaios, but they are not among the eponymous heroes. The statues were made by Pheidias, and they too represent a tithe of the spoils of battle. Afterward the Athenians sent to Delphi statues of Antigonos, his son Demetrios, and Ptolemy the Egyptian; the statue of the Egyptian they sent out of good will, those of the Macedonians because of the dread they inspired.

The description of this monument initially sets two basic historical problems. According to Pausanias, the offering for Marathon is to honor the glory of Miltiades, who is shown as a sort of hero, between two deities: Athena, goddess of his city, and Apollo, god of Delphi. As a result it is impossible to claim that this group was set up immediately after Marathon, during Miltiades' lifetime, like (in all probability) the Athenian treasury.² It is not only because similarly personalized monuments were unknown in the early fifth century; it is also because after Marathon Miltiades was penalized with a heavy fine due to the engagement at Paros (Hdt. 6.136) and was not rehabilitated until the fine was paid, well after his death, by his son Cimon (Hdt. 6.136 and Plut. *Cimon* 4). Thus, we cannot take Pausanias's account literally, despite the emphasis laid on it by Pausanias, who is aware of its paradoxical nature; if the grouping was erected out of a "tithe" from the spoils of Marathan, it can only have been several years after the battle. Pausanias himself corroborates this conclusion by giving us the name of the sculptor, Pheidias. Little as we know of his life, it is nonetheless certain that his earliest works came after the second Persian War.[3] We may join the near-unanimous opinion of the commentators that the Marathon base was set up in the time of Cimon, around the second quarter of the fifth century.[4]

The true difficulty, however, the deepest enigma, is elsewhere. Whatever its exact date, our monument comprises the earliest known representation of the eponymous heroes of the Attic tribes.[5] It is the closest to the time of Cleisthenes' reform, which created the tribes and after consultation with Delphi bestowed on them their eponyms;[6] in any event, it is closer than the group erected in the Agora, whose main part has been discovered by the American excavations and which seems to date from the late fourth century.[7] It is also clear that this monument had a long life for the Athenians, since they took great care to supplement the Cleisthenic eponyms with Antigonos the One-Eyed and Demetrios Poliorcetes, who were so honored in 307–6, and Ptolemy III Euergetes, who probably gave his name to a tribe in 224–3.[8] According to the passage from Pausanias, it can be deduced that this monument, which embodied the spirit of the city of Athens, was missing three eponymous heroes: Ajax, Oineus, and Hippothoön; at the same time, as Pausanias emphasizes, it included three heroes who were not numbered among the "archegetai" (founders) of Athens.[9] How is one to explain the absence and the presence?

Three "supplementary" heroes are present, but who are they? Codros and Theseus are unmistakable, but just a glance at the critical apparatus I have provided shows that, as for the third, neither the manuscripts nor the editors are unanimous: the former seem to waver between Phyleus and the untenable Phileus, while the latter sometimes opt for Phyleus, for Neleus, or for Philaios.[10]

Prior to the Teubner edition of F. Spiro (1903) all editors adopted the reading "Phyleus,"[11] and this "hero" makes an occasional appearance with a reference to the passage from Pausanias.[12] But who is Phyleus? Since he cannot be the son of King Augias, who obviously has no place on an Athenian monument, it was conjectured long ago that he could stand for the eponymous hero of the deme Phylē in the territory of the tribe Hippothontis, which is one of the tribes not represented on the Marathon base. There is no other evidence for such a person,[13] and so this reading only seems to conform to the text of some of the manuscripts.

On the trail of a historical interpretation to which I will return, C. W.

Goettling suggested the correction "Neleus" (1854).[14] The person depicted at Delphi would then be a son of Codros, one of the legendary founders of the Ionian cities.[15] Although this hypothesis evidently had no support from paleography, it met with some success.[16] To be fully justified, however, it would need wholly historical reasons.

Finally, in 1861 Ernst Curtius proposed a much less drastic emendation, reading "Philaios" or "Phileas."[17] In this way the third hero would be the son of Ajax, ancestor of Miltiades the Elder and as a result the adoptive ancestor, so to say, of Miltiades the Younger (Hdt. 6.35; Plut. *Solon* 10). This correction has also met with some approval.[18] Is it possible to make a choice with certainty from among these three solutions? A closer scrutiny of the manuscript tradition will supply the answer. The manuscripts of Pausanias, eighteen in all, were studied for quite a long time, but it is only recently that A. Diller has offered a classification that seems to be altogether convincing.[19] In fact, all our manuscripts derive from a codex acquired in 1416 by Nicollo Nicolli; after his death in 1437, it remained for a century, prior to its disappearance, in the convent of Saint Mark in Florence. Diller has shown that only three of our manuscripts are direct copies of this exemplar: the *Marcianus Venetus Graecus* 413 (Vn) in Venice, the *Parisinus Graecus* 1410 (Pc) in the Bibliothèque Nationale, and the *Laurentianus* 56-11 (Fb) in Florence. Therefore, a critical edition of Pausanias should be made on the basis of these manuscripts alone,[20] and it is easy to see that they have not the reading "Phyleus"[21] but the indefensible "Phileus."[22] The hero Phyleus thus loses what little existence he enjoyed up to now. He stands only on the conjecture of a humanist who knew the name of the son of Augias or on the inattention of a copyist who was led by the person's name in the genitive "Phylantos." It is easy enough to explain the origin of the form "Phileus" by starting from the hypothetical form proposed by E. Curtius, that is "Philaios." From a certain period on, one of the most common spelling errors is to confuse *ai* with *e* due to their identical pronunciation; it is natural for a scribe who was looking at *Phileos* to be led by the nearby proper name *Theseus* into writing *Phileus*.[23] In the present circumstances it is a near-certainty. Indeed a wholly analogous mistake was committed with the name of one of the eponymous Athenian heroes. In all our manuscripts we find the king of Eleusis, Celeos, who has no business being here. It is quite proper that the reading was emended from *Keleos* to *kai Leōs*.[24] Since Phyleus and Phileus are thus excluded and Neleus is very difficult to justify, it is highly probable that on the base at Delphi Pausanias had seen the hero Philaios.[25]

Before going any farther with the analysis and explanation of the

306   passage in Pausanias, it is necessary to clear another preliminary, that of archaeology. Have the excavations at Delphi made it possible to reconstruct, with some degree of certainty, the Marathon base, to determine its exact location and length, to establish the number of statues it held—in brief, to confirm or disprove Pausanias's account as it has come down to us? Regrettably the answer can only be cautious and must take note of the skepticism of the archaeologists themselves. I cannot spend time on the arguments, which anyway largely go beyond my expertise; I will simply restate their principal conclusions.

The diagram I have borrowed from Pouilloux and Roux[26] shows the *probable* site of the Marathon base (no. 5).[27] We must certainly eliminate one of the suggested locations, recess no. 9, whose earliest date is the second half of the fourth century.[28] "It would have been interesting for art historians if the excavators at Delphi had been able to point to at least one stone whose inclusion in the base was definite or even likely."[29] Has this hope been fulfilled? At the end of the major campaign T. Homolle wrote, "There is not a foundation course, nor a stone, nor a scrap of an inscription that could be assigned to this monument."[30] Since then

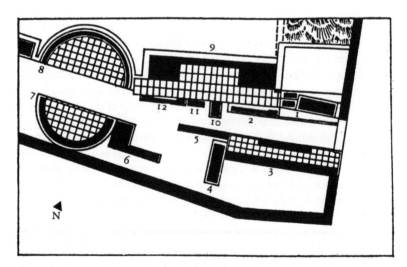

Fig. 4. Delphi: Entry to the Sanctuary of Apollo
1. Corcyrean Bull. 2. Arcadian Base. 3. The Spartan Nauarchs. 4. The "Wooden Horse" of Argos. 5. *The Marathon Base.* 6. The Seven against Thebes. 7. The Epigoni. 8. The Base of the Argive Kings. 9. Anonymous Hellenistic Niche.
10. Equestrian Group of Philopoemen and Machanidas. 11 and 12. Anonymous Bases.

various attempts have been made. For a while H. Pomtow attributed two courses of a limestone foundation to the *West* end of the Marathon base,[31] but the upper course of this block actually marks off a *Northeast* corner and so, as Pomtow himself observed, is more appropriate to the Argive Doureios Hippos (no. 4).[32] The same scholar made a completely different suggestion: to assign to the Marathon base a group of "about fifteen limestone blocks" some of which had slipped next to the base of the Spartan admirals (no. 3).[33] More recently G. Roux has recounted and reexamined these stones; he writes, "In the southeast corner of the peribolos, on the recess of brescia and the Roman agora, I counted twenty-two limestone blocks—I don't boast of having found them all—worked with great care, and supplied with sockets for T-shaped clamps; of necessity they originated in one of the great fifth-century bases situated in the southeast corner of the sanctuary." Recently this site has been the object of excavation,[34] and Viviane Regnot has been kind enough to give me access to the records. Pomtow's fifteen blocks now number twenty-nine. They are "blocks and pillars of light grey limestone, with squared fastenings (T or Γ)." "The location of the find, the identical fastenings and material, and the similarity in the working of the surfaces would lead one to assign these stones to the same monument from the fifth century" that could actually be the Marathon ex-voto.[35] There are four categories of stones of different height, hence at least four courses. There is no cornerstone from the most completely preserved course, whose length had to be about ten meters at the very least. Regrettably, no stone can be assigned to the coping, so that we have no evidence about the arrangement of the statues of Pheidias.[36] One last detail deserves mention: on one of the blocks, which is a cornerstone, "the *visible* vertical face of the smaller side was roughly reshaped later so as to fit into an adjacent monument."[37] G. Roux does not exclude the possibility that this might be a sign of "the lengthening of the Marathon base to accommodate the Hellenistic rulers."[38]

Valuable as such evidence is, we see that it leaves our problem absolutely untouched. In fact the archaeologists had to use the passage from Pausanias as a guide; it was their main point of reference. The dilapidated condition of the southeast section of the sanctuary kept it from shedding any light of its own.

Therefore we must underake a close reexamination of the text of Pausanias. How has it been interpreted until now? The simplest solution was offered by Ernst Curtius (1861):[39] the passage in Pausanias contains a lacuna. To put it another way, the fifth-century monument did not comprise thirteen statues but sixteen—Athena, Miltiades, and Apollo, the ten Athenian eponyms, and Theseus, Codros, and Philaios. In the Hellenistic era, then, there would have been nineteen statues instead of sixteen.[40] As will be seen, we will not retain this solution, yet one of Curtius's arguments merits the most careful attention. How is it possible, he asks, that an official monument of the Athenians left out the tribe of Aiantis, which held the right side of the battle-line at Marathon,[41] on whose territory the battle was fought, and one of whose members was the polemarch Callimachus of Aphidna (as a result of which the tribe enjoyed certain privileges described by Plutarch; *Quaest. conviv.* 10.628a–29a)?[42] How can one claim, we will add, that Oineis, the tribe of Miltiades from the deme Laciadai, was omitted from the ex-voto of Marathon?

This argument can rightly be held up against the theories that postulated a lacuna not in the text but in the monument itself. E. Loewy, for example, alleged that the statues of Ajax, Oineus, and Hippothoön were unchristened in the Hellenistic period in order to be renamed in honor of the Macedonian princes.[43] But, aside from the fact that it is hard to see how bearded eponyms could have portrayed the generally clean-shaven Hellenistic monarchs, we have no evidence before the late Hellenistic period for such "metonomasia" for statues.[44] In a variant of this hypothesis, H. Pomtow believed for some years that in the Hellenistic period the statues of the three missing eponyms could have been replaced, for want of space, by the images of Antigonus, Demetrius, and Ptolemy.[45] But this theory, like Loewy's, is simply absurd, for then the monument would no longer have been what it was exactly intended to be, a depiction of the Athenian eponyms. The latter are only eponyms when shown in a group; when not arranged in a group, they are merely individual heroes without any particular relation to the city.[46] We can also say that if the question of space were the deciding factor—which is doubtful—the Athenians would have used just the three available positions, belonging to Theseus, Codros, and Philaios.

Must we therefore return to the hypothesis of a lacuna in the text? On the contrary, a careful analysis reveals that the monument described by Pausanias was completely coherent and balanced in the fifth century. Our ex-voto looks like an "apotheosis of Miltiades,"[47] and Pausanias's account begins by mentioning Athena, Apollo, and the victorious strategos. We can be virtually sure that these three figures formed the center of the monument.[48] As for the heroes, eponymous or not, the passage divides them into two groups separated by *eti de:* on one side are Erechtheus, Cecrops, Pandion, Leos, and Antiochos, and on the other Aegeus, Acamas, Codros, Theseus, and Philaios[49] (with the last three set apart by

the parenthetical comment that they are not included among the eponyms). So we can accept that on either side of the central group there
stood five Athenian heroes. Such a straightforward conclusion is enough
to suggest that Codros, Theseus, and Philaios *do* represent the three
tribes thought to be absent from the monument, and that they do so in
ways that would allow at least some Athenians to understand the motives
behind such an exceptional shift of heroes.

In fact, this theory is neither new nor revolutionary. It was framed in
1854 by C. W. Goettling,[50] but unfortunately it was based on a text that
was dangerously emended, and it formed part of a system that now seems
indefensible. Goettling was the author of a *History of the Roman Constitution* (1840), which explained the genesis of the Roman constitution by
means of its three "ethnic" components, Latin, Sabine, and Etruscan.
Like many of his contemporaries,[51] the professor gladly resorted to
analogous explanations, although often cautiously, to account for the
enigmas of Greek history. He claimed that Codros, Theseus, and Neleus
(*sic*) were specifically Ionian heroes, since Codros and Neleus were, respectively, the ancestor of ruling families of the Ionian world and the
founder of several cities, and Theseus himself has some Ionian features in
his legends.[52] At the time of Cimon, these three replaced—if not at
Athens, at least on the monument at Delphi—the three heroes who were
specifically Attic: Ajax (who, by the way, was not Athenian), Oineus, and
Hippothoön. The idea is not ridiculous, and it is certainly true that these
legends were used to glorify *syngeneia*, the mythic consanguinity of Athens and the Ionian cities. Hence Smyrna and Miletus had, at a date
difficult to pin down, tribes named "Theseis," although there was none
such at Athens; moreover, Miletus also had a tribe "Oineis," with the
name of one of the heroes missing from Delphi.[53] Goettling's most
important contribution had to do with the composition of the list of
Athenian eponymous heroes; he was the first to point out what he justly
called the problem of "a willful neglect of Theseus" (*eine absichtliche
Ignorirung des Theseus*).[54] Starting from a famous passage in Herodotus
about the hostility toward Ionians of Cleisthenes of Sicyon and
Cleisthenes of Athens (Hdt. 5.66), Goettling used such "anti-Ionianism"
to explain the exclusion of Theseus.[55]

This interpretation, however, cannot be retained. There is nothing to
indicate that Cimon had a policy that was deliberately "pro-Ionian"; in
fact, he is rather more often, and somewhat justifiably, identified as pro-
Spartan. In addition, Goettling's theory has nothing in it to warrant the
replacement, one for one, of three eponymous heroes by three others,
which is precisely what must be explained.

Many years after Goettling's essay, the problem was taken up again by A. Mommsen;[56] although the premises underlying his article have been vitiated, in that he accepted the existence of the imaginary Phyleus, it still marks some essential progress. Mommsen's basic assumption, which is quite enticing, was that the Marathon monument illustrated the battle order of the Attic tribes.[57] The tribe Oineis was represented twice, by its strategos Miltiades and by the hero "Phyleus" whom Pausanias does locate at one of the ends of the monument. Indeed it is likely that Miltiades' tribe, alongside the tribe of Aiantis, held the place of honor in the phalanx at Marathon, for Miltiades waited until it was his turn to be commander-in-chief to launch the attack against the Persian army (cf. Hdt. 6.110). Mommsen perceptively noted that Themistocles (from the tribe Leontis) and Aristides (from the tribe Antiochis) were next to each other in the center of the phalanx at Marathon (Plut. *Aristides* 5), and compared their proximity there to that of Leos and Antiochos on the monument at Delphi. Finally he made the crucial claim that Ajax, being from Salamis, was a foreigner at Athens[58] and that Hippothoön—an Eleusinian who fought alongside Eumolpos against Athens—was scarcely better.[59] Therefore it was natural that they be replaced by Theseus, the king who created Athenian unity, and Codros, the heroic king of Athenian legend. A little later, a closely related theory was advanced by E. Petersen.[60] Miltiades, strategos from Oineis, was in charge of his tribe; as Ajax's son, installed at Athens, Philaios embodied the tribe of Aiantis; as a descendant of the *genos* of the Neleids (which is dear to Poseidon), Codros supplanted Hippothoön, the son of Poseidon; finally, Theseus represented Athens in its entirety. We can say first of all that, with regard to the last claim, it seems completely inconsistent with the analysis of the monument that Petersen himself provides. How can a strategos (Miltiades), placed in a central position, stand for only one tribe? How can one hero (Theseus), placed among the eponyms, be the standard-bearer for a city of ten tribes?

Finally, in 1924 H. Pomtow abandoned his earlier position and, convinced by Mommsen's theory, accepted it while giving it his own interpretation.[61]

I think that it is certainly in this direction that truth is to be found, but in order to pass from theory to proof—at least within the limits imposed by our sources—it is worth taking a detour by way of history and asking what was the significance of erecting *at Delphi* an ex-voto *of Marathon* in the time of *Cimon*.

Marathon used to be simply a battle we could reconstruct with some degree of certainty: the battle of Miltiades and of Callimachus of Aphid-

na, of Athenian and Plataean hoplites, to be commemorated shortly
afterward by monuments such as the Athenian treasury at Delphi and the
posthumous column of Callimachus on the Acropolis.[62] However, it
rapidly became an ideological model, the exemplar of hoplite combat
whose power would last until the end of the fourth century.[63] In the
fourth century, Plato contrasted the glory of the hoplites of Marathon and
Plataea with the shame of the sailors of Artemisium and Salamis (*Laws*
4.107a,d). P. Amandry has recently made a valuable contribution in
showing that a comparable ideological opposition in the fifth century
split admirers of the first Persian War from apologists for the second, the
partisans of Themistocles from the supporters of Cimon, son of
Miltiades. This opposition found perfect expression on one and the same
monument: some fifteen years *after* the inscription of an epigram about
the glory of the combatants at Salamis and Plataea, there was added a
passage extolling the soldiers of Marathon who had had the unique honor
of having stopped the enemy "at the gates" and thus saved the city from
destruction by fire.[64] The Athenian hoplites in action at Marathon and
Plataea numbered about nine thousand, while the fleet employed about
four times more citizens.[65] This is enough to demonstrate the well-
known fact that hoplites do not come from the same social categories as
most of the sailors. At the level of ideology it is clear that Cimon is the
man of the hoplite—and equestrian—class, somewhat like what
Themistocles had been for the fleet. In reality, of course, it is only a
matter of ideology, for the strategos of the Eurymedon, the architect
(after Aristides) of the Athenian Confederacy, would not dream even for a
moment of discarding the new weapon given to Athens by Themistocles.
Cimon himself had set a public example at the time of Salamis by
dedicating the bridle of his horse to Athena (Plut. *Cimon* 5).[66] Within the
ideological sphere, however, on the soil of Athens and Delphi, Marathon
is glorified at the expense of Salamis. P. Amandry has noted that the
epigram for Marathon is not an isolated instance. Pheidias's statue of
Athena Promachos, also from the time of Cimon Pausanias tells us, is also
a "tithe" levied on the spoils from "the Medes who landed at Marathon"
(1.28.2).[67] Toward the end of Cimon's era, it is once again the battle of
Marathon that is depicted on the Athenians' Stoa Poikilē (Paus. 1.15);
still later, to the astonishment of Pausanias, "Aeschylus sensed that the
end was near, and although he had earned so much glory through his
poetry and had fought on sea at Artemisium and Salamis, he omitted all
that and simply wrote down his own name, and the names of his father
and his city, adding that he called as witness to his valor the bay of
Marathon and the Medes who had landed there" (1.14.5).

Lastly, E. Vanderpool identified as part of a trophy for Marathan a column and a monumental Ionic capital, which were discovered on the plain of Marathon in the chapel of Panagia Mesosparitissa. The suggested date, once again, is the second quarter of the fifth century.[68] The sculptural group we are discussing is clearly associated with this whole set of data. Delphi could allow an attempt bolder than what we have described up to now. Although Delphi was not a *center* for propaganda, from which there would be disseminated a *doctrine*[69]—it is hard to see what organization would have invented and maintained such dogma—it was undoubtedly a *site* for propaganda where cities, and sometimes their citizens, could try out new ventures that they would not have risked at home. By organizing the finances for the new temple at Delphi, Cleisthenes and the Alcmeonids secured for themselves a base for returning to Athens;[70] at Delphi, the regent Pausanias dared to boast of being the victor in the second Persian War (Thuc. 1.132); and it was at Delphi that the Spartans, for the first time in their history, portrayed a victorious general, Lysander, being crowned by Poseidon (Paus. 10.9.9–10 and the inscription Meiggs-Lewis 109).[71]

What place does our monument have in all this? That it is primarily a representation of heroes does have some importance for my argument, for there is nothing more malleable than the hero as a religious object in the context of civic worship. What is required of him, basically, is to be present, but he can be molded to conform to the needs of political life in a manner that we would now call artificial. Relying on Delphi, Cleisthenes created the corps of eponyms or Archegetai for the tribes (with their respective priests) and selected the groups of heroes or Archegetai for the demes.[72] Whether or not one takes seriously the anecdote told by Aristotle, according to which the Pythia selected the ten eponyms from a list of one hundred that had been submitted to her,[73] it cannot be disputed that the heroes chosen by Cleisthenes did not all hold the same rank. Some secondary figures benefited from an unexpected "promotion," while others who seemed indispensable were oddly omitted, chief among whom is Theseus.

It has now become possible to fit the ex-voto of Marathon into the history of both Athens and Delphi.[74] The history of the relations between Theseus and Athens is far from simple; although excluded from the list of eponyms, on which both his father Aegeus and his son Acamas are present, he made a remarkable reappearance in the aftermath of Marathon, all the more remarkable because his myth was linked to the region of the Tetrapolis. Such a localization, which could have gone against the son of Aegeus, evidently worked in his favor just after the first Persian War. The sculptural program on the Athenian treasury at Delphi joined Theseus's story with that of Heracles, and the episode of the bull of Marathon had a prominent place there.[75] The clan of Miltiades and Cimon laid claim to this resurgent glory, and perhaps even brought about its revival. It has been alleged that wherever the figure of Theseus appears on the monuments of the late sixth and early fifth century, it should be interpreted as Cleisthenes.[76] This is a useless, indeed absurd theory: "We are not unaware that the family and the party of Miltiades were 'Theseomanes,' but we do not know this about the Alcmeonids."[77] In fact we know that the opposite is true. At least it was Cimon who "discovered" Theseus's remains on Skyros in 476–75, and solemnly established them in the Agora, thereby making the hero the founder (*oikistēs*) of the city (Plut. *Cimon* 8; *Theseus* 36.1; Paus. 1.17.2; Scholia on Aeschines, *In Ktes.* 13).

A particularly valuable piece of evidence about the mythical connections of Cimon's family is provided by the fragments from the first Athenian prose writer, Pherecydes.[78] Pherecydes, as a genealogist of heroes, took an interest in the legends of Theseus and Codros and was well acquainted with their heroic deaths,[79] and he was also preoccupied with legends from Delphi (F 36). Jacoby has shown that, as a unique feature in his surviving work, he carried his analysis of the lineage of Philaios (F 2) (whom he calls Philaias) down to the historical period, indeed to Miltiades the Elder. We know that it was to this family that Cimon was connected.[80] Jacoby drew the legitimate conclusion that Pherecydes was somehow in a client relation to the family of Miltiades.[81]

Hence we find Theseus at Delphi after Marathon[82] and at Athens after Salamis. Must we be surprised to see him appear on two of the major monuments of Cimon's time that commemorate the great victory: our ex-voto at Delphi and the painting in the Stoa Poikilē probably done by Cimon's friend Polygnotus (Plut. *Cimon* 4)?[83] Pausanias saw and described this renowned composition. Next to a depiction of the battle of Oinoē (a victory won over the Spartans on Argive territory during the first Peloponnesian War), and on the same panel that showed the battle of Theseus and the Amazons, "at the very edge of the painting" there appeared the battle of Marathon: "Portrayed there are the hero Marathon, from whom the plain gets its name, Theseus shown as rising from the ground, Athena, and Heracles." Among the combatants are Callimachus and Miltiades, who is so closely linked to Theseus (1.15).[84]

Now we can ask whom Theseus replaces on the ex-voto at Delphi. To me the answer seems unambiguous. The hero of Marathon displaces the king from Salamis, in exactly the same way that, in the ideology of Cimon's time, the hoplite battle won during the first Persian War competes with the great naval encounter of the second. One detail seems to provide corroborating evidence: in the painting on the Stoa Poikilē there is an Ajax—not the lord of Salamis, true, but Ajax son of Oileus, Ajax "the Lesser" who is often confused with his namesake—and he is placed in the humiliating position of facing the kings who have gathered to try him for his sacrilegious attempt to rape Cassandra on the altar (Paus. 1.15.2). At Athens the allusion is subtle, but at Delphi it is more overt. Thus Theseus takes his revenge: omitted from Cleisthenes' list of eponyms, he nonetheless saw his family represented by his father Aegeus and his son Acamas. Excluded from the monument at Marathon, Ajax still appears there in some way through the presence of his Athenian son, Philaios (Plut. *Solon* 10). On the Marathon base, Theseus stands for Aiantis, which had a place of honor in the line of battle; the place of Philaios is even more exalted, because in his position to the far right of the central group he embodies the tribe of Oineis. It seems likely that the obscure Oineus, bastard son of King Pandion,[85] was substituted for by Philaios. True, the deme of the Philaides certainly did not belong to the tribe Oineis but to Aigeis; however Miltiades the Elder, it seems, was already enrolled in what was to become the deme of the Laciadae in the territory of Oineis,[86] and it is certain that this was the deme of Miltiades and his son Cimon.[87] The hero Lacias had a *temenos* there, and nearby honor was paid to Phytalos, who gave hospitality to Demeter and whose descendants, the Phytalidae, welcomed Theseus (Paus. 1.37.2; Plut. *Theseus* 12.1).[88]

There remains the Eleusinian Hippothoön; by process of elimination he can be replaced by no one but Codros. Can we prove this substitution as clearly as we did the others?[89]

The father of Codros was Melanthos, who is mentioned by Pausanias and was, in all likelihood, the eponym of the deme Melainai located in the land of the tribe Hippothontis.[90] I have to admit, however, that this is the only topographic link that can be established between the Athenian king and the tribe he is thought to represent at Delphi. The phratry of the Medontidae, believed to comprise the descendants of Codros, *cannot* be situated in the territory of Hippothontis.[91] Neither can Codros's tomb—located at the foot of the Acropolis, according to an inscription from imperial times (I.G. 2² 4258)—nor the mythic site of his death—near Ilissos (Paus. 1.19.5)[92]—nor the sanctuary he shared with Neleus and Basileus.[93]

One text, however, provides unexpected confirmation of our analysis: it is a passage from the speech *Against Leocrates* (83–88) delivered by Lycurgus after Chaeronea. Lycurgus was both ideologist and archaeologist, blending together learned information and false or forged documentation.[94] Moreover, he was very preoccupied with the Athenian presence at Delphi: he might be responsible for the erection of the famous column with "dancers," whom J. Bousquet has plausibly identified as the Aglauridae.[95] Hence Lycurgus was by no means an immaterial witness. He told the following Delphian anecdote about Codros: A Delphian with the significant name of Cleomantis ("prophet of glory") warned the Athenians that an oracle had advised their enemies that they would capture Athens only if they spared the king, Codros. Codros then decided to use a trick to have himself killed; Lycurgus noted that the descendants of Cleomantis had the right to the honors of the Prytaneum at Athens and then concluded as follows: "Obviously they loved their country with a love different from that of Leocrates,[96] those kings who deceived their enemies, willingly died for their homeland, and sacrificed their lives for the safety of all. Therefore, as a unique privilege they gave their name to the land (τοιγαροῦν μονώτατοι ἐπώνυμοι τῆς χώρας εἰσίν) and earned for themselves divine honors." Let us make certain allowances, beginning with amplification. Evidently Lycurgus was conflating the story of Codros with that of Erechtheus, who, without sacrificing himself, did at least sacrifice his daughter Pandrosos. Lycurgus dedicated a long paragraph to Erechtheus, including a quotation from Euripides (*Leoc.* 99–100).[97] But, I believe, to give the passage its full meaning one must see that Lycurgus was making an allusion to the monument at Delphi on which were portrayed Codros, Theseus, and Philaios, the substitute eponymous heroes. At least that will be my conclusion.[98]

NOTES

1. J. Pouilloux and G. Roux, *Énigmes*.

2. Cf. most recently P. de la Coste-Messelière, *Trésor des Athéniens*, 260ff., where there is a record of the polemic that split French and German scholars. The most complete discussion is still J. Audiat, *Trésor des Athéniens*.

3. Cf. C. Picard, *Manuel, Sculpture* 2.1, 310ff.

4. This had already been well understood by H. Brunn, *Künstler*, 164; I see no element that allows for still more precision. Nonetheless, P. de la Coste-Mes-

selière thinks we may say that the base at Delphi was carved at the same time as the Promachos in Athens (451–48), the latter also sculpted in honor of Marathon (*Musée de Delphes*, 447 n. 2). Relying on Raubitschek's disastrous hypothesis that places Cimon's death as early as 456, E. Kluwe dates the base, with illusory precision, to 460–57 ("Kongressdekret"). Finally we can take note of several untenable opinions: H. Pomtow believes that Pausanias had misread the name of the artist and that the work should have been attributed to Hegias, Pheidias's shadowy master ("Studien II," 95–96; repeated in "Delphoi," c. 1217). By contrast, A. Furtwängler, after some contorted archaeological argument, concluded that the piece could date only from the fourth century ("Zu den Weihgeschenken"). In the same spirit, F. Poulsen made our monument and the "Wooden Horse" into signs of the Athenian-Argive alliance of 414 ("Niche aux offrandes," 422–25).

5. In an article devoted to the passage from Pausanias quoted above, F. Brommer neglected to mention that it dealt with Athenian eponyms ("Attische Könige"). Thus his research, otherwise interesting in its appeal to the evidence of numerous fragments, lost any explanatory value it may have had. On the eponymous heroes, their mythic and religious character, and their iconography, the fundamental work is now U. Kron, *Phylenheroen*. It would be necessary to refer to it on practically every page of this essay; for the Marathon base, see 205–27.

6. Cf. P. Lévêque and P. Vidal-Naquet, *Clisthène*, 50–51, 70–72.

7. Cf. T. L. Shear, Jr., "Eponymous Heroes"; Shear believes that a structure, destroyed c. 350 and located under the middle stoa, represents a trace of the monument built in the last quarter of the fifth century. This monument is described in a variety of texts (e.g., Aris. *Peace* 1183, *Knights* 979; for a summary see R. E. Wycherley, *Athenian Agora* 3, 85–90). Shear is followed by H. A. Thompson and R. E. Wycherley, *Athenian Agora 14*, 38–41. Pausanias describes the monument in 1.5; see also U. Kron, *Phylenheroen*, 226–36.

8. Cf. G. Busolt and H. Swoboda, *Staatskunde* 1, 973–74, and E. Will, *Histoire politique*, 73, 363–64, which includes the discussions about the date of the creation of the tribe Ptolemais. Note that after 224/223 the Athenians stopped attending to the Delphic monument. As a result, it does not reflect either the suppression in 201 of the two "Macedonian" tribes, the creation in 200 of the tribe Attalis, and, under the Empire, of the tribe Hadrianis.

9. In a letter to me from 23 Feb. 1967, G. Roux defines the enigma very well: "I have always been surprised that all ten of the Athenian Eponymous heroes were not there together. When Athenians belonging to the tribes of the three excluded heroes visited Delphi, what could their impression have been? And what could the heroes themselves have thought, these heroes whose favor was otherwise so assiduously courted?"

10. My "apparatus" is meant to be utilitarian and solely an aid to my argument. Naturally I have omitted simple errors of orthography, missing iota subscripts, etc.

11. It is worth noting, however, that although J. G. Frazer uses the reading

"Phyleus" in his translation, in a note and in his commentary he justifies the correction to "Philaios." See *Pausanias* 1, 608; 5, 265–66.

12. Thus in 1941 T. Lenschau described Phyleus as "An Attic hero, his statue being in the Athenian memorial for Marathon at Delphi" ("Phyleus," c. 1016); F. Brommer, "Attische Könige," 152; W. Gauer, *Weihgeschenke*, 66.

13. Cf. H. Sauppe, *De Demis*, 8: *Hunc heroem Atticum, eponymum Phylasiorum, fuisse docent ea quae de statuis ex praeda marathonica Apolloni Delphico consecratis Pausanias narrat.* (This was an Attic hero, the eponym of the Phylasians, as is shown by what Pausanias says about the statues dedicated to Delphian Apollo out of the spoils of Marathon.)

14. "Kynosarges," 17–18. Against the objections of E. Curtius, Goettling resumed and developed his argument in his *Gesammelte Abhandlungen* 2, 163–64.

15. On these legends see M. Sakellarious, *Migration grecque* (index *s.v.* Neleus); for their use in fifth-century politics, see J. Barron, "Athenian Propaganda" and "Religious Propaganda."

16. The theory was taken up by E. Loewy, "Donario," who knows Goettling only indirectly via Curtius's study cited below. Thereafter it moved on into the edition by F. Spiro (Teubner) whose apparatus cites Loewy alone, and then into the "edition" by W.H.S. Jones (Loeb, 1918) that does not even warn the reader that it is a conjecture. It is accepted by A. Furtwängler, "Zu den Weihgeschenken," 396 n. 2, and by A. von Domaszewski, *Attische Politik*, 20. Another proposed emendation, which is perfectly ridiculous, is to move back from *Phileus* to Oineus (E. Berger, "Marathonische Gruppe"). Thus only two eponymous heroes would be missing; but we must remember that Pausanias himself indicates that the three supererogatory heroes are not eponymous.

17. "Weihgeschenke," 366.

18. In addition to the aforementioned opinion of J. G. Frazer, we may note J. Overbeck, *Antiken Schriftquellen*, 117, and especially the more detailed study by H. Hitzig and H. Bluemner, *Pausanias* 3, 547, 678. The text in Hitzig and Bluemner is followers by G. Daux (*Pausanias à Delphes*) and G. Roux (*Énigmes*) but, regrettably, without a critical apparatus.

19. "Pausanias in the Middle Ages," and "Manuscripts." Having tested Diller's classification, I think I can vouch for its effectiveness. It seems to me that his conclusions are not modified, but nuanced, by M. H. Rocha Pereira in her new Teubner edition (1973).

20. The other manuscripts, it must be remembered, could have benefited from good emendations by humanists. This is true, for example, of the substitution of Pandion for the Dion given by our three manuscripts; this emendation has rightly been adopted by all editors since the original Aldine edition of 1516; it appears in the margin of the *Riccardianus graecus* 29 (as I was able to ascertain from a microfilm) and in the manuscripts derived therefrom according to Diller's stemma.

21. This appears only in certain *deteriores*, as I was able to verify: e.g., *Parisinus gr.* 1399.

22. I would like to thank two colleagues: E. Mionni at the University of Padua, who examined the Venice manuscript for me, and M. Papathomopoulos, who inspected the microfilms of both the Venice and Florence manuscripts at the Institut d'histoire des textes. I myself examined *Parisinus gr.* 1410.

23. An argument similar to the one I am developing here was outlined—but only outlined, for want of a rational classification of the manuscripts—by H. Hitzig in a letter quoted by H. Pomtow, "Studien II," 86.

24. As a result, the coordinating conjunction disappears, and this is what might have occasioned the appearance of *houtoi men dē,* which Schubart justly rejected in his edition of 1839. Some *deteriores* added a new *kai,* yielding *kai Keleos te. Keleos* was rightly suspected by the copyist—or the corrector—of *Riccardianus gr.* 29, the same one who is responsible for the excellent reading *Pandion.* The emendation *Keleos = kai Leōs* was first proposed in 1768, with the slip of *Leōn* instead of *Leōs,* by Jacques le Paulmier de Grentemesnil (Palmerius), *Exercitationes,* 435: *Suspicor legendum Pandion kai Leon. Non enim censetur Celeus inter Heroes Eponymos, nihil certius est, omnia enim alia nomina sunt eponymorum qui nomina tribubus Atheniensium dederunt* (I think the reading should be *Pandion kai Leon.* For Celeus is not numbered among the eponymous heroes, and nothing is more certain, for all the other names belong to the eponyms who gave their names to the Athenian tribes). The reading was approved by R. Porson in an appendix to T. Gaisford's *Lectiones Platonicae,* 184; it appears in the editions after Clavier's (1821), but J. F. Facius had already made note of Le Paulmier's emendation in the good Leipzig edition of 1794.

25. The spelling should be *Philaios* and not *Phileas,* as Pausanias himself does at 1.35.2.

26. *Énigmes,* fig. 34. This map is itself a revised and corrected version of the one published by P. de la Coste-Messelière, *Musée de Delphes,* fig. L. I am grateful to my friend P. Lévêque who was kind enough to have this illustration redrawn for me.

27. In the letter quoted above in note 9, G. Roux wrote me: "On the map in *Énigmes* we located this base (5) alongside that for Aigospotami (3). But there is another possibility: base 3 farther to the South, with base 5 lengthened and partly in front of 3 . . . so that it is impossible to calculate even approximately the dimensions of the base."

28. H. Bulle and T. Wiegand, "Topographie," 333ff.; cf. the agreement by T. Homolle, "Topographie 2." This hypothesis is taken up again by A. Furt-wängler, "Zu den Weihgeschenken," and in a more complicated way by F. Poulsen, "Niche aux offrandes." On this niche cf. *Énigmes,* 19–36.

29. J. Bousquet, "Inscriptions," 132.

30. "Topographie 1," 297–99 (erroneously numbered 397–99).

31. Cf. "Studien II," 75 and fig. 5. He was apparently followed by E. Bour-guet, *Ruines de Delphes,* 40, and by G. Daux, *Pausanias à Delphes,* 88.

32. See the map inserted in "Delphoi," c. 1199–1200, and *Énigmes,* 53, fig. 17 and pl. XI, 1–2.

33. "Delphoi," c. 1215.

34. Cf. G. Daux, "Chronique 1965," 899. The excavators were C. Vatin and V. Regnot.

35. This is only a hypothesis; as G. Roux told me in a letter (March 9, 1967), we cannot exclude the possibility that these pieces belong to the Aigospotami base (3).

36. If we are actually dealing with the Marathon ex-voto, it is difficult to assign to its coping the piece of black limestone veined with white described by J. Bousquet, "Inscriptions," 126–29; it had an Attic inscription, as well as two sockets for the feet of a bronze statue. Bosquet's analysis led him to conclude that the statues must have been of moderate height. He calls attention to another block of grey limestone, carrying a decree of proxenia for an Athenian (324/323); Bourguet had thought that this latter stone must have been set into the Marathon base (cf. *Fouilles de Delphes* III, 1, no. 408).

37. *Énigmes*, 54, and pl. XI.4.

38. In the letter quoted above (March 9, 1967). Other references to the archaeological discussions are to be found in Hitzig-Bluemner, *Pausanias* 3, 677–79.

39. E. Curtius, "Weihgeschenke."

40. To the best of my knowledge this hypothesis of Curtius's has been retained only by B. W. Sauer, *Gruppe,* 18–19, and Frazer, *Pausanias* 5, 265–66. Sauer, however, was sensitive to matters of sculptural equilibrium and elaborated on Curtius's theory. He called attention to the fact that the group is symmetrical only if one admits that the three supplementary heroes (Theseus, Codros, Philaios) were balanced by three others. Hence the fifth-century monument would have comprised nineteen statues, and our three unknown heroes would have been replaced in the Hellenistic era by the statues of the three eponyms. This suggestion is clearly incompatible with the hypothesis presented above of a reworking of the pedestal in the Hellenistic period. Most recently, T. L. Shear, Jr., posits again a lacuna ("Eponymous Heroes," 221 n. 112). As U. Kron notes, Pausanias himself indicates that not all the eponyms are present (*Phylenheroen,* 225).

41. On the relation between these facts, cf. G. Busolt, *Griechische Geschichte,* 589 n. 4, and, more generally, "Epaminondas the Pythagorean," p. 62 above.

42. Curtius's remarks deserve quotation: "It is utterly unthinkable that changes so arbitrary would have been allowed on an official monument of such importance and located in Delphi, the place where the ten tribes had received sanction for their names. How could the tribes whose heroes' statues were missing have borne the shame? In particular, how is one to grant the exclusion of Aiantis, a tribe that had reached the pinnacle of fame, and had thus also acquired the privilege that, in public festivals, its chorus would never occupy the last place?" ("Weihgeschenke," 365). This passage refers precisely to the remarks of Plutarch cited in the text.

43. "Donario."

The City, Vision, and Reality

320

44. Cf. E. Petersen, "Marathonische Bronzegruppe," 144 n. 1. Loewy's response does not advance the discussion ("Zu Mitteilungen"). However, U. Kron objects that it is not at all certain that all the eponymous heroes were bearded: Ajax, Hippothoön, and Oineus are often represented with the features of very young men (*Phylenheroen*, 225).

45. "Vortrag," 82–84; "Studien II," 87: "When the Athenians sent the new royal statues to Delphi, three of the ancient Eponyms had to give up their places." In one of his customary shifts, Pomtow explicitly rejected his own hypothesis (cf. "Delphoi," c. 1215–16). Nonetheless, I find it—without attribution to Pomtow—in J. Barron, "Religious Propaganda," 46; it is also finally embraced by U. Kron, *Phylenheroen*, 225.

46. Cf. N. Loraux, "Autochtonie," 12.

47. The phrase is from G. Kato, "En marge," 198.

48. It is likely that Miltiades stood between the two divinities. Unfortunately it is impossible to tell whether the strategos and the gods stood in the front row of the group or in the middle of a rank.

49. The meaning of *eti de* was already clarified by Sauer, *Gruppe*, 19, but it is E. Petersen who has given the most lucid interpretation of the composition of the monument (cf. "Griechische Bronze," 277–78, and "Marathonische Bronzegruppe"). However, Petersen went too far when he made the Apollo of our base into the prototype of the Apollo of Tiber. Following Petersen's lead, Hitzig-Bluemner correctly compares the composition of the ex-voto to that of a pediment (*Pausanias* 3, 678).

50. "Kynosarges."

51. Cf. E. Will, *Doriens et Ioniens*.

52. On these legends, see the prudent conclusions of M. Sakellariou, *Migration grecque*. On the "Ionian" legends about Theseus see, although skeptically, H. Herter, "Theseus der Ionier." An interpretation quite close to C. W. Goettling's (including the correction to Neleus) is still offered by J. Barron, "Religious Propaganda," 46.

53. Cf. L. Robert, "Review of *Didyma*," 673 (which also has the references to epigraphic evidence), and P. Lévêque and P. Vidal-Naquet, *Clisthène*, 111 n. 6. The adoption at Miletus of Athenian institutions and tribal organization seems to be datable to 442 (J. Barron, "Religious Propaganda," 5–6). Did Miletus have a tribe Theseis as early as that?

54. "Kynosarges," 159.

55. For an explanation of this passage that is different from Goettling's, see *Clisthène*, 50–51.

56. "Zehn Eponymen," 451–60. The chronological order that I am following should not give the illusion of a continuous discussion. Goettling's hypothesis is practically unknown and unused except by Curtius alone; Mommsen's article would be introduced into the general discussion only by H. Pomtow in 1924 ("Delphoi," c. 1215–16) whose analysis of it, moreover, is wholly imprecise.

57. About this order Herodotus simply tells us that the tribes followed one another "as they were numbered"—*hōs arithmeonto,* with the Plataeans occupying the left wing (6.3). The passage is open to a host of interpretations.

58. The fact is emphasized by Hdt. 5.66.

59. On Hippothoön see U. Kron, *Phylenheroen,* 177–87. A son of Poseidon, Hippothoön is the grandson of the robber Cercyon who fell to Theseus. On his link with Eumolpos, cf. the anonymous epic poet quoted by Herodian 2.615 (Lenz). Pausanias situates his *heroön* near the ancient border between Athens and Eleusis (1.38.4). For the mythic role of this boundary, see the article, occasionally somewhat fanciful, by C. Picard, "Luttes primitives," 7. Most unusually, the center of the tribe of Hippothontis is located not in Athens but in Eleusis (cf. I.G.2² 1149.153).

60. Cf. the aforementioned articles, especially "Marathonische Bronzegruppe," 144. E. Berger offers a faulty variant on this hypothesis, in which—Phileus being an error instead of Oineus—Theseus embodies all Athens, Miltiades the tribe of Aiantis (even though he belonged to Oineis), and Codros the tribe of Hippothontis, with certain unspecified mythic connections between the last king of Athens and Hippothoön ("Marathonische Gruppe," 25 n. 92).

61. "Delphoi," c. 1216. Pomtow echoes Mommsen in framing the following equations: Philaios (Phyleus) = Aiantis, Theseus = Hippothontis, Codros = Oineis. But Mommsen's only categorical assertion was that, as the hero of Phyle, "Phyleus" embodied Oineis (459).

62. A. E. Raubitschek, *Dedications,* 18–20, with a very dubious restoration. The numerous arguments centering on this inscription and the role of Callimachus as polemarch do not concern us here.

63. See "The Tradition of the Athenian Hoplite," p. 91 above; cf. also N. Loraux, "Marathon."

64. "Épigrammes de Marathon." Similarly, W. K. Pritchett, *Marathon,* 160–68, and G. Nenci, *Introduzione,* 41 n. 46. See also the more general study by P. Amandry, "Lendemain." The discussion has continued long since: cf. especially C. Delvoye, "Art et Politique," and Z. Petre, "Épigrammes de Marathon."

65. Details are to be found in "The Tradition of the Athenian Hoplite," pp. 91–92 above.

66. Still it must also be noted that Cimon brought technical innovations to the Athenian trireme, with the specific goal of allowing a greater number of hoplites on board (Plut. *Cimon,* 12).

67. For the probable date of the work (460–50) see B. D. Meritt, "Greek Inscriptions 1936," 362–80, in connection with I.G. 1² .388 (the accounts of Promachos). Since then G. P. Stevens and A. E. Raubitschek ("Pedestal") have attempted to reconstruct the pedestal of the statue and its dedication, which they date to 480–60. They represent the statue as a memorial for all the wars against Persia. P. Amandry, however, remains skeptical: "The reconstruction of the

dedication and the very identification of the stones are dubious" ("Épigrammes de Marathon," 7 n. 16).

68. "Monument." It was even maintained that the sculptures on the Athenian treasury at Delphi dated from the time of Cimon (cf. G. Perrot, *Journal des débats*, 13 June 1907, p. 2, col. 2); I owe the reference to P. de la Coste-Messelière (*Trésor des Athéniens*, 267 n. 3); while he himself estimates that the sculptures were done in 489, he does not absolutely rule out a later date.

69. See J. Defradas, *Propagande delphique.*

70. Cf. P. Lévêque and P. Vidal-Naquet, *Clisthène,* 40.

71. For a discussion of the placement of this base, cf. *Énigmes,* 16–36.

72. Cf. *Clisthène,* 23–24.

73. Cf. *Ath. Pol.* 21.6 and the doubts expressed in *Clisthène,* 50 n. 7.

74. On the relations between Athens and Delphi, see the summary by G. Daux, who emphasizes their relatively late condition ("Athènes et Delphes," and pp. 61–67 for a useful chronology; for the Marathon ex-voto, cf. p. 44).

75. P. de la Coste-Messelière, *Trésor des Athéniens,* 58–63.

76. K. Schefold, "Kleisthenes," 66.

77. P. de la Coste-Messelière, *Trésor des Athéniens,* 261. I am sticking by this formulation despite the recent outbreak of enthusiasm for Schefold's hypothesis: see C. Sourvinou-Inwood, "Theseus," 99–100; J. Boardman, "Herakles 1" and "Herakles 2;" and C. Bérard, "Récupérer." These scholars have indeed shown that Theseus's career on Attic vases belongs mostly to the time after the expulsion of the tyrants; hence Nilsson was wrong to think of Theseus as an instrument of Pisistratean propaganda ("Propaganda"). However, one cannot base an argument on the vases as if they were a direct expression of the ruling faction and of the city of Athens. When J. Boardman makes Herakles' club a symbol of Pisistratus's bodyguards (*korynēphoroi*), he is talking nonsense ("Herakles 1," 61–62). It is impossible to forget that Theseus is *not* one of Cleisthenes' heroes and that he *is* the hero of Miltiades and Cimon.

78. Cf. F. Jacoby, "First Athenian Prose Writers." The fragments from Pherecydes are cited below according to Jacoby's edition. *FGrH* 3.

79. Cf. fragments 147–50 (*Theseus*) and 154–55 (*Codros*).

80. Cf. the genealogical table in H. T. Wade-Gery, *Essays,* 164 n. 3. The adoption of Cimon Koalemos (the Simpleton) by Miltiades the Elder connects his posterity to the "Philaides."

81. "First Athenian Prose Writers," 31: "Pherekydes not only carried down the pedigree to at least the second half of the sixth century but . . . by making additions to the individual names, he set forth the titles to glory of the Philaid clan." I cannot, however, agree with Jacoby when he invokes the absence of Cimon's name to put Pherecydes' work before Cimon's first *strategia* in 476–475 (32–33). The argument would apply just as well to Miltiades the Younger and would force us to push Pherecydes back much too early. It is unusual enough to see Pherecydes giving the genealogy of a historic personage without making the

additional demand that he do so for a living person. At Athens everyone was aware of the ties that united Cimon to Miltiades the Elder.

82. According to Plutarch *Theseus* 5, at Delphi there existed a so-called "Theseia" in memory of an ephebic rite performed by the Athenian hero.

83. The parallelism between these two monuments' treatments of Theseus was emphasized by H. Herter, "Theseus der Athener," 291–92. In the same article (290) Herter lists all the passages, sometimes quite late, that connect Theseus to the region of Marathon; one of them even claims that Theseus was raised in Marathon (Schol. ad Statius *Thebais* 5.431, 12.196, pp. 284, 474 Jahnke). See also E. Simon, "Polygnotan Painting," and for Theseus at Marathon, A. J. Podlecki, *Background*, 13.

84. The most detailed commentary on this passage and the scarce information we have about the work remains C. Robert, *Marathonschlacht*, 1–45. According to the scholiast on Aelius Aristides 3, p. 566 (Dindorf), Miltiades stretched out his arm and pointed out the Barbarians to the Hellenes. According to Pliny, at least part of the piece was by Panainos (*N.H.* 35.57). On the "epiphany" of Theseus at Marathon, see also Plut. *Theseus* 35.8.

85. On the character and his mythology, see U. Kron, *Phylenheroen*, 188–89.

86. This is the suggestion, supported by good arguments, of D. M. Lewis, "Cleisthenes," 24–25.

87. It was there that Cimon gained for himself a clientele (cf. Aristotle F. 363 Rose). On the tomb of the family of Miltiades' descendants, cf. Hdt. 6.103 and Marcellinus, *Vit. Thuc.* 55; it was located in Koile in the territory of Hippothontis.

88. Cf. F. Jacoby, *FGrH* IIIb, 1, pp. 207–8.

89. Riemann connects the two characters because both are descendants of Poseidon ("Hippothontis," 182).

90. Cf. F. Jacoby, *FGrH* IIIb, II, 50.

91. On the discussions raised by these problems, see M. Crosby, "Poletai," inscription no. 1, pp. 21–22, which provides the prior bibliography.

92. Cf. J. Travlos, *Bildlexikon*, 332–34.

93. Dittenberger, *Sylloge*[3] 93. On the Athenian traditions about Codros, the most detailed analysis is probably that by A. Ledl, *Verfassungsgeschichte*. Codros appears on only one vase of the Periclean era, which is known by his name: Beazley, *A.R.V.*[2] 1268.1: Codros meets the seer Ainetos. It is noteworthy that on the outside of this cup Ajax, Aegeus, and Theseus appear—an interesting conjunction of several of the heroes included or excluded from Delphi, but no further conclusions can be drawn.

94. On this aspect of Lycurgus and his time, see L. Robert, *Études*, 316.

95. "Aglaurides."

96. This is the deserter against whom he is making a case and to whom he returns by some unexpected way, via an archaeological detour.

97. Kron raises the objection that this passage is concerned with "eponyms of the country" (*epōnymoi tēs chōras*) and not eponyms of the tribes (*Phylenheroen*, 224

324   n. 1087). This is an odd objection, since Codros is compared to Erechtheus, the eponym of Erechtheis. For a study of the ideology of the eponyms in the fourth century the most typical text is Dem. *Epitaphios* 34–43, commented on by N. Loraux, *Invention*, 127, 138–42.

98. Must I say that I have not tried to prove that Cimon wished to create Athenian tribes of Theseis, Philais, and Codris? At most the monument at Delphi was a "trial balloon," and if nothing else a sign of both the extreme daring that was permitted at Delphi and of the exceptional flexibility of the world of heroes. There are other such indications, some close to the one we have examined. The study by J. Barron that has already been frequently mentioned ("Religious Propaganda," 35–48) is devoted to some very curious fifth-century documents, boundary-stones from Samos that marked out *temenē* consecrated to Athena *Athē-nōn medeousa*, to the eponyms, and to Ion. The inscriptions sometimes use Ionian dialect, sometimes Attic, and can be dated c. 450–46. Barron thinks that they were a Samian undertaking, but I hesitate to accept this since some of the documents do use Attic. Although I do not grant all his arguments, I am persuaded by his claims that the organization of a cult of "Athenian Ion" and "Athenian eponyms" within the context of an alliance with Athens suggests that these "eponyms" are Ion's four sons (the ancestors of the "Ionian" tribes) rather than the Cleisthenic eponyms. Thus the eponymous heroes replaced by Cleisthenes would have retained an official existence in a Samian precinct put under the patronage of Athens. Or should we conclude that the ambiguity was deliberate?

Bibliography

Amandry, P. "Lendemain": "Athènes au lendemain des guerres médiques." *Revue de l'Université de Bruxelles* (April–May 1961), 1–26.

———. "Épigrammes de Marathon": "Sur les Épigrammes de Marathon." *Théoria, Festschrift für W. H. Schuchhardt*, Edited by F. Echstein. Baden-Baden, 1960, 1–8.

———. "Thémistocle": "Thémistocle: un décret et un portrait." *Bulletin de la Faculté des lettres de Strasbourg* (1961), 413–35.

Amelung, W. "Rito": "Di alcune sculture antiche e di un rito del culto delle divinità sotterranee." *Dissertazioni della Pontifica Accademia romana di archeologia* 9 (1907): 115–35.

Ampolo, C. "La *boulē demosiē* di Chio: un consiglio populare?" *Parola del Passato* 213 (1983): 410–16.

Anderson, J. K. *Horsemanship: Ancient Greek Horsemanship*. Berkeley and Los Angeles, 1961.

———. *Theory: Military Theory and Practice in the Age of Xenophon*. Berkeley and Los Angeles, 1970.

Anderson, P. *Absolutist State: Lineages of the Absolutist State*. London, 1974.

Andrewes, A. "Philochoros": "Philochoros on Phratries." *Journal of Hellenic Studies* 81 (1961): 1–15.

———. "Phratries": "Phratries in Homer." *Hermes* 89 (1961): 129–40.

Apel, H. *Tyrannis: Die Tyrannis von Heraklea*. Halle, 1910.

Arrigoni, G. "Atalanta": "Atalanta e il Cinghiale Bianco." *Scripta philologica* 1 (1977): 9–42.

Asheri, D. "Distribuzioni": "Distribuzioni di terre nell' antica Grecia." *Memorie dell'Accademia delle scienze di Torino*. Turin, 1966.

326 ——————. "Herakleia Pontike": "Über die Frühgeschichte von Herakleia Pontike," *Ergängungsbände zu der Tituli Asiae Minoris nº 5. Forschungen an der Nordkuste Kleinasiens* I. Vienna, 1972, 11–34.

——————. "Mariage forcé": "Tyrannie et Mariage forcé, essai d'histoire sociale." *Annales E.S.C.* 32 (1977): 21–48.

Audiat, J. *Trésor des Athéniens: Fouilles de Delphes II, 4: Le Trésor des Athéniens.* Paris, 1933.

Austin, M., and P. Vidal-Naquet. *Economy: Economic and Social History of Ancient Greece,* 2d ed. Berkeley and Los Angeles, 1977.

Aymard, A. "Hiérarchie du travail: "Hiérarchie du travail et autarcie individuelle dans la Grèce archaïque." *Revue d'histoire de la philosophie et d'histoire générale de la civilisation* 11. 1943; reprinted in *Études d'histoire ancienne.* Paris, 1967, 316–33.

——————. "Mercenariat": "Mercenariat et Histoire grecque." *Études d'archéologie classique, II, Annales de l'Est* (1959); reprinted in *Études d'histoire ancienne,* 487–98.

——————. "Philippe": "Philippe de Macédoine otage à Thèbes." *Revue des études anciennes* 56 (1954); reprinted in *Études d'histoire ancienne,* 418–36.

Aymard, J. *Chasses romaines: Les Chasses romaines des origines à la fin du siècle des Antonins.* Paris, 1951.

Bachofen, J. J. *Das Mutterrecht: Das Mutterrecht.* Stuttgart, 1861. New edition produced by K. Meuli, 2 vol. Basel, 1948.

Bader, F. *Démiourgos: Les Composés du type de Démiourgos.* Paris, 1965.

Bambrough, R. *Plato, Popper: Plato, Popper, and Politics.* Cambridge, 1968.

Barbagallo, C. *Il tramonto di una civiltà; o, La fine della Grecia antica.* Florence, 1924.

Barron, J. "Athenian Propaganda": "Milesian Politics and Athenian Propaganda," *Journal of Hellenic Studies* 82 (1962): 1–6.

——————. "Religious Propaganda": "Religious Propaganda of the Delian League," *Journal of Hellenic Studies* 84 (1964): 35–48.

Bartoli, G. *Explication historique: Essai sur l'explication historique que Platon a donnée de sa République et de son Atlantide et qu'on n'a pas considérée jusqu'à maintenant.* Stockholm and Paris, 1779.

Bellour, R. "Entretien": "Entretien avec Cl. Lévi-Strauss," in R. Bellour and C. Clément (eds.), *Claude Lévi-Strauss.* Paris, 1979, 157–209.

Belmont, N. *Van Gennep: Arnold Van Gennep.* Paris, 1974.

Beloch, K. J. *Geschichte: Griechische Geschichte².* Strasbourg, 1914–1916.

Benardete, S. "Eidos": "Eidos and Diairesis in Plato's *Statesman.*" *Philologus* 107 (1963): 196–226.

Bengtson, H. *Griechische Geschichte: Griechische Geschichte von den Anfängen bis in die römische Kaiserzeit⁴.* Munich, 1969.

————. *Staatsverträge: Die Staatsverträge des Altertums, II, Die Verträge des*   327
griechischrömischen Welt von 700 his 338 V Chr. Munich, 1962. 2d ed.,
1975.

Benveniste, E., *Problems: Problems in General Linguistics.* Translated by M. E.
Mark. Coral Gables, 1971.

————. *Indo-European Language and Society.* Translated by E. Palmer. London,
1973.

————. "Remarks": "Remarks on the Function of Language in Freudian Theory," in *Problems*, 281–88.

————. "Rhythm": "The Notion of Rhythm in Its Linguistic Expression," in
Problems, 281–88.

————. "Tempus": "Latin Tempus," *Mélanges de philologie, de littérature et d'histoire anciennes offert à Alfred Ernout.* Paris, 1940, 11–16.

————. *Vocabulaire: Le Vocabulaire des institutions indo-européennes*, 2 vols. Paris,
1969.

Bérard, C. *Anodoi: Anodoi. Essai sur l'imagerie des passages chthoniens.* Neuchâtel,
1974.

————. *Eretria III: L'Hérôon à la porte de l'Ouest (Eretria, Fouilles et Recherches, III).*
Berne, 1970.

————. "Hérôon": "Topographie et Urbanisme de l'Erétrie archaïque: l'Hérôon," in *Eretria, VI.* Berne, 1978, 89–95.

————. "Récupérer": "Récupérer la mort du prince," in G. Gnoli and J. P.
Vernant (eds.), *La mort, les morts dans les sociétés anciennes.* Cambridge-Paris,
1982, 89–105.

Bérard, J. *Colonisation: La Colonisation grecque de la Sicile et de l'Italie méridionale²*.
Paris, 1957.

Bérard, V. *Calypso: Calypso et la Mer de l'Atlantide. Les Navigations d'Ulysse, III.*
Paris, 1929.

Berger, W. "Marathonische Gruppe": "Das Urbild des Kriegers aus der Villa
Hadriana und die marathonische Gruppe des Phidias in Delphi." *Römische
Mitteilungen* 65 (1958): 6–41.

Bersanetti, G. "Pelopida": "Pelopida," *Athenaeum* 27 (1949): 43–101.

Bertier, J. *Mnésithée: Mnésithée et Dieuchès*, edition and translation. Leyden,
1972.

Bettelheim, B. *Wounds: Symbolic Wounds: Puberty Rites and the Envious Male*, new
ed. New York, 1962.

Beverley, R. *Virginia: The History of Virginia in four parts . . . by a native and
inhabitant of the place*, 2d ed. revised and enlarged. London, 1722.

Bidez, J. *Éos: Éos ou Platon et l'Orient.* Brussels, 1945.

Bisinger, J. *Argrarstaat: Der Agrarstaat in Platons Gesetzen.* Leipzig, 1925.

328   Bleeker, C. J. (ed.) *Initiation: Initiation. Contributions to the Theme of the Study,* Conference in Strasbourg, 17–22 Sept. 1964. Leyden, 1965.

Boardman, J. "Herakles 1": "Herakles, Peisistratos and Sons." *Revue archéologique* (1972): 57–72.

———. "Herakles 2": "Herakles, Peisistratos and Eleusis." *Journal of Hellenic Studies* 95 (1975): 1–12 and pl. 1–4.

Boeckh, A. *Philolaos: Philolaos.* Berlin, 1819.

Bollack, J. *Empédocle: Empédocle, 1, Introduction à l'ancienne physique.* Paris, 1965.

Bollack, J., and E. Von Salin. *Phaidros: Platon, Phaidros.* Frankfort, 1963.

Bourdieu, P. *Esquisse: Esquisse d'une théorie de la pratique.* Paris, 1972.

Bourgey, L. *Observation: Observation et expérience chez les médecins de la collection hippocratique.* Paris, 1953.

Bourguet, E. *Fouilles de Delphes, III, 1: Fouilles de Delphes, III, Épigraphie, 1.* Paris, 1909.

———. *Ruines de Delphes: Les Ruines de Delphes.* Paris, 1914.

Bousquet, J., "Aglaurides": "Delphes et les Aglaurides d'Athènes." *Bulletin de correspondance hellénique* 88 (1964): 655–75.

———. "Inscriptions": "Inscriptions de Delphes." *Bulletin de correspondance hellénique* 66–67 (1942–1943): 124–36.

Bowra, C. M. "Atalanta": "Atalanta in Calydon." *Essays by Diverse Hands* 125 = *Transactions of the Royal Society of Literature of the U.K.* Oxford, 1950, 51–69.

Boyancé, P. "Euthyphron": "La Doctrine d'Euthyphron dans le *Cratyle*," *Revue des études grecques* 54 (1941): 141–75.

———. "Religion": "La Religion de Platon." *Revue des études anciennes* 49 (1947): 178–92.

———. "Religion astrale": "La Religion astrale de Platon à Cicéron." *Revue des études grecques* 65 (1952): 312–50.

Bradeen, D. W. *Agora XVII: The Athenian Agora, XVII. Inscriptions: The Funerary Monuments.* Princeton, 1974.

———. "Casualty Lists," 1: "Athenian Casualty Lists." *Hesperia* 33 (1964): 16–62.

———. "Casualty Lists," 2: "The Athenian Casualty List of 464 B.C." *Hesperia* 36 (1967): 321–28.

———. "Casualty Lists," 3: "The Athenian Casualty Lists." *Classical Quarterly* 13 (1969): 145–59.

Brandenstein, W. *Atlantis: Atlantis. Grösse und Untergang eines geheimnissvollen Inselreiches.* Vienna, 1951.

Bravo, B. "Sulân": "Sulân. Représailles et justice privée contre des étrangers dans les cités grecques." *Annali della Scuola Normale Superiore di Pisa,* Series III, 10 (1980): 675–987.

Brelich, A. *Eroi: Gli eroi greci.* Rome, 1958.

————. *Guerre, Agoni: Guerre, Agoni e Culti nella Grecia arcaica.* Bonn, 1961.

————. "Initiation": "Initiation et Histoire," in C. J. Bleeker (ed.), *Initiation*, 222–31.

————. "Monosandales": "Les Monosandales," *La Nouvelle Clio* 7–9 (1955–1957): 469–89.

————. *Paides: Paides e Parthenoi.* Rome, 1969.

Bremmer, H. *"Kynosarges"*: *"Es Kynosarges."* *Mnemosyne* 30 (1977): 369–74.

Brémond, C., "Message": "Le Message narratif." *Communications* 4 (1964): 4–32.

————. "Postérité": "Postérité américaine de Propp." *Communications* 11 (1968): 147–64; text reprinted in *Logique du récit.* Paris, 1973, 11–47 and 59–80.

Breslin, J. *Prayer: A Greek Prayer.* Pasadena, 1978.

Briant, P. *Antigone: Antigone le Borgne. Les débuts de sa carrière et les problèmes de l'assemblée macédonienne.* Paris: Besançon, 1973.

————. "Laoi": "Remarques sur *laoi* et esclaves ruraux en Asie Mineure hellénistique." *Actes du Colloque 1971 sur l'esclavage.* Paris, 1973, 93–133.

Brisson, L. "Critias": "De la philosophie politique à l'épopée, le *Critias* de Platon." *Revue de métaphysique et de morale* (1970), 402–38.

————. "Instant": "L'Instant, le Temps et l'Eternité dans le *Parménide* (155e–157b) de Platon." *Dialogue* 9 (1970–1971): 389–96.

————. *Même et Autre: Le Même et l'Autre dans la structure ontologique du Timée de Platon.* Paris, 1974.

————. *Platon III: Platon 1958–1975. Lustrum* 20 (1977 [1979]).

Brommer, F. "Attische Könige": "Attische Könige." *Charites. Studien zur Altertumswissenschaft Hrsg. V. K. Schauenburg (für E. Langlotz).* Bonn, 1957, 152–64.

Broneer, O. "Early Athens": "Plato's Description of Early Athens and the Origin of Metageitnia." *Hesperia,* suppl. 8 (1949): 47–59.

Brumbaugh, R. S. *Imagination: Plato's Mathematical Imagination.* Bloomington, 1957.

Bruneau, P. *Recherches: Recherches sur les cultes de Délos à l'époque hellénistique et à l'époque impériale.* Paris, 1970.

Brunn, H. *Künstler: Geschichte der griechischen Künstler.* Brunswick, 1853.

Buffière, F. *Mythes d'Homère: Les Mythes d'Homère et la Pensée grecque.* Paris, 1956.

Bulle, H., and T. Wiegand. "Topographie": "Zur Topographie der delphischen Weihgeschenke." *Bulletin de correspondance hellénique* 22 (1898): 328–34.

Burford, A. *Craftsmen: Craftsmen in Greek and Roman Society.* London, 1972.

Burkert, W. "Kekropidensage": "Kekropidensage und Arrhephoria." *Hermes* 94 (1966): 1–25.

————. *Lore: Weisheit und Wissenschaft. Studien zu Pythagoras, Philolaos und Pla-*

330　*ton.* Nuremberg, 1962; English translation by E. L. Minar, Jr., *Lore and Science in Ancient Pythagorism.* Cambridge, MA, 1972.

Burnet, J. *Early Greek Philosophy*[4]. London, 1930.

Burrow, J. W. *Evolution: Evolution and Society: A Study in Victorian Social Theory.* Cambridge, 1966.

Busolt, G. *Griechische Geschichte: Griechische Geschichte.*[2] Gotha, 1892.

Busolt, G., and H. Swoboda. *Staatskunde,* I: *Griechische Staatskunde,* I[3]. Munich, 1920.

Bywater, I. "Fragments": "On the Fragments Attributed to Philolaos the Pythagorean." *Journal of Philology* 1 (1868): 21–53.

Caillois, R. "Temps circulaire": "Temps circulaire, Temps rectiligne." *Diogène* 42 (1963): reprinted in *Obliques.* Paris, 1975, 130–49.

Calame, C. *Choeurs: Les Choeurs de jeunes filles en Grèce archaïque. I. Morphologie, fonction religieuse et sociale; II. Alcman.* Rome, 1977.

———. "Cyclopes": "Mythe grec et structures narratives, le mythe des Cyclopes dans l'*Odyssée.*" *Ziva Antika* 26 (1976): 311–28.

———. "Philologie et Anthropologie": "Philologie et Anthropologie structurale; à propos d'un livre récent d'Angelo Brelich." *Quaderni Urbinati di cultura classica* 11 (1971): 7–47.

Cambiano, G. "Main": "Le Médecin, la main et l'artisan." *Corpus hippocraticum. Colloque de Mons, septembre 1975.* Mons, 1977, 220–32.

———. *Tecniche: Platone e le tecniche.* Turin, 1971.

Carandini, A. *Archeologia: Archeologia e cultura materiale.* Bari, 1975.

Carrière, J.-C. *Le Carnaval et la Politique.* Paris: Besançon, 1979.

Casabona, J. *Sacrifices: Recherches sur le vocabulaire des sacrifices en grec des origines à la fin de l'époque classique.* Aix-Gap, 1966.

Castoriadis, C. *Imaginaire: L'Institution imaginaire de la société.* Paris, 1975.

Cawkwell, G. "Epaminondas": "Epaminondas and Thebes." *Classical Quarterly* 22 (1972): 254–78.

Chadwick, J. "Dorians": "Who were the Dorians?." *Parola del passato* 31 (1976): 103–17.

Chaignet, A. E. *Pythagore: Pythagore et la philosophie pythagoricienne.* Paris, 1873.

Chantraine, P. "Artisan": "Trois noms grecs de l'artisan." *Mélanges de philosophie grecque offerts à Mgr. A. Diès.* Paris, 1956, 41–47.

———. *Études: Études sur le vocabulaire grec.* Paris, 1956.

———. *Formation: La Formation des noms en grec ancien.* Paris, 1933.

———. "Gauche": "Les Noms de la gauche en grec." *Comptes Rendus de l'Académie des inscriptions et belles lettres* (1955): 344–47.

Châtelet, F. *Naissance: La Naissance de l'histoire.* Paris, 1962.

———. "Temps de l'histoire": "Le Temps de l'histoire et l'évolution de la fonction historienne." *Journal de psychologie* (1956): 355–78.

Cherniss, H. "Review of Gegenschatz": "Review of E. Gegenschatz, *Platons*   331
Atlantis, Zurich, 1943." *American Journal of Philology* 68 (1947): 251–57.
———. *Platon I: Plato 1950–1957, Lustrum*, 4 (1959).
———. *Platon II: Plato 1950–1957, Lustrum*, 5 (1960).
———. "Relation": "The Relation of the *Timaeus* to Plato's Later Dialogues."
American Journal of Philology 78 (1957); reprinted in R. E. Allen (ed.), *Studies in
Plato's Metaphysics*. London, 1965, 339–78.
Clarke, H. W. *Art: The Art of the Odyssey*. Englewood Cliffs, NJ, 1967.
Clerc, M. *Métèques: Les Métèques athéniens*. Paris, 1891.
Cochrane, C. N. *Thucydides: Thucydides and the Science of History*. Oxford, 1929.
Cole, T. *Democritus: Democritus and the Sources of Greek Anthropology*. Ann Arbor,
1967.
Collingwood, R. G. *Idea: The Idea of History*. Oxford, 1946.
Compernolle, R. Van. "Doulocratie": "Le Mythe de la gynécocratie-doulocratie
argienne." *Le Monde grec: pensée, littérature, histoire, documents: hommages à Claire
Préaux*. Edited by J. Bingen, G. Cambier, and G. Nachtergael. Brussels,
1975, 355–64.
———. "Tradizioni": "Le Tradizioni sulla fondazione e sulla storia arcaica di
Locri Epizefiri e la propaganda politica alla fine delle V e nel IV secolo av. Cr."
Annale della scuola normale superiore de Pisa, 3d series, 6, 2 (1976): 329–400.
Connor, W. R. *Theopompus: Theopompus and Fifth Century Athens*. Washington,
1968.
Cook, A. B. *Zeus: Zeus. A Study in Greek Religion*. Cambridge, 1914–1940.
Cornford, F. M. *Attic Comedy: The Origin of Attic Comedy*. London, 1914.
———. *Cosmology: Plato's Cosmology*. London, 1937.
———. *Parmenides: Plato and Parmenides*. London, 1939.
———. *Principium: Principium Sapientiae. The Origins of Greek Philosophical
Thought*. Cambridge, 1952.
Corsano, M. "Sparte et Tarente": "Sparte et Tarente: le mythe de fondation d'une
colonie." *Revue de l'histoire des religions* 196, 2 (1979): 115–40.
Corssen, P. "Sendung": "Die Sendung der Lokrerinnen und die Gründung von
Neue Ilion." *Sokrates* 1 (1913): 188–202 and 235–52.
Coste-Messelière, P. de la. *Musée de Delphes: Au musée de Delphes*. Paris, 1936.
———. *Trésor des Athéniens: Fouilles de Delphes IV, 4, Sculptures du trésor des
Athéniens*. Paris, 1957.
Couissin, P. *Atlantide: L'Atlantide de Platon et les origines de la civilisation*. Aix-en-
Provence, 1928.
———. "Mythe": "Le Mythe de l'Atlantide." *Mercure de France*, February 15,
1927, 29–71.
Crahay, R. *Littérature: La Littérature oraculaire chez Hérodote*. Paris: Liège, 1956.

332   Crosby, M. "Poletai": "A Poletai Record of the Year 367/6 B.C." *Hesperia* 10 (1941): 14–27.

Cuffel, V. "Concept of Slavery": "The Classical Greek Concept of Slavery." *Journal of the History of Ideas* 27 (1966): 323–42.

Cuillandre, J. *Droite et Gauche: La Droite et la Gauche dans les poèmes homériques en concordance avec la doctrine pythagoricienne et avec la tradition celtique.* Paris, 1944.

Cullmann, O. *Christ and Time: Christ and Time: The Primitive Christian Conception of Time and History.* Translated by F. V. Filson. Philadelphia, 1950.

Cumont, F. *Lux perpetua: Lux perpetua.* Paris, 1949.

―――. *Symbolisme funéraire: Recherches sur le symbolisme funéraire.* Paris, 1942.

Curtius, E. "Weihgeschenke": "Die Weihgeschenke der Griechen nach der Perserkriegen." *Gesammelte Abhandlungen,* Berlin, 1899, t. II, pp. 359–74; article dating from 1861.

Daux, G. "Chronique 1965": "Chronique des fouilles." *Bulletin de correspondance hellénique* (1965): 683–1008.

―――. *Pausanias à Delphes: Pausanias à Delphes.* Paris, 1936.

Davies, J. K. *Families: Athenian Propertied Families 600–300 B.C.* Oxford, 1971.

de Acosta, J. *Indias: Historia natural y moral de las Indias* (Séville: 1590); *The naturall and morall historie of the East and West Indies . . .* Translated by E. G. [Edward Grimstone?]. London, 1604. I cite the recent edition *Obras del P. José de Acosta,* Madrid, 1954.

de Certeau, M. "Lafitau": "Writing Vs. Time: History and Anthropology in the Works of Lafitau." *Yale French Studies* 59 (1980): 37–64.

Deribour, M. "Timbres amphoriques," 2: "Réflexions sur les timbres amphoriques thasiens." *Thasiaca, Bulletin de correspondance hellénique,* Suppl. V. Athens, 1979, 269–314.

de Romilly, J. "Cycles et cercles chez les auteurs grecs de l'époque classique." *Le Monde grec: pensée, littérature, histoire, documents: hommages à Claire Préaux.* Edited by J. Bingen, G. Cambier, and G. Nachtergael. Brussels, 1975: 140–52.

―――. *Histoire et raison: Histoire et raison chez Thucydide.* Paris, 1967.

―――. "Progrès": "Thucydide et l'Idée du progrès." *Annali della Scuola normale superiore di Pisa,* Series 2, 25 (1966): 143–91.

Defradas, J. *Propagande delphique: Les Thèmes de la propagande delphique.* Paris, 1954.

Delatte, A. *Études: Études sur la littérature pythagoricienne.* Paris, 1915.

Delcourt, M. *Pyrrhos: Pyrrhos et Pyrrha. Recherches sur les valeurs du feu dans les légendes helléniques.* Paris, 1965.

―――. *Hermaphrodite: Hermaphrodite: Mythes et Rites de la bissexualité dans l'Antiquité classique.* Paris, 1958.

Delvoye, C. "Art et Politique": "Art et Politique à Athènes à l'époque de Cimon." *Le Monde grec: pensée, littérature, histoire, documents: hommages à Claire*

Préaux. Edited by J. Bingen, G. Cambier, and G. Nachtergael. Brussels,   333
1975, 801–7.

Deonna, W. "Cornes gauches": "Les Cornes gauches." *Revue des études anciennes* (1940): 111–26.

———. "Monokrêpides": "Monokrêpides." *Revue de l'histoire des religions* 89 (1935): 50–72.

Despotopoulos, C. "Esclavage": "La Cité parfaite de Platon et l'Esclavage. Sur *République* 433 d." *Revue des études grecques* 83 (1970): 26–37.

Detienne, M. *Dionysos: Dionysos Slain*. Translated by M. and L. Muellner. Baltimore, 1979.

———. *Gardens: The Gardens of Adonis*. Translated by J. Lloyd. Atlantic Highlands, NJ, 1977.

———. "Géométrie": "En Grèce archaïque: géométrie, politique et société." *Annales E.S.C.* 20 (1965): 425–41.

———. "Gnawing": "Gnawing his Parents' Heads," in *Dionysos Slain*, 53–67.

———. *Maîtres de vérité: Les Maîtres de vérité dans la Grèce archaïque*[3]. Paris, 1979.

———. "Panther": "The Perfumed Panther," in *Dionysos Slain*, 20–52.

———. "Phalange": "La Phalange: problèmes et controverses," in J.-P. Vernant (ed.), *Problèmes de la guerre*, 119–42.

———. "Repenser": "Repenser la mythologie," in M. Izard and P. Smith (eds.), *La Fonction symbolique. Essais d'anthropologie*. Paris, 1979, 71–82.

———. "Violentes Eugénies": "Violentes Eugénies. En pleines Thesmophories: des femmes couvertes de sang," in M. Detienne and J.-P. Vernant (eds.), *Cuisine*, 183–214.

Detienne, M., and J.-P. Vernant (eds.). *Cuisine: La Cuisine du sacrifice en pays grec*. Paris, 1978.

Detienne, M., and J.-P. Vernant. *Métis: Les Ruses de l'intelligence. La métis des Grecs*[2]. Paris, 1978. = *Cunning Intelligence in Greek Culture and Society*. Atlantic Highlands, NJ, 1978.

Deubner, L. *Feste: Attische Feste*. Berlin, 1932.

Di Benedetto, V. "Il Filottete": "Il *Filottete* e l'Efebia secondo P. Vidal-Naquet," *Belfagor* 33 (1978): 191–207.

Di Benedetto, V., and Lami, A. *Mistificazioni: Filologia e marxismo. Contra le mistificazioni*. Naples, 1981.

Diels, H. *Die Fragmente der Vorsokratiker*[7], 3 vols. Edited by W. Kranz. Berlin, 1954.

Diller, A. "Manuscripts": "The Manuscripts of Pausanias." *Transactions of the American Philological Association* 88 (1957): 169–88.

———. "Pausanias in the Middle Ages": "Pausanias in the Middle Ages." *Transactions of the American Philological Association* 87 (1956): 84–97.

Dodds, E. R. *Irrational: The Greeks and the Irrational*. 2d ed. Berkeley, 1951.

334   Domaszewski, A. von. *Attische Politik: Die attische Politik der Zeit der Pentekon-*
taetie. Heidelberg, 1925.

Dombrowski, D. *Vegetarianism: The Philosophy of Vegetarianism.* Amherst, 1984.

Dow, S., and R. F. Healey. *Calendar: A Sacred Calendar of Eleusis.* Cambridge,
MA, 1965. = *Harvard Theological Studies* 21.

Ducat, J. "Hilotisme": "Aspects de l'hilotisme." *Ancient Society* 9 (1978): 5–46.

———. "Mépris des hilotes": "Le Mépris des hilotes." *Annales E.S.C.* 29
(1974): 1452–64.

———. "Récits": "Les Thèmes des récits de la fondation de Rhégion." *Mélanges*
G. Daux. Paris, 1974, 93–114.

Duchet, M. *Anthropologie et Histoire: Anthropologie et Histoire au siècle des Lumières.*
Paris, 1971.

———. "Discours ethnologique": "Discours ethnologique et Discours historique: le texte de Lafitau." *Studies on Voltaire and the Eighteenth Century* 151–155.
Oxford, 1976, 607–23.

Ducrey, P. *Prisonniers: Le Traitement des prisonniers de guerre dans la Grèce antique, des*
origines à la conquête romaine. Paris, 1968.

Dumézil, G. *Aspects: Aspects de la fonction guerrière chez les Indo-Européens.* Paris,
1956.

———. *Lemniennes: Le Crime des Lemniennes.* Paris, 1924.

———. *Héritage indo-européen: L'Héritage indo-européen à Rome.* Paris, 1949.

———. *Horace: Horace et les Curiaces.* Paris, 1942.

———. *Idéologie: L'Idéologie tripartite des Indo-Européens.* Brussels, 1958.

———. *Mythe et épopée, I: Mythe et épopée, I.* Paris, 1968.

———. *Religion: Archaic Roman Religion.* Translated by P. Krapp. Chicago,
1970.

———. "Temps et mythe": "Temps et mythe." *Recherches philosophiques* 5 (1935–
1936): 235–51.

Dumont, J.-C. "Aristonicos": "A propos d'Aristonicos." *Eirene* 5 (1966): 189–
96.

Dunn, S. P. *Fall and Rise: The Fall and Rise of the Asiatic Mode of Production.*
London, Boston, Melbourne, and Henley, 1982.

Durand, J.-L. "Délit": "Le Corps du délit." *Communications* 26 (1977): 46–61.

Eitrem, S. *Opferritus: Opferritus und Voropfer der Griecher und Römer.* Kristiania,
1915.

———. "Phaiakenepisode": "Die Phaiakenepisode in der *Odyssee.*" *Videnskabs—*
Selskabet Skrifter. Hist. Filos. Kl., (1904) 2.

———. "Phaiaker": *s.v.* "Phaiaker," *R. E.* 19 (1938): c. 1518–34.

Eliade, M. *Eternal Return: The Myth of the Eternal Return.* New York, 1954.

———. *Nostalgie des origines.* Paris, 1971; partially reprinted from the collection
of C. J. Bleeker, *Initiation;* "L'Initiation et le Monde moderne," 1–14.

Ellinger, P. "Gypse": "Le Gypse et la Boue, I. Sur les mythes de la guerre   335
d'anéantissement." *Quaderni Urbinati di cultura classica* 29 (1978): 7–35.
Farnell, L. R. *Cults: Cults of the Greek States*, V. Oxford, 1909.
————. "Dionysia": "The Megala Dionysia and the Origin of Tragedy." *Journal of Hellenic Studies* 29 (1909): xlvii.
Faure, P. *Cavernes: Fonction des cavernes crétoises*. Paris, 1965.
Ferguson, W. S. "Salaminioi": "The Salaminioi of Heptaphylon and Sounion." *Hesperia* 7 (1938): 1–74.
Fernandez Nieto, F. J. *Acuerdos belicos: Los Acuerdos belicos en la Antigua Grecia (época arcaica y clásica), I, Texto, II, Los Instrumentos materiales de los conventos*. Santiago de Compostela, 1975.
Festugière, A. J. "Arétalogies": "A propos des arétalogies d'Isis." *Harvard Theological Review* (1949): 209–34; reprinted in *Études de religion grecque et hellénistique*. Paris, 1972, 145–49.
————. *Dieu cosmique: La Révélation d'Hermès Trismégiste, II³. Le dieu cosmique*. Paris, 1949.
Fidio, P. de. "Demiurgo": "Il Demiurgo e il ruolo delle *technai* in Platone." *Parola del passato* 26 (1971): 233–63.
Finley, M. I. *Ancient Economy: The Ancient Economy*. Berkeley and Los Angeles, 1973.
————. *Ancient Slavery: Ancient Slavery and Modern Ideology*. London, 1980.
————. "Aristotle": "Aristotle and Economic Analysis." *Past and Present* 47 (1970); reprinted in M. I. Finley (ed.), *Studies in Ancient Society*. London, 1974, 26–52.
————. *Economy and Society: Economy and Society in Ancient Greece*. New York, 1981.
————. "Between Slavery and Freedom": "Between Slavery and Freedom," in *Economy and Society*, 116–32.
————. "Servile Statuses": "The Servile Statuses of Ancient Greece," in *Economy and Society*, 133–49.
————. "Sparta": "Sparta and Spartan Society," in *Economy and Society*, 24–40.
————. *Sicily: Ancient Sicily²*. London, 1979.
————. "Slave Labour": "Was Greek Civilisation Based on Slave Labour?" *Historia* 8 (1959): 145–64; reprinted in *Slavery*, 53–72.
————. *Use and Abuse: The Use and Abuse of History*. New York, 1975.
————. *Ancestral Constitution: The Ancestral Constitution*. Cambridge, 1971; reprinted in *Use and Abuse*, 34–59.
————. "Myth": "Myth, Memory and History," *History and Theory* 4 (1965): revised and expanded in *Use and Abuse*, 11–33.
————. "Utopianism": "Utopianism Ancient and Modern." *The Critical Spirit: Essays in Honor of Herbert Marcuse*. Boston, 1967, 3–20; reprinted in *Use and Abuse*, 178–92.

————. *World: The World of Odysseus*, rev. ed. New York, 1965.

———— (ed.) *Slavery: Slavery in Classical Antiquity*². Cambridge, 1968.

Foley, H. "Similes": "Reverse Similes and Sex Roles in the *Odyssey.*" *Arethusa* 11 (1978): 7–26.

Fortina, M. *Epaminonda: Epaminonda*. Turin, 1958.

Fourgous, D. "Invention des armes": "L'Invention des armes en Grèce ancienne." *Annali della Scuola normale superiore di Pisa*, series III, 6, 4 (1976): 1123–64.

Frank, E. *Sogenannten Pythagoreer: Plato und die sogenannten Pythagoreer*. Halle, 1923.

Fränkel, H. "Ephemeros": "Man's *Ephemeros* Nature according to Pindar." *Transactions of the American Philological Association* 77 (1946): 131–45.

————. "Stileigenheit": "Eine Stileigenheit der frühgriechischen Literatur." *Göttingen Nachrichten* (1924); reprinted in *Wegen und Formen der frühgriechischen Denkens*. Munich, 1955, 40–96.

————. "Zeitauffassung": "Die Zeitauffassung in der frühgriechischen Literatur." *Zeitschrift für Aesthetik* (1931) Beilagenheft; reprinted in *Wegen and Formen der frühgriechischen Denkens*. Munich, 1955, 1–22.

Frankfort, H. *Kingship: Kingship and the Gods: A Study of Ancient Near Eastern Religion as the Integration of Society and Nature*. Chicago, 1948.

Frazer, J. G. *Pausanias: Pausanias' Description of Greece*, 6 vols. London, 1898.

————. *Golden Bough: The Golden Bough. A Study in Magic and Religion*³, Part II (vol. 3). *Taboo and the Perils of the Soul*. London, 1922.

Friedländer, P. *Plato: Plato I*², 2 vols. Translated by A. J. Meyerhoff. New York, 1958–1964.

Froidefond, C. *Mirage égyptien: Le Mirage égyptien*. Paris, 1971.

Frontisi-Ducroux, F. *Dédale: Dédale. Mythologie de l'artisan en Grèce ancienne*. Paris, 1975.

————. "Temps retrouvé": "Homère et le temps retrouvé." *Critique* 348 (1976): 538–48.

Frost, K. T. "Critias": "The *Critias* and Minoan Crete." *Journal of Hellenic Studies* 33 (1913): 189–206.

Fuks, A. "Slave War": "Slave War and Slave Troubles in Chios in the Third Century B.C." *Athenaeum* 46 (1968): 102–11.

Furtwängler, A. "Zu den Weihgeschenken": "Zu früheren Abhandlungen. I. Zu den marathonischen Weihgeschenken der Athener in Delphi." *Sitzungsberichte der philosophisch-philologischen und der historischen Klasse der K. B. Akademie der Wissenschaften zu München*. 1904, 365–70.

Gaidoz, H. "Mythologie comparée": "La Mythologie comparée, un mot d'explication." *Mélusine* II (1884–1885): c. 97–99.

Gaiser, K. *Ungeschriebene Lehre: Platons ungeschriebene Lehre*. Stuttgart, 1963.

Gaisford, T. *Lectiones Platonicae: Lectiones Platonicae*. Oxford, 1820.

Garaudy, R. (ed.) *Mode de production asiatique: Sur le "mode de production asiatique."*   337
Paris, 1969.

Garlan, Y. "Esclaves grecs," 1: "Les Esclaves grecs en temps de guerre." *Actes du Colloque d'histoire sociale (1970).* Paris: Besançon, 1972, 29–62.

———. "Esclaves grecs," 2: "Quelques travaux récents sur les esclaves grecs en temps de guerre." *Actes du Colloque 1972 sur l'esclavage.* Paris: Besançon, 1974, 15–28.

———. *Les esclaves en Grèce ancienne.* Paris, 1982.

———. "Fortifications": "Fortifications et Histoire grecque," in J.-P. Vernant (ed.), *Problèmes de la guerre,* 245–60.

———. *Guerre: La Guerre dans l'Antiquité.* Paris, 1972.

———. *Poliorcétique: Recherches de poliorcétique grecque.* Athens and Paris, 1974.

———. "Timbres amphoriques 1": "Koukos. Données nouvelles pour une nouvelle interprétation des timbres amphoriques thasiens." *Thasiaca, Bulletin de correspondance hellénique,* suppl. V. Athens, 1979, 213–68.

Gauer, W. *Weihgeschenke: Weihgeschenke aus den Perserkriegen.* Tübingen, 1968.

Gauthier, P. *Poroi: Un commentaire historique des Poroi de Xénophon.* Paris, 1976.

———. "Xénoi": "Les *Xénoi* dans les textes athéniens de la seconde moitié du ve siècle av. J.-C." *Revue des études grecques* 84 (1971): 44–79.

Gegenschatz, E. *Atlantis: Platons Atlantis.* Zurich, 1943.

Germain, G. *Genèse: Genèse de l'Odyssée.* Paris, 1954.

———. *Mystique: Homère et la mystique des nombres.* Paris, 1954.

Gernet, L. *Anthropology: The Anthropology of Ancient Greece.* Translated by J. Hamilton and B. Nagy. Baltimore, 1981.

———. "Archontes": "Les Dix Archontes de 581." *Revue de philologie* 64 (1938): 216–27.

———. "City of the Future": "The City of the Future and the Land of the Dead," in *Anthropology,* 112–24.

———. "Dolon": "Dolon the Wolf," in *Anthropology,* 125–39.

———. "Feasts": "Ancient Feasts," in *Anthropology,* 13–47.

———. "Law and Prelaw": "Law and Prelaw in Ancient Greece," in *Anthropology,* 143–215.

———. "Origins": "The Origins of Greek Philosophy," in *Anthropology,* 352–64.

———. "Time": "The Concept of Time in the Earliest Forms of Law," in *Anthropology,* 216–39.

Gernet, L., and A. Boulanger. *Génie grec: Le Génie grec dans la religion.* Paris, 1932. New edition, Paris, 1970.

Gill, C. "Critias and Politicus": "Plato and Politics: the *Critias* and the *Politicus.*" *Phronesis* 24 (1979): 148–67.

———. "Genre": "The Genre of the Atlantis Story." *Classical Philology* 72 (1977): 287–304.

338 ──────. "Origin": "The Origin of the Atlantis Myth." *Trivium* 11 (1976): 1–11.

Glotz, G., in collaboration with R. Cohen. *Histoire grecque, II: Histoire grecque, II. La Grèce au Ve siècle.* Paris, 1928.

──────. *Histoire grecque, III: Histoire grecque, III. La Grèce au IVe siècle. La lutte pour l'hégémonie (404–336).* Paris, 1936.

Godelier, M. "Préface": Préface de M. Godelier (ed.), *Sur les sociétés précapitalistes,* selected texts from Marx, Engels, Lenin. Paris, 1969.

Göttling, G. W. "Kynosarges": "Das Kynosarges." *Berichte über die Verhandlungen der Königlich Sächsischen Gesellschaft* 6 (1854); reprinted in *Gesammelte Abhandlungen* II. Munich, 1863, 156–74.

Goldschmidt, V. *Cratyle: Essai sur le Cratyle.* Paris, 1940.

──────. *Dialogues: Les Dialogues de Platon. Structure et méthode dialectique*². Paris, 1963.

──────. *Paradigme: Le Paradigme dans la dialectique platonicienne.* Paris, 1947.

──────. *Platonisme: Platonisme et Pensée contemporaine.* Paris, 1970.

──────. *Religion: La Religion de Platon.* Paris, 1959; reprinted in *Platonisme et Pensée contemporaine.* Paris, 1970.

──────. *Système stoïcien: Le Système stoïcien et l'Idée de temps*⁴. Paris, 1979.

──────. "Temps logique": "Temps historique et temps logique dans l'interprétation des systèmes philosophiques." *Actes du XIe Congrès international de philosophie,* XII (1953); reprinted in *Questions platoniciennes.* Paris, 1970, 13–21.

──────. "Theologia": "Theologia," *Revue des études grecques* 61 (1950); reprinted and expanded in *Questions platoniciennes.* 141–72.

──────. "Théorie aristotélicienne": "La Théorie aristotélicienne de l'esclavage et sa méthode." *Mélanges E. de Strijker.* Anvers, 1973, 147–63, reprinted in *Écrits,* I, Paris, 1984, 63–79.

──────. "Tragédie": "Le Problème de la tragédie d'après Platon." *Revue des études grecques* 59 (1948); reprinted in *Questions platoniciennes.* 103–40.

Gomme, A. W. *Commentary, I: A Historical Commentary on Thucydides,* I. Oxford, 1945.

──────. *Essays: Essays in Greek History and Literature.* Oxford, 1937.

──────. *Greek Attitude: The Greek Attitude to Poetry and History.* Berkeley, 1954.

Gomperz, T. *Greek Thinkers: The Greek Thinkers: A History of Ancient Philosophy.* New York, 1901–1912.

Goossens, R. *Euripide: Euripide et Athènes.* Brussels, 1962.

Gornatowski, A. *Rechts: Rechts und Links im antiken Aberglauben.* Breslau, 1936.

Graf, F. "Mädchen": "Die lokrische Mädchen." *Studi storico-religiosi* 2 (1978): 61–79.

Griffith, J. G. "Three Notes": "Three Notes on Herodotus Book II." *Annales du Service des antiquités d'Egypte* 53 (1955): 139–52.

————. *Herodotos Historien: Herodotos Historien. Comentaar.* Leyden, 1946.

Grundy, G. *Thucydides: Thucydides and the History of His Age.* Oxford, 1948.

Gschnitzer, F. *Abhängige Orte: Abhängige Orte im griechischen Altertum.* Munich, 1958.

Guarducci, M. *Fratria,* I and II: *L'Istituzione della fratria nella Grecia antica e nelle colonie greche d'Italia,* I and II. Rome, 1937 and 1938 (=*Memorie della classe di scienze morali, storiche e filologiche dell'Accademia dei Lincei,* VI, 6 and VI, 8, 2).

Guérin, P. *Justice: L'Idée de justice dans la conception de l'univers chez les premiers philosophes grecs de Thalès à Héraclite.* Paris, 1932.

Habicht, C. "Falsche Urkunden": "Falsche Urkunden zur Geschichte Athens im Zeitalter der Perserkriege." *Hermes* 59 (1961): 1–35.

————. "Neue Inschriften": "Neue Inschriften aus dem Kerameikos." *Athenische Mitteilungen* 76 (1961): 127–48.

Halliday, W. R. "Xanthos-Melanthos": "Xanthos-Melanthos and the Origin of Tragedy." *Classical Review* 40 (1926): 179–81.

Hansen, W. F. "Journey": "Odysseus' Last Journey." *Quaderni Urbinati di cultura classica* 24 (1977): 27–48.

Harrison, A. R. W. *Law, I: The Law of Athens, I, The Family and Property.* Oxford, 1968.

Harrisson, J. E. *Themis: Themis. A Study of the Social Origins of Greek Religion,* New York, 1962.

Hartog, F. *Miroir: Le Miroir d'Hérodote. Essai sur la représentation de l'autre.* Paris, 1980.

Haussleiter, J. *Vegetarismus: Der Vegetarismus in der Antike.* Berlin, 1935.

Havelock, E. *Liberal Temper: The Liberal Temper in Greek Politics.* London, 1957.

Heidel, W. A. *Greek Maps: The Frame of the Ancient Greek Maps.* New York, 1937.

Herter, H. "Atlantis": "Platons Atlantis." *Bonner Jahrbücher* (1928): 28–47.

————. "Theseus der Athener": "Theseus der Athener." *Rheinisches Museum* 88 (1939): 244–86, 289–326.

————. "Theseus der Ionier": "Theseus der Ionier." *Rheinisches Museum* 85 (1936): 177–91 and 193–239.

————. "Urathen": "Urathen der Ideal Staat"; reprinted in H. Herter, *Kleine Schriften.* Munich, 1975, 279–304.

Hertz, R. "Right Hand": "The Pre-eminence of the Right Hand: a study in religious polarity"; translated and reprinted in R. Needham, *Right and Left,* 3–31.

Hill, G. F. *Middle Class: The Roman Middle Class.* Oxford, 1952.

Hiller Von Gaertringen, F. "Voreuklidische Steine": "Voreuklidische Steine." *Sitzungsberichte Berlin* (1919): 660–72.

Hirvonen, K. *Matriarchal Survivals: Matriarchal Survivals and Certain Trends in Homer's Female Characters.* Helsinki, 1968.

Hitzig, H., and H. Bluemner. *Pausanias: Das Pausanias Beschreibung von Griechenland*, III. Leipzig, 1907–1910.

Hobsbawm, E. J. *Primitive Rebels: Primitive Rebels: Studies in the Archaic Forms of Social Movement in the Nineteenth and Twentieth Centuries*. New York, 1965.

Hodgen, M. T. *Survivals: The Doctrine of Survivals. A Chapter in the History of Scientific Method in the Study of Man*. London, 1936.

Höpfner, W. *Herakleia Pontike: Herakleia Pontike-Eregli, Eine Baugeschichtliche Untersuchungen*. Vienna, 1966.

Homolle, T. "Topographie 1": "Topographie de Delphes." *Bulletin de correspondance hellénique* 21 (1897): 256–320.

———. "Topographie 2": "Topographie du sanctuaire de Delphes." *Bulletin de correspondance hellénique* 22 (1898): 572–79.

Humphreys, S. "Nothoi": "The *Nothoi* of Kynosarges." *Journal of Hellenic Studies* 94 (1974): 88–95.

Huxley, G. "Troy VIII": "Troy VIII and the Locrian Maidens." *Ancient Society and Institutions: Studies Presented to Victor Ehrenberg on his 75th birthday*. Oxford, 1966: 147–64.

Immerwahr, W. *Atalanta: De Atalanta*. Dissertation. Berlin, 1885.

Jacoby, F. "Epigrams": "Some Athenian Epigrams from the Persian Wars." *Hesperia* 14 (1945); reprinted in *Kleine Schriften* I. Berlin, 1961, 456–520.

———. "First Athenian Prose Writer": "The First Athenian Prose Writer." *Mnemosyne* (1947): 13–64.

———. *FGrH: Die Fragmente der griechischen Historiker*, 15 vols. Berlin, then Leyden, 1923–1969.

———. "Geschichtschreibung": "Griechische Geschichtschreibung." *Die Antike* (1926); reprinted in *Abhandlungen zur griechischen Geschichtschreibung*. Leyden, 1956, 1–29.

Jaeger, W. *Paideia*, III: *Paideia*, vol. III. Translated by G. Highet. New York, 1945.

———. *Theology: The Theology of the Early Greek Philosophers*. Oxford, 1947.

Jameson, M. H. "Provision": "The Provision for Mobilization in the Decree of Themistocles." *Historia* 12 (1963): 385–409.

Jaulin, R. *Mort sara: La Mort sara*. Paris, 1967.

Jeanmaire, H. *Couroi: Couroi et Courètes. Essai sur l'éducation spartiate et les rites d'adolescence dans l'Antiquité hellénique*. Lille-Paris, 1939.

———. "Cryptie": "La Cryptie lacédémonienne." *Revue des études grecques* 26 (1913): 121–50.

Joly, H. *Renversement: Le Renversement platonicien. Logos, Épistémè, Polis*. Paris, 1974.

Joly, R. *Genres de vie: Le Thème philosophique des genres de vie dans l'Antiquité classique*. Brussels, 1956.

Kahil, L. G. "Artémis attique," I: "Autour de l'Artémis attique," *Antike Kunst* 8   341
(1965): 20–33.

———. "Artémis attique," II: "Artémis attique." *Comptes Rendus de l'Académie
des inscriptions et belles-lettres* (1976): 126–30.

———. "Artémis de Brauron": "L'Artémis de Brauron: rites et mystères." *Antike Kunst* 20 (1977): 86–98.

Kahn, C. *Anaximander: Anaximander and the Origins of Greek Cosmology.* New
York, 1960.

———. "Menexenus": "Plato's Funeral Oration: The Motive of the *Menexenus.*"
Classical Philology 58 (1963): 220–34.

Kahn, L. *Hermès passe, ou les ambiguïtés de la communication.* Paris, 1978.

———. "Ruse": "Ulysse, la Ruse et la Mort." *Critique* 393 (1980): 116–34.

———. "Ulysse": "Ulysse," in *Dictionnaire des mythologies,* II. Paris, 1981, 117–20.

Kahn, L., and N. Loraux. "Mort": "Mort," in *Dictionnaire des mythologies,* II.
Paris, 1981, 117–24.

Karo, G. "En marge": "En marge de quelques textes delphiques." *Bulletin de
correspondance hellénique* 33 (1909): 201–37.

Kaspar, K. *Indianer: Indianer und Urvölker nach Jos. Fr. Lafitau (1681–1746).*
Fribourg, Switzerland, 1943.

Kember, O. "Right and Left": "Right and Left in the Sexual Theories of Parmenides." *Journal of Hellenic Studies* 91 (1971): 70–79.

Kenner, H. *Verkehrten Welt: Das Phänomen der Verkehrten Welt in der griechischrömischen Antike.* Klagenfurt, 1970.

Kerenyi, K. "Dio Cacciatore": "Il Dio Cacciatore." *Dioniso* 15 (1952): 131–42.

Kiechle, F. *Lakonien: Lakonien und Sparta.* Munich and Berlin, 1963.

Kirchhoff, A. *Composition: Die Composition der Odyssee.* Berlin, 1869.

Kirk, G. S. *Heraclitus: Heraclitus. The Cosmic Fragments.* Cambridge, 1954.

———. *Myth: Myth, Its Meaning and Functions in Ancient and Other Cultures.*
Cambridge, Berkeley, and Los Angeles, 1970.

———. *Songs: The Songs of Homer.* Cambridge, 1962.

Kirk, G. S., and J. E. Raven. *Presocratic Philosophers: The Presocratic Philosophers.*
Cambridge, 1957.

Kleingünther, A. *Prôtos Heurétês: Prôtos Heurétês. Untersuchungen zur Geschichte
einer Fragestellung. Philologus,* suppl. 26. Leipzig, 1933.

Kluwe, E. "Kongressdekret": "Das perikleische Kongressdekret, das Todesjahr
des Kimon und seine Bedeutung für die Einordnung der Miltiadesgruppe in
Delphi." *Wissenschaftliche Zeitschrift der Universität Rostock, Gesellsch. und
Sprachwiss. R.,* 7–8 (1958): 677–83.

Kobler, R. *Weg: Der Weg des Menschen vom Links zum Rechtshänder.* Vienna, 1932.

Koch, E. "Lexiarchicon grammateion": "Lexiarchicon grammateion." *Griechi-*

342   *schen Studien H. Lipsius zum sechzigsten Geburtstag dargebracht.* Leipzig, 1894,
11–17.

Koechly, H. *Cryptia: De Lacedaemoniorum Cryptia commentatio.* Leipzig, 1835. (=
Opuscula philologica I. Leipzig, 1881) 580–91.

Kromayer, J., and G. Veith. *Heerwesen: Heerwesen und Kriegführung der Griechen
und Römer.* Munich, 1928.

————. *Schlachten-Atlas: Schlachten-Atlas zur antiken Kriegsgeschichte* I. Leipzig:
1922; IV. Leipzig, 1926.

————. *Schlachtfelder,* IV: *Antiken Schlachtfelder in Griechenland* IV. (with G.
Veith) Berlin, 1931.

Kron, U. *Phylenheroen: Die Zehn attischen Phylenheroen. Geschichte, Mythos, Kult
und Darstellung.* Berlin, 1976.

Kurtz, D., and J. Boardman. *Burial Customs: Greek Burial Customs.* Ithaca, 1971.

Labarbe, J. *Homère: L'Homère de Platon.* Liège, 1949.

————. "Koureion": "L'Âge correspondant au sacrifice du *koureion* et les données
historiques du sixième discours d'Isée." *Bulletin de l'Académie royale de Belgique,
classe des lettres* 39 (1953): 359–94.

————. *Loi navale: La Loi navale de Thémistocle.* Paris, 1957.

Labat, R. *Monarchie assyro-babylonienne: Le Caractère religieux de la monarchie assyro-
babylonienne.* Paris, 1939.

Lafitau, J. F. *Moeurs: Moeurs des sauvages américains comparées aux moeurs des premiers
temps,* 2 vols. in 4°, then 4 vols. in 12°. Paris, 1724.

Lammert, F. "Katalogos": *s.v.* "Katalogos," *R.E.* 10 (1919): c. 2470–71.

Lang, A. *Myth: Myth, Ritual and Religion.* London, 1901.

Lang, M. "Oral Technique": "Homer and Oral Technique." *Hesperia* 38 (1969):
159–68.

Laroche, E. *Racine nem: Histoire de la racine nem en grec ancien.* Paris, 1949.

Lauffer, S. *Bergwerksklaven: Die Bergwerksklaven von Laureion* 2. Wiesbaden, 1979.

Launey, M. *Armées hellénistiques: Recherches sur les armées hellénistiques,* 2 vols. Paris,
1950.

Leach, E. *Rethinking: Rethinking Anthropology.* London, 1961.

————. "Frazer and Malinowski": "Frazer and Malinowski: on the 'Founding
Fathers'." *Current Anthropology* 7: 360–67.

————. "Lévi-Strauss": "Claude Lévi-Strauss—Anthropologist and Philosopher." *New Left Review* 34 (1965): 12–27; translated by A. Lyotard-May.
Raison présente 3 (1967): 91–106.

Leaf, W. *Troy: Troy. A Study in Homeric Geography.* London, 1912.

Ledl, A. *Verfassungsgeschichte: Studien zur Älteren athenischen Verfassungsgeschichte.*
Heidelberg, 1914.

Le Goff, J., and E. Le Roy-Ladurie. "Mélusine": "Mélusine maternelle et dé-
fricheuse." *Annales E.S.C.* 26 (1971): 601–22.

Le Goff, J., and P. Vidal-Naquet. "Brocéliande": "Lévi-Strauss en Brocéliande,"   343
   in R. Bellour and C. Clément (eds.), *Lévi-Strauss*. Paris, 1979, 265–319.
Legrand, P. E. *Introduction: Introduction à Hérodote²*. Paris, 1955.
Lemay, E. "Nouveau Monde": "Histoire de l'antiquité et découverte du nouveau
   monde chez deux auteurs du XVIIIᵉ siècle." *Studies on Voltaire and the Eighteenth
   Century*, 151–155. Oxford, 1976, 1313–28.
Lencman, J. A. *Slavery: Slavery in Mycenaean and Homeric Greece* (in Russian).
   Moscow, 1963; German translation: *Die Sklaverei im mykenischen und ho-
   merischen Griechenland*. Wiesbaden, 1966.
Lenschau, T. "Phyleus": *s.v.* "Phyleus," *R.E.* 20 (1941): c. 1014–16.
Lerat, L. *Locriens: Les Locriens de l'Ouest*, 2 vols. Paris, 1952.
Lévêque, P., and P. Vidal-Naquet. *Clisthène: Clisthène l'Athénien. Essai sur la
   représentation de l'espace et du temps dans la pensée politique grecque de la fin du VIᵉ
   siècle à la mort de Platon³*. Paris, 1983.
Lévi-Strauss, C. *Raw: The Raw and the Cooked*. Translated by J. and D. Weight-
   man. New York, 1969.
———. *L'Homme nu: L'Homme nu*. Paris, 1971.
———. *Savage Mind: The Savage Mind*. Chicago, 1966.
———. *Totemism: Totemism*. Boston, 1963.
———. "Triangle": "Le Triangle culinaire." *L'Arc* 26 (1966): 19–29.
Lewis, D. M. "Cleisthenes": "Cleisthenes and Attica." *Historia* 12 (1963): 22–40.
Levinson, R. C. *Defense: In Defense of Plato*. Cambridge, MA, 1953.
Lissarrague, F. "Dolon": "Iconographie de Dolon le loup." *Revue archéologique* 1
   (1980): 3–30.
Lloyd, G.E.R. *Magic: Magic, Reason and Experience. Studies in the Origins and
   Development of Greek Science*. Cambridge, 1979.
———. *Polarity: Polarity and Analogy. Two Types of Argumentation in Early Greek
   Thought*. Cambridge, 1966.
———. "Right and Left": "Right and Left in Greek Philosophy," in R.
   Needham (ed.), *Right and Left*, 167–86; revised version of the original pub-
   lication in *JHS* 82 (1962).
———. "Who is attacked?": "Who is attacked in *On Ancient Medicine?*" *Phronesis*
   8 (1963): 108–20.
Loewy, E. "Donario": "Sopra il Donario degli Ateniesi a Delphi." *Studi italiani di
   filologia classica* 5 (1897): 33–38.
———. "Zu Mitteilungen": "Zu Mitteilungen oben s. 144." *Römische Mit-
   teilungen* 14 (1900): 235–36.
Loraux, N. "Acropole comique": "L'Acropole comique." *Ancient Society* 11–12
   (1980–1981): 119–50; reprinted in *Enfants*.
———. "Autochtonie": "L'Autochtonie: une topique athénienne. Le mythe
   dans l'espace civique." *Annales E.S.C.* 34 (1979): 3–26; reprinted in *Enfants*.

344   ———. "Belle mort": "La Belle Mort spartiate." *Ktèma* 2 (1977): 105–20.

———. *Enfants: Les Enfants d'Athéna. Idées athéniennes sur la citoyenneté et la division des sexes.* Paris, 1981.

———. "*Hébè et Andreia*": "Hébè et Andreia. Deux versions de la mort du combattant athénien." *Ancient Society* 6 (1975): 1–31.

———. "Interférence": "L'Interférence tragique." *Critique* 317 (1973): 908–25.

———. *Invention: L'Invention d'Athènes. Histoire de l'oraison funèbre dans la "cité classique."* The Hague, Berlin, and Paris, 1981.

———. "Marathon": "Marathon ou l'histoire idéologique." *Revue des études anciennes* 75 (1973): 13–42.

———. "Mourir": "Mourir devant Troie, tomber pour Athènes. De la gloire du héros à l'idée de la cité." *Information sur les sciences sociales* 17 (1978): 801–17.

———. "Race des femmes": "Sur la race des femmes et quelques-unes de ses tribus." *Arethusa* 11, 1–2 (1978): 43–87; reprinted in *Enfants*.

———. "Thucydide": "Thucydide n'est pas un collègue." *Quaderni di storia* 12 (July–December 1980): 55–81.

Lord, A. B. *Singer: The Singer of Tales.* Cambridge, MA, 1960.

Lotze, D. "Woikees": "Zu den Woikees von Gortyn." *Klio* 40 (1962): 32–43.

———. *Métaxy: Métaxy éleuthérôn kai doulôn.* Berlin, 1959.

Louis, P. *Métaphores: Les Métaphores de Platon.* Paris, 1945.

Lovejoy, A. O., and G. Boas. *Primitivism: Primitivism and Related Ideas in Antiquity.* Baltimore, 1936; reprinted New York, 1965.

Luccioni, J. "Platon et la Mer": "Platon et la Mer." *Revue des études anciennes* 61 (1959): 15–47.

Luce, J. V. *End: The End of Atlantis.* London and New York, 1969. In America, *Lost Atlantis*.

———. "Sources": "The Sources and Literary Form of Plato's Atlantis Narrative," in E. S. Ramage (ed.), *Atlantis*, 49–78.

Lugebil, K. "Staatsverfassung": "Zur Geschichte der Staatsverfassung von Athen. Untersuchungen." *Jahrbücher für classische Philologie,* suppl. 5 (1864–1872): 537–699.

Luria, S. "Frauenpatriotismus": "Frauenpatriotimus und Sklavenemanzipation in Argos." *Klio* 8 (1932): 211–28.

Lyons, J. *Structural Semantics: Structural Semantics. An Analysis of Part of the Vocabulary of Plato.* Oxford, 1963.

Lyotard, J.-F. "Indiens": "Les Indiens ne cueillent pas les fleurs." *Annales E.S.C.* 20 (1965); reprinted and expanded in R. Bellour and C. Clément (eds.), *Claude Lévi-Strauss.* Paris, 1979, 49–92.

Maas, E. "Review of Toepffer": "Review of J. Toepffer, *Attische Genealogie.*" *Göttingische Gelehrte Anzeiger* (1889): 801–32.

Manni, E. "Locridi": "Le Locridi nella letteratura del III sec. A.C." *Miscellanea di*   345
studi alessandrini in memoria di A. Rostagni. Turin, 1963, 166–79.

Manns, O. *Jadg: Über die Jagd bei den Griechen.* Progr. Cassel (1888): 7–38;
(1889): 3–20; (1890): 3–21.

Mansfeld, J. *Peri Hebdomadôn: The Pseudo-Hippocratic Tract Peri Hebdomadôn, ch. 1,
2 and Greek Philosophy.* Assen, 1971.

Marett, R. (ed.), *Anthropology and the Classics: Anthropology and the Classics.* Oxford, 1908.

Margarido, A. "Textos iniciaticos": "Proposições teoricas para a leitura de textos
iniciaticos." *Correio do povo* (Porto Alegre) August 21, 1971.

Marienstras, R. "Prospero": "Prospero ou le Machiavélisme du bien." *Bulletin de
la Faculté des lettres de Strasbourg* 42 (1965): 899–917.

Marinatos, S. *Legend: Some Words about the Legend of Atlantis.* Athens, 1971.
Translation of an article published in Greek in *Krêtika Chronika,* 1950.

Marrou, H.-I. "Civilisation": "Rapport sur l'histoire de la civilisation, Antiquité." *IXᵉ Congrès international des sciences historiques* I. Paris, 1950, 325–40.

———. *Education: A History of Education in Antiquity.* Translated by G. Lamb.
New York, 1956.

Martin, A. *Cavaliers: Les Cavaliers athéniens.* Paris, 1886.

Martin, T. H. "Dissertation": "Dissertation sur l'Atlantide," in *Études sur le Timée
de Platon* I. Paris, 1841, 257–333.

Marx, K. *18 Brumaire: The Eighteenth Brumaire of Louis Bonaparte,* in *Marx and
Engels: Collected Works.* New York, 1979, vol. 11, 99–197.

Masson, O. "Noms des esclaves": "Les Noms des esclaves dans la Grèce antique."
Actes du Colloque 1971 sur l'esclavage. Paris, 1973, 9–23.

Matarasso, M. "Robert Hertz": "Robert Hertz, notre prochain: sociologie de la
gauche et de la mort." *L'Année sociologique* 24 (1973): 119–47.

Mathieu, G. "Éphébie": "Remarques sur l'éphébie attique." *Mélanges offerts à A.
M. Desrousseaux par ses amis et ses élèves.* Paris, 1937, 311–19.

Maurin, J. "Puer": "Remarques sur la notion de *puer* à l'époque classique."
Bulletin de l'Association G.-Budé (1975): 221–30.

Maxwell-Stuart, P. G. "Black Coats": "Remarks on the Black Coats of the
Ephebi." *Proceedings of the Cambridge Philological Society* 196 (1970): 113–16.

Mazon, P. *Travaux: Hésiode. Les Travaux et les Jours,* new ed. Paris, 1914.

Mazzarino, S. *Pensiero storico: Il Pensiero storico classico,* 3 vols. Bari, 1966.

Meiggs, R., and D. Lewis. *Selection: A Selection of Greek Historical Inscriptions to the
End of the Fifth Century B.C.* Oxford, 1969.

Meillet, A. *Langue grecque: Aperçu d'une histoire de la langue grecque⁷.* Paris, 1955.

Mele, A. *Società e Lavoro nei poemi omerici.* Naples, 1968.

Mercier, P. *Histoire de l'anthropologie: Histoire de l'anthropologie.* Paris, 1971.

Meritt, B. D. *Studies: Greek Historical Studies.* Cincinnati, 1962.

346 ————. "Greek Inscriptions 1936": "Greek Inscriptions." *Hesperia* 5 (1936): 355–430.

Merkelbach, R. "Aglauros": "Aglauros. Die Religion der Epheben." *Zeitschrift für Papyrologie und Epigraphik* 9 (1972): 277–83.

Meuli, K. *Odyssee: Odyssee und Argonautika.* Berlin, 1921.

Meyerson, I. "Temps": "Le Temps, la mémoire et l'histoire." *Journal de psychologie* (1956): 333–57.

Michel, P.-H. *Pythagore: De Pythagore à Euclide. Contribution à l'histoire des mathématiques préeuclidiennes.* Paris, 1950.

Mitchel, F. W. "Ephebic Inscription": "The So-Called Earliest Ephebic Inscription." *Zeitschrift für Papyrologie und Epigraphik* 19 (1975): 233–43.

Momigliano, A. "Locrian Maidens": "The Locrian Maidens and the Date of Lycophron's *Alexandra.*" *Classical Quarterly* 39 (1945): 49–53; reprinted with an appendix in *Secondo contributo alla storia degli studi classici.* Rome, 1960, 446–53.

————. *Alien Wisdom: Alien Wisdom. The Limits of Hellenization.* Cambridge, 1975.

————. *Studies: Studies in Historiography.* London, 1966.

————. "Teopompo": "Teopompo." *Revista di filologia e di istruzione classica* 9 (1931): 230–53; reprinted in *Terzo Contributo alla storia degli studi classici e del mondo antico* I. Rome, 1966, 367–92.

————. "Time": "Time in Ancient Historiography." *History and Theory* 6 (1966); reprinted in *Quarto Contributo alla storia degli studi classici nel mondo antico.* Rome, 1969, 13–41.

Mommsen, A. *Feste: Feste der Stadt Athen im Altertum.* Leipzig, 1898.

————. "Zehn Eponymen": "Die zehn Eponymen und die Reihenfolge der nach ihnen genannten Phylen Athens." *Philologus* 47 (1889): 449–89.

Montepaone, C. "Rituale munichio": "Il mito de fondazione del rituale munichio in onore de Artemis." *Recherches sur les cultes grecs et l'Occident* I. Naples, 1979, 65–76.

————. "Arkteia": "L'arkteia a Brauron." *Studi storico-religiosi* III (1979): 343–64.

Moreau, J. *Âme du monde: L'Âme du monde de Platon aux stoïciens.* Paris, 1939.

————. "Review of Mugler": "Review of C. Mugler, *Deux Thèmes.*" *Revue des études grecques* 68 (1955): 363–68.

Morel, J.-P. "Jeunesse": "Sur quelques aspects de la jeunesse à Rome." *L'Italie préromaine et la Rome républicaine: Mélanges offerts à J. Heurgon.* Paris, 1976, 663–83.

————. "Juventus": "La *Juventus* et les origines du théâtre romain." *Revue des études latines* 47 (1969): 208–52.

————. "Pantomimus": "Pantomimus allectus inter juvenes." *Hommages à Marcel Renard II.* Brussels, 1969, 526–35.

————. "Pube praesenti": "Pube praesenti in contione omni poplo." *Revue des études latines* 42 (1964): 375–88.

Morenz, S. "Rechts": "Rechts und Links im Totengericht." *Zeitschrift für Aegyptische Sprache und Altertumskunde* (1957): 62–71.

Moret, A. *Royauté pharaonique: Du caractère religieux de la royauté pharaonique.* Paris, 1902.

Moreux, B. "La nuit, l'ombre et la mort chez Homère." *Phoenix* 21 (1967): 237–72.

Morgan, L. H. "Descent": "Laws of Descent of the Iroquois." *Proceedings of the American Association for the Advancement of Science* 11, II (1857): 132–48.

————. *Ancient Society: Ancient Society; or, Researches in the lines of human progress, from savagery, through barbarians, to civilization.* New York, 1877 [1907].

Morin, E. *Politique de l'homme: Introduction à une politique de l'homme,* followed by *Arguments politiques.* Paris, 1965.

Morrow, G.E.R. *Cretan City: Plato's Cretan City. A Historical Interpretation of the Laws.* Princeton, 1960.

————. "Demiurge": "The Demiurge in Politics: the *Timaeus* and the *Laws.*" *Proceedings and Addresses of the American Philosophical Association* 27 (1954): 5–23.

————. *Plato's Law of Slavery: Plato's Law of Slavery in Its Relation to Greek Law.* Urbana, 1939.

Moscovici, S. *Nature: Essai sur l'histoire humaine de la nature.* Paris, 1968.

Mossé, C. "Archidamos": "Sur un passage de l'*Archidamos* d'Isocrate." *Revue des études anciennes* 55 (1953): 23–35.

————. "Armée et Cité": "Armée et Cité grecque (À propos de Thucydide, VII, 77, 4–5)." *Revue des études anciennes* 65 (1963): 290–97.

————. "Classes": "Les Classes sociales à Athènes au IVᵉ s.," in D. Roche (ed.), *Ordres et Classes,* Colloque d'histoire sociale, Saint-Cloud, May 24–25, 1967. Paris and The Hague, 1973, 23–28.

————. *Fin: La Fin de la démocratie athénienne.* Paris, 1962.

————. "Nabis": "Un tyran grec à l'époque hellénistique: Nabis, *roi* de Sparte." *Cahiers d'histoire* 9 (1964): 312–23.

————. "Périèques": "Les Périèques lacédémoniens. A propos d'Isocrate, *Panathénaïque,* 177 et s." *Ktèma* 2 (1977): 121–24.

————. "Rôle de l'armée": "Le Rôle de l'armée dans la révolution de 411 à Athènes." *Revue historique* 231 (1964): 1–10.

————. "Rôle des esclaves": "Le Rôle des esclaves dans les troubles politiques du monde grec à la fin de l'époque classique." *Cahiers d'histoire* 6 (1961): 353–60.

————. "Rôle politique": "Le Rôle politique des armées dans le monde grec à l'époque classique." in J.-P. Vernant (ed.), *Problèmes de la guerre,* 221–30.

Motte, A. *Prairies: Prairies et Jardins de la Grèce antique. De la religion à la philosophie.* Brussels, 1973.

348   Mugler, C. *Deux Thèmes: Deux Thèmes de la cosmogonie grecque. Devenir cyclique et pluralité des mondes.* Paris, 1953.

Muehll, P. von der. "Odyssee": *s.v.* "Odyssee," *R. E.*, Suppl. VII (1940): c. 696–768.

Mumford, L. "Utopia": "Utopia, the City and the Machine." *Daedalus* 94 (1965): 271–92.

Murakawa, K. "Demiourgos": "Demiourgos." *Historia* 6 (1957): 385–415.

Musti, D. "Locri": "Sviluppo e Crisi di un oligarchia greca. Locri tra il VII e il IV sec." *Studi storici* 2 (1977): 59–85.

————. "Syngeneia": "Sull'idea de *syngeneia* in iscrizioni greche." *Annali della Scuola normale superiore di Pisa* 32 (1963): 225–39.

————. "Valore di scambio": "Per una richerca sul valore di scambio nel modo di produzione schiavistico," in Istituto Gramsci, *Analisi marxista e società antiche.* Rome, 1978, 147–74.

Myres, J. L. *Herodotus: Herodotus, Father of History.* Oxford, 1953.

Needham, R. (ed.) *Right and Left: Right and Left. Essays on Dual Symbolic Classification.* Chicago and London, 1973.

Nenci, G. *Introduzione: Introduzione alle guerre persiane et altri saggi di storica antica.* Pisa, 1958.

Neugebauer, O. *Exact Sciences: The Exact Sciences in Antiquity,* paperback ed. New York, 1962.

Nicolet, C. *Ordre équestre: L'Ordre équestre à l'époque républicaine (312–43 av. J.-C.),* 2 vols. Paris, 1966 and 1974.

Nikitskij, A. "Aianteia": "Aianteia." *Žurnal Ministerstva Narodnógo ProsvešČenija (Otdel po Klass. Fil.)* 43 (January–February 1913): 1–48 and 49–100.

Nilsson, M. P. "Grundlagen": "Die Grundlagen des Spartanischen Lebens." *Klio* 12 (1912): 308–40; reprinted in *Opuscula Selecta* 2. Lund, 1952, 826–69.

————. *Primitive Time: Primitive Time Reckoning.* Lund, 1920.

————. "Propaganda": "Political Propaganda in Sixth Century Athens." *Studies Presented to D. M. Robinson on his 70th Birthday,* vols. 1–2. Edited by G. E. Mylonas and D. Raymond. St. Louis, 1951–1953, Vol. 2, 743–48.

————. "Salaminioi": "The New Inscription of the Salaminioi." *American Journal of Philology* 59 (1938): 385–93.

————. "Ursprung": "Der Ursprung der Tragödie." *Neue Jahrbuch für das klassische Altertum* (1911): 609–42 and 673–96.

Oliva, P. "Helots": "On the Problem of the Helots." *Historica. Les Sciences historiques en Tchécoslovaquie* 3 (1961): 5–39.

Onians, R. B. *Origins: The Origins of the European Thought about the Body, the Mind, the Soul, the World, Time and Fate.*² . Cambridge, 1953.

Oppenheim, A. L. *Mesopotamia: Ancient Mesopotamia: Portrait of a Dead Civilization.* Chicago, 1964.

Orth, F. "Jagd": "Jagd." *R.E.* 9 (1914): c. 558–604.   349

Overbeck, J. *Antiken Schriftquellen: Die antiken Schriftquellen zur Geschichte der bildenden Künste bei den Griechen.* Leipzig, 1868.

Owen, G.E.L. "Place": "The Place of *Timaeus* in Plato's Dialogues." *Classical Quarterly* 47 (1953); reprinted in R. E. Allen (ed.), *Studies in Plato's Metaphysics.* London, 1965, 313–38.

Page, D. *Odyssey: The Homeric Odyssey.* Oxford, 1955.

Pallotino, M. "Atlantide": "Atlantide." *Archeologia Classica* 4 (1952): 229–40.

Panoff, M. *Malinowski: Bronislaw Malinowski.* Paris, 1972.

Panofsky, E. *Iconology: Studies in Iconology.* Oxford, 1939.

Pareti, L. *Sparta arcaica: Storia di Sparta arcaica* I. Florence, 1920.

Parke, H. W. *Mercenary Soldiers: Greek Mercenary Soldiers.* Oxford, 1934.

Parry, A. "Iliad": "Have we Homer's *Iliad?*" *Yale Classical Studies* 20 (1966): 175–216.

Patzig, E. *De Nonnianis Commentariis: De Nonnianis Commentariis.* Prog Leipzig, 1890.

Paulhan, J. *Preuve: La Preuve par l'étymologie.* Paris, 1953.

Paulmier de Grentemesnil, J. Le (Palmerius). *Exercitationes: Exercitationes in optimos fere auctores Graecos.* Leyden, 1768.

Pearson, A. C. *Fragments: The Fragments of Sophocles,* 3 vols. Cambridge, 1917.

Pease, A. S. "Ölbaum": *s.v.* "Ölbaum." *R. E.* 17 (1937): 1998–2022.

Pélékidis, C. *Éphébie: Histoire de l'éphébie attique, des origines à 31 avant Jésus-Christ.* Paris, 1962.

Pellizer, E. *Favole: Favole d'identitá, Favole di paura; storia di caccia e altri raconti della Grecia antica.* Rome, 1982.

Pembroke, S. G. "Family": "The Early Human Family: Some Views 1770–1870," in R. R. Bolgar (ed.), *Classical Influences on Western Thought A.D. 1650–1870.* Cambridge, 1979, 275–91.

———. "Last": "Last of the Matriarchs: A Study in the Inscriptions of Lycia." *Journal of the Economic and Social History of the Orient* 8 (1965): 217–47.

———. "Locres": "Locres et Tarente. Le Rôle des femmes dans la fondation de deux colonies grecques." *Annales E.S.C.* 25 (1970): 1240–70.

———. "Women": "Women in Charge: The Function of Alternatives in Early Greek Tradition and the Ancient Idea of Matriarchy." *Journal of the Warburg and Courtauld Institutes* 30 (1967): 1–35.

Pépin, J. "Mer": "A propos du symbolisme de la mer chez Platon et dans le néoplatonisme." *Congrès de l'Association Guillaume-Budé.* Tours and Poitiers, 1953, 257–59.

Petersen, E. "Griechische Bronze": "Griechische." *Römische Mitteilungen* 6 (1981): 270–78.

———. "Marathonische Bronzegruppe": "Die marathonische Bronzegruppe des Pheidias." *Römische Mitteilungen* 14 (1900): 142–51.

Petre, Z. "Représentation": "Un âge de la représentation; artifice et image dans la pensée grecque du VIᵉ s. av. notre ère." *Revue roumaine d'histoire* 18 (1979): 247–57.

———. "Épigrammes de Marathon": "Eschyle, Salamine et les Épigrammes de Marathon." *Revue roumaine d'histoire* 17 (1978): 327–36.

———. "Architecte": "Trophonios ou l'Architecte. A propos du statut des techniciens dans la cité grecque." *Studii Classice* 18 (1979): 23–37.

Philippson, P. *Genealogie: Genealogie als Mythischeform, Studien zur Theogonie des Hesiod. Symbolae osloenses,* fasc. suppl. VII, 1936; reprinted in *Untersuchungen über den griechischen Mythos.* Basel, 1944, 4–42.

Picard, C. "Luttes primitives": "Les Luttes primitives d'Athènes et d'Éleusis." *Revue historique* 166 (1931): 1, pp. 1–76.

———. *Manuel, Sculpture* II, 1: *Manuel d'archéologie grecque, Sculpture,* II, 1. Paris, 1939.

———. "Marchand d'huile": "Chez le marchand d'huile, le maître charpentier ou le philosophe." *Revue archéologique* 23 (1945): 154–55.

———. "Représentation": "Représentation d'une école de philosophie à Athènes." *Revue archéologique* 16 (1940): 159–60.

Piérart, M. *Platon: Platon et la Cité grecque. Théorie et réalité dans la constitution des Lois.* Brussels, 1974.

Pippidi, D. M. "Luttes politiques et troubles sociaux à Héraclée du Pont à l'époque classique." *Studii Classice* 11 (1969): 235–38.

Plassart, A. "Archers": "Les Archers d'Athènes." *Revue des études grecques* 26 (1913): 151–213.

Pleket, H. W. "Collegium": "Collegium Juvenum Nemesiorum. A Note on Ancient Youth Organisation." *Mnemosyne* 22 (1969): 281–98.

Podlecki, A. J. *Background: The Political Background of Aeschylean Tragedy.* Ann Arbor, 1966.

Poliakov, L. *Aryan Myth: The Aryan Myth: A Study of Racist and Nationalist Ideas in Europe.* Translated by E. Howard. New York, 1974.

Pomtow, H. "Delphoi": *s.v.* "Delphoi." *R. E.,* suppl. IV (1924): c. 1189–1431. (On the Marathon base in particular, c. 1214–18.)

———. "Studien II": "Studien zu den Weihgeschenken und der Topographie von Delphi," II. *Klio* 8 (1908): 73–120.

———. "Vortrag": "Vortrag üer die athenischen Weihgeschenke in Delphi." *Archäologischer Anzeiger* (1902): 80–86.

Popper, K. R. *Open Society I: The Open Society and Its Enemies, Vol. 1: The Spell of Plato,* 5th ed. Princeton, 1966. In French. *Cité ouverte: La Cité ouverte et ses ennemis*. Translated by J. Bernard and P. Monod. I. *L'Ascendant de Platon*. Paris, 1979.

Posner, G. *Pharaon: De la divinité du Pharaon*. Paris, 1960.

Pouilloux, J., and G. Roux. *Énigmes: Énigmes à Delphes*. Paris, 1963.

Poulsen, F. "Niche aux offrandes": "La Niche aux offrandes de Marathon." *Bulletin de l'Académie royale des sciences et des lettres de Danemark* (1908): 389–425.

Préaux, C. "Troupeaux": "De la Grèce classique à l'Égypte hellénistique. Les troupeaux immortels et les esclaves de Nicias." *Chronique d'Égypte* 41 (1966): 161–64.

Pritchett, W. K. *Marathon: Marathon*. Berkeley, 1960.

———. "Marathon Revisited": "Marathon Revisited," in *Studies in Ancient Greek Topography*. Berkeley and Los Angeles, 1965, 83–93.

———. *Topography: Studies in Ancient Greek Topography*, I. Berkeley and Los Angeles, 1965.

———. *War: The Greek State at War*, I². Berkeley and Los Angeles, 1974; II and III. Berkeley and Los Angeles, 1974 and 1979.

Propp, V. *Morphology: The Morphology of the Folk-tale*. Translated by L. Scott, rev. ed. L. Wagner. Publications of the American Folklore Society, Bibliographical and Special Series, vol. 9. Austin, TX, 1968.

Pucci, P. *Hesiod: Hesiod and the Language of Poetry*. Baltimore and London, 1977.

———. "Sirens": "The Song of the Sirens." *Arethusa* 12, 2 (1979): 121–32.

Puech, H. C. "Gnose": "La Gnose et le Temps." *Eranos Jahrbuch* 20 (1951); reprinted in *En quête de la gnose*, I. Paris, 1978, 215–70.

———. "Temps": "Temps, Histoire et Mythe dans le christianisme des premiers siècles." *Proceedings of the Seventh Congress for the History of Religions*. Amsterdam, 1951; reprinted in *En quête de la gnose*, I. 1–23.

Radke, G. *Farbe: Die Bedeutung der weissen und der schwarzen Farbe im Kult und Brauch der Griechen und Römern*. Dissertation. Berlin, 1936.

Ramage, E. S. (ed.) *Atlantis: Atlantis. Fact or Fiction?* Bloomington and London, 1978.

———. "Perspectives": "Perspectives Ancient and Modern," in E. S. Ramage (ed.), *Atlantis*, 3–45.

Randall, R. H., Jr. "Workmen": "The Erechtheum Workmen." *American Journal of Archaeology* 57 (1953): 199–210.

Raubitschek, A. E. *Dedications: Dedications from the Athenian Akropolis*. Cambridge, MA, 1949.

Raven, J. E., *Pythagoreans: Pythagoreans and Eleatics*. Cambridge, 1948.

Rawson, E. *Tradition: The Spartan Tradition*. Oxford, 1969.

R.E., A. F. Pauly, G. Wissova, and W. Kroll. *Realencyclopädie der classischen Altertumswissenschaft*. Stuttgart, 1894 and following years.

352 Reinach, A. J. "Origine": "L'origine de deux légendes homériques. I. Le viol de Cassandre." *Revue de l'histoire des religions* 69 (1914): 12–53.

Reinmuth, O. W. "Ephebic Inscription": "The Ephebic Inscription Athenian Agora, I, 286." *Hesperia* 24 (1955): 220–39.

———. *Ephebic Inscriptions: The Ephebic Inscriptions of the Fourth Century B.C.* Leyden, 1971.

Rémondon, R. "Bilinguisme": "Problèmes de bilinguisme dans l'Egypte lagide (*U.P.Z.*, I, 148)." *Chronique d'Egypte* 39 (1964): 126–46.

Reverdin, O. *Religion: La Religion de la cité platonicienne*. Paris, 1945.

Rey, A. *Jeunesse: La Jeunesse de la science grecque*. Paris, 1933.

Richter, W. *Landwirtschaft: Die Landwirtschaft im Homerischen Zeitalter*. Göttingen, 1968, coll. "Archaeologia Homerica."

Ricoeur, P. "Structure et Herméneutique": "Structure et Herméneutique." *Esprit* (November 1963): 596–627.

Riemann, E. "Hippothontis": *s.v.* "Hippothontis," *R.E.*, suppl. VIII (1956): c. 182–86.

Ritter, C. *Untersuchungen: Neue Untersuchungen über Plato*. Tübingen, 1910.

Robert, C. *Heldensage: Griechische Heldensage*, II. Berlin, 1923.

———. *Marathonschlacht: Die Marathonschlacht in der Poikile*. Halle, 1895.

Robert, F. "Review of Cuillandre": "Review of J. Cuillandre, *Droite et Gauche*." *Revue archéologique* 22 (1944) 2, pp. 127–34.

———. *Homère: Homère*. Paris, 1950.

Robert, J. and L. "Bulletin": "Bulletin épigraphique." The notes refer to the year of the *REG* and to the classification number adopted by the authors.

Robert, L. "Amphithalès": "Amphithalès." *Athenian Studies presented to W. S. Ferguson: HSCP* Suppl. 1. Cambridge, MA, 1940, 509–19.

———. *Asie mineure: A travers l'Asie mineure, poètes et prosateurs, monnaies grecques, voyageurs et géographie*. Athens and Paris, 1980.

———. "Review of *Didyma*": "Review of A. Rehm et R. Harder, *Didyma, 2 Teil. Die Inschriften*, Berlin, 1958." *Gnomon* (1959); reprinted in *Opera minora selecta*, III. Amsterdam, 1969, 1622–39.

———. *Études: Études épigraphiques et philologiques*. Paris, 1939.

———. *Hellenica: Hellenica*. Paris, 1940–1965; Volume X appeared in 1955.

———. "Lesbos": "Inscriptions de Lesbos." *Revue des études anciennes* 62 (1960): 285–315; reprinted in *Opuscula minora selecta*, II. Amsterdam, 1969, 801–31.

———. *Monnaies en Troade: Monnaies antiques en Troade*. Paris, 1966.

———. *Villes: Villes d'Asie Mineure*.². Paris, 1962.

Robin, L. *Platon: Platon*. Paris, 1935.

———. "Progrès": "Sur la conception épicurienne du progrès." *Revue de métaphysique et de morale* (1916); reprinted in *La Pensée hellénique des origines à Épicure*. Paris, 1942, 525–52.

Robinson, D. M. "Bouzyges": "Bouzyges and the First Plough on the Krater of   353
the Painter of the Naples Hephaistos." *American Journal of Archaeology* 35
(1931): 152–60.

Rodier, G. "Politique": "Note sur la politique d'Antisthène: le mythe du Politique." *Année philosophique* (1911); reprinted in *Études de philosophie grecque*. Paris,
1926, 30–36.

Rohde, E. *Psyche: Psyche: The Cult of Souls and Belief in Immorality Among the Greeks*.
Translated by W. B. Hillis. New York, 1925.

Rolley, C. "Thesmorphorion": "Le Sanctuaire des dieux Patrôoi et le Thes-
mophorion de Thasos." *Bulletin de correspondance hellénique* 89 (1965): 441–83.

Rose, H. J. *Handbook: A Handbook of Greek Literature*. London, 1931.

Rosellini, M., and S. Saïd. "Usages": "Usages de femmes et autres *Nomoi* chez les
sauvages d'Hérodote." *Annali della Scuola normale superiore di Pisa*, Series 3, 8
(1978): 949–1005.

Roussel, D. *Tribu: Tribu et Cité. Études sur les groupes sociaux dans les cités grecques aux
époques archaïque et classique*. Paris, 1976.

Roussel, P. "Chlamydes noires": "Les Chlamydes noires des éphèbes athéniens."
Revue des études anciennes 43 (1941): 163–65.

———. "Review of A. Brenot": "Review of A. Brenot, *Recherches sur l'éphébie
attique et en particulier sur la date de l'institution* (Paris: 1920). *Revue des études
grecques* (1921): 459–60.

———. "Principe d'ancienneté": "Essai sur le principe d'ancienneté dans le
monde hellénique du Ve siècle avant Jésus-Christ à l'époque romaine."
Mémoires de l'Académie des Inscriptions et Belles Lettres 43, 2 (1951, in fact 1941):
123–228.

———. *Sparte: Sparte²*. Paris, 1960. (First edition, 1939.)

Rudbeck, O. *Atland: Atland eller Manheim—Atlantica sive Manheim*, bilingual
ed., 4 vols. Uppsala, 1679–1702.

Rudberg, G. *Platonica: Platonica Selecta*. Stockholm, 1956.

Rudhardt, J. *Notions fondamentales: Notions fondamentales de le pensée religieuse et actes
constitutifs du culte dans la Grèce classique*. Geneva, 1958.

Ruschenbush, E. "*Patrios Politeia*": "*Patrios Politeia*. Theseus, Drakon, Solon und
Kleisthenes in Publizistik und Geschichts-schreibung des 5. und 4. Jahrhun-
derts v. Chr." *Historia* 7 (1958): 398–424.

Rüstow, W., and H. Koechly. *Kriegswesen: Geschichte der griechischen Kriegswesen*.
Aarau, 1852.

Saïd, S. "Crimes": "Les Crimes des prétendants, la maison d'Ulysse et les banquets de l'*Odyssée*" *Cahiers de l'Ecole normale supérieure* (1979): 9–49.

Sainte-Croix, G. E. M. de. "Karl Marx": "Karl Marx and the History of Classical
Antiquity." *Arethusa* 8 (1975): 7–41.

———. *The Class Struggle in the Ancient Greek World*. London, 1981.

354   Sakellariou, M. *Migration grecque: La Migration grecque en Ionie.* Athens, 1958.

Santillana, G. de, and W. Pitts. "Philolaos": "Philolaos in Limbo or what happened to the Pythagoreans." *Isis* 42 (1951): 112–20.

Sauer, B. W. *Gruppe: Die Anfänge der statuarischen Gruppe.* Dissertation. Leipzig, 1889.

Saunders, T. J. "Artisans": "Artisans in the City-planning of Plato's Magnesia." *BICS* 29 (1982): 43-48.

Sauppe, H. *De demis: De demis urbanis Athenarum.* Leipzig, 1846.

Schaerer, R. *Homme antique: L'Homme antique et la Structure du monde intérieur.* Paris, 1958.

———. "Itinéraire dialectique": "L'Itinéraire dialectique des *Lois* et sa signification philosophique." *Revue philosophique* 143 (1953): 379–412.

———. *Question: La question platonicienne.* Neuchâtel, 1948.

Schefold, K. "Kleisthenes": "Kleisthenes. Der Anteil der Kunst an der Gestaltung des jungen attischen Freistaates." *Museum Helveticum* (1946): 59–93.

Schmitt, H., and H. Bengtson. (eds.) *Staatsverträge, III: Die Staatsverträge des Altertums,* t. III, by H. H. Schmitt: *Die Verträge der griechischrömischen Welt von 338 bis 200 v. Chr.* Munich, 1969.

Schmitt-Pantel, P. "Athéna Apatouria": "Athéna Apatouria et la Ceinture. Les aspects féminins des Apatouries à Athènes." *Annales E.S.C.* 32 (1977): 1059–73.

———. "Histoire de tyran": "Histoire de tyran ou Comment la cité grecque construit ses marges," in B. Vincent (ed.), *Les Marginaux et les Exclus dans l'histoire.* Paris, 1979, 217–31.

Schmitz-Kahlmann, G. *Beispiel: Das Beispiel der Geschichte im politischen Denken des Isokrates. Philologus,* suppl. 31 Leipzig, 1939.

Schnapp, A. "Immagini di caccia": "Pratiche e Immagini di caccia nella Grecia antica." *Dialoghi di Archeologia.* N.S. 1 (1979): 36–59.

———. *Représentations: Les Représentations de la chasse dans les textes littéraires et la céramique,* thèse de 3ᵉ cycle. Paris I, 1973.

———. "Territoire de chasse": "Représentation du territoire de guerre et du territoire de chasse dans l'oeuvre de Xénophon," in M. I. Finley (ed.), *Problèmes de la terre en Grèce ancienne.* The Hague and Paris, 1973, 307–21.

Schnapp-Gourbeillon, A. *Lions: Lions, héros, masques. Les représentations de l'animal chez Homère.* Paris, 1981.

Schuhl, P.-M. "Épaminondas": "Épaminondas et la Manoeuvre par la gauche." *Revue philosophique* 150 (1960): 529–30.

———. *Formation: Essai sur la formation de la pensée grecque².* Paris, 1949.

———. "Main droite," 1: "Platon et la prééminence de la main droite." *Cahiers internationaux de sociologie* (1946); reprinted in *Le Merveilleux, la Pensée et l'Action.* Paris, 1952, 176–81.

————. "Main droite," 2: "Platon et la prééminence de la main droite." *Cahiers internationaux de sociologie* (1949); reprinted in *Le Merveilleux,* 182–87.

————. "Politique": "Sur le mythe du *Politique.*" *Revue de métaphysique et de morale* (1932); reprinted in *La Fabulation platonicienne.* Paris, 1947, 89–104.

Schwyzer, E. "Eid": "Zum Eid der Drerier." *Rheinisches Museum* 77 (1928): 237–48.

Scranton, R. L. "Lost Atlantis": "Lost Atlantis found again?" *Archaeology* 2 (1949): 159–62.

Segal, C. P. "Antigone": "Sophocles' Praise of Man and the Conflict of the *Antigone.*" *Arion* 3, 2 (1964): 46–68.

————. "Phaeacians": "The Phaeacians and the Symbolism of Odysseus' Return." *Arion* 1, 4 (1962): 17–63.

————. "Temptations": "Circean Temptations: Homer, Vergil, Ovid." *Transactions and Proceedings of the American Philological Association* 99 (1968): 419–42.

————. "Transition": "Transition and Ritual in Odysseus' Return." *La Parola del passato* 116 (1967): 321–42.

Severyns, A. *Recherches: Recherches sur la Chrestomathie de Proclus,* II. Paris, 1938.

Sharpe, E. *Comparative Religion: Comparative Religion. A History.* London, 1975.

Shear, T. L., Jr. "Eponymous Heroes": "The Monuments of the Eponymous Heroes in the Athenian Agora." *Hesperia* 39 (1976): 145–222.

Shimron, B. "Nabis": "Nabis of Sparta and the Helots." *Classical Philology* 61 (1966): 1–7.

Siegel, R. E. "Hestia": "On the Relation between Early Greek Scientific Thought and Mysticism: Is Hestia, the Central Fire, an Abstract Astronomical Concept?" *Janus* 49 (1960): 1–20.

Siewert, P. "Ephebic Oath": "Ephebic Oath in Fifth Century Athens." *Journal of Hellenic Studies* 97 (1977): 102–11.

Simon, E. *Réveil national: Réveil national et culture popularie en Scandinavie. La genèse de la højskole nordique 1844–1878.* Paris, 1960.

Simon, E. "Polygnotan Painting": "Polygnotan Painting and the Niobid Painter." *American Journal of Archaeology* 67 (1963): 43–62.

Snodgrass, A. M. *Rise of the Greek State: Archaeology and the Rise of the Greek State.* Cambridge, 1977.

Société et Colonisation eubéennes: Contribution à l'étude de la société et de la colonisation eubéennes. Cahiers du Centre Jean-Bérard, II. Naples, 1975.

Sofri, G. *Modo di produzione asiatico: Modo di produzione asiatico, Storia di una controversia marxista.* Turin, 1969.

Sokolowski, F. *Lois sacrées: Lois sacrées des cités grecques.* Paris, 1969.

————. *Los sacrées. Suppl.: Lois sacrées des cités grecques. Supplément.* Paris, 1962.

Sordi, M. "Epaminonda": "Propaganda politica e senso religioso nell' azione di Epaminonda," in M. Sordi (ed.), *Propaganda e Persuasione occulta nell' antichità.* Milan, 1972, 45–53.

Sourvinou-Inwood, C. *"Lysistrata, 641–647"*: "Aristophanes, *Lysistrata* 641–647." *Classical Quarterly* 21 (1971): 339–42.

———. *"Review of Paides"*: "Review of A. Brelich, *Paides e Parthenoi.*" *Journal of Hellenic Studies* 91 (1971): 172–77.

———. *"Theseus"*: "Theseus Lifting the Rock and a Cup near the Pithos Painter." *Journal of Hellenic Studies* 91 (1971): 94–109 and pl. 12.

———. *"Votum"*: "The Votum of 477/6 B.C. and the Foundation Legend of Locri Epizephyrii." *Classical Quarterly* 24, 2 (1974): 186–98.

Spahn, D. *Mittelschicht: Mittelschicht und Polisbildung.* Frankfort, 1977.

Sprague de Camp, L. *Lost Continents: Lost Continents: The Atlantis Theme in History and Literature.* New York, 1954.

Stanford, W. B. *Ulysses: The Ulysses Theme. A Study in the Adaptability of a Traditional Hero.* Oxford, 1954.

Stevens, G. P., and A. E. Raubitschek. "Pedestal": "The Pedestal of the Athena Promachos." *Hesperia* 15 (1946): 107–14.

Strauss-Clay, J. "Goat Island": "Goat Island: *Od.* 9.116–141." *Classical Quarterly* 30, 2 (December 1980): 261–64.

———. *Wrath: The Wrath of Athena: Gods and Men in the Odyssey.* Princeton, 1983.

Stroud, R. S. "Theozotides": "Theozotides and the Athenian Orphans." *Hesperia* 40 (1971): 280–301.

Svenbro, J. *Parole: La Parole et le Marbre. Aux origines de la poétique grecque.* Lund, 1976.

———. "Idéologie gothisante": "L'idéologie gothisante et l'*Atlantica* d'Olof Rudbeck." *Quaderni di Storia* 11 (January–June 1980): 121–56.

Swoboda, H. "Epameinondas": *s.v.* "Epameinondas." *R.E.* 5 (1905): c. 2674–2707.

Szegedy-Maszak, A. "Legends": "Legends of the Greek Lawgivers." *Greek, Roman and Byzantine Studies* 19 (1978): 199–209.

Taillardat, J. *Images: Les Images d'Aristophane².* Paris, 1965.

Tannery, P. "Fragments philolaïques": "A propos des fragments philolaïques sur la musique." *Revue de philologie* (1904); reprinted in *Mémoires scientifiques* III. Paris, 1915, 220–43.

Taylor, A. E. *Timaeus: A Commentary on the Timaeus.* Oxford, 1928.

Terres et Paysans: Terres et Paysans dépendants dans les sociétés antiques. Centre de recherches d'histoire ancienne de Besançon. Paris, 1979.

Thompson, H. A., and R. E. Wycherley. *Athenian Agora, XIV: The Athenian Agora, XIV. The Agora of Athens. The History, Shape and Uses of an Ancient City Center.* Princeton, 1972.

Thomson, G. *Aeschylus: Aeschylus and Athens².* London, 1941.

———. *First Philosophers: The First Philosophers,* 2d ed. London, 1961.

Tigerstedt, E. N. *Legend: The Legend of Sparta in Classical Antiquity.* Stockholm, 357
Göteborg, and Uppsala, 1965.

Timpanaro Cardini, M. "Cosmo": "Il Cosmo di Filolao." *Revista di storia della filosofia* I (1946): 322–33.

———. *Pitagorici: Pitagorici. Testimonianze e Frammenti* II. Florence, 1958.

Tod, M. N. *Selection II: A Selection of Greek Historial Inscriptions II.* Oxford, 1948.

Todorov, T. "Récit": "Le Récit primitif." *Tel quel* 30 (Summer 1967): 47–55.

Toepffer, J. *Attische Genealogie: Attische Genealogie.* Berlin, 1889).

———. "Gemeindebuch": "Das attische Gemeindebuch." *Hermes* 30 (1895): 391–400.

Toynbee, A. J. *Problems: Some Problems of Greek History.* Oxford, 1969.

Travlos, J. *Bildlexikon: Bildlexikon zur Topographie des antiken Athen.* Tübingen, 1971.= *Pictorial Dictionary of Ancient Athens.* London, 1971.

Treves, P. "Consenesco": "The Meaning of *consenesco* and King Arybbas of Epirus." *American Journal of Philology* 63 (1942): 129–53.

Triantaphyllopoulos, J. "Varia graeco-romana": "Varia graeco-romana," III. *Flores legum H.J. Scheltema antecessori Groninganae oblati.* Groningen, 1971, 183–92.

Trumpf, J. "Äpfel": "Kydonische Äpfel." *Hermes* 88 (1960): 14–22.

Tylor, E. B. *Primitive Culture: Primitive Culture,* 2d ed. London, 1871.

Usener, H. "Göttliche Synonyme": "Göttliche Synonyme." *Rheinisches Museum* (1898): 329–79; reprinted in *Kleine Schriften* IV. Leipzig-Berlin, 1913, 259–306.

———. "Heilige Handlung": "Heilige Handlung." *Archiv für Religionswissenschaft* 7 (1904): 281–339 (= *Kleine Schriften* IV, 422–62).

Valenza Mele, N. "Hera": "Hera ed Apollo nella Colonizzazione euboica d'Occidente." *Mélanges de L'École française de Rome* 89 (1977): 493–524.

Vallet, G. *Rhégium: Rhégium et Zancle.* Paris, 1958.

van der Loeff, A. R. "De Oschophoriis": "De Oschophoriis." *Mnemosyne* (1915): 404–15.

Vanderpool, E. "Monument": "A Monument to the Battle of Marathon." *Hesperia* 35 (1966): 93–106 and pl. 31–35.

van Effenterre, H. "Clisthène": "Clisthène et les mesures de mobilisation." *Revue des études grecques* 89 (1976): 1–17.

———. *Cité: La Cité grecque des origines à la défaite de Marathon.* Paris, 1985.

———. *Crète: La Crète et le monde grec de Platon à Polybe.* Paris, 1948.

———. "Fortins crétois": "Fortins crétois." *Mélanges d'archéologie et d'histoire offerts à Ch. Picard.* Paris, 1948, 1038–46.

———. *Mallia: le Palais de Mallia et la cité minoenne,* 2 vols. Rome, 1980.

———. "Politique et Religion": "Politique et religion dans la Crète minoenne." *Revue historique* (January–March 1963): 1–18.

358 ———. "Serment": "A propos du serment des Drériens." *Bulletin de correspondance hellénique* 61 (1937): 327–32.

van Gennep, A. "Contributions": "Contributions à l'histoire en France de la méthode ethnographique." *Revue de l'histoire des religions* 67 (1913): 321–38.

———. *Rites de passage: Les Rites de passage.* Paris, 1909.

van Groningen, B. A. *Grip: In the Grip of the Past. Essay on an Aspect of Greek Thought.* Leyden, 1953.

van Houtte, M. *Philosophie politique: La Philosophie politique de Platon dans les Lois.* Louvain, 1953.

Vernant, J.-P. *Myth and Society: Myth and Society in Ancient Greece.* Translated by J. Lloyd. Atlantic Highlands, NJ, 1980.

———. *Myth and Thought: Myth and Thought Among the Greeks.* Boston, 1983.

———. *Origins: The Origins of Greek Thought.* Ithaca, NY, 1982.

———. "Marriage": "Marriage," in *Myth and Society,* 45–70.

———. "Myth to Reason": "From Myth to Reason: The Formation in Positivist Thought in Archaic Greece," in *Myth and Thought,* 343–74.

———. "Myth of the Races I": "Hesiod's Myth of the Races: An Essay in Structural Analysis," in *Myth and Thought,* 3–32.

———. "Myth of the Races II": "Hesiod's Myth of the Races: a Reassessment," in *Myth and Thought,* 33–72.

———. "Myth of Prometheus": "The Myth of Prometheus in Hesiod," in *Myth and Society,* 168–85.

———. "Technological Thought": "Some Remarks on the Forms and Limitations of Technological Thought among the Greeks," in *Myth and Thought,* 279–301.

———. "Work I": "Work and Nature in Ancient Greece," in *Myth and Thought,* 248–70.

———. "Work II": "Some Psychological Aspects of Work in Ancient Greece," in *Myth and Thought,* 271–78.

Veyne, P. *Histoire: Comment on écrit l'histoire.* Paris, 1971.

Vian, F. *Cadmos: Les Origines de Thèbes. Cadmos et les Spartes.* Paris, 1963.

———. "Fonction guerrière": "La Fonction guerrière dans la mythologie grecque," in J.-P. Vernant (ed.), *Problèmes de la guerre,* 53–68.

Vidal-Naquet, P. "Avant-Propos": "Avant-propos de K. A. Wittfogel." *Le Despotisme oriental.* Translated by Anne Marchand. Paris, 1964.

———. "Économie et Société": "Économie et Société en Grèce ancienne: l'oeuvre de Moses I. Finley." *Archives européennes de sociologie* 6 (1965): 111–48.

———. "Flacius Arrien": "Flavius Arrien entre deux mondes," in *Arrien, Histoire d'Alexandre.* Paris, 1984.

———. "Hérodote et l'Atlantide": "Hérodote et l'Atlantide: entre les Grecs et les Juifs. Réflexions sur l'historiographie du siècle des lumières." *Quaderni di Storia* 16 (July–December 1982): 3–76.

———. "Philoctetes": "Le *Philoctète* de Sophocle et l'Éphébie." *Annales E.S.C.* 26 (1971); reprinted in J.-P. Vernant and P. Vidal-Naquet, *Mythe et Tragédie en Grèce ancienne*⁴. Paris, 1979, 159–84.

Vincent, A. "Sacrifice": "Essai sur le sacrifice de communion des rois atlantes." *Mémorial Lagrange*, Paris, 1940, 81–96.

Vlastos, G. "Equality": "Equality and Justice in Early Greek Cosmology." *Classical Philology* 42 (1947): 156–78.

von Fritz, K. "Philolaos": "Philolaos," *R. E.*, suppl. 13 (1973): 454–83.

Vries, G. J. de. *Antisthenes: Antisthenes Redivivus, Popper's Attack on Plato*. Leyden, 1953.

Vürtheim, J. *De Aiacis origine: De Aiacis origine, cultu, patria*. Leyden, 1907.

Wachsmuth, W. *Alterthumskunde: Hellenische Alterthumskunde aus dem Gesichtspunkt des Staats*, 2d ed. 2 vols. Halle, 1844.

Wachtel, N. "Poma de Ayala": "Pensée sauvage et Acculturation: l'espace et le temps chez Filipe Gauman Poma de Ayala et l'Inca Garcilaso de la Vega." *Annales E.S.C.* 26 (1971): 793–840.

Wade-Gery, H. T. *Essays: Essays in Greek History*. Oxford, 1958.

Walbank, F. W. *Commentary: A Historical Commentary to Polybius, II*. Oxford, 1967.

Walbank, M. B. "Artemis": "Artemis Bear Leader." *Classical Quarterly*, 2d series, 31 (1981): 276–81.

Walinga, H. T. "Trireme": "The Trireme and its Crew." *Studies in Honor of H.L.W. Nelson*. Edited by J. Den Boeft and A.H.R. Kessels. Utrecht, 1982, 463–82.

Wallon, H. *Cryptie: Explication d'un passage de Plutarque sur une loi de Lycurgue nommée la Cryptie*. Paris, 1850.

Weber, M. *The City: The City*. Translated by D. Martindale and G. Neuwirth. New York and London, 1966.

Weil, R. *Archéologie: L'Archéologie de Platon*. Paris, 1959.

Welliver, W. *Timaeus-Critias: Character, Plot and Thought in Plato's Timaeus-Critias*. Leyden, 1977.

Welwei, K. W. *Unfreie: Unfreie im antiken Kriegdienst*. Wiesbaden, 1974.

West, M. L. *Orient: Early Greek Philosophy and the Orient*. Oxford, 1971.

Whitehead, D. *Metic: The Ideology of the Athenian Metic*. Cambridge, 1977.

Wiedemann, A. *Geschichte Aegyptens: Geschichte Aegyptens von Psammetik I bis auf Alexander den Grossen*. Leipzig, 1880.

Wilamowitz-Möllendorf, U. von (= Wilamowitz). *Lysistrata: Aristophanes Lysistrata*. Berlin, 1927.

————. *Aristoteles: Aristoteles und Athen,* 2 vols. Berlin, 1893.

————. *Ilias: Die Ilias und Homer.* Berlin, 1916.

————. "Oropos": "Oropos und die Graer," *Hermes* 21 (1886): 91–115.

————. *Platon: Platon,* 2 vols. Berlin, 1920.

Wilcken, U. *Alexander: Alexander the Great,* 2d ed. Translated by G. C. Richards. New York, 1967.

Wilhelm, A. "Mädcheninschrift": "Die lokrische Mädcheninschrift." *Jahreshefte des Oesterreichischen Archaeologischen Instituts in Wien* 14 (1911): 163–256.

————. "Poroi": "Untersuchungen zu Xenophons *Poroi.*" *Wiener Studien* 52 (1934): 18–56.

Will, E. *Doriens et Ioniens: Doriens et Ioniens. Essai sur la valeur du critère ethnique appliqué à l'étude de l'histoire et de la civilisation grecque.* Paris, 1956.

————. *Histoire Politique: Histoire politique du monde hellénistique, I². Nancy, 1979.

————. *Korinthiaka: Korinthiaka. Recherches sur l'histoire et la civilisation de Corinthe des origines aux guerres médiques.* Paris, 1955.

————. *Monde grec: Le Monde grec et l'Orient,* I. Paris, 1972.

Willetts, R. F. *Aristocratic Society: Aristocratic Society in Crete.* London, 1955.

————. *Cretan Cults: Cretan Cults and Festivals.* London, 1962.

————. "Terminology": "Early Cretan Social Terminology." *Epeteris* 6 (1972–1973): 63–74.

————. *Gortyn: The Law Code of Gortyn.* Berlin, 1967. (*Kadmos,* suppl. I.)

————. "Interregnum": "The Servile Interregnum at Argos." *Hermes* 87 (1959): 495–506.

————. "Servile System": "The Servile System of Ancient Crete: a Reappraisal of the Evidence." *GERAS: Studies Presented to George Thomson on the Occasion of his 60th Birthday.* Edited by L. Varel and R. F. Willetts. Prague, 1963.

Wolska, W. *Cosmas: La Topographie chrétienne de Cosmas Indicopleustes.* Paris, 1962.

Woodhouse, W. J. "Mantineia": "The Campaign and Battle of Mantineia in 418 B.C." *Annual of the British School at Athens* 22 (1916–1918): 51–84.

————. "Plataiai": "The Greeks at Plataiai." *Journal of Hellenic Studies* 18 (1898): 33–59.

Wuilleumier, P. *Tarente: Tarente, des origines à la conquête romaine.* Paris, 1939.

Wycherley, R. E. *Athenian Agora, III: The Athenian Agora, III. Literary and Epigraphical Testimonia.* Princeton, 1957.

Yalman, N. "Raw": "The Raw: The Cooked: Nature: Culture. Observations on *Le Cru et le Cuit,*" in E. Leach (ed.), *The Structural Study of Myth and Totemism.* London, 1967, 71–90.

Zafiropulo, J. *Diogène d'Apollonie: Diogène d'Apollonie.* Paris, 1956.

Zeitlin, F. I. "Misogyny": "The Dynamics of Misogyny: Myth and Mythmaking in the *Oresteia.*" *Arethusa* 11, 1–2 (1978): 149–84.

Zeller, E. "Philolaos": "Aristoteles und Philolaos." *Hermes* 10 (1876): 178–92.   361
———. *Philosophie*, II, 1: *Die Philosophie der Griechen*, II, 1. Leipzig, 1889.
Zeller, E., and R. Mondolfo. *Filosofia: La Filosofia dei Greci nel suo sviluppo storico*, I, 2, *Ionici e Pitagorici*². Florence, 1950.
Ziehen, L. "Opfer": *s.v.* "Opfer." *R.E.* 18 (1939): c. 579–627.
Zilsel, E. *Geniebegriff: Die Entstehung des Geniebegriffes.* Tübingen, 1926.
Zimmerman, F. "Géométrie": "Géométrie sociale traditionnelle. Castes de main droite et castes de main gauche en Inde du Sud." *Annales E.S.C.* 29 (1974): 1381–1401.
Ziomecki, J. *Représentations: Les Représentations d'artisans sur les vases attiques.* Wroclaw, 1975.
Zuidema, R. I. *Cuzco: The Ceque System of Cuzco. The Social Organization of the Capital of the Incas.* Leyden, 1964.

Index

Milton Keynes UK
Ingram Content Group UK Ltd.
UKHW030949260724
446093UK00001B/30